GROWTH COMPANY

GROWTH COMPANY

DOW CHEMICAL'S FIRST CENTURY

E.N. Brandt

Michigan State University Press
East Lansing

Michigan State University Press
East Lansing, MI 48823-5202

Printed in the United States of America

02 01 00 99 98 97 1 2 3 4 5 6 7 8 9 10

Library of Congress Cataloging-in-Publication Data

E.N. Brandt
    Growth Company : Dow Chemical's first centuty / E. N. Brandt.
        p. cm.
    Includes bibliographical references and index.
    ISBN 0-87013-426-4 (alk. paper)
1. Dow Chemical Company—History. 2. Dow, Herbert Henry, 1866-1930. 3. Industrialists—United States—Biography. 4. Chemical industry—United States—History. I. Title.
HD9651.9.D6B73   1997
338.7'.66'00973—dc20   97-749
                                                CIP

For Jeannette

CONTENTS

PART THREE: WILLARD DOW
(1930–49)

PART FOUR: THE FIRST BILLION
(1949–62)

PART FIVE: DOW GOES GLOBAL
(1962–78)

PART SIX: THE MODERN ERA BEGINS
(1978–96)

APPENDICES

PREFACE

Herbert Dow founded his chemical company in 1897 in the twilight of the horse-and-buggy age. A century of spectacular change was about to ensue. The horse and buggy would be superseded by supersonic aircraft, handwritten letters by e-mail, and double-entry bookkeeping by computers. Now, a hundred years later, we are about to usher in another fresh, new century, the twenty-first, with all the shocks and marvels of the continuing change that its new technology will bring us.

The fantastic changes of the twentieth century, igniting this mad rush into the future, were brought about by a multitude of factors, one of them the rise of the research-based industrial firm. The subject of this book, Dow Chemical, grew up in that time to become a leading representative of the type—a prototypical "growth company," as Wall Street calls them. Technological powerhouses such as Dow straddled the globe and triggered much of the progress and change of the twentieth century, spending significant sums in a daily, continuing search for better products, better ways to make them, and a better understanding of the science that makes them possible. In ways we hardly fathom, they changed our lives and will change the lives of our children.

Every industry buys and uses chemicals, making them a critical factor in the progress of industry as a whole. The influence of chemical research findings flows out to industry around the globe, and through industry to the world of the consumer, carrying with it the seeds of social and economic change whose connections to the research laboratory we perceive only dimly, if at all.

In this century Dow has grown to be a $20 billion-a-year firm, with operations pole to pole and an impact, in one way or another, on most of humanity. It is one of the world's half-dozen largest chemical firms, and in its 99th year was threatening to overtake DuPont, America's largest chemical company ever since such records were kept.[1] Dow makes about 2,400 different products, most of them unfamiliar to the general public, for it is a "chemical company's chemical company," supplying chemicals to other chemical companies, often in tank car lots. In the 1990s it spends, in a typical year, in excess of $1.25 billion on research and development. Its consumer products, a more familiar facet of the company to the general public—Saran Wrap, Bathroom Cleaner, Ziploc bags—make up a relatively small segment of its business. Dow is one of the wonders of the modern business world, and its story is one the general populace ought to know better.

I fell in love with this company when I joined its staff some 40 years ago, and that feeling has only matured in the years since as I have grown to understand its workings and culture and to appreciate its ethical standards and outlook (invariably gung-ho optimistic) on business and life. I have seen it in times that were wildly prosperous, and in times that were hard and thin; in times when it basked in the public favor (most conspicuously during those long-lost days of trust and confidence in the business community before the war in Vietnam), and in times when it was pilloried mercilessly and almost unanimously in the public press (during much of the time since that war). Through all these vicissitudes it has remained unchanged in its basic personality, though the personnel that make it up have changed constantly, a process that continues even today.

Dow's continuing task is to uncover "the facts," the science, without reference to bias or prejudice, and to put that science to work for the benefit of humankind. As we will see in these pages, its faith in science and technology has frequently gotten it into trouble; for humans are often more strongly moved by emotions than by facts, and the science of a situation is occasionally ignored or forgotten, sometimes for a very long time. Furthermore, what may be the "best" science is often in dispute.

Among the largest American corporations, Dow is the only one, at the end of the twentieth century, that still proclaims itself a "chemical company" in its title, and it is typical of the company that it would decline to change its label simply because being a chemical company was out of fashion.[2] Chemicals are widely misunderstood, feared, even derided today, in spite of the amazing benefits they bring. Without them, however, civilization as we know it could not exist.

Doing proudly what it does best, even when that is greatly unpopular, is one of the unique characteristics of the Dow organization. I am sure it will continue to make chemicals in the twenty-first century, whether that is "popular" or not, trusting that time and common sense will bring chemistry and its wonders once more into acceptance, perhaps even into favor, and that science, in the end, will prevail over emotion.

This history of the first 100 years of the Dow company is not "the" history but "a" history, for no two persons attempting to relate this complex, tangled story would select the same events from among the many thousands of people, products, and places that make it up, and no two people would place the same emphasis on the wealth of material available.

Although chemists, chemicals, and chemical terms perforce enter into it at every point, this is not a "chemical" history. It focuses rather on the people who made up and who make up an extraordinary company. Their stories are full of human interest and they reflect the full range of joy and pathos of the human condition in a particular slice of world history, the chemical world.

I have tended to focus, as you might expect, on the more remarkable people in this company, perhaps most conspicuously its chief executives. That is partly because they form a handy set of mileposts for compiling this particular history—there have been only 10 of them in the century covered—and also because its chief executives have reflected in a striking way the personality and development of the company itself at any given period. Additionally, I have had the good fortune to know and work with 7 of the 10 chief executives of this first century (William S. Stavropoulos, the tenth, began his term of office only at the end of 1995, and I have for obvious reasons not attempted to chronicle his stewardship). Thus, I have dealt here largely with people I have known and with whom I have worked.

As I have researched the history of the Dow Company these last half-dozen years—a good historian must be a good detective—I have uncovered more than a few errors and goof-ups by managers and employees, and many (but not all, of course) are noted in these pages. As you would expect, Dow employees are quite as prone to human failings as any other group of people, and while I occasionally encountered sinful or stupid behavior in them, I found no case where the corporation (as contrasted with an individual within the corporation) knowingly engaged in wrongdoing of any nature. If there is such a thing as a "corporate" conscience, I am convinced Dow has one.

Before we begin, a word to those Dow employees who search these pages for mention of "their" plant, product, or project, on which they may have lavished a lifetime of talent and toil: I ask their indulgence if they find no trace of it here. I have not attempted to compile an encyclopedia, and by no means are all facets of the company treated; to do so would require several volumes more than the fat one I have written. In attempting to encompass 100 years of history, I have been obliged to select incidents and anecdotes that seemed representative of the company's history, rather than trying to be all-inclusive. I could have chosen other products, other people, other places, of course, without altering the main thrust of the story, so I can only apologize to those whose role in Dow has been left out; the slight is unintentional and unavoidable.

Here, then, is the story of a growth company, the story of Dow Chemical's first century, as accurately and faithfully as I can tell it.

Notes

1. By at least one report Dow had actually surpassed DuPont in chemical sales. See "Dow Replaces DuPont to Lead Top 100 U.S. Chemical Producers," *Chemical & Engineering News*, May 6, 1996. This report pegged Dow's 1995 chemical sales at $19.234 billion compared to $18.433 billion for DuPont, but Dow and others disputed these numbers. DuPont's total 1995 sales were $42 billion compared to Dow's $20 billion. The third-ranking U.S. chemical producer was Exxon, with $11.737 billion in 1995 chemical sales.

2. The second-largest U.S. firm with "chemical" in its title in 1995 was Eastman Chemical, a subsidiary of Eastman Kodak, with $5.040 billion in chemical sales. Of the top 50 U.S. chemical producers, only six, including Dow, called themselves "chemical" or "petrochemical" firms.

SOURCES

I was given total access to the records of the Dow Company and no censorship was exercised by the company over my work. I worked out of an office in the Post Street Archives in Midland, Michigan, owned by the Herbert H. & Grace A. Dow Foundation, where I had complete access to the holdings. Most frequently, in fact, I worked in the archives (open to the public in the mornings only) alone and unattended. When I needed materials not in the archives, I requested them, and in no case was refused.

Fortunately, Herbert Dow kept complete records of his activities from the time of his senior year (1888) at the Case School in Cleveland (now part of Case Western Reserve University), and his papers, admirably organized and catalogued almost 50 years ago by Paul L. Parsons Associates of New York City, still form the basic historical record of the company up to his death in 1930. As the company historian since 1983, I was already familiar with these papers before beginning this project.

Incidentally, having studied Herbert Dow and his papers over an extended period, I am convinced that he is one of the more underrated and underrecognized of the major inventors and business figures of American history. This lack of recognition as a national figure occurred, I believe, because he toiled during his entire adulthood in the obscurity of a small backwoods town in Michigan, far from the legendmakers in the East, and because his firm became a "chemical company's chemical company," well known and respected in its own field but virtually unknown outside of it. Herbert Dow worked in the wrong place at the wrong time to capture the attention of the national press, and the renown he deserves as a historical figure still escapes him.

The papers of his son and successor, Willard H. Dow, were also indispensable in the preparation of this work, as were the papers of Leland I. Doan, the fourth chief executive, both held at the archives.

There was no serious lack of material concerning most of the pioneers of the company. The late Ormond Barstow, for example, provided the papers of his father, E. O. Barstow, the "father of magnesium"; I was allowed to rummage for materials in the attic of Charles J. Strosacker, "father of saran," after his death; I met and interviewed such pioneers as Thomas Griswold Jr. and Ivan Harlow—the latter as he was approaching his 100th birthday. Much of my research focused on the more obscure figures of the company's early era, such as Albert E. Convers, the first chief executive of the company, and the early officers of the company who resided in Cleveland, such as Harvey E. Hackenberg, who were tremendously influential in the company's formative years but were then quite forgotten.

I also had available to me a substantial amount of information not available at all to earlier Dow historians. In 1988 Julie Arbury, a great-granddaughter of Herbert Dow, discovered a trunk that had belonged to J. Henry Dow in the garret of the Herbert Dow homestead, and the family made it available to me. It contained correspondence and documents revealing hitherto unknown information concerning Herbert Dow's parents and childhood (J. Henry Dow, 1836-1901, was Herbert Dow's father), and added significantly to our knowledge of the young Herbert Dow.

I also studied the notes and raw materials generated by previous Dow historians, including those of Murray Campbell and Harrison Hatton, authors of "Herbert Dow, Pioneer in Creative Chemistry," published in 1949. Especially valuable was material from Hatton, who following publication of that work began gathering material for a second volume. This project was aborted in 1951 but the materials survived and were greatly useful to me (referred to as "Hatton" in the source notes).

In 1946 Willard Dow projected a company history of his own, with Samuel Carothers of Sunapee, New Hampshire, as ghost writer, a project abandoned when Crowther suffered a stroke and (some months later) died. The surviving drafts of early chapters, the only portion completed, provide valuable insights concerning Willard Dow's view of early Dow history. I also consulted materials gathered by Don Whitehead for "The Dow Story," a history published in 1967, particularly an extensive series of audiotaped interviews of A. P. (Dutch) Beutel. As it happens, I served as Dow liaison and general helper to Whitehead during the time he worked on this volume, not knowing it was to be my apprenticeship for the present work.

My research also led me to the sites of various events significant to the company history, such as Belleville, Ontario, where Herbert Dow was born; Hampton, New Hampshire, where the Dow family had resided since 1643; London, Ontario, site of the airplane accident that killed Willard Dow; Cleveland, Ohio, early home of Herbert Dow and birthplace of the company, where its board of directors met from 1897 to 1918; Freeport and Lake Jackson, Texas, home of Dow's largest manufacturing operations; Horgen, Switzerland, Coral Gables, Florida, Sao Paulo, Brazil, and Sarnia, Ontario, headquarters of Dow Europe, Dow Latin America, and Dow Canada; and other Dow locations around the world.

I derived the bulk of my material for the more contemporary aspects of the company's history, however, from the Dow Oral History Program, funded by the Herbert H. & Grace A. Dow Foundation.

As I began to compile the Dow history, it quickly became apparent that the written record of the company's history was skimpy for the decade beginning about 1970; the papers of C. Benson Branch (president and chief executive, 1970-76) and of his successor, Zoltan Merszei (president and chief executive, 1976-78) were virtually nonexistent. To document this period, I turned in 1988 to oral history, with the help of the Center for History of Chemistry (or CHOC), as it was then known, at the University of Pennsylvania (now the Chemical Heritage Foundation).

In the years after 1988 we ("we" being principally James J. Bohning, deputy director of CHOC for oral history, and myself) completed extensive, fully transcribed and indexed oral history interviews with well over 100 of Dow's top inventors, executives, and managers, as well as other employees in key positions, as part of this program (their names are listed in an appendix). This project grew into perhaps the most extensive oral history program yet undertaken in any major American firm. The wealth of material developed in this way became my key resource for the more modern era of the century that is covered.

A selected bibliography of books consulted, including those by Dow authors on Dow subjects, books touching on Dow by other authors, and unpublished manuscripts held at the archives, is also found in the appendix.

Sources such as the company's quarterly and annual reports; internal and external news announcements; files of company magazines, newspapers, and technical literature; executive speeches; and product literature of all kinds have all been useful. The minutes of the board of directors were consulted in some cases.

Other sources are listed in the notes.

ACKNOWLEDGMENTS

I am indebted to more people than I can acknowledge individually for assistance in this endeavor, but I will try:

The Herbert H. & Grace A. Dow Foundation has generously funded from its inception in 1988 the oral history program that became my principal source of material concerning the modern era of the company. The foundation is also the owner of the collections at the Post Street Archives, to which I have had complete access, and in fact of the archives themselves, housed in a building where Grace A. (Ball) Dow once taught school.

Herbert D. (Ted) Doan, the foundation's current president, has been one of this project's most enthusiastic and helpful supporters since its beginnings (he may in fact have originated the idea, among other contributions), and for his help I am especially grateful. I have referred to him more than once as the "godfather" of this volume, and he is that and more. Herbert H. Dow II, late president of the foundation, was my consultant on matters concerning the Dow family and an unflagging supporter of the project until his untimely death in January 1996.

An Editorial Advisory Committee has guided my work all the way, and these friendly helpers have been both my closest collaborators and harshest critics and hecklers (with the possible exception of my wife, Jeannette). If every author were blessed with such a group of advisors, writing would be a far more rewarding pursuit, and we would be blessed, I am convinced, with better literature. They are: James J. Bohning, longtime head of the chemistry department at Wilkes University, now of the American Chemical Society, my mentor and sidekick in developing and executing the Dow Oral History Program; Thayne R. Hansen, corporate communications director of The Dow Chemical Company, who provided liaison with the company and helped in the production of the book in a hundred different ways; Holmes H. McClure, retired vice-president of Dow's Texas Operations, now president of the Lake Jackson (Texas) Historical Society, an unfailing source of helpful suggestions and support; Patrick P. McCurdy, former editor of *Chemical Week* and of *Chemical & Engineering News*, now editor of *Today's Chemist at Work*, whose knowledge of matters editorial and chemical has been invaluable; and Arnold Thackray, executive director of the Chemical Heritage Foundation and faculty member at the University of Pennsylvania, whose wise, timely, and friendly counsel has been of enduring benefit. Robert W. Charlton served as the capable Dow liaison for the first year or two of the project, until Dow transferred him to Horgen, Switzerland.

Terry S. Reynolds of Michigan Technological University and Lisa M. Robinson of Michigan State University ably assisted with various aspects of the oral history program.

The personnel at the Post Street Archives—Barbara Brennan, Delores Goulet, Margaret R. Lyon, and Kathy Thomas—promptly and cheerfully provided daily help of all kinds.

Mrs. Lois Foster of the Hastings County Historical Society at Belleville, Ontario, helped track down details concerning the Dow family's stay in Belleville and Herbert Dow's birth there. Ansell Palmer of the Hampton Historical Society, Hampton, New Hampshire, provided information on the Dow family's history during many generations in Hampton; and Eric Small and Madaline Castleton of the Seabrook Historical Society, Seabrook, New Hampshire, provided information concerning the family's ties to that locality. Lisa A. Compton of the Old Colony Historical Society at Taunton, Massachusetts, supplied various materials concerning Albert E. Convers, Dow's first chief executive, who was born and is buried there. Marilyn Cook, specialist in the history of Navarre, Ohio, and Don Cooke of the Stark County (Ohio) Historical Society provided materials concerning Herbert Dow's sojourns in the region of Canton, Navarre, and Massillon, Ohio, where he located his first company, the Canton Chemical Company, and later, the Dow Process Company, immediate predecessor of The Dow Chemical Company. Dr. Dennis Harrison, of the Case Archives in Cleveland, supplied various tidbits of information and guided me through the papers of Albert W. Smith and other holdings at that archives. Rebecca M. Johnson and Cheri Widowski of the Western Reserve Historical Society provided background on various of the early Cleveland associates and backers of Herbert Dow.

I appreciate also the contributions of Dr. Ben B. Holder (documents concerning Dr. William F. Koch and William J. Hale); James G. Hanes (miscellaneous documents concerning the Atomic Energy Commission and Dow's stewardship of its Rocky Flats, Colorado, operation); Philip R. Beutel, of Colorado Springs, Colorado (transcript of interviews of his father, A. P. Beutel, by Don Whitehead); James E. (Mickey) McGuire of D'Arcy Masius Benton & Bowles, Bloomfield Hills, Michigan (miscellaneous early Dow advertising materials); Paul K. Graves of the Holyoke Public Library, Holyoke, Massachusetts (research concerning J. Henry Dow's apprenticeship as a machinist at Holyoke); David W. Carnell of the Cape Fear Museum, Wilmington, North Carolina (information concerning early history of the Kure Beach plant of Ethyl-Dow Corp.); David E. Wright of Michigan State University (custodian of the papers of William J. Hale at the MSU Archives); James K. Rieke, of Midland (custodian of the papers of Raymond P. Boyer); Craig McDonald of the Alden B. Dow Archives at Midland (various materials concerning A. B. Dow and other members of the Dow family); Alex Groner, of Poway, California (copy of the unpublished manuscript of "Petrodow," which he authored, an account of Dow's experiences during the Allende regime in Chile); David H. DeVorkin of the National Air & Space Museum at the Smithsonian Institution (permission to use materials from his book, *Race to the Stratosphere: Manned Scientific Ballooning in America*, published in 1989, concerning the Dow role in the exploits of the ballooning Piccard brothers); and Homer L. White, of Pasadena, California (materials concerning early Dow activities on the West Coast).

So many Dow employees extended courtesies and assistance that it is impossible to list them; I have been learning about Dow history from them since 1953. I do want to express special gratitude to James C. Mackey of Dow's Western Division for his oral histories of Dow Western pioneers and for materials from the papers of Dr. Wilhelm Hirschkind; to David M. Young of Dow Chemical Canada, my guide to the history of Dow Canada; to Libia Winslow of Dow Latin America, who greatly assisted my research on that continent; to Babs Babin of Dow's Louisiana Division; to Marcelo Lins and Theo Carnier of Empresas Dow, Sao Paulo, Brazil; and to Leanne Dijak, Karen Willard, Charles A. Infante, and John W. Tysse at corporate headquarters.

Those present and former employees of the company who graciously (and for the most part enthusiastically) gave of their time and abilities to participate in the oral history program are listed in the back of the book; without their help this volume would not have been possible.

I also discussed numerous aspects and incidents of Dow history with a multitude of other people, both inside and outside the company, active and retired, in person or by telephone, and I hope they will accept my thanks and forgive the fact that they are not individually listed here.

E. N. (Ned) Brandt
June 15, 1996
Midland, Michigan

Dow

June 6, 1888—Herbert H. Dow, 22, graduates from Case Institute, Cleveland, Ohio, with a chemistry degree.

1889-90—Dow forms Canton Chemical Company in Canton, Ohio, based on bromine-from-brine process he has invented; the venture fails.

August 12, 1890—Dow and backer J. H. Osborn form Midland Chemical Company based on Dow's bromine process; Dow arrives in Midland, Michigan, on August 14.

January 4, 1891—Dow produces world's first commercial bromine from brine by electrolysis at Evens Mill in Midland.

1893—In policy dispute, Dow is fired as general manager but remains on payroll of Midland Chemical Company

1895—Dow founds Dow Process Company at Navarre, Ohio, and develops chlorine cell and a method of making bleach.

1896—Dow Process Company moves to Midland.

May 18, 1897—Dow Process Company is reorganized as The Dow Chemical Company, with A. E. Convers as president, to manufacture and sell bleach.

World at large

1888—Jack the Ripper murders six women in London.

George Eastman perfects "Kodak" box camera.

1889—Thomas Edison patents motion picture using film manufactured by Eastman.

1890—Rubber gloves used for first time in surgery.

Idaho and Wyoming are admitted to the Union.

United Alkali Co., syndicate of British soda producers, is formed to protect bleach prices in England and abroad.

1891—W. L. Judson invents the zipper.

1892—First cans of pineapple are produced.

1893—Henry Ford builds his first automobile.

1894—Thomas Edison opens "kinetoscope parlor" in New York, forerunner of movie houses.

1895—Wilhelm Roentgen discovers X rays.

Guglielmo Marconi invents radio telegraphy.

1896—Klondike gold rush begins.

First modern Olympic Games are held in Athens.

1897—America's first comic strip, *Katzenjammer Kids*, debuts.

J. J. Thompson discovers the electron.

THE YOUNG HERBERT DOW (1866-97)

I.

It all began in a modest brick house at the corner of Dundas and Pinnacle streets in Belleville, Ontario, Canada, on February 26, 1866. There Herbert H. Dow was born.

The little brick house disappeared long ago. The site is occupied now by a Speedy Auto Glass shop, "Windshields our specialty." On the waterfront a block or so away was the Belleville market, one of Upper Canada's liveliest, where the area's farmers brought their produce and the Dows did their shopping.[1]

Herbert's parents were Joseph Henry Dow of Hampton, New Hampshire, and Sarah Jane Bunnell Dow, of Derby, Connecticut. J. Henry (Sarah always called him "Henry") had come to Belleville in the autumn of 1863, an itinerant 27-year-old bachelor, to work for a struggling young sewing machine company, Irwin & White. As soon as his work position there was established, Henry hurried back to Derby, where his betrothed lived, and on November 24, Thanksgiving Day of 1863 (Abraham Lincoln, dedicating a cemetery in Pennsylvania, had delivered his celebrated Gettysburg Address five days before), they were married. The newlyweds left immediately for the long trip to Belleville.

Strung out along the shore of the Moira River, which empties into the Bay of Quinte on the north shore of Lake Ontario, Belleville was an overgrown village of perhaps 5,000 in 1866. It had been settled largely by British Loyalists who left the United States following the American Revolution, and it was proud of its Loyalist heritage. What brought J. Henry and his mechanical expertise to the busy riverside town was the sewing machine business; there were at least four small sewing machine companies in 1866 Belleville, all competing fiercely to develop a better sewing machine. None of them would be the winner of this contest; the eventual "winner," the Singer Sewing Machine Company, had already opened a sales agency in Belleville in 1866 and was preparing to drive most of its fledgling competitors, including Irwin & White, out of business.[2]

Although he is listed on the 1864 Belleville city rolls as a "carpenter and joiner," Henry was a born tinkerer, and already at 27 had a reputation as a top-notch mechanic and inventor. He had studied higher mathematics at Cooper Union in New York City, one of the nation's finest schools, and he had learned the machinist's trade in several shops in New England, principally at Holyoke, Massachusetts. He was now in charge of the small production crew of Irwin & White, and Stephen J. White, the firm's manager, apparently was also counting on his inventive skills to help perfect their entry in the sewing machine derby. White himself spent much of his time on the road trying to secure orders for the machine. Having Dow on the payroll enabled him to do this. Charles Irwin appears to have been a silent partner.

"I like my situation here very much," Henry wrote Sarah on November 8, 1863, just before their marriage. "Everything was in confusion when I came and it will require months to get it to going right and there is a good deal of trouble and perplexity and anxiety to endure, but after all I like it."[3]

The newlyweds moved into the upstairs front room of a two-story frame house on South John Street and boarded with Martha Furnival, widow of a prosperous Belleville harness maker. Henry had boarded there earlier. Later, when Sarah became pregnant, they moved into the house at Dundas and Pinnacle, rented from a man named Abraham Frost.

The young couple seems to have been happy in Belleville, although Henry was beginning to have serious doubts about the business abilities of his employer. "Mr. White has the blues sometimes," he wrote.

> Until he gets over his blue streaks and goes out and sells machines I shall not have much confidence in the permanence of his business. I expect to have the order to fit up some machines for the fair and which I have got the men at work on countermanded tomorrow. Who in the world can manage a shop to advantage under such a changeable proprietor? I can hardly wonder at it however. The vexations of a credit business are wearing out his patience, his pocket, and his life almost. Protested notes which he has endorsed are worrying him now.

Still, Henry observed to Sarah, "I think Mr. White will decide to go on with the business here . . . so we may as well make up our minds to live in Belleville for another winter at least and I hope for a good many more for I am thoroughly tired of moving about and I am very well satisfied with Belleville and my situation here."[4]

In the summer of 1864, while they still lived in the upper front room at Mrs. Furnival's, the marriage went through its first serious crisis. Sarah, homesick and perhaps ill—she was given to "fainting spells," her sister said—left in August for her first visit home since the wedding. She and Henry agreed on a visit of "a few weeks," and once she had left he quickly defined "few" as three. But August went by, and September and October, and Sarah was still visiting with the Bunnells in Derby and the Dows in Hampton, with no sign of when she might return to the upper front room in Belleville.

Henry spent much of his spare time during these months on church matters, and wrote her faithfully every Sunday evening describing his experiences. He attended church services as many as four times each Sunday, and finally reached a decision. "I think the proper time has come for me to connect myself with some church in Belleville," he wrote Sarah, "and my mind is now settled that it is best for me to unite with the Wesleyan church." His friend Rev. John Climie, he said, "brought me to account for not becoming a member of his (Congregational) church and 'deserting' to the Methodists," but he had made his decision. Henry's "desertion" to the Methodists must have been a great shock to his parents; his father, a lifelong Congregational deacon, and his mother, daughter of a distinguished Congregational clergyman, seem to have considered any other denomination beyond the pale. The relationship between father and son seems to have cooled thereafter.

In November, with Sarah still vacationing back East, Henry decided to take matters in hand. He wrote Sarah, announcing that he would be arriving in Derby to celebrate with her the first anniversary of their marriage; this would give him the opportunity to accompany her back to Belleville, he added, so she would not have to make the trip by herself. It worked; by the end of the month the couple were back in Belleville and the crisis was past.

Henry's impassioned letters to his bride back in Derby do give clues to other problems ahead. Later in life he was to be a notoriously poor manager of funds and to depend heavily on his son Herbert for financial support. At first Henry enclosed $20 in his letters to Sarah, a substantial sum by 1864 standards, but soon the amount began to shrink. "I do not think it is right to give so little in charities," he explained, "and besides that although I never made a positive promise to that effect yet I did resolve years ago that one tenth of my earnings should be spent for other than merely selfish purposes." In another he wrote: "Enclosed is $5.00. I have found a place where that amount was needed and have disposed of it. This is your share to do as you please with. We own all together and will share in giving."

When little Herbert was six weeks old, Henry and Sarah left Belleville for Derby, where the family would live for the next 11 years. Irwin & White seems to have collapsed about this time, and by 1868 it had disappeared entirely.

We do not know very much about this period. Henry worked as a machinist in the area, principally at the Howe Pin Company in Derby, with the assignment of redesigning and rebuilding the machinery to put the pins into papers. This was apparently the first mechanical problem he discussed with young Herbert, just reaching school age. "I used to carry my father's dinner down to the Howe pin factory," Herbert recalled later, and "came to be posted on the advancement in the art of making pins."[5] It was not until 1873, when the boy was seven, that his father enjoyed permanent employment again, this time as superintendent of the Derby Shovel Manufacturing Company, for which he had worked off and on prior to this time. In the meantime two more children were born—Herbert's sisters, Helen and Mary.

Henry quickly became a pillar of the shovel company, and there are reports, handed down in the family but possibly exaggerated, that he "invented everything the firm had for sale." In 1877 the company was bought out by William Chisholm, Henry's boss, who announced that he was moving the entire operation to Cleveland, Ohio—but only if Henry would agree to come with him. Henry readily agreed to move, and spent the remainder of his active career as the master mechanic of what then became the Chisholm Steel Shovel Works. He moved his family to Cleveland in the late summer of 1878. Herbert was 12, and already showing signs of precocity.

In 1876 the great Philadelphia Centennial Exhibition celebrated 100 years of American independence, and Herbert Dow, at the age of 10, decided he wanted to see it. He got a job distributing handbills for a local dry-goods store, put the money he earned into a little bank he made for himself, and financed the trip. He wanted to see one of the marvels of the age, the gigantic Corliss steam engine. The sight of the Corliss engine seems to have impressed him greatly; he was to be "power-conscious" all his life.

From his mother and his maternal grandfather, Capt. Alva Bunnell, of Derby, with whom the small boy spent a good deal of time, he began to learn gardening before he even started school. Within a few years he began to keep a kitchen garden of his own, to contribute to the family larder or, when there were extras, to sell. It was a practice he carried with him to Cleveland and continued on into his college days; some of his high school friends recalled his getting up at dawn to tend to his garden before school started. Gardening became his lifelong avocation.

While Herbert was still at a tender age, his father began the practice of bringing home his mechanical problems and sharing them with his young son. The pin machinery case was only the first. His sisters recalled father and son constantly working on problems together, and these were usually the topic at the dinner table.

Herbert's first solo invention seems to have been an incubator for chicken eggs. The idea for it came from an article in a magazine called *Youth's Companion* concerning the problems of raising ostriches in South Africa. The main problem in incubating eggs, he found, was to maintain a constant temperature in the incubator. He tried to develop a device to do this automatically. Nothing seemed to work for him, but he kept on trying, and on the 40th try he succeeded. Then he discovered that his invention was not the route to riches; he might sell one machine, but that one was then duplicated by its new owner, and he had another competitor in the business. Herbert Dow's response, when he discovered this, was to drop out of the market. He decided instead to market plans to build incubators—the most economical way, he told prospective customers, to acquire one.

His father's major invention—the only one of Henry's that was an unqualified success—was a small, football-sized steam turbine used for many years by the U.S. Navy to power its torpedoes. Herbert is listed as coinventor with his father on two of the six patents covering the device. J. Henry began working on this invention during the time Herbert was in high school and completed it when he was in college. Chisholm became one of his principal financial backers in the venture. Henry confided to Sarah that the turbine was to be the key to their becoming wealthy, but it was not to be. Much of the time, J. Henry was scraping money together to pay the patent attorneys and the fees to patent his device in various countries around the world, and the Dow turbine was never much of a money maker.[6]

Young Herbert, observing his father's struggles, was already learning how, and how not, to make his way in the business world.

II.

The Dows were a proud and distinguished family of Puritan New Englanders. Hampton, New Hampshire, had been their home since 1643. The town was founded five years before the first Dow arrived by the Rev. Steven Bachiler, a Congregational minister, who sailed up the small Taylor River and established his flock at a place the Indians called *Winnacunnet*, "Place of Beautiful Pines." He renamed it Hampton after his parish in England, and it became one of the four founding cities of New Hampshire, together with Exeter, Dover, and Portsmouth.[7]

Most of Hampton's settlers came from Norfolk County in southeastern England, as did the first Henry Dow, progenitor of the Dow family in Hampton. Henry, born in a Norfolk village called Runham in 1608, had friends in the Bachiler group, and in 1637 he sailed for America with his wife, Joane, four children, and a servant girl, intent on catching up with them. When the Hampton townspeople agreed on a plan to lay out farms for themselves in June 1640, they noted that there should be a farm for "Dow, if he come"; but he had not arrived.

Instead, Henry had landed at Watertown, Massachusetts, a few miles up the Charles River from Boston; there in March 1639 the first of his New World children was born. This son was named Joseph, the first of a long line of Joseph Dows (Herbert Dow's father and grandfather both were named Joseph). In June of 1640 tragedy struck: Joane, only 33, died of unrecorded causes. A year later Henry married again, this time to Margaret Cole, of Dedham, Massachusetts. The next year there was fresh tragedy: his eldest son died, not yet 11. Henry Dow then left Watertown with the five remaining children and his new wife and made his way through the 60 miles of wilderness to Hampton, where he bought a house and the farming land his friends were holding for him.

Henry appears to have prospered from the start in Hampton; by 1651, eight years after he arrived, he was a selectman—a member of the five-man town council. At his death in 1659 he was one of three people administering local land grants and highways.

Hampton remained staunchly Congregationalist; city and church were one there until 1803. A tax paid by all citizens supported the minister, whose salary was fixed by the city. Rev. Bachiler, the founder, was much admired by Herbert Dow's grandfather, Joseph Dow, who in 1838 delivered a lengthy paper eulogizing him.[8] Bachiler was 77 when he sailed up the river with his congregation to found Hampton; he married a third time when he was 89, and lived to be 100. Among his descendants were Daniel Webster and John Greenleaf Whittier.

Henry Dow's second son, called Captain Henry, became a distinguished leader of the New Hampshire colony—an attorney, captain of the militia, deputy to the General Assembly, clerk of the House, Speaker pro tem, marshal of Norfolk County, and senior justice of the Court of Common Pleas. He was also a leader in opposing British impositions on the colonists. In 1682 he was named in a writ of arrest for refusing to pay a tax levied by the Crown, but was not actually jailed.

The Dow family quickly began to play a prominent role in the colony. There is a Dow's Hill, a Dow's Meadows, a Dow's River, and a Dow's Lane. Captain Henry became the town clerk in 1681 and was succeeded by his son and grandson. The office of town clerk of Hampton was held in direct descent in the family for six generations and 134 years, down to Col. Josiah Dow Jr., brother of Herbert Dow's grandfather; the post became almost hereditary.

In the late seventeenth century, the Quaker religion made many converts in New England. It "spread like wildfire," as churchmen said, and among the most ardent of its converts were the Dows. By 1666 the Quakers were being actively prosecuted for refusing to pay the tax in support of the Congregational minister, and they began meeting secretly. Joseph Dow became their agent and quietly bought up property in Seabrook, across the Taylor River from Hampton, to which the Quaker group moved a few years later.[9]

During the Revolutionary War one of Joseph's great-grandsons, Samuel, fought at Bunker Hill, and several other descendants served in the Continental forces. When victory was won and the new president, George Washington, made a triumphal tour of New England in the fall of 1789, he stopped in Hampton Falls to greet the Revolutionary War veterans in that area, including the Dows who had served. Another of the long line of Joseph Dows, Maj. Joseph Dow, served in that war with James Monroe, later a president of the United States. When President Monroe in his turn made a tour of New England, he stopped in Hampton on July 12, 1817, to meet with his old friend.

In the fall of 1860, with the Civil War looming ahead, a group of 36 Hampton men, including four members of the Dow family, organized a military unit they called the "Winnacunnet Guards," and informed the governor of New Hampshire they were ready to go if needed. When war actually broke out in April 1861 it was one of the first units called. Joseph Warren Dow was first sergeant of the outfit, and two of the four corporals were Dows. One of these corporals was Jonathan N. Dow, a first cousin of Herbert Dow's father. His monument in Hampton Cemetery proclaims: "He was the first victim of the Southern Rebellion from his town. He died while serving his country as Standard Bearer of the 3rd Regt. New Hampshire Volunteers at Port Royal, S.C." Jonathan, who had been promoted to color sergeant, died February 20, 1862, aged 29. Although his death sounds heroic, Jonathan actually died from what was then called the "wasting fever"—typhoid.

Abram Dow was promoted to sergeant two days later to replace him. Disabled and discharged a few months later, Abram eventually went to Washington to demand that he be allowed to reenlist for limited service. This accounted for his being at Ford's Theater the night Lincoln was shot. Realizing instantly the impact the event would have on history, Abram made his way to the front of the theater, whipped out his knife, and cut off a piece of the stage curtain as a souvenir.

Herbert Dow's grandfather Joseph, the Congregational deacon, graduated from Dartmouth College in 1833 and often styled himself "Joseph Dow M.A."; a master's degree was a mark of distinction then. While he was completing his studies at Dartmouth the preceptor (or principal) of the Hampton Academy left town, and the city fathers invited Joseph to become the new preceptor. Joseph turned them down at first, having other things in mind; in April 1835 he married Abigail French, daughter of the Rev. Dr. Jonathan French, minister of the Congregational Church in North Hampton, a renowned New England preacher, and chairman of the Hampton Academy board. Dr. French was a direct descendant of John Alden, of Mayflower fame; thus Dow descendants from that time are also descendants of John Alden. Joseph Henry Dow, Herbert Dow's father, was born of this marriage in Pembroke, Massachusetts, a few miles from Plymouth Rock, a year later. Joseph brought Abigail and the baby back to Hampton in 1837 and became preceptor of the Hampton Academy, which taught Greek, Latin, logic, and other studies considered necessary to an education in that day.

Joseph Dow, M.A., retired from teaching when he was only 53 to devote himself "to probate and other legal business and to historical study."[10] From family letters he appears to have complained of ailing health most of his life, but he lived to be 82, devoting most of his later years to a *History of Hampton*, finally published by his daughter Lucy in two volumes in 1893, four years after his death.

The careful scholarship of *The History of Hampton* is somewhat marred by the items Joseph Dow chose to omit from it. He does not mention the Quakers, for example, perhaps because of his close ties to the church that persecuted them. In his genealogy he lists the white first wife but omits the Indian second wife of Joseph Dow (his great-great-grandfather's brother), thus eliminating a great number of Dow descendants from his "official" list. In fact, he mentions none of the Dows who moved to Seabrook; he was, after all, writing a history of Hampton.

He also turned a blind eye to one of the more memorable of the Dow ancestors, Eliphaz Dow, a son of the first Quaker Joseph Dow and the first person to be hanged in Norfolk County. Eliphaz (named for Job's friend in the Old Testament) dropped by to visit his brother Noah one day in December 1753. Another visitor to Noah's bachelor quarters was the local blacksmith, Peter Clough. As the three sat by the fire imbibing generous quantities of hard cider, an argument broke out. Peter's cow had been killed, and he accused Eliphaz of doing it. The argument became quite heated, and Peter proposed they step outside and settle the matter with fisticuffs. Eliphaz declined; the blacksmith was a big, burly ox of a fellow. Peter said he'd be outside waiting for him, and staggered out. Eventually Eliphaz also left, and as he did so he picked up a garden hoe standing by the door just in case. Sure enough, Peter came charging at him. Eliphaz swung the hoe and hit Peter on the side of the head, killing him with one blow. Puritan justice was unrelenting; Eliphaz was hanged for this deed the following May 8.

Posterity did not treat Eliphaz kindly. For many years afterward, mothers around the Hampton area told a child who had done something nasty, "Ye have a bit of the Eliphaz Dow in ye."

The Dow family tree was full of fascinating individuals. One of the most remarkable was Brig. Gen. Neal Dow, grandson of a cousin who had moved to Portland, Maine. A tiny man barely five feet tall and a firebrand Quaker, Neal Dow became nationally known as the "Father of Prohibition" and the "Napoleon of Temperance." He began his political career as mayor of Portland. When the Civil War broke out, he was shocked to discover the extent to which soldiers drank hard liquor, used profanity, and played cards. He decided to form a regiment of his own to show that none of these things were necessary to being a good soldier, and advertised that he was forming "Neal Dow's Temperance Regiment," a model of upright deportment for soldiers. The mothers of Maine sent 2,000 of their boys to join him—the "Flower of Maine's Sunday Schools," one newspaper called them—and an overflow of 600 was sent on to other units. This became the famous Maine 13th, from which rum peddlers were chased at bayonet point (or so Neal Dow claimed). Dow himself led prayers and the singing of psalms at evening dress parade. Eventually the Maine 13th, with Neal Dow promoted to general, was assigned to General William Tecumseh Sherman, who became a fast friend of Dow's in spite of his drinking, and they fought together in the Mississippi campaign.

By a stroke of bad luck General Dow was captured by a Confederate raiding party and became the highest ranking Union officer in the notorious Confederate prisoner-of-war camps. After eight months of misery he was exchanged for Gen. W. H. Fitzhugh Lee, son of General Robert E. Lee, who had fallen into Northern hands. After the war Neal continued his lifelong crusade against Demon Rum and wound up his active career in 1880 by running for president of the United States on the Prohibition ticket. He received 10,305 votes, including 7 from Midland County, Michigan. When he was 80 General Sherman sent a telegram: "Tell General Dow that he is now at an age when an occasional glass will do him good." When the two friends had retired to their tent of an evening during the war, General Sherman had sipped whisky; General Dow had sipped water.[11]

III.

When Herbert Dow graduated from the gothic majesty of Cleveland's Central High School in 1884 there appears to have been no question at all whether he would go on to college; that had already been decided. He enrolled at the Case School of Applied Science in downtown Cleveland as though he had been planning to do so for some time, as undoubtedly he had. This budding new school had opened only three years before in the Case family home on the Public Square with 5 faculty and 16 students. In April 1883 the school had broken ground for a permanent building on the east side of Cleveland, where a joint campus with Western Reserve College was planned, but the new building was still under construction when Herbert Dow entered school.

Tuition was $100 per year and this posed a serious problem for the perennially under-funded J. Henry Dow and his son. Henry talked to his employer, William Chisholm, about it, as he often did when he was short of funds. Chisholm, who now resided in a mansion on a stretch of Cleveland's Euclid Avenue called "Millionaires' Row," readily agreed to help, and although the terms of his help are unknown, his financial support did enable the young man to enter Case in September of 1884.

Chisholm was an immensely wealthy and powerful man. His father, Henry Chisholm, had been the primary stockholder and driving force behind the Cleveland Rolling Mill, which in 1868 had begun production of Bessemer steel—one of the first U.S. plants to do so—and had amassed millions manufacturing steel rails for America's expanding railroads. Chisholm and others also organized the American Sheet & Boiler Plate Company, the Union Steel Screw Company, and the HP Horse Nail Company, all of which became divisions of the U. S. Steel Corporation when it was organized in 1901. Some observers put Chisholm in the same league with his friend and fellow Clevelander Andrew Carnegie. When the older Chisholm died in 1881, aged 59, he was succeeded by his son William, the man who had brought the Dows to Cleveland only three years earlier by insisting that J. Henry come with him when he purchased the Derby Steel Shovel Works, renamed it, and moved it to Cleveland.[12]

William did not enjoy the success his father had at the helm of these sprawling enterprises. He quickly had a series of ugly labor strikes on his hands, and he handled them poorly. The elder Chisholm's passing, one authority noted sadly, "marked the end of paternalistic labor relations and of progressive management at the mill." When his skilled workers joined a union and demanded a wage raise and a closed shop one year after he had taken over, William Chisholm flatly rejected their proposals. The workforce walked out. Chisholm responded by bringing in unskilled Polish and Czech workmen from out of town and reopened the mill. This was the beginning of the violence-punctuated "Cleveland Rolling Mill Strikes" of 1882 and 1885. Things came to a head in 1885 when a recession prompted Chisholm to cut wages three times in a year for the workmen he had imported; this was more than even the eager immigrants could take, and the third cut precipitated a series of riots and violence that dragged on for months. In the end, Cleveland Mayor George Gardner ordered Chisholm to restore the wage cuts, an unheard-of move for a mayor, and peace was gradually restored.

Herbert Dow, a schoolboy observing these activities of his financial sponsor, was getting an early education in employee relations.

The Case School also experienced turbulent times during Herbert Dow's years there. He learned his first chemistry in what had been the Case barn, behind the homestead. The second floor of the barn, where hay had been kept for the horses, had been remodeled as the school's chemistry and physics laboratory.

In September 1886, when Dow was entering his junior year, a handsome new building was complete—Case's trustees called it a "technical tabernacle" and spent lavishly on its scientific equipment—and the whole college moved in under the guidance of the school's newly arrived first president, Cady Staley, a one-time ox driver on the wagon trains that crossed the plains to the Pacific, where he had gone seeking gold. Finding none, he had become a professor of civil engineering, and eventually a college president. Six weeks after they moved in and the new term began, there was a muffled nighttime explosion in the third-floor chemistry lab area and the brand-new technical tabernacle burned to a shell in a spectacular fire, destroying the new equipment, the chemistry lab, the library, and all.

The college moved in with Adelbert College, next door on the Western Reserve property, and promptly began to rebuild, but unsettled conditions prevailed for the remainder of Herbert Dow's tenure. Because the fire appeared to have started in the chemistry lab, the trustees decided to move chemistry to its own building and within 90 days had built a temporary frame structure that was the home of the chemistry department for the next six years. Some of his employees later claimed that Herbert Dow, having learned his chemistry in a barn and a shack, never appreciated anything finer than the plainest of working places—and it was largely true.[13]

As Case was organized at this period, the first two years for all students were devoted to training in mathematics, physics, chemistry, civil engineering and drawing, and modern languages (French and German). In the junior and senior years the student elected a course of study in one of the sciences or in civil engineering; in the senior year a thesis was required, reflecting study and investigation of a subject in the student's field of study. Herbert Dow chose chemistry, a new offering, in his junior year, and his friend James T. Pardee, in the same class, chose civil engineering. By now the school had grown to seven faculty and 44 students.

It was the faculty that made up for the shortcomings of these unsettled times. They were a truly remarkable lot. John Nelson Stockwell, Dow's math professor, was a nationally known astronomer, mathematician, and scholar later known as the "dean of American astronomy"; he was also chairman of the Case faculty until President Staley arrived; he hired the first faculty and devised the curriculum.[14]

Charles F. Mabery, Dow's chemistry teacher, was renowned for his skill and enthusiasm and was best known for his work in petroleum chemistry. He published some 60 papers on petroleum chemistry and was known in this field worldwide. One of the first to obtain a doctorate in science at Harvard, he was director of the Harvard Summer School in Chemistry for 10 years before moving to Case. He was also noted for his expertise in electrochemistry, an interest he passed on to Herbert Dow with remarkable results.

Edward W. Morley of the Adelbert staff also taught some chemistry courses at Case and became one of Dow's favorite teachers. He is remembered today mainly for his determination of the ratio of the atomic weights of oxygen and hydrogen in 1896; this became the key ratio for establishing a reliable atomic weight scale. Morley served on the Dow Company's board of directors from 1898 to 1907.

Albert A. Michelson, Dow's physics teacher, was perhaps the most illustrious of the group. In 1878 he was the first to measure the speed of light, and in 1907 he became the first American to win the Nobel Prize in Physics. Albert Einstein said it was Michelson's work that opened the way for his theory of relativity.

Michelson was a strict, no–nonsense teacher in the German academic tradition—no interruptions, no questions. A graduate of the U.S. Naval Academy (he had graduated first in his class of 29 in optics and acoustics, but 25th in seamanship), he always appeared before his class with his mustache carefully trimmed and waxed, dressed in a wing collar, ascot tie, black jacket, and striped trousers.

Another faculty star was John Eisenmann, professor of civil engineering and the architect who designed the Case Main Building. He was a pioneer in structural steel construction in the United States and the designer (with George H. Smith) of the Euclid-Superior Arcade in Cleveland, a "crystal palace" that ranked among the largest glass-roofed structures in the world, second only to the Duomo arcade in Milan.

His sister Mary and his son Alden said Herbert Dow originally wanted to be an architect. This may have been a passing fancy, possibly inspired by his association with Eisenmann. Once embarked on a chemistry career, in his third year at Case, he never looked back.

On June 6, 1888, the faculty and student body gathered at Case Hall in downtown Cleveland and the school graduated the six members of its third commencement class, Herbert Dow and James T. Pardee among them. Dow read an abstract from his senior thesis, "Composition of Salt Brines in Northern Ohio, with Special Reference to Bromine and Lithium Contents," at the ceremonies. The commencement speaker was J. Twing Brooks, president of Western Reserve and a Case trustee. Herbert Dow was proud of his thesis on brine, and proposed to present it to the Cleveland chapter of the American Association for the Advancement of Science, only to be told the organization did not accept student papers. After talking to Professor Mabery about it, he resubmitted the paper as a joint effort by Charles Mabery and Herbert Dow. The paper was then accepted. When it was read to the AAAS in August 1888, Dow appeared alone, presumably smiling, explaining that his coauthor was indisposed.

He had already submitted a first senior thesis in December 1887 entitled "A New Method for Mining Native Copper"; in it he proposed to mine copper by sealing off part of a mine, flooding it with copper sulphate solution, and electroplating copper from the ore onto a copper electrode. It was not one of his better inspirations, and he did not pursue the subject.

In the middle of his senior year, perhaps dissatisfied with the copper mining thesis, he began work on a different thesis, a study of boiler fuels and their chemical composition. During the Christmas break he visited a gas well being drilled near his home to get a gas sample for analysis, and while he was there a driller gave him a sample of a bitter brine he had struck in drilling for gas. This casual incident struck a spark that was to change his life; it was his introduction to salt brines and, although he did not know it, to his life's work. He seems to have grasped at once that there was a sea of chemical raw materials not far below the crust of the earth just waiting to be mined and used, and that he could be the one to tap these riches. In the months ahead he began to visit various places in Ohio to obtain brine samples and to analyze them. This work broadened even more after his graduation, and in the summer following graduation he continued his research, visiting West Virginia, Pennsylvania, and

Michigan, as well as Ohio. The bitter-tasting lithium salts, his first interest, were present in relatively large amounts in the Ohio brines but absent from the Michigan brines, he found. He lost interest in the lithium when he discovered there was little market for it and began to focus on bromine, the main component of many of the patent medicines of the era.

"In the fall of 1888 I accepted a position as professor of chemistry and toxicology in a medical college in Cleveland [Huron Road Hospital, parent of Huron Road College, also known as Huron Street Hospital College], where I had a laboratory and an assistant," Herbert Dow wrote years later, "and I utilized all my spare time in perfecting a process of extracting bromine from brine. This process for extracting bromine appearing to offer better commercial possibilities than the only process I had been able to devise for extracting lithium, caused me to make arrangements in the spring of 1889 with some capitalists in Canton, Ohio, where we started a small plant and began the extraction of bromine from the Canton brine."[15]

At the time of Herbert Dow's work there the Huron Road Hospital was home to the Cleveland Training School for Nurses, the first nursing school west of the Alleghenies. His job was to teach the nursing students chemistry and toxicology, but his primary interest in the Huron Road Hospital was in the laboratory that came with this job; there he could continue his research on bromine. To earn extra funds he also taught mechanical drawing to a night class for railroad shop apprentices.

The young professor nonetheless found time for a full social calendar, most of it centered around the Willson Avenue Methodist Episcopal Church, where his parents were both stalwarts. His father was for many years church treasurer. His mother was an officer of the Ladies' Aid Society and the Woman's Foreign Missionary Society. At one time or another all the members of the J. H. Dow family taught Sunday School there.[16]

Joseph P. Smith, who directed the choir (in which Dow sang), became Herbert Dow's financial backer in his first business venture with the Canton "capitalists." A Cleveland butter and egg dealer, he agreed to invest some of his funds to help his young friend get started. Smith was an older brother of Albert W. Smith, Dow's Case classmate, and Dow had worked in his butter and egg store on Saturdays and vacations to help finance his schooling.

Moses B. Johnson, who always styled himself "M.B.," another pillar of the church, later became the first employee of The Dow Chemical Company. Johnson, chairman of the Sunday School committee, took on the job of building a new Willson Avenue ME Church in the early 1890s, assisted by his two sons. Herbert Dow was so impressed with M.B.'s skills that a few years later, when he looked for someone to build and superintend his new plant, he chose M.B.

Through the young people's group at the church, Herbert Dow met his first serious girlfriend, Mabelle L. Ross, a young schoolteacher who lived with her mother. Mabelle loved going to musical concerts and the opera and to baseball games—she was a fan of an early Cleveland professional team, the Cleveland Spiders—and they began "keeping company." During his time in Canton and Midland they corresponded and he sent gifts, and he would see her when he was back in Cleveland. On a trip back in April 1891 they became formally engaged, and the young swain gave her a diamond ring. It was a bigger diamond than he could afford, in his mother's opinion.[17]

He proposed that Mabelle and her mother take a boat excursion "up the lakes" to Saginaw and visit Midland, but Mabelle put off this expedition with various excuses—"Mamma is not well," she repeated regularly in her letters to him—and the trip never took place.

"Mamma" seems to have been the wrecker of this engagement; she was either unwilling or unable to leave Cleveland, and a wedding date was never set. By the winter of 1891-92, he was cooling fast. "I mean this to be the last winter I shall spend alone in Midland," he warned her. The words were prophetic, for a year later, on November 16, 1892, he married Grace Anna Ball, another schoolteacher, in Midland.

He had met the Ball family soon after arriving in Midland. G. Willard Ball was proprietor of the town's leading hardware store and had other business interests, and Herbert Dow became a substantial customer. Grace, his daughter, was the schoolmarm at the First Ward School, only a few hundred yards from Herbert Dow's place of business. They also met at the Midland Temperance Society meetings they both frequented in the evenings, and over a period of time an attraction began to build.

Herbert told her about his fiancée back in Cleveland, and they agreed to be friends and to treat each other as brother and sister. Their early notes back and forth (often carried by one of Grace's students who had a bicycle) were addressed "Dear Brother" or "Dear Sister." Sometimes Grace signed herself "The First Ward Schoolmarm." When the engagement with Mabelle was finally broken off, the friendship blossomed into romance. (Herbert never got his diamond ring back, by the way, filling Sarah Dow with indignation). They went for walks in "The Pines," as they called it, a wooded area on Main Street between the First Ward School and the Evens Mill, and that was where, a few years later, they built the Dow family home and Herbert Dow established his gardens.

The "capitalists in Canton" were Joseph A. Linville and Jacob Miller, officials of C. Aultman & Co., makers of the Buckeye mower and reaper. Canton was then a center for the manufacture of farm machinery. Linville and Miller (an uncle of Mrs. Thomas Edison) owned an abandoned saltwell at Canton, and Herbert Dow's analyses told him the highest bromine content of the brines he had collected occurred there and at Midland, Michigan.

In 1888 Linville had asked Dow, whom he met as a student collecting brine samples, to keep him informed of his progress with his bromine process; a year later the four men— Linville, Miller, Smith, and Dow—struck up an agreement whereby the 23-year-old professor would try out his new process at the Canton well site, located at the corner of what is now Hartford and Third Street, N.E.

They called it the Canton Chemical Company, and gave young Herbert the title of superintendent. It was to be an experience almost as bitter as lithium for all of them. Miller and Smith had very little to do with the firm; Dow ran the place single-handedly, working, according to the records, even on Christmas Day and New Year's. The first recorded sale, two carboys of bromine, occurred on December 4, 1889. Earlier that year Dow had inquired of

Edward Mallinckrodt Sr., of the Mallinckrodt Chemical Works in St. Louis, about the price and market for bromine. Mallinckrodt advised him to keep quiet about his new process but said he'd buy Dow's bromine, assuming good quality, at 26 cents a pound. Mallinckrodt became his first customer. But sales by the new firm were rare, and such records as survive show only five actual sales in the half year the firm was in production.[18]

The Canton saltwell, worn out and rusty, was 3,000 feet deep. Herbert Dow complained the entire time he was there of problems with the pump, which was so old that parts were not available. Some days he pumped water all day without getting any brine. There was never enough money to pay the bills. Linville was a tyrant. On one occasion Linville discovered that Dow had purchased 3,800 pounds of iron and put it into "the box" (where it combined with free bromine to form ferric bromide) at a cost of more than $30, double what he felt Dow should have paid for it. He ordered the workmen to take the iron out of the box and informed Dow he had sold "over a ton of it that should never have gone into that box . . . we must quit buying and making bills to be paid, until we get squared up. . . . Experience is a dear school, ain't it?" he asked.

Dow wrote Linville:

> I got the iron you refer to at a time when it was absolutely necessary for me to have some if we kept running and at the time the well was doing the very best. I went to every place in Canton where there was any probability of getting iron suitable for us but found none, and I went to every wire works, wire mill, or sheet iron manufactory there is here but could get nothing. Then I went to the junk dealers and in one of their yards found the 3800 pounds I bought; $14.00 per ton was the best figure I could get from them. If you sell any of the iron out of the box you will have to buy more to replace it if you ever intend to run the brine through very fast.[19]

In February 1890 they concluded that the Canton Chemical Company was a failure and closed down the operation. By April they had agreed to swallow their losses and separate as amicably as possible. The final accounting showed that the Joseph Smith/Herbert Dow share of the loss was $1,728.49, and in 1890 that was a lot of butter and eggs.

After this debacle Herbert Dow returned to Cleveland feeling he had earned a degree from the school of hard knocks. He commented later that the only good thing that came out of the Canton experience was that he proved his bromine process would work. Joseph Smith continued to direct the choir, and stopped investing in Herbert Dow's ventures only temporarily; by 1892 he was again backing his young friend.

Crossing Canton off his list, Dow now began to look at Midland, the other location where bromine was most plentiful in the brine. A notebook entry indicates that in a casual conversation with a fellow traveler on a train he learned there was a disused mill available in Midland with a brinewell adjacent to it—just what he was looking for.[20]

He once again sought financial support. He found it in another family friend, John H. Osborn, a Cleveland sewing machine manufacturer who became one of Dow's closest friends, confidants, and advisers over the next dozen years, though he was roughly the same age as Dow's father. Dow named his second son Osborne (1899-1902) in honor of this friend. (John H. Osborn later was superintendent of the National Carbon Company, one of the two companies that merged to form Union Carbon and Carbide Company)

On August 12, 1890, Dow and Osborn formed the Midland Chemical Company as a partnership to make ferric bromide, based on Dow's electrolytic blowing-out method for extracting bromine from brine. As the joke went later, theirs was an ideal partnership: Dow had chemical genius and Osborn had $3,000. On August 14 Herbert Dow arrived in Midland with $100 in cash and a bank draft for $275. He walked up Main Street from the Ann Street station, and before the day was out had leased as his new plant the gristmill he had heard about.

The next day he set about the backbreaking labor of reshaping the mill and its adjacent small buildings to his needs. Five months later he succeeded in producing bromine by electrolysis there, the first time it had been done commercially. The date was January 4, 1891.

The firm's main product soon became potassium bromide rather than ferric bromide, because that was what customers wanted. The major market for it was in pharmaceuticals, primarily as a sedative and stomach settler. He quickly added a second product, "Red Seal Bromine Purifier," sold in pharmacies, mainly as a disinfectant.

In 1892 the little company was reorganized as a corporation, under the same name but now capitalized at $100,000, although only $10,000 worth of the new stock was actually paid in. Herbert Dow promptly borrowed another $10,000 and built a bigger, better bromine plant at a new location—a 10-acre plot he purchased at the other end of Midland's Main Street on the banks of the Tittabawassee River. The plant at the Evens Mill had already served its purpose, and henceforth would be seen mostly in history books and on stock certificates; its picture still graces the Dow stock certificate today. A replica of it built in Midland houses the Herbert H. Dow Museum.

Brought in as board members at this point in addition to Osborn and Dow, who became general manager of the firm, were Thomas Percy, of Ludington, Michigan, a well-driller; W. B. Remington, of Grand Rapids, a mill owner who was elected the firm's president; Willis W. Cooper, a businessman in St. Joseph, Michigan; and Byron E. Helman, of Cleveland, vice-president of Burrows Brothers, Ohio's leading bookstores. Helman, the most significant new arrival, became the largest single stockholder, and when he was elected treasurer, he began to exercise the prerogatives of chief executive and was soon running the business from his desk in Cleveland.

In addition to financial and technical problems, the new firm also ran head-on into the closed society of the U.S. bromine cartel. In 1890 bromine sales were rigidly controlled by this cartel; the entire market for potassium bromide was in the hands of three firms: Powers & Weightman, and Rosengarten & Sons, both of Philadelphia, and Mallinckrodt in St. Louis. The total output of the bromine-producing firms then in business, clustered in 1890 along the Ohio and West Virginia shores of the Ohio River, was under contract to the National

Bromine Company and its agent, W. R. Shields, who had long-term contracts to sell exclusively to the three firms. These firms in turn had an agreement with the Deutsche Bromkonvention, the German bromine cartel, that they would not sell bromides outside North America, in return for which the Germans agreed not to market bromides in North America. The three firms jointly set the wholesale prices for North American bromide sales, sharing the fruits of their monopoly with Shields and the producers on the Ohio River.[21]

As soon as he offered product for sale Herbert Dow heard from Shields, who offered to buy Dow's output of bromine at the same prices he was paying the Ohio River producers; otherwise, he warned, the bottom might fall out of the price of bromides: "I have given your Mr. Helman a copy of the contract. I am willing to buy your product at same price and terms. . . . I am assured by Mr. H. that he will call a meeting of the company and act in the matter. The matter is in your hands. The party who gets the goods will not continue unless all are in, and again I could not hold them together, with anyone outside."[22]

With its recent success Herbert Dow's electrolytic process had made him the most efficient producer in the bromine business; it permitted extraction of bromine from brine without evaporating out the salt (sodium chloride) first. In the traditional process salt frequently became a burdensome and unprofitable by-product. The Dow process extracted the elemental bromine and combined it with potassium in a continuous process. Because of his technological advantage, which also made it easier to meet the pharmacopeia standards of the time, Dow immediately advocated to Helman that his new company operate independently of the cartel. The Midland Chemical Company could supply the entire U.S. market, he told Helman, at a lower price than the Ohio River producers could meet.

Helman did not believe they could sell their product without the cartel and in consequence were obliged to work within it. In an attempt to make his point, Herbert Dow tried to sell bromine himself. "We went all over the country offering it at about 60% of the recognized market value and could not dispose of it although our Bromide was better than the competing article," Dow wrote later. "The wholesale Drug houses told us they had no demand for KBr (potassium bromide) of an unknown make. . . ."[23]

As sales languished and inventories grew, Helman and Dow reached an impasse. Dow was spending most of his time working the bugs out of the manufacturing process and balking like a mule at working with the cartel. Helman felt that accepting the cartel's terms was the only reasonable decision they could make, the only way to stay in business. Osborn agreed with Helman on this point.

Toward the end of 1893, as the squabble continued, Helman fired Herbert Dow and replaced him with Henry S. Cooper, brother of Willis, who had manufacturing experience but not in chemicals. It was the only time in his life Herbert Dow was fired, although nominally he remained on the payroll, apparently at Osborn's insistence, as the company's secretary. Within a few weeks the Midland Chemical Company was selling its output through the cartel, contracting with Mallinckrodt and Powers & Weightman to sell its entire output to them at a fixed and highly profitable price. As part of this arrangement the Midland company agreed to limit its production to a figure that at first amounted to about half its capacity. The contract put it firmly in the hands of the cartel, and from then until the arrangement lapsed, in 1902, there was a running argument with the cartel over the price the Midland company would receive for its product and how much it was allowed to produce. Nonetheless, the arrangement was a workable deal for the Midland Chemical Company, which in 1894 began to show profits and pay dividends. At first the rate was 1 percent per month, then 2 or 3, and occasionally dividends of 5 percent per month were paid out.

Kicked out of the management, Herbert Dow went back to the laboratory bench and resumed his work on processes to extract the chlorine, magnesium, and other useful elements still remaining in the brine stream after the bromine was removed. Helman was pleased with this; "it is just along such lines of working up by-products that we can make money," he wrote Cooper, "our KBr [potassium bromide] as now having paid for all. . . ." Dow was becoming interested in using the chlorine to make bleach, for which there was a growing market, and was encouraged in this direction by Osborn.

A few months later disaster struck. "In the summer of 1893 we built an electrolytic plant for making electrolytic chlorine," Dow recalled later. "This plant was just completed and the current turned on for about an hour when a tremendous explosion occurred which entirely destroyed the apparatus and the building and injured an adjoining building, although fortunately no persons were injured. A meeting of the board of directors was then called, at which the verdict was reached that they did not care to do any expanding. This decision was literally carried out, and for a number of years thereafter all the earnings were paid as dividends."[24] Herbert Dow did not need to read the tea leaves; within a few months he left the firm he had founded three years before.

The "stand-pat" policy adopted by the Midland Chemical Company against the wishes of Herbert Dow was to stand it in poor stead in the long run; it would be merged into another company established by Dow within a few years. Convinced of the rightness of his feeling that open competition in the marketplace was the way of growth and progress, and that a controlled market would lead inevitably to stagnation, he was to be preoccupied with the cartels that prevailed in the business world of the late nineteenth and early twentieth century over most of the next 20 years. Rather than controlling the price and production of bromides through agreement among the competing firms, he argued that finding new uses for bromine was the thing to do; this would serve both to absorb greater production and to bring the price of bromine down, and would also chart the way to economic growth. For the rest of his life he would be looking for new uses for bromine.

We will return to Herbert Dow's wars with the cartels shortly. In the interim, it being clear to him that the Midland Chemical Company would now never pursue his work on chlorine and bleach, Dow looked about for greener pastures. In the spring of 1895 he decided to go to Navarre, Ohio, a village of only 1,100 a few miles from his Canton venture. He moved his wife and new daughter (their first child, Helen, born in 1894) to a neighboring community, Massillon, and leased a piece of land on the flats between the Tuscarawas River and the Ohio

Canal in Navarre. He bicycled to work daily along the canal's towpath, from downtown Massillon to Navarre, a distance of about five miles.

Recognizing that he would need a new company to develop the manufacture of chlorine, Dow once again went back to Cleveland looking for finances. One of those he visited was his student-day friend James Pardee, who had gone to work in the Cleveland City Engineer's office upon graduation and was now the city's engineer of bridges and viaducts. They had hardly seen each other in the intervening years. "On the afternoon of August 15, 1895, we opened Columbus Street Bridge in Cleveland, just completed under my direction," Pardee recalled. "As it swung into place and the gates opened, there stood Herbert Dow, who had come down from Midland to request me to join with him in forming a new company for developing the manufacture of Chlorine by an electrolytic process he had invented."[25]

Pardee became the largest shareholder of the Dow Process Company and the two resumed a lifelong association. Other backers were the faithful Osborn, Albert W. Smith, and Cady Staley. Dow put up $2,000 of his own funds.

In Navarre, which was more of a research than a production operation, Herbert Dow went to work to develop what was to become the Dow cell. "I am proud of that cell," he said many years later, "more proud of that, I think, than anything else I ever did." This was the chlorine cell that was to be the foundation of The Dow Chemical Company. He evolved it using dissolved salt (purchased from one of the Ohio River bromine producers) rather than brine. He bought carbon electrodes, six inches long, from his friend Osborn's National Carbon Company, at three cents a pound. There were 12 carbons to the pound, he remembered more than 30 years later. The cell was 16 feet long and had 70 anodes and 70 cathodes. "When we tried to patent it they told us it was visionary," he said, "and before a patent would be granted we had to take a little cell to Washington which included one carbon and demonstrate it to them."[26]

During the six or seven months he was actually in operation at Navarre, Herbert Dow became something of a legend among the townspeople, who saw him bicycle in from Massillon along the towpath every day and disappear behind the eight-foot board fence he had built around his plant. It had only one door, and there was a night watchman. He had brought with him two Midland men, Elzie Cote and Asa Bacon, both early associates whom he trusted totally. He hired a few local workmen but allowed almost no visitors inside the gate; in fact, sometimes, according to Navarre lore, he would not even allow his own workers inside. He told those who inquired that he was making embalming fluid, and that usually ended the questioning. For those few who gained admittance, he rigged thermometers and pressure gauges to give false readings, and he mislabeled materials and other devices to conceal what he was actually doing.[27]

The work was not without its dangers. On one occasion he was knocked unconscious by an explosion in the testing room that filled the place with chlorine gas. He was saved from serious injury by a workman who kicked the boards out of a wall and pulled him to safety.

He was also experimenting at Navarre with the production of bleach, or "chloride of lime" (calcium hypochlorite). Within a short time he knew exactly how to manufacture it, using the chlorine from his cell. This was to be his next product and his next company. On November 16, 1895, their third wedding anniversary, his wife gave birth to their second child, whom they named Ruth Alden Dow. By the spring of 1896 he seems to have felt his work in Navarre was completed. He had his cell and he had his new product. He closed up the little plant behind the big fence, packed up his family, and moved both the Dow Process Company and his family back to Midland.

IV.

The Dow Chemical Company was founded by an unusual blend of educators and businessmen. Convened at Cleveland's East End Savings Bank in May 1897, the meetings at which the new corporation was organized attracted faculty members from the nearby campuses of Case and Western Reserve as well as Cleveland businessmen and professionals. At the first of these meetings the partners in the Dow Process Company—Herbert Dow, James Pardee, J. H. Osborn, Albert W. Smith, and President Cady Staley of Case—met with Charles A. Post, secretary and treasurer of the East End Bank, and agreed to reorganize the company, seek a large infusion of new capital and incorporate it as The Dow Chemical Company. The company would make bleach using the new cell and process developed by Herbert Dow at Navarre.

Post, who seems to have known most of the key members of the Cleveland business community personally, issued the invitations to this meeting and took the lead in assembling the businessmen. Albert W. Smith invited his faculty friends. This first meeting, on May 4, was followed by a larger one on May 13 at which the stage was set for formal incorporation on May 18.

At the May 13 meeting, George C. Ashmun, professor of hygiene and preventive medicine at Case, was elected chairman, and Abraham Lincoln Fuller, professor of Greek and dean of Adelbert College at Western Reserve, was elected secretary. Some of the others attending were Edward W. Morley, of Western Reserve, at this time president of the American Academy of Arts and Sciences; Sheldon Q. Kerruish, of Kerruish, Chapman & Kerruish, the attorney who drew up the incorporation papers; Luther A. Roby, a mechanical engineer; Dr. Herbert F. Harvey, a dentist; Oliver F. Emerson, professor of the English language at Western Reserve; Charles W. Wason, an electrical engineer; Albert E. Convers, a tack manufacturer; Frank H. Neff, an authority on electric railways who had left the Case faculty to become president of the Electric Railway Improvement Company; Jesse B. Fay, a patent attorney; Edward I. Leighton, president and general manager of the Cleveland Punch and Shear Works Company; and G. E. Collings, of the Cleveland Woolen Mills.[28]

This group agreed to name the new company The Dow Chemical Company, and called for the first meeting of the stockholders to be held May 18. In the interim the rolls would remain open for persons to subscribe for stock. A committee of five was appointed to draw up the articles of association and bylaws—Dow, Wason, Kerruish, Collings, and Post.

At the meeting of Tuesday, May 18, the new company was formally brought into being. Samuel T. Wellman, a steel man and inventor, was elected chairman of the meeting.[29] The assembled stockholders then elected the company's first 11-man board of directors: Wellman, Post, Convers, Collings, Dow, Fuller, Smith, William L. Baker, Pardee, Osborn, and Staley. Fuller, Smith, and Staley were educators. All except Dow and Baker, a Midland banker, lived in Cleveland.

Convers was elected president of the company; Wellman first vice president, Collings second vice president; and Post, secretary and treasurer. Herbert H. Dow became general manager.

Fortunately a copy of the "general remarks" Herbert Dow addressed to these meetings has survived, discovered in 1992 in an old trunk at the Dow homestead. In 1897 Herbert Dow had sent a copy to his ailing father, then in treatment at a tuberculosis clinic in Thomasville, Georgia, to ask his comments on it, and it turned up in J. Henry Dow's trunk, with other letters the old man had tucked away, almost a century later.

"Over $2,000,000.00 worth of Chloride of Lime or Bleaching Powder is consumed each year in the U.S. but none is now made here on the commercial scale," his presentation, or prospectus, began.[30]

> We propose to manufacture it by a new electrical process, in some respects similar to our bromin process that has proven a phenomenal success.
>
> We are the first persons, so far as any records show, to make use of electricity in any chemical manufacture, on a commercial scale, aside from the electroplating of metals. This is quite a different operation and has been in use for many years.
>
> Bleach is made from Lime and Chlorin. The latter obtained from the chlorid of natural salt brines. Chlorin and Bromin are very similar substances and from a commercial standpoint both are peculiar in that there is no tendency towards a decreasing price. The cause is the same for both substances namely that they were formerly manufactured from by-products of other manufactures but these other manufactures have been superceded by new methods in which appropriate by-products are not made.

After a review of the fluctuation of bleach prices over the 1888-97 decade—prices had been up and down, and recently were down—Dow turned to a description of the plant he proposed to build:

> In the design of plant figured upon it will be possible to run 350 days per year without any one individual working more than six days per week. As planned about the only work necessary on Sunday in order to keep up full capacity will be running the engines and boilers. Engineers and firemen will work 8 hrs. each except on Saturday, Sunday and Monday when 2 shifts only, working 12 hrs. each, will do the work. This enables one third of the engineers and firemen to be off duty on Saturday, another third off on Sunday and the remaining third off on Monday.
>
> Our method of making chlorin is extremely simple and does not require expensive apparatus and has been developed to such an extent that we advocate no change whatever even in

size in the proposed new plant. Only an increased number of decomposers [Dow called his cells "decomposers"] will be required. From experience with this apparatus and the very similar apparatus in use for five years in making bromin we are enabled to give costs quite accurately and even approximate the loss by depreciation.

He estimated the new plant would cost $210,000 and make 23 tons of bleaching powder per 24-hour day on 350 days per year. By far the largest single cost item was a "plant to generate 2,000 electrical horsepower and fireproof building complete," at $80,000. His tabulation of building costs for the plant was followed by another detailing his "estimate of daily cost of operating bleaching plant having a capacity of 23 tons per day."

He estimated the cost of a "decomposer" at $5.90, and that of a frame building made of hemlock barn boards for a series of "decomposers" of 90 horsepower capacity—88 foot long, 32 foot wide, and 12 foot high, with a tar roof, painted outside and whitewashed inside—at $180. His plant would need 60 tons of slack coal per day at 70 cents a ton, but he noted that "three mines of unusually good coal have been opened up within one year in the Saginaw Valley and others are being started."

He estimated he would need a staff of nine salaried persons, including himself as general manager at a salary of $500 per month. There would be two superintendents at $2,000 per year, a chemist at $1,000, a bookkeeper at $700, and four engineers—one at $1,000, two at $700, and one at $500 per year. The total annual salaried payroll would be $14,600.

He would need six firemen at $1.25 for an eight-hour day, 21,000 pounds daily of burnt lime at 26 cents, 250 barrels daily at 23 cents each, two teams of horses, and men to barrel the bleach, wash out tanks, handle the lime, and the like.

When he totaled it all up, he estimated the total annual costs of the new Dow Chemical Company at $122,500, including a depreciation schedule he had drawn up, and he estimated receipts at $281,750, assuming production of 23 tons of bleach daily, 350 days a year, sold at $35 per ton (recently the price had been hovering around $36 or $37). That figured out to an annual profit of $159,250, or, in an ideal year, a whopping 56.5 percent profit margin. He knew, of course, that as a practical matter an ideal year would never occur.

J. H. Osborn, who was wintering in Florida, also received an advance copy of Herbert Dow's presentation and quickly expressed alarm. "I think one half the size is large enough to build first, and it would in my opinion be best to cut even that down as low as possible until we had a part actually running and perfected, before building an immense plant which we might possibly find when finished would not be altogether satisfactory. . . . You young men can't afford to have any failures in a big plant but would be better to secure a reputation for carefulness and safety." Osborn was also concerned about showing insider information to the general public. "I think the matter of estimates, etc., should receive careful study and be worked up as fine as possible before we submit them for consideration by outsiders. I would in any event be careful in submitting them anyway, and not do so to anyone unless there was some certainty of their becoming stockholders."[31]

Osborn was also eager to get on with "uniting the two companies into one," and wanted Dow's views on how this could best be done. He warned Dow he was about to undergo a severe test: "Money men will ask at once who is going to manage this thing, and are they capable of handling so large a concern?"

Dow's estimates and the juicy dividends that had been paid out by the Midland Chemical Company were convincing arguments, and the new company's stock was subscribed in good order in Cleveland and Midland.

The original stockholders of the company included most of those who attended the formation meetings, and a few others as well: Professors Frank M. Comstock and Dayton C. Miller, of Case; Stanford Crapo, general manager of the Pere Marquette railroad in Detroit; Professors Charles Harris, Francis Herrick, and Frank P. Whitman, of Western Reserve; John W. Seaver, Cleveland steel executive; John Martin Vincent, of Johns Hopkins, and George F. Wright, of Oberlin College. Another was George Westinghouse, founder of the Westinghouse Electric Company, with whom Herbert Dow had already worked in various power-generating ventures.

The Midland stockholders, in addition to Baker, included Sherman Olmsted, G. Will Ball, S. C. Carpenter, J. C. Graves, James J. and M. A. Savage, Judge Ray Hart, Dr. Frank Towsley, Henry S. and W. W. Cooper, T. W. Crissey, Ewart Gardiner, Stewart B. Gordon, and Norman Parks.[32]

All told, they provided Herbert Dow with $83,333 in new capital with which to build his new bleach plant. It was more money than he had ever had before. His new company, The Dow Chemical Company, was under way.

Notes

1. The main source of information concerning the J. H. Dow family's sojourn in Belleville is J. H. Dow's correspondence of this period (1863-66) with his fiancée and then wife, Sarah Bunnell. Various details concerning old Belleville and the Dow family's stay there were also supplied by Mrs. Lois Foster of the Hastings County Historical Society, Belleville.

2. See Nick and Helma Mika, *Historic Belleville* (Belleville, Ont.: Mika Publishing Co., 1977).

3. J. H. Dow to Sarah Bunnell, November 8, 1863.

4. J. H. Dow to Sarah Bunnell Dow, September 1, 1864. Stephen White had no discernible relationship to Thomas H. White, founder, in 1866, of the more successful White Sewing Machine Company in Cleveland.

5. H. H. Dow to Rev. Joseph W. Naramore, E. Liverpool, Ohio, March 30, 1929.

6. J. H. Dow's extensive correspondence concerning the turbine is held in the Post Street Archives.

7. The major source for the early history of the Dow family in the U.S. is *History of the Town of Hampton, From its settlement in 1638 to the Autumn of 1892,"* by Joseph Dow, 2 vols. (Salem, Mass.: Salem Press, 1893), reprinted with Peter E. Randall, *Hampton, A Century of Town and Beach, 1888-1988*, vol. 3 and James K. Hunt Jr., *Hampton Vital Records and Genealogy, 1889-1986*, vol. 4 (Hampton, N.H.: Peter E.

Randall, Publisher, 1988). The prime source of Dow family genealogy is *The Book of Dow, Genealogical Memoirs*, Robert Piercy Dow (Rutland, Vt.: Tuttle Co., 1929).

8. "An Historical Address delivered at Hampton N.H. on the 25th of December 1838 in commemoration of the settlement of that town, two hundred years having elapsed since that event," Joseph Dow, Hampton Historical Society, Hampton, N.H.

9. Madaline Castleton, *Seabrook, New Hampshire, A Commemorative Book, 1768-1968* (Seabrook Historical Society, 1968).

10. *History of Hampton*, 2:686.

11. See Herbert Adams, "Neal Dow of Maine, Enemy of Rebels and Rum Lovers," *Civil War Times Illustrated*, March 1986, 46-51.

12. David D. Van Tassel and John J. Grabowski, ed. and comp. "Henry Chisholm," *Encyclopedia of Cleveland History* (Bloomington: Indiana University Press, 1987), 182.

13. See C. H. Cramer, *Case Institute of Technology: A Centennial History, 1880-1980* (Cleveland: Case Western Reserve University, 1980); and C. T. (Deac) Martin, *From School to Institute, an Informal Story of Case* (Cleveland: World Publishing Co., 1967).

14. Material concerning faculty members from Case Archives, Cleveland, and Western Reserve Historical Society, Cleveland.

15. Herbert H. Dow, "Why I Came to Midland," *Midland Sun*, Second Development Edition, November 1926.

16. Numerous references, papers of J. H. Dow. See especially *Directory of Willson Avenue Methodist Episcopal Church, Cleveland, 1894-95*.

17. The Mabelle Ross-Herbert Dow corespondence is preserved, as much of it as has survived, in the papers of J. H. Dow.

18. H. H. Dow to Mallinckrodt Chemical Co., February 17, 1889; E. Mallinckrodt to H. H. Dow, February 22, 1889. The surviving records of the Canton Chemical Company are at the Post Street Archives.

19. J. A. Linville to H. H. Dow, February 6, 1890; H. H. Dow to J. A. Linville, February 10, 1890.

20. H. H. Dow, Notebook #13, May-August, 1890.

21. See Margaret C. Levenstein, *Vertical Restraints in the Bromine Cartel: The Role of Distributors in Facilitating Collusion*, NBER Historical Paper No. 49, National Bureau of Economic Research, Cambridge, Mass., July 1993 (based largely on research in papers of Herbert Dow).

22. W. R. Shields to H. H. Dow, December 9, 1892.

23. H. H. Dow to F. G. Trimble, Manistee, Michigan, September 20, 1905.

24. H. H. Dow, "Why I Came to Midland."

25. James T. Pardee, "Dr. Dow the Man," Perkin Medal Award Dinner, New York City, January 10, 1930.

26. "Stenographic Report of Proceedings at Dinner Given in Honor of Dr. Herbert H. Dow at the Chemists Club," New York City, February 27, 1929.

27. Edward T. Heald, *The Stark County Story* (Canton, Ohio: Stark County Historical Society, 1949); William L. Bennett, *History of Bethlehem Township, Stark County, Ohio*, (Canton, Ohio, Stark County Historical Society, n.d.); and Report by Oscar J. Everson of interview with Miss Elisabeth Stough of Canton, Ohio, January 22, 1948. (Herbert Dow had roomed with the Stoughs, 1889-1990).

28. Minutes, "Preliminary Meeting of persons proposing to become interested in a Company to be formed to operate the Dow Processes," East End Savings Bank, Cleveland, May 13, 1897.

29. "Record of the first Meeting of the Board of Directors of The Dow Chemical Co.," East End Savings Bank, May 18, 1897; and "Minutes of adjourned meeting of the Directors of The Dow Chemical Co.," May 20, 1897.

30. "General Remarks," H. H. Dow, May 1897 (original spelling preserved here).

31. J. H. Osborn, St. Augustine, Fla., to H. H. Dow, January 5, 1897.

32. Midland stockholders listed in *Midland Sun*, June 11, 1897. Those of the 51 original stockholders who kept their holdings of the stock became quite wealthy. Biographical and related information concerning these early stockholders was compiled by Horst von der Goltz, 1948, and is preserved in the W. H. Dow Papers at the Post Street Archives.

PART ONE

THE FOUNDING FATHERS

Dow

January 1898—First sales of bleach by Dow.

1900—Midland Chemical Co. merged into Dow Chemical.

1901—Herbert Dow institutes profit-sharing plan with employees.

1902—Dow establishes a second Midland Chemical Co. to make chloroform when Dow board refuses to add second product.

1903—"Bleach war" breaks out between Dow and the British United Alkali Co.

1904—Dow establishes own sales department with Rupert E. Paris as first sales manager.

1905-8—Long bromine war with German cartel, the Deutsche Bromkonvention, nearly renders Dow kaput.

1910—First sales of lime sulfur (calcium sulfide) and lead arsenate sprays mark Dow's entry to farm chemicals business.

1911—Dow begins string of years with unreduced dividends, which continues today.

1913—Dow announces it will go out of the bleach business; it produces its last bleach in July 1915.

1915—With dyestuffs cut off by the war, Dow initiates crash research program, becomes first to synthesize indigo.

July 20, 1916—Dow succeeds in extracting magnesium metal from brine as first large chunk is poured in a Dow lab.

1918—90 percent of Dow production is for war purposes; Dow is nation's largest producer of phenol; Herbert Dow becomes president and CEO.

WORLD AT LARGE

1898—Pierre and Marie Curie discover radium and polonium.

1900—Max Planck formulates the quantum theory.

First flight of German Count Ferdinand von Zeppelin's zeppelin.

1901—J. P. Morgan organizes the U.S. Steel Corp.

U.S. President McKinley is assassinated and is succeeded by Theodore Roosevelt.

1902—United States acquires perpetual control over the Panama Canal.

1903—Orville and Wilbur Wright successfully fly a powered airplane.

1904—F. S. Kipping discovers silicones.

New York woman is arrested for smoking a cigarette in public.

1905—Albert Einstein formulates his special theory of relativity.

1906—San Francisco earthquake kills 700, causes $400 million in property loss.

1908—First Ford Model "T."

Leo H. Baekeland invents Bakelite.

1909—U.S. explorer Robert E. Peary reaches North Pole.

Charles Kettering develops self-starter for automobiles.

1912—1,513 drown as S.S. *Titanic* sinks on maiden voyage.

June 28, 1914—Archduke Francis Ferdinand, heir to the Austrian throne, and his wife are assassinated, starting off World War I.

1915—Germans sink the *Lusitania*.

1916—Woodrow Wilson is re-elected U.S. president, barely defeating Charles Evans Hughes.

1918—Armistice is signed on November 11.

THE TACK MAN

I.

Once the new company was formally incorporated, Herbert Dow set to work with fervor and method. He spent a week or so in Cleveland working out financial arrangements, signing up more shareholders, opening new bank accounts, ordering stationery, and tending to legal odds and ends with Kerruish, the attorney. Then he headed back to Midland and set about buying a plant site.

On June 2 he wrote Post in Cleveland to announce that "I have just closed the deal for a piece of land between the Midland Chemical Co. and the town, and between the Flint & Pere Marquette track and the river, adjoining the Midland & Northern railroad on one corner. I think it is the most desirable piece of land in this locality. It is within the city limits and has one fairly good house on it." He noted that it was "more desirable and somewhat more expensive than the land I originally contemplated buying, but we think it is well worth the money. When I first came back from Cleveland $4,000 was the best figure I could get, later they dropped to $3,500, and today we bought it for $2,500." W. L. Baker, a Midland banker who had become a director of the new company, advised him closely on the negotiations—Dow had wanted to settle when the price fell to $2,800—and had served him extremely well in this deal, he added.[1]

He had further good news: "The carpenters will go to work at the office building in the morning." At the same time Dow had been talking, both in Cleveland and in Midland, to people he wanted to recruit to work for the new company.

One of his first acts was to move some of the employees of the Dow Process Company over to the new payroll. These included Flora M. Thompson, who quickly became the anchor of his front office staff, which until production plants were built was the entire staff. The men, including Dow, were in and out of the tiny office most of the day, seeing to the plant construction, but Miss Thompson seldom left it. She gave them their mail and messages as they came in, and sent out their mail and messages after they had left. She took letters from Dow, Thomas Griswold Jr., M. B. Johnson, James C. Graves, and others of this pioneering band, typed them up and mailed them, and generally acted as mother hen to a restless brood of creative cockerels. She was the company's first woman employee.

"Flo," as she was known to family and friends, was a Midland girl and a contemporary of Grace Ball Dow; they had been in high school together and were to remain close friends for life. Her father, George C. Thompson, was proprietor of Thompson Mercantile Company, a Main Street emporium that sold everything from wallpaper and cigars to schoolbooks. He was also Sunday School superintendent at St. John's Episcopal Church, where both Flo and Grace were Sunday School teachers. The two girls often double-dated; Flo's boyfriend was John C. (Jack) Stahl, a young builder and contractor who built several houses in downtown Midland and then after a while went "out West to seek his fortune." Flo heard from him regularly, but clearly gainful employment was in order for her.[2]

She had a solid background in office skills and management from her experience at Thompson Mercantile, and fit easily into the Dow office. When D. W. Chase, a young bookkeeper, left she added his work to her own, and took on more when another young man in the office, A. R. Wilbur, also left. She worked closely with young Earl W. Bennett, office boy (later a Dow board chairman), part of whose job was to run down to the post office to pick up the mail. By the end of the year 1900 she felt she was doing very well, and she wrote a letter to Herbert Dow pointing out that "I have never yet received a raise in salary" and "it seems to me as though I am entitled to a raise as much as Mr. Bennett." She added: "I assure you to the extent of my ability I will endeavor to give good service, as I have always tried to do in the past."[3]

Eight years passed, and finally in the fall of 1905 she heard from a jubilant Jack that he had made his fortune out West. He proposed that she come out to Los Angeles at once and marry him, as they had been planning for so many years. Flo left almost immediately. Her place as Herbert Dow's secretary was shortly taken over by a reserved, efficient young lady named Clara Turner, always known as "Miss Turner"; she remained Herbert Dow's secretary for virtually the remainder of his career, and in the 1920s took over most of his financial and family accounts.

The Stahls, meanwhile, did well and lived well as building contractors in booming southern California; their next-door neighbor for many years was the celebrated cowboy movie star Tom Mix. Dorothy Dow Arbury remembered visiting the Stahls with her mother and having her picture taken aboard Tom Mix's famous horse, Tony; so did Robert H. Ward, a longtime Dow employee, Flo's nephew.[4]

The Stahls lost everything during the Great Depression; in that time even the movie stars stopped building, and Tinseltown lost its glitter. Jack languished and died. Grace Dow urged Flo to come back to Midland and move in with her when this happened; Herbert by then had also died. Flo did return to Midland but lived with her own family in her declining years, and remained one of Mrs. Dow's closest friends. She died in 1944.

The first employee on the hourly rolls was Frank Publow, "Mr. Publow" as he was known to the Dow children, a laborer hired to help set up the chlorine cells. Publow, like almost all the men who worked in the cell department, chewed tobacco, which the men believed absorbed the stray chlorine gas in the cell room. Margaret Dow Towsley remembered him well:

> He was, I think, the first man in the company to work out in the plant. I remember they said that when Publow was getting old, they went to Dad and said, 'What are we going to do with Publow? He can't do much any more'; Dad told them they could locate him at the gate where the men left, and tell him his job was to check on people to be sure only people that really belonged there were being admitted. So Publow worked there for a long time. While Mr. Bennett was the first office boy and eventually took over the Treasurer's job, Mr. Publow started the work force in the company. Everybody got a kick out of him. When Willard (Dow) went down there to work, Mr. Publow met him at the gate and said, "First I have your dad for a boss, and now here you come to tell me what to do next."[5]

The old-timers who had worked with Herbert Dow when he first came to Midland in 1890—men like Elzie Cote and the Burows brothers, Julius and Albert, and J. J. (Jake) Shattuck—stayed on with the Midland Chemical Company, which continued to make bromine.

Badge No. 1 in the new company was held by M. B. Johnson, the first general superintendent.[6] Johnson had been in the hardware, plumbing, and house contracting business for many years for one of Cleveland's largest hardware firms, Milton Morton. Thomas Griswold Jr. said of Johnson that he was "the best foreman and superintendent" he had ever known. "He knew a day's work; he knew workmanship; he knew what tools should be used and how . . . he was personally skilled in so many construction arts that he never had to ask a man to do a job which he could not do better."[7] Dow had invited M.B. to join him in 1895 at the Canton plant, but Johnson was in the midst of building a new house for his own family in Cleveland at the time and had turned him down.

In May 1897, when Dow sought out his old friend again and told him he wanted him to come to Midland to be his superintendent, M.B. drove a hard bargain. He wrote "Friend Herbert," stating his terms: a salary of $1,800 per year, a guarantee there would be no reduction in this salary the first five years, and a commitment from Herbert to furnish employment to his two sons at $25 and $40 per month, respectively. Dow responded that the salary was acceptable but he had only a one-year contract himself and was thus in no position to give five-year guarantees. He proposed instead that he would help M.B. become a stockholder in the company, something a lot of people were eager to do, he pointed out. He would make no commitment about the two sons either; one of the worst things you could do for a young man was to guarantee him a job no matter how well or poorly he might do it, he said.[8] By June 2 they had reached agreement, essentially on Dow's terms, and on June 5 M.B. sent a telegram from Cleveland saying he would "arrive in Midland next Monday."

Johnson arrived in the midst of frantic activity by the little group in Midland. J. H. Osborn was there from Cleveland, working with Dow on the specifications of the power plant he wanted, its location and details; the carpenters were in the midst of building the new offices and the place swarmed with painters, masons, and laborers; Griswold was trying to lay out the exact plot of the property they had just purchased, "probably a trifle under 25 acres although the County Surveyor made it between 28 and 29 acres," Dow wrote; the new checkbook arrived from Cleveland, and Dow was able to make out Dow Chemical Company checks for the first time; and Dow was trying to prepare the first weekly report that the management in Cleveland had requested of him on costs and production.[9]

With two grown sons, M.B. was by a goodly margin the oldest man in the new company; all the others were younger than Herbert Dow, then 31. Within a couple of weeks M.B. was hiring a lead, zinc, and piping specialist from Cleveland, J. C. Parker, and making arrangements for him to bring lead-burning apparatus with him from Cleveland. Johnson "built the first lead burning outfit at Dow and practiced lead burning evenings until he was able to instruct a $1.50-a-day man to do work in lead burning which had been previously contracted for at $14.00 per day plus living expenses. He was greatly loved by all his associates. He was a most competent buyer and taught us the art of buying. One of his proverbs ran 'Buy in a hurry and pay through the nose,'" Griswold said.[10]

Johnson wrote to Cleveland that the best way to get to Midland in 1897 was "by boat from Cleveland to Detroit, and then take the Flint & Pere Marquette railroad. The train leaves Detroit about 1:20 and arrives here (at Midland) at 5:30 P.M. The boat fare is 50 cents and from Detroit to here by rail costs $3.50 or $3.60."[11] The alternative was to take a Lake Shore & Michigan Southern train from Cleveland to Toledo and switch to the Flint & Pere Marquette to Plymouth. Another F & PM train ran to Saginaw, and a fourth to Midland.

The new plant made its first bleach at the end of November and its first commercial shipment—the first sale by The Dow Chemical Company—in January 1898. Johnson spent much frustrating time negotiating railroad freight rates for these first shipments, most of them less-than-carload, to various places in the United States, including all the way to the West Coast. One of the most difficult places to ship to turned out to be a relatively close customer, the Bardeen Paper Company at Otsego, Michigan. There did not seem to be any way to get a shipment of bleach by rail to Otsego on time, and it was a constant headache. Herbert Dow had negotiated a deal with the railroads, when they were eager to acquire business out of Midland, Michigan, that all rail shipments would be made from Midland by the Saginaw rates; the railroads kept forgetting this, and Johnson had constantly to remind them of it.[12]

Telephone service was atrocious, and this too fell to Johnson to improve. In 1898 there were only 19 telephones in Midland, and very often the town's central exchange would not answer for hours on end. Johnson finally threatened that if the service did not get better Dow would pull out its telephone and rely on the post and telegraph. "If Dow pulls out there are five or six other subscribers that will also pull out," he predicted.[13] The service gradually got better. In addition to his other duties, Johnson carried on correspondence with customers as to shipping dates and quantities, and served as the customer complaint department. His duties steadily expanded, and by the end of the century M. B. Johnson was the overall production and construction chief for the company, taking care of matters as diverse as job applicants, dealings with building contractors, and purchasing.

In the fall of 1900, just as he was hitting his stride and becoming Herbert Dow's right-hand man, Johnson began to feel tired and ill, suffering from a lingering sore throat and a constant cough; working around the chlorine cells seemed to aggravate his condition. Herbert Dow told him to go find some sunshine and take a rest, and on November 12, 1900, Johnson left for Albuquerque, New Mexico, on a leave of absence. It was the twilight of his career. He stayed in Albuquerque a few months, visited a sister in Sterling, Kansas, and proceeded leisurely onward to Cleveland, from whence he corresponded with Dow for a few years, usually saying that he "felt better but still tired," and speaking fondly of the busy days he had known in Midland.[14] Herbert Dow continued his salary for two full years, for which Johnson was extremely grateful, but by 1903 he was lapsing into silence, and then was heard from no more.

Not all of Dow's recruits were winners. A. R. Wilbur, for example, was a close friend and protégé of Post, at whose offices in Cleveland the Dow board meetings were held. He had had experience at Standard Oil Company but had been laid off. Post recommended him glowingly to Dow—"he'll do anything you need done," Post said—and not wishing to offend Post, who had done a great deal and not asked for much, Dow reluctantly asked him to send Wilbur to Midland.[15]

He put him to work in the front office to see what he could do. Dow seems to have been disenchanted with Wilbur from the beginning, but having given his word to Post he tried to keep it. Within a few months Post was writing to Dow, saying: "I only urged you to take him [Wilbur] as I thought he would be a valuable man, after his experience, and because I was extremely anxious to help him. I want you to do nothing that is not for the best interests of the Co. and if he does not earn a better wage do not give it [to] him. . . . Pardon this which is written only in the hope of helping a boyhood friend who has I know many faults and has seen better days."[16] Herbert Dow kept Wilbur on for two more years, but in July 1899, after talking to his old friend Osborn, he fired the man—the first recorded firing of an employee in the Dow Company's history. Post's reaction to this event was mild: a note saying, "I'm sorry you had to let him go."[17]

The first major crisis in the new company had already begun before it made its first sale. It took the form of small explosions, and sometimes big ones, that occurred in the chlorine cells, or "decomposers" as they were then called. These explosions sent chlorine gas rolling through the cell buildings, forcing time-consuming shutdowns, and were so common that reaching full production was impossible. The plant got up to about half its capacity but almost never exceeded that. Dow thought he had solved this problem in Canton, but it turned out otherwise.

As production limped along, the plant was running in the red, and the directors in Cleveland became increasingly alarmed. Herbert Dow reassured them at the board meeting each month that all was well, and adopted an attitude of unwavering optimism. He asked Tom Griswold and Jim Graves (the first chemist he had hired, who had now switched over from Midland Chemical to Dow) to spend their full time on the problem until it was solved, and spent every moment he could spare on it himself; all three were aware that if the problem could not be solved, and solved soon, the new company was unlikely to survive; its cash reserves were dwindling fast.

In November 1897 Griswold married Helen Dow, Herbert Dow's sister, and the young couple moved into the Mary Patrick house, the "fairly good house" on the plant site. Griswold and Graves went to work on the problem around the clock. Graves worked from noon to midnight, and at midnight came to the Patrick house to meet with Griswold. Helen Dow Griswold fixed them a midnight meal, and over the food Graves would tell Griswold what had happened on his shift. At noon the next day the two would meet again at the same place, and Griswold would tell Graves what had happened on the midnight shift.[18]

It was Griswold who eventually came up with the answer; he went down to the drugstore one day and bought some paraffin, the kind used by housewives for canning. He dipped the carbon electrodes in melted paraffin, put them back in the cells, and the explosions stopped. He and his colleagues had surmised some time before that hydrogen gas was seeping through the electrodes to the chlorine gas and forming an explosive mixture. They also found that the pine boards forming the cell structure had become spongy, permitting the passage of electricity. It was relatively easy to replace them, and the problem began to ease. Production soon climbed to the level Dow had planned, and with this the company itself climbed into the black.

Griswold, the hero of this episode, had badge no. 2 in the company, and he was to make many other major contributions to the company's development. Dow had spotted him as a bright student at Case (with the help of Albert W. Smith, his chief "spotter") and had offered him a job at his Massillon plant in the winter of 1895-96. Griswold, then a senior, had turned him down in favor of completing his degree, and after graduation had gone to work for the Brown Hoisting and Conveying Company of Cleveland, running a "rapid coal handling plant" for Brown Hoist on Whiskey Island. On April 20, 1897, he wrote Dow, now the brother of his fiancée, asking about his plans for establishing the new company. He said he was tired of "coming home from work at from 8 P.M. to 5 A.M. looking like a coal heaver and completely exhausted . . . I am looking for a change, the sooner the better." He suggested that what he would really like to do was "the laying out and designing of the new plant."[19] A month later Griswold was in Midland, doing just that.

Griswold, a civil engineer by training, designed most of the early buildings, and laid out water lines, electric lines, gas lines, streets, sewers and drains, and all the other substructure of the plant. He soon came to be called the "chief engineer," and remained in that position for 25 years. His relationship with Herbert Dow was often stormy and had many of the aspects of a love-hate dichotomy, especially as the two grew older.

Griswold was a strong-minded man, and was not above using his relationship with the boss to work his will with employees in the plant and labs; from time to time, Herbert Dow had to sit on him. He had occasional serious bouts of illness, sometimes for months at a time, and indeed Griswold enjoyed poor health for 96 years; at that age he was the oldest graduate of Case and the oldest retiree from Dow Chemical.

Griswold went back to Cleveland for a holiday visit at the end of 1905, and while he was there he visited some of the auto dealerships and garages that were springing up around town, looking at the new model automobiles. At one of them he found a garageman offering his customers gallon jugs of calcium chloride, for laying dust and melting ice, at 75 cents a gallon. He wrote Herbert Dow in great excitement about this discovery, recognizing immediately that here was a product that could readily be made from the Midland brine stream. Each gallon contained four pounds of calcium chloride, he wrote. He included rough sketches of "crystallizing pans" and other ideas for manufacturing calcium chloride in Midland.[20] Herbert Dow was also immediately interested, and that was the beginning of one of the company's all-time top products, one in which it still exercises world leadership today under the trademarks "Dowflake" and "Peladow."

A year later Griswold was designing a carbon bisulphide plant, another new product he proposed. T.G., as he was called, earned 29 patents during his long career in a wide variety of fields; amazingly, six of them were awarded in the 1940s, when he was past 70—during World War II he worked on improvements to the magnesium cells being installed in Texas to extract that metal from seawater—and the last in 1949, when he was nearing 79.[21] Undoubtedly the most important of them all, though, was the chlorine-caustic electrolytic cell known as the DG (Dow-Griswold) cell, patented in 1911; it incorporated the bipolar cell design, a characteristic of Dow cells even today.

In 1902 Griswold refused to sign a standard form releasing his inventions in the line of work to the company, and Herbert Dow told him he would not get a raise in pay until he did. This dispute apparently was at the root of Griswold's applying for a job at the National Carbon Company in Cleveland in 1909. Harvey E. Hackenberg, an official of NCC and also a Dow board member, immediately informed Herbert Dow of this confidentially, saying he thought things "had blown over," and that T.G. was staying at Dow. Herbert Dow wrote Hackenberg that

> We could get along without Mr. Griswold without any great inconvenience if the policy of this company is to always remain the same size it is now . . . in fact, if this were the policy we could probably save some money by cutting off his salary. If, however, the policy of the Dow Company is to be at all progressive in the future, it will be impossible for us to replace Mr. Griswold at any price, as he is now so familiar with our work and our successes and failures that he is able to profit by the results of the past to an extent that makes him a very valuable man to the company. . . . Personally I should regret it very much if Mr. Griswold should leave us, and yet I believe that he would very shortly be earning a much larger salary with The National Carbon Company than he is earning here, and I would not like to be the means of preventing his securing the maximum prosperity that his talents warrant.[22]

A few days later Hackenberg sent a private note to Dow: "Upon my arrival at the Union depot Wednesday morning I met Mr. Griswold and told him frankly that I did not think it to his advantage to take the position at the National Carbon Company and advised him to remain where he is. In any event, the position at the National has now been filled."[23]

In 1924 Griswold suffered what he calls in his autobiography a "nervous breakdown." His wife took him to Henry Ford Hospital in Detroit for what became an extended stay. "He is certainly very ill and tires oh so quickly of anything," Vera Griswold wrote Dow. "He doesn't seem to have the strength to even talk only such a little and the nurse and I visit with him only when we feel he is thinking of himself too much and needs the conversation."[24] Dow wrote her: "I think it would be well to tell Tom that we are not expecting him back here for a year, but expect to keep his name on the payroll, the same as in previous years."[25]

It was about 18 months before T.G. returned to work. George A. Yocum, acting chief engineer in his absence, became chief engineer and Griswold became "consulting engineer" at no change in salary.

Looking about for problems to solve, Griswold found that the company's patent attorneys, Fay, Oberlin, & Fay of Cleveland, were about a year behind in filing patent applications for Dow. John F. Oberlin, partner in charge of the Dow work, refused to move to Midland but suggested to Griswold the organization of an in-house patent department. T.G. had long been the liaison between the company and its patent house. He now promptly organized the Dow patent department, working at first through Fay, Oberlin, & Fay because there was no licensed patent attorney at Dow. To simplify things, Griswold decided to become a licensed patent attorney himself, and the Dow patent department adopted the name Griswold & Burdick, a title necessary for work with the U.S. Patent Office. Edward C. Burdick, Griswold's assistant, succeeded him as patent chief when Griswold again fell ill in 1936. Griswold looked about the Dow staff for patent attorneys, preferring to make patent attorneys out of scientists rather than the reverse. One such he found was William M. Yates, a young chemist who was working for Dr. E. C. Britton in the Organic Research Lab in 1936. Griswold described what happened in his autobiography: "I placed a pad of paper in front of him and said, 'Without notes or references, please write me a few hundred words about something you know, that is, about some one subject.' He began to write and completed several pages. I picked them up and read a beautifully clear description of a research problem with which he had been engaged. I said, 'Yates, you're hired, you can put the inventor's ideas into words.'" Yates later succeeded Burdick as head of the department.[26]

His illness of 1936 forced Griswold to retire from the company, but again he made a remarkable recovery and soon was a consulting engineer once more. He continued some of his activities until he died in 1967. He had been a founding director of the Chemical Bank & Trust Company in Midland in 1916, and continued to serve on its board until 1965; he resigned on his 95th birthday.

In a 1902 photo of the proud crew of Dow's new power plant, assembled in front of the Corliss engine of which Herbert Dow was so fond, there stands a short, square black man, Dow's first black employee. His name was Frederick (Freddie) Highgate, and he was one of the most unusual persons ever to work for the company. His brother Oliver, or Ollie, was a Main Street barber, and their sister Ada, a hairdresser, kept house for Ollie and was the organist at the Episcopal church.

Freddie did not stay long at Dow. He took some chemistry courses but decided he wasn't cut out to be a chemist, and opened up a mail-order business selling shrubbery to the people of Midland. It is said that most of the shrubs, bushes, and trees planted in the town in that era were provided and sold by Freddie Highgate. He had only one sales pitch: "Plant a shrub or a tree and it will be a joy forever."

Freddie gained renown in the town through his philanthropy, most of which went to the First Ward, the poorer section of town alongside the Dow fence line, largely settled by Irish immigrants and known as "Paddy Hollow." Judge Henry Hart, who researched Freddie's story, said Freddie "knew every poor widow and unfortunate family in the Ward, and when the need was acute he brought food, fuel, and paid their debts, as anonymously as possible." Frank Thompson, of Thompson Mercantile, said: "If Freddie saw a poor child on the street without mittens, he went into a store and bought them for him. If he saw or heard of an old person who was ill, he would call and speak a few words of encouragement and the next day a bouquet would be sent. And when he made his purchases he would never tell where the gifts were to go."

Alden Dow remembered Freddie Highgate too: "It seems like he was always walking someplace and, as I remember, he had a peculiar kind of walk, much like Groucho Marx. He leaned forward as if walking against the wind. Wherever he was going, his heart got there before the rest of him did."

Norris Coalwell, a Dow superintendent, remembered being in the local coal yard at closing time one winter day when Freddie came in and bought a 20-cent bag of coal. He threw it over his shoulder and headed out into the snow, to keep some unfortunate warm for the weekend.

Practically everyone who lived in Midland in those years had a story, or several, of Freddie Highgate's deeds. As Judge Hart put it, "To many Midlanders, years ago, Santa Claus was a black man."

When Freddie died, on December 4, 1937, the city council declared a day of municipal mourning. Five white clergymen of various faiths delivered eulogies at his funeral. Persons who remember still tend Freddie's grave in Midland Cemetery, 60 years later.[27]

II.

Herbert H. Dow was the superstar of the new Dow Chemical Company, and Albert E. Convers, president of the company, knew it, but Convers was Herbert Dow's boss, and there was never any question about that, either. Both men liked it that way, although Dow occasionally chafed about Convers's overly close supervision, and their teamwork became steadily more mutually reinforcing over the 33 years they worked together.

THE CHLOROFORM TRUST

As told to succeeding generations of Case chemistry students, the story of how Albert W. Smith invented a new process for making chloroform became a legend: in 1901, the story went, Professor Smith walked into a chemistry lab where students were experimenting with carbon tetrachloride, sniffed the air, and asked, "Who's working with chloroform?" When no one admitted it, he walked to a steel sink, sniffed again, and turning to the lab assistant said: "In a distillation flask, boil carbon tetrachloride and water in the presence of steel shavings for two hours; then separate the chlorinated hydrocarbons from the water, dry, and distill." When he returned he was informed that the method produced a good yield of chloroform.[1]

From this beginning, Smith and another young Case professor, William O. Quayle, set to work devising a process for making a lower-cost chloroform not dependent on high-cost acetone as a raw material. It was also, incidentally, one of the first large-scale syntheses of an organic compound in the United States. Smith, a member of the Dow board of directors, offered the process to his friend Herbert Dow, and Dow quickly decided to build a chloroform plant. He invited Quayle to move to Midland to get it started.

In 1902, as the battle of the bleach was beginning, the infant Dow Chemical Company was so shaky and the chloroform venture so difficult and risky that after much discussion Herbert Dow decided to establish a separate company for it. "Everybody involved thought it had a chance to be a complete failure, and they did not want to annoy the Cleveland directors by adding chloroform to all their other troubles," said Dr. W. R. Veazey, a Case faculty member who also later transferred to the company.[2] The new company was called the Midland Chemical Company, like Herbert Dow's first Midland venture; and to distinguish the two, the chloroform firm (which had a separate existence from 1902 to 1914) is usually called "Midland Chemical Company II." Albert W. Smith, inventor of the process it used, was its chairman.

Quayle seems never to have been comfortable as a production manager. He came to the plant in a dark blue pin-striped suit, high white collar, flowering tie, black patent-leather shoes, and a bowler hat, an unheard-of sight in the rough-and-tumble of the early Midland plant. Tom Griswold recalled that "he would sit in the office but seldom if ever got into the plant itself." From the beginning the plant had troubles: quality problems—chloroform had to be absolutely pure for use as an anaesthetic; an impurity was extremely dangerous and could cause death—and troubles in packaging the product in bottles that tended to break. There were also severe production problems: the plant seemed to produce only about 20 percent of the expected yield. Finally, there were problems with the chloroform trust, called the "Chlorine Products Company," which controlled the market for the product.

The chloroform trust was jointly controlled by three firms: the Roessler & Hasslacher Company, the Albany Chemical Company, and the Charles Pfizer Company. It operated on the same principles as the other cartels of its day. Sales and distribution of chloroform was to be a problem for years, as the trust by turns bullied and cajoled this intruder into its market. Unlike the bleach and bromine combines, however, the chloroform trust never quite declared open war.

To meet this problem Herbert Dow turned to his old friend Adolph Rosengarten in Philadelphia, in whom he had complete confidence, and Rosengarten & Sons became the exclusive distributor for MCC II chloroform. Later, when Dow developed its own sales staff, chloroform was marketed directly by the Dow Company, and in 1914 MCC II was merged into the Dow Company.

In 1908 Quayle told Dow he was leaving; he had not expected to stay in Midland six years, the plant was still a marginal proposition at best, and his wife did not like the town.[3] Dow seems to have been relieved. He immediately asked E. O. Barstow to take over the chloroform operation and see if he could straighten it out. Barstow agreed to do so if the Dow Company would take care of all the correspondence, bookkeeping, and paperwork and leave him free to run the plant, and that was the arrangement.

Barstow started with some detective work to find out why so much chloroform was being lost. He went around the plant and sniffed at pipe joints, and as soon as he smelled chloroform he called in the plumber shop and ordered the pipe repaired. He quickly discovered that he could smell the chloroform only a short time before his nose "wore out," so he got a pipe blowtorch and went around applying it to pipe joints; when he saw a peculiar blue color it meant chloroform was leaking. He soon discovered that the plant was just one vast leak. Barstow then had the whole piping system ripped out and put in an entirely new system with tight joints. Within three weeks after he had taken over the plant it was operating in the black. Barstow ran it successfully for years.[4]

By 1914 it was becoming cumbersome and time-consuming to keep separate books, hold separate meetings, and maintain separate personnel groups for MCC II, and it was quietly folded into the Dow Company.

1. See Robert S. Karpiuk, Dow Research Pioneers, 1888-1949 (Midland, Mich: Pendell Publishing Co., 1981), 24.

2. W. R. Veazey to H. Hatton, June 12, 1950; T. Griswold Jr. to H. Hatton, July 6, 1949.

3. Quayle later joined the Chemical Department of E. I. du Pont de Nemours & Co. in Wilmington. There he died of a heart attack in October 1919.

4. T. Griswold Jr. to H. Hatton, July 6, 1949.

As they looked around the room at the East End Savings Bank that day in May 1897 when they incorporated the company, the Cleveland college and business men who formed the firm had serious misgivings about the mustachioed 31-year-old youngster who had presented such a masterly picture of what he proposed to do. This was his fourth try at launching a company. He had been fired once and had failed twice; fortunately one of the three firms he had founded was making money in 1897, or he might not have been given another chance. Brilliant as he was, they decided the company needed an older, more experienced hand at the helm, and the hand they chose was Albert E. Convers, a man with a solid business reputation and one of the first to subscribe for stock.

Convers, "the tack man," then 39, had ended his formal education after two years of high school to begin a lengthy apprenticeship in his grandfather's carpet tack factory, the Albert Field Tackworks, in Taunton, Massachusetts. Grandfather did him no favors; the boy started at the bottom and learned every phase of tack-making, even how to make tack-making machinery. Then Grandfather switched him to the front office and he learned how to sell tacks and run the business. When he was 23 the old man took him into the firm and it became Caswell, Convers & Company, manufacturers of tacks and fine nails. Grandfather, Elijah S. Caswell, died two years later at age 74, and the young man was left to run the business alone.[28]

Tack-making was a rough, tough, competitive, mass production business in the era after the U.S. Civil War. The tacks weighed as little as 20,000 to the pound, and some of Convers's customers used as many as 50 tons every two or three months. They were used for shoe-making (8 or 10 nails to fix a heel), curtain shades, basket-making, and carpets. Young Convers soon figured out that the faster you made tacks, the more profit you would make.

He ran the tack-making machinery faster and faster until it broke down, then reshaped and strengthened whatever part had broken, and did it again. Before long, his machines ran faster and broke down less often than those of any of his competitors.[29]

In 1887 Convers followed the trend of the times and moved westward. He packed his tack-making machines in a freight car and took them to Cleveland, leaving his widowed mother and family in Taunton but taking with him his closest associates, Charles K. Hill and Charles C. Paine. The company was rechristened the H.C. Tack Company H.C. stood for "Honest Count," the company's motto; Convers prided himself on honest dealings. He traveled from one end of the country to the other selling tacks. His production climbed to 17 tons a day and he was soon one of the most prominent tack men in the nation.

He and his partner had just completed a new tack plant in Cleveland when the recession of 1893 set in. Business went to pieces and they began to have trouble paying their bills. Paine, Convers's partner, panicked one day, convinced that bankruptcy and total ruin were just around the bend, and stormed into Convers's office to tell him so. Convers calmly advised him to take a vacation and insisted on his leaving on one at once. While he was away Convers met with the creditors, reassured them of the soundness of the enterprise, and paid off the bills as rapidly as he could; by the time Paine returned the firm was on the rebound. Convers was not one to cave in under pressure.

By 1897, when The Dow Company was formed, he had a reputation as an unusually savvy and successful businessman. As Herbert Dow's overseer, representing the board of directors and the investors, Convers became an unusual but in many ways ideal foil for the aggressive young chemist in Midland—not a chemist, not a college-educated man, not a soaring ego, just a level-headed, no-nonsense businessman.

Herbert Dow, general manager, ran the business on the ground in Midland and Convers, president, presided over the board of directors in Cleveland, and once a month Dow traveled to Cleveland to meet with the board.[30] In these circumstances much of their business was done by correspondence, and in the succeeding years Dow wrote Convers several times a week, sometimes two or three times a day, reporting on events, asking his advice, answering his questions, explaining why he had done—or not done—this or that. When Dow had critical decisions to make that couldn't wait for a board meeting, Convers would consult with the directors in Cleveland and relay their recommendations back to Dow. Within a few years this practice evolved into what became known as "the executive committee"—Convers, Dow, Hackenberg, Collings, and A. W. Smith—empowered to act between board meetings.[31]

In October 1897, Convers made his first trip to Midland to see the new plant being built and wrote his first formal report to the board of directors. He was accompanied on this trip by Post, the treasurer, the Cleveland banker who had hosted the first meeting of the corporation.

"Your Committee," as they styled themselves in this report,

> takes great pleasure in stating that it is believed that the money you have subscribed has been very economically expended, and that there seems to have been a disposition throughout to accomplish as much as could possibly be done with the least expenditure possible. Your Committee wishes to add further that it is believed that the method of construction of the plant of The Dow Chemical Company embodies the right principle where land is cheap enough to warrant it, which is to have the apparatus set on the ground, using the building merely as a covering to protect the apparatus from the weather. This admits of a construction much cheaper than the building of more than one story would be, and also seems to a certain extent to mitigate damage in case of fire.[32]

The company was not yet six months old and some of its basic principles were already being enunciated—economy in expenditure, economy in plant construction. Later, looking back, Herbert Dow was to recall that "when the Dow Chemical Company was organized I made the remark to Mr. Convers that I did not think we needed much of an office. He immediately complimented me on this viewpoint, and I think nobody doubts Mr. Convers's ability as a manufacturer. He won out manufacturing tacks, which was an old competitive line and therefore an especially hard one for a man to make a fortune out of." A Spartan style of office became a Dow hallmark.[33]

Dow used Convers as a sounding board whenever he had questions for which he did not have an answer himself. When he heard that the Mallinckrodt Company was buying bromine from other sources in spite of a contract by which Dow was to provide all of their requirements, he asked Convers what he ought to do about it. Convers advised that he follow "my general practice" of "letting the culprit hang himself"—let him do it until you have indisputable evidence of wrongdoing. Dow followed the advice and nothing more came of it.

Some years later, when Dow began experimenting with fruit tree sprays in his own orchard, and made them a "showroom" for the company's spray materials, he asked Convers whether the extra expense involved should not be borne by the company. Convers replied that Dow had full authority to charge any extra expense to the company but recommended he discuss the matter informally at the next board meeting to avoid any misunderstanding. Again Dow followed Convers's advice, and again it worked.

Some of the problems he took up with Convers were highly sensitive. About 1902, Herbert Dow asked his key employees to sign a standard agreement assigning "such inventions as they may bring out in the course of their work" to the company. All of them readily signed this agreement except two holdouts—Thomas Griswold Jr., Herbert Dow's own brother-in-law, and E. O. Barstow, his "No. 1 chemist." An angry Dow, as noted previously, told Griswold he wouldn't get a raise in pay until he signed and Griswold, retorting that he preferred it that way, actually went for 10 years without signing and without a pay raise. The problem drifted on and finally came to a head about 1911 when Barstow and Griswold rented a room in town, hired an engineer, and began developing, outside of hours, an apparatus they had worked out for extracting oils and grease by use of carbon tetrachloride. At this point Herbert Dow became genuinely alarmed and asked Convers's counsel in a long, anguished letter.

Convers agreed this was a matter of crucial importance to the company and proposed that the board of directors discuss it fully at their next meeting, devoting the whole meeting to it if necessary. If that were not enough, a special meeting of the board should be called. The upshot of a lengthy discussion was that Griswold and Barstow were told they could either sign the company's agreement on inventions or seek other employment. The two men prepared a counterproposal that called for them to be retained at a salary of $4,500 per year (Griswold's salary since 1902 had been $2,500) and given time to file patents on their carbon tetrachloride extraction process, which they would be considered to have developed on their own time. After some editing (Convers spotted a few ambiguities in the language of their proposal) this became the basis of a settlement.[34] Herbert Dow was relieved. He had been afraid he was about to lose two of his best men.

Herbert Dow's children remembered Convers as a frequent visitor at their house, and one for whom they had great respect. Margaret Dow Towsley said, "I liked him a great deal. He was a dignified man, but a very pleasant one as well." Dorothy Dow Arbury remembered him as "the kind of man that you just liked without even knowing him. I always looked up to him—boy, he was wonderful!"[35]

In March 1916, Convers's wife, Fannie Crane Convers, died—he had married her shortly after coming to Cleveland—and Convers accompanied the body back East to Taunton for burial there. The board of directors meeting was postponed in deference to his bereavement, and Convers wrote a note of appreciation to the directors, saying it gave him what he needed, "something else to think about." The couple had no children, and Convers seems to have been a lonely man after this event. Sometime after the funeral he moved to Brooklyn, New York, where he knew a number of bankers and financial men.

The move to Brooklyn carried Convers away from his daily involvement with Herbert Dow and Dow Chemical, and after a year or so of trying to make it work he proposed that Herbert Dow take over the presidency. His fellow directors were not about to let him off so easily; they promptly created a new position for him, chairman of the board, and so it was that Convers became both the first president and first chairman of the company. From 1918 to his death in 1935, he remained the presiding officer at the monthly board meetings. Curiously enough, there is no record of Herbert Dow ever presiding over a Dow board meeting. This was largely a technicality; the records show that he dominated them, whatever his position.

Pardee and Crider drew up a formal board resolution on this occasion that said:

> Whereas, Mr. A. E. Convers, after serving as President of the Company for 21 years, has been elected its Chairman, Resolved, that the members of this board desire to express by recording in the Minutes of the Company, their sincere appreciation of his fairness in presiding, his unfailing courtesy, and his faithful devotion to the best interests of The Dow Chemical Company for the entire period of his occupancy of the office of President, and to express the hope that as Chairman of the Board our friendly relations may continue for many years to come.[36]

In 1920 he sold his tack company to Atlas Tack Corporation, the largest tack-maker, but by 1924 he was back in the tack business again with Charles Hill, his associate since the Taunton days. Convers also had major interests in the Philippines, where with some of his financial friends he owned 10,000 head of cattle at a ranch on the island of Mindanao and farmed some 243,000 coconut trees. He was also a key investor in the Steelex Manufacturing Company, which made piston rings in a Boston suburb.[37]

In the spring of 1930 an aging Convers wrote Herbert Dow that he was thinking of making Midland his home; after 1918 board meetings were held in Midland, and commuting there from Brooklyn was becoming onerous. Dow responded by inviting him to stay a few days with him and Mrs. Dow during the April board meeting, during which time they would try to arrange this. "It will be a source of satisfaction to local people to know that the Chairman of the Board of the Dow Chemical Company is a local man," Dow wrote.[38]

When Convers came to Midland the two old warriors spent what was to be their last few days together; Herbert Dow was dead a few months later. They looked over the new Midland Country Club being built by young Alden B. Dow, Herbert's architect son, and a suite was set aside for Convers. It became his home during the last years of his life.

On a trip to Cleveland in 1935 he suffered a heart attack, and died a few days later, aged 76. Willard Dow led a delegation of his colleagues to the funeral in Taunton, where he was laid to rest beside Fannie in Mt. Pleasant Cemetery. The "old guard" of Dow was represented by Pardee, Crider, L. I. Doan, Strosacker, and Bennett. The *Midland Republican* on this occasion recalled his "retiring disposition," and how he lived "modestly and quietly," and said he was "a fine friendly gentleman, ruggedly honest, sincere, and kind. He took an immense interest in Midland and contributed liberally to its projects."[39]

Convers's will, after providing for old friends, relatives, and business associates, left the bulk of his $3 million fortune to the Cleveland Foundation, the first of the nation's community foundations. The idea for such a foundation had been conceived by his friend, F. H. Goff, president of the Cleveland Trust Company, and the Convers bequest was one of its earliest major gifts. "Cleveland was his heir," observed the *Cleveland Plain Dealer*.[40] In 1992 the Cleveland Foundation calculated that his contribution was worth $82.9 million in today's dollars.[41]

III.

The business world Herbert Dow entered in the 1890s was hardly animated by a spirit of free enterprise and open competition. As we have seen, the cartel system was still in full sway, and Dow almost in spite of himself became a key figure in the fall of that system, at least as it applied to the U.S. chemical industry, then in its tender infancy. The European producers who had long enjoyed a virtual monopoly in America's chemical business were not about to give up this rapidly growing market without a struggle, and Dow became the focal point of that struggle.

In these early years of his business life Dow was to battle, and defeat, three different combines—the bromine "pool," which controlled the bromine business in the United States; the United Alkali Company, of Great Britain, which monopolized—or felt it had the right to monopolize—the bleach business; and the German bromine combine, the Deutsche Bromkonvention, which dominated the world's bromine markets and had a business arrangement with the U.S. bromine pool.

These organizations carved up the international markets for bromine and bleach, dictated annual production figures for their manufacture, and set the prices at which they would be sold. Newcomers to the market, or mavericks who attempted to circumvent the rules, were dealt with harshly, as Dow was to discover.

The coordinator of the U.S. bromine business in the 1890s was W. R. Shields, a Columbus, Ohio, businessman whose letterhead simply said "Bromine." All bromine was sold through the three wholesalers—Mallinckrodt in St. Louis, Rosengarten & Sons in Philadelphia, and Powers and Weightman, also in Philadelphia—with whom Shields had long-term contracts.[42] Shields would contract to buy all production in the Ohio Valley—at the time Herbert Dow entered the market, the only U.S. area producing bromine—usually for five years ahead. Each producer sold his production to Shields at a price fixed by the contract, the price decreasing year by year as the yearly amount to be produced increased.

The large wholesalers, who were also pharmaceutical manufacturers, stored large amounts of bromine toward the end of the contract period and would then have the producers at their mercy when the time for a new contract arrived. At this time the price of bromine would be depressed, and Shields would set about working out a new contract with the producers.[43] When Shields offered Dow a five-year contract on equal terms with the other producers, Dow wanted none of it, and this led eventually to his being fired, as noted previously.

Henry S. Cooper, Dow's successor at the Midland Chemical Company, promptly signed up with Shields (in early 1894), and the Midland company became part of the Shields "pool" until 1902, when it was merged into the new Dow Chemical Company. When that happened, Dow made arrangements to sell his bromine directly to Mallinckrodt and Powers-Weightman-Rosengarten, cutting out Shields but retaining his freedom to produce as he wished and sell at a price freely agreed upon.

Herbert Dow could do this because his bromine process made him by a significant margin the lowest-cost producer in the business. The Ohio Valley producers were still using the ancient process of drilling a brinewell near a coal mine and using low-grade coal to boil down the brine to obtain bromine; their method was cheap but crude, and in an increasingly sophisticated market, doomed to oblivion. Within 10 years Dow totally dominated the U.S. bromine market and the Ohio Valley producers began to disappear, one by one; by the end of World War I they were almost a memory.

As an officer of the Midland Chemical Company Herbert Dow had frequent dealings with Shields, and the two remained on friendly terms for 30 years, freely exchanging information about the bromine business. Dow rebuffed a suggestion that he hire Shields, who knew more about the U.S. bromine market than anyone else; he did not want Shields to know anything about his manufacturing process, he said.[44]

As the years went by and the Ohio Valley bromine manufacturers faded, twisting slowly in the wind as the new technology took over, Shields fell on hard times. In 1919 Lillie Shields wrote Herbert Dow from Columbus saying her husband was growing old and their income had shrunk to only $68 per month; she hoped Mr. Dow could find it in his heart to provide some source of income for him but not tell her husband that she had written, for he was still a proud man, not asking for charity. Herbert Dow sent the one-time "Mr. Bromine" of the nation a check for $100 and asked him for a report on the current status of the Ohio Valley bromine business, saying he was the best source he knew for such information. Dow also wrote Edward Mallinckrodt of Shields's difficulties and suggested he do something along the same line. Mallinckrodt trumped up an excuse and also sent $100.[45]

The bleach war, in contrast, was a cold, grim price war without much human interest. In 1897 Herbert Dow had convinced the investors of The Dow Chemical Company that the opportunity for a U.S. company to clean up in bleach was unparalleled since there was then no U.S. producer of that commodity. (This situation did not last long; new bleach producers quickly popped up at Niagara Falls and on the East Coast.) He did not mention it much, but the bleach market was controlled by the British combine, the United Alkali Company, who had split up the world market with the big German producers. The British, who under this arrangement controlled the U.S. market, paid little attention at first to the new Dow company, whose initial market was in the Midwest, especially among the paper mills of Ohio, Michigan, and Wisconsin, and in the American West, where bleach shipped from Midland had a considerable freight advantage over product shipped from the East Coast. Only when the mushrooming Dow firm began to push out of its mid-American base did United Alkali swing into action.

The practice then was for American salesmen to call on purchasing agents every fall, feeling out the market. No purchasing agent would sign a contract for the coming year, however, until United Alkali had made its big annual move—a late-fall announcement establishing its price on bleach for the coming year. There then followed a scramble to close contracts for the year ahead; Dow and the other U.S. producers would usually match United Alkali's price and try to "undersell" the British by lower freight rates (the British price was FOB port of entry).

Over the years the price of bleach had drifted down from $3.50 per hundredweight at the time United Alkali was the only supplier to $1.75, the price on which Herbert Dow had based his 1897 business calculations. United Alkali lowered the boom in late 1902 by announcing that its 1903 price would drop to $1.25, from $1.65 the year before. Dow was forced to meet the British price, which then was quickly dropped to $1.04 per hundredweight. United Alkali was now selling at beneath its production costs; it had to absorb a 25-cent import duty per hundredweight in addition to heavy shipping costs.

The timing was devastating for the new company. In 1901 Herbert Dow had launched a $225,000 bleach expansion program, followed by a second, even larger $300,000 expansion, based on his expectations that the price would not fall below $1.65. Under the British combine's pressure the other U.S. producers, all relatively small greenhorns, dropped out of the market; Dow alone refused to do so. By the middle of 1903 the company was $92,000 overdrawn at the bank and had debts of $225,000. The Cleveland bankers complained, but agreed to extend more credit.

Hardly had Dow solved the problem of staying afloat than the British announced their bleach price for 1904 would be 88.5 cents a hundredweight. Dow gritted his teeth and as a counterblow announced that his 1904 price would be 86 cents. In the annual year-end scramble he signed contracts for his entire 1904 production at 86 cents. The United Alkali Company then announced that its 1904 price would be $1.25 rather than 88 cents. That signaled the end of the bleach war, but Dow had already contracted for the entire year at 86. "It seems too bad," Herbert Dow commented, "that we have to bear the entire cost of bringing the United Alkali Co. to recognize outside production."[46]

An important factor in the company's survival was Herbert Dow's dictum that you always used the cheapest local material possible to build a plant. The Dow bleach plant was made of tar, cheap wood, iron, glass, and concrete. Tom Griswold recalled that Herbert Dow used to say the cost of the whole Dow bleach plant was less than the cost of the mercury and platinum in the electrodes of competing concerns at Niagara Falls. Because of design, cheap materials, and inventive ingenuity, Griswold said, the cost of a Dow chlorine cell in the period around 1899 or 1900 was only one dollar.[47]

During the bleach war Dow pushed its sales into the New York/New England area, the heartland of United Alkali's market, and became a national factor in the bleach field. As the price stabilized at around $1.25 in the years following, the company kept expanding its capacity, and Dow began to win recognition as a premier bleach maker.

Then in 1909 a seemingly obscure event—the shipping of the first carload of liquid chlorine by the Pennsylvania Salt Company of Philadelphia—signaled the end of bleach as a product. Early in 1913 Herbert Dow told a meeting of his top lieutenants—Barstow, Griswold, Strosacker, and Bennett—that they were going out of the bleach business. It came as a bombshell to them; bleach, after all, had been the company's first and biggest product, even though sales had of late been slowing down. Bleach, which had long been the best way available to handle "fixed chlorine," was now being replaced by new products, and as they discussed the matter, Bennett recalled later, "it finally grew on everyone that there was no future for bleach whatsoever." They discussed the possibility of selling liquid chlorine but decided the tanks and cylinders necessary to ship it were too expensive a plant investment, and that it was far more attractive to put the chlorine to other uses.[48]

The decision to get out of bleach was quickly put into effect, even though Dow had to turn over some of its long-term contracts to other companies. Dow and his team turned to a search for new uses for their chlorine that led to some of the company's flagship products—calcium chloride (or "Dowflake") and magnesium chloride, which in turn opened the door to a series of products including metallic magnesium, magnesium oxychloride cements, and magnesium sulphate, better known as Epsom salts, of which Dow became the world's largest producer.

Taking the company out of the bleach business established another basic rule in the Dow lexicon: if a product has no future, drop it; don't let it die a slow death. Bennett and others said that perhaps the best thing about the bleach and bromine wars was that they did not happen at the same time. If they had, Bennett was reasonably certain the company could not have survived.[49]

The war with the Bromkonvention was a long and grueling test of wills. It began with a surprise visit from Hermann Jacobsohn, representative of the German cartel, who made a trip to Midland to see Herbert Dow as the bleach war was winding down. The Germans had evidence he had been exporting bromides to Europe, he told Dow. "Don't you know you cannot export bromides?" he asked. Dow said he knew nothing of the sort. Jacobsohn explained that he was sent by his colleagues to make it clear to Dow that infractions of the rules could not be tolerated. The amounts exported may have been small, he said, but if they continued the convention would put two pounds of bromine on the U.S. market for every pound exported by Dow. Feeling it was a bluff, Herbert Dow paid no attention.

Early in 1905 the Germans suddenly cut the price of potassium bromide in half in the United States—from 30 cents a pound to 15—while holding the price at 40 cents in Europe.

Other bromide prices were also cut in half. Herbert Dow was in San Antonio when he got a message to come urgently to St. Louis to meet with a representative of the Deutsche Bromkonvention, who turned out to be Jacobsohn. Jacobsohn told him the price cut had indeed been made as an object lesson to Dow that he should stop shipping bromides to Europe and Japan. Dow, he said, was trying to disrupt the unwritten but historic understanding that the bromide market in Europe and the rest of the world outside the United States was reserved to the Bromkonvention; if Dow did not cease, they would have no alternative but to flood the U.S. market with bromides priced below production cost. The convention could well afford to do this, he said, because it was backed by the financial resources of the German government, and in a long price war the Germans would inevitably be the winners, he argued.

Angered by the German's insolence and threats, Dow refused to change his policies, and after further discussion rose and announced that the meeting was at an end. He had a train to make, he said. Jacobsohn was astonished. "You don't know what you are doing," he told Dow. Dow left for his train.[50]

In spite of his anger Dow now moved swiftly to plot his strategy. He was fully aware that he was embarking on one of the biggest fights of his life. He was also aware that at 15 cents, including a 25 percent import duty, the Germans had less than 12 cents to cover their costs, so that every pound they put into the United States would be a financial drain on them. He was sure he could produce bromides cheaper than the Germans could, and he was also sure the Germans were not in as powerful a position as Jacobsohn pretended.

He instructed Jim Graves, now his plant manager, and Rupert E. Paris, newly appointed as the first Dow sales manager (both of whom had accompanied him to the St. Louis meeting) to run the bromide plant at full production and start stockpiling bromides. He also authorized them to sell 120,000 pounds of bromides on the U.S. market at 12 cents a pound; he wanted the Germans to think he was preparing to do battle with them in the U.S. market.

Actually Herbert Dow had a different plan: to invade the Germans' home market and undersell the Germans in that market, where they counted on continuing to sell at a profitable price, 27 cents a pound. He dispatched Paris to sell 100,000 pounds of bromides in Europe, mainly in Germany.[51] Within a few months he had a 300,000 pound stockpile to sell in Europe, and an entrée to the German market.

This was a German sales agent in Hamburg named Julius Grossman. Because Hamburg was a free port, Dow could ship bromides directly to Grossman; Grossman would remove the American and Dow identification from the boxes and relabel them "J. Grossman, Hamburg, Germany." Carrying the process a step further, he began buying up German bromides in the United States at 12 or 15 cents a pound and shipping them to Germany, where they could be sold on the European market for up to 27 cents a pound. The Germans realized they were losing a lot of money, but they were not sure just how. It took them more than a year to discover what Herbert Dow was doing.

Several of the Dow Company directors expressed alarm at the prospect of another price war on top of the first, but Convers backed Herbert Dow to the hilt. "It would seem to me better to hit the market where it is highest, viz., in Germany," Convers wrote Dow. "If we can only break their home price so that the whole market is unprofitable to anyone but the Dow Co., the price will eventually come up, if we hold the market in that condition long enough."

A few months later he was writing to Dow: "My idea is that we ought to ship Bromide to Germany in such quantities as to completely upset the market there, if possible to do so. . . .It seems as though the only way we could bring Jacobsohn to terms . . . will be to demoralize his market if possible at the point where he is getting his profit."[52]

The two sides settled in for a long war. The Germans cut their U.S. price to 12 cents a pound, and then to 10.5. Herbert Dow must have smiled as he purchased these bargain-basement bromides through a New York agent and shipped them out to Hamburg for sale at more than double these prices; the Bromkonvention was working against itself without knowing it.

In 1907 Herbert Dow took his family on a trip billed as a family vacation in Europe. Installing his family in London, he visited bromine plants in Germany and bleach plants in England, becoming thoroughly convinced by the experience that his plants were producing both products at considerably less cost than those of the Europeans. While he was at New Stassfurt, in Germany, site of the great German potash mines, he was approached by members of the Bromkonvention with an offer: they would pull out of the U.S. market if he would pull out of the European market. Dow turned them down. He also turned them down later in the year when a German delegation came to St. Louis to meet with him, but he made a counteroffer: "Germany for the Germans; the U.S. for the American manufacturers, and the rest of the world on an equal footing." The Germans were furious. Dow wrote Convers that "the Germans could not realize that it was possible for anyone else to make bromides as cheaply as they could."[53]

Some weeks later the Germans asked for another meeting, and this time Dow left the preliminaries in the hands of the corporate secretary of Dow, Harvey Hackenberg. The meeting was set up at the Savoy Hotel in London on November 24. On Hackenberg's advice Dow traveled to London under the sobriquet "Herbert Henry," to avoid publicity. The two sailed from New York to Liverpool and then went on to London.

The Savoy Hotel meeting, at which Dow and Hackenberg met with a quartet of German representatives, again including Jacobsohn, went on for three days without reaching any decision.[54] The Germans insisted that in all "neutral territory"—their term for the world other than Europe and North America—the Germans should have two-thirds of the market. The talks moved on to New Stassfurt and Berlin, but still nothing was decided, and the two Americans sailed for home at the beginning of December.

Although no formal peace treaty was agreed upon, the bromine world began slowly to return to normalcy after these meetings, quite to the surprise of Dow and Hackenberg. The Bromkonvention quietly began to withdraw from the U.S. market and Herbert Dow slowed and eventually stopped his shipments to Germany. The "neutral territory," as Dow had wished, became and remained a freely competitive area. Bromine prices began to rise again, and by the end of 1909 were back at the level where they had started before the Germans declared war.

For the rest of his life Herbert Dow remembered the war with the Bromkonvention as a narrow scrape. The great financial panic of 1907 occurred during this battle, and the financial status of the Dow Company was more precarious than the Germans ever realized.

It was a close call but a resounding victory for the small American company in the Michigan backwoods, which now in only its 12th year had already earned a reputation for not backing down from a fight.

Notes

1. H. H. Dow to C. A. Post, June 2, 1897.
2. Author interview, Robert H. Ward, Flora Thompson's nephew, Midland, November 23, 1993.
3. Flora M. Thompson to H. H. Dow, January 7, 1901. The records show that Herbert Dow purchased Dow stock for her with his own funds prior to this date, although she does not mention this; she was also a stockholder in the Midland Chemical Company.
4. Oral History, Dorothy Dow Arbury, January 18, 1989; Ward interview.
5. Oral History, Margaret Dow Towsley, December 6, 1989.
6. Since Thomas Griswold Jr.'s "start date" at Dow was May 22, 1897, and M. B. Johnson's was June 10, the story that Johnson was "the first man hired" by Dow lacks credence. The employee badge system was installed by Johnson when he assumed office as first general superintendent—and when badge numbers were assigned, lo, M. B. Johnson's name led all the rest.
7. T. Griswold Jr., "Midland in Earlier Days," November 6, 1946, in T. Griswold Papers.
8. M. B. Johnson to H. H. Dow, May 27, 1897; H. H. Dow to M. B. Johnson, May 29, 1897.
9. H. H. Dow to C. A. Post, June 10, 1897.
10. T. Griswold Jr., "Midland in Earlier Days." *Lead burning* is a technical term for the forming or fabrication of objects such as a chlorine cell with lead metal.
11. M. B. Johnson to J. C. Parker, July 28, 1897.
12. See Johnson correspondence with Flint & Pere Marquette Railroad, Bardeen Paper Company, and other customers and railroads, January 1 - December 31, 1898.
13. M. B. Johnson to Frederick A. Forbes, president, Michigan Telephone Co., Detroit, November 18, 1898.
14. M. B. Johnson to H. H. Dow, September 18, 1902; also November 14, 1902.
15. H. H. Dow to C. A. Post, June 11, 1897.
16. C. A. Post to H. H. Dow, October 23, 1897.
17. Ibid., September 11, 1899.
18. T. Griswold Jr., interview, "Griswold's Early Days Recalled," Midland Daily News, October 19, 1960.
19. T. Griswold Jr. to H. H. Dow, April 20, 1897.
20. Ibid., January 14, 1906.
21. See list of Griswold patents, T. Griswold Papers.
22. H. E. Hackenberg to H. H. Dow, June 12, 1909; H. H. Dow to H. E. Hackenberg, June 21, 1909.
23. H. E. Hackenberg to H. H. Dow, June 25, 1909.

24. Vera Griswold to H. H. Dow, July 5, 1924. Helen Josephine Dow, Herbert Dow's sister and Griswold's first wife, died April 18, 1918, during the WWI influenza epidemic, at age 41, leaving him with three underage children. In October 1918, Griswold married Vera Ann Hadsall, 22, a secretary in the headquarters office at Dow. He was then 48.

25. H. H. Dow to Vera Griswold, June 27, 1924.

26. T. Griswold jr., The Time of My Life (Midland, Mich.: Northwood Institute, 1973), 82.

27. See "Early Midland Blacks," *The Midland Log* (spring 1986), journal of the Midland County Historical Society. The author is especially indebted to Judge Henry Hart, retired, for his sketch of Highgate's life in this publication, pp. 21-32.

28. Genealogy and family information, Old Colony Historical Society, Taunton, Mass.

29. See obituary, Albert Elijah Convers, Midland (Mich.) Republican, April 11, 1935.

30. Herbert Dow did not make his first automobile trip to Cleveland until 1911. Through the end of World War I, he traveled on any long trip almost exclusively by train.

31. In its formative days the "executive committee" also at times included James T. Pardee and John S. Crider.

32. Report by A. E. Convers, Pres., and Charles A. Post, Treas., to Board of Directors, October 21, 1897.

33. See H. H. Dow to W. R. Veazey, February 22, 1930.

34. This incident finally ended only in January 1915 when H. H. Dow agreed to purchase the Barstow-Griswold extraction process. See E. O. Barstow to H. H. Dow, January 6, 1915, and accompanying Salary Agreement, Thomas Griswold Jr. Their salaries were set at $5,000 per annum as of January 1, 1915.

35. Oral History, Dorothy Dow Arbury, January 18, 1989; Oral History, Margaret Dow Towsley, with Dr. Harry A. Towsley, December 6, 1989.

36. See J. T. Pardee to J. S. Crider, July 12, 1918.

37. Obituaries of A. E. Convers, *Midland (Mich.) Republican*, April 11, 1935; *Cleveland Plain Dealer*, May 16, 1935; and *Taunton (Mass.) Daily Gazette*, April 9, 1935.

38. H. H. Dow to A. E. Convers, April 4, 1930.

39. *Midland Republican*, April 11, 1935.

40. *Cleveland Plain Dealer*, May 16, 1935.

41. Cleveland Foundation, Cleveland, Ohio, to author, October 15, 1992.

42. The two Philadelphia firms merged in 1904 and became Powers-Weightman-Rosengarten. Adolph Rosengarten of this firm became Dow's lifelong friend.

43. Earl Bennett described the modus operandi of Shields and the U.S. bromine cartel for Harrison Hatton, May 13, 1949.

44. H. H. Dow to H. E. Hackenberg, April 26, 1900.

45. Lillie M. Shields, Columbus, Ohio, to H. H. Dow, April 10, 1919; H. H. Dow to W. R. Shields, April 30, 1919; H. H. Dow to E. Mallinckrodt, April 30, 1919; E. Mallinckrodt to H. H. Dow, May 13, 1919.

46. H. H. Dow to C. Staley, November 4, 1903.

47. Tom Griswold, interview with Harrison Hatton, July 6, 1949.

48. Earl Bennett, conversation with Harrison Hatton and Murray Campbell, December 14, 1949.

49. Earl Bennett, interview with Harrison Hatton, June 13, 1949.

50. Dow was on a trip to the West Coast with his family at the time, primarily to visit the J. H. Osborns, and his family was waiting for him to return from the meeting to go to the train. Dow left the meeting, put his family on the train, and then got off himself at Kansas City, Missouri—the first stop—where through a series of letters, telegrams, and the like he began organizing for his battle with the Deutsche Bromkonvention. This done, he caught up with his family in Los Angeles.

51. The idea of flooding the German market with bromides came from Edward Mallinckrodt, Sr. in whose offices the meeting was held. Mallinckrodt "advised this action and said that he made the Germans withdraw from here some years ago by dumping a lot of bromide in Germany," Dow wrote Convers on February 15, 1905. The idea of buying German bromine in the United States and selling it in Germany was pure Herbert Dow.

52. A. E. Convers to H. H. Dow, April 23, 1905; September 13, 1905; and other dates this period.

53. See lengthy report concerning this trip, H. H. Dow to A. E. Convers, March 13, 1907.

54. It became a Dow characteristic for the company to be represented by one or two persons given full responsibility to speak for the company, as Dow and Hackenberg were at this meeting, opposite a usually larger group not empowered to act without consultation with a higher authority. Dow invited Edward Mallinckrodt Jr. to accompany him and Hackenberg on this occasion, but he declined.

THAT CLEVELAND CROWD

I.

The mindset among the Cleveland businessmen and investors who hatched out The Dow Chemical Company was quite different from that of its employees in Midland; among themselves the Clevelanders frequently referred to the new firm as their "Michigan flyer." They all had other occupations and resources, and if the investment in Midland paid off, so much the better; if it did not, they would still survive. Those on the scene in Midland where the new plant was being grubbed together saw it quite differently, and sometimes spoke rather disparagingly of the captains of finance as "that Cleveland crowd."

Fortunately the Cleveland crowd was a conspicuously successful group of men. They provided not only the funds but the basic business know-how that set the new firm on the pathway to success. Their prototype was probably George E. Collings, a gentleman of the old school who was a remarkable story in himself. Born in an English Hertfordshire village called Clehonger, he set out to seek his fortune in Canada in his middle teens, worked as a clerk for the Canada Southern Railway, and arrived in Cleveland at the age of 17. When he was 30 he founded the Collings-Taylor Company, a woolen goods manufacturer, and he presently also became president of the Cleveland Woolen Mills Company, a manufacturer of blankets, robes, and shawls, his main occupation at the time the Dow Company was formed.

He had big ideas. In 1900 the *Cleveland Press* described his proposal to build a single, huge power plant to "supply all Cleveland with energy." "Geo. E. Collings has worked out a scheme which, if carried out, will revolutionize the present power systems and at the same time abolish the smoke nuisance in Cleveland," the newspaper reported. Electric power at the time was generated by a series of small, smoky, coal-fed neighborhood plants. All large cities eventually adopted the Collings scheme, but he received little credit for it.[1]

Herbert Dow said Collings was the first person to buy stock in the Dow Company, although several others also claimed this distinction. On its incorporation he became a director and one of two vice-presidents of the company (S. T. Wellman was the other), and served as a director and vice-president for more than 44 years.

On August 13, 1941, Collings and James T. Pardee, also a director from the beginning, retired from the Dow board. Each had been an officer and member of the executive committee for many years. Pardee and Collings were awarded the first honorary titles conferred by the company, Pardee being named "chairman emeritus" and Collings "vice president emeritus." Collings reportedly never missed a meeting in 44 years. He was nearing his 87th birthday when he retired. Ailing, he died only six weeks later, in September 1941.

Collings presided over a surprising variety of firms aside from his Dow activities. In addition to his basic business as a woolens maker he was president of Ohio's first sugar beet processing concern, the Continental Sugar Company, which he organized in 1910, and he was also president of the Lennox Chemical Company, in Cleveland, manufacturers of liquid carbonic gas, and of the Cleveland Faucet Company.

In addition to these enterprises he kept up a running correspondence with Herbert Dow. He had a puckish sense of humor: "Regarding a meeting of the Midland Chemical Company," he wrote Dow in 1911, "it is so much farther from Cleveland to Midland than it is from Midland to Cleveland . . . that I suggest holding the meeting here in Cleveland." Commenting on a company financial statement he received from Pardee in which indigo dyes showed a sizable loss, he wrote to Pardee: "Everything looks quite well in the statement except the Indigo, and that looks a little blue."[2]

In 1906 he sent a small cannon to nine-year-old Willard Dow, who wrote back that he was delighted at the prospect of firing it off a few times on July 4. Collings immediately sent off a warning to Herbert Dow: "This cannon kicks a little when it is touched off, and would suggest that you do not allow anyone to go near it; in fact I always got behind a tree myself when sending it off at the house, as I always think there is some danger that a cannon of this size might possibly explode, but I am sure you will use good judgment in the matter as I would certainly dislike very much to have anyone hurt."[3]

Throughout his career he was conscious of his lack of knowledge about chemicals. "I always tell anyone when they ask me anything about the Dow Co. that I have been connected with them for many, many years but I know nothing about chemicals," he told Dow. "Dr. (Albert W.) Smith used to be very severe on me for this. He said I should get down to it and learn some of the things and I think he was right, but I never did."[4]

Pardee, a Clevelander born and bred, became one of Herbert Dow's closest friends and backers. They graduated from Cleveland's Central High School in the same class but did not become friends until they found each other among the 12 young men enrolled in the Case class of 1888 (six of whom graduated four years later).

After graduation Pardee went his own way and in 1893 was appointed engineer in charge of bridges and viaducts, docks and wharves, in Cleveland's City Engineers Department, moving up to assistant chief engineer in 1901. In 1895 he designed and built a double swing bridge, the Columbus Street Bridge, over the Cuyahoga river, the first of its kind in the United States. It was a big success, solving a difficult traffic problem where a major city street crossed a rather sharp bend in the river, and Pardee was then also handed the job of Cleveland river and harbor improvement and launched the first organized lakefront planning for the city.[5]

Pardee remembered many years later that it was on the afternoon of his first great triumph, when the Columbus Street Bridge was inaugurated, that Herbert Dow reappeared in his life. Pardee became secretary-treasurer of the Dow Process Company, which Dow was then forming, and their business association lasted the rest of their lives.[6] When The Dow Chemical Company was formed Pardee continued his financial backing, and by 1910 he was the firm's second-largest stockholder after Herbert Dow.[7] He became a vice president in 1901, corporate secretary in 1916, and when Convers died in 1935, chairman.

When Pardee came to Midland he always stayed with the Dows, and "was more or less part of the family for a long time," the Dow children said. On occasion he would babysit for the Dow children and crawl around on all fours to amuse them. Margaret Dow Towsley said, "he had a lot of fun in him," and that "he's one of my nicest memories of the life at home."[8]

Pardee was a 50-year-old bachelor when he finally married, to Elsa Uhinck of Cleveland, who was 28 and had a twin sister, Eda. Eda had married a high school classmate, Rollin M. Gerstacker, and they had two children, Elsa and Carl. Pardee's nephew Carl was to follow in his uncle's footsteps as Dow chairman a generation later. Pardee never had children of his own but "just doted on" his niece and nephew, Dorothy Arbury recalled.

Pardee had the reputation among his colleagues of having a strong character, a nimble and orderly mind, and a phenomenal memory for the names of hundreds of people. He had a fetish for counting things—the number of steps in a stairwell, the number of persons at a party, the mileage to wherever he was going. He always insisted on good grammar, in public or in private. People in Midland remembered him as an immensely friendly man who used to stop and talk to casual acquaintances in downtown Midland, inquiring how they lived and what they were doing.[9]

Margaret Johnson, who with her husband ran the Dow cafeteria, remembered an incident during the Depression of the 1930s when on a hot spring day Pardee asked Charley Johnson for iced tea, which was not on the menu. Johnson said he would get it as soon as he could, but it took a long time and Pardee asked why it took so long. Johnson explained that because of the Depression they had been ordered to cut back on personnel and did not have nearly enough help. Pardee told him that nonetheless he should get himself another girl to work there. "Well," Margaret Johnson said, "Mr. Pardee was Mr. Pardee, and that was an order, so we got another girl."[10]

Dow frequently used Pardee as a sounding board or release valve for matters that had come up or that he wanted to bring up at board meetings, knowing that he could blow off steam to Pardee, or ask his advice, without his confidence being betrayed.[11]

In his declining years he received a cascade of honors, including an honorary doctorate from Case in 1940. Pardee Hall on the campus was named for him later. When he and Collings retired from the Dow board in 1941 he was already an ill man, and he died of cancer some two years later, on January 3, 1944, at the age of 76.

Elsa Pardee died only nine months later, in the interim having made provision to leave $1 million in Dow stock to establish a foundation "for the care and cure of cancer"; the Pardee Foundation, housed in the Pardees' former Midland residence, today provides a good deal more than that sum annually for the funding of cancer research.[12]

II.

In later years the Dow Company would become one of the most ardent advocates anywhere of an "inside" board of directors—directors drawn from among its own employees, rather than from outside the firm—but in the beginning it was the very model of the "outside" board. Of the 11 original directors who first met on May 18, 1897, only one, Herbert Dow himself, was a Dow employee; all the others were outsiders with other employment.

Furthermore, only one was a Midlander. In the discussions leading to the formation of the company it had been agreed there should be one member of the board representing "the Midland interests," the shareholders residing in Midland. Herbert Dow mentioned this proviso to his father-in-law, G. Willard Ball, the hardware dealer, who proceeded to drum up support for William L. Baker, the largest initial Midland stockholder (aside from Herbert Dow), with $5,000 subscribed. Ball cruised up and down Main Street and gathered 11 signatures from his fellow Midland stockholders nominating Baker (there were only 15 Midland stockholders in all at this point), and in due course he became one of the 11 original members of the board.[13]

Baker, an unassuming but highly successful Midland banker who also had other interests in the town, including a general store, soon became Dow's principal confidant on matters of Midland real estate and banking. He helped Dow decide what property to buy, and often served as his intermediary. Baker's bank, the People's State Bank, became the company's Midland repository. When Dow visited nearby towns such as St. Louis (Mich.) and Mt. Pleasant where there were brine processing firms or other matters of interest, Baker usually went along. It was a great burden to Baker, however, to attend the board meetings in Cleveland—a monthly three-day trip for a meeting lasting two or three hours—and after four years of it he gave it up. Thinking better of it later, he returned to the board in 1907 and served until his death in 1916.

The academic contingent on the original board was headed by Cady Staley, president of the Case School, who served five years until his retirement in 1902. A. L. Fuller, dean of

Adelbert College, another member of the first board, was a respected classical scholar, an instructor in Latin and French, and then for a dozen years professor of Greek at Western Reserve. This is one of the rare instances where a professor of Greek has served on the board of an American corporation. The business world seems, alas, to have been Greek to him; by early 1899 he was writing Herbert Dow that he needed as discreetly as he could to sell the 20 shares of Dow stock he had subscribed for. In 1901 he left the board.[14] The third academic was Albert W. Smith, who was head of the chemistry department at Case. Smith was to remain one of the most influential members of the Dow board for thirty years, and a prime proponent of its research interests, until his death in 1927.

When the board decided to add a 12th member, in June 1898, they chose a fourth educator, Professor Edward W. Morley of Western Reserve, the celebrated chemist of the Michelson-Morley experiment and one of Herbert Dow's mentors—he was then one of the nation's best-known chemists. Morley served as a board member for nine years. He retired and became a professor emeritus in 1906.

Dow seems always to have favored board members who could "bring something to the table," and when Morley was a board member (and even later) Dow felt free to ask his advice on matters related to his chemical expertise. Judge John C. Hale, an elderly jurist who lived with the Albert Smiths, became a director in 1900 and in the dozen years he was a board member frequently served as an informal consultant on bond issues and legal matters; Dow would ask him to look at the language of important contracts, for example. The judge was Albert Smith's uncle, and as Herbert Dow explained it, "as he has no children of his own and Dr. Smith has no Father, he is pretty near the same as Father to him."[15] Jesse B. Fay, a board member from 1902 to 1907, was a partner in the patent law firm that served Dow, and provided expert counsel in the patent field.

S. T. Wellman, chairman of the first meeting of the company's board of directors, was a stout fellow in both senses. He became first vice president of the new company, and as such, heir apparent to Convers as president.[16]

Wellman was a steel man, president of Wellman Seaver Engineering Company, specialists in the building of steel plants, rolling mills, and metallurgical furnaces. He remained a board member until his death in July 1919 except for a four-year period when he was on the West Coast.[17] Not surprisingly, much of the heavy equipment Dow needed, such as the big Berry boilers, a key element in the power system, came by way of Wellman Seaver.

On his death the board passed a resolution recalling Wellman's optimistic nature, which accorded well with that of Herbert Dow. "When at times the affairs of the Company seemed at a low ebb he gave encouragement and pointed ahead to a brighter future," the resolution said. "We shall miss his cheerful presence and his fund of anecdotes gathered from all parts of the world."[18]

By the turn of the century the burdens of secretary-treasurer of the firm were too much for one person, and the board cast about for a recruit to be the secretary of the company; Post was still both secretary and treasurer. John H. Osborn, Dow's faithful backer in the early days and one of his closest friends, had also become one of the original directors. Some years before, Osborn had recommended Harvey E. Hackenberg, one of his colleagues at National Carbon Company, for secretary of the Midland Chemical Company, and Dow had been well pleased with what he had seen of Hackenberg. Now Harvey Hackenberg was prevailed upon to also join the Dow board as its secretary, with Post remaining as treasurer. Hackenberg turned out to be one of the best things that could have happened to the infant Dow Company.

As his first assignment Hackenberg was asked by the board to look at the two firms and recommend whether they should be merged; this request also gave him the chance to get acquainted with the Dow Company, with which up to then he had had no connection. He looked at the books, both in Midland and in Cleveland; inspected the plant in Midland; and wrote a report that went well beyond recommending a merger of the two firms. Hackenberg, an experienced administrator, was shocked by some of the things he saw. The books in Cleveland, made up from reports received from Midland, contained information not known to the people in Midland, and vice versa, he pointed out, and he urged that all the managers should be working from the same fund of information. He therefore recommended extensive changes in the reporting and accounting systems.[19]

This was only the beginning of his services to the firm. Over the following years Hackenberg was the key factor in installing the principles of sound accounting procedures in the new firm, and he greatly improved the kinds of reporting done to keep track of costs. Other improvements initiated by Hackenberg ranged across the entire spectrum of office procedures and controls. For instance, he recommended uniform stationery for the new company instead of each branch or division printing its own; Herbert Dow readily admitted he had a good point, and the change was made.[20]

In 1909 Hackenberg was surprised to find the company's new sales department routinely keeping track of orders, contracts, and correspondence, but not records of call. He wrote a private note to Dow saying, "all well regulated concerns have reports made of all trips made by the salesmen," and sent a copy of the form used at National Carbon Company. By return mail Dow sent him a proposed form asking for his comments. Thus was born the Dow report of call still used (in a modern, electronic form) today.

The maxim that "if you want a good job done, give it to a busy person" applied with full force to Hackenberg. In his basic full-time job he was treasurer of the National Carbon Company, where he supervised, according to Osborn, a staff of 75. He was also in the cement business, serving first as secretary-treasurer and from 1901 as president of the Iroquois Portland Cement Company, which had a plant at Caledonia, New York, east of Buffalo. He was also a banker, and was president of the Lakewood Savings Bank Company, at Lakewood, Ohio. His outside activities were also numerous: in 1912 he served as president of the Cleveland Chamber of Industry, and he was active in the national organization of credit men. In addition to all of these duties, he was secretary and a director of the two chemical companies in Midland. From time to time Hackenberg went through a crisis in which he resigned one or more of these duties, and one of Herbert Dow's problems was to keep Hackenberg from resigning his Dow duties. In 1908 he actually did resign as Dow secretary, having just accompanied Dow to Europe to dicker with the Deutsche Bromkonvention, but after a month or two he was back on the job and things returned to normal.

In 1908 Charles Post resigned as treasurer—the Cleveland banking world was in chaos in the wake of the "Millionaires' Panic of 1907"—and Hackenberg recommended his colleague at National Carbon, John S. Crider, for the job.[21] Crider was to serve as Dow treasurer for 26 years, until Earl W. Bennett took over the job in 1934. Crider remained a Dow director for 42 years, finally retiring in 1950 in his 80th year. He was the last of the Cleveland residents to journey to Midland for the monthly Dow board meetings.[22]

Hackenberg became one of the most influential of the Cleveland directors, often taking over chores that would normally have fallen to Convers, such as Herbert Dow's salary, about which Dow was unhappy for years. Dow's salary had been set at $3,000 per annum and stayed there through the early years of struggle. In 1905 he proposed a new arrangement whereby his salary would be set at 4 percent of the net earnings of the company, and this was approved by the board. This arrangement might have made him wealthy, but with the onset of the pro-tracted war with the Bromkonvention it turned out to be a disaster for Dow, and by 1909 he was asking that this arrangement be amended to provide for a $3,000 minimum—the same salary at which he had begun a dozen years before. The salaries of all the other officers had been doubled in the interim, he pointed out, at his instigation.

In response Hackenberg let him have both barrels:

> In the common vernacular, you make me "tired" in continually referring to the fact that "without solicitation I introduced a motion that doubled the salaries of all the other officers" and "the other officers received an increase and, by comparison, a high salary based on the time spent, without asking for it." The salary that the officers received, before the enormous increase of doubling, was $25 a month, with a small allowance for clerk hire. I will not say anything about the President or Vice President, but so far as the work of the Secretary and Treasurer is concerned, Mr. Crider and myself are putting in time and service to The Dow Chemical Company that would be worth a great deal more to us if spent in other directions, than the small amount of $100 that we receive jointly. We would be only too glad to turn our work over this very minute and are ready to do so if you can get any one else to take the jobs. We are inclined to think you are very unappreciative of what we have done and are doing for The Dow Chemical Co. So far as you are concerned, you made your own salary four years ago and when it did not turn out as you anticipated you commenced kicking and finally demanded that a minimum be fixed, which was done. You then asked to have your salary fixed on the same basis as four years ago but with a minimum of $3,000. This was also done and you are still kicking. Now, what DO you want?[23]

Dow apologized immediately. "It was not my intention to belittle the work that the officers are doing or to criticize the small salary they are receiving," he wrote Hackenberg. "I certainly think you are giving your time and energy to the company for a very small consideration in proportion to the value received, and I regret very much that I gave you a different impression."[24]

Hackenberg was also instrumental in setting up a separate sales department, which took place in 1904; until this time the production of the company was sold entirely through agents—the Fred G. Clarke Company of Cleveland at first, and then the Edward Hill Son & Company of New York, from the beginning of 1903. Jim Graves, who had taken over as plant superintendent with the departure of M. B. Johnson, was the supervisor of this relationship, and was increasingly being called upon to visit customers and take care of correspondence with them. By early 1904, Hackenberg was pressing Dow to "arrange to sell bleach directly to the consumers." Graves, he said, was "too valuable a man at the factory to place upon him the additional burden of doing all the travelling, together with the correspondence and general supervision of the sales."[25]

By the summer of 1904 they were actively looking at candidates. Unfortunately Herbert Dow's top candidate for the job had flown the coop. He was E. O. Cross, an early Dow employee who Dow lamented, was "the only good employee the company has yet lost." Cross had left for the Klondike gold rush in 1902; there he operated a plant to separate gold from ore chemically at a place called Bonanza Creek in the Yukon, being paid $1,800 for a short season as compared to his Dow salary of $1,200 annually. After a season of this he returned stateside, and wound up with the Fostoria Glass Company, of Fostoria, Ohio, of which he was later president. Dow wrote him about the sales job, but Cross was not interested.

In the summer and fall of 1904 Dow, Hackenberg, and others looked at some 12 or 15 candidates, most attracted through a blind advertisement in a New York trade journal. Eventually the choice was narrowed down to Rupert E. Paris, a Saginaw businessman, and in September the company announced that sales of bleaching powder for delivery after January 1, 1905, would be made directly from the Midland office through its "Selling Department," and that Mr. Rupert E. Paris was taking charge of that department. Hackenberg suggested the company carry an ad in the *Oil, Paint & Drug Reporter* with this announcement for a few months, "until the trade has become accustomed to the change in the Selling Department."[26] This modest effort was the first Dow advertising campaign.

Paris lined up the company's bleach contracts for 1905 that fall, and appeared to be doing famously. By 1906 he was accompanying the Dow family to Europe, and he seemed destined for a key role in the firm. He stayed at Dow only a few years, however, leaving when he received a better offer—as general sales manager (and assistant treasurer) of the Oldsmobile automobile firm in Lansing, Michigan.

Dow went back to recruiting a sales manager, and this time zeroed in quickly on the man he wanted, W. H. Van Winckel, an experienced chemical seller in Toronto, where he was secretary-treasurer of Chemical Laboratories Ltd., a small chemical manufacturer and marketer. Van Winckel was the first Canadian hired by Dow and the last sales manager recruited from outside the company. Dow informed Van Winckel before he arrived that his assistant in the Selling Department would be G. Lee Camp, then a shipping clerk; Camp would take over as sales manager when Van Winckel in turn left, at the end of World War I.

Van Winckel picked up smoothly from Paris and began to put together the core of a marketing department. Dow said later that his only criticism of him was that he "preferred to give his time to big deals in New York City rather than attend to a mass of details in Midland," and said, "I think his only reason for leaving us was the thought that he could make a good deal more money in the brokerage business in New York than he could as Sales Manager for The Dow Chemical Company."[27]

In 1911 three Case men—Dow, A. W. Smith, and Charles S. Howe, now its president— approached Hackenberg with a proposition that he give a "short course of lectures" on business accounting to the students at Case, which because of his expertise they felt would be an invaluable service to the school and its students. "I am certain that I have been handicapped all my life by reason of my lack of knowledge along the lines of financial accounting," Dow wrote Hackenberg. "If I had had less chemistry than I did, I would not have been handicapped because I could easily have acquired the lacking information, but I have never been well enough posted on common accounting methods to utilize them."[28] Hackenberg, as busy as ever, thanked them but declined the opportunity.

In the spring of 1916 Hackenberg finally cut the thread, sold out his Dow stock holdings, and resigned as Dow's corporate secretary. The Union Carbide and Carbon Company was to emerge shortly, in 1917, as one of the nation's largest chemical firms, and the National Carbon Company with which he was associated was merged into this major new firm. James T. Pardee became the new secretary of Dow and quickly began to take on a much heavier Dow load than had previously been the case.

Looking back on it many years later, Herbert Dow became nostalgic about Harvey Hackenberg and wrote Pardee a note:

> Years ago when Mr. Hackenberg and I went to Germany he was vastly more experienced than I and I was undoubtedly a handicap to him . . . we have gotten into the habit of thinking that his associates of that time were much more experienced business men than we were, but they never did a business of a million dollars a month as we are now doing. . . . Conditions are entirely reversed and we are now the sophisticated and experienced business people, and on a much larger scale than were the operations of the Company with which Mr. Hackenberg was associated.[29]

Notes

1. *Cleveland Press*, March 31, 1900. Biographical sketch of Collings, *Dow Diamond*, October 1941.

2. G. E. Collings to H. H. Dow, December 21, 1911; G. E. Collings to J. T. Pardee, August 23, 1921.

3. G. E. Collings to H. H. Dow, May 28, 1906.

4. Ibid., August 17, 1928.

5. The chief biographical sources for Pardee used here are *Case Alumnus* magazine, August 1957; *Midland Daily News*, January 3, 1944; *New York Times*, January 4, 1944; *The Brinewell*, Dow employee publication, January 11, 1944; and *Oil, Paint and Drug Reporter*, April 29, 1935.

6. From talk by Pardee, "The Early Life of Dr. Herbert H. Dow," New York, at presentation of Perkin Medal to Dow, January 10, 1930.

7. H. H. Dow to J. T. Pardee, February 3, 1910.

8. Oral History, Dorothy Dow Arbury, January 18, 1989; Oral History, Margaret Dow Towsley, December 6, 1989.

9. From notes prepared by George D. Welles Jr., of Dow, for the archives of the American Society of Civil Engineers, February 11, 1944.

10. Harrison Hatton, conversation with Mrs. Margaret Johnson, June 30, 1950.

11. See, for example, two letters dated March 18, 1909, Dow to Pardee, one marked "Never Sent," and letter same date, Pardee to Dow, marked "Personal." These concerned remarks critical of Dow made by Charles Post at the board meeting that month that infuriated Dow. The company was not paying dividends at the time because of the bromine war. Pardee advised Dow to cool it down. "We have had enough of criticism," he wrote. "The thing we are all after now is Dividends."

12. The Uhinck twins, Elsa Pardee and Eda Gerstacker, both established important foundations: Mrs. Pardee the Pardee Foundation for cancer research and care, and Mrs. Gerstacker the Rollin M. Gerstacker Foundation, named for her husband.

13. G. Willard Ball, 1897; document preserved at Post Street Archives.

14. A. L. Fuller to H. H. Dow, March 9, 1899. See *Catalogue of officers, graduates and students of Western Reserve College and of Adelbert College, 1826-1916* (Cleveland: The Western Reserve University Press, 1916), 7-13.

15. H. H. Dow to J. H. Osborn, February 8, 1899.

16. The titles "first vice president" and "second vice president" were no longer used in the company after World War I.

17. The firm later became Wellman-Seaver-Morgan Company, engineers and manufacturers, Wellman remaining as president. Wellman was in California in 1908-12 with the Noble Electric Steel Company, Heroult, Shasta County.

18. Minutes, Dow board of directors, July 2, 1919.

19. "Report of Examination of The Dow Chemical Company's Business," May 24-29, 1900, H. E. Hackenberg.

20. H. H. Dow to H. E. Hackenberg, March 6, 1909; H. E. Hackenberg to H. H. Dow, March 8, 1909; H. H. Dow to H. E. Hackenberg, March 9, 1909.

21. Crider had a distinguished career at National Carbon Company as secretary, vice president, and general manager. Later, when it was formed, he became a vice president of Union Carbide and Carbon Company. Hackenberg had been secretary of National Carbon and was promoted to treasurer in 1899, being succeeded as secretary by Crider.

22. Herbert Dow bungled the succession to Post rather badly. His nominee to succeed Post as director was E. O. Cross; having Cross on the board would bring in a person very familiar with the chemical business, Dow said. The board then engaged in a protracted discussion of whether it was necessary to be familiar with chemical manufacture in order to be a good director. The Cleveland directors, none of whom had experience in chemicals, were certain it was not necessary, and in the end Dow did not press the Cross candidacy, knowing it would be defeated. When Hackenberg nominated Crider he agreed, and nothing more was said about it.

23. H. E. Hackenberg to H. H. Dow, June 26, 1909, marked "Personal."

24. H. H. Dow to H. E. Hackenberg, June 28, 1909, marked "Personal"; see also H. H. Dow to H. E. Hackenberg, March 18, 1901 and H. H. Dow to H. E. Hackenberg, June 21, 1909.

25. H. E. Hackenberg to H. H. Dow, March 31, 1904.

26. The *Oil, Paint & Drug Reporter* is now known as *Chemical Marketing Reporter*, or *CMR*.

27. H. H. Dow to R. Chandler Snead, New York attorney, March 23, 1920; H. H. Dow to Ralph L. Fuller, Ralph L. Fuller Company, Cleveland, December 3, 1917.

28. H. H. Dow to H. E. Hackenberg, May 13, 1911.

29. H. H. Dow to J. T. Pardee, March 16, 1929. Hackenberg died suddenly of a heart attack in 1923.

THREE
LITTLE GIANTS

I.

At least three of Herbert Dow's early "hires" became legends in the company. Today the main headquarters buildings of the firm in Midland bear the names of these legends. The Bennett Building is the central headquarters building, housing the executive offices and world-wide administrative functions; the Barstow Building houses many of the chemical and related product headquarters, as well as Dow North America; and the Strosacker Building is essentially the capital of Dow's plastics operations.

Earl W. Bennett was a prototype Horatio Alger story, a tiny, skimpily educated youngster who started at the bottom and by talent and hard work made his way to the top. It was he who journeyed to Wall Street to raise money to fuel the growth of a struggling, unheralded small chemical company in a small town in Michigan, and thereby contributed mightily to (and perhaps even enabled) its success.

He was born at White Cloud, Michigan, a lumbering days leftover, in 1880. His father drove horses for the lumberjacks and later became supply superintendent for a lumber camp at Hub, North Carolina. Young Bennett went to work as a lumberjack at age 16 without even graduating from high school. The lumber crews moved to North Carolina from Michigan in 1896, and the Bennetts followed them there. Earl was then barely five feet tall, not exactly the right size for a lumberjack, and when the camp cook died (the crew claimed he choked to death on his own cooking) he asked his father for a tryout as replacement.

For 10 months the teen-aged Bennett was a successful camp cook; the men loved his jelly rolls and cakes. During this time he collected no pay, and when the year ended he took his entire earnings, $450, and headed for Chicago, where he had decided he would enroll in a two-year accounting course at the Bryant Stratton Business College. He completed the course in nine months and took a job at Marshall Field, where he worked for three years, taking night courses in accounting as he went along.

In 1900 he decided on a vacation trip, and because he did not have enough money to go to North Carolina to see his parents he went to Midland, where his grandmother lived and where he had had some of his schooling. While he was in town he heard that the new "bleaching powder works" in Midland was about to double its capacity, and he decided to see if they needed a bookkeeper. His friend Paul Engwis, who already had 10 years' acquaintance with Herbert Dow and was now his "steam engineer," took him in to see M. B. Johnson, who had charge of the hiring. He then talked to Herbert Dow, who said he would hire Bennett as office boy at $360 a year; if he proved he could do the books he would get a raise.

Bennett was making $500 a year at Marshall Field but accepted the offer, reasoning that Dow looked like a fast-growing firm and that "he thought he'd like to grow up with the company."[1] His work as office boy included sweeping out the office, running down to meet the train with the mail, and other such chores, including helping Daniel W. Chase of the Midland County Savings Bank, who was working part-time for Dow preparing the weekly report for Cleveland. Within a short time Harvey Hackenberg in Cleveland was telling Dow he liked what he was seeing in the way of improved accounting and reports, and Bennett was soon off probation. By December 1900 Bennett already had his first raise (to $480 a year), and Dow wrote to Charles Post: "Bennett works more than 10 hours a day and receives compensation of $480 a year. Mr. Hackenberg considers him entirely competent to take charge of the books of the company and we will therefore raise his salary to $600 a year."[2] Bennett became the bookkeeper as of January 1, 1901, and a year later became auditor as well. In 1907 he advanced to assistant secretary and assistant treasurer of the company, working closely over the succeeding years with Hackenberg, the secretary, and Crider, the treasurer.

His lumberjack days had made him athletic and tough, and in the fall of 1900 Bennett resumed what he had done in high school, becoming the star quarterback of the Midland City football team, which traveled about and played neighboring towns. Gilbert A. Currie, who also played on that team, remembered him as "the best quarterback Midland ever had"; another teammate said Bennett "never settled for a four-yard gain when he could get a little more than that."[3] His football career ended when Herbert Dow grumbled that he "hadn't brought Bennett to Midland to play football"; after that season he did not play any more, although he was a major sports fan all his life. He followed and knew personally most of the key football players at the University of Michigan for a generation.

In 1902 a new Baptist minister came to town, the Rev. A. C. Barclay, and as Bennett told it, he met Barclay's daughter Eva in the Sunday School class he was teaching and began to walk her home from church. In July 1905 they were married (by her father), and began a family that eventually numbered eight children, four boys and four girls.

Bennett quickly became an enthusiastic purchaser of Dow stock, making his first buy, 13 shares, in November 1900. During much of his youth the family was rich in Dow stock but poor in cash, and the children later remembered many meals of cornmeal mush.[4] Bennett sold magazine subscriptions during this time to earn extra income, and several slips by which he renewed Herbert Dow's subscription to the *Saturday Evening Post* have survived.

One of Bennett's favorite stories of this time concerned an incident just after the panic of 1907 when his wife called and asked him to pick up a loaf of bread on the way home. Walking up Main Street to the grocery, he realized he did not have a nickel in his pocket.

> I thought of asking the grocer for credit but I was afraid word would get around that Dow was in such bad shape Bennett couldn't even pay cash for a loaf of bread. I walked past the grocery wondering what to do. I said, "Lord, I'm in trouble and I need help." I crossed the street and walked back down Main Street. The wind was blowing leaves along the walk and I saw a ball of green paper roll by. I thought it was the wrapper from a tobacco package, but I stopped and picked it up. I unfolded it and saw I was holding a two-dollar bill. I said, "Thank you, Lord, for answering that prayer."

Bennett added: "Times were never as bad after that, and I never did think a two-dollar bill was unlucky."[5]

Bennett decided that to get ahead he needed to be there when something needed doing, and from the beginning he was the last one in the office in the evening. This worked very well; when Herbert Dow needed something Bennett was always there, and he steadily accumulated more responsibility.

His first significant contribution was to install double-entry bookkeeping. As Bennett explained years later, "Double-entry bookkeeping was not originated with me because it was discovered by the Italians a great many years ago, but most concerns (in 1900) did not have accountants who knew double-entry bookkeeping. Before that we just used counter books, marking down the cash you took in, the cash you paid out. Double entry provided a record of debits and credits."[6]

He progressed steadily, and so did the company, and by the 1930s Dow had a solid record on Wall Street—it had not missed a dividend since 1911—and a growing reputation as a financially well-run company; and the shrewd little man who kept Dow's books in Midland had a growing reputation as a financial wizard. He was promoted to director in 1927, and four years later, when the company reorganized following Herbert Dow's death, Bennett became a member of the executive committee and a vice president of the company, the first person accorded that title since 1914 and the first non-Clevelander. When John Crider stepped down as treasurer in 1934 (after 26 years in the job), Bennett officially succeeded to that job, and when James T. Pardee moved up from secretary to board chairman in 1935, he added the job of secretary as well.

He acquired these responsibilities when Dow was about to enter an era of fantastic growth, growth that would not have been possible without heavy infusions of capital, more than the Cleveland banks who had provided for Dow's needs up to this time were likely to provide. Bennett proved to be the ideal man for the situation. The company's sales in 1934 were $17 million, net income $3.3 million. Seven years later the figures had leaped to $47 million and $9.9 million; invested capital in that period also tripled, from $22 million to almost $70 million, and this in a period of general deflation.[7]

Bennett went to New York soon after becoming treasurer to meet with the key banking houses. As he told it,

> I went to New York cold, without any introductions, and started making the rounds of the banking institutions. I introduced myself and explained that I represented The Dow Chemical Company. Remember, I was only 5-feet-6 and weighed no more than 110 pounds. A good many of these people found it amusing that so small a man should be walking around such a big city talking about credit for a company few of them knew anything about. Our stock wasn't listed in the New York papers. It was quoted on the Cleveland market.
>
> I wasn't able to get through the layers of secretaries and vice presidents in many houses to reach the top men. But I did get a very warm reception and a hearing from Smith, Barney & Co., and from Lehman Brothers. As a result of this trip, we developed a very close relationship with Smith, Barney that lasted through the years.[8]

Charles W. Kennard, who became a partner in Smith, Barney, recalled years later his experiences as a young man in 1934 when Bennett came to Wall Street. The net result was that in January 1935, Smith, Barney began working with Bennett, placing privately for Dow $3,600,000 of 2.5 percent serial notes; this was followed in December 1936 with the first public offering of Dow securities, $5 million in 3 percent debentures. Then, on June 30, 1937, Dow's stock was listed for the first time on the New York Stock Exchange.

"I am sure no other financial officer in the last half century ever made a nickel work harder for his company," Kennard said. "The money for Dow's tremendous growth was raised at the lowest possible cost to the stockholders. The financing history of Dow has always been the right security at the right time.

"Dow through all its existence has been famous for its research—new products and new processes have been the hallmark of Dow through the years. What is not so well known, except in the financial world, is that under Earl Bennett's guidance Dow's financing has been equally imaginative. Earl Bennett was not orthodox in his finance, and because of his creative thinking Dow established bold new patterns of financing." He cited a 1952 issue of $100 million in 3 percent subordinated convertible debentures. "Prior to that time these securities were not fully acceptable in corporate financing, their use being limited mainly to reorganizations of distressed companies. The response of the investment world was fantastic, exceeding even our fondest hopes. Thus a new financing horizon was opened and such securities became a frequently used and acceptable financial tool."[9]

During World War II Bennett became president of Dow Magnesium Company, a firm set up to build plants and produce magnesium for the war effort under government contracts. When peace came he stepped down and resumed his usual Dow responsibilities.

When Willard Dow was killed in a plane crash in 1949 and the company went through a major reorganization, Bennett was 69 years old, an age at which most would have thought about retiring. Instead, Bennett moved on into a new chapter of his life and the capstone of his long career, as Dow's chairman of the board.

He turned over his chores as treasurer to Carl A. Gerstacker, whom he had trained for the job and whom he called "the top financial genius in the chemical industry today."[10] He remained chairman until he was 80, however, turning that position over to Gerstacker (in 1960) as well, and continued as a member of the finance and executive committees of the company until he retired at age 89.

He would not have retired even then except that his eyesight was failing (he was afflicted with glaucoma) and he had to hold papers close to his face to read them. He continued on in his tiny office, which had glass walls above a wainscoting so that he could see and be seen by the Dow financial staff, whose offices surrounded his, and he continued to punch a time clock, as he had from the beginning. When a visitor would ask him why he, as the chairman, still punched a timeclock, Bennett would say, "Why, so I'll get paid."[11] When he retired the board of directors made him honorary chairman for life.

He once said his business philosophy was "live and let live," which as far as he was concerned included the Golden Rule, honesty in competition, ethics, and a multitude of other relationships. Asked what his advice would be for new employees looking to get ahead, he said he had a few suggestions:

- Work hard and avoid worry. Try to clean up everything each day so you can sleep nights.
- Train yourself to love your job, but look forward and learn as much as you can about the job ahead without being nosey.
- When you have a position of responsibility be sure you have someone trained to step into your shoes.
- Above all, keep your nose clean, and believe enough in your company to invest in it.[12]

After his retirement the glaucoma continued to progress and he soon became blind. He and Eva continued to live in the big old house on Main Street where they had brought up their eight children, and where the Barstows and the Pardees were next-door neighbors, just up the street from the Herbert Dow place. Groups of his friends would gather in the evening to play bridge with him, taking turns sitting at the old man's elbow and whispering into his ear what cards he was picking up and telling him what card had just been played. He would then call the card he wanted to play. It was a remarkable feat of memory for a man blind and 93, and he enjoyed it immensely.[13]

With today's retirement rules it will be impossible for anyone ever to break Earl Bennett's record of 69 years of unbroken service with the Dow Company. When he died (on September 18, 1973) the Dow board paused to pay tribute once again: "Earl Bennett always exemplified his basic beliefs that one should be of service to others, put in an honest day's work, and get the maximum of enjoyment out of life; and these are among his legacies to the company," a board resolution said.[14]

II.

As a college student Herbert Dow occasionally visited the Edwin F. Barstow farm at Rockport, on the outskirts of Cleveland, where he earned a dollar or two toward his education by doing farm work. The family had a son, Edwin O. Barstow, 13 years younger than Dow, and through conversations with Dow the boy became interested in chemistry. Dow urged him to go on to the Case School and he did, becoming one of Albert Smith's brightest students.

By the time he was a senior at Case young Barstow (class of 1900) was already on the Dow Chemical payroll at half pay, doing experimental work on ammonia yields in the Case laboratory. When he graduated he went up to Midland and became a full-time employee.

Barstow is remembered principally as the father of magnesium, a field he pioneered for 27 years, but he was also a distinguished scientist and inventor who accumulated 60 patents in his Dow career. He was a chemical innovator who devised processes for many of the products Dow launched, and a community leader who worked tirelessly for the betterment of his city.

Dow often referred to Barstow as his "first chemist," but that seems to have referred to his rank rather than to chronology; Barstow himself always noted that James Graves was the first chemist hired by Dow.[15] He seems in any event to have been the first person to have had Dow's complete confidence in dealing with chemical problems, and his early career was a series of troubleshooting assignments; if a plant was not working right, Dow asked Barstow to take it over.

He began as the chemist in charge of the bleach plant. The first Dow laboratory was "a little shack in a corner of the bleach plant," and Barstow immediately began to spend time there running tests on the plant's product, and doing a little research as well. It was in this "lab" that he worked out the process for his first new product for Dow, benzoate of soda. The Germans were then the sole manufacturers. "Its consumption is increasing very rapidly, although very little attention is attracted to this fact for the reason that none of the users want it known that they employ this material," Herbert Dow wrote. "Some of the very best canned goods manufacturers are using benzoate of soda for preserving their fruits, vegetables, and ketchup, and are commanding a much higher price than their competitors can secure without using this material."[16]

Sodium benzoate was the first food additive and the first controversial product Dow produced. Congress had passed the Food and Drug Act in 1906 and food additives were now undergoing stiff scrutiny, inspired by writings such as Upton Sinclair's novel, *The Jungle*, about unsavory practices in the meatpacking industry. The campaign was led by a pioneering chemist and crusader, Harvey W. Wiley, chief of the Bureau of Chemistry in the U.S.

Department of Agriculture. Dow and the users of sodium benzoate contended that "it is as necessary to use a high-grade preservative today as it was for the Indians to use salt or smoke, and the use of these newer materials is as great an advance as other achievements of civilization." In the end the material passed muster and federal law simply required a statement of the amount of benzoate contained in a food product, clearly printed on the label.[17] Barstow devised an entirely new way to manufacture the material, and it was added to the Dow product list.

How he and Tom Griswold designed production plants such as this one in this pioneering day was described by Barstow later:

> I would sit on one stool and Griswold on the other. I would tell Griswold what I wanted and Griswold would sketch it out right there. Mr. Griswold was exceptionally good at making quick sketches on the spot and putting ideas into drawings. Then Mr. Griswold would go back and make a formal drawing of it. We would consider the whole thing again after he had it drawn up and make any change that seemed necessary. From these corrected drawings the plant would be built.

In this way Griswold designed the sodium benzoate plant, "as he had designed most of the others," Barstow said.

Barstow had vivid memories of many of the hourly paid men he worked with in those days: John Collinson, the "boss carpenter" ("When he first came all the tools he had were a saw, a hatchet, and a hammer, but when he was working for me he could do the fastest rough carpenter job I have ever seen and do it well."); Paul Engwis ("a superb machinist"); Bill Day (another machinist, engineer at the Old Mill, which became the main research laboratory a little later); Elzie Cote and Julius Burows, who had been among Herbert Dow's earliest employees at the Evens Mill on Main street; and Lance Graves, the carpenter shop foreman famous around town as "the only honest spy."[18]

He also had vivid memories of Midland's downtown in these early days, when there were 13 saloons on Main Street, all on the north side of the street. The north side was the "saloon side" and the south side was the "store side"; proper women shopped on the store side, but no respectable woman could be seen on the saloon side—her reputation would be ruined. The older townspeople tended to be pro-saloon, many of them either owning a saloon, working in one, or having a relative who did. The new young men in town—Dow, Griswold, Barstow, Strosacker, and a few others such as Gilbert Currie, and certainly most of those brought to town by Dow, were strongly anti-saloon. There came to be rival factions, and within a few years the liquor issue—was Midland to be "wet" or "dry"?—became the biggest battle in the city.

The "due bill" issue was a second factor dividing the town. Local employers such as the Reardon brothers, William and Thomas, proprietors of Reardon Bros. Mercantile Company and major powers in the county Board of Commissioners, were accustomed to paying their employees in "due bills." They felt Herbert Dow should pay his employees in due bills as well, but Dow insisted on paying his employees in cash. (Due bills were redeemable only in certain stores, such as, for example, Reardon Bros.).

One day Will Reardon visited Herbert Dow and told him the younger element in town was "stirring up a lot of trouble," and that Dow would have to put a stop to it. They were trying to stir up interest in "local option" (a county could vote "dry" if it chose) and do away with the saloons, he said. Dow replied that he did not know whether or not he wanted to do anything about it, but even if he did it would not do any good, because the men would not pay any attention to him on a thing like that. Reardon replied that they certainly would if they worked for Will Reardon; what kind of boss was Herbert Dow, anyway?

A story often repeated concerned the time Barstow, a strapping 6' 2" farm lad, was escorting a young lady down Main Street when an unsteady, half-soused fellow made a scurrilous suggestion to the lady. Barstow, offended, took the lady to a nearby place of security and then returned and gave him a thrashing.

In 1908 the local option issue came to a head, and Midland became a "dry" county after a bitterly contested election. This marked the end of the saloon era in Midland, and Midland was to stay "dry" for 50 years. From then on neighboring Bay City, which remained "wet," was a favorite destination for Midlanders in search of a watering spot.

Overcoming the animosity of some of the Midland population toward the Dow Company was "pretty much a process of evolution," as Barstow saw it. There was never any attempt to tax the company out of the town, although that had happened in St. Louis, Michigan, where Dow bought an old brine-plant site that was no longer being operated. When the city slapped a big tax on the plant Dow sighed and pulled out of town, leaving the plant to the city.[19]

When World War I came, and with it thousands of single young men arriving to take jobs making chemicals for the war, Herbert Dow became concerned not only with housing and feeding them, but with their recreational needs as well. Dow asked the Rev. Myron E. Adams, a Baptist minister who had been one of the leaders in the Midland local option fight a few years before, to look into the situation; Adams had in the interim moved on to the Chicago area. Adams recruited Guy L. Shipps, a friend who had worked with boys' clubs there, and the two came to Midland, where Herbert Dow provided them with offices and salaries.

They first explored the possibility of establishing a YMCA branch in Midland but abandoned the idea when it became clear that a large number of the newcomers were Catholics unlikely to patronize what was perceived as a Protestant institution. Instead they focused on the concept of a community center that would provide a wide range of programs at little cost to the participants.

The Midland Community Center was launched in July 1916 with a fund of $83,735, of which Herbert Dow contributed $37,010 out of his own pocket. Other members of the Dow family contributed $1,760, the Dow Company contributed $22,000, and 73 other persons gave a total of $22,965. Shipps became the first director, and Barstow, who had been a key figure from the beginning, became president of the center's board. He served in this position until 1950, making sure over the years that the center had continuing support and was doing the job it had been assigned.[20] Barstow also at this time became the founder of the Midland Welfare Association, forerunner of the city's Community Fund.

The community center generated a wide range of recreational activities, many of which did not remain housed there but became independent activities: bowling, which became a major activity in Midland; softball leagues; archery clubs; rifle-shooting organizations; and other programs ranging from square dancing to senior-citizen travel all grew out of community center programs.

When the WWI-era building became obsolete and outgrown, Barstow, then in his seventies, initiated a campaign for a bigger, newer community center located close to the residential center of the city. It was dedicated in 1965.

Turning back to his Dow activities, Barstow in 1914 became production manager for the Inorganic Division of the company, which grouped all of the products of the brine stream and represented by far the largest segment of the firm. Before long it was called "Barstow's Division." It was the responsibility of this division to research and develop new products based on brine, and for much of the rest of his career Barstow was supervisor (and usually directly involved in) the extraction of more useful products from the brine—calcium chloride and magnesium chloride, the Dow Epsom salt process, more and better bromine and bromides, and iodine and iodides. Barstow was the inventor of the crystallization process for separating the calcium chloride and magnesium chloride in the brine stream, a key step in these advances.

In 1915 Dow and Barstow began to look into the magnesium chloride component of the brine as a source of magnesium metal—Dow originally saw magnesium simply as a useful by-product—and Barstow began work on an electrolytic cell to produce magnesium. He was to work on magnesium development for the next 27 years.

Through his friend Albert W. Smith, Herbert Dow put W. R. Veazey of the chemistry faculty to work on the problem at Case, and Barstow put a young man named Edward C. Burdick to work on it in Midland. They started work with a small cell using a current of 100 amperes in the basement of the Old Mill, which had now became the main Dow experimental lab. Veazey assigned a Case student, William R. Collings, to work on the problem with him in Cleveland, and Herbert Dow sent them a five-gallon can of magnesium chloride solution. Collings arrived in Midland the next year with a tiny two-inch disc of magnesium he had produced from it for his senior thesis; it was barely a quarter-inch thick, but it was magnesium, and a sensational introduction to his new employer.[21]

Veazey, who in those days taught at Case but spent his summers working in Midland, came to Midland after school was out in the spring of 1916 and with Burdick, Collings, and I. J. ("Charley") Stafford (who did not stay with the company very long) set to work on the first crude magnesium cell, made of welded boiler plate and soapstone slabs. It was easy for them to get small globules of magnesium to emerge from the cell feed and float on the surface, but they could not get them to coalesce in a mass. Encouraged but not content, Herbert Dow told them he wanted to see "one pound of magnesium in one piece," and that became their mission.

At the beginning of July they produced the first ingot, a piece about the size of a baseball, by electrolyzing a fused salt bath. As Veazey described it:

> We had been working at such a determined pace on the problem of getting the small pieces of magnesium to coalesce that when we finally succeeded in getting one whole piece, we suddenly realized nobody had thought about how to cast it or get it out of the cell. Somebody grabbed the first thing he could find, which was a piece of sheet iron. It was heated and bent into the shape of a crude ladle. A piece of pipe was attached for a handle and the piece of magnesium metal was scooped out of the magnesium bath. There was no mold, so we set the ladle on the floor to let the magnesium cool. And that's how we got the first ingot of magnesium.

Herbert Dow took this first piece of magnesium home to show his family. "Some day," he told them, "this will be the biggest thing we have." A few days later it was displayed in the window of Bert Carter's Dry Goods store on Main Street as evidence of the latest triumph of Midland's chemists. On July 20 the four men produced an enormous piece weighing 100 pounds; magnesium metal production had begun.[22]

Barstow said later that if Dow and his colleagues had had a real idea how big magnesium was to be, and the bitter disappointments it was to bring the company, "we would have quit, even though it was against our tradition to quit." "Here we were," he said, "a chemical company used to producing and selling chemicals, and we had gotten into the field of metallurgy, which is as big a thing as chemistry itself, or almost so, and one in which we had no experience. There was no know-how on magnesium available in this country. Nobody knew anything about it, and we had to go ahead and find out as we went along. We could not have had any real idea of the problems involved; nobody did at that time."

He said some people "wanted to quit magnesium almost as soon as we had gotten into it, and there were times when that seemed to be the general opinion, and there is plenty of evidence to prove that those people were right, even today (he was speaking in 1950). However, it was a very fortunate thing for the United States that we did not quit, although it is something no one could foresee at that time."[23]

In 1917 Dow told Barstow to build a magnesium plant, skipping the pilot plant stage; with a war going on there was no time for it. The plant cost $225,000 and was to have a capacity of 3,000 pounds a day. It featured the new electrolytic cell and a number of complex control features, most of which did not work in actual operation. When it was completed, Veazey and another recruit from the Case School, Ralph M. Hunter, started up the plant one night with 32 men, Hunter being recruited from the Indigo plant at the last moment because Burdick and Stafford were not available.

The plant ran about 36 hours before it was closed down; in the end it never ran again, and was eventually scrapped. The chlorine lines were plugging up and spilling chlorine into the atmosphere at a rate of three or four tons an hour. By the time Veazey and Hunter decided to close it down, on the second night of operation, they were the only two left in the plant; the others had all been chased by the chlorine. Veazey said the plant was not a complete loss: they learned many things from it that they needed to know.[24]

Not going through the pilot plant stage had been an expensive proposition. Undaunted, Dow and Barstow set about designing a new plant, with new cells. By the end of the war this second plant, under Ralph Hunter, was successfully turning out 1,500 pounds of magnesium daily.

Barstow became the driving force behind Dow's faith in the light metal, and played a key role in developing the electrolytic process by which it was extracted from seawater beginning in 1941 at Freeport, Texas. That achievement became most significant to the world when the Allies found themselves desperately short of the material at the outset of World War II. Dow quickly became a leader in the wartime push to produce the metal, largely through Barstow's expertise.

After Herbert Dow died, the company was reorganized under Willard Dow, and in 1931 Barstow and Charles J. Strosacker were elected to the Dow board and named vice presidents. Barstow was to serve in these offices until 1958, when he was 79 years old, and when he retired his colleagues elected him honorary chairman of the board. He continued to attend board meetings regularly until his final illness.

Among his farsighted efforts were his concern for air and water pollution, Barstow's Division being the largest generator of pollutants in what became for a time the world's largest chemical plant. When President Harry Truman convened the first "President's Conference on Air Pollution" (on May 4, 1950), in Washington, D.C. Barstow was invited to attend and describe Dow Chemical's program in this field. Barstow traced Dow's activities in air pollution to a Willard Dow order of August 2, 1940, appointing Ivan F. Harlow, a division superintendent and Barstow lieutenant whose responsibilities already included operation of the waste disposal department, as the person responsible for air pollution controls.[25]

The Barstows had six children, five boys and a girl. Only the eldest son, Ormond E., followed in his father's footsteps. He was a top graduate at Case in 1926 and then joined the Dow Company for a long career; he established an instrument research laboratory at Dow and was the company's director of instrument systems and design for many years.[26]

Probably the most famous of the Barstow children was John C., known as Jack, an aviation pioneer who in April 1930 established a new endurance record for gliders, remaining aloft for 15 hours 13 minutes in a Bowlus sailplane at Point Loma, California. Barstow's glider pilot's license was signed by Orville Wright, one of the famous Wright brothers. When Charles A. Lindbergh enrolled to learn gliding at Point Loma, Jack Barstow was his instructor—he was then chief instructor for the Bowlus Sailplane Company—and the two became good friends. Jack came to a tragic end in 1935 when he was killed in a midair plane crash at an air show in Corpus Christi, Texas; he was 29 years old.[27]

Oddly enough, his brother Ormond took up flying 53 years later, at the age of 84, and flew his first solo flight at 85. He was still trying to make up for lost time and had logged 250 flights when he died in 1992, aged 88.

When E. O. Barstow retired from Dow about 150 of his associates gathered at a "surprise party"—he would not have consented otherwise—at the Midland Community Center to honor his 58 years as a Dow chemist. After listening to an evening of fulsome tributes he protested, saying he was "terribly embarrassed. I really don't deserve the things that have been said about me. Many of these accomplishments could not have resulted without the help of a lot of others. They really deserve most of the praise."[28] In the words of H. D. (Ted) Doan, who as the president of Dow presided over several events honoring Barstow, "he did his best to make his company the best company it could be, and his community the best community it could be."[29]

III.

Charles J. Strosacker, the third of the pioneer giants who helped Herbert Dow build the company, was a humble, homely man, and while it is unusual to say that a corporate executive was "beloved," he was the exception that proved the rule. He was "Dr. Stro" to the managers who worked for him, "Uncle Charley" to the men in his plants, and just plain "Stro" to everyone else.

He was born Carl Johann Strosacker in the tiny German community of Valley City, Ohio; when he was in high school his family decided to Americanize their names and he became Charles John. The teacher in their one-room school was a Case School graduate and advised the young man to go there, which he did after a year at Baldwin-Wallace for financial reasons.

In the fall of 1905 Dow asked A. W. Smith at Case to have a couple of his promising seniors do their senior thesis work on a process for making indigo starting with bromine (a quite different proposition from making bromindigo dyes), and Strosacker was one of those chosen by Smith to do this. The indigo work came to naught—Strosacker said later it was probably far too advanced for student work—but it was the occasion of his first meeting with Dow.[30]

At the end of the school year Dow told Smith, "I want two chemists this year, one for the Ontario Nickel Co. up in Worthington, Ontario, the other for the Dow Company in Midland. Because living conditions are pretty poor up in Worthington we are going to pay $70 a month to the man who goes there instead of the usual $60, which we will pay the man who comes to Midland." Strosacker, given first choice, chose the $70 job. The Ontario Nickel project went badly, however, and in the fall of 1907 it was abandoned at heavy financial loss to Herbert Dow, who according to Strosacker had sunk $87,000 into it. Strosacker then went to work for the company in Midland.[31] This occasioned Dow's oft-repeated remark that he "brought back (from Ontario Nickel) the best thing they had up there, a chemist named Strosacker."

Strosacker found himself working in the chloroform plant with Barstow, who had taken it over from William Quayle, and before long Barstow moved on and Strosacker was running it.

While Strosacker was running the chloroform plant an accident occurred in which he narrowly missed being killed. On a Sunday morning, November 6, 1910, about 11 o'clock,

Strosacker, William Alvord, foreman of the carbon tetrachloride plant, and a young helper, Eddie Warren, were working on a still of sulfur dichloride; the agitator in it had stalled out and the chloride had crystallized. They decided to pump in a fresh supply of molten sulfur chloride, thinking to melt the solidified material, but instead a resounding explosion occurred, covering all three with the burning, fuming contents and knocking them unconscious. When they were rushed to medical care the major fear was for their eyes—none of them could see— and an eye specialist was summoned to treat their eyes; it was feared they might be permanently blinded. A few days later all three seemed to be rallying and were thought to be out of danger when to the great surprise of the doctors young Eddie Warren died. He was just short of his 20th birthday.[32]

Strosacker's parents and sister Bertha rushed to his sickbed from Valley City. When they arrived he was able to make gestures but not to speak. Five days after the explosion it was reported that he and Alvord could now see a little, and the two men gradually but fully recovered their eyesight.[33] Strosacker stayed in the hospital in Saginaw until December 22, when he reported to Dow that he could see well enough with "my better eye" to read, although the other eye was still poor. He went home to Ohio for the holidays, and told Dow he expected to be back to work on January 10. Dow told him to stay home as long as it helped his eyes to improve.[34]

The accident seems as a by-product to have generated the notion that Bertha, who stayed with her brother throughout this ordeal, should return to Midland with him and continue to nurse him back to health. Strosacker was then 30 and unmarried. Years later, Bertha settled down in Midland and became her brother's hostess and housekeeper for the rest of her life, until she died in 1942.

Herbert Dow used to joke in informal company gatherings that the greatest failure in his life was that he had not managed to get Strosacker married. Stro had dated various women, including, conspicuously, Herbert Dow's eldest daughter Helen, but Helen went off to the university at Ann Arbor and fell in love with and married her chemistry professor, the dashing young Dr. William J. Hale, the Beau Brummel of the campus.[35]

Dow said Strosacker was "the hardest man to please on salary that I ever ran across."[36] In 1912, after a salary argument with Dow, Stro wrote to General Electric and other firms asking if they had a job for him. Dow was at his wit's end. "His salary has been raised either $200 or $300 per year for each of the past few years and evidently his ideas of salary are reaching a point where we are unable to satisfy him," he said.[37] He asked Smith what he thought about it.

Smith wrote, "I think we can well afford to be liberal to him and to consider his case without reference to anyone else. He is an extra-good man. . . . I have just looked over the list of his classmates and I think few of the chemists of that graduating class are getting less than $2,000, and he was perhaps the best of them."[38]

Strosacker told Dow that sulfur chloride was getting monotonous and suggested he would like to do some original research work; this was soon arranged. In 1915 Strosacker was promoted to production manager, received another handsome raise, and bought his first automobile, a 1915 Dodge deluxe touring car with side curtains. He gave away the bicycle on which he had been coming to work.[39]

At the end of 1916 Strosacker suffered a case of "nervous prostration" and was taken to the general hospital in Saginaw again. "It has affected his feet and legs so that it is difficult for him to walk," Dow wrote Smith. "The doctor states that it is caused by overwork." Stro was the second employee to come down with these symptoms, Dow noted; the first was Coulter W. Jones, called "Bromine" Jones to differentiate him from J. I. Jones at the carbon tetrachloride plant.[40] Strosacker was sent on from Saginaw to a sanitarium in Cleveland for treatment, but wrote Dow he'd be back on the job soon. "Don't hurry returning," Dow wired him. "Your plants are running fine."[41]

The organic chemicals and dyes department, of which Strosacker was now the production manager, was formed in the early stages of World War I when a shortage of dyes, imported from Germany until then, brought Dow into the dye manufacturing business. He had resumed the indigo research Strosacker had begun 10 years earlier, and Dow was now in the dye business.

The organic chemicals and dyes department soon became known simply as "Strosacker's Department," and Strosacker became, with Barstow, one of the satraps of the Dow production world. In the early years, as a production chief who loved research, he set aside a corner of each plant for production control work, and this corner became known as "Stro's Lab." By the time his group of plants was formally named Strosacker's Department these labs had been largely amalgamated, given a building of their own, and had grown into one of the company's larger laboratories.

In the years through the end of World War I this was the usual pattern for laboratory work at Dow: most laboratories were set up for the control of manufacturing processes, were small, and occupied a space in or near the manufacturing facilities. This type of small lab popped up all over the plant, especially during the years of World War I, and when a new product was launched—often enough as the result of work done in some makeshift manufacturing control laboratory—the superintendent would quickly set up a small lab for control purposes inside the plant itself. The research function at Dow thus grew up in intimate relationship to the manufacturing function.[42]

Strosacker himself was credited with 27 patents during his career, most of them jointly with other researchers, and the list of his coinventors is almost an honor roll of Dow researchers: Earl L. Pelton, Robert R. Dreisbach, Chester C. Kennedy, Forrest C. Amstutz, Clarence C. Schwegler, James I. Jones, Sheldon B. Heath, Herbert H. Dow, Thomas Griswold Jr., Harold S. Kendall, and Howard J. Rupright.

During the summer of 1915 Herbert Dow introduced an unusual research technique: he asked rival teams of researchers to work on the same project. The idea proved quite successful and has since been used, at irregular intervals, again and again in Dow history. Because of the desperate wartime demand for phenol, needed for explosives, he put Strosacker and

Dreisbach to work developing a method using brombenzene or chlorobenzene. A rival team of Barstow, Paul Cottringer, and Boyd H. Carr was put to work on a sulfonation and fusion method, and the race began, both teams eager to be the first to develop a process for making phenol.

Dreisbach remembered Strosacker saying to him, "Do you suppose we can have a quart of phenol on Mr. Dow's desk Monday morning?" Strosacker and Dreisbach were the first to get a process, and did put a quart of phenol crystals on Dow's desk Monday morning, and as a result a plant was designed and ordered, but never built. As it turned out, the price of bromine and bromides was going sky high, and Dow decided to sell them as bromides rather than use them as raw materials in a brombenzene process. The sulfonation process was used instead, and a plant was built. Dow shut down the plant using this process at the end of the war, when phenol was a glut on the market, and never used the sulfonation process again.[43]

Dreisbach said that when they made the first phenol, Strosacker was holding a long-handled apparatus one day when it exploded. "He got a little piece of metal on his lip, but he didn't worry about that," Dreisbach recalled. "What he said was, 'Do you smell it? Do you smell it?' It was phenol."[44]

Thus both of the research teams racing for a phenol process came out with their honor and their bragging rights intact.

Stro's rivalry with Barstow never was a problem for either of them, and they remained life-long friends and allies in spite of markedly contrasting styles. As W. R. Veazey saw it, Barstow was

able to spend more money in less time than anyone ever connected with the Dow company, in the line of plant building, but he got a job done and in a hurry, and got it into production, which is sometimes a decided asset, when you know three or four other people are working as hard as they can to get into the market; the fellow who can get you into production "the fustest with the mostest" before all the cream is taken off the product is a wonderful man to have around. Strosacker's approach was quite different. While Barstow was building a new plant he had junked an old one, and as soon as he junked it Strosacker and his men were over there taking the plant apart and putting it together again along their own lines to make something entirely different; here is a production man who can spend almost nothing and still produce chemicals you can sell. Strosacker's department has always been a collection of cats and dogs lying around which nobody knew what to do with. So what happened? If a chemical is supposed to call for 90 percent concentration and Strosacker's apparatus happens to make it over 95 percent, do you suppose it gets shipped that way to the customer? No, they take out the extra 5 percent and combine it with another cat or dog for still another product.[45]

One of the more remarkable facets of Strosacker's style was that he never had an office. During the day he would move from building to building in the plants he managed, and if there were a message for him he would get it from the plant superintendent and use his phone to answer it. He did not want his superintendents to spend their time in their offices either; a good superintendent or manager, he felt, didn't sit in an office and let people bring their problems to him—he was out there on the plant floor making sure no problems were going to occur.

Norris E. Coalwell, who started as a pipefitter and became general plant superintendent, recalled that when he was a pipefitter Strosacker "collared" him one day and told him he was doing a simple piping job in a complicated way. Coalwell said, "Well, this is the way I was told to do it." Strosacker answered, "You can think, why didn't you figure out a better way?"[46]

A story told many times concerned the time Stro was hurrying through the plant and found a man reading a newspaper. "Why aren't you working?" Strosacker asked. "I'm waiting for my partner; he went to get some stuff," the man said. After an argument about why the man wasn't working Stro said, "Well, you go on up to the front office and tell them you've been fired, and you need to make arrangements for your last paycheck." "You can't fire me, Mr. Strosacker," the man said. "And why can't I?" Strosacker asked.

"Because I work for Bell Telephone."

Herbert Dow was primarily an inorganic chemist; Strosacker (and Billy Hale) led the way into the organic field, beginning with the first commercial production of indigo. This trend continued later with the first commercial production of styrene, the first commercial production of butadiene, and Dow's move into the plastics business and the introduction to the world of Styron polystyrene and the saran family of plastics; "Stro's Department" was mainly responsible for Dow's extraordinary expansion into plastics production.

During his career Strosacker was responsible for the commercial introduction and large-scale production of many Dow products: ethylene, the glycols, ethyl chloride, perchloroethylene, monochloracetic acid, ethanolamines, a number of pharmaceuticals, and, as mentioned, the plastics. He also played a key role in the development of Saran Wrap plastic film, Dow's first consumer product.

When his devoted sister died in 1942, aged 59, Strosacker decided she should have a memorial, and he proposed to build a new Presbyterian church in Midland, where she had been a Sunday School teacher for 20 years. He himself had never been a church member as an adult, though he did have a confirmation certificate dated 1896 from the Emanuel Evangelical Lutheran Church in Valley City, the family church.[47]

For the next 10 years (the work did not get under way until the war was over), Strosacker immersed himself in all the details of site selection, architecture, decoration, construction, and furnishing that go with the building of a $1.5 million church, the Bertha E. R. Strosacker Memorial Presbyterian Church. During actual construction he was at the site daily making sure the contractors were doing a good job. The church was completed and occupied in 1953.

After Bertha died Strosacker began to look for companionship and found it in a neighborhood family, Walter and Rosalie Klein and their six children, to whom he soon became "Uncle Charley." The Kleins became almost a second family for him; it was said that he spent more time there than at home.

Walter Klein, who was like a son to Stro, became the manager of the Saran Wrap plant when it was built, and it quickly became clear within the company that anyone who disputed a decision by Klein had a dispute with Strosacker. Klein found he could spend Dow funds virtually as he pleased, and built himself an enormous, sumptuously appointed office in the Saran Wrap plant, far larger and more lavish than any other office in the company, including that of the chief executive. (Strosacker himself still had no office.) The top officers of the company turned a blind eye, not wishing to get into a fight with the revered old man that Strosacker had become.

This awkward situation continued until Strosacker died in 1963, at which time an audit of Klein's books turned up some highly questionable expenditures and he left the company. He moved to Arizona and became a land developer.

In 1954, when the company decided to launch Saran Wrap film nationwide and chose Dave Garroway, host of the original "Today" TV show as spokesman for the product, Garroway and a retinue of Dow, advertising agency, and TV brass arrived on a Saturday morning at the Saran Wrap plant where Garroway was to get acquainted with the product; in that day TV commercials were still done "live." As Walter Klein led Garroway and the crowd of hangers on through the plant they came upon Charles Strosacker, sitting on the floor leaning against a wall; he had a brass valve in his hand, and was studying how it might be made to work better. Klein and Garroway halted and Strosacker got to his feet to be introduced. "Just do a good job for us," Stro said to Garroway. "We've got a good product here." Then he sat down again and returned to work on the valve.

It does not seem ever to have occurred to Strosacker that he might retire, but he finally did when he reached his 80th birthday in 1962. On that occasion, marking both his 80th birthday and his 54th year with the Dow Company, the top managers of the firm insisted that he let them honor him for all his contributions. It was a happy evening for him, full of warm nostalgia, praise, and respect.

Only four months later "Dr. Stro" was unexpectedly and peacefully dead. Much of his fortune was left to establish the Charles J. Strosacker Foundation to carry on the types of philanthropy and good works he had pursued in his lifetime.

Notes

1. Biographical materials, Earl W. Bennett, at Post Street Archives.

2. H. H. Dow to C. A. Post, December 31, 1900.

3. G. A. Currie to E. W. Bennett, January 18, 1960.

4. Oral History, Robert B. Bennett, August 24, 1990.

5. "1900 Brought E. W. Bennett to Dow," *Brinewell*, March 1972, 4-5.

6. Transcript of radio interview of Earl W. Bennett by Clarence E. (Dusty) Rhodes, Mid-States Broadcasting Co., 1962.

7. Figures from Annual Reports of Dow for the years ending May 31, 1935, and May 31, 1941.

8. Interview of Earl W. Bennett by Don Whitehead in 1967, Don Whitehead, *The Dow Story* (New York: McGraw-Hill, 1968), 151.

9. Charles W. Kennard, Smith, Barney & Co., remarks prepared for Testimonial Dinner Honoring Earl W. Bennett, January 18, 1960. (There was a seven-inch snowfall in Midland that day and Kennard failed to reach Midland from New York; his prepared remarks were read by the master of ceremonies.)

10. E. W. Bennett to C. A. Gerstacker, January 24, 1960.

11. Only after Bennett's retirement was the requirement that all Dow employees "punch the clock" upon arrival and departure from the work post relaxed for salaried employees, years after this had occurred at other companies.

12. Interview of Earl W. Bennett by L. H. Woodman, Dow Editorial Services, April 5, 1949.

13. The author was an occasional participant in these soirees.

14. Minutes, Dow Board of Directors, October 4, 1973.

15. Graves, a graduate of Albion College, was hired as a chemist at the Midland Chemical Company in 1896 during Dow's absence in Navarre. He resigned from the Dow Company on January 1, 1910, and established the Saginaw Chemical Company to manufacture bromine, taking with him Arthur E. Schaefer, superintendent of Dow's bromine plant. This resulted in a protracted court case, and hardly endeared Graves to Dow, although they remained friends.

16. H. H. Dow to H. E. Hackenberg, July 21, 1905.

17. Harrison Hatton, Notes on conversation with E. O. Barstow, May 16, 1949. Ketchup, for instance, contained about 0.1 percent sodium benzoate. For a discussion of Harvey Wiley's work, see Ken Reese, "Chemistry, Congress, and Safe Foods," *Today's Chemist at Work* (January 1994).

18. Before coming to Dow, Graves worked for the Saginaw (or Tittabawassee) Boom Company, which during the logging drives contracted to move logs (each marked with its owner's "log mark") down the river from the logging banks far upstream to sawmills situated along the river from Midland to Bay City. The boom company hired "spies" at $1 per day to watch the logs at Midland to make sure the Midland mills didn't steal their logs; and to combat this practice the Midland mills often paid the same spies $2 per day to keep their eyes closed. Graves, who "would have none of this," Barstow said, became known as "the only honest spy." Harrison Hatton, conversation with E. O. Barstow, July 18, 1949.

19. Hatton, Notes on conversation with Barstow, June 23, 1950.

20. Hatton, Notes on Comments on Mss. at Executive Committee, September 16, 1949. See also correspondence, February 7 - July 17, 1916, between H. H. Dow and Rev. Adams.

21. Dorothy L. Yates, *William R. Collings, Dow Corning's Pioneer Leader* (Midland, Mich.: Dow Corning Corp., 1985), 17.

22. Incidents described in Robert S. Karpiuk, *Dow Research Pioneers 1888-1949* (Midland, Mich: Pendell Publishing, 1981), 41-48. For magnesium history see William H. Gross, *The Story of Magnesium* (Cleveland, Ohio: American Society for Metals, 1949), 17-23.

23. Hatton, Notes on conversation with E. O. Barstow, March 30, 1950.

24. Hatton, Notes on conversation with W. R. Veazey, March 22, 1950.

25. E. O. Barstow, address at "President's Conference on Air Pollution," Washington, D.C., May 4, 1950.

26. Oral History, Ormond E. Barstow, July 28, 1988. It should be noted that the only Barstow daughter, Ruth, married William R. Dixon, who became a director and the senior marketing executive of the firm for many years.

27. See Mary Novak, "Barstow Rubbed Shoulders with Lindbergh and Wright," *Midland Daily News*, January 12, 1992, and E. O. Barstow, administrator, "Final report, Estate of John Carlton Barstow," June 19, 1936 (E. O. Barstow papers, Post Street Archives).

28. "Pay Tribute to Dr. E. O. Barstow," *Midland Daily News*, January. 30, 1959.

29. H. D. Doan, "Remarks, Dr. Barstow's Contributions," Midland, April 5, 1965.

30. Herbert Dow returned to this indigo research in 1916 and became the first to manufacture synthetic indigo; see chapter 4, "The Great War."

31. Hatton, Notes on conversations with Charles J. Strosacker, May 23, 1949 and September 22, 1949.

32. See *Midland Sun*, November 11, 1910, for a full account. Herbert Dow canceled a trip to Cleveland to attend Warren's funeral.

33. H. H. Dow to H. E. Hackenberg, November 9, 1910.

34. C. J. Strosacker to H. H. Dow, December 21, 1910; H. H. Dow to C. J. Strosacker, December 22, 1910.

35. Oral History, Dorothy Dow Arbury, January 18, 1989.

36. H. H. Dow to L. D.Vorce, Pennsylvania Salt Manufacturing Company, October 9, 1912.

37. H. H. Dow to A. McK. Gifford, General Electric Company, July 11, 1912. Strosacker became a director of Dow in 1930, a vice president in 1941, and a member of the executive committee in 1949. He received honorary doctorates from Case in 1941 and Baldwin-Wallace College in 1949.

38. A. W. Smith to H. H. Dow, July 10, 1912.

39. Alden Dow said Strosacker "used to rent a super car with driver from Saginaw and take the girls for a ride on Sunday afternoon." He also recalled Stro's love for opera, architecture, and gardening. Alden Dow to C. J. Strosacker, November 15, 1962.

40. H. H. Dow to A. W. Smith, December 28, 1916.

41. C. J. Strosacker to H. H. Dow, January 3, 1917; H. H. Dow to C. J. Strosacker, January 7, 1917.

42. See Hatton, "Report of Telephone Conversation between Earl L. Pelton and F. H. Langell, July 7, 1949." Pelton enumerated about 12 such laboratories in 1917.

43. Hatton, "Notes on Telephone Conversation with R. R. Dreisbach, June 23, 1949, 9 A.M., with F. H. Langell."

44. R. R. Dreisbach to C. J. Strosacker, November 15, 1962.

45. Hatton, Notes on conversation with W. R.Veazey, June 29, 1950.

46. N. E. Coalwell to C. J. Strosacker, November 15, 1962.

47. Various German-language documents from his youth, including baptismal and confirmation certificates made out to Carl Johann Strosacker, are in the possession of the Charles J. Strosacker Foundation, Midland, Michigan.

PART TWO

HERBERT DOW'S LEGACY

Dow

1919—With huge wartime contracts canceled, Dow reduces payroll from 2,000 to 400. Intensive search for uses for magnesium begins. Dowmetal is developed and first set of Dowmetal pistons is made.

1921—Dow launches first national advertising campaign, promoting Dowmetal. On Memorial Day, Tommy Milton wins Indianapolis 500 auto race using Dowmetal pistons.

1922—Sales at postwar low of $4.2 million, compared to $12.2 million at war's end.

1923—Company finds huge potential market for ethylene dibromide in use to make tetraethyl lead antiknock fluid in gasoline.

1928—First Dow plant outside Midland, Jones Chemical Company, is established in northern Louisiana to produce iodine from waste brines.

1929—Growing use of ethyl (leaded) gasoline causes severe shortage of ethylene dibromide; Herbert Dow decides company must "go to the ocean" and extract bromine from seawater.

1930—Herbert Dow awarded Perkin Medal, highest honor for industrial chemistry.

October 15, 1930—Herbert Dow, stricken with liver cancer, dies at age 64 at the Mayo Clinic and is succeeded by his son, Willard H. Dow, 33.

World at large

1919—Peace treaty is signed at Versailles, France; Woodrow Wilson presides over first meeting of League of Nations in Paris.

1920—U.S. Senate rejects U.S. membership in League of Nations.
Nineteenth Amendment gives U.S. women right to vote.

1921—Einstein wins Nobel Prize for physics.
First radio broadcast of a baseball game.

1922—Soviet states form U.S.S.R.

1923—Tokyo and Yokohama destroyed by earthquake; 120,000 killed.
German mark falls to rate of 4 million to one U.S. dollar.

1926—Joseph Stalin establishes himself as dictator of U.S.S.R., beginning 27-year rule.

1927—Charles Lindbergh flies nonstop from New York to Paris, alone, in 33.5 hours.
Airplanes are used to "dust" crops with insecticides for the first time.

1928—First Mickey Mouse films are shown.
Alexander Fleming discovers penicillin.

1929—"Talkies" mark the end of silent films.
Construction begins on the Empire State Building, New York City.
Stock market plummets, beginning October 29, marking beginning of Great Depression.

1930—President Herbert Hoover signs Smoot-Hawley Tariff Bill.

THE GREAT WAR

I.

U
ntil it entered the Great War, World War I, the United States had no interest in chemical warfare, no knowledge of it, no skills in manufacturing chemical weapons or in using them in battle. All of this innocence and ignorance was stripped painfully away in the months following U.S. entry into the war in April 1917, and Dow played a key role in this drama. Herbert Dow was to remember the making of chemical weapons, which the company was now called upon to do, as "the worst thing I ever had to do"; his children remembered anguished conversations over the dinner table about the dreadful demands of duty in wartime. Margaret Towsley, his daughter, said, "Dad and Mother hated the fact that they had to make war gases; I remember that they got old during that time . . . there was apparently no yes or no, you just made it."[1]

Early in October 1917, A. W. Smith, Dow's schoolmate and lifelong friend, received a message from George A. Burrell, assistant director of the U.S. Bureau of Mines, summoning him urgently to Washington; and Smith sped off to the capital. Burrell had just been recalled to government service and put in charge of research related to gas warfare. The title masked his "real" assignment; he was shortly to become Colonel Burrell and to play a leading role in the formation of the U.S. Army's Chemical Warfare Service.

Burrell told Smith the army was moving as rapidly as possible to meet the problems posed by Germany's introduction into the war of gas warfare. With the Germans relying more and more heavily on gas weapons, the United States had decided it must now as a matter of national urgency develop its own knowledge of gas warfare. He asked if Smith could, beginning immediately, devote two-thirds of his time to research on such problems as Burrell and the army would ask him to look into, and suggested a salary of $2,500 per annum for these services. With this preamble he gave Smith two immediate tasks—to find a way to provide antidimming eyepieces for gas masks, just then being developed (they fogged up when put on), and to find a better gas adsorbent for the mask.[2]

Burrell recruited some of the nation's most eminent chemists from campus and industry for his research group. Eventually more than 3,000 specialists were enlisted. The buildings and grounds of the American University in Washington were taken over as headquarters and fitted up as research laboratories; problems were also assigned to the research departments of participating chemical companies. Coordination was quickly established with the chemical divisions of the Allied governments, and new chemical information became common property. Government red tape was virtually eliminated; as soon as the group had a chemical product it felt was of value, a plant design was prepared and construction of one or more plants was started.

One of these "recruits" who played a heavy role in Dow's wartime involvement was William McPherson of the Ohio State University chemical faculty, the army officer to whom the facilities built in Midland reported; he was a captain in October 1917, and ended the war as a colonel a year later. Another was the illustrious William H. Walker, of Massachusetts Institute of Technology, generally considered the father of chemical engineering. Walker signed on as a colonel "for the duration" and was something of a power-behind-the-throne in developing the American gas warfare program; if the renowned German chemist Fritz Haber was the brains behind the German gas program, Walker was as close to being his opposite number as the U.S. program had.

The government had purchased a large tract of land on the Gunpowder River in Maryland as a proving ground for army ordnance, and a portion of this land was now assigned as the site of a government shell-filling plant and chemical works to be called the Edgewood Arsenal. Later, in the summer of 1918, a separate Chemical Warfare Service was established with Edgewood Arsenal as its main facility. By the end of the war plants for making chlorine, phosgene, chlorpicrin, and mustard gas were operating there.[3]

Albert Smith and Herbert Dow were thrust into the U.S. chemical warfare program in the midst of its birthing pains. At that point its activities were shadowy (what it was doing was concealed until the war was over), confusing (the U.S. military had no chemical warfare expertise, so most of the initial leadership was civilian, working in civilian organizations under military rules), changing daily (the full-fledged U.S. Chemical Warfare Service was officially unveiled only four months before Armistice Day), and expanding wildly (it grew from nothing into a full branch of the army within a year); such was the organization the two were now asked to help as their part in winning the war.

Smith recruited his young Case faculty colleague William R. Veazey (later to be a Dow director, research executive, and in his final years research coordinator for the company) and the two immediately went to work on the gas mask problem. This puzzle was never solved to Smith's entire satisfaction, although he felt the U.S. gas mask was the best developed in the war.

Smith then moved on to other military problems, at Herbert Dow's invitation doing much of his research at the Dow laboratories in Midland—work on development of a smoke screen for naval vessels, to help them dodge German submarines, and research on ways to make toxic gases such as chlorpicrin, and tear gases such as bromacetone and xylyl bromide. His first big success was with the latter; within a few weeks Smith had completed plans for a Dow plant to make bromacetone (a tear gas with the military code name "Y-2") and another to make xylyl bromide ("Y-11").

Every day counted. Smith went to the Austin Company and asked how quickly they could build a standard plant building. "Thirty days," they replied. "You'll have to beat that," he told them. "This is war." Construction of the tear gas plants (the two were set up in the same building) actually began in Midland on January 2, and the first product was made on January 21. While plant construction proceeded, Smith was working on a protective coating for metal gas shells, to prevent damage to or leakage of their bromacetone contents.

The tear gas production of the Midland plant was shipped off to military camps around the United States and used to train the troops in the use of gas masks by exposing them to attacks with "real" gas. Smith recalled that in the frantic crash effort to make xylyl bromide at Midland in the severe winter of 1917–18, "considerable" of it was spilled in the ice and snow, and "that particular section of the plant became a very uncomfortable place during the several weeks of spring thaw"; as the product warmed it vaporized, and as Smith observed, "the small amount of vapor given off was entirely sufficient." A lot of tears were shed in the Midland plant in the spring of 1918.

The Germans initiated gas warfare in 1915 by releasing chlorine gas at the front. It was not very effective; a change in the breeze could blow it back on the attacker. With the combatants locked in long-term trench warfare, the Germans introduced new gases from time to time over the succeeding months and improved their release techniques as they developed the "science" of gas warfare with the aid of top German chemists. On July 12, 1917, the Germans introduced a devastating new agent called "blister" gas or mustard oil, or, as it is now generally known, mustard gas. It had a faintly mustardy smell, and in use at the front it caused blindness, raised great blisters, and was often fatal. A famous painting in the British Imperial War Museum shows lines of troops blinded by it, each soldier clinging to the man ahead as they are led away to a first aid station.[4]

That first day it was used, mustard gas blasted a hole five miles wide in the British and Canadian lines at Ypres, and if the Germans had been ready to take advantage of the opening, it might have changed the complexion of the war. Elated with their success, the Germans then concentrated on the production and use of mustard gas, developed by the brilliant Haber, as their main gas warfare weapon.

On February 13, 1918, Burrell called Smith and Dow to Washington and asked them to work on a new problem—to develop a process to make and manufacture mustard gas. The Allies had decided they could not afford to have the Germans hold a monopoly on this weapon and that they too must make it. A crash program was being launched, and again some of the best chemists in the West were being asked to devise a way to make it; because of Smith's outstanding success with tear gas agents they were hopeful he would take on this problem, too, with the utmost urgency. Herbert Dow immediately offered to provide Smith with laboratory space, help, and whatever else was needed in this emergency.

Smith bought a new diary that February 13 in Washington, and kept a separate record of his mustard gas experiences in it over the ensuing months. The diary begins with an account of the meeting with Burrell and his notation: "Decided to make small experiments on this at Midland and if successful to build experimental plant." Within two weeks he had tidied up loose ends on his other wartime projects and had holed up in Midland to begin work on G-34, the military code for mustard gas and the term by which it was henceforth known.[5]

In the next few weeks he worked nonstop on different methods of producing dichlorethyl sulfide—mustard gas—with occasional interruptions for trips to Cleveland and Washington. On Sunday, April 21, he interrupted his work to attend the funeral of Mrs. Thomas Griswold Jr., Herbert Dow's sister Helen, victim of the 1918 influenza epidemic, and then the next day successfully made his first mustard gas in a 110-gallon tumbler that he filled with sulfur chloride and ethylene, the chemical route he had chosen as most practical. Next came the problem of scaling this process up to an 18-foot rotating tumbler 4.5 feet in diameter that would make 5,000 pounds of mustard gas per batch by the same basic method. The first of these big tumblers became his pilot plant, and he was looking ahead to a full-scale production plant that would incorporate a series of such tumblers. The army was estimating its needs at 40 tons per day.[6]

As soon as Smith wired the War Department that he had successfully made G-34, the U.S. Army dispatched troops to take over and operate the modest Midland pilot plant, which now became a branch of the Edgewood Arsenal. Suddenly the plant became a secret military operation, operated exclusively by soldiers, under military guard, in one corner of the Dow plant in Midland.

The first of the troops arrived in Midland from New York on May 12 and began a fortnight's training in operating the plant, taught by Dow personnel under Ivan Harlow, who became the liaison between the military unit and Dow, and his assistant C. G. Smith. There was no place available for the troops to be billeted together in jam-packed wartime Midland, so they were housed with Midland families willing to take them.

Joseph E. Ritzer Sr., one of the soldiers who arrived, recorded in his wartime diary:

May 21, 1918: I finally arrived in Midland about 4 P.M. My first impression was anything but favorable. The Lieutenant met us at the depot with a list of names of people who were willing to room us. I was very fortunate in securing a room with a trained nurse by the name of Miss Murphy. She certainly has made my stay very pleasant, and it certainly seems like a home. The Lieutenant called me on the phone at 7 P.M. I said I was all in, but went down anyway. I worked until 2 A.M. the next morning."[7]

When the soldiers "graduated" from the training course on May 30 and had their picture taken in front of the Educational Building, they insisted that Winnifred Murphy, a popular young lady, join them for the occasion.

With the tremendous influx of new workers—the workforce multiplied from 400 in 1914 to 1,200 a year later, and by the end of the war to 3,000—the incidence of work-related injuries had begun to climb, and Herbert Dow decided an expansion of medical facilities was in order. In the early years he had had an easy-going arrangement with Dr. Frank Towsley, a well-loved Midland doctor who on his daily rounds by horse and buggy would drop by the plant to take care of cuts and bruises. "Doc" Towsley now proposed setting up a "first aid room" at the plant under the care of a full-time nurse, and said he would continue stopping by daily. This facility became the forerunner of the Dow Medical Department. He recommended Winnifred Murphy as the nurse, and she was hired.

In the weeks before the troops arrived, "Doc" Towsley and Nurse Murphy treated the minor burns that occurred during the gas's manufacture and he began to feel he had some familiarity with the treatment of mustard gas burns, though no one in the United States had ever seen such burns before and there was nothing about them in the medical literature.

Old-timers in the chemical plants used to refer to the more dangerous chemicals they worked with as "bad actors," and those who knew about it said mustard gas was the worst they had ever encountered. A drop of it on the skin was enough to kill a person, it was said, although no one had seen such a thing happen. In one incident at the plant a teamster was carrying waste away from the G-34 plant when on a sharp corner a barrel of the waste fell off and the bung popped out, a few drops splashing on the horses. It killed one horse. Dr. Francis B. Lambie, Midland veterinary surgeon, managed to save the other.[8]

Joe Ritzer recounted:

> When we got to Dow Chemical, in 20A building, we started an experimental unit with a metal drum that rotated in a water bath to keep the temperature right. We were running for awhile and then the tank started to leak. It dripped down off the shaft into the water bath below, so I got a wrench to tighten these two nuts up to try to stop the leak and the darn wrench slipped off, and my arm dropped down into the water bath. I got my clothes off right away and scrubbed my arm down good. I didn't worry too much about it because I figured it was just a water bath. Then I went up to supper—we all dined at the Widdifield Hall, which was part of the old Episcopal Church on Larkin street—and pretty soon my arm started itching. By the morning, time for breakfast, this arm was one big blister, full of liquid. So I went down to the first aid at Dow Chemical, and Miss Murphy drained it out and put my arm in a sling. It stayed in a sling for three weeks, and every once in awhile I would go down and she would drain it. It finally dried up and healed.

About the time the soldiers were becoming comfortable with the operation of the big 18-foot tumbler, a tragic accident occurred. Its heavy lead lining jammed up, and seven soldiers were sent into the tumbler to repair it. Albert Smith had set up a rigid step-by-step procedure to be followed in such an event, and this procedure was followed to the letter except that the lieutenant in charge did not insist on his men wearing rubber suits. Smith noted in his diary that "all wore (gas) masks and oilskin suits." The tumbler had been scrubbed and blown clean with forced air for hours. About three hours after they finished the repairs all seven of the soldiers began to feel ill and to show the signs of mustard burns. They were sent to Nurse Murphy at the first aid room.

Joe Ritzer recalled:

> It was up to our gang to clean things up and get the tumbler in shape for the lead burners. Fortunately for me, I was carrying my left arm in a sling at the time suffering the effects of previous burns. So I didn't do any dirty work. At about 7 P.M. the same day [June 26, 1918], the whole bunch on the shift—Speishandler, Hayward, Wikoff, McIntyre, Mendelsohn, Easton, Huntoon—came into the first aid room sick as dogs. It seems they had been burned by the G-34 or mustard gas, which certainly made a sick bunch of boys. It happened at the time when I was at the first aid getting my arm dressed, so I assisted getting the boys to bed. All I can say about the slow recovery of the boys was that it was too painful to put into words, and I have tried to forget this part of it.[9]

A room next to the first aid room was quickly set up as a hospital ward and the soldiers were moved in. They were immediately diagnosed as needing 24-hour care. Herbert Dow told Doc Towsley to give those boys the best of care and to hire as many extra nurses as he'd need to do this. Before they were through Dow had hired seven nurses, brought in mostly from Saginaw. In the circumstances (their injuries were sustained in a secret military installation) the two rooms were declared to be a military hospital, and the army sent in a medical officer to take charge.

The medical officer who arrived was Capt. Lester L. Roos, who proceeded at once to make himself as unpopular as possible. The day he arrived he proposed to Nurse Murphy that they go over to Bay City that evening to get better acquainted (Bay City was "wet"; Midland was "dry"). She declined. Capt. Roos asked if she couldn't find a girl who'd like to go over to Bay City with him. Murphy said she wasn't that kind of girl.

The captain moved into the first aid room, which he took over as his quarters, and had the nurses prepare his meals, sometimes at midnight. Even worse, Murphy and the other nurses were convinced the captain did not know what he was doing medically. The captain was sure that what Doc Towsley had prescribed was completely wrong; Capt. Roos now prescribed round-the-clock saline baths for the patients, a one-hour bath every three hours, done by the nurses. With his arrival the hospital ward became a 24-hour bathhouse.

Eleven days after the accident, on a Sunday evening, one of the soldiers died—Pvt. Walter Marchmont Hayward, known as "March" Hayward. He was 23 years old. His father and his fiancée, Elsie Lewis, arrived on the train from Rhode Island a few hours before he died. When the death of one of the soldiers was announced—"as the result of an accident," the Midland newspapers said—the people of Midland lined the street from the funeral home to the Ann Street Station as the body was taken off to Wickford, Rhode Island, for burial with full military honors. "March" Hayward had become a victim of the German gas offensive without even leaving the United States.

Ten days later another of the men died—Pvt. Julius Speishandler of New York City. Joe Ritzer said, "He was a hard guy to be around. You and I would be talking, and he would bust right in, that type of guy. We gave him a military funeral too."

A third soldier, Pvt. Alan Wikoff, was a touch-and-go case for weeks but finally pulled through and survived. He also was a New York City boy, and both his parents came to Midland during this time. The other four men were less severe cases, and within a few weeks they were all packed off to Ft. Custer, Michigan, for recuperation.

During this time a war-within-a-war was threatening to break out at the military hospital. The nurses seem to have concluded that the constant baths prescribed by Capt. Roos (still continuing, around the clock) were actually helping to kill their patients. This conflict was exacerbated by visitors from the University of Michigan, Dr. A. S. Warthin, a pathologist at the University of Michigan Medical School, and Dr. William Herrmann, also of the medical faculty, who became interested in this splendid opportunity to study at first hand the effects of mustard gas poisoning. Dr. Herrmann moved into the first aid room with Capt. Roos and shared the meals prepared by the nurses. Herbert Dow hurried over when he heard about it and asked Dr. Herrmann who he was; the place was a military hospital and he had strict orders not to allow civilian visitors except immediate family, he pointed out.

The next day Capt. Roos reported that Dr. Herrmann had been commissioned as an army officer by telephone. Herbert Dow took him at his word, but Dr. or Lieut. Herrmann was never seen with any military identification in Midland.

Matters came to a head when Capt. Roos announced he was fed up with all this and was moving his patients to Bay City. This precipitated a major dust-up. Seward Wikoff, father of the most seriously ill of the remaining patients, protested that his boy was being well cared for in Midland and fired off telegrams to Washington declaring that if his son died as a result of being moved he would hold Capt. Roos responsible and demand his arrest. In the middle of the night the captain relented and rescinded his order.

Then an astonishing thing occurred. Capt. Roos's left foot began to swell and to show the unmistakable signs of mustard gas burns. Someone had put a drop or two of mustard gas on his shoe while it sat by his bed in the first aid room.

In the brouhaha that resulted, it did not take long to find out who had done this. It was Winnifred Murphy. Sobbing and brokenhearted, she admitted what she had done. She had gotten the mustard gas, she said, from her friend, Ivan Harlow, the liaison officer between Dow and the military detachment. Her friends among the nurses testified that she was frustrated, exhausted, and furious with Capt. Roos. She told her family years later that it had all started as a joke among the nurses as they were discussing how they could "get back" at that nasty Captain Roos; they decided to give him a "hotfoot."

The military authorities demanded that Herbert Dow fire Winnifred as well as her accomplice, Ivan Harlow. Murphy was indeed fired; no one could defend what she had done, but

Herbert Dow defended Harlow vigorously, feeling him innocent of any wrongdoing. Harlow, who lived to be 100 years old, remained on the Dow payroll another 40 years or more and made significant contributions to the firm's progress, most conspicuously as president of the Ethyl-Dow Corporation.

One of the more amazing aspects of this episode was that the whole thing was hushed up. Nothing appeared in the press; no stories circulated around town. Joe Ritzer, though he was living with the Murphy family, knew nothing about it. Ivan Harlow seems not even to have told his family about it. Outside of a handful of insiders, no one knew it had happened; it was all a military secret, and remained so for 70 years, until a series of sworn statements turned up in the Dow archives. Herbert Dow had asked Joe Bayliss, a notary public who did legal odds and ends for the company, to take statements from the soldiers and nurses and others involved, in case the matter ever came to court.[10]

Within a few days after the incident Herbert Dow received a telegram from Maj. Gen. William D. Sibert, commanding general of the Chemical Warfare Service, ordering an immediate and complete halt to all mustard gas activities in Midland. This included the new full-scale mustard gas plant that Albert Smith had designed, then under construction. It was in fact only two or three weeks from going into production. In the interim production had continued in the pilot plant. This was an amazing order to be issued in the middle of a war in which mustard gas was required by the military and was only being produced successfully in Midland. Smith had visited Edgewood Arsenal, where it was also being made, and recorded in his diary: "conditions there in G-34 very bad. Chart in Col. McPherson's room showed production first 20 days August less than 3 tons/day average." The tiny Midland pilot plant was equipped to make 7.5 tons daily, but the new plant, commissioned by Col. Walker, had been scheduled to produce 20 tons daily, half the army's estimated total need.

Smith and Herbert Dow hurried off to Washington to appeal to Gen. Sibert. They were received with polite frigidity, and were not even able to find out what the case was against them. They knew Capt. Roos had filed a report, complete with photos of his swollen left foot, and that Drs. Warthin and Herrmann had also filed a report at the Captain's request.

That was the end of Dow Chemical's involvement in mustard gas. The Midland product did arrive in France—in what amount is not clear—and the U.S. government was careful to let the Germans know that the first shipment of U.S.-made mustard gas had arrived in Europe. In the end the Midland mustard gas was never actually used in France, nor did the U.S. forces use any mustard gas as a weapon.

In December 1918 A. W. Smith made one last trip to Midland in connection with mustard gas, having been given instructions by Col. Walker to load all remaining G-34 in Midland in barrels and ship it off to Edgewood. On December 19 Smith and Lieut. J. W. Van Arnam, who had been the production officer, began loading the G-34 into barrels and moving the barrels onto railcars. They finished the job on a Saturday morning, December 21, and locked up the three boxcars for shipment to Edgewood. Then they met with Herbert Dow, E. O. Barstow, Ivan Harlow, Joe Bayliss, and Gilbert Currie to discuss the remaining cleanup needed, and how to avoid river contamination. The whole lot of the mustard gas made in Midland was buried at sea a few years later.

After Christmas Smith went to Washington and on December 30 handed in his resignation from the service of the U.S. Bureau of Mines, effective January 1, 1919. On the last day of 1918 he went to Baltimore to take his leave, and when he called on Col. McPherson found him in conference with Herbert Dow and Earl Bennett about the wartime bromine wells contract. In the afternoon Smith paid a farewell call on Col. Walker. After supper, he took the 7:08 P.M. train homeward. It was finally over.

Winnifred Murphy continued working as a nurse around Midland for a few years, and then married a Dr. Mullins and moved to Sacramento, California, where she had five children and lived a reasonably happy life. Her intended joke on Captain Roos seems to have provided the excuse for making mustard gas exclusively at the Edgewood Arsenal under military supervision, and while he never said so, Herbert Dow was probably just as happy it turned out that way.

II.

To cut off the enemy's trade by sea, in 1915 the British Navy blockaded German ports, and this soon virtually halted German shipments of all kinds, including chemicals, to the United States and the West.

Realizing that many of the chemicals vital to a war effort would soon be in short supply or no supply at all in the United States—and the bulk of America's chemicals still came from German sources at that period—Herbert Dow began to beef up his facilities to produce these materials as rapidly as possible. The first of these was phenol, used to make explosives. He proceeded to double his capacity for phenol, and then doubled it again. By the time the war was over he had boosted the company's phenol production from 1 ton to 30 tons per day and Dow was the nation's largest producer, with 35 percent of U.S. capacity. To make phenol and other wartime products he needed more caustic soda capacity, and more chlorine, and thus he cranked this up as well.

In addition to the bromine used for tear gas manufacture, large quantities were needed for medicines, photography, and other uses, and in particular for mining salts, a mixture of sodium bromide and bromate critical to the nation's mines. Chlorine was needed for chloroform, the major anesthetic of the day (a million pounds of chloroform was shipped to the army for surgical use), for carbon tetrachloride and sulphur chloride (10 millions pounds of carbon tet was used to make smokescreens for naval and battlefield use), and for monochlorobenzene (the company shipped 2 million pounds of it for making explosives). Most of the company's contributions to the war were based on Herbert Dow's main chemical building blocks—chlorine, bromine, and caustic soda.

The greatest triumph of pure chemistry achieved by Dow during the Great War was the synthesis of indigo, the blue in blue jeans, the dyestuff used in larger volume than any other, which up to then had been a German monopoly. Herbert Dow had himself worked on the synthesis of bromindigo back in 1906, but after a few months had dropped the project. With the blockade of Germany in 1915 he picked up where he had left off.

This time he called in Dr. Lee H. Cone of the University of Michigan, who left his Ann Arbor faculty position and went to work on the problem in temporary quarters set up near the Dow Midland headquarters building. Cone brought Howard J. Rupright, another young organic chemist, with him, and although Cone returned to teaching after a couple of years, Rupright remained with Dow for 34 years, chiefly as a production superintendent.[11]

While Cone and Rupright were working out the synthesis of indigo, the Germans undertook a colorful, highly daring venture by shipping a small quantity of indigo into the still officially neutral United States by submarine. An unarmed merchant U-boat, the *Deutschland*, evaded the British blockade and on July 9, 1916, pulled into Baltimore harbor with its cargo. This attention-getting incident caused a tremendous sensation in the United States but Herbert Dow was not impressed.

He wrote to Charles H. Herty, president of the American Chemical Society, who was coordinating the efforts to obtain tariff protection for dyestuffs from Congress, saying:

> It is my personal opinion that the "Deutschland" was sent here as a part of German industrial strategy, to prevent the establishment of a dye industry in the United States, and the action of Congress in delaying the tariff on dyes is probably exactly what the Germans anticipated would be done. The coming of the "Deutschland" has therefore affected the dye situation in the following ways: It has made capital timid about investing money in dye plants. It has raised the hopes of dye users that dyes would come regularly to this country and therefore prevent the dye users from actively engaging in dye manufacture. It has raised the hope among Congressmen that their constituents would get dyes, and therefore relieve them from the pressure of enacting legislation favorable to American dye manufacturers, and has made the present infant dye industry in the United States afraid to go forward boldly in this line of manufacture, as they had started to do. All of which works to the benefit of the German dye manufacturer in a very effectual way.
>
> When the "Deutschland" first arrived, it looked strange to me that the German Government should permit a vessel so valuable to them at this critical time, and a crew so competent and much needed by the exigencies of war, to be diverted from the pressing needs of the Navy and allowed to engage in peaceful commercial pursuits.

Herty told him his comments were "exactly what I needed" for his presentations to Congress.[12]

Cone and his colleagues succeeded in synthesizing indigo after some 18 months of work, and Dow shipped the first synthetic indigo made in the United States in March 1917, breaking the German monopoly. Du Pont and National Aniline and Chemical Company soon also produced synthetic American indigo.

The Indigo Lab, as Cone's "temporary" group became known, became a hatchery for stellar research personnel. Rex Ward was one, Chester C. Kennedy another, Ivan A. Kenaga a third; all started in the Indigo Lab and became topflight laboratory directors with the company.

Indigo also became the vehicle for Dow's first venture into the Orient. The Chinese were (and are) the world's biggest market for indigo, and Dow was shipping indigo there before the war was over through the Wah Chang Trading Company in Shanghai. In 1919 Herbert Dow considered building an indigo plant in China, but decided against it. Dow indigo pails and drums were red and bore a special "chop" or trademark registered by the Chinese government for the company's products in China. This was the Dow Flying Tiger Chop, the flying tiger being China's historic symbol of national strength.[13]

Another material made only in Germany until the blockade was magnesium, which was now required for star bursts and incendiary flares by the military and had great potential in other uses. Herbert Dow immediately perceived that because of its lightness—a third lighter than aluminum—it could become the major metal used in making airplanes. As has been related, he put his number one chemist to work on that problem.

After the war the company received all manner of plaudits for its wartime contributions. Some, such as James Sweinhart of the *Detroit News*, went so far as to say that "Dow was the salvation of the country."

"For years," Sweinhart wrote in the *News* (April 7, 1921),

> Dow, singlehanded, had waged a war with the German government, with the home chemical market as the background. Somehow he managed to survive. It is well for the country that he kept courageously on—for when the war came and chemicals were needed in unprecedented quantities to be used for high explosives and other needs, Dow was the salvation of the country. Dow did just what Germany had planned to do for a generation. Germany had figured that, if she were to develop a great military establishment, she must find some use for it during peace times. It could not stand idle. Her reason for endeavoring to corner world control of dyes and chemicals was not only commercial—it was military; for the same raw materials that make dyes and chemicals make explosives. Overnight, Germany changed her dye and chemical plants to explosives factories. Dow did a similar thing. . . . When the war began and German chemicals were cut off from export, the U.S. chemical industry forged ahead. Before the U.S. entered the conflict, the Dow company had been manufacturing on a large scale for the Allies, and hence was in a position to go into major contracts for the U.S. government.[14]

One day in 1918 Herbert Dow did some doodling in his office at the north end of the headquarters building. He emerged with a rough sketch of what became the Dow diamond, the company's trademark. Legend has it that employees on the shipping docks had begun years before to mark barrels of outgoing product with a scrawled "Dow" inside four slashes that made up a crude diamond shape, and it is likely that efforts along this line inspired the ultimate shape. Doodles in hand, Dow walked through the office and stopped to talk to Roscoe K. (Rocky) Snow, a young salesman who was manager of the new pharmaceutical sales group. Angela Post, secretary to sales manager G. Lee Camp, who sometimes typed up Herbert Dow's correspondence, was also there, and the three worked over the sketches together. Angela: "I take the credit for the serif on top of those W's. I always contended the "O" was too small and didn't go with the rest, but they did adopt the change I suggested on the W's. Mostly it was worked out between Dr. Dow and Rocky."

The Dow diamond trademark was immediately adopted and swiftly became the universal Dow logo, known around the world. It first appeared in rather crude form in an advertisement in the *Oil, Paint & Drug Reporter* on September 9, 1918. By January 1919 it had evolved to its present essentially unchanged form.[15]

III.

At the end of the war Herbert Dow paused to tally up the contributions of his company and was more than satisfied that Dow, both man and company, had done more than its share toward Allied victory.

Mustard gas was surely the most dreadful, demanding, and dramatic of these efforts. The Dow Company, he noted in a summary of the company's contributions, "did this work without any definite promise of being recompensed, and up to this time (early 1919) the United States has found no way to reimburse the Dow Company for its experimental work."

Herbert Dow was called to Washington for consultations at various times during the war, and the company made chemicals for the Allies well before the United States entered the war. "Shortly after the United States had declared war, it became very apparent in Washington that one thing greatly needed in this country was the production of chemicals which entered into warfare, and for the maintenance of safety and health," he wrote. "It was soon apparent that there was a very great shortage of three basic raw materials, namely chlorine, caustic soda and bromine, for upon these three products depended the maximum output of high explosives, toxic gases, and medicinal preparations." [16]

Chlorine formed the base for chloroform (Dow furnished the government with about one million pounds of chloroform during the war), carbon tetrachloride, and sulfur monochloride, all used in the manufacture of products for warfare (sulfur monochloride was a basic component of mustard gas). During the war Dow made 30 million pounds of chlorine, placed it at the disposal of the U.S. government, "and they directed as to what use it was to be put." The company's bromides were heavily used by the photographic branch of the army, and bromides were also used in large quantities for shellshock patients.

Carbon tetrachloride (Dow produced 22.9 million pounds during the war) was used as a fire extinguisher and solvent and in the manufacture of war materiel. Large quantities converted into chlorobromomethane were used to generate smokescreens for warships and on the battlefield.

All of the U.S. caustic soda manufacturers, including Dow, placed their entire output at the disposal of the government during the war, and the government took 35 million pounds from Dow at a price of 3.5 cents per pound; on the open market caustic soda sold during the war for as high as ten cents a pound.[17]

As the leading producer of bromine, Dow furnished several hundred thousand pounds of bromine to the government for tear gas and lachrymators, and this material was so important to the government that it established at Midland the U.S. Bromine Reserve. Under this wartime program Dow built a powerhouse and drilled 17 brine wells to produce major quantities of bromine for the government, and a contingent of soldiers was sent to Midland to guard these installations, which were part of the Midland Branch of the Edgewood Arsenal (which also included, as a separate unit, the mustard gas operations). This work was supervised by Maj. Marion G. Donk, commanding officer of the Midland Branch. Donk, a New Yorker, became a lifelong friend of Herbert Dow. After the war Dow purchased these facilities from the government.

The major part of the phenol Dow made during the war was used in the manufacture of the high explosive, picric acid (the common name for trinitrophenol). Dow furnished the government some 11,750 tons for this purpose. The U.S. government's wartime contract with Dow called for thirty tons per day, the plant's full capacity.

Herbert Dow was proud of this contract, considering it a tribute to the Dow Company's efficiency. In awarding such contracts the government considered the number of men a plant required for a given output and the economy of raw materials with which the plant could be operated, and chose the most efficient.

The biggest customer for Dow phenol before the United States entered the war was the French government, which nitrated it to trinitrophenol, the main battlefield explosive used by the French. Large amounts also went to Japan, where it was made into picric acid sold to the Russians.[18]

Dow's wartime products varied. Acetic anhydride, of which Dow was again the largest manufacturer, was used as a varnish in the making of airplane wings, making the wings moisture-proof, fireproof, and stronger. In addition to supplying small quantities of magnesium metal, the company made cellulose acetate (from cotton and acetic anhydride) for the production of nonflammable motion picture film; cellulose nitrate, from which film was then made, was highly flammable. During the war the government also directed Dow to continue to produce and market its usual quantity of insecticides for the preservation of fruit crops so that the fruit supply of the country could be maintained at a high level.

The company provided war materials to every important military and war-related branch of the government—to the Ordnance Department, the Aircraft Division, the Chemical Warfare Service, the navy, the American Experimental Station, and the Medical Supply Department—as well as to such agencies as the International Red Cross and Belgian Relief.

Herbert Dow was also proud that his workforce now numbered 2,300, for whom the company had during the war built more than 300 houses and maintained a large boarding house called the Stag Hotel, which accommodated 150 men. Housing the influx of new employees was an acute problem throughout the war. One of Midland's largest hotels, the three-story brick Madill House, burned in January 1916, and that made things even worse; more than 60 of Dow's employees were rooming there.

"Families are now living under the grandstand at the baseball grounds," Dow wrote Convers. "One family is in the weighing shanty of the sugar beet company, and practically all the barns and woodsheds around town are housing people." He asked for board authorization to spend up to $100,000 to buy land, lay out streets, and build housing for employees. It was the forerunner of several such projects.[19]

For the first time Herbert Dow considered hiring women to work in the plant, but decided against it. "The manufacture of heavy chemicals is materially more of a man's job," he said. "At present there are no young ladies employed in the plant," he told an inquirer. "The question of using young ladies . . . has come up several times, but one of the great objections is that our plant runs nights the same as daytimes, and it would not be advisable under conditions that are likely to obtain, for young ladies to do this night work."[20]

Building of the Stag Hotel took off some of the housing pressure. "The Stag Hotel," he wrote, "was conducted in so sanitary a manner that there was no epidemic during its operation." That must have caused him a twinge. Two of his immediate family members had been carried off by the terrible influenza epidemic of 1918, the epidemic to which he referred—his sister Helen, wife of Thomas Griswold Jr., and his daughter Helen, wife of Dr. William J. Hale.

Between these losses and the trauma of producing mustard gas, his children said, it was the worst time of his life.

When the war was over, Midland, like the rest of the world, erupted in glee and relief. At 7:30 A.M. on November 11, 1918, the Dow factory whistle sounded out over the city. The news had actually reached the town at 4 A.M., but there had been two previous false reports that it was over so the whistle-blower waited until the news was finally confirmed. "That long blast was the sweetest tone the old Dow whistle ever tooted," the *Midland Republican* reported, "and it was soon followed by all the other whistles, bells, and horns in the city." Angela Garrett remembered that "Grover Ritenour got a Dow truck and took all the office girls around town. We had a wonderful time."

There was no work at the Dow plant that day, except those on operations that couldn't be shut down. Everyone went downtown to celebrate in what the newspaper called "the biggest, wildest, shootin', tootin', sonofagun, noisy celebration" that anyone could remember, a "jubilant bedlam." Effigies of the Kaiser were buried, burned, and hanged. In the evening there was a patriotic meeting attended by more than 2,000 persons. Among the speakers was Herbert Dow, who expressed appreciation to the workforce for their hard work and forbearance and their contribution to the war effort. Then everyone went over to the Pythian Temple on Ashman Street (which later became Midland's City Hall) for a big dance party to close out the evening. The next day all selective service schedules were canceled in Midland, to the great relief of 38 draftees who were scheduled to leave for their military service. The Great War was over.[21]

Notes

1. Oral History, Margaret Dow Towsley, December 6, 1989; Oral History, Dorothy Dow Arbury, January 18, 1989.

2. Smith had become head of the Case chemistry department upon the retirement of Charles Mabery; simultaneously he was a Dow director, from 1897 until his death in 1927. Smith kept separate diaries of his military work in World War I, one (October 1917-February 13, 1918) concerning his work in toxic gases, and the other (February 13, 1918-October 2, 1918) devoted to his work on mustard gas. Both are held at the Case Archives, Case Western Reserve University, Cleveland.

   U.S. Bureau of Mines involvement came about because the Bureau maintained a branch laboratory at Pittsburgh to investigate poisonous gases in mines, at that time the only U.S. government facility dealing with poison gases in any form.

3. *The Story of the Development Division, Chemical Warfare Service*, a history published by General Electric Company, 1920. (Much of the early development work of the CWS was done at the Nela Park, Cleveland, facilities of GE's National Lamp Division).

4. See, for example, Maj. S. J. M. Auld, *Gas and Flame in Modern Warfare* (New York: Doran, 1918).

5. From A. W. Smith's wartime mustard gas diary, see note 2 above.

6. The use of ethylene to make mustard gas was Dow's first production and use of that material, of which it became one of the world's largest manufacturers. The ethylene was produced by dehydration of ethanol over superheated kaolin in a unit called the Morrison Generator, named for Charles N. Morrison, who with his fellow Dow engineer George Yocum developed it.

7. Oral History, Joseph E. Ritzer Sr., April 19, 1991.

8. "Circumstances of accident in which two horses owned by Charles Denison, a contractor, employed by The Dow Chemical Company, Midland, Michigan, to haul toxic gases and liquids, were burned and one horse killed," affidavit by Earl W. Bennett, asst. treasurer, November. 1, 1918.

9. Joseph E. Ritzer Sr., WWI Diary, Post Street Archives.

10. Affidavits by Nurses Rose Morrow, Katherine McFadden, Eva C. Venner, Winifred Coady, and Marie O'Connor, and statements by 21 soldiers in the mustard gas detachment at Midland, including those directly involved in the June 26, 1918, accident who survived it—Pvts. Wilmot J. McIntyre, Ephraim A. Mendelsohn, Robert P. Easton, and Maxwell C. Huntoon, and Seward Wikoff, father of the still seriously ill Pvt. Alan Wikoff—are among Joseph E. Bayliss' voluminous records of his investigation of this incident. The U.S. Attorney General looked into the matter, based on charges made by Drs. Warthin and Herrmann and Capt. Roos, but did not prosecute. Bayliss's draft of a lengthy brief defending the Dow Company also survives.

    Also, "Confession by Winifried [sic] Murphy," 2nd Lt. Gerald Thorp to Capt. B. B. Wright, Development Division, Chemical Warfare Service, Nela Park, Cleveland, Ohio, undated, c. September 1, 1918. Murphy confessed to Clarence E. Rice, newly appointed director of Dow's health and safety department and her supervisor, and Rice asked her to repeat her story to Lt. Thorp, which she did.

11. Born Lee Holt, he was adopted by the Cone family and became Lee Holt Cone. After his adoptive father died, however, he resumed the name Lee Holt.

12. Dow and Herty carried on an extensive correspondence during the summer of 1916, when Herty was testifying before Congress on the question of a tariff to protect the new U.S. dye industry. See especially H. H. Dow to C. H. Herty, August 12, 1916, and C. H. Herty to H. H. Dow, August 2, 23, and 24, 1916.

13. See "Carrying Indigo to China," *Dow Diamond*, January 1948.

14. "Dow Company Called U.S. Salvation in World War 1," *Coleman* (Mich.) *Tribune*, May 10, 1945, summarizing article by James Sweinhart, *Detroit News*, April 7, 1921. For Dow's outlook early in the war see "Address made by H. H. Dow at Shepherd, Michigan, during Mr. G. A. Currie's campaign for Congress," 1917, Post Street Archives.

15. Oral History, Angela Elias Post Garrett, August 30, 1985; *Oil, Paint & Drug Reporter*, September 9, 1918 et seq.

16. The main source for this section is a long memorandum in Herbert Dow's papers, "Activities of The Dow Chemical Company During the Period the United States Was at War With Germany and Austro Hungary," undated and unsigned, early 1919, prepared as a reference for talks, correspondence, and other uses.

17. During the war the U.S. government commandeered various supplies needed for prosecution of the war. At the outbreak of the war there was a severe shortage of caustic soda, and the manufacturers, including Dow, voluntarily put their entire output at the disposal of the government. The government then indicated its needs; the manufacturers allotted what remained to their regular customers. It was thus never necessary to commandeer caustic.

18. H. H. Dow to J. H. Osborn, June 24, 1916; H. H. Dow to Gilbert A. Currie, May 19, 1917.

19. H. H. Dow to A. E. Convers, February 25, 1916.

20. H. H. Dow to James N. McBride, Michigan Agricultural College, July 15, 1918; H. H. Dow to Helen Seeley, Ann Arbor, Michigan, June 3, 1920.

21. *Midland Republican*, November 12, 1918.

THE ROARING
TWENTIES

I.

At the end of World War I Herbert Dow decided not only that he would enter the metals field in a big way, but that his first campaign in this field would amount to little less than an attempt to revolutionize the motorcar industry.

Stuck with a sizable backlog of magnesium on his hands when the war ended, he decided to inaugurate a serious magnesium research program. The Dow Company, this decision signaled, was in the metallurgical business to stay. Dr. John A. Gann, one of W. R. Veazey's Case students, was assigned in August 1919 to inaugurate research focusing on magnesium alloys and fabrication techniques, a break with the way it had been done previously and the birth of what was henceforth called the Metallurgical Laboratory—"the Met Lab." Up to this time metallurgical research had been done in the Electrochemical group under Louis Ward, a cells expert and inventor who had been a key figure in most of the new cells developed in Midland; Ward's group reported to Barstow, and was to continue a string of spectacular improvements in the Dow cells on into the 1920s.

Over the succeeding years, under the guidance of Barstow, the Dow Company tried patiently to develop uses for magnesium—wherever its lighter weight would be an advantage—that would make it a viable product and pay back the heavy research costs of presses, fabricating and machining methods, and the like, that the company was bearing. Magnesium was used to make furniture frames and luggage frames; it was used to make skis, baseball bats, canoes, and wheelbarrows; it was used to make airplane parts, lawnmower housings, and cooking griddles; it was used to make propellers for planes and boats, gardening tools and hand tools of all kinds, and landing mats for portable airfields. Wherever its lighter weight was a help, magnesium was tried, with Dow encouraging the effort and usually footing the bills.

The great bulk of these uses were abandoned after a brief try, but a few stuck and provided a modest market for the material; there were years when Dow came close to making a profit on magnesium. It was only during World War II that this effort paid off for the nation, when magnesium became a vital contributor to the masses of planes produced by the United States for the war effort.

The vehicle Herbert Dow chose for the introduction of magnesium to the U.S. market was Dowmetal pistons—pistons made of magnesium, a third lighter than aluminum. Sold not as original equipment but as replacement parts, these pistons would give an automobile new pep, added speed, and greater efficiency, he argued. As the principal moving part in the engine, their extreme lightness would make better use of gasoline; the pistons would move with less effort by the motor, and make the whole vehicle move more briskly than ever before.

This was the reasoning behind Dow's bold foray into the automotive field. Once the pistons had proven themselves as replacement parts the automakers would jump on the bandwagon and they would become standard in the industry, he expected.

In the late summer of 1919 a laboratory report landed on the desk of E. O. Barstow concerning Alloy No. 98. It was one of a series of lab tests of every imaginable alloy of magnesium, and No. 98 seemed to be what Barstow and his colleagues had been looking for in relation to strength, fatigue, corrosion resistance, and other characteristics. It contained about 6 percent aluminum and 0.5 percent manganese.

When additional tests confirmed these findings, No. 98 was adopted as Dow's basic magnesium alloy and was dubbed "Dowmetal." It was under that name that it was presented to the world, for the word magnesium, to much of the public, meant the danger of fire—it had been used in large quantities in the war just past for battlefield flares, an important and often critical matter in trench warfare, especially at night.[1]

Dow and the Searight-Downs Manufacturing Company of Detroit, a small die-casting specialist, agreed to establish a new company, the Aircraft Parts Company, to make pistons of Dowmetal in Midland.[2] Sales and administration remained in Dow's hands, and the firm began making magnesium pistons for Ford cars and Oldsmobiles, and a widening range of other automobiles as time went on. The Dow Company signed up local garagemen across the nation to sell and install the pistons, and undertook its first national advertising campaign to laud the advantages of the product and persuade auto owners to visit their local garage and have the pistons installed.

The pistons lent themselves particularly well to promotion in the auto-racing field, and every year some of the entries in the Indianapolis 500 auto race were equipped with Dowmetal pistons. Tommy Milton, the 1921 winner at Indianapolis, used Dowmetal pistons, piloting Louis Chevrolet's new eight-cylinder "Frontenac" around the course at an average of 89.62 miles per hour. Milton's win was a great coup for the company and the product. "The semi-pro Ford drivers from the central part of the state have long known (Dowmetal's) worth and used it in their racing Fords," a Detroit newspaper reported at the time.[3]

"It seems to me that we should stay in the racing game with the best men, like Louis Chevrolet, as long as we can do so without incurring any more expense than the supplying of the pistons, which is our present arrangement with them," Herbert Dow wrote to Smith.

"They are working right around the limit of endurance of every known substance adapted to use in their engine, and if we had a metal twice as good as we now have, they would still work it to the extreme limit and prove its limits by failures."[4]

Exploration of the use of the pistons in aircraft had already begun. The development effort soon spread to motorboats and marine engines, to trucks, to generators, and to centrifugal pumps—wherever pistons were used.

Beginning in 1922 the pistons were used with success in racing boats. Gar Wood, the speedboat king, became a customer, and Edsel Ford bought some to put in a boat he was building to try to beat Gar Wood. Horace Dodge of the Dodge Brothers put them in his racing boat, too.

Herbert Dow also became aware that the Dowmetal piston had already attracted at least one strong competitor: the Griesheim firm in Germany, which had begun marketing pistons in Europe made of Elektron, a different magnesium alloy (it contained 13 percent copper) developed by the Germans during the war. The Fiat car in Italy and the Renault in France both contracted with Griesheim for Elektron pistons. Herbert Dow was unperturbed. "The particular alloy that the Griesheim people use according to our tests is very much inferior to the metal we are using as shown by a fatigue machine, and in other respects is no better," he said. "I am very sure that we have a superior product."[5]

Competition became fierce, with Elektron winning the races in Europe and Dowmetal the races in the United States. For six months in 1922, Dow reported with satisfaction, every important auto race in the United States was won by cars using his pistons. The Targa Florio hill-climbing race in Sicily was won by a Mercedes equipped with Elektron pistons. The Milwaukee Regatta was won by a boat with Dowmetal pistons.

Dow made detailed tests comparing the Elektron alloy, of whose composition he was informed through their U.S. representative, with Dowmetal, and developed new alloys, Dowmetal D and Dowmetal T, his "new racing alloy," for higher compression engines.[6]

Thousands of Dowmetal pistons were made, sold, and used in those roaring, prosperous days of the 1920s. Just as Herbert Dow began to think he had a real winner, however, it began to fizzle out. What killed the Dowmetal piston was introduction of high-compression automobile engines, according to Veazey, one of the pioneer Dow researchers in the field. Dowmetal was not strong enough to withstand the high temperatures of high compression engines, and aluminum once more became the standard material in this use.

Looking back on it in 1950, Veazey said Dow could hardly have chosen a more difficult challenge than pistons for launching new uses for magnesium, because of the extremely fine tolerances needed in machining and manufacturing; but once the project was launched, he said, Dow was stuck with it.[7]

In 1927 the company decided to begin pulling out of the field, and eventually that meant the Dowmetal piston was being tossed on the trash heap of history, although pistons were still made and sold until the World War II era. Harley-Davidson motorcycles, for example, used magnesium pistons until that time; after that they disappeared. Ironically enough, by that time magnesium technology had advanced to the point where the pistons would have been completely feasible, even in ultra-high-compression engines, but no one was interested; Dowmetal pistons had had their day.

It was not a complete loss, however. In his view, Veazey said, the main thing to remember about the piston era of magnesium history was that it introduced magnesium alloys to the metal-working industry and introduced the Dow Company to the needs and peculiarities of the metalworking industry. In brief, a start was made on getting the metal-working industry and magnesium together.

II.

Research remained Herbert Dow's passion, and no place symbolized the changes being wrought by him in mid-Michigan better than the Old Mill Laboratory, a ramshackle relic of the lumbering era that became his early research headquarters. It was situated on the site of an 1852 log cabin built by John Larkin that had been the first structure put up by pioneer settlers in Midland County.

The Larkin cabin had been succeeded by a lumber mill, the Peters Bros. Hoop & Cooperage Factory, employing 35 men and producing 385,000 barrel hoops a week.[8] In the early days of the Dow Company it was known as "the Remington mill," being then the property of W. B. Remington, the mill owner who was one of the original directors of the Midland Chemical Company and its first president.

As Herbert Dow looked about for a place to do some research (and without funds to build a laboratory), the Old Mill seemed to be the only place around with any spare room, and he transformed it into his chemical research facility; it soon became a beehive of men looking for the way to the future in the oldest building around. Here most of the early work on electrolytic cells and the brine stream was done. It was in the basement of the Old Mill that magnesium metal was first extracted from the brine stream in 1916, and it was here that the Epsom salts process was developed, the work on magnesium oxychloride cements was done, and calcium chloride was hatched out as a product.

The Old Mill was also the scene of the first safety meeting in the company. Herbert Dow felt there were too many accidents happening, and one day he asked Tom Griswold to get all the men together and talk to them about plant safety. Griswold stood on top of a five-foot scaffolding at the Mill to give his talk, waving his arms about and raising his voice as needed for an open-air meeting. He became so absorbed in what he was saying that he took a step in the wrong direction and fell off the scaffolding, landing on a pile of boards underneath. Griswold was unhurt, but that broke up the safety meeting.[9]

Over the years the Old Mill Laboratory was home to some illustrious Dow researchers: Paul Cottringer, Sheldon Heath, Kelvin Smith (Albert W. Smith's son, later one of the founders of the Lubrizol Corporation in Cleveland), Ray Dulude, Lester Johnson, and Arthur C. White. In the 1920s others moved in: Forrest Minger, G. F. (Brick) Dressel, Ormond

Barstow, A. A. Asadorian, Ivan Kenaga, Porter Hart, William R. Collings (who became the first president of Dow Corning Corporation), and John A. Gann.

Wrenched out of the lumbering era to become the scene of cutting-edge chemistry, the Old Mill was surely one of the most colorful laboratories in U.S. chemical history. It was unbearably hot in summer and freezing cold in winter. On one wintry day Don L. Gibb, later Dow's plastics sales manager but then a young researcher at the Mill, submitted a requisition for "one Eskimo suit." (He did not get it.) The floor was springy white pine and full of holes that had been punched through for previous research projects. This made it hazardous to work on the ground floor but it was even more hazardous to work in the basement because tobacco chewers on the ground floor often used these holes in lieu of spittoons.[10]

The Old Mill was finally razed in 1976, long after it had taken its place in Dow legend. The operations that had been housed there had long since been moved out and renamed the Chemical Engineering Laboratory (which performed inorganic chemical research), and the Mill was being used as a storage shed, a useful place to the end.

In those pre-WW1 days of struggle against the European cartels and U.S. business combines Herbert Dow could hardly afford well-appointed laboratories but remained gung ho for research. When Mark E. Putnam came to Dow in 1916, Dow showed him an abandoned chlorine cell building and told him it was to be his research laboratory. Putnam, who had been teaching chemistry at the Case School, asked Dow what direction he thought that research ought to take. "You've been teaching chemistry," Herbert Dow said. "You should know what to work on."

Putnam chose to work on the salicylates, and that took the company into acetylsalicylic acid (better known as aspirin), methyl salicylate (oil of wintergreen), phenyl salicylate (salol), and other products.[11] The company became perhaps the world's largest manufacturer of aspirin (it was never clear whether Dow or Monsanto was number 1 in aspirin at a particular time, and it probably depended upon which had most recently added production capacity), although Dow never sold any under its own label. As with so many products, it sold the chemical raw material to firms who made and marketed the end product, thus moving toward its ultimate niche in the economy as the "chemical company's chemical company."

Putnam's research directions from Dow were often cited as a shining example of research freedom at Dow, but Putnam said that was not it at all. Herbert Dow was asking for advice, he said, and if Dow had disagreed with his choice of the salicylates he would simply have asked him to work in some other field.

The company had been dipping its toe into organic chemistry from time to time for some years now in spite of its inorganic beginnings, and Herbert Dow, in spite of his training and success as an inorganic chemist, began to be concerned about his own inadequacies and those of the company generally in this field. In the winter of 1917-18 he organized what he called "the Carbon Club" with his new son-in-law, Dr. William J. Hale.[12]

The "Club" met weekly in the Education Building to hear Hale lecture on organic chemistry; Hale gave ten lectures that winter. Rather than label it a general course in organic chemistry, which it was, Hale and Dow called it the Carbon Club (carbon being present in all organic compounds); this made it easier for veteran managers such as Dow himself to attend. Otherwise in that day they would have risked becoming a laughingstock for "going back to school." The Club was popular and short-lived, and like Caesar crossing the Rubicon, symbolized the point at which the company crossed the threshold into the field of organic chemistry, which was to dominate the chemical world for the rest of the century.

Billy Hale presented a more advanced and concentrated series of lectures to a group of Dow employees, again including Dow himself, during the summer of 1918. About 30 attended the course, which met five times a week for five weeks. By its conclusion Dow was convinced the company must expand aggressively into the organic field, but he was not sure how.

As he was pondering these problems, family tragedy struck. Helen, who had delivered her first child, Ruth, during the spring, was struck down by the deadly influenza epidemic of 1918 in mid-October of that year, and died. She was only 24. Her death completely shattered the young husband and he took an indefinite leave of absence from his faculty post at the University of Michigan. For the moment he moved to Midland, where he was joined shortly by his widowed mother, who came to help care for the baby. The grief-stricken Hale told his father-in-law he did not think he wanted to go back to Ann Arbor, and Herbert Dow asked if he would like to stay and organize an organic research laboratory at Midland. After some thought, Hale said yes.

In March 1919 the first basic research laboratory was established at Dow under the direction of Dr. William J. Hale. In Dow terminology it was the first "independent" laboratory—independent of production functions and production managers.[13] Its beginnings were modest; it occupied a 15-foot by 25-foot corner of the minor bromides plant, next to facilities for making calcium, strontium, and lithium bromides. The location was chosen because Hale wanted to be close to the Education Building, where he expected to spend a good share of his time, and the bromine plants were only a stone's throw away.

The young professor began to make changes almost immediately. He found the scientific literature resources of the company entirely too meager, so he began building a scientific library, obtaining a $10,000 fund from the board of directors with which to buy books. The library he founded became one of the world's finest industrial libraries.

He also found there was no Midland branch of the American Chemical Society where he could indulge in the scientific discussions he loved, so he immediately set about organizing the ACS Midland Section. It held its first meeting on December 2, 1919, with Herbert Dow as first chairman, Putnam as vice chairman, and Hale as councillor. The other members of the first executive committee were C. C. Kennedy, secretary-treasurer; Tom Griswold Jr., and Ivan Harlow.

Hale worked alone in his corner of Minor Bromides until September, when the first chemist hired for the laboratory arrived from Ohio State University. He was William H. (Bill) Williams, who embarked on a long and distinguished career at Dow, first as one of the inventors of the Dow phenol process and later as a major production manager, becoming the head of what was known as "Williams's Division," which made benzene-based products.

In October 1920 Hale recruited for the new lab his former assistant at Ann Arbor, Dr. Edgar C. Britton, then acting head of the Michigan chemistry department, who had been one of his brightest students. Britton was to become one of the company's most renowned organic chemists (See "Chemist's Chemist").

In 1922, at Herbert Dow's request, Hale, Britton, and Williams took up the problem of synthesizing phenol. Dow had already turned over Dreisbach's notebooks from the bromobenzene process worked out during World War I to Williams, Dreisbach having left Dow for an interlude at another company (he returned to Dow later). With this as a starter the Organic Research Lab soon scored one of its biggest successes, devising the Dow phenol process, based on chlorobenzene, by which the company was to dominate the phenol business for a generation.[14]

Williams said that on a trip to Nazi Germany in 1936 he found the Germans at I.G. Farben openly manufacturing phenol by the Dow process, which in fact they unabashedly called the Dow process. Dow had not taken out a patent on the process in Germany, "but at that time it wouldn't have made any difference anyway," Williams said.[15]

This early success of the organic research laboratory must have encouraged Herbert Dow greatly in the establishment of independent laboratories, for he was soon pursuing this route in other chemical fields. Hard on the heels of his establishment of the organic lab came the founding of the "Met Lab." There was no metallurgist on the Dow staff at the time, so Dow and Veazey selected John Gann, a young newcomer who was working at the Old Mill for Barstow, learning the plant processes, and asked him to become one. Gann had a Ph.D. in chemistry from the University of Goettingen.

It was not the first nor the last time a complete career switch would be proposed to a Dow employee, but Gann, trained as a colloid chemist, quickly decided to take on the challenge. He started by studying all the available literature on magnesium metallurgy, most of it in German, where magnesium had been made since 1886. He set up a lab on the downriver side of the basement in the Education Building and began to acquire testing apparatus. His first recruit was Leo B. Grant, who was working at a machine shop in Detroit, and Grant soon became his right-hand man. Grant later became the first magnesium sales manager and then served as manager of Dow's New York office.

Another early recruit was Manley Brooks, who became a lab helper (at 17 cents per hour) in 1920 while enrolled in college and worked in the Met Lab when he was not in school. He became a permanent employee only in 1928, after earning a degree in metallurgy. Brooks became a specialist in foundry work and eventually was recognized as the leading U.S. expert on this subject; he was widely known as "Mr. Magnesium Foundryman."

The story is told that Herbert Dow came into the magnesium foundry one day in 1926 and began to show some of the foundrymen the right way to cast Dowmetal pistons. The superintendent, a crusty old Dutchman named Hugo Schmidt, watched this for a bit, and

CHEMIST'S CHEMIST

When he laid aside the rumpled white lab coat that was his trademark for the last time, Edgar Clay Britton closed one of the most brilliant careers ever recorded in chemistry. The number of patents on which he was listed as inventor or coinventor added up to 354, the all-time record for the Dow Company.[1]

Britton became a chemist by accident. On the train to Wabash College in Indiana, where he was a student, he fell into conversation with an upperclassman who urged him to take at least one course in chemistry from Prof. James B. Garner, a campus favorite. Britton did and was entranced. He dropped all thought of following in the footsteps of his father and becoming a lawyer, and when Garner switched to the University of Michigan, Britton followed him, and graduated in chemistry in 1915.

He went on to Ph.D. work in organic chemistry under Prof. William J. Hale and became an instructor at Ann Arbor. When Hale left for Midland to found an organic research laboratory for Dow and invited him to join him, Britton did, and became Hale's assistant. Early in this experience he and Hale worked out what became known as the Dow process for the synthesis of phenol, which gave Dow dominance in that field for many years; and when Hale left for Washington, "Doc" Britton, as he was always known at Dow, became the lab director. That was in 1932.

Britton said that in 1928 Herbert Dow stopped him as he was going into the library one day and asked whether he would like to become a production manager. Britton told him he loved research, was trained for research, and thought he could make his best contribution to the company in research. Dow nodded and moved on, and that brief conversation was the last time anyone asked seriously whether he had other ambitions. He worked in the company's organic research laboratory, today known as "the Britton Lab," for 42 years.

His 354 patents cover an astonishing variety of products, ranging from plastics, dyes, pharmaceuticals, synthetic rubber, and silicone products to weedkillers, insecticides, fungicides, and preservatives. His insecticides and herbicides opened up a new era in agricultural chemicals. The first tank car of pure butadiene shipped during World War II was manufactured by a process he invented, making possible the manufacture of synthetic rubber. The first high-temperature insulating resin was pilot-planted in his laboratory, pre-dating the formation of the Dow Corning Corporation (on whose board he served for 18 years).

His prodigious memory is recalled in *Dow Research Pioneers*:

"Doc" Britton was an avid reader of scientific publications and his retentive memory could recall the volume and page of articles concerned with almost any problem his associates could have. . . his reading generated a multitude of ideas. He went into each laboratory in his building every day to talk with his people. If a new project was to be started, he would not only state the problem or objective, but also almost always specified a plan of attack and a probable means of solving the problem . . . he was a real scientist and a teacher.[2]

His research colleagues noticed that he never accused them of botching an experiment. "Maybe we didn't run the experiment properly," he would say. "Maybe we ought to try it this way."

One of his favorite long-term projects concerned the essential amino acids, and he pioneered the synthesis of eight of these protein building blocks.[3] He was convinced they would one day become important food additives for men and animals. Only one of them, methionine, now widely used as an additive in poultry feed, became a volume product for Dow.

To demonstrate his faith in the future of the amino acids he often lunched on peanut-butter-and-methionine sandwiches, made with homemade bread containing the amino acid lysine.[4]

Starting out in a corner of the minor bromides plant, the organic research laboratory pushed the minor bromides out into other manufacturing facilities within a few years and continued to grow. When a modern new laboratory was finally built in 1953 it was dedicated as the Edgar C. Britton Research Laboratory, the first time a building had been named for an individual in the company's history. In 1952 he served as president of the American Chemical Society (in which he had been active since 1917), the only Dow employee ever elected to that office.

In 1956 he was the recipient of the Perkin Medal, the highest honor in industrial chemistry, and he was only the second Dow employee ever accorded that honor, Herbert Dow being the first. "I believe the chemist was put on this earth to provide materials for man's use," he said in his Perkin Medal address. "If every chemist had this thought in mind, be he teacher or researcher, and made it part of his idealism, our progress would be astounding."

"I have always considered myself a scientist, and in all questionnaires classify myself as a chemist," he said. "I think and feel like Pasteur when he said in Orleans in 1867, 'Nothing is more agreeable to a man who has made science his career than to increase the number of his discoveries, but his cup of joy is full when the result of his observations is put to immediate practical use.'"

"The least one can do is to hope that the results of his work will be useful to mankind at some future date."[5]

1. Thomas A. Edison, with 1,093 patents, is considered the U.S. titleholder.
2. Robert S. Karpiuk, *Dow Research Pioneers, 1888-1949*, 71-72.
3. The eight are valine, methionine, threonine, leucine, isoleucine, phenylalanine, tryptophan, and lysine.
4. John R. Halsey, "Michigan Profiles—Edgar Clay Britton," *Michigan History Magazine* (May-June 1992): 46-47.
5. Edgar C. Britton, "Journeys in Research" (Perkin Medal Address), New York, September 14, 1956.

when he had had enough he picked Herbert Dow up bodily and carried him out the door to his car. "And from now on youse do not tell my men what to do," he told Dow.

Herbert Dow, guessing what would happen next, went over to the clockroom and waited. Schmidt arrived shortly, heading directly for the employment office to draw his last pay, when Dow stopped him, asking, "Where are you going?" Schmidt said, "I quit." Herbert Dow said, "Get back down to the foundry and run it like you're supposed to, and if I ever come back down there or anybody else tells you how to run the foundry, you do the same to them." Schmidt went back to the foundry.[16]

Within a month of the time he began work as a tyro metallurgist Gann had begun to supply new alloys for automobile pistons, which became the main use for magnesium in the postwar era. The pistons were produced on ordinary hand lathes; automation had not yet made its appearance. The price of magnesium fell from $5.00 per pound in 1915, just before Dow produced its first metal, to 20 cents per pound during WWII.[17]

Dow's Main, or Analytical, Laboratory grew out of the control labs in the various production departments, which ran quality checks on the products being made. Ivan Harlow, who joined the company in 1909, was the first person to serve as chief analytical chemist of the company, in fact if not in title.

Harlow said when he arrived in Midland

the paper people were questioning the bleaching concentration of the product . . . the chemist preceding me they let go—his results weren't right and I can only guess. He had a whitewashed hood, and I suspicioned he put his stuff in there and didn't cover it, and stuff dropped into it and he got wrong results. The first few months I worked, H. H. came out after a period of time. He never walked into a room, he banged into it, and he says, "You are doing all right on the analysis work. We sent everything to Penn State for analysis, and they checked." I told him Penn

State was pretty good if their results checked with mine. He was really interested in the lab, H. H., and necessarily so.[18]

Within a few years Harlow had become Barstow's "right-hand man," but the small analytical lab, now under Edward A. De Windt, still reported to him. At the end of World War I Harlow and Barstow hired a soldier who had just mustered out of the Chemical Warfare Service, Alonzo W. (Al) Beshgetoor, and Beshgetoor became the dominating personality in the Analytical Laboratories for the next 40 years, taking over as lab director from De Windt in 1926. Under Beshgetoor the laboratory expanded steadily in size, functions, professionalism, and stature, and the laboratory became a pioneering force in the analytical field.

Many of the company's most prominent chemists and researchers came out of the Analytical Laboratories. "Mr. Harlow both gave and received," Beshgetoor said. "He gave requisitions for new men, and he 'took' men, and many others did, too." The early water pollution work and, later on, air pollution work was initiated in the lab, and Hans A. Reimers became the resident specialist in this field. This work was taken over by Thomas J. Powers in 1934 when a separate Pollution Control Department was established.

Joe Ritzer, who had originally come to Dow during World War I to make mustard gas, worked in one corner of the lab at glassmaking assignments. Edgar Britton was a skillful glassblower and initiated Ritzer to this work. This became the start of a Glass Fabrication Lab, headed up by Ritzer, who trained others in the art and moved three times to larger quarters over the years as the lab grew to include some 25 artisans in glass.[19]

In 1928 Herbert Dow asked his friend L. G. (Lee) Morell to return to Dow and organize an X-Ray and Spectroscopy Lab, principally to support the Met Lab in its analyses of magnesium alloys through the newly introduced techniques of X ray and spectroscopy. It was housed in the same building as the Met Lab.[20] Another small lab that began early was the Indigo Lab, which continued the dyestuff research work begun in 1915 on into the 1930s.

By 1928 these labs were all well in place and Dow had an organized and growing research establishment, most of its principal components having been put in place in the decade following World War I. With research in place, the company was poised for the future.

III.

"The war after the war," Billy Hale called the long-running tariff debate that raged on the American scene from 1917 to 1922. In the end, after many words had been spilled, it resulted in passage of the Fordney-McCumber Tariff Bill of 1922. Hale saw the battle pitting an adversary "intent upon destruction of all American industry, against another intent upon casting out these foreign agents and building up an America for Americans only." This foe of U.S. industry, he said, was the German exporter of chemicals to the United States, and "his goal of goals is the subjugation of America to Germany, whereby our country will be made the great source of supply of raw materials for German industry."[21]

THE IDEA MAN

He was born Hans Josef Grebe (rhymes with Phoebe) in the German Rhineland in 1900, eldest of the 12 children of a German machinist and farmer. In 1914, convinced a war was coming, his father shipped him off to an uncle who had a restaurant in Cleveland. He arrived in New York on March 17. Long afterward he remembered that the uncle, who had come to New York to meet his boat, took him to Fifth Avenue that day to see the St. Patrick's Day parade.

"What's this, foreigners are allowed to march in this country like that?" he asked his uncle. "Yes," said the uncle, explaining that he was now in a free country, one that respected ancestry as well as merit. "The greatest thing that ever happened to me was to feel really at ease in a foreign country," Grebe said.[1]

When war did break out, his teachers at Cleveland's East Technical High School changed his name to John. He conquered the English language rapidly, becoming a popular classmate, a reporter for the school paper, a debater, and class valedictorian. In the high school yearbook he was described as "our dear enemy." Then he enrolled at Case as a physics student, and his potential as an original thinker was soon noted by Veazey, his chemistry professor, who told Herbert Dow about him.

In the spring of 1924 Herbert Dow returned to Case to receive an honorary doctorate. Grebe was in the graduating class, and Dow sought him out and hired him. "Herbert Dow was anxious to get people at the top of the class in any field," Grebe said. "It didn't matter whether it was biology, anything, just so they were the top students."

"When I got to Midland, Dr. Dow came and visited with me and said, 'What is it that you would like to do?'—not 'I have this and that to be done.'" Dow told him that after this first summer he would not be under other supervision like the other new employees. Grebe said, "That's all right, but are you sure I would know what's needed to be done?"

In the course of their talk Grebe told him that "the only thing that is obviously badly needed here is something that keeps the bromine plant from making such a horrible stink every few hours. It makes everything around here corrode to have that bromine spit out of the top of a vent." He recommended installation of an instrument he knew of at a cost of about $250.

Dow ordered the instrument but there was hell to pay, Grebe said:

> H. H. Dow had overridden the plant manager and bromine-producing individual. He had done something they didn't understand or even know about and that would be charged against them. H. H. Dow knew that it was an urgent thing because there was $10 to $20 a day going up in the air and corroding away equipment and facilities and making people sick in the city whenever the wind came from the East, which was not often.

Soon as I had that instrument installed and working, Barstow and Harlow made a special point of coming to me and saying, "John, you've been here only half a year and you've done something that we've needed all these years. Now what else is there that we should do?" That's how nice they were, they were completely cooperative from that point on.

Grebe was a man after Herbert Dow's own heart, an idea man. Like Dow himself, he had a new idea every morning. Recognizing this, Dow gave him a free hand from the beginning. As his first project Grebe selected "Application of Automatic Control to Chemical Reactions," working on some ideas he had for converting batch processes to continuous ones. In the next 40 years his work would put Dow in the forefront of the automation of chemical production. Grebe established what was known at first as the "Physics Department" (which was Grebe alone), and later as the Physics Laboratory, occupying a corner of the big room in the Educational Building that also housed the infant Met Lab. In early 1926 Grebe hired a couple of laboratory assistants—George W. Bugbee and Wesley Dove—and then in the fall of that year his first technical man, Ray H. Boundy, a newcomer from Case just beginning at Dow.

Grebe borrowed Boundy from the main lab "for a couple of days," to help run some data on a pilot plant for making Dowtherm heat-exchange compounds. The two days stretched into two years, and then into two decades; Grebe and Boundy became perhaps the most renowned research duo in Dow history. Boundy's main job, as he said later, was to sift through the ideas that Grebe generated and "pick out those that were good from those that weren't."

Herbert Dow often dropped by to discuss his ideas with Grebe. Boundy said Dow's ideas were usually excellent but that on one occasion when he did not think the idea was very good he was surprised to find Grebe enthusiastic about it. When Dow had left, Boundy asked him why he had been so excited, and Grebe gave him a lecture he never forgot: "Ideas are among God's most precious gifts," he told Boundy. "Without them we would still be living in the Dark Ages. They separate man from all other creatures. Listen carefully and keep an open mind. Perhaps you can convert a bad idea into a useful one. Be enthusiastic while you can. Tomorrow, after you have slept on it, will be a better time to judge."[2]

"Ideas," Grebe said, "have a way of cropping up suddenly, but never unexpectedly. They rarely arrive until you are thoroughly prepared to receive them—even, sometimes, after you have grown weary waiting for them. When you have explored and probed and tested and studied and discarded, then, click! It is often as if they came from outside the mind when you have become, in a sense, prepared and strong enough to grasp them."

Grebe said he did not "insulate" his ideas. "I find talking over a project with others enhances its value, develops its progress more swiftly, focuses light on obscure aspects. No mere man should walk alone among ideas. Sometimes the very young scoff at help, thinking they can draw on their own unchallenged wisdom to teach the whole world unassisted. But the loneliness of such an attitude soon palls."[3]

Grebe enjoyed an unprecedented amount of freedom, and Willard Dow told Grebe years later that "my dad told me to let you do what you please." As a lab director he reported directly to Herbert Dow, and later to Willard Dow, an unusual arrangement then and unheard of now for a laboratory director.

It is difficult if not impossible to distinguish between the accomplishments of John Grebe and the Physics Lab as a whole, filled as it was with top-flight personnel, but the results speak for themselves. Boundy listed 25 major accomplishments for the lab during Grebe's tenure, including invention of many of the major products the company makes today—polystyrene plastic (Styron); and later on, high-impact polystyrene; Styrofoam plastic foam; Saran and its relatives, including Saran Wrap; bromine from seawater; iodine from brine; Dowtherm heat exchangers; automatic control systems for chemical production; vinyl chloride (the monomer from which polyvinyl chloride is made, and also the primary component of saran); ion-exchange resins for water softeners and other uses; Ethafoam expanded cellular polyethylene and its relatives; and a host of other products and processes.

Boundy was justifiably proud of the lab's accomplishments but he admitted there were also among them some "bummers," as he called them, projects that did not turn out well. One was a project to measure the electrical resistance of the earth over large areas and at great depths as a shortcut to locating brines with the highest salt and bromine content (which turned out to be only marginally useful); another was a plant to manufacture low-cost metallic sodium (used by Dow in making indigo), and to use sodium as an electrical conductor—why use all that irreplaceable copper when the sea is full of sodium, the reasoning went. A sodium-filled conduit from one of the power plants to an electrochemical cell building was built at considerable expense; it worked but was a great nuisance and was abandoned a couple of years later.

Ernie Mitchell remembered a Physics Lab meeting called to discuss butadiene at which Grebe said there was something else he'd like to talk about—an idea he had to develop a new source of magnesium. Why not breed oysters so they laid down magnesium carbonate rather than calcium carbonate in their shells? Grebe asked. With the right diet this could possibly be done, he said; Dow could then harvest the oyster shells as a magnesium source. Before the meeting was out he had reassigned Mitchell to a new job—developing magnesium-bearing oysters. "When my boss, George Hebbard, found out about it he was absolutely furious," Mitchell said. "He and John had a hot session, and I was reassigned to butadiene."[4]

The Physics Lab had the huge advantage of recruiting its operatives during the Depression years of the 1930s, when virtually every other chemical firm had stopped its hiring procedures entirely. With almost no competition for the graduating seniors, Dow was able to attract the top people it wanted. Many of them went into the Physics Lab, whose alumni list is almost a Who's Who of Dow. In 1929 Herbert Dow hired Dr. Sylvia G. Stoesser, the first woman Ph.D. chemist hired by Dow, and she became the chemist of the Physics Lab and the pioneer among Dow's corps of women researchers.[5]

Grebe had some unusual rules for his laboratory, which used the multidisciplinary approach and had all sorts of specialists working together, rather than specialized engineers working with specialized engineers and biology specialists working only with biology specialists. He introduced what he called "idea cards"—anyone with an idea about something was to write it down and put it up on the bulletin board, signed and dated; then the idea was discussed among colleagues or in lab gatherings. This promoted openness of discussion and was valuable in filing patents; and everyone in the lab knew what everyone else was working on. A sign tacked up over his door said, "For every successful idea there are 100 who claim they had that idea long ago."

He also promulgated what was called, at Dow, "the Grebe rule," which stated that the researcher could spend 10 percent of his or her time working on projects or ideas that the researcher preferred; the other 90 percent was to be spent on projects assigned by the company. The saran family was one result of the 10 percent portion of the Grebe rule.

To encourage openness of discussion he laid out the laboratory so that the inhabitants had to walk past their colleagues to get anywhere. There were frequent (and famous) lab picnics at Grebe's place out on the river, about six miles out of town. In 1925 he had brought over his parents and most of his family from Germany; Herbert Dow had promised to give them jobs.

In 1943 he became the youngest person ever to receive the Chemical Industry Medal for outstanding contributions in the field of chemical research, and in 1946 he received the Hyatt Award for plastics. During most of World War II he was a consultant to the Office of the Rubber Director. By the end of the war, however, watching the development of nuclear fission, Grebe was convinced that the wave of the future, the next real development in the chemical industry, would be the peaceful use of the atom, and he began actively to explore this field.[6]

In 1946-47 he attended, "on loan" to the U.S. government for nine months "for training and work on the application of nuclear energy to the industrial operations of this country," the first reactor school at Oak Ridge National Laboratory, Tennessee.

The experience launched him on a new career as a nuclear scientist, and he was soon designing atomic reactors for submarines as a government assignment. In 1953 he established the nuclear and basic research laboratory back at Dow and began to study the possibilities of nuclear power as an energy source and in other uses for Dow's operations. In 1950 Dow formed a joint venture with the Detroit Edison Company for this purpose, and Grebe became its chairman on the Dow side. The company was soon involved in operating a plant for the Atomic Energy Commission as well. In 1954 he was a civilian observer at the Bikini atoll in the Pacific ocean when the first H-bomb was exploded; by this time he was beginning to be well known to the fathers of the atomic age, and vice versa.

Grebe had spent two solid months at Oak Ridge working on the mystery of the basic structure of matter, one of the basic riddles of physics and a question that had haunted him ever since his freshman year at Case. It was the first time he had found time for intensive research on this problem, but to his disappointment found no answer that he was willing to defend in a forum of his peers. After that he pondered the riddle of the universe in his spare time. Before he was through he had spent more than 2,000 hours with paper, pencil, and tinker toys, working on his own concept of what holds the atomic nucleus together.

With the tinker toys he constructed atomic models and tried to visualize the arrangement of points of induction of the fundamental particles. Finally, in September 1957, he said, "the fact that I didn't have the answers irritated me so much I decided to give all my time to the riddle. Since then, my wife has played second fiddle to an atomic model." For six months he spent most of his waking hours on this problem. Two days before Christmas he came up with "the first satisfying answer," a key ratio between two fundamental particles of the atom. A second key ratio came to him suddenly, late one night in a New York hotel room after a science conference. "This second answer showed us that the individual unit that appears to be the basis of matter can appear as doubles and quintuplets," he said. The resultant mathematical formula "determines facts on masses of these particles that appear to be the building blocks of all matter. We found a beautiful, simple system of order."

In working on this problem, he found that he would get "completely fagged mentally" in three hours, and that his best hours were late at night or early in the morning. Sometimes he would leap out of bed at 5:30 A.M. and begin work without even waiting for coffee. He relaxed by walking along the banks of the Chippewa River near his home or playing with the youngest of his five children, James, then 12.[7]

He retired at age 65 and moved to Sun City, Arizona, with his wife, who had been Hazel Holmes, Willard Dow's secretary, when he married her in 1929. Ray Boundy felt Grebe was disillusioned by this time that the peaceful use of the atom had never materialized in the United States "and this is the thing that he was sure was going to happen."

"The primary reason for the success and the accomplishments of the physical research laboratory was John Grebe," Boundy said. "He was so uninhibited, he was so creative, and he listened to everybody's ideas to the extent where I just suspect that without John Grebe, or without a John Grebe, the physics lab never would have been as successful as it was. Some of us were good listeners, and that probably made a difference. But you can find good listeners a lot easier than you can find really creative people who were technically as uninhibited as John was. This is the conclusion of the group who worked in that lab, not my conclusion alone."

Boundy said also that he doubted John Grebe would be hired in a big company today, "and I also doubt that John Grebe would choose to work in a big company. So one of the big hurdles you have to get over is how do you do research in a big company and make everybody in that research organization feel that they are just as important and just as responsible as in a small company? Once a big company finds a solution to that I think they have it made."

One of Grebe's inventions, a screen that keeps out sun and insects but permits light and a one-way view, is seen frequently in public buildings around the world. Called "KoolShade," it was invented by him in 1934-35. The Dow Company did not choose to go into the sunscreen business, but one of Grebe's colleagues, Walkley Ewing, decided to make and sell the product and organized the KoolShade Corporation in Glendale, California, with a manufacturing plant at Fajardo, Puerto Rico. KoolShade is seen in such places as Dodger Stadium in Los Angeles and the National Library in Rome, Italy.[8]

Grebe was also the father of the Dowell division of Dow, holding 21 of the basic patents that buttressed its oilwell stimulation services. He was a director and vice president of Dowell from its formation in 1932 until his retirement in 1965.

John Grebe died peacefully in Sun City at the age of 84. Hazel Grebe told a reporter that he was still expounding new ideas to the last, "but unfortunately he no longer had a laboratory in which to work on them."

---

1. Quotations in this section from Oral History, John J. Grebe, 1982.

2. Oral History, Ray H. Boundy, September 9, 1988.

3. Katharine Tuttle, "Scientist Also A Philosopher," *Midland Daily News*, October 29, 1958.

4. Oral History, J. Ernest Mitchell, May 4, 1995.

5. See Ray H. Boundy and J. Lawrence Amos, eds. *A History of the Dow Chemical Physics Lab*. Dr. Wesley C. Stoesser had come to Dow earlier in 1929, and soon volunteered to drive Mrs. H. H. Dow to church on Sunday mornings. He told Mrs. Dow that he and his fiancée, Dr. Sylvia Goergen, were unable to marry because the company did not hire women in research. Hearing this, Herbert Dow

told him to get married; there would be a job for his wife in Midland. She was assigned to the Physics Lab because it was the only research lab with access to a ladies' restroom.

6. Some of his colleagues said Grebe took part in the 1942 University of Chicago experiments that first achieved nuclear fission, but this is unconfirmed by the available evidence. In his role as advisor to several government science groups he was probably aware of and may have discussed these matters with some of the participants, however.

7. "Quantum Mechanic and a Riddle Solver: Werner Heisenberg and John Josef Grebe," *New York Times,* April 26, 1958.

8. "Shade Makes a Hit in Front Office," *Los Angeles Times,* April 23, 1967.

The tariff war was Herbert Dow's first and only serious foray into national policy, and while many of the major chemical companies fought for passage of a protective tariff—Allied Chemical, du Pont, Mallinckrodt, and Monsanto were all active and prominent in the campaign—Dow became the chemical industry's key player in the drama through an unusual set of circumstances.

In November of 1916 Dow's principal legal counsel, Gilbert A. Currie, was elected to Congress to represent the Michigan district including Midland, and he soon became a close ally of his longtime friend and fellow Republican, Cong. Joseph W. Fordney, who represented the neighboring Saginaw area. Fordney became chairman of the House Ways and Means Committee that November as the Republicans captured control of the House, and when Warren G. Harding was elected president of the United States four years later one of his chief campaign promises was tariff protection for U.S. industry. "Joe" Fordney was then duly charged with drawing up a tariff bill, and went to work on one with his friends Currie (now freshly out of Congress after two terms) and Herbert Dow; informally they became his chief advisers on Schedule A of his bill, governing chemicals, oils, and paints. A lumberman by training with little formal education and no knowledge of chemistry, Fordney was eventually able with a little coaching by Currie to bluff his way through the debate on the House floor when it dealt with chemicals.

The Saginaw congressman had asked Herbert Dow for his suggestions on chemical tariffs as early as January 1917, when he wrote Dow that "it is thought advisable that we should prepare and introduce a tariff measure of some kind."[22] Over the next half dozen years their correspondence and meetings on the subject seldom languished. Sen. Reed Smoot was also anxious to introduce a tariff bill at that time, and also wanted to talk to Herbert Dow about it.[23]

Dow was quickly initiated into the arcane world of politics, appearing before congressional committees and subcommittees of various kinds and making numerous trips to Washington to discuss tariff questions with members of Congress. He also pressed James Pardee into service (Pardee was the company's representative in the Capital during the war) and Pardee became the company's representative to the various industry and government groups studying the complex tariff question. As a pulpit for himself Dow accepted the chairmanship of the tariff committee of the American Drug Manufacturers' Association, which had offices conveniently located for him in Detroit. Dow's experience with Herr Jacobsohn and the German bromine cartel and the German effort to put him out of business in the 1905-9 era became something of a cause célèbre in Washington, and Herbert Dow was asked again and again to repeat the story for wavering Congressmen.

Under the Democratic administration of Woodrow Wilson and with the nation at war, the tariff bills went nowhere, but with the election of Harding in 1920 the tariff question moved overnight to the front burner. In one headline episode, Pardee, appearing before the House Ways and Means Committee early in the new administration, was asked about the German "Yellow Dog Fund"; it was one of Joe Fordney's favorite anecdotes, which he had heard from Herbert Dow.

Jacobsohn had told Dow that "we have in Germany what we call a 'yellow-dog' fund, to which the manufacturers contribute one half and the Government the other half, and when we find it necessary to put an industry out of business in the United States or in any other country in the world we use that 'yellow-dog' fund and undersell you and put you out of business, and I advise you to get out of Germany." Fordney reported that there was $25 million in the fund at that time (1905). Pardee assured the congressmen that Fordney's version of the story was "substantially correct."[24]

Herbert Dow, stating his own views on the tariff, said:

> I am satisfied that every chemical made in Europe is absolutely controlled by a trust except during occasional periods of commercial warfare, and so far as Germany is concerned, it looks as though all the producers of chemicals were now combined in one company—the I.G. [Farben]. I also believe that their policy is to throttle competition by ruthless methods, and there is such a tremendous advantage in manufacturing a chemical on a big scale that if any one company once gets a preponderance of the business in any specific line, they can usually hold their advantage over all competition. However, the advantage of large-scale production is much greater in the United States than in Germany, for the reason that we have learned how to operate much larger units than are customarily employed in Europe. Our locomotives and freight cars are an example . . .
>
> It is the popular idea that the firm with the lowest costs, quality being equal, can command the market. This is what I thought before our fight with the German Bromine Trust. I now know that this will not put us on a par with the German producer; in addition to a low cost, we must have an impregnable fortress in the same way Germany has, so that we cannot be attacked in our home market. Under these circumstances we can confidently design and build plants on a larger scale and with greater economies than will be possible in any foreign country. The principal reason why we could excel is because we would start out by having the biggest market in the world and more than a fighting chance of getting a good share of the remainder, whereas our German competitor would start out with the positive assurance of the

German market, which in most cases is relatively small, and the poor Englishman starts out without the assurance of any market at all.[25]

As a young man Dow had started out as a "free trader"; during William McKinley's campaign for the U.S. presidency in 1896 (McKinley's campaign slogan that year was "Peace, Prosperity, and Protectionism") he consistently took the free trade view in opposition to McKinley. McKinley won in a landslide, and one consequence of his victory was passage of the Dingley Tariff of 1897, the highest in U.S. history; it imposed tariffs averaging 57 percent on the value of goods imported into the United States.

The Dingley Tariff had taken bleach off the "free list" and imposed a duty of 0.2 cents per pound (bleach was then selling for 2.25 cents per pound), an impost that Herbert Dow came to appreciate enormously when the British United Alkali Company cartel tried to put him out of the bleach business. Looking back on it, he felt the tariff had saved his bacon in both the battle of the bleach and the bromine wars, and for the rest of his life he was a confirmed protectionist.

He argued in answer to the main argument against tariffs—that they would raise prices—that tariffs would actually reduce prices on products in the United States, citing as an example novocaine, which as a prewar German monopoly had been offered to U.S. dentists at $1,600 a pound. The Dow company made novocaine for a time after World War I and marketed it at $16 per pound—1 percent of the prewar German selling price. "Every one of the similar compounds that were controlled by German monopolists before the war are now selling for from 1 percent to 10 percent of their former price," Dow pointed out, "and this situation was brought about by what was equivalent to an infinitely high tariff, namely the World War, followed by an absolute embargo."[26]

Another critical factor in the equation was wages; German wages were pitifully low after the war. In the postwar era the German chemical worker was earning a wage of about 45 cents per day, compared to an average in the United States for chemical workers of $5 per day.

"There is not a chemical manufacturer in America but knows that all the chemicals made in Germany are normally controlled, and that the price these German trusts make in America is just what the traffic will stand without destroying their control, no more and no less, and that under a protective tariff it will not stand as much of a price as it will under free trade, because the American chemists are more willing to take the risk of a trade war with a foreign monopoly when the foreigner is handicapped by a tariff, than when no handicap exists," Herbert Dow said.[27]

Dow and his colleagues worked closely with Cong. Nicholas Longworth of Ohio, chairman of the subcommittee that wrote the chemical schedule, and with the two Michigan senators, Charles E. Townsend and Truman H. Newberry. Dow had several meetings with Sen. Boies Penrose of Pennsylvania, one of the powers in the Senate, leader of the faction that President Wilson called the "group of willful men" who engineered the rejection of U.S. participation in the League of Nations.

THE "DIZZY DEAN" OF CHEMISTRY

In 1919 Dr. William J. Hale, Herbert Dow's son-in-law, bought a farm near West Branch, Michigan, in the jackpine country northeast of Midland. An enthusiastic hunter, he raised ruffed grouse, sometimes called "partridge" or "pats," at this unusual "farm," and took his friends there on hunting expeditions. West Branch became a mecca for the nation's leading organic chemists, who in the autumn would doff their lab coats, deck themselves out as hunters, and head for Midland. Hale's guests did little damage to the grouse population on the whole, even though those on his property tended to be quite tame, but they did a lot of talking during these forays, as chemists will, about chemistry.

In the fall of 1925, on one of these trips, Hale and Charles H. Herty, one of his cronies, a soft-spoken Georgian and a leading authority on cellulose chemistry (president of the American Chemical Society, 1915-16), sat down on a log and in the course of a conversation evolved the philosophy of "chemurgy." Hale coined the term much later from "chemi" and "ergon," the Greek word for work, signifying "chemistry at work."[1] They had come upon a rusting combine sitting beside an old barn and paused to discuss why a farmer would want to own a combine, an expensive piece of equipment that he used only a few days a year.

Neither could reconstruct the conversation later, but it became a discussion of the growing problem of surplus farm produce in the United States; out of it evolved the idea that farm surpluses should be used as chemical raw materials rather than destroyed. Hale's central idea was that surplus corn and other grain should be converted into alcohol and mixed with gasoline, and he became the pioneer and chief proponent of what is today called "gasohol." A popular after-dinner speaker, he was soon promoting the notion of gasohol in speech after speech. Herty, as a result of this conversation, wrote a series of articles in scientific journals warning of the approaching problem of farm surpluses.

Hale also wrote a long article entitled "Farming Must Become a Chemical Industry," in which he said only organic chemistry held any promise as an answer to the farm problem and predicted that "we (the U.S.) shall be importing large quantities of grain in ten years (because chemurgy will use so much of it)." It was later recognized as the first organized presentation of the idea that became chemurgy, but no one wanted to print it. Eventually some forgotten angel suggested to Hale that he send it to Henry Ford. Hale did, and forthwith received a telegram asking, "May we publish this immediately in the *Dearborn Independent*?" The telegram came from William J. Cameron, editor of the *Independent*, a newspaper owned by Henry Ford; Cameron was later famous for his weekly commentaries, heard nationally on the Ford Sunday Evening Radio Hour.

Then things began to happen. Cameron's office was flooded with requests for reprints of the Hale article. Extra copies were printed in leaflet form but requests continued to pile up. The Chemical Foundation agreed to take over the job of complying with these requests, and quickly exhausted a press run of 500,000 copies. "That was the beginning of the chemurgic movement," Herty said.

Hale steadily gained notoriety as a public speaker and as a prophet of things to come. During 1925 he was invited to participate in an early radio broadcast series called "Radio Talks on Science," sponsored by Science Service and the National Research Council, of which Hale had become a member, over Washington radio station WCAP. Introduced as one of the great living organic chemists in America, Hale was asked to imagine the "Prophecy of a Chemist."

Because his prophecies were later set down in print, they are on the record.[2] Hale predicted in 1925 that:

- highways and airways would become serious competitors of railways, and trucks would compete for the short-haul business of the railroads;
- air transport lines would compete for the long-haul business of the railroads;
- alcohol would be blended with gasoline to make a more efficient fuel for high-compression motors;
- airplanes would become the strongest arm in military combat, and Germany would lead this development;
- America would run head-on into a major problem—surplus farm crops;
- while only 15 percent of the 1924 corn crop had gone into factories rather than stomachs, the day would come when 50 percent would go to industry, which would return the by-products to farmers for fattening stock;
- oats would be raised for their hulls and the kernel would be used as a by-product for cereal production; and
- a depression was coming that would be cataclysmic to agriculture.

It was a dazzling performance; all of these things came true. By 1939, for example, the Quaker Oats Company was at times using oat hulls as the raw material for furfural (in 1925 it had been a useless laboratory curiosity), producing oatmeal as a by-product.

A newspaper woman compared his record for accuracy of prophecy with that of baseball's Dizzy Dean, who also had a remarkable record for "calling his shots," and dubbed him "Chemistry's Dizzy Dean," a name which stuck.

In 1935 another of Hale's cronies, Francis P. Garvan, president of the Chemical Foundation, convened the first Joint Conference of Agriculture, Industry and Science at the Dearborn Inn in Dearborn, Michigan, in the shadow of the Ford Motor Company. It met here at the invitation of Henry Ford, whose experiments with the soybean made him the most prominent philosophical ally of the chemurgists. Ford made brief appearances at the meeting. Garvan, describing how Ford researchers had converted soybeans into some 30 industrial products, cited this as proof that "agriculture may be wedded to industry with chemistry serving as the wedding ring."

Garvan became the first president of the National Farm Chemurgic Council, formed at this meeting, and annual conferences of the movement continued until World War II. A history of the chemurgic movement calls Hale, Herty, and Garvan its founders.[3] Other leading pioneers were Wheeler McMillen, an editor and writer who became chief of the Farm Chemurgic Council after Garvan's death, and Leo M. Christensen, of Iowa State College, the early champion of "power alcohol."[4]

Garvan died in 1937 and Herty in 1938, and the movement began to run out of steam. By the end of World War II its leaders were gone or aging—Hale himself was 70 in 1946—and it never regained its vigor of the 1930s.

Billy Hale had moved on into other fields by then and was pursuing the commercialization of some of his inventions. Following extensive research on chlorophyll he had developed a green chewing gum, incorporating chlorophyll, that he called "Phyllets" and packaged in a little green and orange box. His daughter Ruth remembered them vividly:

> He was bound and determined that everybody should chew Phyllets. Chlorophyll was good for you, and would make your breath fresh. He didn't advertise; he put it in a drug store down on K Street and Connecticut Avenue (in Washington, D.C.). I will never forget; he had me and Wiley (Wiley T. Buchanan, her husband, who some years later became President Eisenhower's Chief of Protocol) one day, standing there on the corner handing out these damn Phyllets to anybody that came by. He said, "Just pass them out." We did it. After that he said, "Oh, no, I just can't be bothered advertising. This man Mr. Wolf has offered to buy me out." So Mr. Wolf bought him out and those are now Clorets. He would have made a fortune on Clorets had he stuck with the Phyllets, but he didn't. He never worried about anything like that. Mr. Wolf began to advertise, and it was everywhere; later you still saw it on television; you see chlorophyll advertised everywhere. But my father never believed in advertising. If the thing sold itself, it sold; if it didn't, you just couldn't worry about that. He could invent it, but in the sales department he was awful, terrible. He just didn't know about it.[5]

He also put chlorophyll into cigarettes called "Hale" cigarettes, made of light green paper with a chlorophyll filter tip. His slogan for them was "Inhale with Hale." He experimented with chlorophyll toothpaste but never brought out his own brand. He tried chlorophyll-treated chocolate, for people allergic to chocolate, and chlorophyll coffee, for people allergic to coffee. None of it went over. He did have some success with a chlorophyll cigar called the "Crest" cigar. "That was the only one that caught on for awhile, for a few years," Ruth Buchanan said. "After he died I would still get a check for something like $15 once in awhile for the Crest cigar, made by Larus Brothers in Richmond, Virginia."

Hale's notorious lack of business sense, combined with an outstanding talent for deviltry, made him at times an outright danger to the Dow Company. He tended to speak or write as though he carried the full force of the company behind him, and after a while Willard Dow asked him to write his letters on his own private stationery, not on the company's letterhead.

At the company he felt free to walk into any office or any meeting at any time. If the topic was interesting he might stay and join in; if not, he would leave. On one occasion he walked into a meeting with the Ciba Geigy Company, which had become sales agent for Dow's production of indigo and dyes when the company decided dye-making would never be more than a sideline for it. After weeks of negotiations the text of an agreement between the two firms was being read out as prelude to signing of the contract. When the price of indigo that had finally been agreed upon was read out, Hale reached over and patted Willard Dow's arm. "Willard," he said, "these people are our friends; we can give them a much better price than that, now, can't we?" In the midst of the sizzling discussion that followed, Billy Hale got up and left.

Hale's widowed mother moved to Midland after his wife Helen's death and helped him raise his infant daughter. "You're a big girl now," grandmother Hale told the little girl, "and we have your Daddy to take care of. Your Daddy is brilliant. He's sort of a genius, a brilliant scholar, but he doesn't have much common sense. So we have to help him behave. When he does erratic things, we have to straighten him out because he just doesn't think like normal people. He's too busy with his work."[6]

Among other eccentricities, he refused to drink coffee for breakfast, or any other time; the best thing to take at breakfast, he said, was beer.

Like many American chemists of his generation he had gone to Germany to earn his Ph.D., and the experience had led him to consider the Germans superior in chemistry and most other things. His admiration for things German was sometimes carried to outrageous lengths. Even in the 1930s, when Hitler had taken power and war was approaching, Hale did not conceal his Germanophilia. He acquired a reputation as a Nazi-lover, and at one time was listed in a major magazine as one of America's leading Nazi sympathizers. There is no record of his doing anything in a political sense in furtherance of these feelings, but he built a reputation that was outright embarrassing to Willard Dow when in 1946 Willard and the company were accused of collaborating with the Germans to hold down U.S. war preparedness. Hale, in fact, was convinced the Germans would win the war.[7]

He was also convinced the Japanese would win. On June 18, 1942, he told a meeting of the Michigan Bankers Association in Detroit that only a combination of Germany and Russia could beat Japan, that "we are now engaged in an inter-racial war between the yellows and the whites," and that "this time the yellow race will win." The bankers were shocked; so was the press and public. "The Midland Metal Merlin has a habit of opening his mouth and walking away and leaving it uninhibited by any contact with his head," one *Detroit Free Press* editorial writer commented. "Outside his specialized field of organic chemistry few men have revealed a greater capacity for not knowing what they are talking about."

Hale enjoyed the notoriety and continued to hobnob with such jet-setters as Louis Bromfield, the novelist, and James A. Farley, Franklin D. Roosevelt's campaign manager and postmaster-general. After the war he went on a three-day tour of Germany with another friend, Gen. Anthony C. McAuliffe, the hero of Bastogne, on what had been Hermann Goering's luxurious private railway train.

Douglas MacArthur was "the one man who could bring the U.S. out of the mire," he believed. After the death of Arthur MacArthur, the general's brother, Hale often squired his widow Mary. But he never remarried. "To him," his daughter said, "Helen was still with him. She was always there and I don't think he could stand the thought of marrying anybody else. As a substitute for my mother, he just threw himself completely into his work. He worked every night. Always. He never went to bed before midnight; he was always up late. In contrast, all of the Dows were early-to-bedders—they all went to bed at nine or ten o'clock. He never could really understand that."

Philip T. Rich, editor of the *Midland Daily News*, said that during "the smog siege" in California, Billy Hale telephoned the governor of the state and asked him to call together a group of scientists, and offered to sit down with them. "As far as I know, this meeting never took place," Rich said. "Too bad it didn't. Billy Hale would have outsmogged the smog if you gave him a chance."

Hale, he said, "could stir up more arguments in two blocks of walking than any man on earth. And he liked to walk. He could make a series of statements that blazed in the sky like meteors, but he could add his positive assertions in sessions which gave strength to the whole belief. He never went half-way."

Hale defended his argumentativeness by saying that he wanted to stir people up, "and make them think about things." "That was his favorite pastime," his daughter said. "He was an unforgettable man, a great showman, and lived on controversy," Rich said.[8]

1. The term "chemurgy" first appeared in print in Hale's book, *The Farm Chemurgic* (Boston: The Stratford Co., 1934).
2. *Scientific Monthly*, February 1926.
3. Christy Borth, *Pioneers of Plenty* (Indianapolis and New York: Bobbs-Merrill Co., 1939). Borth, a *Detroit Free Press* writer, was a friend of Hale's and unofficial historian of the chemurgic movement. Garvan received the American Chemical Society's Priestley Medal in 1929, the only nonchemist ever so honored.
4. Wheeler McMillen was given a special award by the U.S. Department of Agriculture in 1991, when he was 98, the award ceremony being attended by Hale's daughter, Ruth Hale Buchanan. He died in Virginia a year later.

   For Henry Ford's role in the chemurgic movement, see David L. Lewis, *The Public Image of Henry Ford: An American Folk Hero and His Company* (Detroit: Wayne State University Press, 1976), 282-87.
5. Oral History, Ruth Hale Buchanan, June 13, 1991. Hale virtually gave away "Phyllets"; "Mr. Wolf" paid him $100 for the patent.
6. Ibid.
7. Oral History, Gertrude Winfield, May 23, 1994.
8. Philip T. Rich, editorial, *Midland Daily News*, August 9, 1955

Gil Currie, Billy Hale, James Pardee, Herbert Dow, and on occasion other Dow representatives went about the country giving speeches in support of the tariff. Hale was the most violent fire-eater of the lot: "Prosperity is not returning and never will until the tariff is made a law," Hale said in his standard speech. "Those German propagandists who go around bewailing and pretending that Germany never can pay off her indebtedness unless her goods are sold in America are our lowest types of criminals. England, France, and Italy have taken great care to protect themselves. Have we no right to protect ourselves, or must we be made the grand dumping ground? To Hell with everything German! Down with all German importers!"[28]

Currie became the chief "buttonholer." In that day bills were argued man-to-man, and political buttonholing was the common and accepted way of discussion; in fact, said Currie, "nobody ever thought there was another way of passing a bill at that time." When the bill was debated Currie would be standing in the cloakroom listening, and would occasionally sally out on the floor to "straighten things out" with Nicholas Longworth or Joe Fordney, even though he was no longer a congressman himself.

The chemical industry needed the tariff desperately, Currie and the others said. If the Germans had been admitted to the U.S. market without any correction in the tariff, they would have had such a tremendous advantage that there would have been no opportunity for the Americans to produce anything but the heavy inorganic chemicals. Before the war Germany had produced about 90 percent of the world's pharmaceuticals and coal-tar chemicals and it expected to return to this status in the postwar world.[29]

Edgar C. Britton pointed out that the German chemical industry had come through the First World War intact—in contrast to the destruction it suffered in the second—and in many fields of chemistry was about 50 years ahead of the U.S. industry in know-how and experience. What the U.S. chemical industry was asking for was a few years of protection until it was sufficiently grounded in the organic field to compete with the rest of the world.[30]

That was what the chemical industry was finally granted by the Fordney-McCumber Tariff Bill when it was signed by President Harding on September 20, 1922. Duties on the organic chemicals were set particularly high—the only really high tariff barrier in the bill, most experts thought—but it was specified that they would be reduced (from 60 percent to 45 percent) at the end of three years, which duly occurred in 1925.

Most analysts felt that the Fordney-McCumber tariff was a great achievement for the future of the American chemical industry in affording the industry some catch-up time to develop the infant organic chemical facilities it had rushed into during the war. The chemical world was never the same again; it never returned to the prewar status, and the tariff was one of the main reasons.

Looking back on that period a few years later, in the full proud ebullience of the flapper age, Billy Hale dissolved in lyric praise for what he called "the Great Tariff." "We live today under a tariff of the most benign influence," he said in 1928.

> Had there not been sufficient protection afforded certain of our industries at the close of the War we would have lost the progress then attained, but thanks to the emergency tariff, followed immediately by the Fordney-McCumber tariff, protection for all industry was set upon a high plane.... If those who would criticise the tariff could only comprehend in a small way what this enormous field of organic chemistry means to the American people they would realize that the Fordney-McCumber tariff was written under masterly guidance and with a vision truly prophetic. . . Fordney and McCumber were the creators of an industrially independent America and through bringing into existence the Great Tariff of 1922 assured our nation of continued prosperity the like of which has never been known before in the history of the world.[31]

That was the spirit of "the roaring Twenties."

The "great tariff" also left the Dow company with a solidly protectionist outlook that was to last for nearly half a century. Leland I. Doan was still trying to explain the company's protectionist stance in 1958, when the free trade movement was sweeping across the world and trade barriers were widely seen as an archenemy of progress.[32] By that time the company had become one of the last of the die-hard protectionists.

The company's distinguished chief economist, Dr. Lewis E. Lloyd, was for many years one of the chief protagonists of protectionism. He argued for it on into the 1960s, and taught the tenets of the doctrine at a local university after he retired in 1972.[33] It was only when the company moved boldly abroad in the middle 1960s and became one of the leading international firms of the world that it changed its tune. Then its love affair with tariff protection began to be a liability and an embarrassment, and it was quietly dropped and finally forgotten.

Notes

1. These flares incorporated a finely divided, powdery form of magnesium; solid magnesium does not burn.

2. See contract between Dow and Searight-Downs dated August 13, 1919.

3. W. D. Edenburn, "Small Engine Does Not Reduce Speed in 500-mile Race," *Detroit News*, June 5, 1921.

4. H. H. Dow to A. W. Smith, October 4, 1921.

5. H. H. Dow to E. E. Keller, Standard Screw Products Company, Detroit, May 18, 1922.

6. See H. H. Dow to Charles L. Nedoma, Engineering Dept. Secretary, Cadillac Motor Car Company, Detroit, June 16, 1922, marked "Confidential."

7. Harrison Hatton, Notes on conversation with W. R. Veazey, March 22, 1950.

8. *Portrait and Biographical Album of Midland County, Michigan, 1884* (Chicago: Chapman Brothers, 1884), 351-53, 398.

9. Hatton, Notes on conversation with F. H. Langell and R. R. Dreisbach, June 23, 1949.

10. Hatton, conversation with E. Barstow, June 23, 1950.

11. Bayer's patent on aspirin expired in 1917, which was one attraction for Putnam; it was also, looking ahead, a peacetime outlet for phenol. Dow was one of several firms (including Monsanto) who rushed into aspirin manufacture at this juncture.

12. Hale, professor of organic chemistry at the University of Michigan, and Dow's eldest daughter Helen, a student in one of his classes, were married in February 1917.

13. Prior to this time all laboratories reported to some production manager. The Old Mill Laboratory, for example, was Barstow's responsibility.

14. For Hale's description of this research, see William J. Hale, "New Processes for Phenol and Aniline," in *American Chemical Industry, A History*, ed. William Haynes, vol. 4, appendix 36 (Reinhold, 1954), 534-36.

15. Harrison Hatton, Notes on conversation with William H. Williams, March 29, 1950.

16. Robert S. Karpiuk, *Dow Research Pioneers, 1888-1949* (Midland, Mich: Pendell Publishing), 97-98.

17. "50 Years in Magnesium," *Dow Metal Products News* (Midland, Mich: Dow Metal Products Dept., July 1966), 6-9.

18. Oral History, Ivan F. Harlow, March 12, 1984. Harlow was 99 years old at the time of this interview.

19. A. W. Beshgetoor to Jack D. Eadie, Public Relations Dept., The Dow Chemical Company, January 16, 1967, a handwritten 14-page account of the history of Dow's Main Laboratory. See also Oral History, Joseph E. Ritzer Sr., April 19, 1991.

20. Morell (the "L. G." stood for Le Grand, French for "The Great") had been superintendent of schools in Midland from 1907 to 1912. In 1916, when chemists and engineers were in severe shortage because of the war, Herbert Dow asked him to organize and direct a training program at the plant; the

"Educational Building" was built to house those activities. Morell earned a Ph.D. in physics before returning to Midland for a third time, in 1928, as a lab director.

21. "The War After the War," speech delivered by William J. Hale several times, 1921.

22. Joseph W. Fordney to Herbert Dow, January 26, 1917.

23. Smoot later gave his name to the infamous Smoot-Hawley Tariff Act of 1930, often seen as a major U.S. policy blunder and one of the root causes of World War II. Dow met with him but the two never became more than casual acquaintances. See C. Cyril Bennett, publisher of *The Observer* magazine, Washington, D.C., to H. H. Dow, January 18, 1917.

24. *Congressional Record*, January 29, 1918, 1482-83. Also "German Yellow-Dog Fund," *American Economist* (New York: American Protective Tariff League, February 4, 1921).

25. Herbert Dow to George E. Roberts, vice president, The National City Bank, New York, August 25, 1921.

26. Dow was one of six U.S. companies licensed to make and market novocaine after World War I under German patents taken over by the Alien Property Custodian and administered by an organization established for the purpose called the Chemical Foundation. The license fee was 5 percent of sales. The product was not sold as "Novocain," its German patent name, but as "procaine," the name assigned by the Chemical Foundation.

   When Dow applied to the foundation for a license to manufacture novocaine in May 1919, several companies objected; Dow was making all the intermediates required and selling them to other companies. The foundation's advisory committee recommended refusal of the Dow application. Herbert Dow protested angrily that the foundation was "playing favorites," in violation of its charter. Six months later, the Dow request was granted.

27. Herbert Dow to Roger W. Babson, Wellesley Hills, Mass., October 21, 1922.

28. Hale, "The War After the War."

29. Hatton, Notes on conversation with Gilbert A. Currie, April 28, 1950.

30. Hatton, Notes on conversation with Edgar C. Britton, May 9, 1950.

31. William J. Hale, speech, "The Great Tariff and the Future of Michigan," March 24, 1928.

32. See Leland I. Doan, "Foreign Trade in a Changing World," speech to the Economic Club of Detroit, February 24, 1958.

33. Lewis E. Lloyd, *Tariffs: The Case for Protection* (New York: Devin-Adair, 1955) is a comprehensive statement of the protectionist position.

HERBERT DOW:
THE LEGEND

I.

All sorts of stories were told about Herbert Dow during his lifetime, and even more after his death in 1930. Anyone who knew the company, worked at the company, or lived in the community during his lifetime had a fund of them, some of them personal experiences, some heard from friends and neighbors. "Herbert Dow stories" have been repeated in company gatherings in the years since and have become a cornerstone of the company's culture, closely related to its reputation for doing things differently—"the Dow way." Some of them bear repeating here, for they illustrate pointedly what made Herbert Dow tick and the kind of personality on which the firm was built.

W. R. Veazey, who knew and worked closely with both of them, once compared Herbert Dow with Albert W. Smith, the distinguished head of the chemistry department at Case. "Smith was the serious, completely accurate type of student who took copious, exact notes and always made a brilliant record on exams because he gave the teachers back exactly what they had given him," Veazey said. "Herbert Dow was the opposite. I don't imagine he spent a quarter of his time in school paying attention to what was being taught. He would use a professor's lecture or remarks as a springboard for going off on some tangent of his own. Therefore he was a very poor student by the usual teaching standards. When exam time came, he would have to get together with Smith to find out enough about the course to be able to pass the exam."[1]

He was opposed to and irritated by dogmatic statement in any form, whether in the classroom, in a preacher, in a scientific textbook, or wherever he might run across it, Veazey said. Dow's longtime friend Professor U. P. Hedrick, director of the New York Agricultural Experiment Station (at Geneva, New York) and one of the nation's leading experts on apple growing, told him apples could be grown successfully only in heavy, clay soil. "As soon as he heard this Herbert Dow determined to grow apples in the sand on his property, just to prove Hedrick was wrong." And he did, Veazey said.[2] Eventually he could grow apples in this sandy soil that could win a prize anywhere.

If authoritative chemical sources said it couldn't be done, Herbert Dow wanted to do it. The English chemists refused to believe Dow could make bromine from seawater—the chemistry involved just was not possible, they said. Telling him it was impossible was a challenge to him.[3]

"Just let me outline a typical day with Herbert Dow," Veazey said.

He might call you into the office and say, "Say, Veazey, why don't you go to work on so-and-so and see if you can't make something out of it. And you know, it just occurs to me that if you were to try this process instead of that process, you might get something, and, oh, I've never talked to you about this before, but why don't you see if you can't think of some way to make all the apples on a tree ripen at the same time." Then, without any further ado, Herbert Dow might say, "Let's go up to the house; I want to show you something." So he would take you to the house and show you a painting he had just bought in Detroit or New York or some-place. Now, you didn't know anything about paintings, but he would talk to you about them and you would talk to him, and in the course of that talk he might suggest four or five things, and then you would go out in the orchards, because something he had said about the paintings suggested something in the orchards. There he might show you a whole row of trees which had been grafted in a special new way. That might suggest seven or eight things for you to work on in connection with grafting trees, chemical sprays, and the like. This might bring up something he wanted to see down at the magnesium plant, so you would drive back to the plant. Before you were there very long he might say, "Let's go see Jack Frost," and you would climb into a car and drive forty miles south to see a farmer who had some unusual infestation of a parasite or bug in his orchard. Herbert Dow would tell you to go to work on that, too, and a week or so later you would be back down there with a spray and probably trying every chemical you could think of to see how it worked.

You weren't supposed to do anything about most of the suggestions he made, Veazey said.

What Herbert Dow wanted you to do was take the ideas he had given you, look at them, pick out the two or three best ones, and get to work on those. You might think he was rattling this stuff off so fast to so many people he might forget all about it in a few days, but that was a booby-trap a lot of people fell into. He had a memory like an elephant and would come back in a week or ten days after giving you this flood of instructions and ask you what you had done about the idea for using sodium instead of copper as a way of conducting electricity from the powerhouse to the cells. "You remember we talked that over," he would say. "A pipe filled with sodium, you remember." Now we might just have mentioned that in passing while we were going from the magnesium plant to Frost's farm, but he knew, and you were supposed to know after looking over the other suggestions, that the idea of working on sodium as an electrical conductor had the best implications for the Dow company and therefore was what you should work on. If you didn't pick a good one, or one he wanted, Herbert Dow would ask why you had wasted time on that fool thing when the other thing he told you about was much better.[4]

From Herbert Dow "there was a new idea every morning," Tom Griswold said.

Maurice Thompson, an engineer, remembered Herbert Dow coming into a building and noticing that the windows along one side of the room were extremely dusty. Without a word Dow walked over to the windows and with a finger traced a letter on each window in the row. When he had finished the windows spelled: J A N I T O R.

He seemed to notice everything and to have an idea about everything. Thompson remembered working in the early engineering department, which was in a big, open, upstairs room. The room was "noisy as could be," he said. One day Herbert Dow noticed the noise level and after some thought had some cross-shaped pieces of wallboard made and hung from the ceiling as sound baffles. It was an improvement but "hardly a masterpiece of acoustical engineering," Thompson said.[5]

Many employees remembered him asking unexpected, out-of-context questions. Thompson remembered Herbert Dow asking, "out of a clear blue sky": "How many cubic feet in a bushel?" Probably, Thompson said, he was considering some problem where he needed to know that.

Merle Newkirk, longtime head of the Power Department, said Dow would come in and ask: "Mr. Newkirk, how much is your labor costing you an hour?" or "How much total steam did you generate a year ago yesterday?" Newkirk said he began to carry a small notebook with every conceivable kind of power record in it, because he might be standing in line at the cafeteria and have Herbert Dow ask him: "Newkirk, how many kilowatt hours did you get last week?"

The quickest way to get in trouble with Herbert Dow was to tell him when he suggested some project that it could not be done. "You always said you would try it, and strangely enough, it worked more times than you expected," he said.

Newkirk said Herbert Dow saw him in the cafeteria one day and said, "Come to my office after lunch." Dow told him he should buy some Dow stock. Newkirk said he couldn't, on his salary, but Dow told him to go see Mr. Bennett; he would take care of that. Bennett explained how they would take a little out of his salary to pay for the stock until it was paid for, and that was how Newkirk bought his first ten shares of Dow stock. The story is typical of that generation of Dow pioneers, many of whom from humble beginnings became wealthy men by investing in the company's stock.

One day Newkirk was out in the plant with Dow, who pointed toward the Pot House. "What are we going to do about that?" he asked Newkirk, pointing to heavy smoke coming out of the Pot House chimneys. "I don't know, Mr. Dow," Newkirk said, "It's not my department, anyway."

"Look here," said Dow, "that is The Dow Chemical Company just the same as this plant. You are the combustion expert around here, so go down there and find out why they are sending so much coal out as smoke, and see what you can do." Newkirk went down to see the Pot House foreman, who said it was the worst problem they had, and he would be glad for suggestions. The problem, Newkirk said, was that the men would "Wabash the stoker"— fill it to the brim—and then let it burn down again. "Out of this we designed something very close to the sprinkler stoker, which solved that problem," Newkirk said, "but the main point of this story was that Herbert Dow wanted everybody's ideas and efforts on any part of the plant where an improvement could be made."[6]

Many of the Herbert Dow stories focused on his horror of wasting money. Griswold said that "what was unique about the Dow Company was that crazy old Dow used scrap carbons, cheap white pine and tar to build an electrolytic chemical plant. Anybody else trying to do something like that would have used expensive crockery, porcelain, platinum, mercury, glass, rubber, things like that. Crazy Dow did not have that kind of money, even to think of buying things like that, so he turned to what was there, and the amazing thing is that it worked."[7]

Veazey explained:

He was away off in the woods, far from sources of cheap power such as there were at Niagara Falls, and he had to take on the making of chlorine as cheaply or more cheaply than they did at Niagara. The way he did it was probably the most unique thing in the chemical history of that time. Wood sold for from $16 a thousand for the very best obtainable down to $3 a thousand for cheap hemlock or culled pine. The $3 wood was so poor that the lumbermen used to say that if you laid it down it would roll up into hoops all by itself. The buildings and cells of his first chlorine plant were built of the $3 lumber, not the $16 variety. This is the first way Herbert Dow made up for the fact that his power could never be as cheap as Niagara Falls power if he had to import coal over long distances.

Veazey said the first cells were 16 feet wide for a reason. The reason: the cheap lumber Dow was buying was cut in 16-foot lengths, and if he made the cells that wide he would not waste lumber or labor in sawing it to fit.[8]

Willard Dow remembered his father saying that Coulter Jones would be a good man to send down to Louisiana to build an iodine plant because Jones would work with a lot of junk and old rusty pipes. That way everybody would think he was crazy and pay no attention to what he was doing, which was exactly what Herbert Dow wanted.[9]

Margaret Johnson, who with her husband, Charles, ran the Stag Hotel (built by Dow during World War I to house the influx of new employees), said she and Charley once got into a tiff with Herbert Dow about the price of teapots. Dow happened to see the invoice for some graniteware teapots that cost a dollar apiece and he told Charley he had never heard of a teapot that cost a dollar. The next time he was in Chicago Herbert Dow went to Marshall Field's and priced teapots, and brought back a list showing sizes and prices, the most expensive one being 35 cents. Mrs. Johnson then explained to him that while china teapots at 10 cents apiece might last as much as three meals before being broken, a graniteware teapot would last a couple of years and therefore was much cheaper. At that, Herbert Dow said he guessed she was right.[10]

Once Herbert Dow was making telephone calls from a pay booth at the Grand Central Station in Detroit and ran out of nickels, which calls then cost. He had a dime and two calls to make, so he asked the operator if he could put in the dime and make two calls. She said he could and he inserted the dime, but something happened and he was cut off, could not make his calls, and lost his dime. When he got back to Midland Herbert Dow wrote the president of Michigan Bell Telephone about the incident and his dime was refunded.[11]

Tom Griswold Jr. said his mother-in-law, Herbert Dow's mother, told him that as a small boy, when he was trying to build or make something and it broke or didn't work, Herbert would say, "That is just what I wanted," and he would go on to rebuild it or make something a little different. "Now I ask you," said Griswold, "how can you stop a man like that?"

Alden Dow, Herbert's son, said his father told him an inventor must have the attitude that whatever he sees, it is just the thing he is looking for. "If the inventor is looking for pipe and the first thing he sees is some bamboo trees, he assumes that bamboo trees are exactly what he wants and sets about finding ways to use bamboo for pipe. No matter what the material is, the real inventor will exhaust all the possibilities in this first material before moving on to consider something else." Making use of what was at hand was fundamental to his father's thinking, Alden Dow said.[12]

Herbert Dow could not tell a story or a joke and seldom tried, although he appreciated hearing a good story immensely, and he had very little sense of play, Alden said; he could not remember his father playing with his children. "I don't think he knew how," Alden Dow said. "He had never done it." He did remember a period when Griswold and his father got one of his sisters to play the piano and the two of them would sing. "The singing was pretty terrible, but loud," Alden remembered.

He was quite susceptible to seasickness, and Alden Dow remarked that immediately after returning from Japan his father set about inventing a seasickness remedy, and patented one.

His father might or might not come home for lunch, Alden Dow said, but he never talked at meals. There were times, he said, when his father came home to lunch, ate, and went back to the plant again without saying a word; sometimes the whole family would be sitting around the table, all talking except his father. This seems to have vexed Mrs. Dow considerably. Alden Dow recalled her throwing a piece of bread at him and asking: "Why don't you say something?"

Often in the evenings he played solitaire, but his main form of recreation, his children remembered, was digging holes. On a Sunday morning he would get up early, take a shovel and a pail of water and disappear into the garden or orchard. When he found a tree that was not doing well he would start digging around it; in a day or two he would have topsoil brought in to fill around the tree and give it new nourishment. In the meantime Mrs. Dow would ready the children and shepherd them off to Sunday School at the First Presbyterian

Church downtown; when they returned she would send a child or two out to look for Father. "After much looking about we would stumble on his coat, which he had taken off someplace to do some digging; next we might find the pail, and finally the hole, and down inside would be Father digging," Alden Dow said.[13]

He said he suspected "that the going might have been tough at the plant and Father wanted to get away to think out a problem." Margaret Towsley, Herbert Dow's daughter, said the same thing: that her father "on Sundays, if he was worried, almost always went out and decided someplace in the orchard had to have a ditch; so he'd proceed to dig a ditch."

He had been a devoted churchgoer as a young man but almost never went to church when he grew older. "Herbert Dow objected to being forced to listen to a sermon without being able to argue with the ministers, many of whose views he disagreed with rather violently," Veazey said.[14]

In his older days he was very hard of hearing, a trait that ran in the family. Margaret Towsley said:

> One thing I inherited from Father were bad ears; it's gone straight down the line. Dorothy and Willard had bad ears. Alden was deaf the last few years. I don't know as Dad would have admitted he was as deaf as he was. But I remember Willard coming home from directors' meetings and he'd say: "Most of the time the directors are saying, 'What was that you said?'" Because everybody had gotten hard of hearing and they didn't have any help, any hearing aids.[15]

In the evening, Griswold said, Herbert Dow would sometimes go out in the yard or orchard with a big jackknife and prune branches off bushes and trees. In the World War I period he often chewed rubber bands, a habit that annoyed the family. On a Sunday evening he liked to play checkers or chess with Griswold or his son-in-law, "Billy" Hale.

He spent a great deal of time doing "picture puzzles," especially a favorite early jigsaw puzzle he had of about 250 pieces. He did this puzzle at various times of the day—the same puzzle, over and over again—with a stopwatch to determine when his faculties were at their peak. One day he had just finished the puzzle when Grace Dow brought him a cup of tea. After the tea he did it again, and discovered his time was better after the tea. This proved to him that a tea or coffee break was a good thing, and after that he often had a cup of tea at about four in the afternoon.[16]

He did not often argue with his employees, but it happened occasionally. One day E. O. Barstow came in to see him and said he wanted to get something straight: that he was building and operating a plant and trying to do his best at it, but that Herbert Dow simply had to leave him alone and let him do what he was trying to do without interfering all the time, introducing new ideas all the time. After the argument, that was the way it worked out, Griswold said.[17]

Griswold thought Dow's outstanding characteristic was that "he didn't know he could be beaten." Actually he was beaten but he didn't know it, Griswold said, so "he carried everybody else along with him," referring to the 1892 experience with the bromine plant; Herbert Dow had tried to use potash made locally from ashes, and it was a very crude product, high in impurities and a commercial disaster. (In 1899 or thereabouts he switched to German potash, which did not have to be re-refined).

The family members who worked at the company often gave him problems. Griswold said he and Dow argued constantly from the time he came to Midland. Once Herbert Dow was stopped on Main Street by Clarence Macomber, president of the bank. "Say, what's the matter with that son-in-law of yours, Dr. Hale?" Macomber asked. "We keep sending him OD notices but he keeps on writing checks." Dow said he'd look into it, and when he saw Hale asked him about it. "OD means 'Overdrawn'?" Hale asked, and erupted in laughter. "I thought it meant 'On Deposit'. I thought someone was putting money in my account I didn't know about, so every time I got an OD notice I went out and spent it."[18]

Ivan Kenaga and Arthur W. Winston Jr. worked on an early process for making Epsom salts (magnesium sulfate) from the brine stream, but for a long time met with disappointing and frustrating results. Kenaga said they finally told Herbert Dow they were writing up a final report recommending the project be written off as a failure. Dow refused to accept this and instead insisted they keep right on working at it—and in the end he was vindicated because they finally "made a go of it" and it became a highly successful product. In fact, Dow Chemical became the world's biggest manufacturer of Epsom salts. "No one could compete with us," Kenaga said.[19]

Dr. Joseph H. Sherk, the Dow family doctor, told about a man who in the process of moving from one rented house to another in the town left an unpaid water bill of $1.50 at his previous address. Instead of telling him about it or sending him the bill, the landlord garnisheed the man's wages for $1.50. The custom was that if a man's wages were garnisheed he had to see the employment manager, C. E. Rice. As the man was standing in front of the clockroom with the garnishee slip in his hand, Herbert Dow came by and asked what he was waiting for. The man said he was waiting to see Mr. Rice. "What about?" Herbert Dow asked. "About this garnishee slip." "Well, let's look at it," Herbert Dow said. He took the man to the legal office and quickly had the whole matter straightened out. The man actually got some money back from the landlord for his impudence in garnisheeing his wages without presenting a bill first. It illustrated several things about Herbert Dow, Dr. Sherk said—his interest in his men and his interest in problems big or small; if something needed doing, no matter how much trouble it was, he just went ahead and did it.[20]

Leo Johnson, a painter, was sent to the front office one day in the 1920s to paint numbers on the curb so that reserved parking places could be provided for the top managers. While he was doing this Herbert Dow came along and asked why he was doing it. Leo explained that the managers were having trouble getting a parking place near the office, so reserved places were being marked. "You just paint out those numbers right now," Dow told him. "If those fellows can't get here early enough to find a parking place they can park downtown."[21]

Dow liked to go down to the clockroom now and again to watch the comings and goings at shift changes, usually looking like he was staring off into space but actually aware of everything that was going on. He spotted one man who always managed to be entering the clockroom at the exact moment the whistle blew the end of the shift. Finally he stopped him one night and said: "I want to congratulate you. You're the only man I know who is right at the clock at whistle time." Another time he looked out the window of his office and saw a man reading a newspaper. He went out and fired him on the spot.[22]

Mark Putnam told of a man who had stolen a lunch pail full of heavy spikes and was leaving the plant with them when he ran into Herbert Dow at the gate. In his anxiety he stumbled and dropped the pail, which fell to the ground, spilling spikes at Dr. Dow's feet. "For heaven's sake!" the man said to Herbert Dow as he bent to gather them up. "Some joke makers have filled my pail with spikes." Herbert Dow did nothing to the man, but was highly amused at his alibi.

Putnam said that on a hot summer day two men were loafing in front of a large electric fan when Herbert Dow unexpectedly came by. "It was generally known that Herbert Dow was death on loafers," Putnam said, "so as Dr. Dow went by, one of the men looked very attentively at the fan and said, 'Well, now it's working just fine.'"[23]

In the early days parking a horse and buggy was a different matter. Herbert Dow once left his horse and buggy tied up in front of the office and accepted a ride home with someone else. About midnight he realized his horse was still down at the office, without any feed. He got out of bed, went down to the office, and brought the horse home.

He lived through the transition from horse and buggy to the automobile age but was never completely comfortable behind the wheel of an automobile. "The world's worst driver," Alden Dow called him; he was as likely as not to drive all the way to the plant in low gear. He bought his first car, a 1913 Ford roadster, when he was 47, and the children said he would sometimes forget, pull back hard on the steering wheel and cry "Whoa!" when he wanted to stop, to their great amusement. The Ford roadster parked under the portico at the main office became a Dow landmark; it meant Herbert Dow was there.

When he was growing older and deafer he had a minor accident, colliding with another car while he was driving down to the Michigan State Fair at Detroit. He emerged unscathed, but Grace Dow became increasingly worried about his safety on the highways. She asked Willard to sell the car and eventually he did, getting himself in deep trouble with his father. "It's still a good car," Herbert Dow said. In his final years he suffered the indignity of being driven about by others.

One matter he insisted on was that the expensive chemical balances around the plants and labs should be put away in their cases when they were not in use; chlorine and other corrosive substances would ruin them well before their time. Once Albert Smith spent a summer in Midland and Herbert Dow asked him to give a lecture to all the lab men about the importance of putting the balances away. A day or two after the lecture Herbert Dow came into a laboratory and saw a balance case wide open. "Harlow," he said, "who did this? I just had Smith give a lecture about this and I want to know who left this case open." An hour or so later Ivan Harlow reported that as far as they could determine the last person to use that balance was Dr. Smith. "My, my," said Herbert Dow, and walked off.

John Sinclair, long-time superintendent of the Well Department, said sometimes in the early years their orders came from Fred N. Lowry, the plant superintendent, and sometimes they came directly from Herbert Dow to Charlie Potter, his right-hand man on brine wells, first superintendent of the department. When the order came from Herbert Dow, Charlie would tell John, "Now, this is right from the man with the whiskers."[24] (C. W. Markus, the purchasing vice president of Eastman Kodak, with whom Herbert Dow visited regularly, said that with his close-cut beard Dow very much resembled General U. S. Grant).

In those early years Herbert Dow knew everyone by name. He spent at least half his time in the plant. If you were working on something new you understood that Dr. Dow would be in sooner or later to talk to you about your work, and he might come to visit at any hour, day or night. Veazey recalled a time when he was working on a project that was going very poorly. He had been up working on it nonstop for a couple of days and at 2 A.M. was lying asleep on a board. He suddenly became aware that Herbert Dow was in the plant, but did not bother to get up off the board. Finally, Dow came over and asked him why he didn't get up like the others had. Veazey replied that, well, everything was now running all right. Dow said, "Well, I guess that's as good an answer as any." He was always frank but reasonable, Veazey said.[25]

Howard Nutting, an organic chemist who later organized the Central Research Index (a repository for Dow research reports), remembered chatting with Herbert Dow in the cafeteria, where Dow usually had lunch. Dow was griping about the cafeteria being used only three times a day, trying to think of something to do with it in the hours it was not being used, but he could not think of anything very smart. Finally, after thinking about it a long time, he said, "Well, I guess in that respect it's not as bad as a church, at that."[26]

Some, including Veazey, felt Herbert Dow did not like to look things up in a reference book. "If you have to look it up in a book," he told Veazey, "it's too late; it's already been done." W. H. Williams, a top production manager, understood it differently: "Herbert Dow would tell a man to do something but would get irritated if he looked it up in a chemical book, because Herbert Dow himself had already looked it up and knew it was in the book; he would not have told the man to try it out if he thought it wouldn't work." Herbert Dow believed completely in the experimental approach to chemistry and to science in general, Williams said, and he would not trust any explanation, even one he read in a book, until it had been checked by someone he knew and trusted in the lab. "The way you could really get in a fight with Herbert Dow would be to say something could or could not be done because you had read thus and so in a chemistry textbook."[27]

Alden Dow said his father's primary dictum was to get to know a problem thoroughly before ever going to a book to get information about it; the idea was "don't read first; find out what you are looking for and then read," he said. "If you go to a book first, that will slant your whole thinking about a problem; if you think the problem through first, the ideas you get from the book will fit into your picture, instead of you fitting into the book's picture."[28]

His was indeed a complex personality. Dr. Sherk felt he was clearly a genius, and most of those who knew him agreed with the doctor. Veazey felt he was "all his life a great big boy, maybe 13 years old, bubbling over with energy." He did not set out to create the Dow Company, Veazey said, but he wanted to do certain things and it was inconceivable to him that he could not do them. Herbert Dow had unlimited confidence in his own ability to generate ideas that would work—but it also happened that he was right. The Dow Company, the building up of Midland, the raising of capital, and other accomplishments were merely by-products or things that he did incidentally because he found he had to do them to get the things he wanted, Veazey said.

F. H. (Heinie) Langell, another engineer, said his belief in exploiting the chemical elements—bromine, chlorine, iodine, magnesium—rather than compounds, was critical, the stuff of legends.

It was to Veazey that Herbert Dow made one of his most often quoted statements. Veazey came to Dow with charts and data showing that an idea Dow had asked him to pursue would not work. Veazey had plumbed the idea thoroughly and showed Herbert Dow all his test data. When he had finished, Dow turned his back on him and stood looking out the window, talking about his work on his apple trees. Then he turned around and said, "Veazey, do you realize I can find a hundred men who won't put my ideas to work?" The remark, Veazey said, registered his disappointment, and his feeling that perhaps another person using another approach might have gotten a more positive answer. There was nothing impossible in his mind.[29]

Ralph Hunter said that when he and Veazey were trying to get into production of magnesium during World War I, Herbert Dow would come around and ask what had gone wrong. "You told him, and then he would say, 'All right, don't make those mistakes again,'" Hunter said.[30]

During World War I Herbert Dow sent Joe Bayliss out to show a state appraiser through the plants. When the appraiser had finished several days of work he told Herbert Dow he had bad news for him—he had to raise the tax appraisal of the plant by $550,000. Herbert Dow asked, "Why not make it a million?" Bayliss thought Dow was being sarcastic, but Dow explained to him: "If the state gets the added tax money we will get some of it back, indirectly, but we would get little or nothing if the federal government got the money." Bayliss said he thought any other industrial leader "would have raved."[31]

Gilbert A. Currie, Herbert Dow's legal adviser, said some of the early pollution problems were extremely difficult because of the Midland plant being located on a relatively small stream, the Tittabawassee. One July night the men in the plant telephoned to tell him that the dyke around the phenol plant had broken and dumped the plant's entire stock of phenol waste into the river in one load. It was a major emergency. Currie called the city of Saginaw immediately so they would turn off their water intake until the phenol had gone out into Lake Huron, and took over as the emergency coordinator.

The next morning Herbert Dow called Currie to his office and took him down to the river, saying he couldn't see what they were so excited about because if there had been so much phenol in the river there would have been dead fish there, and he did not see any. Currie told him four boatloads of men had been following the phenol down the river to get the dead fish before somebody else saw them. "Hmmm," said Dow.

A few minutes later newspaper men arrived, and Herbert Dow told Currie to go out and talk to them. "You know, don't you," Currie told him, "that whatever I say will have to be said in the company's name and will probably be printed." "Go out and talk to them anyway," Herbert Dow said.

Herbert Dow came into Currie's office once with a bill from Allis Chalmers, asking him to take care of it. "The engine we got from them didn't come up to specifications," he said. Not understanding power terminology, Currie spent time with the engineers in the plant, determining what the specifications had been and where the engine had fallen short. Then he met with the Allis Chalmers people, who produced correspondence to show that, true enough, the engine had not come up to specifications but that Herbert Dow had asked that a number of things be altered according to his own design and had insisted on those changes. Allis Chalmers, Currie concluded, had a convincing case why the engine was not up to specifications.

Currie reluctantly went in to explain to Herbert Dow that the Allis Chalmers case was convincing. Dow sat for a minute saying nothing, and then suddenly said, "Write them a check." And that was all.[32]

He believed in the "fundamental basic idea" that "wherever possible a man should keep in as close contact with his job as possible." "A man who tries to run a job from the golf links is not as successful as a man who is in closer touch with his job," Herbert Dow said.

To illustrate this principle he cited an event in which he was himself involved:

A good many years ago [he was writing in 1930] I went out to the bromine plant and saw it was shut down. I found most of the men were on the roof. I went up and found they had a trap door open at the top of a coke tower that was plugged with iron hydrate . . . this layer of iron hydrate was only on the top layer of coke and they understood the necessity of getting in there and taking out a few inches from the top of the coke. I stuck my head through the door and there was a considerable odor of bromine and the men claimed they were waiting for the air to clear up. I was satisfied that the amount of bromine was not more than it had been customary for me to soak up on many occasions, and I presumed the foreman . . . was equally familiar with the amount of bromine the men could absorb without injury. So I told him I thought it was up to him to set the example by going down and taking out the first pail of coke. He started to climb down the ladder and when his head got inside the door he immediately changed his mind and came out again. He said there was altogether too much bromine in the tower. So I took my coat off, threw it to one side, went down myself and told them to pass down the tools. I filled one pail full of coke and they pulled it out, and by that time the ladder was full of men trying to get down to help me, and very promptly enough coke was removed to permit free access of air . . . and the trap door was closed and the plant started again.

If I had not gone up on the roof, and if I had not known by experience how much bromine irritation a man can stand before it becomes a serious matter, that plant might have been shut down all day and several hundred dollars lost thereby. I supposed the foreman himself knew his job much better than he did, but he knew it better after that experience than he did before.

In the same letter he set down another of his basic rules: "I am no believer in an engineer having an oiler. He no sooner gets this oiler than he sits down and the oiler becomes the man who is in intimate contact with his job and therefore knows his engine best, and the engineer proceeds to be the equivalent of a man sitting in the office."[33]

A cantankerous machinist named Rose worked in the machine shop. Herbert Dow came in one day when Rose was in the midst of a long metal cut on a lathe, and the floor was covered with turnings. Seeing the litter, Dow asked Rose why he didn't clean up the mess. Rose, quick on the trigger, said: "I'm busy making this cut, I've got work to do. Clean it up yourself." Dow disappeared and then reappeared with a broom and shovel and swept up the turnings. When it was done he went off again without another word. Rose, largely as a result of this incident, became one of Herbert Dow's warmest admirers.[34]

Now I ask you, as Tom Griswold said, how can you stop a man like that?

II.

According to their daughter Dorothy (Arbury), Herbert and Grace Dow were both "very keen on art." "I don't think they ever went on a trip in their lives that they didn't go someplace and look at paintings. She used to take us to the Metropolitan Museum practically every time we went to New York; that was just part of going to New York. There was always something she had to look up." The family home in Midland is crowded with paintings they chose together.

"They bought every one of those individually," Dorothy Arbury said. "She studied the matter; she didn't go around and say, 'That's a pretty picture,' and buy it. She studied the artists, and then went looking for their pictures."[35]

In May 1919 Herbert Dow received a chance letter from a British artist, Arthur Henry Knighton-Hammond, who had been painting factory scenes at the British Dyestuffs Corporation, asking whether Dow would be interested in commissioning some paintings of his plant in Midland. Dow responded that he had never thought of doing that, but would consider it.

Later that year, visiting the National Chemical Exposition in New York City, Dow saw some paintings done for the National Aniline & Chemical Company, found them attractive and good advertising for the company, remembered Knighton-Hammond's letter, and wrote saying he was interested. By the end of the year he had agreed to hire the artist for six months (at a fee of $5,000 plus travel) to paint at the Midland plant.[36]

Knighton-Hammond, then an unknown talent but today considered an outstanding British artist—"the finest painter in watercolour of our time," in Augustus Johns's opinion—

sailed on the *Mauretania* for New York on April 14, 1920, and was met in New York by Ralph Dorland, manager of Dow's New York sales office. The artist's diary of his trip to America provides a fascinating glimpse through British eyes of Dow and Midland in 1920. He took most of his meals at the Dow cafeteria, bought a Ford sedan (for $1,035), and took driving lessons from "young Dow" (Willard). Dorothy Arbury recalled that he ran the car into the ditch when a bird appeared on the road in front of him: "he didn't know the bird would get out of the way." On Thursdays Earl Bennett took him to Rotary Club luncheons, and on one occasion he described his work to the club. He went to tea with the Griswolds, and socialized with the Barstows, Putnams, Pardees, Curries, and Doans, but mostly with Mr. and Mrs. Dow; he and Herbert Dow had many a "cosy chat" after supper. He mounted a showing of his work at the Midland Community Center in October, toward the end of his stay, and sold a large number of oils and watercolors to eager Midland buyers.[37]

The prolific Knighton-Hammond produced about 30 oils in his time in Midland, as well as miscellaneous watercolors and sketches. Most of them were plant scenes that he and Dow chose, and a few were river scenes and scenes in Herbert Dow's orchards and gardens. Dow's favorite, which he said was picked out "with considerable unanimity . . . as the best one in the collection," was a scene in the heart of the plant at a place where the railroad formed a Y. "This picture is largely in reds and browns, and shows some exhaust steam coming out from the adjoining building," he said, "a feature that has been favorably commented on by one or two artists, including the head of the art department of the University of Michigan."[38]

For 20 years or more the Knighton-Hammond paintings were featured in Dow product catalogs and advertising literature. Herbert Dow presented one of the paintings to the Chemists' Club in New York, another to the New York sales office, and hung most of the rest around the headquarters building. Some of them wound up in the offices of various executives, and a few disappeared over the years as those executives retired, but most of them have survived and today grace the walls of the Herbert H. & Grace A. Dow Foundation.

Alden Dow, then a teenager, watched Knighton-Hammond as he worked and was fascinated with the way he could make a horse appear on the canvas "with just a few strokes of the brush." Some of the national art publications of the time, seeing Knighton-Hammond's work at Midland, praised Herbert Dow as "a patron of and pioneer in industrial art."

A few years later Herbert Dow brought another artist to Midland, and again the choice was accidental. On his annual visit to the Michigan State Fair in about 1924—he attended chiefly in those years to inspect the apples, pears, and other fruit exhibits, and was an officer of the Fair—he saw a poster advertising a lecture by the Detroit artist Paul Honoré, painter of a large mural in the Michigan State Capitol and other works. Dow dropped in and sat in the back of the audience, and when the lecture was completed approached the artist and said he had a commission for an artist up in Midland. Would Honoré be interested?

The commission in Midland was to paint exterior murals on the Midland County Courthouse, for which ground was being broken that fall, using a new magnesite stucco technique devised in the Dow laboratories. Honoré was immediately intrigued—murals were his strong suit—and was hired as the artist for the murals, both exterior and interior.

Oddly enough, Honoré had studied in London for a year with Sir Frank Brangwyn, a renowned British artist whose work Honoré admired and who became his mentor. Brangwyn was a close friend of Knighton-Hammond; Knighton-Hammond's portrait of Brangwyn hangs in the National Portrait Gallery in London. Indeed, the styles of Honoré and Knighton-Hammond had much in common, although Knighton-Hammond favored earth tones and Honoré's palette featured more violent tones—turquoise, mauve, chartreuse.

At the end of World War I there was universal agreement that the ancient Midland courthouse had to be replaced, but the County Board of Supervisors had trouble agreeing on the size and cost of a new building, which required approval by the electorate. Herbert Dow finally offered to pay for an architect and for the decoration of the building, as well as other major contributions, if the supervisors would allow him to choose the architect and the design. The supervisors gladly accepted, and a bond issue was approved by the voters.

Herbert Dow felt his new magnesite stucco had the potential to become a widely used material for public buildings, and wanted an example to show the world how it lent itself to tasteful and artistically decorated surfaces; the Midland County Courthouse was to be a show-piece for marketing this concept.[39] He chose a Cleveland architect, Bloodgood Tuttle, who proposed a courthouse design resembling a Tudor mansion that was soon adopted.

Honoré (1885-1956), best known for his murals and woodcut book illustrations, is usually given credit for developing the new (and short-lived) art of plastic mosaic painting; he was the first artist to use the new technique, and experimented for several months with Donald L. Gibb, of Dow's Magnesium Oxychloride Research Lab, before starting the actual murals on the courthouse. "The new dyes and artistic materials, developed from Midland County's underground salt beds, have all the brilliance and working ease of oil or marble mosaic and the weather-resisting qualities of granite. With it is combined a beauty and utility unequaled for exterior paneling and relief work," one art magazine reported.

The murals cover all four sides of the building (they were restored in 1994) and tell the history of the county, with Indians, traders, and lumbermen in life size. Honoré used local models (Dr. Anderson Arbury, Herbert Dow's dentist son-in-law, for example, posed as a lumberjack holding an ax), but unfortunately no record of the models was kept.

Honoré was somewhat eccentric, a 12-cup-a-day coffee drinker, a notoriously careless dresser, and a hater of social functions. His automobile was easy to identify; he kept it in a barn, where pigeons and chickens used it for a roost, altering its color scheme drastically.[40]

He was also a highly competent and accomplished artist, and his work at the courthouse was widely acclaimed. Magnesite stucco as an external mural base never caught on, and while it was used in many ways, chiefly as a flooring material, the courthouse remained the only major examplar of another Herbert Dow dream—outdoor murals in rural America.

III

Throughout the summer of 1930 Herbert Dow had been feeling poorly, and his stomach was acting up. As Dorothy Arbury said, "he'd always had trouble with his stomach. He couldn't eat apples, he couldn't eat this, he couldn't eat that and the other thing. He went up there (to the Mayo Clinic in Rochester, Minnesota) to find out what was wrong." Dr. Sherk urged him to go to Mayo for "a complete check-up," and offered to go with him.[41]

On September 1, Dr. Sherk and Herbert and Grace Dow left for the Mayo Clinic, and doctors began their "observation" of him, running tests of all kinds, a procedure that took a full month. Willard Dow and other family members would come and stay a few days during this time, and then return home.

In early October the doctors recommended exploratory surgery, and on October 10 their explorations resulted in the discovery of "a portal obstruction at the liver," preventing the free flow of blood through that organ. The report came back to Midland that he had withstood the operation well and that the doctors were optimistic and hoped for rapid improvement. Relieved, Dr. Sherk and Willard Dow flew back to Midland the next day, Willard going on to Washington, D. C., where "Mother" Hale, Billy Hale's mother, was also seriously ill.

On Sunday evening, October 12, Dow worsened and lapsed into a coma. The family was summoned to his bedside Monday morning, and by Monday evening they were told there was no hope. At Detroit a fast train for Chicago was held for 14 minutes by an official of the railroad to permit Willard Dow to make a connection from Cleveland. Alden Dow scrambled to Rochester from New York. Mr. and Mrs. L. I. Doan were located in New York and caught a train for Cleveland; Mary Dow, Herbert's sister, was located in Muskegon, Michigan; Margaret Dow, instructor in the University of Michigan's University School, went to the new airport near Ypsilanti, got a private pilot to fly her to Chicago, and took a night train to Minneapolis.[42]

Herbert Dow died of cirrhosis of the liver on Wednesday, October 15, 1930, at 64.

"I was there before Dad died," Margaret said, "but he didn't know anybody by then; he'd been in a coma for several days. We came home on a private train which carried the family. Dr. Sherk was there, too. The train came in at the old Michigan Central, and they had cars for us and took us downtown, and people were lined up on the street." "They had Dad down in the sun room at the house, and we got flowers. Flowers came day and night, and Mother just adored this. That was the only thing she thought was wonderful, to get all these flowers. . . ."[43]

Notes

1. Harrison Hatton, Notes on conversation with Dr. W. R. Veazey, June 12, 1950.
2. After numerous experiments, Dow succeeded by banking the sandy soil around an apple tree up to the first crotch, or about five feet deep. The method produced show apples but was not very practical for the general orchardist.

3. Hatton, Notes on conversation with Dr. W. R. Veazey and (later) Dr. E. C. Britton, October 12, 1949.

4. Hatton, Notes on conversation with Dr. W. R. Veazey, June 29, 1950.

5. Hatton, Notes on conversation with Maurice Thompson, engineer, August 1949.

6. Hatton, Notes on conversation with Merle Newkirk at the West Side Power House, May 2, 1950.

7. Hatton, Notes on conversation with T. Griswold jr., May 4, 1950.

8. See note 4 above.

9. Hatton, Notes on conversation with Dr. W. R. Veazey and Dr. Willard H. Dow, March 28, 1949. (Note: Conversation occurred three days before Willard Dow was killed in a plane crash near London, Ontario)

10. Hatton, Notes on conversation with Mrs. Margaret Johnson, June 30, 1950.

11. H. H. Dow to manager, Michigan State Telephone Co., Detroit, Michigan, May 12, 1910.

12. Hatton, Notes on conversation with Alden B. Dow, June 22, 1949.

13. Hatton, Notes on conversation with Alden B. Dow, April 19, 1950.

14. Hatton, Notes on conversation with Dr. W. R. Veazey, May 18, 1949.

15. Oral History, Margaret Dow Towsley and Dr. Harry Towsley, December 6, 1989.

16. Oral History, Dorothy Dow Arbury, January 18, 1989.

17. Hatton, Notes on conversation with T. Griswold Jr., November 8, 1950.

18. Gertrude Winfield, private communication to author, 1994.

19. Hatton, Report of telephone conversation between Ivan A. Kenaga and F. H. Langell, July 7, 1949.

20. Hatton, Notes on conversation with Joseph H. Sherk, M.D., June 27, 1950.

21. Richard S. McClurg, private communication to author, 1990.

22. Hatton, Notes on conversation with Robert R. Dreisbach and F. H. Langell, June 23, 1949.

23. Hatton, Notes on conversation with Dr. M. E. Putnam, September 16, 1949.

24. Hatton, Notes on conversation with John Sinclair, Well Dept. superintendent, and F. H. Langell, July 19, 1949.

25. Hatton, Notes on conversation with Dr. W. R. Veazey, June 16, 1949.

26. Hatton, Notes on conversation with Dr. Howard S. Nutting, February 21, 1951.

27. Hatton, Notes on conversation with William H. Williams, June 9, 1950.

28. See note 12 above.

29. Hatton, Notes on conversation with Dr. W. R. Veazey, June 16, 1949. The project, Veazey said, involved making caustic soda anhydrous by electrolysis.

30. Hatton, Notes on conversation with Ralph M. Hunter, June 13, 1949.

31. Joseph E. Bayliss to Leland I. Doan, May 22, 1952.

32. Hatton, Notes on conversation with Gilbert A. Currie, March 21, 1950.

33. H. H. Dow to W. R. Veazey, February 22, 1930.

34. See note 12 above.

35. Oral History, Dorothy Dow Arbury, January 18, 1989.

36. Correspondence, May 8 – December 24, 1919, between Herbert Dow and A. H. Knighton-Hammond.

37. Arthur Henry Knighton-Hammond (1875-1970), "Transcript of his 1920 diary relating to his trip to America," Post Street Archives.

38. H. H. Dow to A. H. Knighton-Hammond, December 18, 1923.

39. See *Plastic Magnesia Cements* (Magnesium Oxychloride Research Laboratory, The Dow Chemical Company, 1920 [revised 1921, 1922, 1927]), especially chap. 11: "Colored Magnesia Stucco and Plastic Mosaic," 101–8.

40. Doris A. Paul, "Life and Works of Paul Honoré," based on research by Dr. Richard Murdoch and Dr. William Gamble (unpublished ms., 13 pp.), Post Street Archives.

41. Oral History, Dorothy Dow Arbury, January 18, 1989.

42. *The Midland Republican* (Extra Edition), October 15, 1930.

43. Oral History, Margaret Dow Towsley, December 6, 1989.

PART THREE

WILLARD DOW

Dow

1931—Dow and Ethyl Corp. form Ethyl-Dow Company "for the purpose of manufacturing bromine from sea water."

1932—"Great Depression" deepens; Dow cuts payroll by 250 and reduces salaries 10 percent.

1933—Bromine-from-seawater plant begins rising at Kure Beach, North Carolina.

1935—Cliffs Dow Chemical Company, for manufacture of wood chemicals, is incorporated at Marquette, Michigan.

June 26, 1937—Dow stock listed on N.Y. stock exchange.

1938—Dow acquires Great Western Electrochemical Company at Pittsburg, California, expands to West Coast.

1940—Dow purchases land near Freeport, Texas, begins to build plant.

January 21, 1941—First ingot of magnesium from seawater is poured at new Freeport plant.

1942—Second large magnesium plant is rushed to completion at Velasco, Texas, for war needs.

1943—Dow Corning Corporation, joint venture with Corning Glass, is formed to manufacture silicones for wartime military needs.

1944—Willard Dow testifies before Truman Committee to refute charges Dow conspired to control magnesium prices.

1947—Company establishes Brazos Oil & Gas Co. subsidiary to explore for and produce oil and gas for company needs.

1948—Dow experiences first Midland strike in history; compromise with United Mine Workers is reached after four-week work stoppage.

March 31, 1949—Willard Dow is one of five killed in a Dow company plane crash near London, Ont., and is succeeded by Leland I. Doan.

World at Large

1931—Mrs. Hattie Caraway of Arkansas is first woman elected to U.S. Senate.
Thomas Edison dies.

1933—Adolf Hitler appointed German Chancellor.
Prohibition is repealed.

1935—FDR signs Social Security Act into law.
German chemist Gerhard Domagk discovers Prontosil, the first sulfa drug.
Wallace H. Carothers of Dupont invents nylon.

1937—500,000 Americans are involved in sitdown strikes, September 1936-May 1937.

1938—40-hour work week established in U.S.
Hitler marches into Austria.

1940—Congress passes Selective Service Act, U.S. begins mobilizing.
Food rationing in Great Britain. Germany intensifies U-boat warfare.

1941—Japanese attack Pearl Harbor.
Edwin McMillan and Glenn Seaborg discover plutonium.

1942—First computer is developed in U.S.

1943—Penicillin is introduced and streptomycin is discovered.

1944—Allied "D-Day" landings in Normandy push Germans back toward Germany.

May 8, 1945—Germany capitulates following Hitler's suicide April 30, ending war in Europe.

August 6, 1945—U.S. drops atomic bombs on Hiroshima this date, on Nagasaki August 9; Japan surrenders August 14.
Vitamin A is synthesized.

1946—Adm. Richard E. Byrd explores South Pole.

1947—Bell Laboratory scientists invent the transistor.

1948—Congress approves Marshall Plan, authorizing $17 billion in aid to rebuild Europe.

1949—"Cold war" begins; North Atlantic Treaty Organization (NATO) pact signed in Washington.

SEVEN

YEARS OF EXPANSION

I.

Willard Dow was 33 when his father died, young enough to be the son of almost any one of his colleagues on the company's board of directors; the next youngest member was 47. As the board considered the succession to Herbert Dow, it became clear they were uncomfortable turning the helm over to their junior member, even though he had spent the last 10 years learning the job. Perhaps an "interim" management would be in order, it was suggested.

Albert Convers, still the chairman at 72 and quite deaf—he had an early model of a hearing aid installed at his place in the boardroom but it was not much help—came to the rescue. He spoke of the 33 fruitful years he had worked with Willard's father and said he would be pleased to serve the son as adviser—as he had the father—if his fellow directors wished, to assist in the transition to a new chief executive. Now that he was a resident of Midland, this would be a natural and pleasurable activity for him, he said. With that reassurance, the succession went smoothly.

Willard Dow immediately took over, and for the rest of his days there was no question who was at the helm of The Dow Chemical Company; it was Willard. He was a roaring success as chief executive, and a model for those who followed. Years later the headquarters complex of the company was named the Willard H. Dow Center in his honor. During his time as chief he took the Dow Company out of the backwoods of Michigan and put it in the front ranks of America's blue-chip companies, a process Herbert Dow had already begun in his twilight years.

It began with iodine, the company's first venture out of Midland. The Michigan brines did not contain more than traces of iodine, and Herbert Dow had mentioned his disappointment at this to several colleagues, including Coulter W. (Bromine) Jones. Jones told him iodine occurred in the salt springs and wells of his native Arkansas and that he himself had experimented with iodine in that area as early as 1904. Dow assured him that if a good iodine source ever turned up down that way he was interested.

_151_

Jones, the company's first "razorback"—he had come to Dow from the University of Arkansas in 1908—had ambitions to strike out on his own, and every time he went back to Arkansas he looked for iodine. In 1912 he proposed a formal iodine search program in Arkansas, Louisiana, and Oklahoma, run by himself, and intimated that he would like to work up a proposal for a Dow iodine plant in that region, expecting to be its superintendent. Herbert Dow said he'd think about it, but with the war coming on, the matter lay dormant for 16 years in spite of Jones "jogging" him about it from time to time.[1]

Jones was an unusual man. During WWI he suffered a nervous breakdown, and it was several years before he fully recovered. He ran for the state legislature from Midland and was elected, becoming the only Democrat in the Michigan legislature during a Republican heyday. When he returned to Dow he became superintendent of its bromine operations, and was called "Bromine" Jones to distinguish him from J. I. Jones, superintendent of the carbon tetrachloride plant.

In the early 1920s, when the Ethyl Gasoline Company told Dow about the gigantic amounts of bromine it was going to need for Ethyl gasoline, Herbert Dow sent Jones to investigate oil wells in Arkansas, Texas, Louisiana, and Oklahoma, and Jones found several bromine-bearing oil well brines as possibilities. He also brought back a sample of water from the Gulf of Mexico that Herbert Dow used to check on the possibility of extracting bromine from the ocean, a problem he was also now looking at seriously.[2]

In 1928 Jones finally found what he was looking for—an abandoned oil well with brine that contained 37 parts of iodine per million. Herbert Dow told him to go ahead, and the Dow Company set up its first subsidiary, the Jones Chemical Company, near McDade, south of Shreveport, Louisiana.

Built of junk and cheap timber, the Jones plant was a disreputable looking place and hardly an immediate success. Jones proved to be an eccentric business manager, and the little plant's production of iodine was erratic at best. Eventually W. R. Veazey and Willard Dow went down to McDade on an inspection trip, to see about improving production. They decided Jones needed a large new brine tank, so they started early the next morning for Shreveport, 25 miles away, to find such a tank.[3]

"We got into Jones's car," Veazey said.

He had a transformer built into the car and he plugged an electric razor in and proceeded to shave himself while he was driving, looking into the rearview mirror to see what he was doing. There was no particular reason why he had to shave right then, because he often did not bother to do that for days on end, but this morning he had an urge to do it.

A few miles down the road, Jones got out to look at an alfalfa field a farmer was harvesting. He and the farmer stood by the fence, bargaining to see if Jones would buy that alfalfa, for a couple of hours. Jones had no idea what he wanted to do with the alfalfa; he just liked to bargain.

We finally got to town about the middle of the afternoon, and we picked out a tank that looked good, and then Jones said, "that one is rather expensive," and asked whether they had one that was secondhand, and the bargaining started all over. By this time Willard Dow was getting very fidgety and had had about all he could stand, and he finally said to the man running the shop that we would take that tank over there; it was the only way he could ever have got Jones out of the place.[4]

The Jones Chemical Company limped along for a few years, and Jones improved the process, but in the end Ivan Harlow determined that it was actually losing money; it was costing more to pump the brine and dispose of it than Dow was receiving from finished iodine. About this time Jones discovered oil well brines in California that were much higher in iodine content than the Louisiana variety, and in 1932, at the behest of A. P. Beutel, who had become Willard's assistant, the whole operation was moved to Seal Beach, California, next to the Signal Hill oil field in the Los Angeles area.

This reincarnation of Dow's first-born subsidiary was called the Io-Dow Chemical Company, and with a brand new plant, a new process, and a greatly improved raw material source (the brine ran 66 parts per million iodine), it was soon a success.[5] When brines at nearby Venice, California, proved to contain more than 100 parts per million iodine, a second plant was built at Venice. The two plants soon became the dominant force in the U.S. supply of elemental iodine and potassium iodide; they provided about 90 percent of U.S. domestic production and supplied more than half the U.S. market, the remainder being imported, principally from the Chilean sources that had dominated the market totally before Dow's entry.[6]

The five acres on which Io-Dow was located, wedged between the oil field and the Pacific Ocean, soon was making products more broadly attuned to the West Coast market, and its employees acclaimed it Dow's tiniest manufacturing plant, and the first outside of Midland.

The expansion of product line came about through the hiring of J. F. ("Kage") Kagy, recipient of a research fellowship established by Dow at Iowa State University in 1931. After leaving Iowa State, Kagy went to the University of California Citrus Experiment Station (at Riverside, California) to study under Dr. Alfred M. Boyce, and it was Boyce who discovered "DN," an insecticide effective against the citrus red spider mite, a major pest in the California fruit fields. Through Kagy's intermediary it became a Dow product, and was made at Seal Beach.[7]

Io-Dow then became the Iodine and Insecticide Division of The Dow Chemical Company, with M. F. (Fred) Ohman as general manager. Ohman was sent to Seal Beach from Midland on a two-month assignment to try to improve the operations of the iodine plant, and wound up staying 30 years. When the Great Western Electrochemical Company merged with Dow on January 1, 1939, these operations became the Seal Beach plant of Dow's Western Division.

Years later the city of Los Angeles decided to develop Venice as a yacht harbor and marina, and prevailed upon the oil companies to close their wells there, thus cutting off Dow's supply of oil field brine and putting the company out of the iodine business. Dow sued the city of Los Angeles, and the court found in favor of Dow; the city thereupon offered to settle out of court for $100,000, half of the amount Dow was claiming, and Dow accepted the offer. In 1964 the Seal Beach iodine plant was shut down.

Iodine production was transferred to Midland. With its experience in Arkansas and California, the company now had the technology to extract the traces of iodine in the Midland brine profitably. Furthermore, modern measuring devices showed the Midland brine had about the same level of iodine content as prevailed at McDade, Louisiana. Iodine had come full circle.

In the late 1920s Herbert Dow, always on the alert for by-products or waste products that could be used to make new products, decided he could use the hydrogen from his chlorine cells to make ammonia, at that time in great demand. The Roessler & Hasslacher Chemical Company, at Niagara Falls, was anxious to acquire more ammonia, and an arrangement was worked out with that firm whereby a new firm, the Midland Ammonia Company, was established.

Midland Ammonia, with Ralph Hunter as manager and W. P. (Bill) Schambra as superintendent, built a small plant in Midland, converted excess hydrogen to ammonia, and shipped the product to Niagara. When R & H was merged into Du Pont de Nemours in 1931, the arrangement was continued. Midland Ammonia was the forerunner of Dow's joint venture companies.

At the end of World War I, Dow had found itself with more bromine than it knew what to do with. Other bromine producers were in the same fix, and marginal producers such as those in the Ohio Valley simply shut down. Dow mothballed the 17 wells it had drilled for the U.S. Bromine Reserve during the war. In desperation, Herbert Dow proposed a prize of $50,000 be offered to anyone who could discover and establish a new volume use for bromine, and the board authorized such a prize. The prize was never awarded, because about this time ethylene dibromide (or EDB) came along.[8]

EDB was to require more bromine than Herbert Dow had ever dreamed of producing, and put him on the path to extracting it from the ocean. Charles F. Kettering, inventor of the automobile self-starter, and Thomas Midgley Jr., later the inventor of the Dupont product Freon, had been looking since 1916 for a way to prevent auto engines from knocking, a universal and troublesome automotive problem. Others were also looking; Henry Ford, for example, had a candidate called the "Knocknocker." In 1921 Midgley came up with a gasoline additive, tetraethyl lead, eventually the winning candidate, and called gasoline containing it "Ethyl gas." It was so effective that it soon put all the other antiknock compounds out of business. But tetraethyl lead, or Ethyl, required a scavenging agent to prevent the formation of carbon deposits, and the GM Research Lab commenced testing literally hundreds of compounds for this use.

Herbert Dow sent Charles Strosacker to Dayton, Ohio, where this research was being conducted, with some compounds for testing and to talk to the researchers about what they were doing. "Be sure to tell them to try bromine," Dow told Strosacker.

On July 18, 1923, Dow wrote Kettering that he was sending him more bromine compounds to try out, adding that the Dow work on fire extinguishers showed that the bromine compounds—carbon tetrabromide, bromoform, and the like—were much more efficient fire extinguishers than the chlorine compounds "and it might be that these compounds would also be more efficient in preventing knock."[9]

One of Dow's products, EDB, was already high on Midgley's list and in the end it became the winning candidate as a scavenger agent, but there was a problem: no one in the world could produce the quantities of bromine that would be needed if EDB were used; the optimum mix for the Ethyl gas additive was two parts EDB to three parts tetraethyl lead.

In January 1924 Kettering and Midgley came to Midland to see Herbert Dow; he was away so they talked to Willard Dow and Leland Doan. Their tests were now completed and they knew EDB was the answer to their problem, they said, and they had decided also that Dow was the best supplier of EDB. How could they work with Dow on the problem? Their visit led to a first contract by which Dow agreed to supply the Ethyl Gasoline Company 100,000 pounds of EDB per month at 58 cents a pound.

Kettering and Midgley talked of what Herbert Dow called "wild numbers" if Ethyl gas caught on with the motoring public. In August Kettering and Midgley returned to Midland to urge a crash program on Dow; they now wanted 600,000 pounds of EDB a month. The wild numbers were already becoming reality.

Dow drilled more wells to meet this challenge, and he also began actively to investigate the question of taking bromine from the ocean. This was to be his last and most daring piece of research, though he left it uncompleted.

When Willard Dow became president, one of the first things he looked at was the Ethyl situation. EDB had become one of the company's biggest products, although sales were essentially restricted to one customer. Willard therefore proposed to the Ethyl Gasoline Company that it join Dow in forming a jointly owned company, "for the purpose of manufacturing bromine from seawater." When Ethyl accepted, the firm became technically the first of Dow's joint ventures, founded early in 1931 as the Ethyl-Dow Company. EDB became the largest-volume bromine compound in history and Ethyl-Dow the largest producer.[10]

Thus only a few months after Willard Dow become the company's president he was setting a pattern. In spite of the fact that the world was engulfed at the time in the worst economic depression in history, he was bent on the aggressive expansion of the Dow Company. Later on, Midland was known as "the town that didn't know there was a depression," and basically it was true; there were slowdowns and slack periods, but for the most part Willard Dow and the Dow Company remained essentially untouched by the financial chaos around them.

In the depths of the depression Willard Dow launched another bold new venture, the Dow Well Service, soon to be called the Dowell Division. Early in 1932 John Grebe had some visitors from Dow's neighbors, the Pure Oil Company, who operated oil wells in the Midland area. They had heard Dow was experimenting with the acidizing of brinewells to improve their capacity to hold debrominated brine; by such a system Dow could extract chemicals from the underground brine and return what was left back to the well. How were they doing this, the visitors wanted to know? Grebe told them about some new inhibitors Dow had devised to prevent acid from eating away the iron well casings.[11]

After a series of meetings it was arranged that the Dow inhibited acid system would be tried on a Pure Oil well to see whether it would improve the flow of oil. The first trial took place on February 11, 1932. Pure Oil chose for the test its Fox No. 6 well in Chippewa Township, Isabella County, about 20 miles west of Midland, a failing well scheduled for abandonment. Grebe and Ross Sanford, superintendent of brinewells for Dow, prepared the inhibited acid and it was trucked to the site by Robert Quinlan, a lab assistant, who was met at the well by John Mayfield and Robert T. Wilson of Pure Oil. They had put an open-top steel tank on the derrick floor for the test but there was no opening in the bottom of it, so Mayfield went home and got a garden hose, and they siphoned the acid into the well. They pumped a half-dozen barrels of oil down after it, using a nearby oil field pump. This done, they went home to wait for the acid to do its work.

Another dose of acid was administered the next day, and Fox No. 6 then produced as much as 16 barrels of oil a day; before the treatment it had been producing 6 a day. On a second test, the acidizing treatment improved the yield of a well producing 30 barrels a day to 125 barrels a day. The third trial was even more sensational. Pure Oil's Root No. 2 well had produced some 700 barrels a day when completed three years before but had tailed off to 90 barrels a day at the time it was acidized. After 500 gallons of acid treatment it delivered 800 barrels of oil a day, 100 more than it had at inception.

The news of these spectacular results sped through the oil industry like wildfire, and Pure Oil and Dow Chemical both raced to file applications for patents on the process. Grebe and Sanford filed a patent (No. 1,877,504) on the treatment of wells with chemicals containing corrosion inhibitors; Pure Oil's Richard H. Carr filed a patent on the technique of introducing chemicals into oil-producing strata. Both were received at the Patent Office on June 30, 1932.

Overnight the demand for oil well servicing began pouring in to Dow. Companies all over the country, from the Midwest to Texas, wanted the immediate help of the Dow Well Service, as it was called. As a result, the company initiated its first major market study; in the summer of 1932 Dow men fanned out across the continent to the oil areas of the United States and Canada to determine whether well treating of this kind would be of interest to oilmen, and if so, how interesting. Sent out on this mission that summer were Jack Chamberlain, C. N. Morrison, Ronald L. Lowry, Allen Salisbury, J. Larry Amos, Milton E. Lefevre, Charles A. Fink, and Lawrence W. (Bud) Lee, most of whom later became prominent in the company.

As a result of these investigations the company incorporated a new subsidiary, Dowell Inc., on November 9, 1932, with a board composed of Willard Dow, Leland I. Doan, Russell L. Curtis, Sherman W. Putnam, Dutch Beutel, and John Grebe. Beutel was assigned to organize a staff and purchase whatever the new company would need in the way of equipment and machinery, and Putnam, a brother of Mark E. Putnam, was assigned to organize a sales and marketing organization.[12] Beutel and Willard Dow hired N. Russell Crawford, an accountant in Bay City, Michigan, to be the manager, and Crawford was soon splitting his time between Midland and Tulsa, Oklahoma, where a headquarters office was established; in 1932 Tulsa was the heart of the oil business.

The new firm ended its first year with 35 people on the payroll, performed more than 1,000 oil well treatments in that year, and on sales of $312,000 paid $29,000 in royalties to Dow and had another $29,000 in net profit. The next year it logged 2,000 treatments. By the early 1950s it was a highly profitable venture; in 1953, after 20 years in business, it had $26 million in sales and $4.2 million in earnings.[13]

The Pure Oil Company felt strongly that the first patent issued to Dow should have been issued in its name as well as Dow's, since the two firms had worked together in the original development, and asked for a royalty, but Dow insisted that the idea had originated in Dow's laboratory (and John Grebe's head). In June 1933 the two firms agreed on a limited partnership in Dowell for Pure Oil, with Pure Oil holding 15 percent of the stock, and the matter was settled amicably on that basis.[14]

Not so amicable was Dowell's early tussle with Earl Halliburton, a celebrated figure in the Texas oil fields, whose oil wells were among the first treated by Dowell. Dowell leased rights to the Grebe-Sanford patent to a few oil companies for a royalty of $5.00 per treatment, a practice that was quickly abandoned. Halliburton jumped into this business but refused to pay any royalty, and began to sell the same service to others as an addition to the large business he was already doing cementing oil wells. Dow sued for infringement of its patents, and Halliburton countersued, contending the Grebe-Sanford patent was invalid. It was a complex case, and when it was heard in the District Court of Bay City, Michigan, became the longest sitting on a single case ever held in the district; the court sat from July 10 to September 20, 1941 on the case. The decision was then appealed all the way to the Supreme Court, which finally delivered its ruling in 1947.

In the end Dow lost the case, and the Supreme Court declared the Grebe-Sanford patent invalid. Dow thought it got "a very poor decision" in the case. Donald L. Conner, the lead Dow attorney, said Dow "could see no connection with the historical cases" that Halliburton and his attorneys dug up in which others had attempted, unsuccessfully, to increase oil production by injection of acids. By the time the suit was over Dow had so many patents in the acidizing and well treating field that the loss of the Grebe patent was not too serious, Conner said; the important point was that Dow did not lose its original technological lead in this field.[15]

The first well treatment acid inhibitor, a mercaptan, was developed in the Physics Lab by Jack Chamberlain and his colleagues. It worked, but smelled so bad that people avoided trucks carrying it, and work began on a substitute. Dr. Sylvia Stoesser was the key inventor of the second-stage inhibitors, and is listed as the coinventor in five key Dowell patents.[16]

In the depths of the depression Willard Dow led the company into still another new field, wood chemistry, a move that took the company to Michigan's Upper Peninsula. Dow had been purchasing charcoal from the Marquette, Michigan, plant of Cleveland-Cliffs Iron Company (or CCI) to make carbon bisulfide. The Marquette plant also made ethyl alcohol, acetic acid, and other chemicals as by-products in the production of its main product, charcoal.

CCI decided to sell off some of its subsidiaries and concentrate on its basic iron ore business at about the same time the Dow company was looking for a source of material for a new plastic material it was developing, ethyl cellulose, for which the Dow trademark is Ethocel. When CCI informed Dow (and other firms) it wanted to sell its Marquette plant, Dow was immediately interested.

Billy Hale and E. C. Britton had been urging upon Willard Dow the need to inaugurate research for a new plastic material, especially one based on cellulose. Work on ethylcellulose began in 1933 in the Organic Laboratory, and in 1934 Dow organized a new and separate Cellulose Products Division under William R. Collings.[17]

Britton was interested in this connection in the Scholler process for converting wood to ethyl alcohol, and in 1934 he and E. T. Olson, manager of the CCI Marquette plant, and A. O. Reynolds of CCI went to Germany to consult with Dr. Scholler, inventor and owner of the process. They came back with an exclusive U.S. license for the process, intending to use it at Marquette.

The conjunction of these events resulted in the birth on April 1, 1935, of a new corporation, the Cliffs Dow Chemical Company, owned two-thirds by Dow and one-third by CCI. Dow poured more than a million dollars into renovation of the CCI Marquette plant, which closed down because of the depression in 1930 and then reopened in 1933. CCI hired Olson, a chemical engineer from New York and inventor of an improved process for making activated charcoal, as manager.

Willard Dow was hailed as a savior by the "Yoopers," the Upper Peninsula being a chronically depressed area that hit a new economic low during the depression. The firm's payroll soared as high as 550 during the renovation period and later settled at around 350.

The employees were a mix of Swedes, Finns, Italians, French, and Cornishmen (called "Cousin Jacks") and this caused occasional problems. The Finns, expert woodcutters, insisted on speaking Finnish to each other and this led to bickering and fights that the foremen had to settle; the others were sure the Finns were talking about them. Eventually the problem was settled by adding a second lunchroom to allow the Finns to eat by themselves.[18]

When Cliffs Dow came into being in 1935 only 35 hardwood distillation plants remained in existence in the United States, and a mere 15 were active; there had been about 100 of them at the turn of the century, supplying charcoal for the making of pig iron. A few of these plants had produced chemicals as by-products—acetic acid, calcium acetate, wood alcohol, ethyl alcohol—but charcoal was always the primary product, as it was at Cliffs Dow. "Cliffchar" charcoal was a Dow product for many years.

The Scholler process was installed to make ethyl alcohol, with Allan F. Olson as supervisor, in a plant promptly dubbed "the whiskey plant" by the employees. But after two years of effort it became apparent that while the process was feasible it was uneconomical at U.S. prices, and the project was abandoned. The "whiskey plant" never produced whiskey, and what was worse, only a few thousand gallons of ethyl alcohol, and eventually was sold for scrap; it was an experience, one Dow supervisor said, "bad enough to drive you to drink."

There was never any shortage of raw material across Upper Michigan—hard maple, beech, birch, hickory, and other hardwoods—but frequently there was a shortage of manpower to cut and deliver wood to the plant. Year after year more than 400 people all across the peninsula cut and delivered "chemical wood" to Cliffs Dow. In the 34 years that Cliffs Dow operated, from 1935 to 1969, the amount of wood converted to charcoal and chemicals was 2,722,000 cords, enough cordwood piles to reach from Marquette to London, England.

To make ethyl alcohol available for industrial use and prevent circumvention of the alcohol tax laws by "revenuers," the U.S. government prescribes various formulas for making it undrinkable. The most widely used of these formulas calls for adding five gallons of denaturing grade wood alcohol to each 100 gallons of ethyl alcohol, and denaturing grade wood alcohol was one of the products of Cliffs Dow. As the various wood distillation plants closed down around the United States the Cliffs Dow Chemical Company finally became the sole remaining U.S. manufacturer of denatured wood alcohol.

R. Wesley Jenner, president of Cliffs Dow from 1960 until it closed in 1969, said a decision by a Chicago court "killed" the wood charcoal business. About 1960 the Great Lakes Carbon Corporation, Husky Oil Company, and other firms began marketing "barbecue briquets" made of West Virginia waste coal, North Dakota lignite coal, and other materials. In competition with higher-priced wood charcoal these products performed poorly and did not sell well, and Great Lakes Carbon decided to label its product "charcoal briquets." The Wood Charcoal Association promptly filed a complaint with the Federal Trade Commission and the case was heard in Chicago.

"By the use of semantics experts from the University of Chicago, Great Lakes was able to prove to the satisfaction of the court that the terms 'char' and 'charcoal' are synonymous, and the court permitted it to continue using the label 'charcoal briquets,' even though the source was West Virginia coal," Jenner said. "This proceeding opened the floodgates for every briquet producer to add all sorts of materials to charcoal briquets. Most present-day briquets are inferior even without the addition of adulterants. Old-style high-quality wood charcoal cannot compete."

Cliffs Dow was the last wood distillation plant in the United States. It closed in 1969.[19]

II.

They were unblushing opportunists, the Easterners who established the firm that became Dow's Western Division. For the first 22 years of its history it was known as the Great Western Electro-Chemical Company, founded January 10, 1916, at Pittsburg on the Sacramento River north of San Francisco, the first electrochemical firm west of the Mississippi; it became the western arm of Dow in 1938.

In the topsy-turvy world of 1915, with the outbreak of World War I totally disrupting world markets, this band of optimists found it easy to get orders for caustic soda, suddenly in heavy demand and hard to find; the European sources of many of America's chemicals had been cut off by the war. They set up an office and began to take all the orders they could line up, both in the United States and abroad, confident they would find caustic somewhere to fill them. They knew quite a bit about caustic, having been employed by the Hooker Electrochemical

WIZARD OF THE WEST

"There are three ways to lose money," Doc Hirschkind liked to say, "women, horse races, and research. The first two are the more enjoyable but the last is the more certain."

Wilhelm Hirschkind was born in the little town of Baiersdorf, near Nuremberg, Germany, in 1886, but left for the United States when he was 26 to become one of the legends of Dow Chemical research and the dominant figure in its Western research organization for a generation. In 1907, "only after serious parental remonstrations," he said, he entered the small, quiet Institute of Technology at Karlsruhe to study chemistry seriously, drawn by the reputation of the celebrated chemist Fritz Haber which had attracted students from around the world.

He liked to tell of having been one of the select group who witnessed the birth of synthetic ammonia in June 1908, when Haber first succeeded in making ammonia from air and water in the laboratory, and then in July 1909, when he demonstrated his synthesis of it to representatives of the big chemical firm BASF. "Had it not been for this development assuring Germany's independence of Chilean nitrate, World War I might not have taken place," he observed.[1]

"The great man to whom we owe this process and who more than anyone else safeguarded mankind from starvation received the Nobel Prize (in 1918) but otherwise very little," Hirschkind lamented. "BASF paid the contractual amounts under their agreement with Haber during the inflation period of the early 1920s. For an invention which feeds the world, he was paid with a wheelbarrowful of worthless paper!" In the Karlsruhe graduating class photo of 1909, when Hirschkind received his Ph.D., he stands just behind "the great man."

Sixty years later he participated in the dedication of a new synthetic ammonia plant built by the Best Fertilizer Company at Fresno, California. Recalling his presence at the first operation of Haber's pilot plant, which "was capable of making one gram per minute of ammonia," Hirschkind said he was glad to participate in the dedication of the new plant "utilizing the very same process" with a capacity to manufacture one metric ton per minute. "In my lifetime I have been fortunate to witness this scale-up factor of one million," he said.[2]

In 1912 Hirschkind came to New York as a delegate to the International Congress of Applied Chemistry. Offered an instructorship at the University of Illinois, he accepted and became a U.S. resident for the remainder of his life. His stay at Champaign was brief; "apparently I am not cut out to be a teacher," he said. In early 1916 he became a chemist for the Natural Soda Products Company, at Owens Lake, California; "Owens Lake at that time was an impressive body of water containing about half a dozen salts eagerly waiting to be extracted."

Later in 1916 he accepted a post with the newly minted Great Western Electro-Chemical Company, which was just opening an alkali chlorine plant at Pittsburg, California. Great Western then organized a caustic-manufacturing company of its own at Owens Lake, the California Alkali Company, with Hirschkind as chief chemist.

"Nobody could have been more enthusiastic than I was over the possibilities of recovering compounds from natural brines and I seriously believed that the ammonia-soda process had a formidable rival," Hirschkind said. In 1922 he returned to Pittsburg, greatly disappointed and disillusioned, at the end of what he called "my desert period—all my painstaking efforts on separation of borax and potash never material-ized."[3]

In 1920 he visited Herbert Dow in Midland to discuss the bleach-making process Great Western had purchased from Dow, which did not work well under the California sunshine. The Dow process did not require refrigeration chambers, and Herbert Dow told him the process worked perfectly in Midland during the cool part of the year but was not operated in the summer months because the chlorine was used in other products at that period. He had merely sold to Great Western, at their request, he said, the technology he was using, without any guarantee as to process or operation. He could not, he added, take any responsibility for the much longer summer season in California. After that visit Great Western gave up on the Dow bleach process and switched to one that used refrigeration chambers.

When Hirschkind returned from Owens Lake in 1922 he discovered that Great Western was looking desperately for outlets for its chlorine. It had built a zinc chloride plant, but in the postwar period use for this product was tailing off (it was used to preserve railroad ties), and the price of zinc chloride had dropped so low that it was not profitable to make it from metallic zinc.

Hirschkind began work on a process to separate zinc from ores by flotation, which would lower the cost of this product greatly. In 1923 a silver lining opened in the clouds: the Mineral Separation North American Corporation of San Francisco, owners of the only valid flotation patents, built an ore flotation plant and developed the use of alkyl dithiocarbonate, or xanthate, as a new collector. The use of xanthate increased their recovery of lead, zinc, and copper sulfides and other minerals by a considerable margin. Mineral Separation badly wanted a supply of this material but there was none—xanthates were at the time barely more than a laboratory curiosity. They asked Great Western whether it could make this material. Hirschkind tackled the problem immediately.

By late 1923 he had successfully produced xanthates in the laboratory, and in 1924 Great Western began producing them commercially. He began with potassium ethyl xanthate and went on to a string of similar compounds. They were given "Z" numbers—xanthate Z-3, Z-4, Z-6, Z-200. Eventually, 12 of Hirschkind's lifetime 32 patents concerned xanthates, and Great Western became the leading producer, at one time making about 70 percent of the world's supply. Xanthates became one of the leading ways to extract minerals from lower grade ores worldwide.

Another good thing happened to help Great Western out of its slough of despond in the early 1920s: the pulp and paper industry, a heavy user of chlorine, was launched and quickly boomed in the Pacific Northwest, in Oregon, Washington, and British Columbia. "If this had not happened at this critical juncture," Hirschkind said, "the Great Western Company might have been doomed to failure; as it was, the pulp and paper industry grew so rapidly that it not only absorbed all the bleaching powder we could manufacture but also all the liquid chlorine as fast as we could enlarge our installations."[4]

Hirschkind became the firm's research director in 1924. During tough times the owners frequently offered to pay him in stock instead of cash, and he usually accepted. When Great Western was acquired by Dow Chemical and his holdings were converted to Dow stock, he found himself a wealthy man.

By 1928 the firm was making 35 tons of chlorine a day for the paper industry, enough to supply most of the needs of the mills. It discontinued making zinc chloride in 1925 and stopped making bleach in the early 1930s.

All of these tribulations made Great Western a research-conscious company, years before the celebrated California research communities came into being.

Probably the greatest technical triumph of his career as a research director was the photochemical chlorination of methane. In lay terms this meant chemists were able to take methane, or natural gas, which was available in the oil fields in immense quantities, and at one stroke produce from it several useful chemical compounds—methyl chloride, methylene chloride, chloroform, and carbon tetrachloride. Much had been written in the chemical literature about the possibility of doing this, but it had never actually been done. This process was so closely related to Dow's business and so economically advantageous to it that it was one of the main reasons Dow became interested in acquiring Great Western. Later Hirschkind, Robert G. Heitz, W. E. (Bill) Brown, Robert D. (Barney) Barnard, and T. E. (Tom) Davis developed the so-called pertet process for thermal chlorination of methane, which produces carbon tetrachloride and perchloroethylene.

It has been reported that in early 1938, when Willard Dow for the first time met Hirschkind, who by then was being called the "wizard of the West," he admired him so greatly that he determined that Dow should acquire the Great Western Company in order to avail itself of the services of Hirschkind.[5] As in most cases of this kind there is some truth in the report, but it was almost certainly only one factor in the merger of the two companies, consummated in 1938. On January 1, 1939, Great Western became "the Great Western Electro-Chemical Company division of The Dow Chemical Company." As time went on this was shortened to "Great Western" Division, and then to "Western Division." Hirschkind continued as research director.

In 1945 the U.S. government invited Hirschkind to become one of a small group of scientists to investigate German industry under the auspices of the U.S. Army's Chemical Warfare Service. Hirschkind, serving as a "simulated colonel," looked into the rocket propellants and other wartime accomplishments of the German chemists, including the nerve gases they had developed but never used. Later he was fond of telling stories of his career as a "capon colonel."[6]

Two years later the U.S. Atomic Energy Commission asked Dow to assist in a uranium recovery program. U.S. uranium production was insignificant at that time; the U.S. supply was brought in from abroad. There were low-grade deposits of uranium in the United States but no economic way to recover it. Hirschkind's experience with the xanthates made him a logical candidate to investigate this problem, and he did, working with the phosphate rocks of Florida and the western states where uranium occurs, and with the South African gold ores. He worked out a successful method using anion resins to extract uranium from these ores.

In 1949 Hirschkind presented a summary of the U.S. work on uranium recovery to a joint meeting of the Atomic Energy Commissions of the United States, Canada, and Great Britain in London, and the AEC asked Dow to send an expert to South Africa to work on uranium recovery from the tailings of the gold mines there. Robert Olson, one of the principal researchers on the Dow process (with Herbert Kerlinger and John Dewey) was dispatched to Johannesburg, where he spent 18 months helping start a uranium recovery industry. Subsequent work by Hirschkind and his colleagues produced a much improved solvent extraction process that replaced it and was generally adopted for uranium recovery.

By the early 1960s the United States was by far the largest uranium-producing country in the free world, mining and processing some 25,000 tons annually.

Hirschkind's stunning success in developing mining chemicals continued in the 1950s when Western Division researchers under David J. Pye tested hundreds of chemical compounds, looking for more efficient flocculants, the agents that suspend molecules of minerals from the muds in which they are usually found and enable their extraction. This research led to a water-soluble polyacrylamide polymer that Dow sold under the trademark Separan.

Separan flocculant is used in copper, lead, zinc, potash, iron ore, and other mining operations; in sand, gravel, and cement production; in pulp and paper mills; in waste treatment; in clarifying river water; and in dozens of other places. It has been dramatically effective in increasing the efficiency of uranium ore processing in South Africa, Colorado, and other locations.

When he was 65, in 1952, Hirschkind stepped down as research director and became a consultant and science advisor to the company's president in Midland. At retirement time he had been meeting in both the United States and Europe with Prof. Karl Ziegler, director of the Max Planck Institute at Mulheim, Germany, who was working on a process for making polyethylene plastic. In 1954 on a subsequent trip to Europe Hirschkind went to see Ziegler again, having heard rumors that he had finally succeeded. "This was confirmed when I reached Mulheim and I found out to my sorrow that the rat race had already begun with several American firms having been there before me," he said later. Ziegler showed him how his process worked, and "this was the first linear polyethylene made at low temperatures and atmospheric pressure which I had ever seen."

Hirschkind returned to Midland at once, "to convince the company of the importance of this process," and a month later was back in Mulheim, accompanied by Dow's Arthur E. Young. In short order they succeeded in arriving at an agreement with Ziegler "for a rather high down payment and a royalty agreement," and Dow became the fourth of an eventual eight American licensees of the Ziegler process.

Dow dispatched a team to Mulheim to learn the process as soon as the agreement was signed, headed by Earl D. Morris and including J. M. (Levi) Leathers, Giffin D. Jones, Harvey D. Ledbetter, and Mark R. Kinter. That put Dow in the polyethylene business and significantly broadened its range of plastic products.

Hirschkind was also responsible for Dow's association with Melvin Calvin, a Nobel Prize chemist whom he had followed since Calvin had been a 30-year-old assistant professor of chemistry at the University of California, Berkeley, in 1941. Hirschkind signed him on as a consultant to Dow in 1946 when he and Dave Pye became interested in the possibility of Dow manufacturing an oxygen-bearing chelate Calvin had developed. In the end Dow did not manufacture the compound but Calvin continued as a Dow consultant for the next 35 years. During those years he was a constant visitor at the Dow Western research laboratories at Walnut Creek, California, only a few miles from Berkeley, where he worked with Dow researchers on a diverse array of projects.

Calvin, who won the Nobel Prize in 1961 for his work on photosynthesis, also served on the Dow board of directors for much of this time, from 1964 to 1981, except for a one-year lapse. He was one of the earliest "outside" (or non-Dow) directors.

In his years as consultant and advisor to Dow President L. I. Doan, Hirschkind roamed the world looking for opportunities for Dow. He made an extended trip to South America in 1953; he made several trips to Israel, investigating the possibilities of mining chemicals from the Dead Sea; and he became a roving ambassador of the company to the leading European chemical companies. On one of these trips he visited the Spanish chemical company Unquinesa at Bilbao, the first Dow person to do so; the company later merged with Dow to become Dow-Uniquinesa, keystone of Dow's important business relationships in Spain.

Hirschkind died in Lisbon, Portugal, while on a business trip for Dow when he was 85 years old. In deference to his age he had given up skiing but he still continued to ride horseback at the California ranch he and his wife, Nell, had purchased many years before.

Hirschkind said there were only two kinds of research: good research and bad research. Basic to good research, he said, was expending the necessary effort first to get a good method of analysis. "You'll have to have it before you're done so you might as well benefit by it at the start," he said. "It will save you much trouble and pain." Another rule was to purify your raw materials rather than just your final product. A major reason for his success in chlorinating methane, according to Bob Heitz, his successor as research director for the Western Division, "when others had spent dozens of man-years on failures, was that he insisted on purifying his methane gas first."

Another rule for good research, he felt, was to "study the fundamental chemistry of a process after your initial exploratory studies convince you to make substantial commitments to develop it." Hirschkind put Jim Mackey of the Western Division to work on the fundamentals of Ziegler polymerization, for example, at a time when both Midland and Texas were racing to get into production as fast as possible, Heitz pointed out, and this work "led to Dow's solution process for polypropylene and for linear low density polyethylene."[7]

---

1. Wilhelm Hirschkind, "Fifty Years in Industrial Research," paper presented before Dow General Research Committee, Midland, May 10, 1965.

2. Personal communication to author, James C. Mackey, October 12, 1994.

3. Wilhelm Hirschkind, autobiographical notes dated June 25, 1943.

4. Hirschkind, "Fifty Years in Industrial Research."

5. Robert G. Heitz, "Our Research Heritage," talk for "Inventor's Day," February 23, 1988.

6. One of the great sorrows in Hirschkind's life was the loss of one of his two sons in the war. His younger son, Robert Roy, a U.S. Navy pilot who had been a Pacific Coast skiing champion, was killed in 1943.

7. Heitz, "Our Research Heritage." See also "Biographical sketch, list of publications and discussion of professional accomplishments of Dr. Wilhelm Hirschkind, candidate for the American Chemical Society Award in Industrial and Engineering Chemistry," 1956, Post Street Archives.

Company at Niagara Falls, New York, and they appear to have assumed that failing all else they could probably fill the orders they were taking through their old friends at Niagara Falls.

One of their efforts to find a source of caustic paid off. John F. Bush, leader of the group, a former vice president of Hooker, called on Morton Fleishhacker, president of the Great Western Power Company in San Francisco, and proposed to build an electrochemical company in the Bay Area as a major customer for his power company. Fleishhacker, who was looking for major buyers of power, liked the idea so much that he went to his utility friends in San Francisco and Detroit and raised $1 million to finance the enterprise, and the Great Western Electro-Chemical Company soon came into being. Fleishhacker was its president, Bush vice president and general manager. Bush, Beach & Gent, the original group of caustic sellers, became sales agent; Frederick H. Beach and Ernest V. Gent had been Bush associates at Hooker. They brought in Carl W. Schedler from Hooker to be the plant superintendent.

Bush had rights to the Allen-Moore chlorine cell used at Hooker and the project moved swiftly. By July 1, 1916, the first of these cells was installed and began to produce chlorine and caustic. The new firm began filling the orders the founders had piled up. There was one immediate problem, however: the company had ample sales for the caustic it was making, but almost no customers for the chlorine it was also producing, and there was no way to turn off the chlorine. Bush decided to transform the chlorine into a salable product—bleaching powder. To make bleach, he needed to buy a process, and he bought what was then considered the best process in the business: Herbert Dow's process. That was the beginning of the association between the two firms. Soon Great Western was exporting bleach to Japan, India, Norway, and Sweden—but it still had too much chlorine.

While it struggled with this problem, the little company expanded rapidly. It hired two young chemists to develop new uses for chlorine; one of them was Dr. Wilhelm Hirschkind, who was to become one of the legendary figures of Dow history. In 1917 the capitalization was raised to $2.5 million and plants were built to make liquid chlorine, sulfur chloride, carbon tetrachloride, and potassium chlorate. Later that year the capital was increased to $5 million and capacity was increased again. In 1921 two more products were added, zinc chloride for wood preserving, and hydrochloric acid.[20]

The arrival in the Pacific Northwest of the pulp and paper industry, heavy users of chlorine, eventually solved the problem of the surplus chlorine in the late 1920s, and Hirschkind found another major outlet with the expasion of the firm into mining chemicals.

Dow had been interested in establishing a plant on the West Coast as early as 1923, when Herbert Dow sent Tom Griswold Jr. to explore the possibilities; the heavy freight charges for carrying chemicals over the Rocky Mountains made a California producing unit desirable. It was not until 1938, however, that the company became truly eager to acquire a West Coast persona. Once the idea of a Dow–Great Western marriage was broached, there appear to have been no serious objections on either side; the merger was logical and amicable.

Willard Dow sent Russell L. Curtis, who had been assistant general sales manager to Leland I. Doan in Midland since 1930, to be general manager of the new division of Dow, and

Robert G. Heitz left Midland to become Hirschkind's assistant (and eventual successor) in Western research. Curtis became a Dow board member in 1948 and spent the remainder of his long career as Dow's West Coast vice president.

Leland A. ("Young Lee") Doan, son of Leland I. Doan, Herbert Dow's eldest grandchild, was another transplant to the West Coast. He began as a Dow salesman in San Francisco in 1941, became assistant general manager under Curtis in 1955, and succeeded him as general manager in 1959.

When Great Western built its first cell building at Pittsburg, it erected a research laboratory alongside it and initiated a research program that had a remarkable record of success from the beginning. Among its successes over the next half century, in addition to mining chemicals, Separan, and the uranium recovery process (see "Wizard of the West") were:

- Pyridine chemistry. Robert Heitz asked Howard Johnson, one of the West's top chemists, to attempt the direct chlorination of pyridine, a coal tar substance with a nauseating odor but highly useful chemically. The textbooks said this was extremely difficult—the known methods only produced large amounts of tar. Johnson, who became one of the company's most highly honored research scientists, succeeded in doing this and thereby opened up a whole new field of chemistry to the world, and to Dow chemists in particular.

  In short order Dow chemists produced a host of new biologically active, pyridine-based chemicals—sold under the trademark Dursban, Tordon, Dowicil S-13, Reldan, and others. The Dursban and Tordon brands were the spearhead of a new generation of safer and more selective pesticides.

- N-Serve. Another of the pyridine products, this product holds ammonia fertilizers in place in the soil, slowing their loss until they can do their work. N-Serve began with work by Cleve Goring at Seal Beach and became another important contribution to agricultural chemistry.

- Vikane fumigant was widely used for fumigating homes on the West Coast and in Hawai'i, Vikane, discovered and patented by Dow in Midland in 1957, was originally dropped because the production process was ecologically poor. A group working under Robert D. (Barney) Barnard developed a new low-temperature, high-pressure process in Pittsburg and it became a successful product. The Vikane plant was Dow's first using fluorine chemistry.[21]

- Zoalene coccidiostat was developed by a group of Dow Western researchers headed by W. E. (Bill) Brown, Guy Harris, and Bryant Fischback. This product revolutionized the poultry business by making it possible to raise chickens on a large scale without risking catastrophic losses from coccidiosis, a major poultry disease. With this disease under control, chicken became the most economical form of animal protein available, and the status of chicken changed from Sunday dinner for the prosperous to everyday food for the masses, available in fast-food franchises across the land. (Unfortunately, as happens with chemicals from time to time, Zoalene was later supplanted by even better coccidiostats and is no longer in production.)

Another outstanding new product group to emerge from Dow Western research was that based on hollow-fiber technology. In the 1930s, Bob Heitz had read somewhere that caribou hairs are hollow, providing maximum thermal insulation with minimum weight. If that was true, he reasoned, hollow fibers might be useful in other ways. He patented his early work on the idea in 1941. The Dow Western laboratory resumed work on hollow fibers in 1957 when it tackled the freshwater-from-seawater problem. This work was started by Ascher Opler, a brilliant young chemist who saw that hollow fiber was an excellent way to perform separation processes.[22]

The intricacies of making tiny hollow fibers required several years to solve; fashioning the spinnerette dies needed to spin them, for instance, was a tricky task. Dow contracted with the U.S. Office of Saline Water to develop a water treatment unit using this technology, and Dow's freshwater-from-seawater know-how was developed in its California laboratories.[23]

It quickly became apparent that hollow-fiber technology also had potential in an unrelated but not really distant field, kidney dialysis. Could hollow fibers become the basis of an artificial human kidney? It was an exciting possibility, and Heitz and his colleagues decided to find out.

Work on the development of an artificial kidney began in 1958 under the direction of one of Dow's outstanding researchers, Phyllis Oja (later Phyllis Oja Jones). Dr. Richard Stewart of Dow's medical department in Midland also became a key researcher in this field and tested the first hand-assembled artificial kidneys on animals beginning in 1963.

On August 3, 1967, a landmark in human health was reached—the first kidney dialysis using the artificial device was performed on a human patient at the University of Michigan Hospital in Ann Arbor. It was successful, awakening new hope for the world's kidney patients.

Although it has never been reluctant to explore uncharted territory, Dow by this time had begun to realize it was wandering away from its basic business of making chemicals, and it began looking for a partner. In 1969 the Cordis Corporation of Miami, Florida, manufacturer of implantable pacemakers for heart patients became that partner, and the two firms formed a joint venture, the Cordis-Dow Corporation. Cordis-Dow took over the job of making the disposable artificial kidney and continuing research in the field.

By 1980 more than 100,000 persons throughout the world depended on artificial kidneys for their dialysis treatments, about a quarter of them using the Cordis-Dow device. Cordis-Dow became a world leader in this field, with plants in Concord, California; Miami Lakes, Florida; and Roden, the Netherlands.[24]

Life in the Western Division of Dow had always been "like family," some of the employees said—they worked together, played together, liked and respected each other—and it was known as a good place to work. It had been organized since 1937 as Local 23 of the International Chemical Workers Union, ICWU. That made it all the more surprising when its record of labor peace was smashed with a long, costly, ugly strike in 1969. Through unusual circumstances this strike led to Pittsburg becoming an all-salaried, nonunion plant.

A key person in this episode was Barney Kriner of the fire & plant protection department, vice-president of Local 23. The strike, Barney said, was caused by two people with clashing, incompatible personalities—Alex Aguirre of the Latex plant, president of the union local, and Fred L. Peacock, Dow's industrial relations chief. For two years they faced off against each other, and ultimately the strike resulted.

It was a time of raging unrest in the division. In early 1967, in the midst of protests against the war in Vietnam, many of which had begun to surface on the college campuses of California, Thomas E. (Tom) Brown had been sent to Pittsburg as assistant general manager. He was a cigar-chomping "hatchet man," assigned to cut back the workforce by at least a quarter, which he did in a few months' time. Nothing of the sort had ever happened in Dow's Western Division before. The workforce was shocked to its core. Morale plummeted. When "Young Lee" Doan retired in 1969 and E. C. (Red) Staehling arrived as the new division general manager, he had a strike on his hands in no time at all and was soon operating the plant with only salaried personnel.

When the strike was launched, Staehling met with the personnel of Kriner's department and told them that since they were security forces they were being given salaried status, as the law provided, and the assignment of protecting the plant. Kriner, the striking union's vice president, unexpectedly found himself a salaried man looking out the fence at his picketing friends.

The strike was a lengthy affair, filled with minor violence, and the settlement was generally unfavorable to the union. When it was over, the rival United Mine Workers union in Midland saw an opening and set out to woo Aguirre, who had gotten into a wrangle with his superiors in the ICWU. With his help the UMWA began to sign up workers to petition for a move from the ICWU to the UMWA.

They brought signed UMWA cards to Jim Campbell, who had replaced Peacock as chief of industrial relations, but Campbell told them they would have to go through the National Labor Relations Board (NLRB). The NLRB then called an election in which the ballot provided three options: Stay with the ICWU, move to the UMWA, or not to belong to a union. Encouraged by A. T. (Al) Look, who had succeeded Staehling, the Dow managers decided to campaign actively for a "no union" vote, which would be a vote for Dow. Their principal strategist became the new salaried man Barney Kriner, who knew everyone in the plant and, more critical to the election, his or her sentiments concerning the union question. Wayne Hancock and Charles (Charlie) Bailey, labor relations specialists, came in from Midland to help.

When the votes were counted the UMWA received 111 votes, Dow (no union) 101, and the ICWU 23, but there was no majority among the three so the NLRB called another election 30 days later between the UMWA and Dow, eliminating the ICWU. Another hurry-up campaign for votes began, with Kriner still chief strategist for the company. In the second election the vote was Dow 118, UMWA 115. In the interim, however, one of the supervisors committed an unfair labor practice: he promised a man a promotion or a raise if he voted for the company rather than the union.

The NLRB called a third election "to clear the air." Before it could take place, however, Dow went ahead on the basis of its close win and switched the workforce to salaried status—

eliminated time clocks, allowed workers to drive their cars into the plant, and began treating them as salaried employees. That, Kriner said, "killed the union"—the employees loved it. In the third election Dow received 141 votes, almost double the UMWA vote, and that ended it; Pittsburg was now an all-salaried operation.

Aguirre became a District 50 UMWA official, but stayed with Dow until his retirement, eventually becoming a supervisor and, said Kriner, "a good one." Kriner became captain of the plant's Fire Department and a longtime participant in Dow's "Road Show" programs, which ran from 1973 to 1982. The "Road Show" programs were designed to show Dow supervisors how to make unions unnecessary; Kriner was often one of the star speakers.

"A union's success is a company's failure," Kriner told Dow managers. "People look for guidance and they want somebody to take care of them, and if management will not take care of them, that's when they go to unionism; if management can learn to take care of the people, then unionism is not needed."[25]

The Western Division grew only modestly over the years, compared to the rest of Dow. A new polystyrene plastic and Styrofoam plant was built at Torrance, California, in 1952, but that was unusual. As Dow Western people observed the company build giant chemical complexes in Texas and Louisiana in the 1940s and 1950s, and in the 1960s and 1970s all over the world, however, and as the West Coast boomed and California became the most populous of the United States, the dream of a major California chemical complex began to take shape.

California, Dow Westerners felt, should take advantage of the oil that had been discovered up in Alaska, which could be transported by oceangoing tanker down the Pacific coast and transformed into chemicals to serve the chemical and plastic needs of the massive, growing West Coast market. These materials would be cheaper because, again, the heavy cost of shipping them across the continent and over the Rockies would be eliminated.

Dow had now for many years been the largest integrated chemical manufacturer in the West, and they reasoned that it was a logical progression to plan and build the petrochemical complex the West Coast now required. In spite of their research successes they were still only the fourth largest division in Dow USA, and they told anyone who would listen that they were tired of inventing new things for other Dow locations to make; when was it going to be Dow Western's turn for major growth?

"Here was an opportunity," said Look.

There were no plants on the West Coast to make these products—vinyl chloride, and the petrochemical line that Dow makes in Texas, styrene, ethylene, propylene, acetone. The question was whether you could get through the environmental laws and restrictions on the Coast. I couldn't see where the problems were any more difficult than some of the problems Dow had had in Yugoslavia or Canada. I'd had some contact with the guys in Canada that were trying to get approval for plants. With the flack they were getting from the Canadian government, I couldn't see where it was any more impossible for us to do it than it was to do some of the things that we were spending 5 to 10 years to accomplish in Canada or Europe.

In February 1975 Dow announced it would build a 13-unit, $500 million petrochemical complex in Solano County, across the river from Pittsburg. The plan was to break ground in 1976, begin actual production by 1978, and complete the whole complex by 1982. Ethylene and propylene would be piped under the Sacramento River to Pittsburg, where the company had operated since 1916, and the Pittsburg facility would be greatly expanded. It would be the first major petrochemical facility west of the Rockies, capable of supplying 40 percent of the plastics feedstocks used in the West.

Dow took an option on a 2,700-acre sheep farm across the river, accessible to deep-water shipping; it would use 600 of these acres for its Solano County complex. As principal raw materials it would use the salt which was in ample supply in the Bay Area, which Dow purchased from the Leslie Salt Company, and 40,000 barrels per day of naphtha, a by-product of refineries distilling the crude oil arriving from Alaska; there were several refineries in the Bay Area.

"We had a good reputation on the West Coast on environmental questions," Look said.

We did not discharge into the Sacramento or into the bay. We were "off the river," that is, we did not discharge anything into the river. We planned for the new complex to be a completely zero-effluent plant, incorporating the most modern technology available. You could do this by using thermal ponds. On the average, if you put water in a pond in that area the level of the pond would drop about 14 feet in a 12-month period, the net loss by evaporation. In contrast, if you put water in a pond in Freeport, Texas, it would be 20 feet higher at the end of a year because there was that much gain in water versus the evaporation. So at Pittsburg we cut back as much as we could on water use and then built the ponds to evaporate it.[26]

To build this model of an environmentally advanced plant, Dow would need 65 different permits: 5 at the federal level, 40 from state agencies, and 20 at the local level. Dow formed a project team to undertake the task, with A. A. (Al) Gunkler as chief engineer, Beckee Beemer as environmental coordinator, Robert E. Perry as documentation chief, and Jack Jones in charge of obtaining permits. They estimated this process would take about nine months, or 280 days, before construction could begin. Jones, who had long been the division's government relations manager, was well known at the statehouse and in local government and had been talking informally during the planning period to local county officials, to the Bay Area Air Pollution Control District (BAAPCD), to local environmental groups such as the Sierra Club and the Planning and Conservation League, and to state officials. The environmental groups seemed to be quite comfortable with the proposal, he felt, seeing it as a local rather than a state issue. At the outset Jones was relaxed and confident about obtaining the 65 permits, and when Solano County gave the project a preliminary go-ahead Dow quickly exercised its option and purchased the Solano site outright for $6 million.

The project was to be one of the first major industrial developments reviewed under the new California Environmental Quality Act, which required an Environmental Impact Report, or EIR (as do federal laws). Solano County asked Dow to contract with a private firm to produce the document because it did not have the personnel to do it; and Dow chose a well-respected consulting firm, J. E. Gilbert & Associates, to produce the EIR. Later this was described as a major blunder by opposing environmental groups, to whom it smacked of impropriety.

Opposition quickly began to form, sparked mainly by the Sierra Club, which formed a "North Bay Task Force" aimed at stopping the Dow project. Its key members were Cynthia Kay, a local environmentalist, Nick Arguimbau, a Sierra Club attorney, and Michael Storper, a geographer at the University of California Berkeley. Storper became organizer and fund-raiser for the group.

"The possibility of a major industrial complex rivaling some areas of the eastern United States makes one shudder," Storper wrote in a Friends of the Earth publication. "Solid industry along both banks of the Sacramento River, vast increases in shipping, and pollution deadly to fragile Suisun Marsh. Large residential communities in now-rural areas. Higher taxes to pay for the problems that are inherent in urbanization—higher crime rates, environmental deterioration, increased demand for social services. These problems are supposedly the 'price' we must pay for economic security, for more goods, and services."[27]

Dow had run head-on into the no-growth school of environmental thinking. On December 19, 1975, just under the legal deadline, the Sierra Club, Friends of the Earth, and a San Francisco group called People for Open Space filed suit against Dow and Solano County to halt the project, challenging many aspects of the proposal.

From there things went downhill for Dow. The deputy secretary of the California Resources Agency, an umbrella department that included most of the state agencies from which Dow needed permits, wrote a long letter to the U.S. Corps of Engineers asking it not to grant a permit "until the State is satisfied that the potential environmental problems can and will be adequately resolved." It seemed clear that the state of California was not going to grant permits for the project quickly nor easily.

Look and other Dow personnel had had meetings with Governor Jerry Brown to brief him on the project and solicit his support for this important industrial development, and he had at first encouraged them, but the governor now seemed totally uninterested in the project. "Jerry Brown decided to run for president of the United States," Jones said.

Most of his key people who could make things happen were preoccupied by the candidacy. So the burden fell to the California Resources Agency, which was headed by Claire Dedrick. She had been a vice president of the Sierra Club and brought Sierra Club politics with her into public office. The Corps of Engineers had started its procedures and to the amazement of us all, Claire Dedrick sent her chief deputy down asking the Corps not to act because the state had a lot of unanswered questions which the state really had no jurisdiction to look into. The Corps said to us, "Gee, we could go ahead as a matter of law, but as a matter of policy we don't want to proceed if the state takes a position as strong as it has." We knew we were in trouble. The questions were quite impossible. Totally philosophical questions. You couldn't answer them with facts.

The Dow people tried to reach Governor Brown without success. "The governor felt he had dealt with this issue and that he had helped it when we got the EIR through quickly," Jones said. The matter dragged on into 1976, when Dow had expected to begin construction. In March 1976 the California Office of Planning and Research held a public technical briefing on the project. In April the Corps of Engineers issued a draft environmental impact statement for it. In June the CRA sent a formal 14-page letter to the Corps of Engineers objecting to the project, and in July the BAAPCD issued a preliminary denial of Dow's application for air pollution permits, which it then confirmed in August.

The project was now heading rapidly toward the ash heap. In August Dow promoted Al Look to general manager, and later president, of its Dowell subsidiary, and he was replaced by Ray Brubaker, whose instructions were to "either get the project moving or pull the plug." Brubaker filed an appeal of the BAAPCD denial of air pollution permits and asked for a meeting with Jerry Brown.

Brown and several of his cabinet-level personnel met with Brubaker and others and listened to the Dow complaints, which were mainly that they could not get a "go" or "no go" decision from the state for their project. The governor agreed to hold consolidated state hearings on the matter, which were convened in December 1976 and ran several days. He promised there would be a yes or no decision within 30 days after the hearings.

A good deal of the state's hearing was so far afield from the matter being considered that it left the Dow representatives slack jawed. "Boy, it was a circus," Jack Jones said.

There was a vice president from Dow. He was sitting in the audience and Dennis Banks—the Indian guy—got up there and the whole hearing panel stood up at reverent attention and Banks babbled something in a singsong sort of way and the hearing officer that night—former chief legal counsel for the Environmental Defense Fund and at that time chairman of the Water Resources Board—looked at him and said, "Would you favor us by translating those beautiful words into English?" And Dennis Banks said, "Oh well, sure—the water is blue and clean, and the sky is pretty and may the buffalo forever roam," or some real innocuous thing like that. You'd have thought these guys were having an orgasm up there.

Well, this guy from the home office looked at me and his eyes turned glassy and he said, "Unbelievable!" He gets up and walks out of the room, so I ran out to calm him down. He said, "Jack, let's withdraw from the proceedings right now." I said, "We can't. We've got to go through with this. At least the governor hasn't reneged on his promise of a decision up or down within 30 days yet."

Bill Press, head of Jerry Brown's Office of Planning and Research at the time, said:

It was every bit as zany and dramatic as you imagine. My first premonition of trouble came when I heard the sound of tom-toms coming from the corridor outside the hearing room. Knowing what must have been going through the minds of Dow executives, I had a hard time keeping a straight face through the presentation. I was astonished to look around me when the song was finished and see several panel members with tears streaming down their faces. How do you explain that in Midland, Michigan?

The hearings concluded on December 18. On January 9, the governor's legal counsel, Tony Kline, presented Dow with an opinion that said he agreed with California attorney general Evelle Younger that the material from the hearings would have to be treated as new environmental information and that Dow would have to go back and start all over again through the EIR process. But, said Kline, they would try to expedite it. "You gave us a commitment to make a permit decision yes or no," Jack Jones said. "We can't honor that commitment," Kline said.

"It was about that time we decided we were not going to make progress and decided to quit," Brubaker said, and he recommended to top management in Midland that the project be dropped. "With no positive results to show after spending two and a half years and $4.5 million to get four permits out of 65, I had to cut my losses."

On January 18, 1977, Dow announced it was canceling the project. "The permitting process for new facilities is so involved and expensive it is impractical to continue," its press release explained.

The company had delayed its announcement 24 hours at Governor Brown's request. As it happened, he was in New York City that day holding a press conference in which he described a series of new measures to attract business and industry to California.

The Dow announcement was a bombshell. The California environmental organizations celebrated a great victory. This was followed quickly by a chorus of outrage that welled up from the labor unions who had expected to see new jobs open up in Solano County, from the chambers of commerce looking for development, and from California industry looking for expansion. The wind shifted. Who to blame for killing the Dow project became a favorite topic for California politicians. Governor Brown and the environmentalists were favorite targets.

"We cannot blame Dow or any other company for pulling out of California," said State Assemblyman Dan Boatwright; "Red tape and bureaucracy are killing business." State Assemblyman John Knox said, "Every time we have a problem in California, we create a new government unit to issue a permit."

Pete Wilson, then mayor of San Diego, later governor and presidential hopeful, was one of the leaders attacking Brown. "This decision will probably cost California thousands of jobs once Dow's decision becomes common knowledge around this country and other business and industries are further discouraged from locating to our state," he said.

Alan Stein, secretary of business and transportation in the Brown administration, said the state was right to set up tough environmental regulations, and that he thought the Dow proposal would get state approval if resubmitted. Paul Oreffice, then president of Dow Chemical USA, would have none of it. "You are assuming the chemical industry is coming here to destroy the environment," he told Stein. "No industry in the world has spent more money than the chemical industry of the United States to clean up the environment. I submit to you there is a problem with attitude in state government in California. We have other states in this country that live with the same Environmental Protection Agency rules but have an entirely different attitude."[28]

The Solano County project was dead. Dow's Western Division went back to business as usual.

<h2 style="text-align:center">III.</h2>

Albert P. (Dutch) Beutel never let anything slow him down. Some of his Dow colleagues felt his drive to overcome the obstacles in his path, and to win out in spite of them, was the secret of his success.

He came to the Dow company in 1916 rather by accident after meeting Tom Griswold Jr. in the smoking car of a train headed for Chicago. In the course of this casual meeting Beutel (pronounced Boy'tel), then 22, told Griswold that as assistant engineer of the Robert Gage Coal Company at Bay City, Michigan, he traveled about the east central Michigan area where the company had five or six small mines, surveying and planning the firm's explorations for coal and designing its mine layouts. Griswold told him if he ever needed a job to call him; perhaps he could find something for him at Dow. "There's no use wasting time on the Michigan coal business," Griswold commented.[29]

The coal seams in the Michigan mines, long since abandoned, were seldom thick enough for a man to stand up in, averaging perhaps three feet in depth and often narrowing to half that; frequently the miners had to grub out the coal lying on their bellies. In such close quarters it was almost never possible to shore up the ceiling, so there were many cave-ins; it was brutish and extremely dangerous work. The coal company "lost lots of men," they said. Living in St. Charles, a village south of Saginaw, Beutel roomed with the village blacksmith and his wife in a house with an outhouse out back—quite a comedown, he said, for a city boy born in Cleveland who had worked his way through the Case School of Applied Science.

In St. Charles Beutel met and wooed his future wife, Belle Armstrong, daughter of a couple who ran the local shoe store, but she informed him that "if you don't get out of the coal mines I'm not going to marry you. I don't want to be a widow at 22." Beutel, who had already been in what he called "a couple of smash-ups down in the hole," one of which left him with a permanent limp, promised to look for another job.

The day before their wedding Griswold phoned him and said, "Get over here to Midland. I want to talk to you about working here." Beutel protested that he was getting married the next day and leaving on his honeymoon. "Oh, to hell with the honeymoon," Griswold said. "Not me," said Beutel.

After the wedding trip Beutel kept his promise to Belle and hired into the Dow engineering department as a draftsman. The department then consisted of six men, including Griswold as chief engineer.

That was the beginning of a 55-year career with Dow during which Dutch Beutel left an indelible imprint on the company and on the U.S. chemical industry; Beutel was to lead the migration of the U.S. chemical industry to the Gulf Coast. During his career the Gulf Coast became, from scratch, host to the world's heaviest concentration of petrochemical operations.

A key early move in his career came in 1921, when Herbert Dow sought him out and told him there had never been any real engineering in the Dow plant piping system, which had grown up haphazardly and was now becoming quite messy, and asked him to take on the assignment of designing new piping systems and getting the plant's pipelines and their accessories in shape. He was soon heavily involved in the postwar expansion of the company's brinewell and brine-gathering system, which in those years pushed its pipeline fingers out to a 20- or 30-mile radius of Midland, almost to Mt. Pleasant on the west, to St. Louis on the southwest, and to Saginaw on the southeast. Central Michigan was brinewell country.

As superintendent of the Pipe Shop, Beutel began to work more and more closely with young Willard Dow, and he acquired an intimate knowledge of the Dow production complex as he ran pipelines about the plant and out to the increasingly far-flung brinewells. He also began to acquire a reputation for getting things done well and on schedule.

By the time Willard Dow took over the reins of the company in 1930, Beutel was its chief troubleshooter. When the Jones iodine plant in Louisiana ran into problems, Willard sent Beutel down to straighten it out, which he promptly did. When the iodine operation moved to Long Beach, California, in 1932, Beutel helped design the new plant and went to California to build it. He began on July 6, and the plant produced its first oaken keg packed with iodine on July 29 before the plant was even completed; from groundbreaking to completed plant took only six weeks. The speed of the thing caused a furor in Midland; no one had ever heard of a feat like that before, and Beutel's reputation was made. Beutel said later: "1932 was a damn good time for quick deliveries because business wasn't too good. I think I got more reputation than I deserved. It was a quite simple process."

He became a peerless construction ramrodder. When the first bromine-from-seawater plant was built at Kure Beach, North Carolina, Willard Dow sent Beutel to speed up the process. When he arrived there in August 1933, construction crews were still clearing the site of trees. Beutel had the plant up and operating in January 1934, only 150 days after construction began.

He was also rapidly becoming Willard Dow's second-in-command. In 1931 his title was Assistant to Willard H. Dow; early in 1932 it became Assistant to the President; later that year it was Assistant General Manager (Willard Dow was GM). In 1932, when the Dowell oil well treating subsidiary was formed, he was one of its principal organizers, and he became its president for 28 years.

Once or twice a year Beutel made a trip around the Dowell treating stations, which were scattered through the Oklahoma, Louisiana, and Texas oil country, sometimes accompanied by Willard Dow, to "keep the boys at the different stations on their toes." In Texas the two saw natural gas being "flared off"—burned—in prodigious quantities, just to get rid of it, in the production of oil. "You could read a newspaper by the gas flares, driving from Houston to Freeport at night," Beutel remembered, "and it was all going to waste." This was their first look at what would become the Texas Gulf Coast Chemical Country a few years later.

The problems of running the bromine plant at Kure Beach were mounting. "The costs were running too high," Beutel explained. "We were paying almost a cent a kilowatt for our power. We were in the hands of the people at Hopewell, Virginia, for our chlorine, which was high-priced, high-cost delivered. The sulfuric acid we were buying from the fertilizer people, which they made as a by-product—they were not really in the acid business—was also too damned expensive. We had to bring our soda ash up the Cape Fear River by ship and lighter it to shore. There was no railroad and it was an isolated unit."

G. F. (Brick) Dressel, Beutel's assistant, estimated they could make bromine at a good location along the Gulf Coast for perhaps half the cost at Kure Beach, without these problems, and the pressure began to build to "do something." With Hitler on the rampage in Europe, war was in the offing. And Dow "had to get out of Midland for magnesium," as Beutel put it—it could no longer rely on extracting it from the Michigan brine stream in the quantities it needed. The demand for bromine and magnesium, for both of which Dow was the principal U.S. source, was rising rapidly. The research work on the magnesium-from-seawater project was nearly complete, and it was time to decide where it should be located.

In late 1938 Beutel and Willard Dow went on a trip along the Gulf Coast to reconnoiter possible plant sites, starting at New Orleans and driving all the way to Brownsville, Texas, at the Mexican border. Corpus Christi "looked pretty good" to them as a plant site; Freeport got only a secondary look because it was behind a levee. Brownsville, Port Isabel, adjacent to it, and Ingleside were also candidates.

A team of Dressel, Roy Osmun, assistant superintendent of the Kure Beach plant, and Joe Bayliss, who had helped pick the site near Wilmington, was dispatched to sample seawater up and down the coast of Louisiana and Texas for bromine content. Their conclusion: it was not a very good place to build a bromine plant because of fresh water from the rivers flowing into the Gulf; the bromine content in consequence was diluted to about 56 parts per million compared to 67 (considered the normal ocean water level) at Wilmington. A deepwater seawater intake would be important.

The studies went on for most of a year. The Austin Company was engaged to survey the "industrial qualifications" of the candidate cities along the coast. Its report was delivered April 10, 1939, and Willard and Beutel asked Austin for a second study focusing on Freeport, which was completed at the end of September.[30]

At the end of the year Willard Dow proposed to the Dow board that it meet for its January 1940 meeting at the Driskill Hotel in Corpus Christi; the purpose: to choose the site for a new Dow plant in Texas. As it happened, the board met there in the midst of a sudden freezing "norther," and peered through a freezing rain at Corpus Christi, which was favored by some of the directors despite the fact that they had to stop every half mile to scrape ice off their windshields. They then moved up the coast for a look at Freeport, where the norther had already passed through and the sun was shining. Finally they met in Houston to make a decision. The decision was no longer in doubt: Freeport was the place.

Freeport had everything they were looking for, they decided—cheap natural gas as an energy source (45 percent of the gas in Texas was within 100 miles); easily available LPGs and other petrochemical feedstocks; great banks of oyster shell in neighboring Galveston Bay as a source of calcium carbonate (or "lime"); an abundant supply of fresh water from the Brazos River; salt domes and sulfur within easy reach (the Bryan Mound salt dome was only three miles from the proposed plant site); ocean port facilities whenever you wanted to put them in; a bounteous supply of low-priced land (although most of it was "salt grass" prairie); and a local community eager to welcome new industry.

"Willard and I were strong on Freeport," Beutel said later.

We had finally come down and looked things over and it looked like a natural. If you look at a map of Texas you'll see that this is the only place along the coast where the mainland juts out into the Gulf. There's no sand bar or reef—no sand-built island, then a lagoon, then the mainland. In obtaining your seawater and disposing of it, the lagoon is something you would have to get across; it represented costly engineering problems. The Freeport Sulphur Company had developed a new river, which had been written up in Ripley's "Believe It Or Not"—they built a bridge across a dry place, then diverted the river down through it, and it cut off the harbor channel so Freeport Sulphur could bring their boats in there.

The new channel of the Brazos River, which had been dug in 1932, made it possible to take in ocean water at the old river mouth, extract its magnesium and bromine, and then discharge the stream back to the ocean at a point several miles down the coast, thus avoiding the possibility of reprocessing the same water.

It was not all peaches and cream. The first time Willard and Beutel went to Freeport they stayed at a venerable old Freeport hostelry, the Tarpon Inn. "I'd been there before; Willard hadn't," Beutel said.

I knew one thing—to shut your damned suitcase or the next morning it would be full of cockroaches. When Willard woke up the next morning and reached in his suitcase for a clean shirt a dozen cockroaches jumped out, and oh, you should have heard him howl. "Why didn't you tell me?" he said. "I didn't think about it," I said. When we got back to Midland I said, "You'd better unpack your suitcase out in the yard." When we drove up to his house he did exactly that, and Martha came out and said, "What are you doing?" He said, "I'm shaking the cockroaches out of my clothes." "Don't you come in the house," she said.

The Dow board authorized $18 million for a plant at Freeport, and hired the Austin Company for the engineering. "We didn't have enough Dow engineers," Beutel said. Through Austin the company bought a first parcel of land, 800 acres, at $100 an acre. "We decided we couldn't carry this load as far as our own construction and engineering were concerned, so we hired the Austin Company to fill up the incremental load."

A team of engineers and process personnel was assembled in Cleveland to start designing the Freeport development on the drawing board, but communication between Cleveland, Midland, and Freeport was difficult, "so in the spring of 1940 we moved them to Houston, Texas, in the loft of the M & M Building," Beutel said. "Most of these fellows were put up in hotels and apartments there, and the last and final stages of the engineering were carried on there at the M & M Building."

The magnesium plant came first. "The drive was on for more magnesium for flares and incendiaries and airplanes, and we started building the chlorine plant and the magnesium plant and the power house and five boilers," Beutel said.

Things moved so fast. We built 18 million pounds per year capacity in there, which was quite a slice. We were busy working on that when the British came along and asked us to build another increment of magnesium capacity for them. Britain was already at war, of course, and badly in need of magnesium for planes. So we drew a line through the plant and said, "from this point to this point is yours." We set aside so many cells in the mag cell building for them, set aside so much equipment in the brine-treating plant for them; in other words, a slice of our plant was built and paid for by the British, with our option to buy it back at the end of the war.

By the middle of March a 66,000-volt power line to the plant site was completed in jig-time by Houston Lighting & Power Company and on March 28, 1940, the *Freeport Facts* newspaper reported in a banner headline, "Construction Equipment Is Arriving." George M. McGranahan came down from Midland to be the new plant manager, and George W. Greene to be the plant engineer.[31]

"Those were the days of boots and mud," Beutel said. "I never went to work without my boots on, and I was dirty all the time. It was so hot; you'd get your arms on the table, you'd be perspiring, and the engineers were worse. They were having a hell of a time making drawings because their damp elbows and arms stuck to the tracing cloth. Air conditioning hadn't become vogue at that time."

Dow began hiring people. The first group, Beutel said, was "a bunch of cotton pickers." Gradually, people from the north came in, "but I'd say this in defense of the cotton pickers," Beutel said, "They developed into the best operators. They were farmhands and they were intelligent, resourceful people."

As was usual with Beutel-built plants, the Freeport plant went up fast and efficiently. The bromine-from-seawater plant (built for Ethyl-Dow) was completed on schedule in 1940. The chlorine-caustic plant started up a few days before Christmas, and the magnesium-from-seawater plant came onstream on January 21, 1941, followed closely by the lime plant, which used oyster shells as raw material. These were the core of Dow's Texas Division and together with the next group of plants built, the ethylene dichloride and glycol units, became known as Plant "A," cradled in a circling loop of the Brazos River.

January 21 was a historic date at Freeport—it marked the first time man had successfully mined the oceans for a metal—but also the beginning of a crisis that could have been disastrous. "We started out nicely," Beutel said.

> The cells were up to production, but all the time, without knowing it, we were concentrating boron, and the more boron we got in there the less mag we were producing per cell. The cells were supposed to be making 1,000 pounds a day; instead we were making 100 pounds. Willard Dow would call up and ask, "What's your production?" We'd tell him and he'd say, "What's the matter with you guys down there?" I'd say, "Well, there's something in this brine and our salt that's not making anything but sludge. Some mysterious material in there is inhibiting the production of mag." "There's nothing mysterious about chemistry—all you have to do is find out what the hell it is," Willard said. "Well," I said, "that's what we're trying to do—find out what the hell it is."

Beutel called E. O. Barstow and said, "Ed, come down and help me out. I'm in misery down here." Barstow said, "I'll be right down." Every morning Beutel and Barstow would go out to the plant where the trouble was and map out the day's attack on the problem.

Beutel said later that he had to take the blame for the problem.

> I told the boys, "Look, lime is much more costly than seawater, and we've got the whole Gulf of Mexico in there, so underlime the seawater; make your lime go as far as you can." We sent samples to Midland, to the Western Division, to every lab we had in the country, to help us out. The British were clamoring, and the sales department was clamoring for production.

Ralph Hunter, Dow's magnesium cell expert in Midland, and Vernon Stenger, a top analytical chemist, were the heroes of this episode. Stenger made a complete analysis of Gulf water and found it contained four parts per million of boron—a remarkable piece of analysis in 1940—and Hunter, studying Stenger's report, began to suspect that might be the problem.[32]

Hunter sent Charles Wiles, a new man in the magnesium cells group, down to Main Street to get 10 pounds of borax. He bought it at Thompson's Mercantile Store, and they added borax to the cell bath. The next morning—it was a Sunday—Hunter asked Frank Latoski, one of the dippers, to check on Cell 24. A few minutes later he asked him, "Frank, what have you got?" Latoski groaned. "It's full of sludge, Ralph," he said, unhappy because he was going to have to remove a ton of it. Hunter went to look at it and then called Barstow in Freeport. "I've got it," Hunter reported happily, "It's boron!"

Once the problem had been identified the solution was relatively easy; it was to overlime the cell feed—to add too much lime to the seawater rather than too little, as Beutel had instructed. The problem quickly cleared up, and the boron crisis was over.

There were other crises, but none that seemed as big. In September 1941 a 120-mile-an-hour hurricane roared through south Texas, knocking out the power, tipping over 20-foot-high Dorr tanks, blowing out the windows, tossing shrimp boats up on shore, and flooding the new plant. "It was pandemonium," Beutel said. The plant was shut down for six days, and then got going again.

Housing the droves of new employees and construction workers pouring in was another crisis. There was no place to rent in the town. People arrived in trailers; some lived in tents until they could find something better.

In the meantime the plant kept expanding. After the Japanese attack on Pearl Harbor a second magnesium plant was quickly ordered by the government, which suddenly realized that it was going to have to make a lot of planes and, except for Dow, did not have the magnesium with which to make them. The Dow Magnesium Corporation was formed to administer wartime magnesium contracts with the government and the second magnesium plant was built at a neighboring village called Velasco, which soon became known as Plant B. The Velasco plant had a capacity of 54 million pounds and was built with Beutel's habitual dispatch in six months.

By Pearl Harbor, the Texas Division of Dow was producing bromine, magnesium, chlorine, caustic soda, ethylene, ethylene dichloride, ethylene glycol, and propylene glycol, and had its own power plant.

Beutel went to Washington for help in housing the people he was bringing in to build and operate these plants, and this resulted in the construction of a temporary housing area called "Camp Chemical," a town that was thrown together in two months at a cost of about $4 million. It was the largest city in Brazoria County for a time, but in 1945 it was bulldozed down without a trace and large chemical plants were built over the one-time town. Camp Chemical was one of the rare temporary wartime structures that was actually destroyed once the war was over. "I was afraid it would end up as a slum area," Beutel said. "So we got permission from the government and they gave me authority to tear it down and sell it."

Dowell's business was depressed because of the war, so Beutel brought in a group of Dowell executives from Tulsa, including N. R. (Russ) Crawford and Leroy Smithers, later to be the top executives of Dow Canada. "I just gave Crawford the job of building Camp Chemical," Beutel said. "We built some 5,000 shacks out of pine lumber. We built a complete shopping center, post office, recreation hall, barracks for the single people. At one time we had 12,100 people in the area. We had to build roads in there; we had to build garbage incinerators and everything that went with it."

The houses were built using an early pre-fab technique. Standardized exterior panels were built and bolted together, and partitions were then put in to mark off kitchen, living room, and two or three bedrooms, depending on the model. Because of the shortage of gasoline and the lack of good roads, Dow installed a horsedrawn stagecoach that circulated around the area providing transportation for the residents.

Willard Dow asked his young architect brother, Alden B. Dow, to design the basic houses for this venture, and Alden quickly accepted the challenge, becoming the designer of practically everything the company built in the area, aside from the chemical plants. Alden was reluctant to see the company build very much rough-and-ready temporary housing, and he and Beutel quickly came up with the idea of establishing an entirely new city, one that would still be there after the war was over, for the permanent residents.

At the site, they quietly purchased a sprawling, disused antebellum plantation a few miles from Freeport, and some contiguous property. The old Abner Jackson plantation sat astride a charming little lake, Lake Jackson, and their new town, they decided, would also be named Lake Jackson.[33]

Beutel and the Dow brothers explored the area on horseback, and Alden Dow was charged with laying out the town and designing its major features. He built himself an office in what was to become the central city and spent the rest of the war at the task. Today a monument to Alden and Dutch near the spot identifies them as the city's fathers.

Alden Dow designed his city for 5,000 people—it reached that level within 10 years—but it has now expanded to about five times that number. Its pattern of curving and gently meandering streets—Alden felt a building or street should always promise new vistas as you explored it, not showing all of itself at first glance—was new for that time, but give it a sense of modernity today.

He called the streets "ways," and with a pixie sense of humor called many by names such as "This Way" and "That Way." The townspeople loved the idea; a street that leads to a church today is called "His Way." He designed a half-dozen basic home models, and residents were given a choice of these designs. The project was begun early in 1943, and by the end of that year the first resident had moved in.

The area surrounding the lake was laid out in larger, more expensive lots and became known as Lake Jackson Farms. Beutel built his own house there, on the shore of the lake next to the old Abner Jackson plantation house. Over the succeeding years it was visited by most of the celebrities who came to that part of the world, including presidential candidates such as John Connally, Ronald Reagan, and Lyndon Johnson.

The complex grew at an unbelievable pace. Hurricanes hit regularly—in 1943, in 1945, and again in 1949—but they were no match for Dutch Beutel and his fury to build. A second chlorine unit and a second power unit were added before 1942 was out; a 42-bed hospital was built; and carbon tetrachloride and triethylene glycol plants were added. A Thiokol rubber plant (used for tire retreads during the war) was built in 1942 and halted a year later, three weeks short of start-up, without ever operating, when the supply of styrene-butadiene synthetic rubber became adequate. In 1944 Freeport began shipping chemicals out by ocean vessel, opening a new chapter of the company's history, for it inaugurated shipment by ocean carrier to destinations all over the world.

When the war was over Beutel asked the Dow board of directors for authorization to purchase a company airplane. It was a three-day train trip to Midland from Freeport, he explained, "and I want to get here before I forget what I'm mad about." He bought a Beechcraft twin-engine plane, initiating the era of corporate aircraft for Dow.[34]

During the war the FBI sent a special agent to Midland to conduct loyalty checks on Dow executives with German names or connections—Strosacker, Grebe, Beutel, and others. "They put us through the wringer," Beutel said. All received a clean bill of health. Later on, when Beutel needed a chief of security for the Texas Division, he went to the FBI and hired away from them the agent who had put him "through the wringer," a man named Al Deere. "I admired the way he went at it," Beutel said. Deere spent the remainder of his career as the Texas Division security chief.

In the same way that Herbert Dow built the Midland plant on cheap pine lumber, Dutch Beutel built the Texas plant on cheap gas. Beutel said that when the plant was growing so rapidly in the early 1940s his staff calculated they had to have 30 million cubic feet of natural gas daily and he went to see Jim Abercrombie in Houston, the proprietor of the Old Ocean gas field. Abercrombie told him, "the price of gas is too cheap, and I'm not going to sell any until it gets higher priced." Beutel, perplexed, stood on the corner of Main and Texas, wondering where to go next. He thought of Glenn McCarthy, who had some gas in the Angleton field, enough to last the plant perhaps a year by the geologists' estimates. Beutel walked over to McCarthy's office and asked his secretary if he could see him. McCarthy came out, and Beutel told him he needed 30 million cubic feet of gas. McCarthy said, "How much do you want to pay for it?" Beutel replied, "I don't want to pay anything for it." "That's ridiculous," McCarthy said. Beutel said, "Oh, I know it; I was just kidding. How about a cent a thousand?" McCarthy then asked, "Well, when do you want to take it?" "Just as soon as I can get a pipeline built," Beutel replied. "Okay," McCarthy said. "Send your lawyers up and we'll draw up a contract." That was it, Beutel said later. "For years, that line took care of 30 million cubic feet of gas and got me out of a hell of a hole at the time."[35]

Beutel's reputation as a hard-driving, tough-to-satisfy manager grew larger as he grew older. "Before he ever came to Texas he had the reputation in Midland of being a holy terror," said Earle Barnes, who became his successor in Texas in 1961.

> People would tremble at his name. He'd walk through the plant and see some guy sitting on his lunch bucket and say, "You're fired; get the heck out of here." He was very feisty, and he would really chew people out. He had a couple of guys that he would regularly chew out in front of everybody in the operating committee. But he always would go back and pat them on the back and do something. He explained once, "They're my boys, and I may whip them once in awhile," but he was very loyal to his people; he always defended them. All he wanted was a real successful operation, and he was very rewarding to everybody. He's a real legend in The Dow Chemical Company. It would never be the company it is today if he hadn't pushed for that Texas operation.[36]

David Rooke, Beutel's assistant for two and a half years, said he was, a terrible guy to work for; it was a roller coaster ride every day. He was a nuclear reactor that was always on the verge of going critical. His drive, his motivation, was so tremendous, and that paranoid personality . . . Beutel could be as smooth, as sophisticated and charming an individual as you have ever seen, and he could also be the meanest supervisor you have ever seen. Beutel was a real driver. I've never seen such brutal behavior as from Beutel. At the operating board he would decide to take off on somebody and he would pace up and down with that gimpy step, shouting. He would call you everything that he could think of and then it was over with.

Rooke said that at one such séance he picked on one of the operating board members mercilessly and then when the meeting was breaking up, called after him, "Wait a minute—I want to talk to you." "He then proceeded to give the man a hell of a good salary increase and complimented him on the way he was doing his work."

"You just have to know that this was Beutel," Rooke said. "This was Beutel the driver who could push thousands of people to better achievement."

At the first meeting of Beutel's operating board he attended, Rooke was taken aside by Walter Roush afterward. "David, I saw your face while Beutel was chewing out Nels Griswold," Roush said.

You're going to see a lot of this. Today you didn't get it, but if you really become a part of the group you will get your turn in the box, so just prepare yourself. This is just the way the guy is. He has to let it out and we are the place where he can let it out, and you just take it. You saw Nels not come to his own defense even once; Nels has worked for Beutel for a long time. If he starts chewing you out, just let it go, listen and say, "Yes, sir." Then it will end at a reasonable time; if you even act like you're going to argue with him, you'll double or triple the volume and the time. But don't let that bother you—he does that to everyone. He just has to.

After one especially difficult day, Rooke said, he was thinking, "Why do I continue to work under these stresses?" Then, he said, "I got in the car and drove home past miles of Dow plants and I said to myself, 'Who am I to be critical of Beutel? I couldn't have done that. I've just got to find a way to learn what is good about this guy and how he can have this kind of unbelievable achievement, so I can be better myself. At the same time I've got to learn not to abuse my people the way he does.'"

As Rooke analyzed it, Beutel's philosophy was: "Every day, I must prove to The Dow Chemical Company that they made the right decision to hire me to work today. I've got to earn what they're paying me. I can never have the attitude that I did this wonderful thing last year, so therefore I can coast. What did you do today? What are you going to do tomorrow?"

When Rooke became Dow's Texas Division general manager in 1968, Barnes, then president of Dow U.S.A., told him: "David, let me give you two bits of advice. One, you've got the best job in the company (Rooke agreed). Two, Beutel created a spirit of achievement down here—don't kill it. That's my advice to you—don't kill it, nurture it."[37]

Perhaps the most oft-told story about Beutel concerned the toilet facility in his office. Beutel did not like going down the hall from his office to the men's room, and decided he wanted his own facility. He had a small screened-in porch in a corner of his office, and he called in Harlan Sherbrook, his maintenance and construction chief, and told him he wanted the porch made into a private restroom. For a time nothing happened; it was a period of intense construction activity. One day Beutel called in Sherbrook and pointed to the screened-in porch. "Harlan," he said, "I've waited long enough. I'm going to be coming in here at 7:30 tomorrow morning and I'm warning you right now that when I get here I'm going to defecate [Beutel used a more graphic term] right in the middle of that porch. There had better be something there to catch it." Next morning the porch was closed in and the plumbing had been installed.

On a trip to Germany he was looking for a place to dispose of some litter when a door-man took it and disposed of it for him. This trivial incident gave him a new awareness of the cleanliness of the German countryside and the frequent litter of American countrysides. When he returned to Texas, he moved some wheels and the Keep Brazoria County Beautiful Association was established.

Carl Gerstacker said Beutel was known principally as a builder but that his greatest contribution to the company was developing men. "There's hardly an enterprise within the Dow corporate structure that doesn't have a man with a Beutel brand on him filling a responsible managerial position," he said in 1966 on the occasion of a gala dinner celebrating Beutel's 50th anniversary with the firm.

The most celebrated of the "Beutel babies" was a small lab group recruited during the war by Earle Barnes to work in Texas Division organic chemical research. Barnes himself, after succeeding Beutel at the helm of the Texas Division, finished his career as Dow's board chairman. The four men in his early lab group were Joel Monroe (Levi) Leathers, who became a director and manufacturing chief of the parent company (and a legend in his own right); Holmes H. (Mac) McClure, who followed in their footsteps as Texas Division general manager and completed his career as Dow's vice president for Gulf Coast operations; Malcolm E. (Mac) Pruitt, a research and development vice president of the company, for whom the company's main research complex in Midland is named; and John H. (Johnny) Brown Jr., who had a distinguished career as a researcher and lab director.

Beutel became a director of the company in 1948 and remained in command of the Texas operations until 1963, by which time it covered 3,000 acres and was the largest basic chemical processing plant in the world. In 1963, when he was 70, he moved rather reluctantly to Midland to take on a new assignment—to organize a government affairs department for the company, and to serve on the executive committee. "Everybody felt that Dow was missing a marketing opportunity for government business," Earle Barnes said, "and Beutel had some real good contacts in Washington. Lyndon Johnson was vice president and very soon to be

DOW IN THE OIL PATCH

The road to success for a petrochemical company such as Dow runs right through the oil patch. That is where its raw materials, or feedstocks, come from, as well as the fuel gases that provide a key energy source.

The company was pushed in the direction of petrochemicals—the entire chemical industry was pushed in this direction—by the products being invented in the 1930s in its research arm, especially the Physical Research and Organic Research Laboratories, which had been established at the end of World War I. But it was not until it began to make styrene, its first mass-production hydrocarbon, in the late 1930s that it made the formal plunge into petrochemicals.

The ancestry of a separate Dow Hydrocarbons and Energy operation—in the 1990s a $2 billion a year business—goes back to A. P. (Dutch) Beutel, father figure of the company's Texas operations. From the time he arrived in Texas in March 1940 he fought for the idea that Dow should be an active player in the oil and gas business and rely as little as possible on the oil companies for its energy and petrochemical feedstock supply—if possible, not at all. This soon became company policy.

Some disappointing early experiences may have kindled Beutel's desire for independence in energy. The Hamman gas field just south of Bay City, Texas, was the first supply source Beutel signed up with in Texas; the company's first pipeline was quickly laid from this field to Freeport, and gas began flowing from Hamman to Dow, 39 miles away, in October 1940, to fuel the first magnesium-from-seawater plant. The contract with Hamman Oil and Refining Company, owners of the field, called for delivery of 30 million cubic feet of gas per day for 20 years, at the astounding price for modern-day observers of 2 cents per thousand cubic feet for the first 10 years. The Hamman deliveries never did reach 30 million cubic feet a day, peaking at 24 million in 1942 and declining rapidly thereafter to extinction in January 1946, so that the 20-year contract lasted barely five. Nelson D. Griswold and J. P. Bryan of Beutel's staff said later they were convinced "the Hammans knowingly contracted to sell gas to Dow that they did not have."[1]

In those early days Beutel and his team were able to buy gas for as little as a half cent per thousand cubic feet; gas was a nuisance by-product of oil production and often was "flared off"—burned as a waste product. Beutel realized this situation would not last and began to push for long-term contracts at the fire-sale prices.

In 1941 gas deliveries began from the much closer Anchor field, owned principally by Humble Oil and Sun Oil, 20 miles from Freeport, under a 10-year contract with the well-known Texas oilman Glenn H. McCarthy, who sold gas to Dow for a cent per thousand. The reserves here, verified more closely than the Hamman field had been by Dow, were estimated at 107 billion cubic feet.

The swift expansion of the pipeline network from surrounding gas fields to the Freeport area continued in 1942 with a line to the Old Ocean field, 31 miles away; the Dow Magnesium Company contracted for 100 million c.f. per day for 10 years at 2.5 cents per thousand, for use as fuel gas. A second contract between Dow and Dan Harrison and Jim Abercrombie of the J. S. Abercrombie Company provided for another 85 million c.f. at the same price.

An ethylene pipeline was built from the Carbide and Carbon Chemical Company at Texas City to the new styrene plant at Velasco in 1943, and a propane line was laid from the Katy recycling plant in the Katy gas field, 70 miles from Freeport, in 1945. Brine lines were run from the Bryan Mound salt dome to Freeport, and from Stratton Ridge to Plant "A"; chlorine and ethylene lines were run from Plant "A" to Plant "B"; and soon the pipeline maps were beginning to look like a spaghetti bowl.

At the end of the war Willard Dow and the Dow board decided to set up the gas and oil operations as a separate business, and on December 18, 1946, the Brazos Oil and Gas Company was incorporated in Texas with Beutel as president, Griswold as vice president, Bryan as secretary, and David J. Landsborough as treasurer. The company's charter was "to store, transport, buy and sell oil, gas, salt, brine and other mineral solutions and liquified minerals; to produce oil and gas, and to do all things incident thereto."[2] Bart DeLaat was appointed the first general manager in August 1947, and offices were set up in the City National Bank building in Houston. The company hired a few veterans of the oil fields—Loy J. Munger and H. (Doc) Cherry were the first—and opened for business.

In the spring of 1947 Dow bought its first oil field through the new Brazos company, the Collegeport field in Matagorda County, Texas, paying the Pure Oil Company, Continental Oil Company, and others $2.4 million for it. The first well drilled by the company itself was begun December 10, 1947, on the Collegeport property; it came in as a gas well in January, 1948.

Brazos quickly began to make noises all over the oil patch. It started operations in California in 1949, building the first privately owned pipeline system in northern California, with producing properties in Isleton and River Island. In 1950 it expanded to Michigan and drilled 29 wells in the Rose City area.

By 1962 Brazos pipelines covered 1,000 miles in nine counties of Texas alone, bringing natural gas, ethylene, and LPGs (liquefied petroleum gases) to Freeport. The lines were so far-flung that they had to be patrolled by plane—a green Cessna 180 flown by pilot Fred Pearce, accompanied by a patrol scout.

By then the company was called the Brazos Oil and Gas Division of The Dow Chemical Company; it had been merged into the parent company in 1955, at least in part because there were beginning to be jokes and questions about just how big the

Texas Division of Dow was—Brazos was now operating in places as far afield as Ohio, Louisiana, and Wyoming. Later it went into Oklahoma, Colorado, Kansas, Nebraska, Florida, and New Mexico. Beginning in 1965 it went offshore in the Gulf of Mexico and the Louisiana offshore area, and drilled wells in the Netherlands and Libya.[3]

Beutel remained president of the Brazos operation until 1966, when he celebrated his first 50 years with Dow. DeLaat was succeeded as general manager by O. W. Lyons in 1952, and he in turn was succeeded in 1958 by Richard A. Beutel, Dutch's youngest son. Luther Evans, a veteran Dow manager who had been one of Beutel's assistant general managers in Texas, became the general manager in 1967. Macauley Whiting took over corporation-wide oversight of all of Dow's hydrocarbon and energy activities in 1966, and by 1974 had reshaped the division as the Oil & Gas Division of Dow Chemical USA, with headquarters remaining in Houston.

Whiting, conscious of being a non-Texan and nonoilman, recalled how the direction of the operations began to change at this period. "Unfortunately we seldom found oil or gas in the holes that Dow drilled," Whiting said.

So we went through an organizational planning exercise. I said, "Fellows, we're not going to be in this activity very long if we don't get successful. We have been singularly unsuccessful at picking winners. If you can't convince me that we can, in fact, do that then we're out of business." That was really traumatic for these guys to hear, although they were expecting it. We finally worked it out. There were lots of people outside Dow who had proven capability to find oil, and there were lots of them who would give Dow a very good deal in return for Dow putting up the money. The thing to do was to back people who knew how to find the oil. We wound up selecting Texas Oil & Gas and Freeport MacMorran, or MacMorran as it was then. By screening and finding the ones who were extremely good we increased the holdings of Dow reserves tenfold in a very few years with a remarkably low budget. It was just a golden technique; that was the way for Dow to acquire oil and gas reserves and in my judgment it still is the right way for Dow to build reserves, using the proven talents of successful oil finders.[4]

Earle Barnes remembered an incident when he was general manager of the Texas Division of Dow, about 1964:

Brazos Oil and Gas didn't really make any great discoveries, but Shell found a gas field right offshore Freeport. They were a long way from their refinery; we thought it would be a great opportunity if we could buy the whole output of this field from them. I remember going to the executive committee meeting and presenting my case for buying this gas for 17 cents a thousand, and Beutel opposed it on the grounds that if we bought this gas (the output of Shell's field), this would hurt Brazos Oil and Gas and take away a lot of their incentive for looking for gas. He thought there were lots of other opportunities and it would be better if Brazos found it. That was one of the few times that we ever ran into a conflict, Beutel and I, after I was no longer working for him.[5]

When the worldwide oil crisis struck—the Arab oil embargo that lasted from October 1973 to June 1974—Dow plants continued to run at near capacity throughout the embargo. Dow at the time controlled 50 percent of the pipelines that carried fuel and feedstocks to the company's plants, and produced 80 percent of its own power. Ben Branch gave much of the credit for the foresight that put Dow "in control of its own destiny" in this crisis to J. M. "Levi" Leathers, who had been preaching the twin advantages of (1) having your own oil reserves and (2) initiating a serious energy conservation campaign.[6] Fuel and hydrocarbon costs tripled and quadrupled in the five years before 1974, but for several years Dow was able to operate on oil and gas that it had contracted for at precrisis prices, a program that Leathers had conceived and engineered.

Another hero of that triumph over adversity was Robert S. Spencer of the Physics Lab. As Whiting described it:

> About 1968 we asked Bob Spencer, one of those brilliant analytical brains, to do a forecast of the cost of oil and gas in the future. He said that long term it's not going to be at all determined by the cost of producing oil and gas from the ground; it's going to be determined by the marginal cost of finding new reserves. He may have been the first in the industry to see this. Gas was selling for 25 cents a thousand cubic feet at the time. Out of his analysis he came up with the conviction that $2 a thousand was the cost of finding gas, and there was no way anybody was going to stay in business selling gas for 25 cents and paying $2 to replace it. We said, "Right, but this insight will never be accepted by the Texas Division." We found out which businesses in Dow the price of the hydrocarbon raw material was important to. Gerry Decker, in his nonthreatening fashion, went around and talked to all the business managers about that, and in the course of a year converted all of the business managers to the notion that natural gas was going to cost a dollar a thousand cubic feet or more in the future, and they better do their business planning on that basis. The business managers came back and said, "We're doing our plans that way, but our plans can't be implemented unless the marketing people believe it." So then we took another year talking to all the marketing people in the energy-sensitive products, and at the end of that year the marketing people

said, "You're right, but we can't do anything about it unless our customers believe it." So in Year Three Decker was on the road almost all year talking to the customers about how we weren't going to raise prices today but it was absolutely inevitable that the price of chemical products had to be raised. That was 1972, and in 1973 the great oil crisis came along; hydrocarbon prices went through the ceiling. You know whose customers were ready to accept the price increase—Dow's. That was also the year in which Dow became the most profitable chemical company in the world, by sheer coincidence.[7]

In 1972 Dow had begun operating the Wanda Petroleum Company, a gas liquids processor that it purchased from Ashland Oil, Incorporated, and became 30 percent owner of the Oasis Pipeline Company, operator of a big 36-inch pipeline from west Texas to Houston, to insure a long-term gas supply for Freeport.

It also had been studying other sources of energy—coal, lignite, nuclear, geothermal. In 1972 the Atomic Energy Commission issued a construction permit to Consumers Power Company to build a nuclear plant at Midland. In 1974 the company bought an interest in the Magma Power Company at Los Angeles, whose subsidiary, Magma Energy, Incorporated, was then the only U.S. marketer of energy based on geothermal power, and initiated a program to develop geothermal energy sources based on that company's technology. Robert E. Reinker, a veteran Dow production executive, became its first manager of Geothermal Operations.

In Canada the company teamed up with Dome Petroleum, one of Canada's largest exploration firms, to develop new sources of oil and gas in western Canada. This program was successful in finding new reserves, assuring long-term supplies of natural gas for use as feedstock and fuel at the Fort Saskatchewan site, a $1.5 billion world-scale petrochemical project it was building in Alberta. "The Fort" went into production in 1980.

A measure of the company's success in the oil patch was provided in its 1981 annual report. Forty years after its first venture into the field it noted that at the end of 1981 its proven oil and gas reserves amounted to 40.5 million barrels of oil and 702.5 billion cubic feet of gas, in the United States and Canada.[8]

The end of Dow's career as its own well driller and oil producer arrived shortly thereafter with startling swiftness. On September 30, 1982, Dow sold its U.S. oil and gas holdings to the Apache Petroleum Company (or APC) for $402 million. In exchange Dow received first rights to feedstock supply and agreed to purchase 75 percent of the gas produced from the properties. The agreement also covered the funding of future drilling. Paul Oreffice, then the chief executive, spoke of the need for "flexibility" of hydrocarbon and energy supply. He also spoke of the intensive campaign to reduce the company's debt load, which had reached a high of $5.2 billion in 1980 and was now down to $3.8 billion.

The heavy load of hydrocarbon costs began to ease over the succeeding years. In 1981 it had amounted to 37 percent of Dow's costs; by 1986 it was down to 25 percent. The company was changing its strategy, and the curtain was falling on Dow's career as independent player in the oil patch.

1. N. D. Griswold and J. P. Bryan, Report, "Gas Requirements and Supply," Texas Division, The Dow Chemical Company, June 30, 1947.
2. *Dow and the Oil Patch, a History of Brazos Oil and Gas 1946-1974*, booklet, Oil & Gas Division, Dow Chemical USA, 1974.
3. Ibid.
4. Oral History, Macauley Whiting, August 13, 1990.
5. Oral History, Earle B. Barnes, October 22 and November 11, 1988.
6. Annual Report, The Dow Chemical Company, 1973.
7. Oral History, M. Whiting,
8. Annual Report, The Dow Chemical Company, 1981.

president, and there was a lot of Texas influence in Washington. They wanted Beutel to get into that."[38]

Beutel stumped back and forth from Midland to Washington to Freeport for the next few years, thrust into the unfamiliar role of supersalesman, putting Dow on the map as a government supplier; the U.S. government had become the world's leading purchaser of almost everything, including chemicals. He finally retired in January 1971, and became a director emeritus after 55 years with Dow. Then he went back to Lake Jackson Farms; he said it was time to get his neglected cattle ranch straightened out.

In November 1972 he celebrated his 80th birthday. A week later he had a heart attack, and a week after that he was dead.

After he retired, the Texas Division renamed its big, rambling administrative building the A. P. Beutel Center and put up a bronze plaque in its lobby that reads: "Dr. A. P. Beutel, executive of The Dow Chemical Company for 55 creative years, 1916-1971. Initiator of the chemical industry's move to Texas and the Gulf Coast. Founder, among others, of Dow's Texas and Louisiana Divisions, organizer and president of Dowell. Forceful leader, tireless pioneer, dauntless builder."

He was full of honors and distinctions—vice president of the board of Texas A & M University, director of the First City National Bank of Houston, and regent of Lamar State College of Technology. "A very few men are truly great," the *Brazosport Facts* newspaper said in a farewell editorial. "He was one of them."[39]

IV.

Soon after Pearl Harbor day there was an urgent telephone call for Willard Dow. C. D. (for Clarence Decatur) Howe, Canada's Minister of Munitions and Supply, was on the line from Ottawa, wanting to know if Dow would help the Canadians meet the rubber supply emergency brought about by the lightning Japanese takeover of the Far East rubber sources. Canada would be in desperate straits without rubber, so it was moving as speedily as possible, he said, to build its own facilities to make synthetic rubber. Would Dow be willing to provide Canada its styrene know-how in this emergency, as it was doing for the U.S. government, and would Dow be interested in building a styrene plant in Canada as part of a Canadian project? Willard Dow immediately expressed enthusiasm for the idea and said the Dow company would help in any way it could.

That conversation was the beginning of Dow Chemical Canada, Inc. In February 1942, a Canadian government delegation came to Midland, led by John R. (Jack) Nicholson, Deputy Comptroller of Supplies, to meet with Dow and his colleagues. An operating agreement was signed on May 1 inaugurating Dow's cooperation with Polymer Corporation, the crown corporation newly organized as the parent firm in the rubber project. The charter of incorporation was issued in Ottawa on June 5, and the first meeting of Dow Chemical of Canada's board of directors convened in Midland on July 2.[40]

Plans closely following the lines of Dow's Midland styrene plant were hastily drawn up and several acres of the 130-acre Polymer plant site on the St. Clair River at Sarnia, Ontario, were assigned to the unit. On August 2 bulldozers moved in and began clearing the heavily wooded styrene plant site.

Willard Dow became the first president of the fledgling firm, with Leland I. Doan as secretary and George Hemmerick as treasurer. The other three directors—Earl W. Bennett, Mark E. Putnam, and C. J. Strosacker—were elected vice presidents. This board served through the war years. N. Russell Crawford arrived in January 1946 to become the second president of the firm.

Hemmerick, the first Dow Canadian, had been Dow's sole representative in Canada since 1926; he was a close friend of Leland and Ruth Doan's. (Leland Doan's second wife, Millie, was a sister of Mrs. Hemmerick.)

John Hacking, a Dow Canada pioneer, said Hemmerick "only had one product to sell, which was calcium chloride [used for settling road dust]. He came from Kitchener [Ontario], and he knew everybody there. Every spring, he had a great Dow Company party and had the road superintendents in from all over. They would sign contracts and he'd go back to Toronto until the next year. The competition in Windsor couldn't touch it; he had the whole market sewn up."[41]

Hemmerick, a civil engineering graduate of Queen's University, Kingston, had been an engineer for the highway department in Ontario before going to work for Dow, and claimed credit for having introduced super elevation to Canada on Ontario's first major highways. He inherited the job of general sales manager when Dow Canada was formed, but stayed in his Toronto office, where he was joined in 1946 by Crawford. The Toronto office soon came to be called "the three musketeers" by those in Sarnia (the third musketeer, with Crawford and Hemmerick, was Blanche E. Hewitt, executive secretary to the president, who had worked in the sales department at Midland before moving to Canada), and so it remained until one day in the late 1950s, when George Hemmerick dropped dead of a heart attack at the office.

John L. Smart, another Dow Canada pioneer, recalled Hemmerick's phenomenal memory: "He remembered people's names like you wouldn't believe. With people he hadn't seen for two or three years he would come out with some comment like, 'remember when we were talking about this subject?' He would pick up a conversation two or three years old. He had no real knowledge of chemistry, chemical engineering, or industry, but he was a good sales-man."[42]

Paul D. Scott remembered Hemmerick similarly: "All he did was sell calcium chloride for roads, attend all funerals and take a bottle of liquor along, and attend all weddings and take a bottle of liquor along. He was a high-class guy, but not exactly the present Dow sales type."[43]

Three operating companies were established to make up the Canadian rubber production team, one of which was Dow Canada, whose task was to build and operate a styrene monomer plant. The second was St. Clair Processing, a subsidiary of Imperial Oil, the name by which Standard Oil was known in Canada, whose task was to produce the butadiene and build and operate the service units. The third was Canadian Synthetic Rubber Ltd. (or CSR), a consortium of the big rubber companies—Goodyear, Goodrich, Firestone, and Dominion—whose responsibility was to design and build the polymerization facilities for making SBR, Styrene-Butadiene Rubber, from these components. Polymer Corporation was the overall coordinating firm.

Five thousand construction workers were hastily brought in, most of them French Canadians, to build the plants, and the early days were not without friction. "Up to this time there had been only one company in Sarnia," John Hacking said, "and that was Imperial Oil.[44] If you didn't work for Imperial Oil, you ran a grocery store. I was at a cocktail party one night, and the wife of one of the vice presidents told me, 'This was a nice place until you people came.' When the French Canadians walked down the street, the local people took a very dim view of them; they were set in their ways. Until then, French Canadians had been strangers in Sarnia."

Construction was to continue at a frantic pace in Sarnia for the next 10 years as the quiet river town was transformed into Canada's "chemical valley."

Hemmerick, as Dow's senior man in Canada, began looking for people. He hired Bernard A. Howard away from his job with an automotive firm in Sarnia to be Dow's accountant; Howard became a board member and the long-time treasurer of Dow Canada. As bulldozers began clearing the site for the plant in August and September of 1942, Steve Starks, Dow's recruiting expert, came over from Midland and Hemmerick and Starks began systematically to recruit engineers to work for Dow Canada.

The interviews took place in Hemmerick's small office at 159 Bay Street, Toronto. Within a few weeks they had hired 11 young Canadians to be the supervisors and technical experts for Dow Canada, and sent them off to Midland for training in styrene plant operation. Their training took place over a nine-month period while the plant was being built.

Paul Scott, one of the 11, said:

They were training a lot of people to run styrene plants in Midland at the time. They were training for Velasco, Texas, and they were training for California. They were training for Midland, too, because we were building a fair number of these plants for Rubber Reserve. I was there nine months. They did a lot of very, very basic stuff, which to me was a waste of time because I knew more about it than probably the guy who was doing the training. Various types of valves, a couple of control valves, welding, cutting with a torch physically with one of those outfits on, insulation work, general plant activities, with some time spent primarily in the styrene plant.[45]

Dow Canada grew from that core of pioneers. Within 10 years most of the 11 had moved into positions of leadership in the organization: Scott and Smart, classmates at the University of Toronto, became works manager and assistant works manager, respectively. Hacking, also of the University of Toronto, became superintendent of the styrene unit. Jack E. Harris, of the University of British Columbia, became works engineer. Jeffrey F. (Tup) Gilbert, of Queen's University, became superintendent of the chlorine, caustic, and brine treating plants built a little later. Fred Bremner, of the University of Toronto, became director of the central laboratory.

Five American technicians came over from Midland to help Dow Canada get started; Canadians, it had been agreed with the Canadian government, would take over the operations as soon as they could be trained. George W. Hooker, a brilliant, balding young group leader in the Physical Research Lab at Midland, was picked to be the leader of this group and became the first works manager of the Sarnia operation. With him went Stephen C. Stowe, his colleague in the Physics Lab, who became superintendent of the cracking and finishing stills in the styrene plant, and Roe E. Withrow, superintendent of Saran Polymerization in Midland, who became superintendent of the ethylbenzene unit in Sarnia. The first styrene was produced on July 15, 1943.

The plant was originally designed to produce 10,000 tons of styrene yearly, but it was not long before this capacity was regularly exceeded. During the second year of operation the Dow people were even able to convert one of the two ethylbenzene units to cumene (isopropylbenzene) production, critically needed for aviation fuel to improve its octane rating and as an antiknock. More than 10,000 tons of cumene was produced in addition to maintaining styrene production.

George Hooker, the Sarnia pioneers agreed, was an unusual person. "He was a very competitive person," Smart said. "He of course wanted to be the first in Canada to produce styrene. We were getting steam through pipelines that were almost half a mile long and the line was insulated only partway, but George insisted that we start up. So we fired it up, and we kept pushing the temperature higher. Eventually, the lining of the fire box collapsed, and the metal fell in. We had to rebuild the fire box. After that we got the lines insulated, which wasn't Dow's job."

"You have to understand the personality," Smart said. "George never played golf until he was in his late thirties or forties. He made up his mind he was going to win the club championship. He spent every minute he could in his backyard swinging a golf club. Two or three years later he won the golf championship. No one could ever divert him from what he wanted to do or from what he thought. I don't think they ever satisfied him, or could ever satisfy him. He left the company."[46] (In 1946 Hooker became manager of the General Chemical Company of Allied Chemical and Dye Corporation).

Hooker seems to have been well liked by the hourly employees of Dow Canada. When it became known he was leaving a letter dated March 25, 1946, was sent to Willard Dow, "from the hourly paid employees of Dow Chemical of Canada, Ltd.," signed by 58 of them, protesting Hooker's departure and asking if he couldn't be kept in his position. Willard Dow replied that "we have to keep our implied promises to the Polymer Corporation, to Jack Nicholson specifically, and through Jack to the . . . Canadian Government" to replace the loaned U.S. technicians with Canadians as soon as practicable. Hooker's post as works manager was taken over by Scott, who had been working as his assistant.

Well before the war was over Willard Dow was talking of a permanent Dow operation in Canada, not just a wartime emergency operation. He invited some of the Canadian trainees to his home in Midland in 1942 and talked to them about it. "This was his pet project," Scott said. "He wanted to build a plant outside of the United States. At one meeting Dr. Dow specifically told George Hemmerick and Mark Putnam and myself that he wanted to build a plant in Sarnia as Dow's first outside of the United States. He said it was going to be a peculiar venture because the country and the market weren't big enough, compared to the U.S. market."

The size of the operation was already a problem. "Dow Texas just laughed at the type and size of plant we had; they just laughed. Dr. Dow, in my personal opinion, had a vision of the Dow empire as it is today, all over the world. We used to kid that the only reason Dr. Dow wanted to get the Americans back to the States is that he didn't want Dutch Beutel to take over Canada as part of the Texas Division."[47]

About 1944, Smart said, "Dow decided they were going to build plants in Canada and have their own operation in Canada, as opposed to the government rubber operation. They employed the Austin Company to do some studies. They surveyed possible sites here (in Sarnia), around Hamilton, and in some other places, but because some operations and organizations already were here, they decided to expand here."[48]

When the war was over, C. D. Howe, now Canada's Minister of Reconstruction, was asked what the future of Polymer Corporation was going to be in the postwar era, and he responded that Polymer would carry on; and since Dow Canada was part of Polymer, the message was that it was expected to carry on, too. The Dow Company began to look for land. It found a 113-acre tract adjacent to the Polymer plant and purchased it in 1946 from the Dominion Alloy Steel Corporation. It purchased 60 acres more from Polymer. Willard Dow and his board of directors already knew that they wanted to build a plant to convert the styrene they were making at Sarnia into Styron—polystyrene plastic—to serve the Canadian market.

Up to this time polystyrene plastic was made in batches by the "can" process: the monomer was poured into an 80-pound tin and immersed in a water vat where it polymerized. Once polymerized it was taken out, smashed up with sledge hammers, and ground up. By the end of the war Dow researchers were ready with plans for a continuous process plant, and Dow Canada became the "guinea pig" for the first continuous process polystyrene plant. The first product came through the grinders in February 1947, and the plant was a smashing success.

The Monsanto company won the postwar race to be the first peacetime maker of polystyrene in Canada, bringing a "can" plant onstream in Montreal well ahead of Sarnia in the fall of 1946. Bert Hillary, who was then superintendent of plastics operations in Sarnia, said "it hurt us very badly because they were six months ahead of us, but their product wasn't as good, being made by the old can process, so we were able to whip the pants off them. That was one of my objectives, to squash Monsanto. I'm a competitive cuss when I get mad."[49]

The Styron plant went onstream in 1947, a new glycols plant in 1948, a chlorine/caustic plant in 1949, and a solvents plant in 1951. Dow Canada sales grew from $2.3 million in 1947 to $11.2 million in 1949 and $21.1 million in 1951, three-quarters of it produced in Sarnia, the remainder shipped in from Midland.

By the end of the war Willard Dow had decided he needed to put a new man at the helm in Sarnia. It was growing like a mushroom, and he was unable to give it the time it needed. On a swing around the Western states he had met his old friend Russ Crawford, who was running Dow's styrene plant at Los Angeles, and on October 25, 1945, he wrote Crawford offering him the top job. "This company needs a man who is willing to spend the time and live in Canada and see the operation develop and grow," he wrote. "Would you be interested in taking over the job as President of the Company? . . . The whole thing is a pioneering project, with everything more or less starting from scratch, but there is a bigger picture involved than appears on the face of it."[50]

Crawford became president of Dow Canada as of January 2, 1946, and moved to Toronto. He brought with him Leroy D. Smithers, with whom he'd been associated since 1936, first at Dowell, in Tulsa, Oklahoma, then for a brief stint at Freeport, and finally at Torrance, in the Los Angeles area. Smithers became the works manager at Sarnia, and the three musketeers set up the headquarters office in Toronto. "I didn't know it at the time," Smithers said, "but first they asked Sam Ludington to go over to be the works manager at Sarnia; then they asked somebody else, but I've never been able to find out who. I guess they finally ran out of candidates."[51]

Smithers said, "Russ and I were just like brothers. He was much older, but we were just like brothers. He would slap me around once in awhile, but he'd take a lot of guff from me, too; it wasn't just a one-way street. We liked each other and we knew that. I think it was sort of a fore-gone conclusion I'd be there in some capacity, but as works manager I wasn't particularly well qualified. Fortunately I found out that a works manager doesn't have to know an awful lot of chemistry. We got along all right. Willard Dow said once that he thought it turned out real well."

"Russ knew everybody in the Canadian government," Smithers said, "and all the prominent businessmen, particularly the ones in Toronto. We had a staff house in Sarnia, and he would come and spend a long weekend at least once a month and go over everything that was being done. This was in a time when the plants were finished and not only operating well, but looking pretty decent. Russ wanted a very neat-looking plant. He was criticized at times for spending too much money on getting the plants neat. Russ always thought that if you planted a few green shrubs around the plant, it showed you weren't losing too many chemicals to the atmosphere."

Smart said Crawford was also responsible for getting the Dow name in front of "the industries we were interested in serving, like the pulp and paper industry." The old Dow Canada railway cars, he said, "had a big Dow Canada maple leaf logo on them, with Dow Chemical of Canada Limited in large letters on the side of the cars. The idea was to get Dow recognized by Canadian industry. I think he hoped these Dow billboards on wheels, sitting on railway tracks in the backyards of the industry people when something was delivered to them, would keep the name in front of a lot of people."[52]

"ICI [Imperial Chemical Industries], which was then CIL [Canadian Industries Limited, a joint venture of ICI and Du Pont], had a monopoly on sales of products like caustic and chlorine to anybody and everybody in Canada. We had to push them aside, and we did in a remarkably short period of time."

With only about 170 acres of land on which to build, Dow Canada was soon cramped for space. "Jack Nicholson and the Polymer people sold a strip of a hundred acres to Sun Oil, and Sun was going to building a refinery on it," Smithers said.[53]

It was going to be an awfully closely built area with Imperial Oil and Polymer and Dow and Sun all in that strip. Russ and Willard and others said, "We've got to buy that Sun property, not only for expansion but for other purposes." Russ called me one day and said, "Get Sun out of there." So I went down to Philadelphia to meet their people. All those guys with Sun are real nice guys. They told me that in truth the property they had in Sarnia was a bit too small for them, but that they weren't going to move unless we could find them a larger property on the river. The only possibility of doing that, and they knew it, was to deal with the Indian reservation in Sarnia. "If you can get some of that Indian reservation for us, we'll sell you our property," they told me.

I really didn't know how those reservations worked. The tribe owns the property, but the Indians themselves can get what they call locatee rights. They could hold those locatee rights as long as they lived, but they could never sell them because they have to get approval from the tribe. So if you want to buy any property, you have to buy off the locatees, and after you've reached an agreement with the locatees, then you've got to go to the tribe and offer them a price they think is reasonable. The meetings went on for a year or a year and a half. Every now and then I'd see some Indian marching down the hall, and he was looking for Mr. Leroy because there was something he didn't like. They did finally agree to sell, at a big price; Sun paid $10,000 an acre for 250 acres. It turned out Sun got a pretty good deal, but they thought they got screwed; they always said I could have gotten a better deal.

One night I was away and the front doorbell rang. Rosie [Mrs. Rosalie Smithers] went to the front door and there was a great big Indian. He had a little statue. He said the tribe had decided to give honorary membership to Mr. Smithers. So they agreed it was a big price, too, at that time. The Indians were always very nice to me.[54]

When Crawford retired in 1956 and went to live in Palos Verdes, California, Smithers succeeded him as president. He was to hold the office for 15 years, the longest tenure of any Dow Canada chief executive. Toronto remained the firm's marketing headquarters, but Sarnia now became the corporate as well as the manufacturing headquarters.

By an unusual turn of events Smithers became the first Dow Canada chief executive who was a Canadian citizen. In 1960 Canadian Prime Minister John Diefenbaker invited Smithers to join a Canadian group he sent to Europe to study the impact of the European Common Market on Canada, and after the trip Smithers made a lengthy tour of Canada speaking on that subject. Two years later Diefenbaker wanted to appoint him to a national Productivity Council he was forming, and Smithers accepted.

"It turned out I couldn't be a member of that council as an American citizen," Smithers said, "so they sent a man right down to Sarnia to swear me in. It was very simple. I got to be a Canadian citizen without making much effort. As it turned out it wasn't very long after that that John Diefenbaker was whipped, and Lester Pearson, who succeeded him, didn't want a Productivity Council. That's how it happened."

The growth of Dow Canada continued through the 1960s. The company built a chlorine-caustic plant at Thunder Bay, Ontario, to serve the Great Lakes Paper Company, and a phenol plant at Ladner, B.C., near Vancouver, its first foray to the far west, to serve the plywood industry. Neither was very successful, and the phenol plant was eventually sold. More significantly, Dow Canada began looking for a site for a major chemical complex, and settled upon a location at Fort Saskatchewan.

Smithers felt the expansion at Ft. Saskatchewan "was probably the most history-making operation in Dow Canada history." John Smart, he said, "was the one that really scouted that area for more than a year, and he would narrow these sites down and then take me out and show them to me. We and a lot of other guys finally decided that Fort Saskatchewan would be the best location. It was close to the oil and it was right on top of a huge bed of salt. I think it's probably a better site for a plant now than Sarnia."[55]

Smart said the move was motivated by a long-range view of where the petrochemical industry might shift from the Sarnia area. "In Canada," he said, the petrochemical industry started in the Montreal/Shawinigan area. Salt was brought to these operations. A lot of the industry was based on acetylene from calcium carbide. Then ICI-CIL installed a plant in Windsor, where they eventually had unbelievable subsidence. A steel-and-brick building housed their chlorine compressors. When the subsidence took place, the center of the subsidence was two or three hundred yards from the building. The whole clay surface began to move, and the building split in two; one half of the building moved about 25 feet away from the other half. I looked at it because we thought we might have the same problem here in Sarnia. After that we moved all our wells from the manufacturing area to farmland three or four miles away. Ft. Saskatchewan was based on the availability of salt, gas, and ethylene.[56]

Then Dow bought Bradshaw's, a converter/packager operating in Toronto. "I don't know what got us into that one," Smithers said.

We saw this beautiful converting plant that Dow had bought in the States, located in Cleveland, called Dobeckmun. We decided we had to have something like that, so we bought Bradshaw's. It was kind of decrepit. It was in a part of Toronto that was hard to get to, and we went out to the edge of town and bought some property and built a brand new plant. Have you ever watched a converting plant? It's just fantastic the way these big rolls of plastic go through these machines and they cut them into little containers for razor blades, and all that sort of thing. But you never could make any money out of it.[57]

That was another business that Dow got out of.

The company used part of the Bradshaw property to build a polystyrene foam plant, which turned out to be very successful. At the same time it built a second polystyrene foam plant at Varennes, just outside of Montreal, which operates entirely in French, and is also a big success.

Dow Canada also became interested in locating a major chemical complex on deep water. Smithers said, "the best location for that in Canada would be in the Canso Straits, out in the Maritime provinces. We bought some property out there, and toyed with the idea of putting in a caustic-chlorine plant and maybe build a plant to produce some hydrocarbons. Clyde Boyd was excited about that for awhile, but it finally dropped out of the picture. It's not feasible."

Another enterprise was Rio Tinto Dow, a small venture near Toronto operated jointly with the Rio Tinto mining firm, prime mover in the Blind River uranium area, in the late '50s and '60s. Dow researchers had developed a process for extracting thorium, which coexists with uranium, from the waste liquors of the Rio Tinto uranium operation. Eager to solidify its position in mining chemicals, Dow had been doing research in flotation chemicals. A small pilot plant, about the size of a dining room table, was set up and successfully used the solvent extraction technique to produce a good quantity of thorium. But the plant never proceeded beyond the pilot plant stage. Smart said, "it turned out that the little pilot plant was going to produce all the thorium we were ever going to sell. We were going to sell it to Coleman for lanterns and that sort of thing, and we did, but basically there was no market for the stuff. There's just not enough hunters these days to support it."

Smithers recalled: "Rio Tinto Dow was just dissolved. Ted Doan called me one day and said, 'Roy, we've decided we're spending too much time on that, and we don't want to split our efforts. We're pulling out of it.'"

Fast as it was growing, Dow Canada was quite aware that Dow Texas was growing even faster, and that comparisons between the two were inescapable. A Texas visitor to Sarnia once called the Sarnia plant "Dow Canada's chemistry set." Smithers said,

> It seemed inevitable to me that a little country with 10 percent of the population of the United States couldn't really be considered very important. No matter what they did and no matter how well they did it, it still didn't make much impact on Dow's earnings. Once in a while I used to hear that Dow Canada ought to join the Dow Chemical Company. There was something to that because the Canadians did consider themselves different. They did not want to be a second Texas, no matter how hard you tried to sell them on the concept that it (Dow) was just one big happy family. This was before Dow had any operation much anyplace else, and it was impossible to convince them that they were to operate exactly like Texas when we were operating under different laws and in a different environment.

It stuck in the craw of Dow Canadians if they were treated differently from Dow Americans. When the Dow employee stock purchase plan was introduced in 1948, Dow Canada could not participate; there were legal problems in extending it beyond the U.S. border. Dow Canada missed the first two such annual plans before the legal problems were solved, and Dow Canadians have participated in the program since that time.

In 1969 Smithers joined the parent company board of directors. "Carl Gerstacker called me one day and said he wanted me to come over, and he said, 'I'm not going to bawl you out about anything this time,'" Smithers said. "When I got there he said they had decided to elect me to the board. I said, 'Well, that's what I always expected.' By that time I was really an old-timer. I had more seniority than most of those other guys on the board; I was sixty years old. That was before I had stumbled on mercury; I didn't have any black marks against my name."[58]

The mercury episode brought Dow Canada more front-page notoriety than it had gained in all the 27 years preceding it. Coming on the heels of the napalm controversy, which had kept Dow in the public eye almost constantly for three years, it caused deep groans in the headquarters offices of the company in Midland. The top officers of Dow felt they had been spending entirely too much time in those years fending off protesters and newshawks, and that it was high time they got back to running a chemical company.

It began when a Swedish graduate student, Norvald Fimreite, published a research paper showing that mercury, deposited in a body of water, could be taken up and accumulate in the bodies of fish as highly toxic methyl mercury compounds. This had not been known before;

indeed, the chemical engineering textbooks taught that for safety reasons spilled mercury should be flushed into the nearest body of water, where it sank to the bottom and remained inert. Fimreite's paper was also the first explanation of the mechanism that was causing the Minamata disease in Japan, where heavy eaters of fish from Lake Minamata had become victims of severe mercury poisoning.[59]

At about the time this paper was being published in English, in the summer of 1969—it had originally been published in a Swedish-language technical journal and went unnoticed—Smithers and Scott had decided to institute a program to button up on mercury losses from the chlorine plants. Len Weldon, Dow Canada general counsel, explained that

> they knew we were losing quite a bit of metallic mercury into the river. They decided to revamp the whole mercury system and put in more traps and screens. This was quite an active and comprehensive program to control and contain the mercury we were losing. However, the environmentalists wouldn't believe this. Back then, the government of Ontario didn't have a ministry of the environment. [It created one early in 1970.] That kind of problem was supposed to be looked after by the local sewerage supervisor. So there was no such organization. What was going on was going on solely on the initiative of management, not because government had said or threatened anything.
>
> Then our people became aware that the government was doing sediment sampling in the bed of the river downstream from our plant. We also became aware that the governments of Ontario and Quebec were meeting to discuss what could or should be done about the mercury problem in the St. Clair River. In March, the whole thing blew wide open. The government of Ontario accused us of a number of things, but in the summer of 1970 what received the most attention, certainly in the United States, was that the attorney general of Ohio brought a motion in the Supreme Court of the United States for leave to start a lawsuit in that court against Dow because of mercury pollution. That was a real bombshell.
>
> We had class action claims against us by groups of people in lower Michigan around Detroit; we had individual claims against us by individual fishermen from Lake Erie; we had a class action suit brought against us by a group of fishermen in Ohio; commercial fishing had been suspended and they were claiming loss of livelihood.[60]

In Midland, Ben Branch told the Dow board he wanted to abandon "all of our mercury cell activities," and take a book loss on them of $39 million. "That was Dow's unilateral decision," Branch said. "We were not going to take a chance that this could adversely impact the environment. As far as I know, we were the first ones to take any action of this sort, and it was under no pressure from anybody except our own conscience."[61]

"The following spring," Weldon remembered,

> Bill Groening and I sat at the counsel table in the Supreme Court of the United States as the Attorney General of Ohio argued his case that he should be allowed to start a lawsuit against

us in the Supreme Court. The Supreme Court rejected his request, and that put an end to that one.

The Ontario case dragged on for several years. The Ontario government kept changing their counsel. We were aware that the government was being told by their counsel that there was no basis in law for the government's claim. As the regulatory body, the government could regulate; they could do all sorts of things. They could even take away our license to manufacture chemicals. But there was no basis in law for the government of Ontario to sue us because of fish and wildlife. They could prosecute us, but they couldn't sue us in civil court for the mercury in the fish. Eventually, we became aware that the counsel for the government told the attorney general that he had no place to go with the case. We finally settled it for a relatively small amount of money.

Smithers recalled that prior to the mercury dust-up Dow Canada had regularly had an expert come in and take samples of the bottom of the St. Clair River, but mercury was not even on the checklist. "We were so certain that everybody was right, that mercury under water doesn't do anybody any harm, and that it is only when it evaporates into the air that it does, that it wasn't even in our minds at that time," he said.

When the mercury "bombshell" hit, Dow Canada had immediately closed down its mercury cells and buttoned up all the outlets to the river. "That was the best thing to do, the only thing we could do," Smithers said. "We couldn't let that stuff go into the river. I'm not sure to this day that we were the only contributor around there. I think there were a lot of other sources of mercury. But we were certainly the most visible and took the brunt of it."[62]

Bert Hillary, now the company's research manager, organized a trip to Europe to look at the latest research. "I took some senior technical men over to Sweden and Finland to get first-hand knowledge of what was up-to-date and what the Swedes thought," Hillary said.

The Swedes were the most important ones; they'd had the problem longer than anyone else, and they had done the key research. They were very helpful and very open and willing to share their knowledge. There were two from Midland and two from Sarnia who went on that trip— Howard Spencer from the Biochemical Laboratory, who handled the medical end of it; Bob Moolenaar from the Physics Lab, the technical strength on the mission; Jack Bristol, a chlorine man from Thunder Bay, a good, knowledgeable plant man; and myself. The Hillary Mission Report recommended a lot of things, but most importantly that Dow get out of the mercury cell business, as it soon did.[63]

Dow Canada was by far the largest mercury customer in Canada at this period, and mercury cost $76 per flask (a dollar a pound) and increased to more than $700 per flask over the 15-year period the company operated mercury cells. Paul Scott said:

Herbert H. Dow in 1897, the year he founded The Dow Chemical Company. He was 31 years old.

J. Henry Dow (1836-1901), Herbert Dow's father, a tinkerer and inventor dogged by financial difficulties.

Sarah Jane Bunnell Dow (1838-1909), Herbert Dow's mother.

Moses B. Johnson had Badge #1 in the Dow company. It helped that it was he who established the badge system.

Thomas Griswold Jr., Badge #2, married Herbert Dow's sister Helen and became a key figure in his brother-in-law's company.

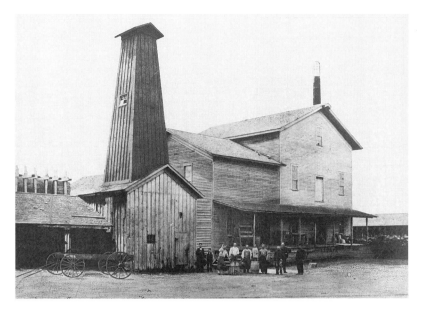

The Midland Chemical Co., Herbert Dow's first Midland venture, in the disused Evens Flour Mill which he leased, was founded August 12, 1890. Facsimile of this photo appears on Dow Chemical Company stock certificates.

The Dow Process Co., predecessor firm to Dow Chemical, located on the Ohio Canal at the southwest edge of Navarre, Ohio, July 8, 1896. The eight-foot fence was designed to protect the secrecy of the process Herbert Dow was developing here.

Dow headquarters group gathers around Albert E. Convers, first company president, 1901. Left to right: Herbert H. Dow, E. O. Cross, Fred N. Lowry, Convers, Joseph E. LeFevre, James C. Graves, D. Richardson, Earl W. Bennett, Thomas Griswold Jr., M. B. Johnson. Lowry succeeded Johnson as general plant superintendent.

The front-office staff, 1916, poses during a party marking departure of Rupert E. Paris, first sales manager of the firm. Left to right, first row: May Barclay Chichester, Gertrude Callahan, Carrie Smith, Winifred Thayer Morris, Mary Burrows Horton, Catherine Goodwin; second row: Clyde Bordner, Vera Hadsall Griswold, Roena Graves Lawn, Ethel McKay Yocum, Clara Turner (H. H. Dow's secretary), Frank Nelson, Carl Barnes. Back row: William Nash, William Bay, J. P. Holmes, Perley Wayne, Arthur Beckert, Joseph E. LeFevre, Thomas Griswold Jr., Herbert H. Dow, Charles Hunsaker, Arthur N. Patriarche, Fred N. Lowry, Norman A. Best, G. Lee Camp. Camp was Paris's successor.

Edwin O. Barstow, "father of magnesium."

Charles J. Strosacker, "father of saran."

James T. Pardee, early Dow backer, later Dow chairman.

Albert W. Smith, Dow's "connection" at Case.

"Graduation" photo of U.S. Army troops sent to Midland to manufacture mustard gas, at completion of their training period, May, 1918. Two of these men were killed in a tragic accident a month later. Joseph E. Ritzer is in middle of top row, slightly hidden. Nurse Winnifred Murphy, first Dow medical staffer, tended their mustard burns daily and the troops insisted she be part of the photo. The officers, seated, are Lieut. G. W. Van Arnam and Lieut. Gerald Thorp.

First Dow "Sales Meeting and Dinner", at the Midland Community Center, April 7, 1920. The four seated at right are Lee Doan, asst. sales manager; G. Lee Camp, sales manager; Ivan Harlow; and Earl W. Bennett. Seated, front row, left, J. E. LeFevre, purchasing director; Tom Griswold Jr.; and (fourth from left) Fred Lowry; seated, front row to right of post, E. O. Barstow, Sherman W. Putnam, and (with mustache) Ralph E. (Doc) Dorland, manager, New York office. Seated to left of flowers is Charles J. Strosacker. Standing, second from left, is Mark E. Putnam. Standing, fifth from right, Herbert Dow; standing sixth from right, John A. Panter. (Others not identified).

William J. Hale, the "Dizzy Dean of chemistry."

John J. Grebe, the "idea man."

Edgar C. Britton, "chemist's chemist."

William R. Veazey, a key Dow research director

Willard H. Dow, Herbert Dow's son and successor, president and CEO 1930-49, for whom the company's headquarters complex is named.

Ralph Hunter (Dow's senior electrochemical expert in Midland) kept telling us from day one that we should do something to recover the mercury, not from an environmental point of view but from an economic point of view. The reason we put mercury cells in first was the fact that we didn't have enough chlorine requirement to build a caustic evaporator. So we put mercury in; Dow wanted to see how a mercury cell operated. We had two small diaphragm plants (which don't use mercury), and then we built a large one, a thousand tons a day, in Sarnia, and got rid of the mercury cell plants both in Sarnia and in Thunder Bay.[64]

Before the mercury episode Dow Canada had been involved to some degree in the napalm and Agent Orange protests that raged in the late 1960s. Neither product was made in Canada, but many of the Canadian campuses were sympathetic to the anti-Vietnam War cause, and a substantial number of American university students went to Canada to escape the draft; Dow Canada became a focal point for these protests in Canada. Len Weldon recalled one such incident vividly:

At five o'clock one morning a time bomb went off in front of my house. It scared the devil out of the family; it was quite a serious thing. This was in November 1968. It shattered the glass, damaged the roof, and did other damage. It was a very loud explosion; people heard it all over the city. People were phoning the police station thinking one of the plants had blown up.

I think there were reasons I was a target. I was on city council then, and I was very well known in the community as a council member. The police uncovered evidence that the people who planted the bomb had been organizing to put bombs at the houses of some of the other Dow people as well. I lived in the city, in a quiet residential street, so it was just a fluke; my house probably represented the easiest one to get at.

The police were pretty sure who had done it, a group of students at the University of Waterloo, near Kitchener, Ontario, about 100 miles east of Sarnia. However, they could not get enough evidence to lay any charges.

There was an interesting sequel to it. A few months later I was sitting at my desk in Sarnia and I got a phone call from Hal Andresen, the manager of our Toronto regional sales office. He was from Denmark. Andresen said, "Len, I need some advice. I've got three people standing in front of my desk and they're telling me they're going to blow the office up unless I sign a document saying that Dow will stop making napalm. What should I do?" I told Hal, "Well, keep talking for a couple of minutes until I think of some way to handle this." He kept chattering away, making idle conversation, and then he said, "Look, we've got to do something. These guys are still here." Our office then was on the eighth floor of a big office building in downtown Toronto. While we were talking I suddenly remembered that the headquarters of the Metropolitan Toronto Police Department was in an office building about 200 yards away. So I told Andresen, "Hal, tell these guys the Toronto police have been notified, and they have three minutes to get out of the office." I assumed people involved in that kind of work would know where police headquarters was and that they'd think it wasn't an idle threat. He told them that, and they immediately got out of there.

Many years later, around 1985, I was talking to our security man in Sarnia, and telling him this story, and he started to laugh. He had not been with the company during the 1960s. He told me, "About a month ago I was in Toronto talking to the police department about some security problems, and the guy I was talking to told me this same story. He said he was one of the three people standing in front of Hal Andresen's desk at the time. He was an undercover policeman who had been put into the organization." So some 17 years later I heard the sequel; there was a policeman standing there.[65]

The strain of all these events had begun to tell on Roy Smithers; the last few years of his tenure were difficult for him, as well as for Dow Canada. Smithers himself said:

I had asked Ben (Branch) three years before to fill in behind me in some way; I'd been there too long. You don't realize how it begins to get you down. This was even before mercury. I was just tired. I don't think they should ever let a guy be president of any of their operations that long again. You're called on continuously to speak, to be at two places at the same time, and you don't know whether you're doing right to turn them down or accept. I was very much ready to retire.[66]

"There were a lot of problems, like the mercury crisis, and we made a number of corporate acquisitions, some of which went badly," Weldon said. "Roy was under an enormous amount of pressure toward the end of his term. I think it affected his personality and his style of management. The last two or three years he was here, I felt unhappy more frequently than I had previously. Roy was a victim of events. The company and he were overtaken by quite a number of serious things that were very difficult to manage. I think Roy started to suffer from the strain and in the last couple of years he had a great deal of difficulty."[67]

Virtually everyone in Dow Canada expected that Smithers would be succeeded by Paul Scott, who had been his alter ego and right-hand man since 1950. When Scott was sent to the Harvard University Advanced Management Program in 1970 it was widely perceived as a prep course for taking on the top job. Scott said,

I was too old to take that course. I was just worn out because from the time I finished school all I'd been doing is building plants, starting plants up, operating plants, going through the national crises, and what I wanted was to get away from things. I had planned to retire when I was 55. I was supposed to be a candidate to replace Smithers. For years prior to (Smithers's retirement) I was supposed to do an awful lot of world traveling in Dow so that my Dow profile worldwide would be higher than it was. I'd worked in Texas, I worked in Midland twice, but it was still pretty low. I didn't do that, probably because I was negligent, and to make a long story short I was not appointed president.

They brought Clyde Boyd in, who was a very good selection for the job because they wanted a new face, new ideas, and a lot of changes. It would have been almost impossible for me to have put those into effect, having worked with some of these people for 30 years. They wanted to change several people who had not been winning any popularity contests in Midland. The concept was that Dow Canada was no longer going to be a separate entity where they had their own freedom, more freedom than Europe had, more freedom than anybody else in the whole corporation had. That wasn't going to be the case. They were going to be part of the company, and there was going to be a broad exchange of people coming into Canada from other parts of Dow, and going out to other parts. There was very, very little of that during Smithers's tenure. The reason I went down to Harvard was that they thought I should go somewhere. Actually, I was scheduled to move to Midland and take Dave Schornstein's job, as manager of organics, when he moved down to Coral Gables to take over Dow Latin America. But I had a sick mother here in Sarnia and I knew I was going to take early retirement, so I asked to be relieved of that, which was not received too well. I knew there was no way I could make some of the changes that Ben Branch, in particular, wanted made in the Canadian operation. It just wouldn't work that way and I didn't have the support in the States that somebody like Clyde Boyd, who had come up through the system, had. He did anything he wanted over here in Canada, whereas I'm sure I couldn't have.[68]

On March 11, 1971, Clyde H. Boyd was named president of Dow Canada, and a new era began. Dow Canada would never be the same again. [Smithers became board chairman on that date and retired two years later, on his 65th birthday]. The charge started with a housecleaning. By one authoritative count, of the top management group of 18 persons, only 3 were still in place two years later.

"The autonomy that we had disappeared out the window," Scott said. "The informality that we had gone to a lot of trouble to build up with regard to management meetings every Monday or every second Monday, which were very informal, almost coffee sessions, became very formal meetings with formal presentations and big slide presentations, which were just excellent and should have been done, no question about it. But we had not done it, favoring a more family type of Sarnia operation." One of Boyd's early acts was to eliminate the traditional Dow Canada emblem, the Dow diamond superimposed on a maple leaf, in favor of the plain Dow diamond used by the company worldwide.

Like the parent Dow Chemical Company, Dow Canada has had its share of controversial personalities. Boyd, who was one of them, was both admired and reviled during his tenure in Canada. Scott recalled:

He was received pretty much as a cold potato. Some people said he was just a breath of fresh air, and some people, if they're honest with you, would say they hated his guts. Clyde was a tough nut; he was a real pro. He gave up his family life for Dow Chemical. His family just went to hell. He went seven days a week, 24 hours a day, as most of us in Dow Canada were doing, but we made sure the family came in somewhere. This is not a kick against Clyde because I think we got along fine. We're entirely different people. He was very, very detailed; very, very technical; very analytical. I've been trained that if you haven't got time for all that stuff you're going to have to skip over it and make a decision and if you're right 52 percent of the time you're a success, and if you're not right, we'll move somebody else in.

We had been pretty much spoiled because promotion worked from within here. Without Dr. [Willard] Dow saying it, I think that's what he wanted. He didn't want people from another area coming into a different country. But the moment Clyde came, almost automatically there was a floodgate opened up where it became a much better company. Communications were better, we were better received in Midland, we were received with almost open arms on almost any subject. And there was a lot more interchange of people, talent coming here, talent leaving here, as part of a worldwide network. Canada is now a Dow family company instead of a little subsidiary in Canada wagging the tail.[69]

One of the more traumatic departures was that of John Smart. He and Boyd had been at odds for years, ever since Smart had recommended against expansion of an operation in Texas then headed up by Boyd. "He apparently took this as a personal matter," Smart said. "When he came to Sarnia he said he didn't want to work with me. I was essentially turfed out."[70] Smart, who was 55 at the time, went to work for Bechtel Canada and spent two years in Japan as representative of that firm.

By the time Boyd left Sarnia—he was tapped to be president of Dow Europe in the fall of 1975, after only four and a half years there—the transformation was largely accomplished; Dow Canada had become part of the worldwide Dow Company. A world-scale chlorine/caustic unit had gone onstream in Sarnia, and Ft. Saskatchewan was launched on a major expansion program that would also make it a world-scale chemical producer. Dow Canada was on a new track, becoming a player in the international chemical markets.

The controversial Boyd was succeeded by the equally controversial Robert E. Naegele, a hard-driving, colorful Ohioan who had been serving as general manager of the company's combined agricultural and organics department in Midland. He was later remembered in Sarnia for such unusual habits as wandering about the headquarters in his stocking feet.

"Canada had been a closed-door operation until Clyde Boyd arrived there," Naegele said.

Nobody here (in Midland) knew what was going on; nobody there (in Sarnia) wanted them to. Clyde got part of that started (on the road to change), and he also ran into some potential opportunities for Dow Canada to expand. None of them had been put together by the time I arrived. We spent over a billion dollars in three years in Canada. That was a lot of money. I think that's more money than had ever been spent on any one project in the company before then. We put in world-class ethylene crackers in Alberta. We built them and ran them, but we had to allow somebody else to own them because that was part of getting the permit. We let a Canadian company own the ethylene plant; we built the downstream facilities.

We built a pipeline that ran to Sarnia; it was the longest chemical pipeline in the world, 1900 miles long. You slugged propane and ethane, and we slugged ethane down there and took off cuts of ethylene, then ethane on both sides and propane in the middle. They'd take propane off, and they'd take ethane off for fuel or upgrading, and we'd get the ethylene in Sarnia. Fort Saskatchewan became a major production facility; until then, it had been a little caustic soda and chlorine facility.

Clyde had opened the door a little, but the Canadians still were quite standoffish to the rest of the company. They still hadn't accepted how good they could be. I saw that the mission of building this organization was to convince these people they were extremely capable folks, capable of doing a lot more than they'd been doing, and to convince them to trust the rest of the company. We tried very hard at that and I think we accomplished most of it, except for Cliff Mort. Cliff was very instrumental in getting Dow going, but he had things so complicated and interwoven that it was extremely difficult to follow where he was going. He was the vice president of development and was the main person in the negotiations that put together the partnerships that built Western Canada [Western Canada Division, which also included the Ladner Works, had been established in the Boyd era]. Cliff did leave the company; he became a director and consultant for Nova, in Sarnia.[71]

Weldon felt that

when Boyd came, we needed Clyde Boyd. The situation desperately needed someone with his strength and perseverance. Somebody had to make a lot of changes, which he did. Once the changes were made, you needed somebody to create harmony and a sense of direction and a pulling together. Again, to the credit of the people in Midland, Bob Naegele was exactly the person; you couldn't have found a better person. He was personable; he was good-natured; he was willing to stand back and let everybody do their job.

A lot of people aren't comfortable with, "Well, go ahead and do your job. You do it whatever way you want." They like to be told how to do their job. If you were that kind of person, Bob Naegele was not your guy, but if you were willing to take on the risk of doing your job the way you thought it should be done, if you enjoyed the freedom to operate, then Bob Naegele was the perfect individual.[72]

Naegele had an inexhaustible repertoire of jokes and stories, many of them off-color, with which he would regale company meetings and social events, in the process scandalizing many of the Dow Canada wives. Scott recalled: "Naegele didn't win many popularity contests because he was pretty vulgar. Particularly the wives didn't like him."

When Naegele was named Dow Canada president at the end of 1975, Zoltan Merszei was named board chairman. As it turned out, the Canadians were not to see much of Merszei; a few months later he became president and CEO of the parent company. Merszei had come to Canada after WWII as a Hungarian refugee, and had taken Canadian citizenship. Smithers recalled his arrival in Dow Canada:

Zoltan just marched into Russ Crawford's office in Toronto one day, introduced himself and said he could speak any language. He wanted a job, and Russ hired him. He stayed in Toronto awhile, and then Russ called me and said, "I want Zoltan to come down and meet all the guys at Sarnia, and I want him to stay there two or three months and get acquainted with what's going on." Then he went back to Toronto where he worked in the sales office and he was very successful. He was damn good. Clayton Shoemaker found Zoltan and demanded he be transferred to the export department, so he went to work for Clayt Shoemaker. Zoltan just went from there. He always said he was coming back to Canada, but he never did.[73]

In November 1979, the company made tall headlines again through its involvement in the largest evacuation that ever occurred in Canada, after the great Mississauga train derailment. Dow Canada had a couple of tank cars of chlorine on a freight train that was heading into Toronto at about 60 miles an hour one night when it derailed in Mississauga, a Toronto suburb. The derailment was caused by a defective lubricating system on a tank car that did not belong to Dow. The train piled up with tank cars one on top of the other. Several of the cars carried propane, and one of them caught fire. The Dow chlorine cars were damaged and were leaking, and to make matters worse, several propane cars were piled on top of the Dow chlorine cars, and they were on fire.

"This happened right in the middle of a community of 300,000 people on the edge of Toronto," Weldon said.

The police declared a state of emergency; 300,000 people were evacuated from their homes. They closed off the whole area, and it took two or three days just to put out the fires; they couldn't start to do anything about containing the leaky chlorine cars until the fires were put out. It was a terrible mess. It was a big event politically, socially, environmentally, and in every other way. We established a Dow communications center and it was there for perhaps a month. We sent a team of emergency people to deal with it, and it's not an overstatement to say that the leader of the Dow team was heroic; he went through the burning propane cars to investigate what could be done about the chlorine cars.

When everything was back in order again the fire department of the region gave a private testimonial dinner to the courage of our Dow team, on its own. It was a very impressive affair. The only people who went were the firemen and our workmen who had been directly involved. They presented them with firemen's helmets, and they were most flattering in their praise of the way our people had performed.

It was a massive, and I think the largest and most successful evacuation of a municipality ever.[74]

Naegele was succeeded in 1980 by Jim Hay, the first native-born Canadian to head up the company. In that same year the Canadian company reached a major milestone—it hit $1 billion in annual sales for the first time. A series of world-scale plants went onstream in the West to produce chlorine/caustic, vinyl chloride monomer, and ethylene oxide and ethylene gly-col. The company opened a West Coast Distribution Center in Vancouver to supply Dow's Pacific area markets.

"There was a great amount of enthusiasm when Jim became president," Weldon said. "He was not only popular as an individual, he was respected. Everybody was quite happy with Jim, because they felt he would be able to adapt corporate policy, to whatever degree was neces-sary, to the Canadian business environment. Jim was one of those people who grew into his job. With every promotion Jim received, he became better after the promotion. He had unlimited ability to expand and develop."

Hay and the company were immediately faced with major problems. In 1981 the Canadian government clamped price controls on the Dow company's products, and everyone else's, through what was called the Anti-Inflation Board, and imposed taxes on its feedstocks, and everyone else's, through the National Energy Program. By 1982 an economic recession was in full swing across Canada. As a result, much of Jim Hay's tenure as CEO was given over to cost-cutting programs to cope with the triple whammy of the AIB, the NEP, and the recession.[75]

In January 1983 Hay moved on to a Midland job as vice president for energy and hydro-carbon supplies for the parent company, and James D. Hembree, a group vice president, came to Sarnia as its new president. Hembree, in the words of one Sarnia observer, "was a square peg put in a round hole," who, "never quite seemed to fit the job." He continued the fight to boost profits and emphasized "doing it right the first time."

Hembree decided the president of Dow Canada should have an official residence, and pro-ceeded to build an enormous one. Dow Canadians found this an odd idea, something no Canadian would do, and the "residence" was laughed to an early death. Hembree elected to take early retirement in January 1986, at age 57, and was succeeded by David T. Buzzelli, the company's public affairs vice president in Midland.

Buzzelli's experience in public affairs immediately became useful because the Canadian com-pany was facing a new environmental crisis, one of the strangest in the company's history, referred to by newspapermen and the public as "The Blob." The word came from the title of a Steve McQueen horror movie of the time and from a government scuba diver who was doing sediment sampling in the St. Clair River in front of the long string of plants, including Dow, known as the "chemical valley," in 1984. "Somewhere in the general area of our plant, in the bed of the river, the diver found a small block of river sediment in a soft lump," Weldon said.

It seemed like an accumulation of heavy oil or grease or something like that which had col-lected a bunch of sand in it. He didn't find anything else in the area; he just found this one thing, which was somewhat larger than his hand. His report appeared in the early spring of 1985 and he used the term "blob" to refer to this. The only explanation most of us could think of for the later reference to "blob" was that Dow was being accused of putting perchloroethylene, a dry cleaning fluid, into the water at the time his report came out. The diver who had done the inves-tigation issued his report at the same time the report on our perchloroethylene contamination came out. Some reporter picked up the word "blob" from this report and used it to refer to the perchlor situation. It had nothing to do with the situation at all; it had to do with the discovery the year before. That's how the blob problem came to be identified in that way; and of course, the word "blob" is much easier to use in a newspaper headline than perchloroethylene. (In August, 1985, Dow Canada had accidentally spilled about 5,000 gallons of perchloroethylene into the river, had admitted it, and within days had begun a cleanup process.)

It was a horrendous thing. We had some criminal charges laid against us, the first ones we had ever had in Dow Canada history.[76]

When they went to court, Dow Canada pleaded guilty to the charges of spilling perchlor brought against it by the Ontario Ministry of the Environment. The company offered to continue its cleanup efforts, and by the spring of 1986 had cleaned most of the river bottom by a vacuuming process it developed.

"Buzzelli was very popular and did a tremendous job to repair the bad reputation we had as a result of this so-called blob," Scott said. "He was very generous with money, and he just did a tremendous job in the community. I think a lot of people were sorry to see him go."[77]

By the 1990s—Denis Wilcock, a Briton, came from Dow Europe to succeed Buzzelli at the helm in 1990, and Graham Sweeney, a South African, took over in 1993—Dow Canada was reaching maturity and vigor. In 1972 it had moved into a handsome new headquarters building outside Sarnia, the Modeland Centre, to which other units were added over the years—part of the new Dow Canada that had emerged in the Boyd era. Situated off the highway in a landscaped park, it set a new tone for the company. Bert Hillary, who picked the site and was involved in its development, also was a key person in the development of the Dow Canada art collection, which has brought the company recognition as one of the leaders in the collection of Canadian art.

"The architects were making some good suggestions," Hillary said,

and we traveled around looking at art with them, Boyd and myself and the architects. It developed into a collection of Canadian art, and a very good collection. I thought that if we were going to do business in Canada we should have Canadian art hanging around, including Eskimo and Indian pieces, rather than Mexican art or something else. My wife, Sylvia, was my mentor; she has a fair amount of good formal education in art.

We did all the selecting of the nearly 200 pieces of art in the Modeland Centre. It grew from there. We selected some for the offices in Horgen (Dow Europe headquarters in Switzerland). After that, in all of the Canadian offices and some of the plants. Some of the individuals in Midland wanted some of this art, too.

After Hillary retired in 1976, he and Sylvia moved to London, Ontario. "We enrolled in the university and decided to take art, and we've taken every art course at the University of Western Ontario."[78]

In 1992 Dow Canada began a new chapter of integration into the world at large with the establishment of Dow North America, which combined Dow's operations in Canada, the United States, and Mexico a full two years before the establishment of NAFTA, the North American Free Trade Agreement. Established in Midland, the North American Area took over many of the functions of the previously separate national headquarters.

The Modeland Center, headquarters of Dow Canada, began to shrink rapidly and by the mid-1990s its population had been halved, to about 400. Dow Canada was meeting the grim realities of international competition.

Roy Smithers, key figure in the first half-century of Dow Canada, died in Boca Raton, Florida, in September 1991. Asked a few months before his death how he felt Dow Canada was doing, he said: "I think they're doing better than any other chemical company in Canada."

Notes

1. C. W. Jones to H. H. Dow, September 30, 1912.
2. H. H. Dow to A. E. Convers, April 2, 1928.
3. See Harrison Hatton, Notes on conversation with Willard H. Dow, March 28, 1949.
4. Hatton, Notes on conversation with W. R. Veazey, January 24, 1951.
5. W. H. Dow to M. C. Schwartz, Louisiana State University, March 29, 1944.
6. Sheldon B. Heath, Director, Chemical Engineering Laboratory, The Dow Chemical Company, "Io-Dow Makes the United States Self-Sufficient in Iodine," *Pacific Chemical and Metallurgical Industries*, November 1937, pp. 7-9. See also Karpiuk, *Dow Research Pioneers*, 473-82.
7. DN (2-cyclohexyl-4,6-dinitrophenol) was produced in several formulations called DN Dust, DN Dust D-8, DN Dust D-4, and DN Dust D-8 with Cryolite. The active ingredient was made in Midland and shipped to Seal Beach for compounding. It should also be noted that Kagy originated the Dow K-List; experimental chemicals sent to him at Iowa State for analysis were listed as "K-1," "K-2," etc.
8. Hatton, Notes on Conversation with W. R. Veazey, October 31, 1950.
9. H. H. Dow to C. F. Kettering, president, General Motors Chemical Co., Dayton, Ohio, July 18, 1923.
10. See Whitehead, *The Dow Story*, 103-9. For an account of the search for an antiknock compound, see Williams Haynes, "Petroleum and Tetraethyl Lead," *American Chemical Industry: A History*, 4:390-406. See also Hatton, Notes on conversation with Charles J. Strosacker regarding Ethylene Dibromide history, May 15, 1950.
11. According to Donald L. Conner of the Dow Legal Department, at this first meeting the Pure Oil visitors said they wanted to treat one of their wells with hydrochloric acid but their boss had said no, the acid would ruin the casing. On the spur of the moment John Grebe said, "Why not inhibit the acid?" Within a few minutes Grebe had worked out figures showing how much damage would be caused by various amounts of acid inhibited by various means.
12. Articles of Incorporation of Dowell, Inc., November 9, 1932; Minutes of first meeting of board of directors of Dowell, Inc., November 12, 1932.
13. Minutes of meeting of board of directors, Dowell, Inc., May 7, 1953.

14. Ibid., June 28, 1933.

15. Hatton, Notes on Conversations with Donald L. Conner, January 26 and 29, 1951.

16. Oral History, Sylvia G. Stoesser, August 17, 1990. See also Robert S. Karpiuk, *Dow Research Pioneers, 1897-1949*, 239-48, 363-91.

17. Hale had been having long conversations about cellulose with his close friend Charles H. Herty, a cellulose chemist, and these appear to mark the origin of Dow's interest in this field, which ultimately led it into plastics.

18. See "Cliffs Dow Chemical Company, Personal Experiences of Gilbert J. Ward, 1936-1945," unpublished ms., October 22, 1991, Post Street Archives.

19. See R. Wesley Jenner, "Cliffs Dow Chemical Company, A Narrative of Background, Formation and Operation," paper presented to joint meeting of Sigma Xi Club, Northern Michigan University, Marquette, Michigan, and the Marquette County Historical Society, June 27, 1979; and miscellanous materials from James Runyon, Allan F. Olson, and other former employees of Cliffs Dow Chemical Company.

20. Haynes, *American Chemical Industry: A History*, 3:21-22. Bush had studied the possibility of a West Coast chloralkali plant for Hooker several years before leaving the firm. He retired shortly after World War I and became executive manager of Presbyterian Hospital, New York. Bush, Beach & Gent dissolved in 1924.

21. Oral History, Robert D. (Barney) Barnard, February 21, 1989.

22. Oral History, Robert G. Heitz, September 26, 1988.

23. Much of this material is derived from Gib Gray, ed., *Dow in the West, 1916-1976* (Pittsburg, Calif.: Dow, 1976).

24. *Dow Western* (employee publication) 6, no. 9 (Jan.-Feb. 1980).

25. Oral History, Barney Kriner, September 19, 1988.

26. Oral History, Alfred T. Look, October 2, 1990.

27. Michael Storper and Barbara Des Rochers, "Can a Quiet Agricultural County on the Sacramento River Find True Happiness With a Huge, Messy Chemical Plant?" in *Not Man Apart*, newsletter of Friends of the Earth, March 1976.

28. Christopher J. Duerksen, *Dow vs. California, a Turning Point in the Envirobusiness Struggle* (Washington, D.C.: Conservation Foundation, 1982) includes a chronology and much other useful information concerning this episode. The author is particularly indebted for the quotations from Jack Jones, now deceased, who was interviewed extensively by Duerksen.

29. Beutel citations in this section are derived from Oral History, Albert P. (Dutch) Beutel, transcription of a series of interviews by Don Whitehead, 1967.

30. "Survey of the Industrial Qualifications of Cities of the Gulf Coast Area," The Austin Company, April 10, 1939, and "Survey of the Industrial Qualifications of Freeport, Texas" Noel H. Hick, The Austin Company, September 30, 1939, Post Street Archives.

31. McGranahan, the company's highly regarded assistant chief engineer in Midland, was promoted to Texas Division plant manager but Beutel retained the authority, and when a few months later Beutel moved permanently to Freeport, McGranahan became one of his assistants. After the war McGranahan left the company and joined Glenn McCarthy's Shamrock Oil Company in Houston.

32. Oral History, Vernon A. Stenger, April 13, 1993. Stenger maintained that T. Melville (Mel) Hess first detected the presence of boron in the cell feed using emission spectroscopy, and that his role has been insufficiently recognized. See also the account of the boron episode in Karpiuk, *Dow Research Pioneers 1897-1949*, 571-74.

33. Much of this material is derived from documents held by the Lake Jackson Historical Association in Lake Jackson, especially in its A. P. Beutel Room, where material concerning Beutel has been assembled.

34. Oral History, Earle B. Barnes, October 22 and November 11, 1988.

35. Oral History, A. P. Beutel.

36. Oral History, E. B. Barnes; See also Oral History, David L. Rooke, October 3, 1990; Oral History, Holmes H. McClure, October 1, 1990.

37. Oral History, D. L. Rooke.

38. Oral History, E. B. Barnes.

39. *The Brazosport Facts*, November 28, 1972.

40. *The First Ten Years, 1942-51, Dow Chemical of Canada, Ltd.*, booklet distributed at annual shareholders meeting, Sarnia, Ontario, September 5, 1951, and *The Story in Figures*, supplement to this booklet for directors only. Also consulted for this section were *Dow Maple Leaf*, employee publication (1947-73), esp. *Special Commemorative Edition*, July 1963; *Dow Canadian* (1972-81) and *Dow Canadian Dimensions* (1985-91), company magazines; *Chem West* (1977-81) and *Insider* (1985-91), employee publications, Western Canada Division; *Information Handbook*, Dow Chemical of Canada, Ltd., 1975; and Vic Dudek, *The First 50 Years: Dow Canada 1942-1992* (Sarnia, Ontario: Dow Chemical Canada, Inc., 1992).

41. Oral History, John M. Hacking, August 22, 1990.

42. Oral History, John L. Smart, August 22, 1990.

43. Oral History, Paul D. Scott, August 20, 1990.

44. See R. M. McPherson and R. W. Ford, *A History of the Chemical Industry in Lambton County* (Sarnia Section, Chemical Institute of Canada, March 24, 1964). Oil was struck by one Charles Tripp at Oil Springs, now known as Petrolia, 10 miles north of Sarnia, in 1855, several years ahead of Col. Drake's first well in Pennsylvania, in 1859, as Canadians delight in pointing out. Seven refineries sprang up in the Oil Springs area and the first refinery was built in Sarnia in 1871. By 1900 the Imperial Oil Company Ltd. was operating Canada's largest refinery at Sarnia, based on this field.

45. Oral History, P. D. Scott.

46. Oral History, J. L. Smart.

47. Oral History, P. D. Scott.

48. Oral History, J. L. Smart.

49. Oral History, Bertrand B. Hillary, August 21, 1990.

50. W. H. Dow to N. R. Crawford, October 25, 1945.

51. Oral History, Leroy D. Smithers, January 29, 1991.

52. Oral History, J. L. Smart.

53. Oral History, L. D. Smithers.

54. Ibid.

55. Ibid.

56. Oral History, J. L. Smart.

57. Oral History, L. D. Smithers.

58. Ibid.

59. The Chisso Corporation, a Japanese chemical firm, disposed of mercury wastes into Lake Minamata, about 560 miles southwest of Tokyo, from 1953 to 1960; in subsequent years hundreds of persons in the neighboring village of Minamata died and thousands fell ill after eating fish in this area from what became known as "Minamata disease." Investigations into the disaster eventually revealed the connection with mercury. Suits against Chisso dragged on in the Japanese courts until a final settlement in 1996.

60. Oral History, E. Leonard Weldon, August 21, 1990.

61. Oral History, C. Benson Branch, November 12, 1988.

62. Oral History, L. D. Smithers.

63. Oral History, B. B. Hillary.

64. Oral History, P. D. Scott.

65. Oral History, E. L. Weldon.

66. Oral History, L. D. Smithers.

67. Oral History, E. L. Weldon.

68. Oral History, P. D. Scott.

69. Ibid.

70. "Turfed out" is a Canadian expression meaning to be ejected from an organization in the same way a divot is removed by a golf club.

71. Oral History, Robert E. Naegele, August 6, 1990.

72. Oral History, E. L. Weldon.

73. Oral History, L. D. Smithers.

74. Oral History, E. L. Weldon.

75. Oral History, James M. Hay, May 27, 1994.

76. Oral History, E. L. Weldon.

77. Oral History, P. D. Scott.

78. Oral History, B. B. Hillary.

EIGHT

RESEARCH TRIUMPHS

I.

It was perhaps the most remarkable decision of Willard Dow's career, one of the most fortuitous of the company's first century, and he made it instinctively, without a lot of thought, and never wavered after he had made it. In the depths of the Great Depression, he decided to expand the Dow research establishment despite all indications that the opposite was the more prudent course.

The depression was just beginning to bite hard when Willard Dow succeeded his father at the helm of the company late in 1930. Many of the nation's industrial establishments were closing down their research organizations (and other overhead groups) as the bottom fell out of the financial system. Some put their research on a starvation diet; all of them battened down the hatches against the economic storms that were raging. It seemed to fly in the face of wisdom to maintain, let alone build up a costly research organization, but Willard did—and the company is still benefiting today from that decision and the range of new products that resulted.

It was the miracle decade of the chemical industry. E. I. du Pont perfected nylon and Teflon; Owens-Illinois and Corning Glass Works developed fiberglass; Imperial Chemical Industries perfected polyethylene; the Geigy Company in Switzerland developed DDT. Dow's research also came into a kind of Golden Age in the 1930s, producing inventions that propelled it out of the Michigan backwoods and into the front ranks of the business world. It was one of those rare conjunctures of the stars when "truly original ideas that had a major impact on society came to fruition in a given time and place," as Keith R. McKennon, research director from 1985 to 1990, described it.[1]

McKennon felt there were several key factors underlying this sudden flowering of creativity. One was active top management support and involvement; the company's research laboratory directors reported directly to Willard Dow, who was both director of research and chief execu-

_215_

tive of the company, a rare combination in that day, and unheard of since. Lab directors could hire more help, buy major kinds of equipment, or incur unusual expenses simply by getting a go-ahead from their friend Willard.

For another thing, Willard Dow tolerated eccentricity to an extraordinary degree. There was no code of behavior, no dress code, no standard approach to problem solving. Doing things differently was not only tolerated, it was encouraged.

McKennon said Bobby Dreisbach, one of the key inventors of Styron plastic, once rushed out of the lab to attend the annual company picnic, the Dow Field Day, and when the start of a footrace was announced realized he had forgotten his running shorts and shoes. "Undeterred and unabashed, Bobby stripped to his underwear and ran in the race (and almost won it)," McKennon said. "In other places and times, Bobby Dreisbach would have been reprimanded and perhaps even fired for running around in his underwear at a company picnic, but there was never any question of that with Willard Dow."

Another factor was the availability on the job market of top talent. Campus recruiting of scientific personnel all but ceased during these depression years, and Dow had virtually free choice of the top graduates on the campuses of those years, particularly in the Midwest, where the company did the bulk of its recruiting. Ray Boundy, the company's first vice president of research, dedicated his history of the Physics Lab, where many of the new discoveries were made, to Willard Dow, "who had the vision, courage, and resolve to increase greatly the company's research when the cost was low and the best technical graduates were available."

Much of this creative explosion occurred around the person of "the idea man," John Grebe, director of the Physics Lab. Grebe, although his senses of discipline and organization were close to nil, was nevertheless a brilliant lab director, McKennon felt. In modern times he would be more likely to be put in some position where he would be relieved of administrative duties and encouraged to concentrate on his ideas.

"We didn't do anything in that lab that didn't get Grebe's approval first," Dr. Sylvia Stoesser said. "And the crazier it was, the better Grebe liked it. He'd say, 'We have to have a meeting.' And we'd say, 'Uh oh, what's this going to be about? It's going to be about something John wants done that we know is just about impossible to do, but he wants it done. And he treats it like it's the most wonderful thing in the world to be working on that.' That was Grebe. And you worked on it. Truly."

Stoesser remembered that "one time he wanted to have his house heated with a solvent. Did you ever hear of diphenyl? He thought it was a good idea to heat the whole house, including doing the cooking, with diphenyl oxide, which wasn't something that would burn easily. You could heat it to a high temperature and use it to heat your house, and then turn it off; that's what John's idea was—you could use it hot. Oh, John had a lot of ideas, and he got a lot of people working on them."[2]

Most of the nation's business was in a freefall, but Dow's business slumped for only two or three years, the workforce shrinking by 27 percent in that period, and then recovered strongly:

Dow Chemical employment and sales figures:

1930—2,400	$ 16	million
1931—1,950	13.5	million
1932—1,750	12.5	million
1933—2,140	11	million
1934—3,000	17	million

As Dow's prosperity grew (sales and employment both surged continuously upward for many years after 1934), so did the research budget and Willard Dow's devotion to it. In 1936, beginning to feel the pressure of his many duties, Willard decided he needed an assistant to give full time to research activities, and he persuaded William R. Veazey to leave Case, where he was chairman of the Chemical Engineering Department, to take that position, with the title of "research coordinator." The research budget grew from $936,000 in 1937 to $1,744,000 in 1940 and $2,263,000 in 1941.[3]

Veazey, who had studied at Johns Hopkins under Ira Remsen, the discoverer of saccharine, had been a Dow consultant since 1915 (he usually spent his summers in Midland, working with the research staff) and a Dow board member since 1927; he had succeeded Albert W. Smith in that position as the spokesman for research on the Dow board.

The arrival of Veazey in Midland marked the beginning of an attempt to organize and coordinate the research effort across the company, as compared to a series of independent laboratories (most of whom continued to emphasize their "independence" for years afterward) and a series of production-controlled and -oriented laboratories, who worked together only through the managerial finesse and fiat of the top executive. The unification movement was completed only after 1950 and the death of Willard Dow, the retirement of Veazey, and the appointment of Ray Boundy as the firm's first research V. P.

In the heady days of the 1930s, as the nation struggled to recover from the worst depression in its history and Hitler and Mussolini prepared for war in Europe, Dow research devised the product base on which the company was to build for the rest of the century. Among the developments of this period, listing in the interests of brevity only the accomplishments of the Physics Lab:

- Automatic controls. John Grebe's first assignment at Dow in 1924 (he chose it himself) was "Application of Automatic Control to Chemical Reactions." Over the succeeding decades the Physics Lab under his direction developed in-plant systems for measuring and recording acidity, electrical conductivity, oxidation potential, specific gravity, infrared spectrum, and other variables, and developed equipment to control these variables.
- The Dowtherm products. Dow developed these products as heat exchangers for high-temperature heat transfer.
- Ferric chloride. Researchers developed uses for this compound for etching copper and for coagulating the solids in sanitary sewage systems.

- Dowell, Inc. The lab developed methods to increase the productivity of gas, oil, and brine wells, and established the Dowell subsidiary to provide these services.
- Waste disposal bacteria. Dow discovered and cultivated bacteria that eat phenol, and employed them in waste disposal processes.
- Ethylene research. Dow developed processes to produce ethylene (and higher olefins).
- Styrene. The company synthesized styrene from benzene and ethylene, at the start of World War II the only commercial process for making styrene in the United States. Most of the styrene used in making synthetic rubber during and after the war was made by this method.
- Styrofoam. Styrofoam expanded polystyrene, developed during World War II for the U.S. Navy as a flotation medium, is now made around the world and has thousands of uses.
- Pertet process. The direct chlorination of hydrocarbons to make carbon tetrachloride, trichlorethylene, perchlorethylene, and hydrochloric acid. Among other advantages, this process (also worked on in Dow's Western division) made dry cleaning methods more economical, safer, and more accessible to the average customer.
- Bromine from seawater. This technological triumph is described in some detail in section III
- Styron. The Physics Lab developed Styron, Dow's brand of polystyrene plastic, the company's number 1 sales item for half a century, and high-impact polystyrene, the first commercially successful method for increasing the toughness of polystyrene.
- PVC. The lab developed the method for making vinyl chloride, the basic material used to make polyvinyl chloride and related plastic products.
- Saran. The lab developed vinylidene chloride, which is copolymerized with vinyl chloride to make Saran.
- Saran Wrap. The company's first consumer product, it has become a familiar item in many of the world's kitchens.
- Ion exchange resins. Dowex and related resins are used in water purifiers.
- Magnesium from seawater. The lab developed the process for extracting magnesium chloride from seawater, using ion exchange, as the basis for magnesium production.
- Polystyrene fine fibers. The lab developed a method for making one-micron pure polystyrene fine fibers used during World War II to mold lightweight aircraft housing transparent to radar waves. Although it was later replaced by another material, this was the original housing material for radar and was credited at the time with making radar possible.
- Butadiene. The lab developed the sulfur dioxide process for purifying butadiene, to make the purest butadiene then available.
- Synthetic acetylene. Acetylene lost out to ethylene as a chemical building block, but its synthesis remains a chemical landmark.
- Ethafoam. An expanded cellular polyethylene, used extensively in furniture cushions, mattresses, and the like.
- Methods for making divinyl benzene, vinyl toluene, methyl styrene, and chlorostyrene. These compounds were critical in the manufacture of other items such as special rubbers or to the production of other chemicals; most were considered critical to the war effort in World War II by the War Production Board.[4]

The Stratonauts

In the early 1930s an odd assortment of men and organizations set out to explore the stratosphere, which at that time man had not yet reached. They succeeded not only in setting new world altitude records but in opening the door, although they did not realize it at the time, to modern space research.

The main players came in twos—Belgian scientists who were twin brothers, two U.S. military services, two Nobel Prize-winning academics, and two U.S. industrial firms. The twin brothers were the Piccards—Auguste, who taught physics at the University of Brussels, and Jean, who taught chemistry at various universities in Europe and the United States. The military services were the U.S. Army and U.S. Navy, each nurturing a struggling young air force at that period, who vied through these years for the world's altitude record and the prestige of having been the farthest aloft. The Nobelists were Robert A. Millikan, president of the California Institute of Technology, and Arthur H. Compton of the University of Chicago, who had a long-standing dispute over the properties of cosmic rays; they believed measurements in the stratosphere would settle their debate.

The companies were the Goodyear Zeppelin Company, a subsidiary of Goodyear Rubber, which had a deep interest in ballooning and outstanding know-how in the design and fabrication of balloons, and Dow, leading producer of magnesium, lightest of the structural metals. The catalyst that brought them together was the 1933 Chicago World's Fair, with its theme, "A Century of Progress."

Auguste Piccard had been interested in ballooning since the early 1920s, and in 1927 persuaded King Albert I of Belgium to establish the Belgian National Fund for Scientific Research (Fonds National de la Recherche Scientifique). The FNRS funded record-making balloon ascensions by Auguste in 1931 (on May 27), when he ascended 51,775 feet (9.81 miles) in a balloon launched at Augsburg, Germany, accompanied by Paul Kipfer as assistant, and in 1932 (on August 18), when he established a new record of 53,152 feet (10.07 miles), accompanied by the Swiss physicist Max Cosyns.

In the spring of 1932 the Chicago Fair organizers asked Auguste Piccard if they could exhibit the gondola from his 1931 flight at their fair, and when he broke his own record a few months later they asked if they could display the second gondola as well. Then they got an even better idea; why not organize a balloon flight by Piccard from the fair site itself and attempt to set a new altitude record, bringing great and enduring glory to the fair, and no little publicity? Piccard came to America in 1933, bringing his first record-breaking gondola with him for display, to talk about it.

American high-atmosphere exploration had been shut down since 1927, when Capt. Hawthorne C. Gray, an American balloonist and space pioneer, had been killed setting an altitude record (42,470 feet, or 8.04 miles, on November 4, 1927). Now Piccard's U.S. tour kindled interest again, and as an added factor, the Soviet Union was also getting into the space race.

On September 30, 1933, the Soviets reported a new altitude record had been achieved by three of their ballonists (G. Prokoviev, E. Birnbaum, and K. Gudunov), at slightly over 18 kilometers—more than 60,000 feet—and the U.S. vs. U.S.S.R. space race began; it was to continue for most of the century.[1]

Up to this time all the gondolas used in these balloon ascents (including the Russian) were made of aluminum. In February 1933 Willard Dow was called by Irving E. Muskat, a young chemist on the Century of Progress science staff, who was looking for help with the balloon project. Would the Dow Company, he asked, be interested in providing a gondola made of magnesium for the new Piccard flight? Willard Dow was immediately interested, told him Dowmetal was just the thing they were looking for in this use, and that Dow was probably as well equipped as anyone in the world to make a gondola of the material. If Dow made the gondola, Muskat responded, "it would be an achievement of which every American could be proud."[2]

Dow quickly agreed that the company would provide the gondola for the Piccard flight at no charge, and it became the first of three the company would make for the record-shattering balloon flights that took place in 1934 and 1935. He called in his magnesium fabrication expert, Edward H. (Ed) Perkins, and the company immediately set about making a gondola, or as the Piccard brothers called it, "la cabine."[3] It was a sphere seven feet in diameter (the second gondola was 100 inches in diameter and the third nine feet), and when it was completely outfitted weighed almost exactly 700 pounds; the naked gondola weighed only 360.

Jean Piccard came to Midland to inspect the gondola in May 1933, and revealed in a talk before the Midland Rotary Club that either he or his brother would fly in it in early July from the World's Fair in Chicago, accompanied by the U.S. Navy's crack pilot, Lieut. Cdr. T. G. W. (Tex) Settle, who was licensed to fly anything from a glider to a zeppelin.

Perkins and the specialists at the Dow Met Lab fashioned the spherical gondolas of 10 pieces of magnesium each, three-sixteenth of an inch thick—eight slices that fit together like an orange peel, with a circular piece at each end.

The interior was primitive by late twentieth-century standards, with simple open shelves for cosmic ray and radio equipment (conversations with the stratonauts were broadcast over NBC radio) and barometers and gauges. The space for passengers was about four feet square and six feet high. On a shelf overhead was a thermos of coffee and a paper bag containing fruit and sandwiches. Tex Settle flew in his Navy dress uniform, but took along a heavy fur coat.

The World's Fair authorities decided the flight would leave from Soldiers' Field, Chicago, and they sold tickets for the launch at 40 cents each. By early July everything was in readiness, but Chicago was living up to its reputation as the Windy City and the flight was put off the whole month, waiting for decent weather for ballooning. In the interim, Jean Piccard, who had never been aloft in a balloon in his life, a matter of considerable concern for the others involved, reluctantly withdrew and became "ground pilot" for the flight, saying in a news announcement written for him that the reduction in weight would give Commander Settle, who would fly alone, a better chance at a new record.

At 3 A.M. on August 5, preceded by seven hours of World's Fair pageantry, and watched by a Soldiers' Field crowd that by that hour had shrunk from 50,000 to perhaps half that many, Tex Settle finally gave the signal and the Century of Progress balloon lifted slowly into the sky in the glare of giant spotlights. "Settle Up!" cried wags in the crowd, "Settle Up!"

Their laughter soon went sour. The balloon went straight up about 5,000 feet and then began veering sharply to the west under the pressure of winds not apparent at ground level. Settle quickly began to "valve off" hydrogen gas, but the valve stuck and the balloon began to sink. Settle began releasing ballast, trying to get the balloon to rise again, but it came to earth in a railroad yard a mile or two from its starting point. The gondola bounced high on the railroad tracks and came to rest. Settle, except for his pride, was unhurt.

Ed Perkins and his wife, sitting in the front row at Soldiers' Field with Mrs. Fay Settle, rushed with her to the nearest telephone, in the cage where the gondola had been stored. Being told where the balloon had landed, they roared off to the railroad yard with a motorcycle escort, and saw the reunited and unharmed Settles embrace.[4] Hundreds of souvenir seekers arrived to tear pieces from the balloon, and it was only saved from total destruction by the intervention of a Marine launch-crew detachment headed by Maj. Chester L. Fordney.

Settle wanted to "have another go at it," but Jean Piccard opposed this passionately; Settle would only bungle it again, he said. He had a better idea: the next flight should be made by himself, he proposed, accompanied by his wife, Jeannette, a Chicago native, as copilot.

Perkins quickly repaired the gondola, and Goodyear repaired the balloon. Perkins and Willard Dow tried to convince Jean Piccard that exploring the stratosphere with his wife was folly. "Why should you and Mrs. Piccard risk your life for a venture of this type?" Willard wrote Piccard. "I should like to urge you to give up the thought of such a proposed trip. There are many others, such as the Navy Department, who make it their business as well as their pleasure to make these 'dare devil' hops and why not leave it to them to explore these regions?"[5]

Dow, now one of the key financial backers, and the Navy insisted the second flight should be an "all-Navy" flight, with Settle accompanied by another Navy man chosen by the fair authorities, and in the end their view prevailed. Selected as Settle's teammate was Maj. Fordney (who was Navy), who had rescued the balloon from oblivion.[6] Again the weather refused to cooperate, and although everything was in readiness no flight could take place, to the great dismay of the World's Fair authorities; the fair was scheduled to close November 12, which it did while the weather continued bad.

Settle and Fordney had been arguing in favor of flying from the Goodyear-Zeppelin Airship Dock at the Akron, Ohio, Municipal Airport, which had a balloon hangar and up-to-the-minute launch facilities. The Chicago interests, obviously, argued in favor of Chicago. Two days after the fair closed, clear weather was forecast in Akron, and Fordney promptly packed up the gondola, the balloon, and the equipment, and rushed it all to Akron.

At 9:30 A.M. on November 20 Settle and Fordney soared aloft from Akron in a smooth flight, and the U.S. Navy recaptured the altitude record the Soviet Union had set two months before. The new record was 61,237 feet, 18.665 kilometers, 11.59 miles. It was later calculated that they had eclipsed the Russian record by only 500 feet, but eclipse it they had.

Floating eastward, with Settle piloting the balloon and Fordney operating the instruments, they landed late in the evening in a southern New Jersey marsh only 40 miles from the Atlantic Ocean. They had no equipment to survive a water landing, and would certainly have perished if they had reached it. They stayed with the balloon that night, and at dawn the next morning reached a farm a few miles away and announced their success to the world.

Amazingly, among the first persons to reach them were Jean and Jeannette Piccard, who were at their home in Delaware near the landing site, where they had been following the flight as closely as they could. (Jean was now working for the Hercules Powder Company) "We went over there and Jean waded through several feet of water till he reached the gondola," Jeannette wrote a friend. "Then he stripped and swam the bayou to get to the balloon itself. It was in beautiful condition . . . we went home delighted that our own prospects were so good."[7]

Jean and Jeannette Piccard persisted in their dream of flying into the stratosphere, and after considerable wrangling with almost everyone else concerned, including Willard Dow, Ed Perkins, and Art Winston (director of Dow's Met Lab), they climbed into the balloon's gondola at the Ford Airport in Dearborn and headed for the stratosphere on October 23, 1934. Piccard had painted out the previous names on the gondola, including that of Dow (Willard Dow having agreed that it now belonged to Piccard), and painted in his own name and that of Grunow Radio and People's Outfitting Company, two new sponsors he had found. The Piccards had argued with Willard Dow about various changes in the gondola the couple had devised and asked him to make, at Dow's expense; Dow finally told them he wasn't going to make any more changes.

The scientific data brought back from the Piccards' flight was almost useless, but they reached the highly respectable height of 57,579 feet, or 10.9 miles; not a new record but enough to make the record books, and higher, to Jean's immense satisfaction, than his twin brother Auguste had ever flown.[8]

In the interim the U.S. Army Air Corps had been watching the Settle-Fordney accomplishments of the U.S. Navy with growing envy. Capt. Albert W. Stevens, chief of its photography laboratory at Wright Field, in Dayton, was one of those arguing that the army was overdue to resume the flights that had been halted after Capt. Gray's death. Maj. William E. Kepner, who became the commander of the army's next flight, said later that the Settle-Fordney flight provided ample precedent for the Army Air Corps to enter the balloon race to the stratosphere. "If beating the navy record was not enough," he said, "there was the national prestige and attention, and more importantly, the considerable serious scientific study already done at Wright Field in high altitude research."

Capt. Stevens, a friend of Gilbert H. Grosvenor, president of the National Geographic Society, had often provided him with aerial photographs for the *National Geographic* magazine, and had provided cameras for the Settle flight. Now he proposed to the National Geographic Society that it sponsor a new balloon flight to the stratosphere with a new, larger gondola, a new, much larger balloon, and army logistical support. In December 1933, the NGS agreed to sponsor a new flight, to be called *Explorer*, and contributed $25,000 for its expenses. Dow agreed to build a new, somewhat larger Piccard-type gondola (100 inches was the diameter finally decided upon), and Goodyear agreed to build a mammoth new balloon, five times larger than the *Century of Progress* balloon; its capacity was three million cubic feet, compared to 600,000 for the *Century of Progress*.[9]

The *Explorer* flight ascended from a natural bowl-shaped formation, dubbed the "Stratobowl," located in the Black Hills near Rapid City, South Dakota. The crew was composed of Kepner as pilot, Stevens as scientific observer, and Lt. Orvil A. Anderson (shortly promoted to captain) as assistant to both; Kepner and Anderson were considered (by Stevens, the organizer) the army's best balloonists.

Explorer rose from the Stratobowl at dawn on July 28, 1934, and climbed uneventfully to 60,613 feet, 18.475 kilometers, 11.48 miles. At that altitude they discovered some small rips in the balloon above them, and they decided immediately to descend. As the balloon rose it expanded under the diminishing air pressure, and the hard-frozen fabric began to crack and tear, a problem that plagued the balloonists throughout these flights. When the *Explorer* had descended to about three miles it began to

Interior of the early space capsule designed by Dow Chemical engineers, in which a world's altitude record was set, featured such amenities as a shelf holding a sack of fruit and a thermos of coffee. The seven-foot-high gondola was a combined radio station, scientific laboratory, and a home for two pilots. (Drawing from Chicago Daily News, Aug. 4, 1933)

rupture; the crew decided to bail out. Moments after they had climbed out and taken to parachutes, the hydrogen-filled balloon bag, mixing with atmospheric oxygen, exploded. The gondola crashed on the flatlands near Holdrege, Nebraska, and was completely destroyed. Kepner, Stevens, and Anderson were unhurt. The barographs survived, and revealed that the army had failed by a narrow margin—about 600 feet—to surpass the navy's Settle-Fordney record.

Fortunately the gondola, balloon, and the rest of *Explorer* had been insured by Lloyd's of London, easing the financial loss greatly. There was immediate discussion of another try. This was quickly endorsed by George H. Dern, secretary of the War Department, and others, and plans for *Explorer II* began promptly.

NGS asked Dow to put together another gondola, and Art Winston put his crew in the Met Lab to work again.[10] This one was larger—nine feet in diameter—but weighed less, only 637 pounds compared to 700 for the 1934 gondola. The manhole openings were enlarged to 20 x 22 inches, two inches larger on each side than *Explorer I*; the ballonists of *Explorer I* had had excruciating difficulty getting out of them wearing parachutes. There were also no more shelves; Winston, who was in charge of installing the instruments, bolted them directly to the walls. Dow researchers had now developed a better technique for pressure testing the gondolas; they filled the completed sphere with water at 45 pounds pressure per square inch, and any leaks were immediately visible. Another major change in the preparations for *Explorer II* was a switch to the more expensive helium gas as the buoyant agent instead of the ever-dangerous hydrogen.

In 1935 the Stratobowl was again chosen as the liftoff site, but there were many delays in the launch; the wait for ideal weather went on for months. Orvil Anderson recalled a ditty written during these delays, sung to the tune of "Home on the Range":

> Home, home in the Bowl
> Where the Soldiers and Scientists play,
> Where ever is heard, the discouraging word,
> "There'll be no inflation today."

The weather finally cooperated in November, although it was cold, and on November 11 a two-man crew of Anderson and Stevens piloted the *Explorer II* as it rose out of the Stratobowl with a 6,800-kilogram payload that included almost 1,000 kilos of scientific instruments. Three and a half hours later they were 20 kilometers off the ground, and they reached 22.066 kilometers (72,395 feet, or 13.71 miles), their maximum, 15 minutes later, staying at 22 kilometers for an hour and a half and taking scientific readings. Stevens and Anderson had set the new world altitude record, and it was to remain the record for 21 years, until the new space age dawned with the Soviet launching of *Sputnik*.

Stevens wanted to go up again, and for several years lectured and raised funds for another flight. "We could go to 82,000 feet, or possibly even 85,000," he felt. But the armed services had lost interest; there was a war heating up in Europe. The National Geographic Society signaled vigorously that it was through with this type of effort as well. It cut up the *Explorer II* balloon into a million bookmarks, which it distributed to its faithful membership. The gondola of *Explorer II* went to the Smithsonian, where it is still on display. The manned ballooning phase of the space race was over.

As it turned out, the scientific data harvested by the flights, while useful, was hardly revolutionary and did not shed very much light on the major problems of the day, although most of the balloonists had agreed that the primary purpose of all the flights was the gathering of scientific data. Millikan and Compton and the other cosmic ray debaters—Millikan provided instruments to measure cosmic rays for virtually all of the balloon flights until 1935—plotted in new points on curves they had already plotted, or without fanfare junked their plots because they did not agree with the new data. Most of the cosmic ray data was determined by scientists working with their feet on the ground.

1. See David H. DeVorkin, curator, National Air & Space Museum, Smithsonian Institution, *Race to the Stratosphere: Scientific Ballooning in America* (New York: Springer-Verlag, 1989). Citations by permission of the author.
2. I. E. Muskat to W. H. Dow, *Century of Progress Papers*, University of Illinois, Chicago Circle.
3. From Piccard Family Papers, Manuscript Division, Library of Congress.
4. *Chicago Daily News*, August 5, 1933. Perkins left Dow (and the gondola work) at this period to establish his own successful magnesium fabricating firm, Brooks & Perkins, in Detroit. His place as Dow's liaison with the Piccards and scientific ballooning was taken by Arthur W. Winston, who in 1935 became director of Dow's Metallurgical Laboratory.
5. W. H. Dow to Piccard, September 23, 1933. Piccard Family Papers, Library of Congress.
6. Fordney was the son of Cong. Joseph W. Fordney of Saginaw, with whom Herbert Dow had worked to produce the Fordney-McCumber tariff measure a dozen years before.
7. Mrs. Jean Piccard to William Rosenfield, November 28, 1933. Piccard Family Papers, Library of Congress.
8. For a detailed description of Mr. & Mrs. Jean Piccard's flight see DeVorkin, *Race to the Stratosphere*, chap. 4.
9. For details of the first Explorer flight, see "The National Geographic Society-U.S. Army Air Corps Stratosphere Flight of 1934," Stratosphere Series No. 1, 1935, NGS Contributed Technical Papers, including a paper, "The Design and Construction of the Gondola for the 'Explorer,'" by A. W. Winston, Experimental Engineer, The Dow Chemical Company. See also Capt. Albert W. Stevens, "Exploring the Stratosphere," *National Geographic Magazine* 66, no. 4 (October 1934): 397-434.
10. See A. W. Winston, "The Design and Construction of the Gondola for 'Explorer II,'" in "The National Geographic Society-U.S. Army Air Corps Stratosphere Flight of 1935 in the Balloon 'Explorer II,'" Stratosphere Series No. 2, 1936, NGS Contributed Technical Papers, and Capt. Albert W. Stevens, "Man's Farthest Aloft," *National Geographic Magazine* 69, no. 1 (January 1936): 59-94.

II.

Dow entered the plastics business rather by accident because it had too much of two common chemicals, caustic soda and ethylene. It is today a world leader in the field.

The key process of the Dow Company is the electrolysis of salt brine, the method by which, as high school chemists know, electricity is used to split common salt and water into chlorine and caustic soda, or sodium hydroxide. Dow has long been the world's premier practitioner of this process and the largest manufacturer of both chlorine and caustic. Dow does not sell chlorine per se, but instead processes it into hundreds of chlorine-containing products, which it does sell. It markets the workhorse chemical caustic soda (simply called "caustic" within Dow) by the tankcar load, or uses it as it does chlorine to manufacture other chemicals.

In the astronomic volumes in which it makes these two items, the company frequently has too much of one or not enough of the other, and the "chlorine-caustic balance" is a constant problem for the company. During the depression days of the early 1930s the company was short on chlorine but long on caustic, and Willard Dow asked his research directors to find ways to use the excess caustic.

Edgar Britton, at the Organic Lab, was reading some German references one day and noted that it took several pounds of caustic to make a pound of cellulose ethers. Since Dow also had an excess of ethyl chloride, he reasoned that it might be well to look into the possibility of making ethyl cellulose, a product with many potential uses, using both of these excesses. Willard Dow agreed enthusiastically, and work on the product began in late 1933 in Britton's laboratory, cheered on by Billy Hale, who had long been interested in cellulose chemistry. In this roundabout way Dow embarked on the manufacture of its first plastic because it had too much caustic.

Within six months Britton and his staff had devised a process for making ethyl cellulose using liberal quantities of caustic and wood pulp as raw materials. Willard Dow decided that Ethocel, as Dow decided to call it, would become the company's entry in the plastics derby, which with the earlier success of bakelite, the first mass-produced plastic, was about to begin.

Willard went at it with a frontal assault, in spite of the fact that the world was in the depths of the Great Depression, launching Dow's cellulose business as a full division of the company, the Cellulose Products Division (CPD), reporting directly to himself. He chose William R. Collings, the young man who had arrived from Case some years before with a nugget of magnesium in his hand, to be its chief. The CPD had its own sales, technical service and development, basic research, product research, engineering, and production groups, all under one roof, and was thus the ancestor of later Dow product groups, except that in its case production was also part of the organization and reported to the same general manager.

Believing in backward integration of raw materials, Willard Dow also hired a forester, Phelps Vogelsang, to plant fast-growing hybrid aspen in the Midland area as a future source of cellulose. The company soon had three plantations around the area, one of them where

Northwood University now stands. Prof. W. O. Hisey of Syracuse University spent a summer in Midland designing a pulp mill to process these trees when they reached maturity.

Britton, meanwhile, had been exploring wood chemistry in Michigan's Upper Peninsula, and when the opportunity opened to acquire the Cleveland Cliffs property in the Upper Peninsula with its ready-grown forests, Willard Dow jumped at the chance—and the newly planted Midland aspen plantations came to naught. (It also turned out that for reasons of purity it was better to use cotton linters than wood pulp as the raw material.)

Collings's search for cellulose chemists led him directly to Syracuse University's New York State College of Forestry (now called the College of Environmental Science and Forestry), the leading center for that study. In the succeeding depression years four professors came to Midland from that school, led by Floyd C. (Pete) Peterson, who had taught many of the students who also began to flow to Midland from Syracuse—43 by one count. Peterson became the CPD's technical director.

Dick Swinehart, an early (non-Syracuse) recruit to the division, said much of the early research was done using small reactor vessels called "bombs," metal cylinders that held about two gallons of liquid, built with inch-thick steel and held together with gaskets and bolts. "At times, I ran the bombs. Other times, Al Maasberg ran them," said Swinehart. "Officially, he was working on ethyl cellulose, but unknown to top management he was also experimenting with methyl cellulose."[5]

Ethocel was developed just in time to be used extensively during World War II; servicemen became familiar with it as the plastic used to make canteens in that war, and it was also used for telephone headsets and mouthpieces, control knobs, dust goggles, and airplane parts. Tents, sleeping bags, and clothing were sprayed with it to make them water and chemical resistant. It had many other uses, but gradually settled over the years after the war into a niche as a specialty plastic material not widely known to the general public.

George Greminger recalled one major miscalculation with Ethocel.

> The ethyl cellulose plant was built on the assumption that we were going to sell "Ethorayon," a fiber. We had a complete spinning and weaving operation set up in the pilot plant. Many of our wives and daughters were wearing underwear made with this material and they liked it. It had a very nice soft, silky drape. The problem was that the irons at that time had only one setting, for cotton, and if it was ironed at the temperature for cotton it would melt the material. The textile industry was very conservative and weren't about to change. It finally took Dupont with nylon to get them off their butts. We were probably 10 years ahead of the time when our material would have been successful.[6]

Albert T. Maasberg, who eventually became the research chief of CPD, began to think methyl cellulose had even more potential than Ethocel. "We were officially concentrating on improving the quality of ethyl cellulose at that time," Maasberg said, but Shailer Bass, Floyd Peterson, and I decided we'd make a few samples of methyl cellulose to see how this would fit into our overall program. Collings, of course, was concentrating on ethyl cellulose and its uses and he took a dim view of these methyl cellulose experiments in the beginning; he thought they would detract from the effort on ethyl cellulose. Shailer suggested we not report my experiments until I had something, and that I stay out of Bill's way; so we did it very quietly to start with. But I'll say this for Bill, after we proved it was a potential product, he supported it.[7]

Methocel, Dow's trademark for methyl cellulose, became a major Dow product, much bigger than Ethocel, and a half-century later was being supplied to the world from plants in Midland, in Louisiana, and in Stade, Germany. That it became a product in spite of initial management opposition, because a researcher followed his nose rather than his superior's explicit instructions, is another example of a frequent occurrence in the company's history, and a mark of Dow's strength.

Methocel is not a plastic material; Ethocel is. Methocel, however, has thousands of uses as a thickener, binder, film former, and suspending agent. It has been called "the invisible product," and is used in adhesives, agricultural chemicals, ceramics, chemical specialties, construction products, foods, paper products, pharmaceuticals, cosmetics, and latex paints.[8] In the pharmaceutical industry, for instance, it has long been used in "controlled release" tablets; in foods, it is used to stop cakes from falling, pies from boiling over, and sauces from running. George Greminger, who spent much of a 47-year career at Dow developing uses for Methocel, had 35 patents covering Methocel uses.[9]

Swinehart said Methocel brought back the nickel cigar after World War II. "Cigar prices had risen to ten to twenty cents because a high-quality tobacco leaf was required for the wrapper and there was a lot of waste," he remembered. "We developed a methyl cellulose film that allowed cigar makers to use less expensive tobaccos in their wrappers and once again produce nickel cigars."

The entire staff of the Cellulose Division gathered annually at a "Buck, Bear, and Beef Brawl," an evening of high jinks held at the end of the Michigan deer hunting season. Successful hunters were expected to contribute to the provender. The highlight of the evening was the annual awarding of degrees by "Kollings Kollege of Sellulosic Knowledge," which recognized noteworthy achievements and snafus of the preceding year. Anyone who was a part of the cellulose ether business, operator or executive, was eligible for these degrees, and they were presented with full pomp and ceremony. The "Kollege" was an outgrowth of a training course instituted by Collings that had become known as "Kollings Sellulosic Kollege, Where Students Go to Hell for Knowledge." In later years the "Brawl" was replaced by a much more sedate "Methocel Open."

In 1943, Willard Dow asked Collings to become the first general manager (and soon first president) of the Dow Corning Corporation, a pioneer firm in silicone manufacture formed as a wartime joint venture by Dow and Corning Glass. Collings worked for both Dow and

Dow Corning while the new firm was gelling. When he left Dow he took a third to a half of the Cellulose Products Division with him, including Shailer L. Bass, his assistant, who later became his successor and the second president of Dow Corning. The dynamic group that Collings had assembled to organize Dow's first plastics venture became the nucleus of the first firm in the silicone business.

Polystyrene plastic, which Dow calls "Styron," also grew out of efforts to use an excess product, in this case ethylene. It was to become the runaway No. 1 best-seller of Dow's first century, and like Methocel, it survived management efforts to kill it.

In 1931, with a new ethylene plant coming onstream, Willard Dow told the research groups that the company would soon be long on low-cost ethylene; could they find a way to use excess ethylene? Robert R. Dreisbach of the Physics Lab, a brilliant inventor but one of the most eccentric persons who ever worked for Dow, sat down and drew up a chart, with ethylene on one side and every reactive chemical he could think of on the other. In between he charted such questions as: Does it react with ethylene? What might be formed? Could it be sold? One of the chemicals he considered was benzene, which would react with ethylene to make ethylbenzene; ethylbenzene could be hydrogenated to form styrene monomer; and styrene could be polymerized to form a plastic material that might have great usefulness.[10]

Within two years, more than a third of the Physics Lab staff was actively working on styrene, and in the fashion that had been inaugurated by Herbert Dow, a rival group in the Organic Research Lab was also working on it. Edgar Britton's group came in second in this race. "[Such rivalry] was expensive, but a way of life that Willard Dow exercised," said Walter Roush, who worked at the other end of the lab bench from Dreisbach at the time. "The Britton process was getting poor quality and poor yields. Earl Pelton was set up as the referee, and he studied both processes and the decision was to go with thermal type cracking," the Dreisbach approach.[11]

Dow began to produce styrene commercially on June 12, 1935, and by that September was making styrene of 98 percent purity. The Dow process was the first and most successful method of making styrene, and a few years later was the method that enabled the United States to meet the widespread need for it that arrived with World War II; when the U.S. rubber supply was cut off by the Japanese in the Far East and the country was forced to shift to synthetic rubber to replace it, the U.S. Rubber Reserve program chose the Dow process to meet the greatest share of the need for styrene for styrene-butadiene rubber.[12]

In the early days, polystyrene was a "poor country cousin" in the Dow plastics firmament. The Cellulose Products Group believed and preached that ethyl cellulose would become the world's largest volume plastic because the raw material, cellulose, was plentiful and cheap. "It is my recollection that the top management of the company favored Ethocel because of the logic of the arguments that could be advanced in its favor," Ray Boyer said.[13]

On at least four occasions Willard Dow ordered the research groups to stop all research on styrene. On one of those occasions Larry Amos, a key styrene researcher, went to Strosacker to talk to him about it. "You keep working on it," Strosacker told Amos. "I'll find the money to pay for the research."[14] On another, Dreisbach went to see Earl Bennett and said, "We can't just stop, because we know we're right. Can't you do something to help us?" Bennett said, "Bobby, I've got my orders too. I've got orders to close the account number. But I'll tell you what you can do. You can go back and think up a name other than styrene. Continue working on styrene, but under another name. I'll issue you a new account number."[15]

The low point in the history of Styron came in the summer of 1937, a few months after the first styrene monomer plant came onstream with Richard S. McClurg as manager. Dupont had placed one of the first large orders for it (5,000 pounds), Bakelite had negotiated to purchase styrene from Dow, and Monsanto was interested, so Strosacker had authorized the building of a modest plant to make about 500,000 pounds a year.

Unfortunately, just as the plant came into production sales suddenly dried up, and the product began to pile up. It was being packed in 55-gallon drums, and with no other storage available, several hundred drums were stored out in an open field behind the Physics Lab. As summer came on the drums began to heat up and there were serious concerns that they might explode. This problem was solved by spraying water over the drums to keep them cool, and adding an inhibitor to each drum.

Boyer said Strosacker's rivals in the plant watched this process with glee, "because Stro had bought the styrene monomer thing, hook, line, and sinker, and built a plant with no market . . . he was considered by many to be a fool who had made a colossal mistake." Larry Amos said Bill Williams, a key production superintendent, confronted him one day and said: "You young whippersnappers certainly have a white elephant on your hands." The drums lay out in the field being sprayed, for about six months, according to Roush's records.[16]

Dow's answer to this debacle was to initiate a crash program to produce polystyrene from the styrene. The company would make and sell polystyrene plastic, it was decided, in addition to styrene monomer. The Physics Lab crew moved full speed ahead with a polystyrene program, and the company quickly had its second entry in the plastics field, and as it turned out, its biggest and most successful.

A few years later, when the war arrived and styrene became vital to the nation's ability to wage war, Strosacker and those associated with him were suddenly heroes.[17] The humiliating 1937 field of 55-gallon drums was slowly forgotten—a later generation would not even know what it had meant—but photos and paintings of that field hung in Dow's plastics offices for many years, a nightmare that turned into a field of dreams.

"Research is to see what everybody else has seen, and to think what nobody else has thought," said Albert Szent-Gyorgyi, the Hungarian chemist who discovered Vitamin C. The discovery of saran, the third of Dow's major plastics, illustrates his point.

The discovery was made by a student named Ralph M. Wiley who was working in the Physics Lab as a lab helper. A chemistry major at Antioch College in Ohio, he was working in a cooperative program that involved work in industrial laboratories sandwiched in with classroom work. He had been assigned to Jack Reilly, a free-spirited Dow researcher who could not stand restraints and despised writing reports.

On a Monday morning in 1933 Wiley was washing up test tubes as usual when he noticed one with a thin white coating from a material that had evaporated over the weekend; to his surprise the coating was impervious to any of the solvents or reagents he had and could not be washed out of the tube. Reilly was intrigued as well, and instead of throwing the test tube out they reconstructed how the coating had come about, and Reilly suggested that Wiley accumulate enough of the material to enable them to identify its chemical structure.

When he had done so he found it was a material called 1,1-dichloroethylene, unsymmetrical dichloroethylene, or vinylidene chloride. A Frenchman named Henri Victor Regnault had noted its existence in a report dated 1838, but almost nothing was known about it.

By December 1934, Wiley, now a graduate chemist working full-time as Reilly's assistant, had prepared a few grams of the white powder and sent them to the Main Lab for analysis. He got a note back from Al Beshgetoor saying they had not been able to find a solvent for it so the material's molecular weight could not be determined. Wiley was to continue his research on the material for 10 years. Their first name for it was "Dow Eonite"; in the "Li'l Orphan Annie" comic strip of the period, an eccentric scientist had produced with Daddy Warbucks's support a completely insoluble and indestructible material called "Eonite."

That was only the first name for what became saran. Reilly, whose independence and work habits became more than John Grebe could take, transferred in 1935 to Strosacker's Lab and Wiley continued his work on Eonite, which he was now calling "Venalloy." (There were also "Venalloy B" and "Venalloy C.") Later it was called "Vec," shorthand for vinylidene chloride; and it was also known for some time as Experimental Plastic B-1500.[18]

In its early development it proved to be easily extrudable into filaments or strands. Its first use was as fishing line, and fishermen in the lab fished with it with enthusiasm until they discovered that in cold water or cold weather it became brittle and broke. That was the end of saran fishing lines.

In 1940, the first year saran went on the market, a furniture manufacturing concern, the Heywood-Wakefield Company, was looking for a replacement for natural rattan for seating, one less likely to snag the seats of men's trousers or lady's silk stockings, and it commissioned the Irvington Varnish and Insulator Company to furnish it with samples of rattan-like materials. Irvington asked Dow for a 50-pound sample of B-1500, and then came back with a 400-pound order for a full test. Firestone Tire and Rubber Company, which was developing rubber padding to deaden the clattering noise of trains, became Heywood-Wakefield's sales agent for railway seating. Firestone arranged with the Long Island Railway Company (the New York City subway system), to run some tests in their cars, and through this labyrinthine route the first big market for experimental plastic B-1500 suddenly opened up—as a seating material.[19]

Firestone at this point was demanding a name for the product—it was gearing up for a major advertising campaign for the seating—and Bill Goggin (Goggin and Alden Hanson were researching ways to fabricate with it) spearheaded a crash campaign to find a suitable trade name. It was agreed that the name should have no more than five letters, have no cur-

Gold from Seawater

In the spring of 1934 rumors raced coast to coast that Dow was mining gold as well as bromine from the seawater it was processing in North Carolina. The gossip sheets of the day said so. Know-it-all experts said Dow was doing it but could not admit it, because such a process would wreck the gold standard and might seriously disrupt the world power structure. Willard Dow was finally obliged to issue an official disclaimer. He told the company's shareholders at their 1934 annual meeting that the company had indeed accomplished a technological marvel by extracting bromine from ocean water, but it was only a rumor that it was also extracting gold.

"We are not extracting gold nor do we anticipate we will extract it in the near future," he said. "The fact that we handle tremendous volumes of water in the plant may seem a justification that in the future other valuable products will be produced from the water but at the present time, we have no plans for extracting gold."[1]

What Willard Dow did not tell them was that the company had in fact conducted serious experiments that year to see whether it could be done and was now satisfied that it was not economically feasible. L. C. (Jack) Chamberlain Jr., a bright young research chemist in the Physics Lab assigned to the bromine-from-seawater project, was the principal researcher. Since the idea was "a bit far-fetched," Chamberlain said, it was added to other miscellaneous work he was doing at the Wilmington location— experiments on solar heating of brine, checking the effects of brine disposal to the river, and the like—so that no specific budget was allocated for the work on gold.

Dow's Magnesium Lab in Midland had done some experimenting to verify Haber's analyses (the celebrated German chemist Fritz Haber had worked with seawater and developed a technique for removing gold from a known solution) and their work cast some doubt on Haber's results. The Mag Lab chemists asked Chamberlain to do larger-scale tests.[2]

Chamberlain's main experiment on gold recovery was run in a series of open-topped drums, which each day were filled with seawater. Iron salt and sulfide solutions were added, and the resulting precipitate was stirred through the solution and left to settle. The next day the precipitate was recovered, the drums were filled again, and the process was repeated. After many tons of seawater had been so treated, the accumulated precipitate was harvested and the precipitate roasted down to a small pellet.

In Midland the pellet was reduced to the metallic state. It was quite tiny by then and had a silver luster, Chamberlain said. Spectrographic analysis showed it was 60 percent gold and 40 percent silver. The amount of gold in the pellet calculated out to about $5 worth of gold per day that might be collected from the vast amount of water being processed through the plant. "This was much less than Haber's findings, maybe one one-hundredth or one one-thousandth as much," Chamberlain said years later. "It was quite discouraging, and nothing further was attempted."

"About the time the pellet was reduced to the silver-gold mixture," Chamberlain remembered,

I was buying a wedding ring and obtained John Grebe's permission to have the hard-won speck incorporated into the ring I was to give Esther. Having obtained permission I hurried out to the chap who had been refining the pellet, only to be told he had just lost it. He had tried to burn off enough silver to bring out the gold color. The flame had sputtered and blew the speck of metal off the plate and onto the floor, never to be found again. End of pellet; end of research on gold from seawater.

The rumors persisted for years. One weekend, a busload of economics students from a New York City college drove up to the Dow plant at Kure Beach unannounced, "and began asking questions about how much gold we were recovering," Chamberlain said. "They had heard the rumor and thought the operation might seriously affect the market value of gold."

The company also received letters from persons proposing various schemes and processes "for making gold out of anything from tapwater to sand." When he wrote his memories of the episode, in 1958, Chamberlain noted that "Esther's wedding ring is worn so thin I'll probably have to buy her another soon, and still no gold from seawater."

Chamberlain and his colleagues also put up charcoal "gold traps" in the process streams at Kure Beach, and these were sent off for analysis, but no gold was ever picked up in them, either.[3]

As a practical joke, some of the researchers gilded a small ingot of magnesium to resemble gold and went in and laid it on Willard's desk one day. "We've finally done it, Willard," they announced. "This gold was extracted from seawater." Willard looked startled, but as soon as he picked it up he knew it was magnesium. Willard enjoyed the joke as much as anyone, and the incident was still being laughed about at company gatherings many years later.

---

1. W. H. Dow, "A Report of the Fiscal Year May 31, 1933 to May 31, 1934," June 27, 1934.
2. After World War I Haber tried unsuccessfully to extract gold from seawater, hoping via this method to pay off the reparations imposed upon Germany by the Versailles Treaty. He too found that previous analyses of gold in seawater had been greatly overestimated. See Dietrich Stoltzenberg, *Fritz Haber: Chemiker, Nobelpreistrager, Deutscher, Jude* (Weinheim, Germany/New York: VCH, 1994).
3. L. C. Chamberlain Jr. to C. M. Shigley, "Gold from Sea Water," April 7, 1958. The literature at that time showed seawater containing two parts per billion of silver and gold, enough to be significant for Chamberlain's experiment. With modern measuring methods it is now known that seawater actually contains only 10 parts per trillion of gold.

rent meaning in either English or any other language, and be easy to remember—something like Dupont's nylon or Eastman's Kodak.

John Grebe devised a five-scale slide rule, each scale having the 26 letters of the alphabet, to produce an infinite number of five-letter words by moving the scales. That produced a host of five-letter words, but none that anyone liked. From the hundreds of names suggested, Goggin chose 10 that appealed most to him and circulated the list to some 200 people chosen at random in the Dow telephone book, asking their preference. That did not produce a winner either.

One morning Goggin received a wire from the Firestone salesman handling the railway seating business. It said simply, "Why not call it Saran? - Stedman." Goggin showed it to several Dow executives, and they all liked the name. Later in the morning he met Willard Dow in the hallway and he also approved. The name "Saran" was immediately adopted, copyrighted as a registered trademark and quickly inserted in the advertising that was to go into *Fortune* and *Time* magazines and other publications.

Years later, Firestone decided to go into the business of extruding saran and was unhappy that Dow and licensees of Dow were using "their" name, "Saran." Dow reminded them that the name had been offered with no strings attached, and that it was available to Firestone as well, nonexclusively, as a licensee. As a result, Firestone never used the name, but chose its own trademark, Velon.[20]

Like many of its siblings in the Dow product mix, saran was the object of at least one effort to kill it. One of the production superintendents, hearing of a couple of small explosions that occurred in the research lab (no one was hurt), told Willard Dow research on it should be stopped; it was too dangerous. This time Willard paid no attention. Saran went on to become the plastic probably most firmly identified with Dow in the public's mind.[21]

From these workaday events of the 1930s—Edgar Britton looking at German reference material, Ralph Wiley finding a test tube he could not wash, and Charles Strosacker suffering the humility of a field of 55-gallon drums no one wanted—came the vastly successful Dow plastics business whose products touch almost everyone in the world daily.

By the mid-1990s Dow was able to claim that it "ranks among the world leaders in the production of plastics, offering the broadest range of thermoplastic and thermoset materials of any manufacturer." Dow plastics, it noted, are used in appliances, automobiles, building and construction, electronics, flooring, furniture, health care, housewares, packaging, and recreation.[22]

III.

As we have seen, Herbert Dow began to think of using the ocean as a mine in 1924, when Ethyl gasoline was developed and brought about a demand for more bromine than Dow was making or could possibly make from brine—and Dow at the time was making roughly 90 percent of the nation's bromine.[23] Indeed, Thomas Midgley of General Motors, inventor of the antiknock compound, told Dow there "wasn't enough bromine in the world" to take care of the need.

Dow decided first to see how much more bromine could be squeezed from the mid-Michigan brine that had been his source of bromine for more than 30 years. After some experiments in the summer of 1924 he wrote the company treasurer, John S. Crider, that there was perhaps an alternative to drilling a huge number of new brinewells to obtain more bromine. "We have just made some tests to see how good an extraction (of bromine) we can get under extreme conditions and have been able to reduce the bromine to a point where it is running 40 percent of the amount in the oceans. This would seem to indicate that we could extract bromine from the oceans and recover 60 percent of the bromine in ocean water," he wrote. "However, bromine made in this way would not be cheap," he added.[24]

Dow, E. I. Du Pont de Nemours, and Midgley all went to work on the problem. The Du Pont Company's idea was to mount a plant to extract bromine from seawater on a cargo ship, using technology developed by Midgley's research group; the ship would put to sea, process seawater, extracting bromine from it, and return to port with a cargo of bromine, just as a fishing vessel would return with a cargo of fish.

In 1925 Du Pont's ship, the S.S. *Ethyl*, made its only voyage. An account of the trip records that it was only a limited success, "the problems stemming in part from the fact that many of the chemists and engineers aboard were too seasick properly to attend their duties."[25] The high amount of organic matter in seawater seems also to have been a problem. In any event, the S.S. *Ethyl* did not sail again, and research along other avenues by both parties continued.

By 1928 Herbert Dow was full of confidence that the problem could be solved. "If sometime in the future a real big demand for bromine arises, we will build a plant on the Atlantic Ocean or some other ocean and take it out of ocean water," he wrote to Prof. Alfred H. White, a friend at the University of Michigan. He spoke of experiments using water with only a quarter as much bromine as there is in the ocean, "so that we have a demonstration on a manufacturing scale and know how to apply it if necessary." The method was not economical, he warned, "unless the quantity should go into thousands of tons, in which case we might get an unprecedentedly low cost on account of the big scale of the operations."[26]

Sales of Ethyl gas and use of bromine (in the form of ethylene dibromide) continued to boom, and by the end of 1929 Herbert Dow was actively planning a plant to extract bromine from seawater. He sent Joseph E. Bayliss, his jack-of-all-trades, to the Gulf of Mexico to look at possible plant sites and get measures of salinity at these sites, and in February 1930 Bayliss sent samples of ocean water from the Gulf near Corpus Christi—the highest salinity he found—for Ivan Harlow and Brick Dressel, who were doing most of the lab work. In March Harlow and Dressel set up glassware apparatus for the process, which was little more than an adaptation of Herbert Dow's old blowing-out process, adjusted for seawater rather than brine, and by April 1 they had it in continuous operation. Joe Bayliss sent them a 55-gallon drum of seawater later in April. In May they scaled up to semi-plant operation, and on June 3 a full tank car of seawater arrived in Midland and was run into the semi-plant area, the first of several used in these experiments.

Much of the work was done with "synthetic seawater"—dilute Midland brine—and the experiments were then verified with the actual seawater shipped up from the Gulf of Mexico. That spring Herbert Dow sent Roy Osmun, another veteran, to look at seawater bromine plant sites on the East Coast as well. On his first trip, June 4-13, 1930, he inspected the area from Cape Fear to Cape Lookout.[27]

Herbert Dow fell ill and died in the midst of these preparations, but they went on without a hitch as Willard Dow smoothly took over. In February 1931 Arthur A. (Art) Asadorian and Francis H. (Heinie) Langell completed a report providing the data for constructing a plant. Kure (pronounced "curry") Beach, North Carolina, not far from Wilmington, was selected as the site. Then construction was held up as the Great Depression hit, people stopped driving their cars as much, and the demand for ethylene dibromide plummeted. Ground was finally broken in July 1933, and the first ethylene dibromide was made from seawater in the new plant on January 10, 1934.[28]

As with other major projects, Herbert Dow had two research teams working on the problem. Grebe said that in February 1930 Herbert Dow came out to his lab and asked if they could take bromine out of seawater. "We told him yes, and told him how it could be done," Grebe said. "He said not to work on it until the people then working on it had a chance to succeed." In June Grebe talked to Harlow "about working on this seawater thing, and told him we wouldn't work on it if he thought they were going to feel we were butting in on their project." Harlow said to go ahead, because they wanted anything they could get, and "we went ahead then and had the answer in a few days." Harlow deserved a lot of credit for "this broad-minded attitude," and in general a great deal of credit for working out the ocean water process, Grebe said.

Grebe recalled, "we tried our process and it worked. Herbert Dow came over to the lab and personally worked a 100 cc sample of synthetic ocean water through the process with me. Just as soon as he smelled the bromine he was satisfied. Later, when it was reported on three separate occasions that the process would not work, he did not give up; he had smelled it himself and knew it was there."

Grebe proposed using a potentiometer in the process, a device that makes continuous recovery of the bromine possible. Bromine can be recovered from seawater only in a very narrow range of acid-chlorine concentration, Grebe explained, and too much chlorine or too little acid converts the bromine to bromate, which cannot be recovered; the potentiometer helps maintain the stream in the recoverable range.[29]

Dow leased property on the Cape Fear Peninsula, a spit of land 17 miles south of Wilmington, with the broad Cape Fear River on one side and the Atlantic on the other. Salinity tests of the water here ranked it the second highest Bayliss and Osmun had encountered. During the Civil War, federal troops had thrown up earthworks at Kure Beach in their attack on Ft. Fisher on this peninsula, and these 1865 earthworks became one side of the plant's seawater holding pond, covering several hundred acres. The seawater intake was on the Atlantic side, and the debrominated water was released into the river, a tidal estuary.

Dressel and Glenn Cantwell built a pilot plant on the site, and when the full 10 million-pound-a-year plant was built, Dressel became the manager. Capacity was boosted to 22 million pounds in 1936 and to 40 million in 1938, and the process was changed and improved repeatedly. By then Willard Dow and Dutch Beutel were looking for a major new plant site, and Kure Beach was not it. In 1940, facing the staggering demand that a war would bring, a new EDB plant was built in Freeport, site of Dow's new Texas Division, incorporating all of the best features of the Kure Beach plant, and that became the home base of the Ethyl-Dow Corporation for the rest of its corporate life.

Kure Beach ran as a production facility until the end of the war, and was phased out in 1946 and closed down.

Situated on a peninsula as it was, the Kure Beach plant had to be serviced by water—reaching it by highway was difficult, and by railway impossible—and the vessels it used were the beginning of what was jokingly called "the Dow navy." In 1934 Earle MacLaughlin of Dow's engineering department bought an old wooden-hulled ship, the *Vanessa*, and refitted it to handle chemicals both in tankage and as deck cargo, and it plied back and forth from the plant to the Wilmington harbor daily. As the plant expanded, the *Vanessa*, which until its rebirth as flagship of the Dow navy had been a rumrunner, was replaced in 1936 by the *Edco* (for Ethyl-Dow Co.), a tug that hauled a big new barge back and forth to the harbor.[30]

Dow leased a rundown old beachfront hotel, "The Breakers," about two miles from the plant, and most of the Dow employees and their families stayed there. It was quickly discovered that the place had previously been a brothel, and one of the men complained he could not sleep for thinking of what might have gone on in his room. Its big dining room was called the "Edco Club."

Monroe Shigley, who became plant manager in 1936 after Dressel was transferred to manage the Cliffs-Dow plant in Michigan, was one of the few who lived in a separate house. He remembered showing Willard Dow about the plant one day when he came upon his favorite operator, who was cleaning shrimp, a practice strictly forbidden on the job, instead of tending to the pumps. He rebuked the operator severely and at length; and when he was through the operator said, "Well, it's this way. Your wife called me a little bit ago and said she was having Dr. Dow to lunch, and could I please get her some shrimp?"

Fishing about the place was forbidden too, but at night interlopers would sneak in and fish anyway. One night Shigley had the Plant Protection crew surprise them, and the surprise was Shigley's; among the lawbreakers they caught were the mayor of nearby Carolina Beach, one of that city's councilmen, and the Baptist minister.

Among the visitors to the plant were British and French engineers who came to acquire know-how so that they could build wartime plants to make bromine from seawater in Europe. Three British engineers from Imperial Chemical Industries came to Kure Beach, led by William Venn, studied the process, and then built two wartime plants on the British coast, one at Land's End managed by Venn. During the war Venn and others frequently had to leave their posts to man antiaircraft guns located around the plant. Jacques Coulon came from

Etablissements Kuhlmann in France to do likewise, and Morris McGowan, who spoke some French, and Bill Schambra conveyed the process information to him and designed a plant that was built at Port-de-Bouc, near Marseilles.

The Ethyl-Dow Company was eventually displaced by research that made the Arkansas brinefields the prime source of bromine. This technical advance was accompanied by the demise of tetraethyl lead, the single largest user, and the firm was dissolved in 1969. In its time it processed more than six cubic miles of seawater from the Atlantic Ocean and the Bay of Mexico, and extracted from them more than 2.4 billion pounds of bromine.

It was also one of the most profitable of Dow's ventures. Willard Dow told Shigley that in the late 1930s Ethyl-Dow was accounting for 25 percent of Dow Chemical's total profits.[31]

Notes

1. Keith R. McKennon, "Foreword," in Ray H. Boundy and J. Lawrence Amos, eds., *A History of The Dow Chemical Physics Lab* (New York: Marcel Dekker Inc., 1990), 4. See also Oral History, Keith R. McKennon, June 9, 1993.

2. Oral History, Sylvia Goergen Stoesser, August 17, 1990.

3. As a percentage of sales, the Dow research budget ranged from 3.65 to 5.78 percent during Willard Dow's tenure.

4. See Boundy and Amos, eds., *A History of The Dow Chemical Physics Lab* for fuller listings of these accomplishments and details of their discovery.

5. Oral History, Richard W. Swinehart, March 22, 1988.

6. Oral History, George K. Greminger Jr., March 21, 1988.

7. Oral History, Albert T. Maasberg, March 25, 1988.

8. Stanley Mason, "Methocel, the Invisible Product," *Elements* (English edition) no. 5 (1972).

9. The most detailed extant history of Methocel is a technical paper, DPE-81-013, by George Greminger, Dow Central Research Index, 1988, classified as Dow Confidential Information.

10. "Styrene" in Boundy and Amos, eds., *History of the Dow Chemical Physics Lab*, chap. 9.

11. Oral History, Larry Amos, Raymond F. Boyer, Walter Roush (reminiscences of early polystyrene history), recorded at Dow R&D meeting, "the Cadillac conference," at Cadillac, Michigan, July 27, 1976.

12. Ray H. Boundy and Raymond F. Boyer, "History," in Sylvia M. Stoesser, ed., *Styrene, Its Polymers, Co-Polymers and Derivatives*," chap. 1, ACS Monograph Series (New York: Reinhold Publishing Corp, 1952).

13. Raymond F. Boyer, "Anecdotal History of Styrene and Polystyrene," *Journal of Macromolecular Science* A15, no. 7 (1981): 1411-34. Boyer mentions one of Dreisbach's hobbies in this paper: insect collection and classification in terms of their genitals.

14. Karpiuk, *Dow Research Pioneers*, 262-63.

15. Whitehead, *The Dow Story*, 145-46.

16. Oral Histories, L. Amos, R. F. Boyer, W. Roush. Strosacker was one of the rare persons who could have ignored Willard Dow's orders and still survive as an employee.

17. Boundy and Boyer, "History."

18. Max Key and Eugene E. Perrin, "The Saga of Saran" (unpublished manuscript, 1983), Post Street Archives.

19. Stanley D. McGregor, "A History of Saran," unpublished manuscript, "Assembled as a special project in Dow Corporate Research and Development," 1968, marked "Restricted: for use of Dow employees only."

20. Key and Perrin, "Saga of Saran."

21. Oral Histories, Ralph M. Wiley, April 14, 1993 and May 6, 1980.

22. Dow Annual Report to Stockholders, 1993.

23. See memorandum, "Extraction Sea Water Bromine—Historical Matter," Thomas Griswold Jr., August 31, 1933, Post Street Archives.

24. H. H. Dow to J. S. Crider, July 30, 1924.

25. Joseph C. Robert, *Ethyl, A History of the Corporation and the People Who Made It,* (Charlottesville: University Press of Virginia, 1983), 114.

26. H. H. Dow to A. H. White, University of Michigan, April 5, 1928.

27. Harrison Hatton, Notes on conversation with Roy H. Osmun, May 11, 1950.

28. Hatton, Notes on conversation with F. H. Langell, May 8, 1950.

29. Hatton, Notes on conversation with John J. Grebe, May 12, 1950. Also, Hatton, Notes on conversation with Ivan F. Harlow, Grayton F. Dressel, and Francis H. Langell on Early Ethylene Dibromide-Ethyl Corp. History, May 10, 1950.

30. See Karpiuk, *Dow Research Pioneers*, 392-417. The Cape Fear Peninsula had long been a favored location for the production of illegal "North Carolina Corn" liquor and was frequently visited by revenue agents. Carolina Corn, said humorist Irwin S. Cobb, "had all the qualities of swallowing a lighted lantern."

31. Much of this account is derived from Oral History, Claire Monroe Shigley, June 15, 1989.

NINE

WORLD WAR II

I.

On December 6, 1941, a Saturday, Willard Dow and Dutch Beutel took an overnight train out of Detroit for Washington. They had an appointment with the secretary of war, Henry Stimson, to push construction of a mammoth new 72-million-pound-a-year magnesium plant at Freeport. With war clouds gathering, both government and Dow were becoming anxious to begin construction.

Late the next morning, picking up a newspaper in the club car, they learned that the Japanese had attacked Pearl Harbor. As Beutel recalled it, years later:

> We went to the secretary's office and he said, "I know I've got a date with you, but you know what happened yesterday. See the undersecretary. Whatever he agrees with you gentlemen is all right with me." So we went in to see the undersecretary, Robert Patterson, and he said, "Gentlemen, we've been wrangling about this magnesium plant down in Freeport all summer." I said, "Yes, and don't blame it on us. We're ready to start this thing. Now you're going to ask us to make up all the lost time you guys lost making up your minds as to what you wanted to do." I wasn't a bit polite. Willard looked at me as if he thought I was nuts. The undersecretary said, "Well, how long is it going to take you to build that plant for $52 million?" "About two years," I said. He said, "You're crazy. We've got to have that stuff tomorrow. What's the earliest time you can build it?" I said, "Well, I wouldn't attempt it in less than a year." "That's not good enough," he said. "We need it in six months." I said, "You want me to weep? You guys have lost a whole year fiddling around with this; now you want us to kill ourselves trying to do the impossible." Patterson said, "Fellows, we're in a war. If you're at all patriotic, you'll go back and try to build it in three months." I said, "Impossible. I also think six months is out of reach. We'll try, but I won't promise you anything in less than nine months, and we have got to have the best damn priori-

ties there are." He said, "You'll get them." I said, "Well, I hope to hell we do." He said, "Well, what is it going to cost to build it in nine months?" I said, "God only knows." "Give me a figure," he said. I pulled an envelop out of my pocket and I sat there thinking to myself, "What should I add to the cost estimate to do the job in nine months"; that was way off in the deep blue yonder. I thought, "Well, I'll just add another $10 million," and I said to him, "I'm going to give you a ballpark estimate. I don't think we should start it for less, and if we run over, you're going to pay the bill. But I think we can build it in nine months for $62 million dollars." Patterson said, "All right, $62 million is fine with me. I'll send you confirmation tomorrow." That was it, and we said our good-byes. We got a telegram the next morning authorizing us to proceed, signed by him. Willard damn near kicked my hind end when we got out of that office. He said he thought I was going berserk.

As it turned out, Beutel's estimates were not too far out of line. The plant was built in eight months for $56,326,000.[1]

By Pearl Harbor Day Dow had already largely converted to wartime manufacture. Already some months earlier an Office of Production Management official had described Dow as "the No. 1 defense plant in the nation," and its reputation as such had grown rapidly. As events were to prove, the Dow Company was well ahead of its industry and its government in the matter of war preparedness. During the years 1937-41 Dow was by far the fastest growing of the nation's large chemical firms, averaging 26 percent in annual growth during a period when one expert estimated growth for the top ten firms in the industry at an average of 3.2 percent yearly, and much of Dow's growth was in products that were to be key to the war, such as magnesium and styrene.[2]

Beutel's complaints about government foot dragging reflected Willard Dow's own frustration at dealing with Washington. In February 1941, shortly after the first Freeport magnesium-from-seawater plant had gone into production, Willard had proposed to Washington that provision be made to boost U.S. magnesium production to 100 million pounds annually, and he offered to expand the Dow facilities, with Dow money, to accomplish this, providing the government take the output. The offer was not accepted. As late as December 1940 the government estimated its need of magnesium for 1941 at 14 million pounds and pointed out that Dow already had this capacity—the Freeport magnesium plant's rated capacity was 18 million pounds. By June 1942, as it turned out, the OPM, the U.S. government's wartime production authority, was calling for a hike to 400 million pounds of capacity, and then to 600 million; by the end of the war the United States had actually built capacity for 580 million pounds.

A second major Dow involvement in the war involved the U.S. supply of synthetic rubber. The modern military, it was said, "runs on rubber wheels," and virtually all of the U.S. supply of natural rubber was at that time coming from rubber plantations in the Far East; synthetic rubber had not been fully developed, although much work had been done on it in Germany.

In 1940 a short-lived Goodyear-Dow Corporation had been formed with the object of developing, designing, and building a plant to produce synthetic rubber; the world's supply of natural rubber from the Far East was already in precarious shape. The two companies combined their knowledge and resources and in January 1941 proposed to the government a plant to produce 10,000 tons of Buna-type rubber annually. Even this modest proposal was not accepted, and it was 1942 before the government had a synthetic rubber plan in place.[3]

At the outbreak of the war Dow was the only U.S. producer of styrene, which it had begun making in 1937. (It had been the only U.S. producer of magnesium since 1927.) Buna-S rubber was made of the two chemicals styrene and butadiene, and Dow was also the principal developer of the latter. In the emergency brought on by Pearl Harbor, Dow quickly agreed to provide its know-how to the government, and this know-how was made available for the construction of styrene plants by other companies as well—Monsanto, Koppers, Carbon and Carbide Chemicals Corporation, and Polymer Corporation, Ltd., at Sarnia, Canada, newly established as the synthetic rubber arm of the Dominion of Canada.[4]

Government styrene plants were built by Dow itself at Velasco, Texas (next door to the magnesium plant), and at Los Angeles. More than 96 percent of the styrene produced at all of these plants was used for synthetic rubber production.

Aside from magnesium, which made lighter, swifter airplanes, and styrene, which made the tires, there were dozens of other Dow products that contributed to the war. A few examples:

- Thiokol rubber. Produced by Dow for the Thiokol Corporation, which marketed it. Thiokol rubber was a synthetic rubber devised by Thiokol in the late 1920s. During WWII it was manufactured because of the critical rubber shortage and used primarily for retreading tires. A government plant to boost Thiokol production was built by Dow in Texas but canceled in April 1943 when it was 85 percent complete and three weeks from start-up; the synthetic rubber program by this time was a roaring success. The United States was by then sending tires to the Soviet Union under the wartime Lend-Lease program.

- Saran. Fresh out of the Dow research laboratories, this product was used for insect screens by the military in tropical jungle climates; it was cheaper and more effective than ordinary metal screen in these uses because it did not rust or rot. One of its early uses was as a film wrapping for ordnance and supplies being landed on the beachheads. This was its first use in film form. Shoe innersoles made of saran were used in tropical climates, inserted in "jungle boots" to prevent fungus foot diseases. Civilian uses for saran were developed only after the war was over.

- Hexachlorethane. The principal ingredient of military smoke screens, it was made by Dow in Midland, Pittsburg, and Freeport.

- Butadiene. Dow was the first U.S. producer of butadiene, in 1940, but made it as a by-product of ethylene manufacture and never itself went into production of butadiene per se. Dow did discover how to purify crude butadiene to make it usable in synthetic rubber production.[5]

- Phenol. During World War I Dow was the nation's largest producer of phenol, the basis of picric acid and explosives in general and vital to other activities, such as the refining of oil and the manufacture of pharmaceuticals, germicides, and fungicides. After World War I Dow scrapped its phenol plant, developed and perfected a new process, and was by WWII again top dog in the manufacture of phenol, most of which was devoted to the war effort. The company was one of the leading shippers of phenol to America's allies under the Lend-Lease program.

- Impregnite. During World War II a big Chemical Warfare Service (CWS) plant was hurriedly built and operated in Midland. It occupied a series of buildings constructed on 10.4 acres of Dow property and kept under heavy guard. Behind those walls was manufactured a mysterious product referred to as "CC2." The workforce were forbidden to talk about what they were doing outside the plant. Only after the war was it revealed that the plant had been making "impregnite," a material used to treat combat clothing to make it resistant to gas warfare agents, especially mustard gas and Lewisite.

The Midland CWS plant was one of four identical plants around the United States. The original and model for the other three was a Du Pont installation. For 14 months—February 1943 to April 1944—the Midland impregnite plant produced high-quality product at full capacity. By then the military forces had bigger stockpiles of impregnite than they wanted, and the plant was put on standby. It never operated again. It was reported that the troops who landed on the beachheads of Normandy wore clothing treated with impregnite in case the Germans launched a gas attack. During its brief active life the Midland CWS plant was given army and navy "E" Awards and two Star Awards recognizing excellence in performance.

As the CWS plant was being closed down, in the spring of 1944, the new Dow Corning plant, also built to provide wartime products, was just going into operation. Many of the early employees of the Dow Corning Corporation were Dow employees who had been working at the CWS plant.[6]

One of the "miracle products" that came out of WWII was radar, and Dow scientists played a significant role in making radar possible—another story that emerged only after the war. As radar was being developed, in Great Britain first and then at the Radiation Laboratory of the Massachusetts Institute of Technology, a seemingly insurmountable obstacle appeared. An aircraft's radar antenna, mounted in a saucer-shaped rotating reflector, had to be securely protected, but this cover, or "radome," had also to be transparent to the waves sent out and reflected back, and it had to be physically strong, able to withstand tremendous air pressure and the shock of gunfire from the plane's armament. All manner of laminated wood and plastic materials were tried, but no material with the necessary specifications was found.

Dow researchers came up with an answer to this problem with a material called "polyfiber," which the company had originally developed in 1940 as a proposed filling for gas masks. Polyfiber was a matting, or batt, of extremely fine fibers of polystyrene, laid end to end and heated to form a large, thin-walled molding. Polyfiber radomes were used in the pioneer days of radar but were soon replaced by a new type of fiberglass plastic sandwich developed at MIT.

Although it was soon forgotten, the impact of polyfiber in making radar workable was considered by some writers one of the company's top contributions to Allied victory. Allen Shoenfield of the *Detroit News* wrote that "if the good folk of Midland were a bit more boastful of the scientific marvels that issue from the giant plant of the Dow Chemical Company they could erect, with perfect justice, a monument in the public square bearing the legend: 'In this city, in 1943-44, the Battle of the Atlantic was largely won and the might of new chemical achievements was added to the military strength of America.'"[7]

Another of Dow's more significant contributions to the war was a top secret project involving Ethocel, the first plastic made by the company. Donald L. Gibb, wartime manager of Dow's Plastics Engineering Division, told company officials that "this project is so secret that even our men who are cleared to discuss it know little of its complete ramifications, and yet this product, which we have worked on for ten years or more, may very conceivably affect the final outcome of the war."[8]

Only at the conclusion of the war did Dow learn that "Project A," as it was called, involved development of a shell fuse that could be adjusted to detonate within any desired distance of its target; this was in fact the first effort to produce what came to be called "smart bombs" half a century later. With such a shell it was no longer necessary to make a direct hit with an antitank or antiaircraft gun. An umbrella of shells could be fired that would explode whenever a tank, plane, or other target came near them. The World War II work on this was done by the Naval Ordnance Laboratory of Johns Hopkins University, aided by University of Michigan physicists, working in an old gravel pit outside Ann Arbor, Michigan. Dow's contribution was made through its Ann Arbor Laboratory, established in 1936 as the Consulting Engineering Division, the company's first research facility outside of Midland.

The "brain" of the shell was a miniature radar set inside the fuse that sensed its nearness to the target. To operate properly the fuse case had to have certain physical and electrical properties. Dow's researchers sucessfully developed a fuse case from an Ethocel material even though they didn't know what it was for. "We were told only that the project was one of great military importance and we worked on it for long periods almost entirely in the dark," Gibb wrote.

Efficient work under such conditions is very difficult, but we were so impressed with the necessity for secrecy that our work continued and increased until we had perfected a compound which had . . . properties judged satisfactory for the end use. The importance of this work finally was made known to us only about the conclusion of the war when we were told that the particular formulation was adopted and used in the construction of the body of the VT [variable time] fuse, a development probably second only to the atomic bomb in importance. This work again was undertaken first by individuals in our organization who were free to do so because of the liberal research policy the company follows and later because even though we had no opportunity to judge its value we had Dr. Willard Dow's specific approval to press the matter to a successful issue.

The VT, or proximity fuse, as it soon came to be known, was introduced to use late in the war and was given much of the credit by military men for the Allied victory in the Battle of the Bulge.

In at least one case the freedom of research espoused by Willard Dow led to solutions to military problems that involved no sale of Dow products at all. During a visit to Wright Field, Ohio, one of the major air force development bases, a group of Dow men heard about the military's desperate search for a self-sealing gas tank, and they immediately took it on as a project, starting out with Dow products that appeared to fit the bill but eventually coming up with a proposal for such a tank in which no Dow products were used at all. The net result was the development of Doron, a plastic glass-cloth laminate, and the chief of the Quartermaster Corps telephoned Willard Dow to congratulate him on Dow's achievement. The company was offered a research contract on the material but Willard Dow chose to continue work on it at company expense without a contract, reasoning that in that way any invention that came out of it would belong to Dow, not to the government.

One of the most challenging technical problems of World War II was that encountered by aircraft operating in searing desert heat and flying high into the subzero temperatures of the stratosphere; the extreme variations in temperature caused constant engine breakdowns. One answer to this problem was a material from Dow called Styraloy, a rubbery plastic that combined flexibility at subzero temperatures with excellent electrical properties. It was used extensively by the military for military telephone and radio facilities.

Another response, with considerably longer-lasting effects than Styraloy, which after the war became little more than a laboratory curiosity, was development of the Dow Corning Corporation, formed by Dow and Corning Glass Works in February 1943 for the development and production of silicones. The earliest Dow Corning products were fluids for high and low temperature use, chemically resistant greases, insulating resins and lubricants. The silicone fluids combined unusually low freezing points and high heat stability, and were water repellent and chemically inert. They made possible the operation of engines such as aircraft motors at higher temperatures—175° to 200° Celsius—than had previously been possible; planes could now fly higher and faster.

Dow did not make mustard gas during World War II, although there were recurrent rumors that it did, rumors nourished by the military authorities. When Maj. General William N. Porter, chief of the Chemical Warfare Service, came to Midland on December 29, 1942, to award two Army-Navy E flags to the company, he devoted his speech to U.S. preparedness for gas warfare.

The United States was ready to retaliate "in whatever quantities necessary, anytime, anyplace," if the Axis nations resorted to gas warfare, he told his Midland audience. "The fact that gas has not been used against us yet is no reason to suppose it will not be used when the enemies' position becomes desperate," the general said. "They certainly have no scruples against it."[9]

After that speech, made at the Dow headquarters itself, it was difficult to convince the public that Dow was not again making mustard and other gases, as it had during World War I, but had to keep it a secret, as it had before.

In the fall of 1943 the company distributed to all employees a booklet detailing, as well as could be done publicly, their role in the war. Entitled *Your Job and Victory*, it carried a message to Dow employees from Maj. Gen. Lucius D. Clay, then director of materiel for the army, famous later as the commandant of Berlin. "Guns, planes, tanks, bombs and shells are the headline weapons of this war," the general told Dow employees, "but behind them all lies the magic of chemistry. Not a single soldier or a single fighting weapon could survive upon a modern battlefield without the equipment that chemical workers and technicians have furnished. War, like peace, is fundamentally the history of chemistry in action. . . ."

"The final decision of this war will come, as always, on the battlefield itself," he concluded after discussing the role of magnesium and other Dow products, "but behind that final patch of land, on which the last Axis soldier will be beaten into unconditional surrender, will lie the chemical laboratory which prepared the way for his defeat."[10]

For the Dow workforce, those were strong words and strong medicine. They knew the war was also being fought on the home front, and that they were a powerful force on the side of the Allies.

II.

For Willard Dow the high point and low point of World War II came only nine days apart. On January 21, 1941, the first ingot of magnesium made from seawater was poured at Freeport, Texas, and one of his father's dreams became reality. It was one of the greatest chemical engineering feats of all time, and after all these years of preparation, and the dedicated work of many brilliant men, the Dow Company under Willard Dow's leadership had finally pulled it off. For the first time, man was mining the oceans. It was a historic event, magnificent in its timing, with war looming and the need for magnesium about to multiply, as it did by the war's end, a hundredfold. Dow people were elated with their success, and the date was long to be remembered.

Their joy was brief. On January 30 the U.S. Justice Department, over the signature of Thurman W. Arnold, assistant attorney general, handed down charges of conspiracy against Dow, charging that the company had conspired with the giant German firm I. G. Farbenindustrie to hold down magnesium production in the United States in the prewar era, thus contributing to U.S. unpreparedness for the war. Dow, it declared, had agreed with the Germans to limit its production to 4,000 tons a year.

Willard Dow was stunned and incredulous. How could anyone believe such a lie? On what was it based? Was this the thanks you got from the American government for being the only U.S. entity that had done anything to provide a reliable U.S. source of magnesium?

This "infamous charge," as he termed it, was based on a contract, the "Alig contract," that Willard Dow and his colleagues had never heard of until these accusations. "It is alleged,"

Willard later explained to the Truman "Watchdog" Committee (which catapulted Sen. Harry S. Truman into the vice presidency, and from there to the presidency),

> that I. G. Farben and Alcoa entered into an agreement by which an American company known as the Magnesium Development Corporation ("MDC") was formed. To this company the I.G. transferred its production and fabrication patents. A production patent has to do with the making of magnesium metal, a fabrication patent with alloying and working the metal after it is made. . . . None of us in our company ever heard of this contract between the I.G. and Alcoa, known as the Alig contract, until we were charged in an antitrust criminal action with having agreed to limit our production to 4,000 tons a year. . . . Dow was not a party to the Alig contract and knew nothing of it, and the [4,000 tons a year] limitation did not apply at all to the I.G. fabrication patents which are the only ones in which Dow was ever licensed. The charge, you see, is utterly baseless.

Further, there never was a shortage of magnesium in the United States, Willard Dow said.

> The fact is that there was never a real—as opposed to simply a theoretical—shortage of magnesium up to the time of filing the indictment against Dow by the government. Every requirement was met by Dow in 1940. Every requirement was met by Dow in 1941. These were all met out of resources provided by Dow. Since then there have been no real shortages except as the actual supply is compared with the rated capacity, and that has been due to the failure of other Government-owned plants. Dow has operated at better than full rated capacity and has done the job assigned by the Government.

The Justice Department, said Willard Dow, "in effect said that the defendants had prevented the United States from having a full supply of magnesium and that the best way to get more magnesium was to take the chief supplier out of his factories and put him in court."

On October 15, 1941, he telephoned Thurman Arnold in Washington. Notes taken at the time record the gist of the conversation:

> Dr. Dow stated that he was disturbed over the fact that on next Tuesday, October 21, the Department is going to set the case down for trial next April unless all parties indicate their willingness to enter into a plea of nolo-contendere assuming that a satisfactory decree and fines could be worked out. Dow said that it was impossible for the Dow Company to make magnesium and at the same time defend an Anti-Trust suit. Arnold said it is necessary to do both and that the Department could not nolle pros our case on the above grounds. Dow asked for an adjournment of our case until after the emergency. Arnold said that this could not be done. He said that if they did it for the Dow case, he would have to postpone all the cases until after the emergency. Dow said why shouldn't they do this. Arnold suggested that his advice was for one individual to plead and no doubt satisfactory fines could be worked out at a later date.

Willard Dow, saying he was "given the choice of serving his nation or serving himself," pleaded nolo contendere on April 15, 1942, and the final decree stipulated that the defendants "asserted their innocence of any violation of law," and that "neither consent (to the decree) nor this decree shall be evidence, admission or adjudication that they have violated any statute of the United States. . . ." He accepted the decree, he said, on the understanding that it was a compromise of convenience so that he could "get on with his work."[11]

It was only in 1944, on March 6, that Willard Dow finally found the opportunity to defend himself fully against these charges. He appeared before the Truman Committee (formally called the Senate Special Committee Investigating the National Defense Program) to present a detailed 76-page exposition of Dow's experience in magnesium and submit to questioning by the committee.

In the intervening three years the company's reputation had suffered greatly, as had that of several other companies similarly charged; World War II was hardly a time to be accused by the Justice Department of collaborating with the enemy. For all those years the company had a black cloud hanging over it, even though the case had been concluded with the nolo contendere plea, and newsmen and government officials regularly took potshots at the company. It was the first sustained assault on the Dow reputation in its history, and it prompted Willard Dow to establish a public relations department (called the editorial services department until 1949). He engaged a special writer, Samuel Carothers III, of Sunapee, New Hampshire (who had ghost-written a book for Henry Ford some years before), to gather the facts on magnesium and craft what became his 76-page presentation to the Senate committee. He hired another writer, Louis H. Woodman, editor of a small local newspaper, the *Freeland* (Michigan) *Star*, to draft speeches and news releases.

One of the early news releases of the company was issued in Washington on the date of Willard Dow's appearance before Senator Truman, March 6, 1944. It said:

> Vigorously attacking the Department of Justice as the authors and spreaders of a smear campaign linking his company with a German cartel, Willard H. Dow, president of The Dow Chemical Company, today told the Truman Committee in a special session called on magnesium: "The Department of Justice has at various times and in various places tried to force into the Dow war record certain charges growing out of peacetime operations. It pretends these charges are proven facts. By deduction, it claims both The Dow Chemical Company and the nation were less able than they should have been to meet the magnesium needs of the war emergency. Every act complained of by the Department of Justice as against the public interest was actually in the public interest and, if anyone impeded the magnesium program—it was not Dow.
>
> "The Dow Chemical Company," said Dr. Dow, "has been unfairly treated. It has served the nation in spite of and not because of the Government. The magnesium program of the Government, and consequently the service of supply to the Allies, was made possible by the foresight of The Dow Chemical Company in having ready the facilities for production when and as the materials were needed.

"In 1942, the critical year in magnesium production, Dow produced 84.2 percent of all the magnesium output in the country and the Dow 'know how' produced 91.2 percent.

"The alloying and fabrication program of the Government, and consequently the use of the metal in airplane building, was made possible only because of the independent research and developments, through the years, of The Dow Chemical Company."[12]

When the Truman Committee issued its report a week later it conceded the key point, saying: "Dow Chemical never has been a licensee of Magnesium Development Corporation production patents but only of fabrication patents, under a cross-licensing agreement. Therefore, Dow Chemical was never limited in the volume of its production."

It added some high praise for the company:

The magnesium plants owned or operated by The Dow Chemical Co. and the magnesium plants for which The Dow Chemical Co. acted as consultant and adviser reached 100 percent production within 5 to 7 months from the start of operations. Other companies, new to the magnesium field, with processes heretofore not utilized in this country, took a longer period to reach capacity operation, and even at the present time there are a few of the projects which are still experiencing production difficulties and have not reached capacity operation. The extent to which magnesium operations were met is due in no small part to the established production of The Dow Chemical Co. and the speed with which additional projects using the Dow process were brought into production.[13]

This seemed to put to rest the allegations against Dow, although they cropped up for years afterward.[14] In the postwar era Dow's romance with the world's lightest structural metal continued in full bloom. As the years went on the company expanded its production facilities at Freeport and became the world's largest producer. It gradually withdrew from the fabrication side of "Maggie," as the employees of the magnesium facilities liked to call her, leaving that to other firms. The sole exception was a Dow plant in Denver producing fabricated magnesium for Samsonite luggage.

By 1991, when Dow Magnesium celebrated its 75th anniversary, the company had a capacity of 90,000 metric tons of magnesium, 30 percent of the world's total magnesium capacity, and was still the world's largest producer.[15]

Notes

1. Oral History, Albert P. (Dutch) Beutel, transcript of interviews by Don Whitehead, 1967.
2. *Chemical Industry Survey, 1943 Edition* (New York: Merrill Lynch, Pierce, Fenner & Beane). See also *Moody's Manual of Investments*, 1942.
3. See "Performance Record of The Dow Chemical Company in the War Effort," compilation by Donald D. Hall, assistant to the general manager, January 9, 1945.

4. Dow received a royalty of 1/8 cent per pound on styrene monomer made by firms using the Dow process.

5. Dow's know-how in butadiene was made available through an agreement with the government entitled "General Information on Exchange and Use of Technical Information relating to Butadiene," February 5, 1942.

6. Hall, "Performance Record of The Dow Chemical Company in the War Effort."

7. Allen Shoenfield, "Midland Acclaimed for Radar Miracle; Dow Improvements That Helped Win Battle of Atlantic Revealed," *Detroit News*, November 10, 1945.

8. Undated memorandum, Donald L. Gibb to D. K. Ballman, 1945.

9. "U.S. Alert to Gas War; 'E' Award for Dow Chemical Points Readiness Against Foes' Last-Effort Attack," *Detroit Times*, December 30, 1942.

10. *Your Job and Victory*, employee booklet, 1943.

11. Willard H. Dow, statement to the Truman Committee, U.S. Senate, March 6, 1944. This statement was reprinted by the company as "Dow and Magnesium," together with extracts from the cross-examination and from the report of the committee. The defendants in the case included Alcoa and MDC as well as Dow. Earl W. Bennett, president of Dow Magnesium Corporation, a wartime Dow subsidiary, was also named.

12. News release issued by Dow at Washington, D.C., March 6, 1944.

13. Report of the Senate Special Committee Investigating the National Defense Program (the "Truman Committee"), March 13, 1944. See also account of these matters in Whitehead, *The Dow Story*, 176-83.

14. Sen. Estes Kefauver, for example, was still accusing Dow in connection with these matters during his run for the U.S. presidency in the 1950s.

15. "Dow Magnesium Business Celebrates 75th Anniversary," *Dow Today*, no. 13 (February 8, 1991).

THE STYLE OF
WILLARD DOW

I.

Willard Dow liked to quip that he arrived in this world just in time to get the Dow Company started. He was born in January 1897, a few months before the firm was incorporated, the third child and first son of Herbert Dow's family, and was named for his grandfathers, G. Willard Ball and J. Henry Dow.

When he was 10 he received his first chemistry set, whereupon he got a pail of brine from somewhere and began to experiment with the brine and the chemicals in his new set. His father set up a home laboratory for him, and while he was still a child he became familiar with chemical work. There seems never to have been a question, at least for father and son, but that Willard was destined to be his father's successor at the helm of the Dow Company.

He was always "Willard" to his colleagues in the community and the company, of whatever station; he grew up being called "Willard" by them and remained Willard to the end of his days. After he became president of the company, one of his friends came into his office and addressed him as "Mr. Dow." With a smile he asked, "Ted, where do you get this 'Mr. Dow' business? I'm still Willard."

He was his own man, even at a very young age. He acquired his own automobile (a Ford touring car) in 1912, when he was a 15-year-old high school student; a year later his father bought one too.[1]

In the early 1920s Herbert Dow received a quite unexpected message from Saginaw General Hospital that Willard had come safely through an operation for appendicitis. In consternation the family sped off to the hospital. There Willard explained that since most of his brothers and sisters had already had operations for appendicitis, he felt he might someday suffer a like attack, and he had decided to have this source of possible affliction removed when he was not overly pressed for time.[2]

He was anything but a couch potato, but he was not an athlete either. He became a casual golfer, but called it "a monotonous pursuit," and never played very much. He liked variety in his recreation—ice skating, dancing, and murder mysteries; rose growing, softball, and color photography. As a teenager he and the other boys in his neighborhood set up a wireless set in the Dow barn.

In the fall of 1915 he followed his sister Helen to the University of Michigan and enrolled in chemical engineering. She introduced him to Dr. William J. Hale, whom she was shortly to marry, and Willard became a regular visitor to Hale's laboratory, where they discussed "some of the more complex chemical problems." In due time Willard finished his chemistry courses "with flying colors."

In the summers he worked at the Dow plant back in Midland, getting acquainted with various operations, and he labored at some of the toughest and dirtiest jobs in the plant. He did a stint on the "tar gang," which applied tar to the chlorine cells, and came home so dirty that it drove his mother to distraction. She had a shower installed near the back door and insisted he take a shower every night before he was allowed in the rest of the house. Another summer he worked in the phenol plant, where his hands also got black, but by then Willard had figured out what to do about it. Bobby Dreisbach, who was running the phenol plant at the time, said Willard "before leaving on a Saturday afternoon would wash the black off his hands with an 18 percent caustic soda solution. This would get rid of the black alright," Bobby said, "but it would just about get rid of his hands too."[3]

In 1919 he graduated with a degree in chemical engineering and went to work full-time, serving first as assistant to Hale in the organic research laboratory. "Our first joint efforts," Hale said, "were devoted to improvements in the manufacture of chloroacetic acid, a forerunner in the production of indigo. Though the ideal course of this process was quickly determined it seemed to Willard Dow that the practical results were not readily forthcoming. All of which I explained to him could not take effect until the plant operators themselves had come to the realization that they had made the discoveries. True to this prediction, when we left that department these discoveries all came into realization. From this simple experience, Willard Dow has never forgotten that if you want a thing done, be sure that the man who is to do it is thoroughly convinced he is the originator of the idea. So far has this characteristic pervaded Willard Dow's mind that he practically refuses to have his name on an application for a patent to cover discoveries in which he has played a great role."[4]

In 1921 he married one of his Midland high school classmates, Martha Pratt, who had a degree from Western Michigan College of Education (now Western Michigan University), and was teaching French and Latin at the Mt. Pleasant (Michigan) High School. She was an extremely intelligent woman, energetic, hard-driving, insistent that things be done right, and, Macauley Whiting, her son-in-law, said, "a really fine complement for Willard, whose approach was generally a lot softer than that. His thought processes were a lot more immediate, whereas hers were much more concerned with what the effect of what we do today would cause out in the future."

Martha Pratt Dow was frightening to other women, Whiting said. "My mother was in awe of her, just because of the strength of her personality, and some other people were somewhat uncomfortable with her because of this power that just exuded from her, an energy that she exuded, never, never sitting still. She had a box of chocolates and when she was working real hard at something and she'd accomplish something, as a reward she'd go and give herself a chocolate. That accomplishment syndrome was so important to her."[5]

In 1922 Willard became a director of the firm, and in 1926 his father made him the official heir apparent by appointing him as his own assistant—Assistant General Manager. It was perhaps his most difficult assignment, because for four years his job was to follow his father around like a shadow. A shadow is not expected to express an opinion, and neither was Willard. His title, said Leland I. Doan (his brother-in-law and successor as president of the firm), "was little more than a facade . . . but it permitted him to become familiar with every aspect of the conduct of the business. The elder Dow frequently questioned, but seldom advised. 'How much,' he might ask suddenly, 'do you know about the operation of Plant X?' If the son admitted he knew little or nothing, he would remark dryly: 'Don't you think it's about time you found out?'"

On one occasion Herbert Dow was asked by an old associate why he didn't spend more time with the young man, teaching him. "One day," Dow said, "he will have to stand on his own feet. I don't want him accustomed to leaning on me."[6]

The day for Willard Dow to stand on his own feet came earlier than anyone had expected with Herbert Dow's death on October 16, 1930. To the Dow board of directors of 1930—which included Grace Dow, his mother, who had become a director two years before, and seven men old enough to be his father—Willard Dow must have seemed the most callow, wet-behind-the-ears kind of adolescent, even though he was 33.[7] Willard himself was saddened and stunned by the sudden loss of his father. Both the country and the company were at a turning point.

At the 1930 annual meeting of stockholders (on June 25) chairman Convers had observed that a stock market crash "usually precedes a business depression by four to six months," and that "you don't have to read the market reports to learn that dividends have been passed by some companies and cut by others." The Great Depression lay just ahead, but in spite of the storm clouds, the Dow Company had enlarged its business, done more business, and made more money than any year before, Convers said.[8]

Herbert Dow, at that meeting, had been busy denying the rumors that Dow was about to merge with what was referred to as "a large Eastern chemical concern" (E. I. du Pont de Nemours). These rumors were fueling great interest in the company's stock.[9]

"The big thing in Willard's life and particularly in Martha's life was the crisis that occurred when H. H. Dow died," according to Whiting.

It seems just routine that Willard was the guy who should take over, but in the eyes of Willard and Martha there was a very great debate about whether the company should continue as an independent company or whether it should be sold to Du Pont or somebody else for a very high price. It must have been awfully tempting at that time for a lot of people. The sense of it I got was that Martha was the one to whom this was very important. Willard never spoke quite so much about their fight to keep the independence of the company at that time, and their alliance with Grace Dow. The feeling they gave was that the three of them would really assure the independence of the company.[10]

Du Pont had made a bid to buy a controlling interest in the Dow company in 1927; after several clandestine meetings the matter had ended with a note from Herbert Dow to R. R. M. Carpenter, vice president of Du Pont, saying: "We are now able to state that the principal stockholders of the Dow Company do not desire to sell an important part of their common stock." That ended the Du Pont proposal, except for persistent rumors in the press. When Willard Dow became president in 1930 the question considered by the Dow board was whether to go back to Du Pont and reopen the negotiations.[11]

At the October meeting that considered the succession, these questions were discussed, including the possibility of an interim arrangement pending negotiations with Du Pont. Convers came to the rescue, as has been related, with an offer to serve as the young man's senior adviser on the scene in Midland; the notion of an overture to Du Pont was rejected; and Willard was elected as the new president and general manager of the company.

Although all the signals said a retrenchment was in order, the chemical industry was spoken of as "depression-proof," and Willard seems never seriously to have considered that idea. Amazingly, he acted, and the company with him, as if there were no depression to worry about; and it worked. Midland became known as "the town that didn't know there was a depression." The company made some of the greatest research discoveries of its history, and indeed of American industrial history, in the depths of the depression.

A. P. (Dutch) Beutel, who was closely associated with Willard Dow throughout Willard's 30 years with the company, said one of his most amazing traits was that he was "a wonderful listener." He had learned the habit of listening to people and letting them talk themselves out, which is one of the hardest things an executive has to do; many never learn to do it, Beutel said.[12]

Both Herbert and Willard Dow were always asking questions, Beutel said. "The way Herbert Dow did it was perhaps a little more obvious, and he had quite a different manner from Willard Dow's approach, but when you stop to think it over, you realize there wasn't so much difference after all."

Willard had a store of jokes and loved to tell them. They tended to be the "shaggy dog" type of story. One of his favorites concerned the dog that played the piano in partnership with a mouse who stood on the piano and sang. The amazing part of it was that the mouse really couldn't sing a note—the dog was a ventriloquist.

Midland was a small town and Dow was a small company. Willard knew everyone in town, and everyone knew Willard. One of the local characters was Freddy Odekirk, a mentally handicapped young man who could be seen hauling a wagon around town on which he carried his lawnmower. He wore pants, a vest (no undershirt or shirt, but a vest), and a derby hat. One of Freddy's chores was to bring home the milk, and one day he took some wires and devised a gadget that could be placed over the neck of the old-style glass milk bottle and, when lifted, would tighten; he could then carry two bottles of milk with one hand. His friends at Tom Dunn's candy store on Main Street kidded him about the gadget and one of them asked, "You know Willard Dow, don't you?" Freddy said, "Sure. Willard Dow is my friend." "Why don't you go down and see him and get your gadget patented, so no one will steal your idea?"

So Freddy walked into the lobby at Dow headquarters and told the receptionist he wanted to see Willard, and shortly was sent to his office. Willard looked at Freddy's gadget, and then phoned Bruce Fayerweather in the patent department and asked him to come to his office to talk to Freddy Odekirk about a patent. One was applied for over the signature of Edward C. Burdick, Dow's chief patent attorney, and the U.S. Patent Office in due time granted Freddy Odekirk a patent, which Freddy ecstatically showed the gang at the candy store who teased him all the time. It was probably the proudest moment of Freddy Odekirk's life.[13]

Willard Dow combined the functions of chairman, president, general manager, and director of research during most of his time as chief executive. The research lab directors all reported to Willard, along with everyone else; he was deeply involved in virtually every detail of the company's business. He was renowned for his prodigious memory and his ability to recall the detail of conversations conducted months before. "Sparked with a keen sense of humor, his genial casual manner all but conceals an amazingly retentive mind with an acuteness for detail that makes it nearly impossible for a Dow employee ever to 'get the jump on the boss,'" *Chemical & Engineering News* reported.[14]

When he was in his early forties his hair turned rapidly white, and he became known as "the silver fox," a term that always made him smile. During his tenure the company's sales multiplied by more than 10 (from $16 million in 1930 to $200 million in 1949) in spite of the Great Depression, World War II, and postwar adjustments. The company emerged from the backwoods of Michigan to become a major force in the U.S. chemical industry.

Willard continued the philanthropies of his father, and added a few of his own. At the end of 1941 he learned of severe problems at Ferris Institute, a small school in west central Michigan where in a wave of patriotism large numbers of students had joined the armed forces, leaving less than 50 tuition-paying students on the campus; as a result the school could not meet its payroll and was about to close its doors. Willard gave the school a check for $10,000. With this timely help it met its payroll and survived what was perhaps the most life-threatening crisis of its existence.[15]

Willard began to pile honors upon honors, receiving honorary doctorates from the University of Michigan, Michigan Technological University, and Illinois Institute of Technology in rapid succession. He became the first American industrialist to receive the Chandler Medal, conferred by Columbia University for distinguished achievement in science and industry (1943), and received the Gold Medal Award of the American Institute of Chemists (1944), and the Chemical Industry Medal for "conspicuous service to applied chemistry" (1946). In November 1946, *Science Illustrated* nominated him as its "Man of Science." The magazine said "the secret of Dow success" is "spending 65 to 70 cents on research for every dollar paid to stockholders—and 15 research laboratories, all directed by Dr. Dow himself."[16]

At the AIC Gold Medal banquet, Mark Putnam, who introduced him, said that

practically all of the projects which have been developed by The Dow Chemical Company during the past 14 years have been worked out under his personal guidance—enterprises such as the extraction of bromine from seawater, iodine from oil well brine, ethyl cellulose from cellulose and ethyl chloride, styrene and polystyrene, chemical servicing of oil wells, and magnesium from seawater. Whereas Herbert Dow created the essential idea, Willard Dow has nourished and built that idea to greater and greater proportions. . . . Without Dow's recovery of bromine from the sea, there could be no flood of 100-octane gasoline for the United Nations.

These events prompted Willard to express his philosophies, and brought forth some of his most memorable speeches. They reflect a deeply religious man, a strong proponent of rugged individualism, and the conviction that the opportunities in chemistry are boundless. "There is always room out in front," he said, "room for all without crowding, and work for generations to come."[17]

II.

Pollution control was a problem for the company from the beginning. Chlorine, the active ingredient of the bleach that was its main product, was difficult if not impossible to contain in the equipment of 1897, and while Herbert Dow did all he could to avoid losing any (he much preferred to sell it), there were often windborne whiffs of chlorine around the town, especially in the vicinity of the plant and around "Paddy Hollow," the Irish neighborhood across the railroad tracks.

Any time a cow died in the vicinity, the owner wanted to believe the cause was chlorine gas, and the company was constantly involved in lawsuits of this kind; people in the neighborhood frequently claimed their yard and shrubbery was being blighted and killed by chlorine, and Gil Currie, Dow's attorney, believed many of these suits were instigated by the town's liquor interests, who were convinced Dow wanted to put them out of business. Herbert Dow finally planted some bushes and shrubbery inside the company fence to prove they would grow there and that stray chlorine wasn't hurting anything, Leland Doan recalled.[18]

Gilbert Currie said the general reasoning of the suits was that chlorine escaping from the Dow plant combined with moisture in the air to form hydrochloric acid, and the acid precipitated out of the air onto trees, plants, screens, and the like, damaging them. The suits were finally decided in favor of the company, he said, but to clear up all questions about it Herbert

"Curing" Cancer

During the time Willard Dow presided over Dow Chemical there was a great shining hope that a simple cure could be found for cancer, and many a young chemist of that day dreamed of finding it.

Among them was James V. Sheridan, who joined Dow's Analytical Lab in 1935 with a chemistry degree from Carnegie Tech (today's Carnegie-Mellon University). On September 6, 1936, the young chemist had a dream. He "saw a round circle with bars across it like venetian blinds, all the colors of the rainbow," he said, "with molecules moving in and out of it, coming close and receding." When it all settled down he recognized the molecular structure of tetrahydroquinone, and understood that it was a cure for cancer.[1] "That dream was a miracle, a gift from God," said his wife Estelle.

Sheridan told Willard Dow about the dream, and said he wanted to begin research on it. "What would you need?" Willard asked. Sheridan said that beyond Willard's authorization to work on it he'd need about $150 to buy cancer strain mice.

Willard thought a minute and said, "Jim, I'm not going to give you that $150. If I do you'll probably spend the rest of your life on this and my advice to you is not to go down that road. If you do, in the end they'll just tar and feather you—they'll crucify you. Don't do it."

Disappointed but not discouraged, Sheridan set up a lab in his own basement, bought equipment and mice with his own funds, and conducted experiments on his own time. The more he worked at it the more encouraged he became. In 1937 he became one of two chemists (Bill Yates was the other) in the first group trained in-house to become patent attorneys by Bill Groening of Dow's legal department, a five-year program. He continued his experiments on his own during this time. "Tests Show Possible Cure for Cancer," said a 1941 article in the *Midland Daily News*. "Startling Results Obtained by Dow Patent Attorney in Two Years of Experimentation."[2]

At the end of World War II, Sheridan, by then a general attorney for the company, left Dow "because I couldn't work on my project at Dow" and went to work for a cancer institute in Detroit. He continued to get a paycheck from Dow for a full year after he left. "Willard Dow was such a wonderful man," he said.

For the rest of his career Sheridan continued to pursue his dream, working for a succession of cancer research organizations and falling back on his legal skills when the research money ran out. He called his material "Entelev"; it was also known as Jim's Juice, Crocinic Acid, Sheridan's Formula, JS-114, JS-101, and 126-F. In 1984, when he was 72, he turned it over to a younger colleague, Edward Sopcak, who began manufacturing it under the name "CanCell."[3]

Over the years he had all kinds of trouble with his cancer cure—fights with government and medical authorities, and court injunctions against making or selling it. "Why did God give this miracle to a chemist," Estelle Sheridan asked, "and then give him only dummies to work with?"

At age 82, his own health failing, Sheridan still remembered his dream of 58 years before in vivid detail, and was convinced his material would also work on the AIDS virus. He said he had heard from a man in Africa that "it works like a charm on AIDS." "What's the matter with people?" Estelle Sheridan asked. "It seems like they just don't want a cure for cancer or for AIDS."

In 1945, when he was still with Dow, he was called to Willard Dow's office and introduced to Dr. William F. Koch, who also had developed a purported cancer cure. Willard asked him to "check into" Koch's cure. Sheridan soon also became one of three attorneys defending Koch at a Food & Drug Administration trial in Detroit, Sheridan in charge of "the chemical side of it." Dr. Koch promised to work with him on Sheridan's cure once the trial was over, but this never happened, and the two parted on decidedly unfriendly terms later.

Its association with Dr. William Frederick Koch was one of the more embarrassing events in the Dow company's first century. Koch, one of the great medical quacks of the twentieth century, was best known as inventor of the "Koch Shot," an injection that allegedly cured cancer. Koch claimed his treatments also cured polio, asthma, arthritis, and other maladies, as well as various diseases of cows and horses.

Dr. William J. Hale introduced Koch to Willard during the early days of World War II. Willard was anxious to find a cure for the common cold at the time, and Koch's work was immediately interesting to him. Hale had known Koch in Ann Arbor, where both had been on the faculty of the University of Michigan and Koch had earned B.A., M.A., and Ph.D. degrees. Koch was an instructor in histology and embryology at Ann Arbor, from 1910 to 1913, and then became professor of physiology at the Detroit Medical College (1914-19), where he earned a medical degree. It seems never to have crossed Billy Hale's mind that a man with credentials of this sort could turn out to be a fraud.

As early as 1918 Koch had been tinkering with a cancer cure, and by 1926 he had come up with one. He called it "glyoxylide," and administered in a single hypodermic shot it cured, he said, whatever ailed you. By the beginning of World War II he had built a nationwide network of some 80 doctors who purchased the glyoxylide from his Detroit laboratory (at $50 a shot) and then administered it to their patients for whatever the market would bear—up to $500 a shot.

A government prosecutor at one of his trials described him as "the smartest, brightest quack in the United States." Typical of the medical findings in respect to the Koch shot was this one, contained in the official report of a hearing before the Wayne County (Michigan) Medical Society: "In no instance have we found a case where the diagnosis of cancer was absolutely established (by pathological tests) and where no other form of treatment had been used, in which a cure or any decided benefit had been obtained."

Koch, like Sheridan, carefully collected from his customer network accounts of cures effected with his treatments, which he then trumpeted in his literature. When he was haled into court by the Food and Drug Administration, as he increasingly was, or called upon to defend his practices before his fellow M.D.s, as he also frequently was, he produced these testimonials, and his friends in the client network were always ready to testify in his behalf.

Dr. Koch also carefully cultivated the backing of religious groups. The introduction to one of his principal promotional brochures, "The Koch Treatment" (1951) said: "The discoveries of Dr. Koch are regarded by multitudes of religious folk as a gift of God to our day and generation. Dr. Koch is himself a Bible-believing Christian. His attainments as a scientist have confirmed rather than mitigated faith in God and the Word of God. History will record him as one of the great benefactors of mankind."[4]

There is evidence that at least a few of Dr. Koch's network of doctors paid their preacher friends $50 for each patient referred to them.

Ignored were such cases as the bereaved Chicagoan who asked the *Chicago Tribune* about Dr. George Franklin Smith, Koch's outlet in Chicago. He said he had paid Dr. Smith $50 down to treat his severely ill wife and had signed a contract for the remainder of the $325 total he was to pay. His wife had one treatment and died three days later. Did he still have to pay the remainder of the contract, he wanted to know?

Koch was surely one of the most controversial figures of his time. There were those who called him "the world's greatest living chemist" and "the discoverer of a new science which charts the future course of the medical profession," and there were those who saw him as a crook and a fraud. Koch printed only one testimonial to his ability on the cover of "The Koch Treatment." It said: "Dr. William Frederick Koch is the modern Pasteur," signed by "Dr. William Hale, Dow Chemical Company."

When Dr. Hale brought his old friend with the impeccable credentials to Willard Dow, Dr. Koch explained that he was being opposed by the American Medical Association. Each cancer patient paid the medical profession an average of $7,500, he said, just to die. The AMA did not want to lose this major source of income, of course, and they were therefore opposing his cancer cure by all the means at their disposal, fair or foul, he told Willard.

He asked Willard for a little help. He needed, he said, completely unbiased and scientific analyses of his treatment that would stand up to any opposition, in any court of law. Could Willard provide him, in the interests of a suffering humanity, a bit of laboratory help?

Willard called in Sheridan, and within a short time was one of Dr. Koch's biggest fans. "As far as I am personally concerned," Willard wrote in 1946,

> I consider him one of the outstanding scientists in the medical profession, and he is so far ahead of the thinking of his profession that he is naturally being ridiculed. . . . The mere fact that Dr. Koch has a treatment definitely affecting virus diseases is of itself sufficiently important that it ought to be analyzed from every angle by the medical profession. As I understand it, his treatment of the virus type of cancer will run anywhere from 40 to 60 percent cure. If he had a 10 percent cure, it would be something the medical men ought to look at, but the ways of the world are strange, and new ideas are slow in developing. I think we all have an opportunity to see something new aborning in Dr. Koch's work. . . .[5]

Dr. Koch was quick to capitalize on Willard Dow's endorsement. Doctors giving the Koch shot were soon letting their clients in on a little secret—glyoxylide was made by the Dow Chemical Company (which of course was not true) and was fully endorsed by the president of that firm.

Willard had a cow named Rosie who had mastitis, and he asked Dr. Koch to treat Rosie. "Although the record of mastitis cure is of the order of better than 90 percent, we have had a great deal of difficulty getting her cured," he wrote an interested farmer, but "I have all the faith in the world she is going to be cured. . . ."[6]

Dr. Koch used Dr. Hale's office when he was in Midland (Hale was seldom there at this period), and often administered "Koch shots" to patients there. He was also provided the technical help he had asked for, which seems to have been a frustrating experience for the Dow personnel involved. As Dr. Harold H. Gay, director of the Dow medical department, wrote in response to an attorney's inquiry in 1953, "I am not by any means sure that these 'shots' were ever the same twice and there seems to be some evidence that there was usually insufficient chemical material of any kind to make a valid analysis."

Gertrude Winfield, Hale's confidential secretary, kept Dr. Koch's records of his Midland patients, and often went out with him on patient calls. She soon also became his fiancée, Dr. Koch's wife having died. "Before I knew it we had between 300 and 400 patients," Winfield said, "and they never paid anything of course. There was never any charge."

Koch would work all day in his office in Detroit and "then about four o'clock in the afternoon he'd drive up here to Midland (about 130 miles) and we would start to see patients," she said. "Sometimes I'd get home around five o'clock in the morning. Then I'd take a shower and come back to the office to work for Hale."

In the end they broke off the engagement. "Koch wanted to live in South America and I had no idea of living in South America," she said.[7]

Louis C. (Bud) Rubens, who became one of Dow's most distinguished research scientists—one of only six accorded the title of "research fellow," the highest research rank in the company—saw the Koch controversy a little differently. "The truth was probably somewhere between the two extremes," he said. Rubens, then a young research chemist, was asked by Willard Dow to help Dr. Koch, and did. Occasionally he would go down from Midland to the Detroit Club, one of Billy Hale's favorite haunts, to meet Dr. Koch.

The shot seemed to work in many cases, Rubens said, but no genuine clinical trials of it were ever made. "I concluded that Dr. Koch and his colleagues did not really want stringent clinical tests; keeping the flow of money coming in, that was the important thing." Dr. Koch was working on the principles of homeopathic medicine, and many of these remedies (such as bee stings for arthritis) were extremely difficult to evaluate, Rubens felt.[8]

The connection with Dr. Koch became increasingly embarrassing to the company as the Food and Drug Administration continued to indict him for mail fraud, mislabeling, and the like, and there was also growing opposition to the Koch connection within the company. Much of this was concentrated in the company's own medical department. Harold Gay, its director, a plainspoken man, referred to Dr. Koch as "Dr. Hoax," and called him "an unadulterated quack." Willard Dow maintained his loyalty to the man to his dying day, however.

"Dr. Dow was a very open-minded person who was able to jump the hurdles of prejudice in an attempt to get at facts," Dr. Gay wrote later. "He was very research-minded and immediately became interested in Dr. Koch and his alleged treatment for cancer. His interest was undoubtedly stimulated by the fact that his own father had died of cancer of the liver. Until Dr. Dow's death, Dr. Koch was able to prey upon his credulity and sense of fairness and collected a number of letters written by Dr. Dow which Dr. Koch now (1953) quotes in part and misquotes as a testimonial for his treatment."[9]

When Willard Dow died, Mark Putnam, who then became executive vice president of the company, quickly persuaded the new president, Leland I. Doan, that Dow should immediately and firmly distance itself from Dr. Koch and his work. Putnam called in the people who had been working with Dr. Koch, one by one, and told them there would be no more work for or company connection with Dr. Koch. Most of the records of the relationship were destroyed at that time.

That was the formal end of Dow's assocation with Dr. Koch, who in the interim had apparently decided to quit while he was still a free man and left for Brazil, where he worked with the Brazilian government agriculture department, promoting the Koch shot as a cure for mastitis in Brazilian cattle. The Food and Drug Administration filed an action by which he would have been arrested the moment he set foot on U.S. soil again. A few years later, having settled down with a new Brazilian wife, he died of a heart attack. "He thought she had money, and she thought he had money, and neither one did," Gertrude Winfield said. "They deserved each other."

For many years afterward, Dow field salesmen and representatives would be asked about buying Koch shots from Dow; many people were convinced they were a Dow product. Even today an occasional query is received by the company. A recent request for a supply of the material came from an AIDS researcher, for example. Had Dow ever thought of trying the Koch shot as a remedy for AIDS victims, he wanted to know? How could he make some?

---

1. James V. and Estelle Sheridan, interview by the author, March 2, 1994. The preferred material was 4, tert-butyl orthoquinone, according to L. C. Rubens (see note 8 below).
2. "Tests Show Possible Cure for Cancer; Startling Results Obtained by Dow Patent Attorney in Two Years of Experimentation," *Midland Daily News*, May 31, 1941.
3. See Louise B. Trull, *The CanCell Controversy: Why Is a Possible Cure for Cancer Being Suppressed?* (Norfolk, Va.: Hampton Roads Publishing Co., 1993), an account of the work of Sheridan and Sopcak.
4. Gerald B. Winrod, *The Koch Treatment* and companion volume, *The Koch Treatment Relieves Suffering* (Wichita, Kans.: Christian Medical Research League, 1951).
5. Willard H. Dow to Laurence B. Thatcher, Imlay City, Michigan, June 21, 1946.
6. Ibid.
7. Oral History, Gertrude Winfield, May 25, 1994.
8. Oral History, Louis C. Rubens, August 19, 1986. (Rubens prepared compounds for testing for both Sheridan and Koch.) Also, Rubens, private communication to the author, June 1994.
9. Harold H. Gay, director, Dow Medical Department, to Frederick Ornsteen M.D., Chelsea, Mass., August 25, 1953.

Dow bought the land along the plant fence (the present Bay City Road in Midland) and leased it back to people who wanted to live there, with a proviso in the lease that the company was not responsible for damage caused by escape of chemicals from the plant.[19]

The problem became even more severe when the company began making phenol in 1915. Unlike most of the chemicals Dow had been making, phenol and the chlorinated phenols dissolve in water and cannot be settled out of the water, as can insoluble or poorly soluble waste. About a year after Dow began making phenol, fishermen downstream began to complain that their fish tasted bad, and it was soon clear that phenol was the culprit. This prompted the practice of "ponding"—running the phenol plant waste into large holding ponds that were later dumped into the river at flood stage or high water, when they would be quickly and thoroughly diluted. A dike was built around the phenol plant to contain the phenolic waste there until it was diverted to one of the ponds.

In the early 1920s, when introduction of the new Hale-Britton phenol process began to thrust Dow into world leadership as a phenol producer, phenol became an even bigger waste problem. The company then began to separate different kinds of wastes and develop different treatments for different wastes; up to then there had been only one category of waste. This was a pioneering move.

By 1931 the Midland plant had 600 acres of waste ponds and had on staff its first waste disposal engineer, Alvin M. (Al) Edmunds, a chemist from the University of Minnesota. From 1928 to 1935, Edmunds was in charge both of waste disposal and of research to determine how to dispose of wastes efficiently. He was responsible for releasing waste from the ponds during high water flow in the river and would then follow the release to Saginaw, taking river samples along the way. At the Saginaw water intake (a big new Saginaw Waterworks was completed in 1929) he would close the gates, and after the waste flow had passed would open them again.[20]

As phenol production soared to new heights the plant outgrew the ponding system. When the system was installed the phenolic wastes had amounted to 200,000 gallons daily; now they amounted to two million gallons a day. In 1934 the state of Michigan sent Milton Adams, director of the state's Stream Control Commission, and his engineer, Thomas J. Powers, to talk to Willard Dow and the company about wastewater problems on the Tittabawassee River. Where Dow had once been a small company on a small river, it was now a very big company on the same small river.[21]

The basic problems were water taste and odor and fish taste, the toxicity to fish of the wastes, and calcium and magnesium salts, which could cause water hardness. Two years later Dow hired Powers as its first water pollution professional, and June 1, 1936, is generally acknowledged as the beginning of a formal pollution control program in the company. Edmunds and Powers became the forerunners of a long line of pioneering Dow professionals in this field—among them Charles Sercu, Stan Mogelnicki, Jim Teal, Charles Querio, E. S. (Bud) Shannon, and others.

Powers went to work for Al Beshgetoor in the Dow Main Laboratory and tackled the phenolic waste problem first. Edmunds had begun some experiments with a species of bacteria that seemed to thrive on phenolic waste, and this quickly proved to be the most efficient way to deal with the problem. In June 1937, Dow began construction of the first large-scale biological plant designed to destroy phenols.

Identified as *Achromobacter Cruciviae*, the tiny bacteria that love phenol had been studied closely by the Dow Biochemical Laboratory under Don Irish and had been selected for this job. The system consisted of a trickling filter 142 feet in diameter containing cinders (later it was blast furnace slag) about 10 feet deep, through which the phenolic waste was filtered. It took about 15 minutes for the waste to filter through, during which time the bacteria "ate" the phenol. With major refinements, this basic system is still used today. The 1937 model took care of 18 million gallons of phenolic waste per day.[22] The plant was expanded in 1940 and again in 1942.

To back up its phenolic waste disposal system the company instituted daily taste tests to verify that the system was working. Fish grown in various riverwater samples, including samples of Dow waste disposal plant effluent, were served to a taste-test panel at two sessions daily, at 11:30 A.M. and 4:30 P.M. The panel gathered in the Dow cafeteria at these hours and each panelist tasted and rated about 20 samples.

In 1947 the fish-tasting was expanded to include other Dow waste effluents, and fish were brought in from the Saginaw River and Bay. Roy Osmun was in charge of catching the fish, the envy of his coworkers because he was actually "paid to go fishing." Perch, the most important commercial and sports fish in the area, was chosen as the test species.

For years these tests served to tell Dow whether it was doing a good or a bad job on its waste stream. The data were later provided to the U.S. Public Health Service under the first industrial research contract the USPHS ever signed with an industrial firm.

Ivan Harlow, the first supervisor of waste control in the company, insisted on a regular river sampling and analysis program that has been maintained by Dow throughout the years. As a result, Dow has for most of the last century known more about the Tittabawassee River than anyone else, public or private.[23]

During World War II the demands on the waste system soared again, and in 1943 Barstow, Harlow, and Powers began to plan for a newer, bigger general waste disposal plant. After months of research experiments, construction began in March 1945 and the plant went into operation a year later. It was one of the world's largest and most modern industrial waste treatment systems; the waste plant itself was big enough to handle the wastes of a city the size of Albany, New York.[24]

Some years later Dow went a step further with the development and introduction of a plastic packing material called Dowpac that replaced the cinders or slag used in trickling filter systems, which were then coming into general use. It had the advantages of light weight, uniformity of shape, and excellent aeration. Dowpac became a regular Dow sales item in 1958 for use in sewage and industrial plants of all kinds.[25]

Dow was thus one of the leaders in bringing industrial waste control to newer, higher standards.

Dow's "CIA"

I n the 1940s, at the onset of the Cold War, large research-minded companies such as Dow became very conscious of the threat of infiltration by Communist spies intent on ferreting out their secrets and turning them over to the godless Soviets. When it turned out that spy Klaus Fuchs had filched the secret of the atomic bomb and given it to the Soviets, it removed any lingering doubts they may have had, and many companies installed security forces to guard against this evil. Usually the corporate security chief worked very closely with the chief executive, and some became extremely powerful. Harry Bennett, virtual dictator of the Ford Motor Company for some years through his influence on the aging Henry Ford, was a model of the type.

Willard Dow did not want his company to be infiltrated any more than anyone else did, and his "Bennett" was a rather inoffensive, colorless man named Russell A. Post. Post never held anything approaching the power of Bennett, and he lasted a relatively brief time, but in his day he was the most feared and despised personage in The Dow Chemical Company.

His title was "Personal Assistant" to Willard Dow, but since Willard was chairman, president, general manager, and research director of the company, all rolled into one, that was a very big stick. He also had a position as chairman of the Dow Athletic Committee, and from that post he quietly but firmly ruled over the professional and semiprofessional sports teams the company fielded.

His job was to keep Willard Dow informed of anything that was going on in the company that he thought Willard should know about. He also began to build up a security function in the company, to check on possible Communist connections by employees and institute measures to prevent Communist infiltration into the company.

Soon Post was dispatching his own representatives to the various divisions of the company and building a network of men whose job was to feed whatever intelligence they could gather back to him. This operation became known among employees as "the CIA," for the U.S. Central Intelligence Agency.

Jim Dunlap, personnel manager of the Western Division, recalled that he had met a bright, energetic young mail carrier in Midland named Eddie Fales. The next time they met Eddie Fales came out from Midland to be the security manager of the Western Division, representing Russell Post's operation. Eddie told Jim life in the security division of the company was the main line to success and power; it was the coming thing. The power went straight to the top, to Willard Dow.

Bob Heitz, long-time research director in Pittsburgh, said Fales was a pleasant young man, "and we were too busy trying to make things work to pay any attention" to that kind of thing. The problem was the idea that the management believed you were not telling them something and "they were going to sneak around behind your back and find it out."[1]

When Willard Dow died in a plane crash in 1949, Post locked Willard's office and posted a guard at the door with orders to admit no one without specific authorization from him. Leland I. Doan and Mark E. Putnam, the newly elected president and executive vice president of the company, came down the hall and were going into Willard's office when the guard informed them he could not allow them to go in. Doan and Putnam inquired who had given that order. "Mr. Post," said the guard. "Thank you," said Lee Doan.

Doan and Putnam walked back to the boardroom, where the directors were in recess, called them to order, and proposed a resolution dismissing Russell Post from all of his functions in the company. They thought it preferable, in the circumstances, they explained, that this action be taken by the full board rather than by one or two of the directors. Then they proceeded to Post's office and fired him, and went back and told the guard he could go find something else to do; Mr. Post was no longer with the company. Post had the distinction of being the only employee fired by a unanimously adopted resolution of the board of directors.[2]

"It showed what kind of folks were on the Board of Directors at the time," Heitz said. "The first chance they got they completely rejected the idea that a company should have a CIA."

---

1. Oral History, Robert G. Heitz, September 29, 1988.
2. Mark Putnam rarely talked to his family about events in the company, but he did tell them of this incident. R. William Caldwell to author, October 1992.

III.

One Sunday in 1936 a male choir group at the First Presbyterian Church sang an anthem that impressed Leland I. Doan, the Dow sales manager, so much that he praised it to Frank Whaley, one of the choir members and a kingpin of calcium chloride sales. Whaley told his colleagues about it (several were members of the same choir), and out of their conversation came the idea of a Dow male chorus. "There are lots of first-rate singers around Dow, men who love to sing," the group in calcium chloride sales told Whaley. "Why not get them together?"

Whaley took the idea to Willard Dow, who made him an offer. If there was enough interest, he said, the company would provide a place for a men's chorus to meet, rent a piano, and pay a director—up to $60 a month. Whaley put notices up in the clockrooms inviting "men who like to sing" to an organizing meeting; 47 showed up at the first meeting, and 80 at the second. They elected Whaley their president and invited Prof. J. Harold Powers, head of the music department at what is now Central Michigan University, to be their director. The new chorus gave its first public performance at the 1936 Christmas tree-lighting ceremonies at the Midland County Courthouse.[26]

Out of this beginning grew one of the most extensive music programs ever carried on in industry. The Dow Male Chorus became only the first of a number of employee performing groups that eventually included a symphony orchestra, a girls' chorus (the male chorus was called the male chorus but following the usage of the time the female chorus was called "the girls' chorus"), a boys' choir, a madrigal group, and a choral society.

Finding a part-time choral director to come to Midland was difficult, and in 1943 Willard Dow, responding to a petition from the Male Chorus, decided to engage a full-time music director; with this the Dow music department was born. Spurred on by rapid wartime growth in the employee population and the demand for family-type entertainment close to home—gasoline rationing made travel a luxury—the music department soon became a major vehicle for employee recreation and community participation in Midland.

Willard Dow and the Male Chorus lured Dr. Theodore M. Vosburgh, associate professor of music at Albion College, to Midland to organize and direct the Dow music program. Over the next half century Vosburgh became "Mr. Music" in the Midland area. Vosburgh, a graduate of the Eastman School of Music, had studied orchestral conducting with such luminaries as Leonard Bernstein and choral conducting with such as Fred Waring.[27]

Willard Dow bought an old Nazarene church that was for sale near the Dow headquarters and remodeled it as the Dow Music Building.

The Dow Symphony Orchestra had been born in 1936 as the Midland Civic Orchestra with Dr. Vernon A. Stenger, a pioneer analytical chemist at Dow (for whom an annual award for achievement in analytical chemistry is now named), as its first conductor. "I was the only one around who had any conducting experience at all," Stenger said, "so I agreed to do it until a better candidate could be found." Stenger was not only a crackerjack analytical chemist but a crackerjack oboist, and played oboe and English horn in the orchestra for more than 50 years.[28]

In 1944 the Dow music department staged its first big show, a performance of the Gilbert and Sullivan operetta *H.M.S. Pinafore*. Before long the department had expanded to four professional musicians, and more than 500 employees and family members were participating in its programs. Wilford Crawford, who had been music director of the Midland Public Schools, became assistant director of the department.

From the start all these activities were open to members of the community except the Men's Chorus, which until 1957 insisted on remaining strictly a Dow employee organization. Around 1950 Earl Ziegler of Plastics Technical Service, then president of the chorus, anonymously penned a theme song for the group; once it was adopted by the chorus, Ziegler admitted he had written it, and "Men of Dow" became their signature song.[29]

In 1952 Vosburgh took the 100-man chorus on a 3,000-mile concert tour of Oklahoma and Texas, giving 11 concerts in eight days, mainly at Dow plants. "This trip (was) thoroughly successful in building greater community spirit and in helping to bring our Dow family represented in other divisions closer together," Leland I. Doan, then the president of Dow, said.[30]

After the concert at Freeport, Texas, 17 men from the magnesium cells department came to the management and asked if they could have help in starting a chorus of their own. "We are besieged by other industries with requests for information and suggestions on how to organize musical groups among their employes," Harold S. Kendall, assistant to the president and supervisor of the music department, told a reporter.[31]

The music program in the Texas Division, under a full-time music director, John W. Robbins, developed to include a concert band, a dance band, and a string band, and cooperated with the Freeport Community Choral Club. In the Western Division, the music department included a band and a Dow chorus. Before it realized it, the company had become the nation's leader in industrial music. While many companies had choral groups, none had programs of the breadth and diversity of Dow's.

The concerts were always free, and open to whoever came. Concertgoers insisted they wanted to contribute something, so after awhile a collection was taken at each concert and put into a fund called the Midland Music Foundation. The first year the proceeds were given to the Midland Hospital, but after that the funds were used to provide prizes (principally music scholarships) for an annual music competition among the community's children.

It was not difficult to join the music programs. Luman Bliss, a member for almost 60 years, said auditions consisted of singing a couple of songs for the director. "All the director really wanted to know is that you knew enough about music not to ruin the chorus," he said.[32]

The severe recession of 1958 brought the first major jarring note to the music program; in that year Dow experienced its worst financial crunch in many years and the company reduced its personnel population by 10 percent across the board; costcutting became the order of the day, and the music department was an obvious target. The Dow Symphony was the first casualty, and it quickly (and successfully) became the Midland Symphony.

In the spring of 1961 Lee Doan announced that the company was going out of the music business but would help the groups involved make the transition to community organizations. A "Steering Committee" was appointed to guide the reorganization effort. The Midland Music Foundation was reorganized and expanded to take over a leadership role, and the company for a token payment leased the Music Building to the foundation. Ted Vosburgh became music director of the foundation and also of the new Delta College in the Midland area. The foundation quickly launched an advance sale of tickets for the next season. In spite of grave misgivings by many of the participants the transition from company to community music programs proceeded quite smoothly.[33] By early 1961 Doan said the symphony, for example, was a better orchestra than it had been three years before.[34]

The instant popularity and success of the music program in the 1930s and 1940s made Willard Dow and his colleagues wonder whether other employee-oriented programs might be in order. With the Dow "Field Days" suspended for the war, he asked Steve Starks to survey recreation needs in the Midland area. What would Dow's employees like to have available to them, he wanted to know.

Starks canvassed employees and community leaders and reported that the major lack in the Midland area was for sports programs, both sports of the kind people could themselves participate in and spectator sports—it was virtually impossible in wartime to travel to professional and collegiate sports events, and there were not any available in Midland. The employees also wanted sports programs for their children; they wanted their kids to know how to play golf and softball, and to learn to bowl and swim.

Early in 1944 Willard hired Gordon A. MacDonald as the company's first director of athletics. (Other large companies in small towns, such as the Phillips Petroleum Company at Bartlesville, Oklahoma, also established sports programs at this time.) MacDonald, a star athlete from Bay City, Michigan, had become the highly successful director of athletics at Alma College, some 40 miles from Midland. His first assignment at Dow: to establish a Dow basketball team.

MacDonald set out to recruit and coach the best college basketball players he could find, and they were given Dow jobs in addition to their athletic chores. "Slim" Wintermute, who had led the University of Oregon to a national collegiate championship in 1939, became the team's captain and leader. A 6' 7-1/2" center, Wintermute had a devastating left-handed hook shot and a job in Dow's plastic sales department. Another star was Daniel (Danny) Smick, 6' 5," who had starred in three sports at the University of Michigan; Danny became editor of a new employee publication, *The Brinewell*. John (Doc) Wright was recruited from Indiana University, and Ray Patterson from the University of Wisconsin; Patterson at the time held the Big Ten scoring record for a 10-game season. Keith Carey came from Alma, Charles (Red) Caress and Robert (Bob) Igney from Purdue, William (Smiley) Johnson from Wisconsin, and Harvey Martens from George Washington University.

Under Coach MacDonald, the team won 22 and lost 5 in the 1944-45 season, and had 33 wins and five losses the next year. One of its losses (46-43) was to the legendary Chicago Monarchs, a black team of that segregated day in pro sports, and the team lost three out of four meetings with its nemesis, the Ft. Wayne, Indiana, Zollner Pistons (who later moved to Detroit and became the Detroit Pistons), that year's world and national professional league basketball champions. At the American Basketball Congress' first tournament, held in Atlanta in 1946, the Midland team came in fourth, and Wintermute and Smick made the all-tournament team.[35]

The "Chemical City ACs" did so well in the industrial basketball league that they "turned pro," under Dow company sponsorship. Midland, Michigan, became the smallest town in the United States with a professional basketball team.

According to G. Robert Baker, who came to Dow as a softball pitcher during WWII and remained 40 years, becoming the longtime president of Dow Japan,

In the years during the war, Dow sponsored a very outstanding industrial basketball team, and they played against some of the best industrial teams in the country. The Dow basketball team won an awful lot of games, and they went to the National AAU and played well there too. Then it was decided that Dow should become a professional team so they could begin to charge admission. Maybe that was a mistake. They bought the Youngstown [Ohio] franchise in the old National Basketball League. With it came some new players that the Midland people did not know, but readily and quickly accepted. However, the remnants of the Youngstown team that came were not strong enough to carry the load in the National Basketball League. After two or three years the company decided that they were really not a professional basketball sponsor, so they dropped it about 1949. At that time I was helping [Richard C.] Dick Pendell [Jr.], publicity director for the basketball team. After the basketball team was dropped, emphasis was shifted to the softball team.[36]

The softball team, a major power in the softball world for many years, also came out of the Dow Athletic Club (or Dow AC) program, which had an executive committee composed of Russell A. Post (who had become personal assistant to Willard Dow), chairman; Steve Starks; and Tom Kanary, a former golf pro who later succeeded MacDonald as Dow athletic director. MacDonald coached the team but soon turned these duties over to Jimmy Walsh, a 5' 6" veteran of the softball wars who was working in Dow's marketing department, and Walsh became the team's chief scout, spark plug, and strategic brain.

Baker remembered:

I became the publicity manager and business manager as well as a pitcher and sort of assistant coach on the softball team. We had five pitchers; I was No. 5. There were three catchers and a total of 23 ballplayers. We averaged 110 games per year and traveled about 80,000 miles a year in a Dow AC bus. The team won the World's Championship of softball four times. The team had a number of players who were perhaps the greatest players in America, many of whom have made state Hall of Fame teams and the National Softball Hall of Fame teams. Our greatest pitcher was Al Linde; he's in everybody's Hall of Fame. Clyde Dexter was probably the greatest left-handed pitcher in the United States at that time; he's in the Hall of Fame. Bobby Wright was a catcher. Dick Dudzik was a third baseman. Jack Kett was one of the greatest hitters in softball. Those five guys are probably on everybody's All-American team or everybody's Hall of Fame team. The interesting thing to me has been the fact that after the softball team was disbanded in 1955, all of the people who played had jobs. They stayed (with Dow) and they worked. Very few of the softball people left Midland.[37]

A survey made in 1976 showed that 18 of the ACs were still working for the company.[38]

When the Dow ACs won the world championship in 1951, Midland's population was about 15,000 but attendance at the home games often went over the 5,000 mark. As Jack Kett's wife, Marie, telephone clerk at company headquarters, recalled, "there was shuttle bus service to Emerson Park and game schedules were listed in the paper. The crowd was so big, bleachers were set up in addition to the stadium and you had to go an hour early to get a good seat."

Why did the ACs disband in 1955? Jimmy Walsh said, "Well, it was a combination of things. Competition, for one—there wasn't any locally. It got so we had to travel so much and so far and this caused problems . . . we needed new talent, and times were changing. The company was growing and there were new policies."[39]

The preeminent softball team in Texas Dow was the Lake Jackson Gators, organized in 1946, who had many successful years, including a state championship season in 1947.

In their spare time Willard Dow put some of the well-known athletes on his teams in those years to work at a "Junior AC" program designed to teach children between the fourth and twelfth grades the rudiments of baseball, touch football, basketball, tumbling, boxing, wrestling, swimming and diving, and other sports. Children became members of the Junior ACs by earning 25 merit points—given for attendance, cooperation, cleanliness, leadership, athletic ability, and progress—and with another 25 merit points earned a Junior AC emblem to wear on their sweater or jacket.

Leagues were organized in many of these sports, and the youngsters of Midland were soon benefiting from athletic coaching that would have been the envy of many a youth. The program also prompted the building of more and bigger sports facilities in the city; there were not enough softball diamonds and swimming pools to accommodate the demand.

Not only did these programs build a foundation for excellence in competitive sports in Midland—still known today as a strong sports town—but in the years ahead amateur sports competition would become a trademark of Dow installations everywhere. Dow organizations usually fielded softball teams, soccer teams, and bowling teams representing the company at the local level, and they always worked hard and played hard.[40]

The professional-level basketball and softball teams that once represented the company became a thing of the past, but Midland is still represented today by a top-notch fast-pitch softball team, the Midland Explorers, and remains a hotbed of softball. The Dow AC program evolved into a Dow recreation department that organized employee leagues in bowling, golf, and other sports. Interest in employee sports and athletic competition, and a belief in the value of a sense of play, became part of the company's heritage.

In spite of all the Slim Wintermutes and Al Lindes, and the numbers of fans they had, the greatest sports hero of the men in the Midland plant of the 1930s was undoubtedly Jimmy Adamick (or Adamcik), a Midland boy who worked for a time in the plant and then launched a professional boxing career. His fights were followed avidly, punch by punch, by his former coworkers at Dow as he climbed the heavyweight boxing ranks toward the top. Adamick had 42 wins, including a phenomenal string of 31 consecutive knockouts, and only one loss, when he met Roscoe Toles at the Olympic Stadium in Detroit on September 28, 1938, in what sports reporters viewed as a tune-up for an Adamick match with Joe Louis, the reigning world heavyweight champion. Toles scored a stunning upset knockout of Adamick, who was severely injured in the fight. He was in a coma for 33 days, and never fought again. The company magazine, the *Dow Diamond*, carried pictures of the disastrous Toles fight with the comment, "Out, but Midland hopes not for good."[41]

Disaster was also in store for Willard Dow. By 1949 he was "Mr. Everything" at Dow and at age 52 at the peak of his career. When he scheduled a March 31 trip to Massachusetts Institute of Technology, at Boston, where he was a member of the corporation and his son Herbert H. Dow II was a student, timing it to coincide with a visit to MIT by Winston Churchill, it seemed routine enough, but it was to be his last flight.

Margaret Dow Towsley, his sister, remembered telephoning Willard from Ann Arbor the evening before the trip. "The last thing I remember of Willard," she said,

> was that Ranny's class in high school ["Ranny" is the nickname of her eldest daughter] had to make a field trip, and they wanted to go up to Midland to see the plant. I called Willard the night before the accident to find out if this class could go up to the plant. Willard was so excited over the fact that he was going to sit next to Winston Churchill and he was going to have a chance to talk to Winston Churchill. I always thought it was too bad the accident couldn't have happened on the way home—funny thing to talk about, but you always wish they could have had their last desire.[42]

Flying over Ontario toward Boston, the plane encountered freezing conditions and fog and the wings began to ice up. Frederick C. (Blackie) Clements, a veteran pilot, headed for the nearest airport, at London, Ontario, but crashed a few miles from it. Ernest (Ernie) Dobinson, a young farmer, was the only eyewitness. "It was a cold March day and it was sleeting that morning, as I remember," Dobinson said. "I was heading out to the barn with my little dog when I heard a plane motor right overhead. A second later there was a big boom, then everything went quiet. I saw flames streaking across the ground and I ran over to where the plane had crashed, with my dog at my heels. The plane was burning, and as I got there I saw a man standing out on the ground by himself. He seemed dazed. He pulled up his pantleg and showed me a big scratch on his leg. From what I could make out he was wondering, couldn't understand how he could get out of a crash like that with just a scratch on the leg. Then other people began to arrive."[43]

The dazed survivor was Calvin A. (Tink) Campbell, vice president and chief counsel of the company. When he was taken to the London hospital the "scratch" on his leg turned out to be a crushed heel. The five others on the plane were killed in the crash: Clements and his copilot, Arthur J. Bowie; Willard and Martha Dow; and Campbell's wife, Alta. Campbell said he tried desperately to pull his unconscious wife from the crash but was driven from it by the flames and intense heat, and "just got out in time."

Many eulogies were written for Willard Dow in the following days, but one of the most memorable was an editorial in the *Wall Street Journal*. "The nation has lost much more than a leading industrialist and more than a successful scientist," the *Journal* said.

Dr. Dow, head of one of the world's great chemical enterprises, was not the sort of man who is popularly glorified these days. Probably 99 percent of the people of the country have never heard of him. Yet if the score were added up correctly, it probably would be found that he had done more to make and to preserve the United States than many a more noted figure.

He inherited the control of a small but rich business, but he was not in the least interested in living on income. He went to work and he worked harder than most of his employees all his life. He increased the size of the original business tenfold by creating new things. These in turn created thousands of jobs not only in his own firm but in scores of new industries that grew like trees from the seeds of new products.

As a consequence, the United States was able to fight the last war with synthetic rubber and with the light metal magnesium, essential for incendiaries and airplanes. Dow was the first to perfect a process for making styrene, one of the two essential chemicals needed to synthesize rubber. When war broke out he had an efficient plant ready and running, in which he planned to make plastics. The rest of American industry carried on, but without Dow there might have been a disastrous delay.

When American business looks for a man to typify the best it can show, it may well point to Dr. Dow.[44]

Notes

1. Fourteen was then the minimum legal age for automobile drivers. Willard's first automobile was a 1912 Ford touring car; his father's was a 1913 Ford runabout.
2. William J. Hale, "The Personal Side of Willard Henry Dow," Speech introducing Dow at New York award dinner, September 30, 1946, Post Street Archives.
3. Harrison Hatton, Notes on conversation with F. H. Langell and R. R. Dreisbach, June 23, 1949.
4. Hale, "The Personal Side of Willard Henry Dow.".
5. Oral History, Macauley Whiting, August 13, 1990.
6. Leland I. Doan, *Willard Henry Dow (1897-1949), President of The Dow Chemical Company* (New York: The Newcomen Society in North America, 1950).
7. Why Grace Dow became a director in November 1927, following the death of Will Pardee, whom she replaced, has been a subject of much speculation. Herbert Dow once said it was a temporary expedient because the person he had in mind as a director was not available at the time. Others have speculated that Herbert Dow knew he did not have long to live and felt the presence of Grace Dow among the directors (and her vote) would reinforce his message that Willard was to succeed him, regardless of his age. A more compelling reason was the 1927 Du Pont proposal to buy a controlling interest in Dow; this would have been a tantalizing proposition for the elderly Cleveland board members, who were a majority, and Herbert Dow may have wanted to add to the board a vote he could reasonably rely on.
8. "Much Interest in Annual Meeting of Dow Co. Owners," *Midland Republican*, June 26, 1930. Dow's 1930 earnings were $20.40 per share, adjusted to compare with $18.55 the year before. The actual

earnings were $4.08 per share, but in June 1929 the stock had split five for one; in December 1929 a further 5 percent stock distribution was made.

9. "Dow Earns $4.08," *Cleveland Press*, June 26, 1930; "Dow Chemical Holds Up Well," *Cleveland Plain Dealer*, June 27, 1930.

10. Oral History, M. Whiting.

11. See account of this episode in Whitehead, *The Dow Story*, 117-18.

12. Oral History, Albert P. (Dutch) Beutel, transcript of interviews with Don Whitehead, 1967.

13. From Judge Henry Hart, "We Remember Willard," talk at ceremonies formally naming the Dow headquarters complex the Willard H. Dow Center, October 20, 1983.

14. Aubrey D. McFadyen, "Willard Henry Dow," *Chemical & Engineering News*, June, 1948.

15. Minutes, board of trustees, Ferris Institute, Big Rapids, Michigan, January 9, 1942, and February 18, 1942. When the school, now called Ferris State University, celebrated its centennial in 1984 it remembered the incident and invited the then chairman of Dow, Robert W. Lundeen, to be a keynote speaker.

16. *Business Week*, October 26, 1946 (Willard Dow's portrait on cover). *Science Illustrated*, November 1946 (also a McGraw-Hill publication).

17. See particularly his Chandler Medal address, "Rediscover the Rainbow," delivered at Columbia University, New York City, May 20, 1943.

18. Hatton, Notes on conversation with Leland I. Doan, July 11, 1949.

19. Hatton, Notes on conversation with Gilbert Currie, July 28, 1949.

20. Karpiuk, *Dow Research Pioneers*, 129.

21. Hatton, Notes on conversation with Thomas J. Powers, April 24, 1950.

22. See "Down the River—The Success of Dow's Quarter-Million-Dollar Phenolic Waste Disposal Plant Hinges on the Strange Appetite of a Little Bug," *Dow Diamond* 1, no. 6 (August 1938): 133-36.

23. Karpiuk, *Dow Research Pioneers*, 604-10.

24. "Waste Disposal, the Dow Way," *Dow Diamond* 9, no. 4 (July 1946): 1-7.

25. "Nature Gets an Assist," *Dow Diamond* 21, no. 3 (October 1958): 27.

26. John C. (Jack) Spencer, chorus historian, "History of the Dow Male Chorus," in *Tenth Anniversary Concert Program*, Dow Male Chorus, February 19-20, 1947.

27. Commemorative Section, Golden Jubilee Celebration 1943-1993, *Midland Daily News*, September 8, 1993.

28. Oral History, Vernon A. Stenger, April 13, 1993.

29. "50 Years of Song," in concert program, Dow Male Chorus/Men of Music, May 17, 1986. "Men of Dow" used the tune of a song called "Friendship," by W. E. Haesche, copyright G. Schirmer Inc., New York. The text of "Men of Dow":

> A band of voices, men of Dow,
> We greet you with our music now,
> With hymns and folksongs, parodies,
> And love songs' tender melodies.
> Then rousing, stirring songs of power
> And long-loved classics fill the hour.

The thrill is ours, of voices free

Together raised in harmony.

The men of Dow stretch forth a hand

To all their friends throughout the land,

We hope to bring you joy and smiles,

For friends count neither time nor miles.

It's true that songs can be the core

Of firmest bonds forevermore;

And so we sing, our goal in sight,

To keep the diamond ever bright.

(The "diamond" was, of course, the corporate symbol, the Dow diamond).

30. "Music in Industry," *Dow Diamond* 10, no. 1 (January 1947): 12-15.

31. Quoted in *The Keynote*, publication of the Associated Male Choruses of America, Inc., 28, no. 3 (April 1952).

32. Carol Farrand, "Men of Music Roots Reach to the '30s," *Midland Daily News*, September 11, 1989.

33. See H. S. Kendall to L. I. Doan, "Cessation of Music Activities," June 13, 1961.

34. L. I. Doan to J. D. Ronda, Lockheed Aircraft Corp., Sunnyvale, California, January 10, 1961.

35. "The AC's, Athletic Ambassadors of Good Will," *Dow Diamond* 9, no. 2 (March 1946): 14-19.

36. Oral History, G. Robert Baker, March 13, 1991.

37. Oral History, G. Robert Baker. For general information and history concerning the Dow AC's, see Marie Kett, "Softball Memories," *The Midland Log*, journal of the Midland County Historical Society (summer 1984): 2-30.

38. Diana Manges, "Whatever Happened to the Dow AC's?" *The Eastern Scene*, publication of the Eastern Division of Dow, Strongsville, Ohio, 3, no. 6 (Nov.-Dec. 1976) and 4, no. 1 (Jan.-Feb. 1977).

39. Diana Manges, "Whatever Happened to Dow AC's?" (*Midland Daily News,* October 9, 1976.

40. "Athletics for Juniors," *Dow Diamond* 10, no. 5 (September 1947): 26-31.

41. "Out—But Midland Hopes Not For Good," *Dow Diamond* 2, no. 1 (October 1938): 4. See also Dorothy Langdon Yates, *Salt of the Earth, a History of Midland County, Michigan* Midland, Mich.: Midland County Historical Society, 1987), 258.

42. Oral History, Margaret Dow Towsley and Dr. Harry A. Towsley, December 6, 1989. "Ranny" (Margaret Ann) is now Mrs. John E. Riecker of Midland.

43. Ernie Dobinson, interview with the author, June 26, 1992.

44. "Dr. Willard Henry Dow," editorial, *Wall Street Journal*, April 1, 1949.

PART FOUR

THE FIRST BILLION

Dow

1951—Dow contracts with Atomic Energy Commission to operate AEC plant to produce A-bomb "triggers" at Rocky Flats, Colorado.

Dow Chemical International and Dow Chemical Inter-American are organized to promote the company's business abroad.

1952—Asahi-Dow Ltd., first joint venture abroad, is formed in partnership with Asahi Chemical Industry Co., Ltd. to produce saran in Japan.

1953—Saran Wrap, first consumer product, is launched nationally in the United States.

"Marine Dow-Chem," first-of-its-kind tanker, designed to carry liquid chemical cargoes, is launched at Quincy, Massachusetts.

May 26, 1954—World's biggest magnesium rolling mill, at Madison, Illinois, is dedicated in honor of E. O. Barstow, father of magnesium.

1955—Nederlandsche Dow Maatschappij (NDM) is organized in Rotterdam as Dow's gateway to Europe.

1956—Dow acquires site at Plaquemine, Louisiana, and begins to build major new chemical complex.

1957—Dow acquires Cleveland-based Dobeckmun Company, a leading packaging firm, as hub of a new packaging division.

1959—L. I. Doan appoints Ben Branch president of Dow International with mandate to build Dow's business abroad.

1960—Company introduces 24 new products, including Rovana drapery fiber; Zoalene coccidiostat for the poultry trade; and Handi-Wrap household wrap.

World at large

1950—North Korean forces invade South Korea and Korean War begins.

1951—U.N. forces under General Douglas MacArthur push N. Koreans back to the Yalu River but Chinese troops attack; Truman fires MacArthur.

1952—George VI of England dies and is succeeded by his daughter, Queen Elizabeth II.

United States explodes first hydrogen bomb at Eniwetok Atoll in the Pacific.

1953—Korean armistice signed at Panmunjom, July 27.

1954—Dr. Jonas Salk begins inoculating schoolchildren with antipolio serum.

1956—Fidel Castro lands in Cuba with a small force intent on overthrowing dictator Fulgencio Batista.

Mao Zedong launches "Great Leap Forward," puts more than half a billion Chinese into 24,000 "people's communes."

1957—USSR launches *Sputnik I* and *II*, the first earth satellites, inaugurating the space age.

Mackinac Straits Bridge, world's longest suspension bridge, opens.

1958—United States establishes NASA to administer a program of scientific exploration of space.

1961—United States breaks off diplomatic relations with Castro-controlled Cuba.

Space race is hot as Soviet Cosmonaut Yuri Gagarin orbits earth in a two-ton spacecraft, followed by Alan Shepard making first U.S. manned space flight.

1962—Cuban Missile Crisis erupts over installation of Soviet missiles there.

ELEVEN

POSTWAR GROWTH

I.

Five days after the fiery crash that killed Willard Dow a somber board of directors gathered to choose his successor. There was not much discussion; there were only two serious contenders—Dutch Beutel, Willard's longtime deputy, builder of the Dow empire in Texas, and Leland I. (Lee) Doan, general sales manager for the past 20 years. Beutel knew he had two strikes against him: he was unrelated to the Dow family, and his reputation for ferocious attempts to move the company to the Gulf Coast, piece by piece, had alarmed many in Midland. After the adoption of a resolution eulogizing their late departed leader, Doan quickly became the unanimous choice.

"There has to be a lot of sharing of this burden," Doan told them. Before the meeting was out Willard Dow's many duties had been assigned to three persons and a committee. Earl Bennett, who had been thinking about retirement (he was 69), instead found himself chairman of the board, the capstone of a career he had begun as office boy almost half a century earlier. Mark E. Putnam, the hardworking, no-nonsense production chief, became general manager.

Willard's portfolio as research director was handed to an Executive Research Committee headed by the veteran board member W. R. Veazey, assisted by star researchers E. C. Britton and Raymond F. Boyer. To round out the new management team, Carl A. Gerstacker, assistant director of purchases, was promoted to treasurer, replacing Bennett; Calvin A. (Tink) Campbell, general counsel, was promoted to secretary, replacing Doan; and Beutel and Russell L. Curtis of the Western Division were promoted to vice presidents.

Lee Doan, then 54, was a relaxed, gregarious, friendly man who had found his niche in a sales career. He had been born the son of a physician in North Bend, Nebraska, but Dr. Ira Doan died when Lee was nine and life became difficult for the Doan family. Hester Doan took her brood to Ann Arbor, Michigan, where she found a job as housemother. Young Lee ran a newspaper route, scrambled through Ann Arbor High, and went on to the University of Michigan.

In 1916 he took a job at the Michigan Bell Telephone Company and then at Easter 1917, following a campus romance, he married fellow student Ruth Alden Dow, Herbert Dow's second daughter, and accepted his father-in-law's invitation to work at the Dow Company.[1]

He did not seem to fit in either the chlorine cells or engineering departments, so in 1918 Herbert Dow shifted him to the embryonic sales department to work with G. Lee Camp, and there he blossomed. Four years later he was assistant general sales manager, and when Camp retired in 1929 he became manager. By the mid 1930s he was recognized as one of the most astute chemical marketers in the business.

Now, thrust suddenly into the top position in the firm, a position he had neither expected nor sought, Lee Doan was shattered. In an emotional first speaking appearance before an assemblage of employees—the April 27 annual bowling banquet at Frankenmuth, where Willard Dow had been scheduled to hand out the awards—he stated his misgivings.

"I am not Willard Dow," he told a hushed gathering. "I could not be Willard if I tried. I'm going to be Lee Doan and I will do my very best. I hope my performance will measure up to your expectations and earn your respect."

"We were all dispirited," Carl Gerstacker said as he recalled the scene years later. "It was a time of extreme gravity for our company; in fact, some people wondered whether Dow Chemical would survive this crisis. Lee Doan picked us up off the floor and led our company to unprecedented heights of achievement and prosperity."[2]

The company rallied quickly behind its new leader, and then a few months later another personal tragedy struck. On a New York trip Doan was dining with Ruth in the Persian Room of the Plaza Hotel one Saturday evening when she folded her arms on the table, put her head down upon them, and was dead of a massive heart attack.

Ruth Dow Doan, who had worked quietly in many community enterprises but always shunned the limelight, occupied a unique place in Dow history; she was daughter, sister, wife, and mother of successive Dow chief executives.[3] Three days before her death she had jokingly been introduced at a Midland Chamber of Commerce dinner as "the boss of the boss of Dow Chemical."

Dow employees took it upon themselves to offer encouragement. More than 5,000 of them in Midland and Bay City signed a letter that was brought to Doan's office by a delegation led by Frank Jacobs of the calcium-magnesium department, Patricia Yack of standards, and Ross Gordon of the service station. "Dear Mr. Doan," the letter said,

> As you near the end of your first year as president of our company, you may be looking back with deep regret over the series of tragic personal and community losses which have been packed into so brief a period. It may well be that the burdens of your office by now seem mighty heavy indeed.
>
> As president, you are one Dow employee among many thousands of Dow employees proud of the name. We are all bound together by the fact that our hopes and ambitions and future security are to a great degree interwoven with the future success of this our Company. . . . You

and Mr. Bennett and Dr. Putnam and the rest of our management have done a wonderful job of operating the company following the tragic death of Dr. Willard H. Dow. We want to express our sincere appreciation of a job well done.[4]

Doan, surprised but delighted, could only say, "I'm simply overcome." Shortly he sent out a note expressing to the men and women of Dow his "sincere human appreciation for the pat on the back," and his "determination to deserve this vote of confidence."

Eleven months after Ruth's death Lee Doan married again and left on a honeymoon trip to Hawai'i. His new bride was Mrs. Mildred ("Millie") Mellus, widow of a Brighton, Michigan, physician. They had been introduced by George Hemmerick, sales manager of Dow Canada; Millie was Mrs. Hemmerick's sister.

While he was honeymooning he received an urgent message from Owen J. Cleary, state party chairman, and others in the Michigan Republican organization. They felt he would be the strongest candidate they could field, so would he run for regent of the University of Michigan on the Republican ticket? "When your friends and your university say they need you, how can you say no?" Doan asked. He was suddenly in the midst of what was to be his only political campaign, and the only run for public office by a sitting chief executive of the company.

It promised to be a tough race. At their state convention the Republicans nominated the Ann Arbor attorney Roscoe O. Bonisteel, an incumbent, and Doan. The Democrats nominated Murray D. Van Wagoner, a popular former governor of the state and also an incumbent, and Wheaton L. Strom, an Escanaba attorney, the lone candidate from the Upper Peninsula.

Doan received some key endorsements, especially from the *Detroit Free Press*—"although he is a newcomer to politics his vast business and administrative experience makes him a logical choice for the Regency," the paper said—and Bonisteel and Doan won handily.[5] Doan was soon involved in the selection of Harlan Hatcher as next president of the university, succeeding Alexander G. Ruthven. When he stepped down after eight years he was called a model university regent.

He remained active in Republican Party affairs throughout his career and was an enthusiastic supporter of Dwight D. Eisenhower. He was Michigan chairman of the nationwide series of January 20, 1956, "Salute to Pres. Eisenhower" dinners, for which the main speakers in Michigan were Gen. James H. Doolittle and Arthur Summerfield Jr., Ike's campaign chairman and postmaster general. It was a period of strong Dow relations with the White House; in addition to Doan's involvement, Wiley T. Buchanan was Eisenhower's chief of protocol (Mrs. Buchanan was Billy Hale's daughter and Doan's niece).[6]

II.

Under Herbert Dow's leadership the company had grown to $16 million in annual sales from a standing start as he prodded constantly through the years for another new product and another new plant. Under Willard Dow, following the same formula, sales had grown from $16 million in 1930 to $171 million in 1949. By 1949 Dow was the fourth largest U.S. chemical company and growth was the gospel of the company, its second nature. Lee Doan, as he took over, had observed this process under both Dows and hardly needed a compass to tell him the direction the company should take.

In the first five postwar years the company spent a total of $223 million for expansion, far beyond anything it had ever spent before, but Doan and his colleagues decided the opportunities before them were even greater than these sums could encompass and that this rate of growth was not half enough.[7] The war in Korea began in the summer of 1950, and in May 1951, with Dow's magnesium and other products now in heavy demand by the military, Doan told the Cleveland Society of Security Analysts that Dow was planning on $100 million in expansion in the next fiscal year and that "we expect to spend $100,000,000 a year for the next five years."

This investment could be classified as defense spending if the government so decided, "but this doesn't mean that all of this will make things that will go to Korea," Chairman Bennett said. "The essential needs of the nation to keep on a defense footing will make it necessary for some of the products to be used in this country."

At least half of the first-year $100 million would be spent in Texas, Doan said. "Texas has been good to us and we can't let Texas down." There was jubilation in the boomtown of Freeport, where the government had just reactivated standby magnesium facilities to supply war needs.

Bennett told the analysts most of these funds would be generated by retained earnings but that he expected the company would have to raise at least $70 million and possibly as much as $120 million from outside sources. Just a year later, true to his prediction, on July 23, 1952, Bennett accepted a check for $100,425,000 from Charles W. Kennard, partner in the New York investment banking firm of Smith, Barney & Company, the proceeds of a sale of $100 million in 30-year, 3 percent convertible subordinate debentures. It was the largest public offering of the securities of a chemical company to that time. The company was seeing big; in the year newly completed its sales had amounted to a mere $407 million. It had just received certificates of necessity from the government to build plants costing $265 million.[8]

Treasurer Gerstacker predicted that by 1956, through the cash pickup from depreciation, retained earnings, and yearly stock sales, Dow would be generating about $100 million annually. He turned out to be right.

As the Texas Division raced to keep up with this accelerated program, it began to be plagued with a new problem—labor troubles. The diversity and scope of its operations and their pell-mell growth had spawned some 23 different Freeport-area union locals with which the company now had dealings. As union leadership groups jockeyed for position and bragging rights, it seemed to Beutel that at any given moment at least one of the locals and more often several were threatening a strike.

A frustrated Beutel stormed and grumped and cajoled, but nothing happened. He put his staff to work on schemes to combine the locals into larger units to simplify working with them, but it was slow and time-consuming work. Over a period of several years the 23 became 6. When the division was closed down by strikes two years in a row, in 1955 and 1956, at a time when chemical prices were at a premium, Beutel decided he'd had enough. An alternate supply source was needed.

He had been quietly exploring for some time the possibility of a second big Dow Gulf-area plant, this one on the Mississippi in the Louisiana area. From there Dow's big-volume petrochemical products could be barged up the river and serve the American heartland as far as Chicago. The Texas Division shipped to the East Coast but hardly touched this market.

Now he gave the go-ahead signal. Beutel had already asked Nelson D. Griswold and John R. (Jack) Stein, two of his key deputies, to find a site for the new division, looking especially at the Mississippi north of New Orleans where there was a growing cluster of petroleum refining and chemical activity.[9]

The Griswold-Stein team turned up three main possibilities: at Port Allen, across the river from Baton Rouge; at Plaquemine, 10 miles south of Baton Rouge; and at Donaldsonville, another 15 miles south. An intensive site study recommended Plaquemine as the best of the three, and on June 4 the company exercised its option on a 1,700-acre site there for about $1.1 million. Dow had already purchased a second, 133-acre site at the Napoleonville salt dome, the best salt dome in the area, 23 miles from Plaquemine, which became the source and site of salt brine operations for the new division.[10]

Plaquemine (a Cajun French word meaning "persimmon") sits in Iberville Parish on the west bank of the river—almost all of the industrial growth up to then had been on the east bank—in a wide, sweeping loop of the Mississippi called Australia Point. The plant site straddles this point, with river frontage on both its north and south sides, although the river loops 12 miles between the two points.

The key property here had been the Union Plantation, once part of a sprawling sugarcane empire operated by Andrew H. Gay and his descendants. The Gay interests had purchased the plantation at a tax sale during the Civil War, and from 1875 to 1928 it was operated as a prime sugar-producing property with up to 600 employees. At its heart was a gracious but run-down old plantation house, which became the first Dow on-site office and was later restored by the company as a social center.

On September 18 Dow and local officials gathered in a field on the old plantation to break ground for the new division, of which Stein had been appointed general manager. Beutel did the honors, climbing onto a bulldozer and tearing out a deep gash in the black loam as cameras snapped and the onlookers cheered.

Stein faced no easy task. Lee Doan's first announcement of the new division had spoken of a $20 million investment. That was soon scaled up to $45 million, and when the full array of plants was finalized it stood at $75 million, the biggest single expansion the company had attempted since 1940.

Beutel and Stein recruited a cadre of 38 from the Texas Division, and by early fall virtually all of them had packed up their families and moved to Baton Rouge, taking over temporary Louisiana division offices in the Commerce Building there. Their assignment, Stein told them, was to build a new chemical complex—7 major projects, 35 minor ones—and to do it by April 1958. The first products, vinyl chloride and propylene glycol, were to come onstream late in the first quarter of 1958 and the remainder in the second quarter.

The major projects were a power plant, caustic, chlorine, ethylene, glycol, and vinyl chloride facilities, and chlorinated solvents. The 35 "minor" projects ranged from brine-pumping facilities and pipelines from the salt dome to a sewage system and the construction of wharves on the Mississippi.[11]

The Texas transplants invaded Cajun country eagerly and began to get acquainted with what was for most of them a strange new culture, accompanied by an often baffling political system. Early in the year Lee Doan and other Dow executives, aware of this problem, had met in Baton Rouge to discuss their project with Louisiana Gov. Robert F. Kennon and his colleagues and open up communication channels with the state government.

This turned out to be a judicious approach. As an incidental to the process Doan found himself being commissioned an admiral in the Louisiana Navy, "since Dow Chemical also operates ships," Governor Kennon explained. The governor also sent the pipe-smoking Doan some of "the famous Perique pipe tobacco," a highly spiced variety produced only in Louisiana. "Be cautious" in using it, he advised.[12]

In spite of some unexpected obstacles, the foundling Louisiana Division came close to meeting the wildly optimistic scheduled proposed by Stein. The first fruits of the new plant were shipped the last week in July 1958. "The start-up of our vinyl chloride production unit has been most successful and satisfactory," Stein proudly reported on July 30. "A finished product that met market specifications was being turned out on the seventh day after the first raw materials were fed into the process system."[13]

There was one jarring note in the success of that summer of 1958 as production units came smoothly onstream in Louisiana: the start-up time collided with a sharp recession that had begun late in 1957; sales of chemicals and most other products were in a nosedive. The Louisiana division was ready to go, but the bottom had fallen out of the chemicals market.

Pondering this problem, the Dow board of directors decided to go ahead and start up the production units that were ready, but asked Plaquemine to do it without hiring additional personnel. No hourly paid, union-eligible employees had yet been hired, although the salaried cadre had grown to about 200 persons.

It was an enormous undertaking, but the 200 new-model Cajuns not only started up the new plants but actually ran them for months. Staff and services were cut to the bone to put maximum muscle in the operating units. Clerks worked as operating engineers, accountants as shift foremen, research chemists as material handlers.

When late in 1958 the nation began to recover from the recession, the division's people began to say, jokingly at first but seriously after a while: "We don't need hourly help; we can run this place without them." Stein and John (Jack) Harvey, the industrial relations manager, began to study whether and how the division might be made an entirely salaried operation, with no hourly paid structure at all.

A search turned up no chemical manufacturing plant of comparable size in the United States where such a system was used. An entirely salaried operation was so unusual that it was often difficult to explain it to the Dow management, but Stein asked Midland, could he try it out as an experiment? Given the green light, the Louisiana Division become the first all-salaried operation in the company—indeed, of its size, in the industry.

The experiment was such a rousing success that it became a general template for the company, although most major divisions of the company still have (and enjoy good relations with) unionized employees. When the Dow Badische Company was formed in 1959 (owned jointly by Dow and the German firm BASF [Badische Anilin- und Soda-Fabrik]) it too became a salaried operation. So did the Oyster Creek Division established at Freeport in 1967.

Dow plants at Pevely, Missouri; Dalton, Georgia; Magnolia and Russellville, Arkansas; Allyn's Point, Connecticut; Fresno, California; Licking River, Ohio, and others were salaried operations. Following the Dow lead of 1958, other companies moved into the Baton Rouge area with salaried operation plants. When the employees of the company's Western Division at Pittsburg and Torrance, California, voted in 1972 in a formal election for "no union representation," thus voting out their union, the Western Division of Dow also became a salaried operation.

The Louisiana Division, formally dedicated November 5, 1958, with Doan as the principal speaker, has become known as one of Dow's top performers. Everett Jacob, a later general manager of the division, said: "It's people—our people. The salaried operations concept is a people thing."[14]

In 1974, by which time it had grown to include 14 production plants and was already double its size of 1958, the Louisiana Division began a major expansion program, adding a big naphtha cracker and using naphtha as feedstock for an additional array of products. The expansion used 2,000 construction workers, added 500 new salaried employees, and lasted three years. It cost more than $165 million.[15]

With demand for magnesium spurred on by the war in Korea—defense needs had pushed U.S. production of the metal to 130,000 tons annually, most of it from Dow—Doan and his colleagues continued their optimistic view of its potential. Dow was now producing from seawater in Texas about 75 percent of the world's magnesium. In the postwar years, 1947-1950, the metal had enjoyed a boomlet, its popularity climbing steadily for aircraft and auto parts, aluminum alloys, portable tools, trucks and trailers, and rust-preventing anodes for cathodic protection.[16]

Hubert (Hoop) Fruehauf, manager of the magnesium department, J. Donald Hanawalt, the technical director, and other Dow experts felt the metal was at a crossroads. Major growth of market for the metal was being held back, they said, by lack of facilities to roll magnesium sheet, a basic need for fabricating almost anything from magnesium metal. Therefore Dow would have to build such facilities.

In late 1951 they bought a disused mill at Madison, Illinois, across the river from St. Louis, and began to outfit it as the company's new Madison Division, a $40 million magnesium fabrication plant. The world's first facility for the mass production of magnesium mill products, it would include the first large-scale magnesium sheet mill and the largest extrusion facilities for the metal. The company contracted to purchase a 13-ton extrusion press from a firm in Duisburg, Germany, that had already spent eight years designing and building it; it would take four more years before it was completed and installed at Madison. It was 250 feet long and could produce extrusions up to 80 feet long.

In April 1953 the Dow board of directors visited Madison for the first time and viewed a scale model of the gigantic press they were buying. On May 26, 1954, the mill was dedicated in honor of E. O. Barstow, the "father of magnesium," then 75 and in the twilight of an illustrious career.

The main speaker was Donald A. Quarles, assistant secretary of defense, who paid tribute to Dow for pioneering magnesium production. "Our strength for security depends primarily on a strong industry, always taking advantage of new technology and always advancing," he told the assembled representatives of the military, the government, and industry.

Doan, who presided, noted that the plant could easily mill 100 million pounds of magnesium annually compared to the four million that could be turned out at the Dow facilities in Midland. "The United States now has the greatest magnesium facilities in the world," Doan said. "No other nation has a magnesium industry of remotely comparable size and aggressiveness, and nowhere is magnesium as cheap as it is in the United States. In fact, no other country has a substantial commercial industry to act as a base for military need in time of emergency."[17]

Madison, Doan said, should be "the biggest stimulus to the use of magnesium yet." He hoped to be able to sell the full capacity of the plant within five years, he told a reporter, "but since it is the first operation of its kind it is difficult now to estimate the economic factors."[18] He was delighted when the first mass-produced magnesium consumer item, Samsonite luggage (Jesse Schwayder, president of Samsonite, said magnesium frames made the line 25 percent lighter), was introduced in January 1955.[19]

When an armistice was reached in Korea, he continued to express optimism. "I would expect the armistice in Korea to have about the same effect as 1945, if anything on a smaller scale," he said, "with some economic recession for the short term but better conditions for the long term. The greatest danger may be psychological; if business gets panicky the country could think itself into serious trouble."[20] To another reporter he predicted a fivefold growth of the chemical industry between 1950 and 1975.[21]

Saran Wrap, following a long period of development, was finally introduced to the American housewife in October 1953, just after the Korean conflict was over. This celebrated product was developed at Dow during World War II when the U.S. Army asked industry for a cheap material in which to wrap arms and equipment to be moved from ship to shore in beachhead invasions. Ralph Wiley, the inventor of saran plastic, tried it out as a film material, and the result was the forerunner of Saran Wrap. The wartime version was oily and ugly and dull green in color, but it had the qualities the military was looking for and it became a basic wartime wrapping material, especially for invasion situations.

In the postwar period Wiley and others refined it further, developing it into a smooth transparent film, and it began to be apparent that it was not only a useful industrial film but a premier household wrap as well. Dow began selling it to industrial firms in big commercial rolls 40 inches wide, but was not in the kitchen wrap business and decided not to enter that business. Two enterprising Dow employees, Carroll R. (Curly) Irons and Russell C. Ludwig, asked for permission and began making and packaging household-size rolls from the big industrial rolls at their homes; they called it "Clingwrap." It was an instant hit with Midland housewives and Dow began to have second thoughts; perhaps the company should enter the consumer products field after all.

Eventually, renamed Saran Wrap, it became the company's first product designed for the supermarket shelves, and the company quickly found it had a tiger by the tail. Selling Saran Wrap off a store shelf was nothing like selling a carload of caustic or plastic granules, so Dow, the chemical company, began to educate itself in this strange new field of selling products to the housewife. It did this by hiring people who knew how to do this, but the tuition was expensive.

William R. Dixon, the Dow marketing manager, reasoned that television was the logical vehicle for launching Saran Wrap nationally, in part to establish name recognition, but mainly because "you had to show the housewife how to use the stuff, and TV was ideally suited to that purpose." In the fall of 1953 the product was introduced on the *Today Show* (then hosted by Dave Garroway), the *Kate Smith Show,* and the Sid Caesar-Imogene Coca vehicle, *Your Show of Shows.*

But Dixon wanted a program that would clearly be Dow's own, that would be identified as "the Saran Wrap show," and he began to look for one. In those pioneering days of television a sponsor often purchased an entire program, a big step up from simply buying units of airtime.

He found it in *Medic*, developed by a young television writer, James Moser, who had been working in the medical files of the Los Angeles County Medical Association, developing a program portraying and based upon actual medical cases. Dixon signed to air *Medic* on NBC.

On August 20, 1954, the company invited the press, medical leaders, community leaders, and food brokers throughout the country to a nationwide closed-circuit television preview of the program. "We have reached the final step in the buyer-seller relationship, that of marketing a product directly to the consumer, and with it the necessity of reaching out directly to millions of American people," Lee Doan told this audience, noting that up to then Dow had sold its products principally to other firms—"we ourselves did not sell or manufacture products from them under our own trademark." In *Medic*, "I believe we have found a vehicle of such caliber that it will not only serve our necessity but will additionally satisfy our sense of social responsibility," he said.

Millard J. Hooker, the company's advertising manager, recalled years later that there was one major flaw in *Medic's* dazzling success that fall. "Only Dow, a newcomer to the medium, would have been naive enough to put a brand-new program on the NBC network opposite a relatively new CBS program starring Lucille Ball and called *I Love Lucy,*" he said. "*Lucy* was the top show on television."[22]

For those who tuned in, *Medic* was the hit of the 1954 fall season, plowing new ground by presenting dramatized medical cases on TV for the first time; in the years ahead these would become a staple of the TV diet. The first program (September 13, 1954) starred three new faces—Richard Boone, Lee Marvin, and Beverly Garland—unknowns then but all destined for long and glorious screen careers. The craggy-faced Boone played Dr. Conrad Steiner, program host and sometime protagonist in the series.

Late in the year, Doan went to New York to accept a Sylvania TV Award honoring *Medic,* which was named "the outstanding program on TV" that year by a committee that included such luminaries as Deems Taylor, its chairman, Ethel Barrymore, James A. Farley, and industrial designer Raymond Loewy. Also receiving awards for it were Moser, its creator and writer, and Dr. Phillip Sampson, president of the Los Angeles County Medical Association.[23]

The little screen did its work. By 1958 the 200 millionth roll of Saran Wrap, enough to go around the world 38 times, was on its way to someone's kitchen.[24]

III.

It was John Grebe, guiding genius of Dow's Physics Lab, who led the company into the atomic age. At the end of World War II, having been an official witness of the Bikini A-bomb explosion in the Pacific, he and others from Dow had spent most of a year at Oak Ridge National Laboratory in Tennessee studying potential peaceful uses of the atom; "Atoms for Peace" was the order of the day, although nothing much was to come of it except protest, turmoil, and frustration. He led a Dow group in a joint study with the Detroit Edison Company and the Atomic Energy Commission, exploring the possibility of a nuclear reactor to produce electrical energy; and in 1953 became the company's first director of nuclear research and development and founder of its Nuclear and Basic Research Laboratory.[25]

The Soviet Union exploded its first atomic bomb in 1949, shocking the world out of its socks and heating up the cold war, which had begun a year or two before and was to drag on for another 40 years. The U.S. Congress responded by authorizing a major expansion of American nuclear weapons capability, and a representative of the AEC came to Midland shortly after that to see Lee Doan. The AEC had been screening various companies privately, he said, and had decided it wanted Dow to manage a top-secret project the AEC had in mind involving research, development, and production connected with the nuclear arsenal.

It was not the AEC's first invitation to Dow to get involved in its programs; Dow, the AEC pointed out, was in fact the only major chemical company not directly involved in its activities, in spite of the substantial expertise of Grebe and others. The AEC had in recent years invited Dow to take on a nuclear waste research program and to operate the chemical separations plant and a reactor at Arco, Idaho. The company had politely turned down the three invitations.

Doan learned almost nothing about what the government was actually asking Dow to do on its fourth try (it was all hush-hush) but Grebe urged him to accept—"we can't keep telling them no forever, and this looks like a good project," he said—and Doan did. He assembled a group chaired by Mark Putnam to guide the project, and they started (once they had security clearances) by visiting the Los Alamos (New Mexico) atomic facility, where much of the work of developing the A-bomb and H-bomb had taken place, for exploratory studies. When they returned to Midland, Putnam called in F. H. "Heinie" Langell, a veteran Dow chemist who had gone to Oak Ridge with Grebe, and asked him if he would like to manage this big new project. Langell accepted.

The assignment was to select a site and build a nuclear production facility to make the plutonium triggers for American nuclear bombs, although this information was known to only two or three people in Dow at the time, and they were forbidden to talk about it. Langell began selecting a cadre of Dow people to help with the project and joined the AEC team that was looking for a site himself. The AEC wanted the most isolated site it could find, he discovered, although utilities, workforce, rail service, and other necessities must be available.

The task force looked at seven sites and chose among them a desolate spot in the Rocky Mountains between Denver and Boulder, Colorado. Maps showed it as Rocky Flats, and the facility that sprang out of the rocks there became known as the Rocky Flats Division.

The final decision to locate at Rocky Flats was made in a secret meeting in the old Olin Hotel in downtown Denver. The extremes to which the group went to insure secrecy were at times close to hilarious, Langell said, but "that was considered necessary at the time." When they were out on the street, they were not to speak to each other or give any sign of recognition, he remembered, "as though we were playing roles in some bad spy movie."

The AEC called a press conference in Denver to announce its intentions: it would build a $45 million facility at Rocky Flats, and it would be managed by Dow, but everything else about the place was secret. Fencing with reporters, the AEC said that yes, there were military applications to the product to be made there but no, it would not be a bomb "as such." Yes, the employees would handle radioactive materials. About 2,000 workers would be employed in the construction period. Plutonium was not even mentioned.[26]

Construction crews from the Austin Company arrived on the ground shortly and the plant was up and operating by the end of 1951, although it was 1954 before everything was complete.

Langell recruited Lorne H. (Matty) Matheson, another Dow graduate of Oak Ridge, to occupy the key post of technical director. Matheson, Canadian born and educated, had been hired by Grebe in 1929 while he was earning his Ph.D. in physics at the University of Michigan, and the two had worked together ever since. An FBI agent, R. L. (Mike) Carroll, was hired to handle press relations, which consisted chiefly of explaining that the place was classified secret, and to manage an employee publication, which could not mention what the place was doing. For the Dow transfers, accustomed to open communication on any topic, it was a weird place to work.

One of the early local recruits was Leroy Hampton, a University of Colorado pharmacy graduate who was working in a Denver pharmacy at the time for $85 a week. He dropped out to Rocky Flats to pick up a job application, and after a nine-month wait for security clearance was hired in July 1953 (at $425 a month) as assistant to Dick Woodard, a Dow chemist who had been at Oak Ridge and was now in charge of the Rocky Flats chemistry group. Their group's job was to separate the uranium, and later plutonium, from something else, often, Hampton, said, "a lot of crud."[27]

Hampton, with Woodard's encouragement, plunged into uranium chemistry, earned a master's degree in chemistry, and when Woodard moved on to another assignment became the chief "uranium chemist" at Rocky Flats, serving in that capacity until 1967. Hampton's hiring marked another landmark in the company; he was the first black professional employed by Dow. Most of the early employees at Rocky Flats considered it, at best, "a Godforsaken place." They lived in Boulder or Golden or Arvada and drove out into the mountains on roads "that would shake your car apart," to work they couldn't talk to anyone about outside the fence line. The wind whistled across the flats at up to 75 miles an hour, blowing a kind of grit that got in your teeth and blasted the paint off your car.

Nevertheless the Rocky Flats Division accomplished its mission faithfully and well. It was different from all other Dow divisions in that Dow managed the plant on the basis of a contract with the AEC, and Dow was paid a modest annual management fee beyond its expenses. "Rocky Flats was a burden we had to carry," one executive said. "Dow wasn't used to getting someone else's approval for anything we did."[28] In spite of this the company usually enjoyed the best of relationships with Seth R. Woodruff Jr., the congenial manager of the AEC's Rocky Flats Area Office, and his AEC colleagues.

By the nature of its work, dealing with plutonium, one of the deadliest elements in the universe, handling it daily in glove boxes, the division had to be exceedingly safety-conscious, and it was; it achieved one of the top safety records in the company. In June 1960 Lee Doan visited Rocky Flats to present it with the President's Safety Award, which was being awarded for the first time. Doan had established the award for the Dow unit showing the greatest relative improvement in its safety record, or for any unit that reached five years or 5 million man-hours without an injury. Rocky Flats had then worked more than 8 million hours without a disabling injury, almost three years, from 1957 to 1960.[29] It went on to achieve one of the best all-time safety records in industry—more than 15 million hours without an injury.

In the early 1950s the company was expanding almost everywhere except in Midland, and by about 1954 it was clear that a reorganization of the company's home base was overdue. The production facilities there were becoming not only antiquated but arthritic. Midland occupied a unique place in the firm; it was the oldest facility and the home plant, and also corporate headquarters, but no one had specific responsibility for its well-being, renewal, and growth. Mark Putnam, as general manager of the company, was almost totally absorbed by this time in administrative work at the corporate level, with little time to concern himself with Midland activities, and he increasingly left these to Ed Barstow and Charles Strosacker, who were concerned with their own fiefdoms but did not perceive that they had any plantwide responsibilities.

When a contract with the Midland labor union (Local 12075, largest local of the United Mine Workers' catchall District 50) was signed in 1953 it was still Lee Doan who signed on behalf of the company, although division managers had been responsible for such contracts in other locations of the company for some time. Managers and superintendents in Midland grumbled that "Texas is running away with the company"; when a new plant was built, it was almost automatically built in Texas because Dutch Beutel had little competition at the board level. Russell L. Curtis was a board member and vice president representing the Western Division and brought in far more modest projects for board approval than Beutel did, but Midland, for whom all the board members were, in theory at least, responsible, had become a corporate orphan. The need for separation of corporation and division was becoming apparent.

Another problem was that Midland's managers had grown old—the Strosackers and Barstows, the Harlows and Schweglers had been around for 40 years and more. To organize a separate Midland division and breathe new life into it, Putnam chose one of its brightest young managers, William H. Schuette, then plastics production manager, and told him he was going to be the first general manager of the division—if he could get it constituted.

Schuette (pronounced "shoe´-tee") faced an extraordinarily difficult task. He was a young man (41 in 1953) being pole-vaulted into a general managership over men in their 60s and 70s long established in their positions and prestige. Furthermore, separating out the production and administrative functions was not simple; it was not at all clear whether some groups (and individual employees) belonged in the division or in the corporate, administrative, organization; many did both, and no one had ever worried about it before.[30] The legal department, for instance, did not distinguish between legal work done for the local production facilities and the corporation; production coordination routinely coordinated production both within the Midland complex and in the company at large.

Bill Schuette turned out to be not only an able organizer and diplomat, but also a brilliant manager. He introduced new concepts of management to the firm—"appropriate frugality" and "management by objective" were two of them—and was soon promoted to the board of directors, where he faced the old bull of the woods himself, Dutch Beutel, who had been having his own way with plant locations in the company since World War II. Schuette recognized that the Midland Division's rebirth required the stimulus of new products and production facilities, but Beutel had no inclination to slow down in Texas, and in the late 1950s the two had some memorable face-offs in the boardroom over this subject.

"Schuette died at age 47 of a heart attack," Ted Doan recalled some years later. "A month before that we had a board meeting in which the Texas Division and the Midland Division got into a shouting match. Schuette turned absolutely livid. He was red-faced because he was so angry at the discussion that was going on. A month later he was dead of a heart attack."[31]

Working almost entirely behind the scenes, Schuette waded into the tangled undergrowth of overlapping responsibilities and personalities that had grown up in Midland, won acceptance for the new concept of its management (i.e., two levels of authority in Midland), and began chiseling out a new organization. At the end of 1955 the Midland Division (today called the Michigan Division) came officially into being.

Schuette also proved to be a builder in the classic Dow mold. First, to provide a Midland area petroleum source, he negotiated purchase of the Bay Refining Company, at Bay City, which refined Michigan crude to gasoline products marketed at stations in the central Michigan area; as a result, for several years Dow found itself in the gasoline business, with a string of stations marketing Bay gasoline. Bay Refining was hardly a major refiner, with only $25 million in annual sales, but Schuette's objective was not to put Dow into the gasoline business; he needed petroleum and refining capacity as underpinning for his main undertaking, the creation of a totally new division to provide basic capability for Midland in the petrochemicals field.

With these elements in place, Midland would once again, he calculated, be fully competitive in almost any product with the Texas Division or any other Dow location. At Bay City he built the Saginaw Bay Division, which used Bay Refining products as feedstocks. The new division was dedicated in mid-1959. Although modest in size it was the largest petrochemical complex in the United States east of the Mississippi and north of the Ohio, producing as its key products ethylene and polyethylene, the raw material (for example) of such items as Handi-Wrap, produced in Bay City.

Schuette also wanted to take advantage of the newly inaugurated St. Lawrence Seaway, which made the Great Lakes accessible for the first time to oceangoing freighters. He built a new Dow Marine Terminal at Bay City, and in May 1958 the *Christel Heering*, a Danish vessel out of Copenhagen, became the first ship to dock at the new terminal. It took on a load of Dow chemical cargo and sailed for Rotterdam via the St. Lawrence route.[32]

Another new division that year was the Dow Industrial Service Division, or DIS, with headquarters in Cleveland. It took over a highly specialized field—the chemical cleaning and conditioning of industrial equipment such as boilers. Its specialized services were soon to be much in demand by the nation's space program. DIS was a spin-off from the Dowell Division, which had begun to offer industrial cleaning services 20 years before.

The cascade of new ventures continued. Perhaps the biggest gamble of them all was the company's plunge into the textile business. Dow researchers, like those in every chemical company in the world, inspired by Du Pont's spectacular success with nylon, Orlon, and Dacron in the late 1930s and the 1940s, were looking for a textile of their own.

After the war Dow had staked its first claim in the field by forming a joint company with the National Plastic Products Company to explore the possibilities of saran as a textile. The new firm, the Saran Yarns Company, had a plant at Odenton, Maryland, where it made saran staple, which showed promise in upholstery fabrics and rugs.

Pushed by a veteran textile man, Ephraim Winer, the Saran Yarns president, saran scored a big success as a hard-wearing, colorful automobile seat cover, and saran seat covers began popping up everywhere—in the New York subway system, in trains, in the big new auto-mobiles coming out of Detroit—and it had several years of popularity in the early 1950s. In 1951 Dow doubled its capacity to produce the material, just before coming a cropper. What did saran seat covers in was the ubiquity of the cigarette; careless cigarette ashes landing on saran would burn an unsightly and unrepairable hole in it, and Dow chemists could not quickly come up with a flame-resistant variety. Saran seat covers almost literally flamed out.

Willard Dow had sent G. W. (Bill) Stanton, a veteran researcher in Strosacker's group, to the Western Division in 1948 to head up a group that worked there to find a new textile fiber. Their eventual discovery was based on a polyacrylonitrile process developed by Stanton that produced an acrylic fiber he called "Zefran." (In some blends it also had the names "Zefstat" and "Zefchrome.")[33]

Zefran acrylic fiber had great promise—"good initial whiteness, good bleachability, good dyeability, resistance to rot," said the lab reports—and Lee Doan and his colleagues began to get excited about it. Should they get into the race? Du Pont had its horses, and Union Carbide had Dynel; Chemstrand had Acrilan, American Cyanamid had Creslan, Tennessee Eastman had Verel. Should Dow saddle up with Zefran? Textiles had always been a notoriously unstable and cycli-cal product, up one year and down the next, Doan knew, but the temptation of big profits was too much, and in the summer of 1956 the Dow team got into the saddle and bought a site on the James River near Williamsburg, Virginia, conveniently located to the textile markets. "Sure it will be rough for awhile," Doan said, "but if we have something good to offer, we have to offer it. Zefran is good. We feel that synthetic fibers will be a big item for us in the future."[34]

The James River plant went into production two years later, in July 1958, under the man-agership of Arthur E. Young, a British-born Dow veteran, with Amos L. (Mose) Ruddock as marketing manager. Doan and Donald K. Ballman, the company's sales director, were still opti-mistic about Zefran when they visited the plant a year later.[35]

Unfortunately, the textile market continued to experience its wild swings and Zefran, while a resounding technical success, never did well in the market. After a few years Dow combined its textile operations with those of BASF, the German chemical giant, which had also entered the textile race late, and after a few more years it sold its half of this joint ven-ture, the Dow Badische Company, to BASF. As gracefully as it could manage it, Dow was out of the textile business.

The great bulk of Dow's postwar expansion was built upon the company's own products. In an era where many of the nation's largest firms were growing by merger, Dow did very lit-tle of this, although in 1955 it had purchased Versenes, Inc., a small manufacturer of chelating agents, and the Columbia Oil Shale and Refining Company, holder of a major oil shale field in Colorado. Its first major acquisition of the 1950s was the Dobeckmun Company of Cleveland, which was merged into Dow by the terms of an agreement signed by Doan and Thomas F. Dolan, Dobeckmun's president, on August 30, 1957.

Dobeckmun—the name was coined from Dolan, Becker, and Munson, the names of the three founders—brought Dow fully into the packaging materials field, which it had been exploring for several years as it introduced plastic films and related materials to that industry. Dobeckmun's best-known product was Zip-tape, the tiny red tape opener on cellophane cigarette packages, chewing gum, and hundreds of other products. It also produced a metallic yarn called "Lurex," a full line of gift wrapping papers, and other packaging materials and industrial laminates. It had plants in Cleveland; Bennington, Vermont; and Berkeley, California. The combined Dobeckmun and Dow packaging products became Dow's Packaging Division.[36]

In 1960 Dow began beefing up its pharmaceutical capability with the acquisition of Allied Laboratories, another moderate-sized firm with annual sales of about $30 million. A stock swap was involved (two-thirds of a share of Dow for a share of Allied) that made the cost about $45 million. As with Dobeckmun, Dow later sold parts of Allied, or Pitman-Moore Co., the dominant piece of Allied's collection of businesses, that did not fit into the Dow lineup—the Allied line of veterinary products and the Campana Company, makers of Campana hand lotion.

In 1958 Doan had introduced Tom Dolan of Dobeckmun to the annual meeting of shareholders; in 1961 he introduced Kenneth F. Valentine, president of Pitman-Moore, to the meeting. Valentine told the shareholders that in spite of accusations to the contrary, pharmaceuticals were one of the best bargains the American consumer had available. It was a speech that could have been made any time in the next 35 years.

IV.

Spectacular as the growth of the company was in the 1950s—in 1957 it was building three major new divisions at once, in Louisiana, Virginia, and Michigan, and in 1960 alone it introduced 24 new products—there were other developments afoot that would one day overshadow this growth completely: the early glimmerings of serious Dow interest in the international field.

In 1950, totally absorbed in its domestic expansion, Dow was barely aware of a world beyond North America. Its sales abroad amounted to only 5 percent of the total; the average for the U.S. chemical industry was 8 percent.

In 1951 Lee Doan had visitors from Japan who wanted to talk about fishing nets. Kagayaki Miyazaki and Manabu Enseki of the Asahi Chemical Company, Japan's largest chemical firm, explained to him that the Japanese from time immemorial had made their nets of cotton and ramie, an Asian plant fiber, both of which Japan imported. They had been experimenting with nets made of saran filaments and found them to possess great advantages over ramie. Would Dow like to build a production plant in Japan to provide raw material for such nets? Asahi would provide the capital, Dow the know-how, and the company would be jointly owned.

Doan was interested, and sent L. C. (Jack) Chamberlain to Japan to look into it. Chamberlain recommended acceptance of the Japanese proposal, and in 1952 Asahi-Dow Ltd. was established, Dow's first joint venture abroad. A plant was built at Nobeoka, Japan. The firm languished in its first years—saran fishnet was not a large-volume seller—but with the addition of styrene and Styron plastic in 1956 the firm became a prosperous affair and the rock on which Dow was to build a solid, long-term relationship with the Japanese.

It was in retrospect an incredible about-face, the founding of Asahi-Dow. The Japanese visitors could not even obtain visas to enter the United States and had to wait in Toronto for several days while Dow attempted to clear their visit with Washington. Enseki had been first secretary of the Japanese Embassy in Washington at the time of Pearl Harbor and his visit to the United States was news in itself. The war was recent enough that there was still a deep resentment of the Japanese in Midland, and Strosacker, among others, said he did not even care to talk to them.

"We had an unusually isolationist group in the management of the company at the time," Ted Doan said. "My father was an isolationist. Don Williams, who was head of sales, hated the Japanese. Tink Campbell was an absolute isolationist; Gerstacker was an isolationist."[37] Despite these factors and his isolationism, Lee Doan felt it was a good, sound move, and the Dow company, amazingly, became one of the first U.S. companies to establish a joint venture with the Japanese in the postwar era.

Late in 1951, Dow studied some attractive new tax concessions the U.S. government was offering firms willing to risk their capital to build U.S. trade abroad—"trade, not aid," was Harry Truman's and Washington's slogan at this period—and as a result Dow quickly organized two new foreign-trade subsidiaries, Dow Chemical International and Dow Chemical Inter-American. Clayton S. Shoemaker, who had been managing export sales in Dow's New York office, one of those urging Dow's export expansion, became president of Dow Chemical International (or Dowintal, as it became known), and was soon off on an extensive globe-trotting mission to begin organizing Dow sales offices abroad. Within a year he had opened new offices in Brussels, Hong Kong, and Montevideo. These were to be the seedpods of Dow Europe, Dow Pacific, and Dow Latin America.

In the beginning the new Dowintal employees were order takers and pushers of surplus product. Lee Doan was greatly pleased when by 1960 the foreign sales of the company amounted to 10 percent of the total, double the percentage of ten years before.

The company's outlook changed rapidly, however. By 1960 Dow had 15 offices in 13 foreign countries, 16 subsidiaries in 11 countries, and 9 associated companies in 8 countries (excluding Canada). Sales abroad climbed from $11 million in 1950 to $86 million in 1960.

"Prior to World War II, and even in the years immediately after it, Dow was inclined to use foreign markets as a means of disposing of surplus production," Lee Doan explained. "If we were in short supply, our customers had to find other sources. Naturally, we did not build very substantial relationships."

Analyzing the reasons expansion overseas was becoming attractive, Doan emphasized the postwar development of mass markets. "The formation of the European Economic Community creates a new mass market of some 160 million people, a market opportunity suited to our aptitude for mass production," he said.

Additionally, many sectors of the world are in need of and willing to accept American manufacturing, processing, or marketing know-how—and in many cases American capital.

Economic activity in the so-called underdeveloped countries has been growing rapidly. The war-ravaged countries of Western Europe bounced back much more rapidly than anyone expected. They have capital, energetic industries, purchasing power, and their standards of living are rising more rapidly than ours. All these things spell opportunity and necessity for the movement of American industry abroad which were largely not present before.

The problems for firms such as Dow going abroad were basically four, he said, "the four D's"—distance, duties, dollars, and discrimination. The "duties" problem involved not only customs duties themselves but quotas, import licenses, and other devices countries used to restrict imports, he said. The "dollar" factor was that many countries had regulations favoring the import of nondollar over dollar goods, dollars often being scarce. "Discrimination is partly natural," he said, "the inclination to buy from neighbors rather than strangers in far-off lands, but is in some cases arbitrary."

One of the key factors moving Dow overseas was the steeply rising cost of research, which doubled between 1950 and 1960, while prices held relatively steady. "It has become more difficult to support a large research program and more difficult to recover research costs," he said.

A research project which might have been attractive 10 years ago cannot be justified today because of the disparity between its probable cost and the return that can reasonably be expected from it. But what if the returns that can be expected from a research project are suddenly doubled? Then research costs can be justified. Since domestic markets cannot be doubled, it is logical to expand our markets overseas.

Getting more return on our research is one of the principal reasons we have been stepping up our activity in world markets and establishing operations of various sorts in foreign countries.

Another attraction was higher profit margins. "We find that on the whole the percentage of net return on invested capital is considerably better in foreign countries than it is in the United States." Then, too, there was Dow's commitment to a policy of aggressive growth, he added. "We have never been content to simply grow with the economy."[38]

One of the early Dow outposts in Europe was Nederlandsche Dow Maatschappij (or NDM), a chemical terminal in the Dutch port of Rotterdam called the Botlek, which Dow established in 1955. It became the main transshipment center for Dow exports arriving in Europe in those early years.

By the late 1950s Doan was leading the charge overseas himself. In 1959 he made a European tour that included a visit to the company's new plant at King's Lynn, where he was greeted by Dr. Walter E. Ripper, managing director of Dow Agrochemicals Ltd. Not only had Herbert Dow's ancestors come from that part of Norfolk, Doan said, but his own ancestor, John Doane, had left Norfolk for America in the seventeenth century.

"Nowhere have I seen better farms," Doan told the East Anglians. "Nowhere have I observed agriculture more scientifically conducted than in this county, which is one of the important larders of England. The agricultural chemicals we shall produce in King's Lynn you will find of considerable assistance in this task which you perform for England so well."

Dr. Ripper responded: "I want you to feel completely happy about the fact that American money, know-how and enterprise will play a major part in bringing to this English town an extremely important new industry." He also said he believed local people would "soon be saying that Dow was a British company, that it was too East Anglian to be anything else, and that anyone could see that Dow was an East Anglian name anyway."[39]

Doan also got acquainted with a Spanish grandee, the Conde del Cadagua, board chairman of the Union Quimica del Norte de Espana (or Unquinesa), at Bilbao, a leading Spanish manufacturer of chemicals and plastics with whom Zoltan Merszei, Dow's manager in Europe, and others in Dow had become acquainted. In 1960 Unquinesa was acquired by Dow and became Dow-Unquinesa, the company's flagship in Spain. In 1961, when he made a farewell seven-week swing around Europe, the longest of his career, Doan and Ben Branch, the president of Dow International, were decorated by the Spanish dictator Francisco Franco who conferred upon Doan the Spanish Grand Cross of Civil Merit, the highest civilian honor available for a person not a Spanish citizen.[40] Branch, whom the Caudillo seemed to consider a somewhat lesser mortal, received the Order of Isabel Catolica, Commander Grade.

All this was merely prologue to Dow's future in Europe. When the Dow plant at Terneuzen, its biggest in Europe, was dedicated in April 1965, with Prince Bernhard of the Netherlands officiating, Lee Doan returned to Europe once again and helped his successors celebrate the gala occasion, strolling along the avenue to the Dow plant, now named "Herbert Dow-Weg." It was nice, he told a friend, to "get a look at what I helped get started."

V.

When a severe economic recession hit in late 1957, just as Dow was at the peak of the biggest wave of expansion spending in its history, the timing was disastrous for the company. Sales figures had been climbing rapidly, quarter by quarter, since the end of World War II, spiraling upward from $200 million in 1949 to $628 million in 1957; now suddenly they were in free fall. For the first time in the memory of many employees, sales were less than they had been a year before.

In that same period of time the employee population had doubled, from about 13,500 to 27,000. Dow recruiters combed the nation's leading campuses each winter and spring, seeking out the brightest and best. Faculty members at many of the country's finest chemistry and chemical engineering schools regularly steered their top graduates toward Dow, well known as a growing company and a good company to work for.

The Dow board of directors was caught in a vise between the surging upward push of spending for payroll and expansion and the downward push of income as sales plummeted.

What to do? Some of the building could be "stretched out," they decided—slowed down—but about 80 percent of it could not be stretched without incurring heavy losses; contracts had been let.

The board gritted its teeth and for the first time in the history of the company ordered a general reduction in personnel. Each department, companywide, it decreed, would reduce its personnel by 10 percent. Department chiefs would accomplish this by evaluating the performance of each individual in the work group and dismissing those that fell to the bottom of the ratings. The whole process was to be completed within a matter of 90 days. Furthermore, there was no campus recruiting by Dow in the spring of 1958.

It was not a happy spring for the employees of Dow Chemical. The process was called "Black Friday" (it was unveiled on Friday, May 23), or "the bloodbath," or simply, as time went on and it became a memory, as "1958"; employees who went through it simply said, "1958," and other employees knew exactly what that meant. It was a harrowing, traumatic experience for everyone concerned. Robert J. House, Midland Division controller at the time, remembered people crying in their offices after the announcement.

One of the long-term results was a close rein on hiring procedures; the hiring of new personnel was rigorously controlled from 1958 on. Each department had an "Authorized Personnel Level," or APL; no new hire could be made without a corresponding APL.

Carl Gerstacker and other top managers swore the company could not afford and would never have "another 1958," and for a quarter of a century afterward the company avoided general reductions in staff. Its executive group took pride in the company's ability to withstand economic downturns without a corresponding downturn in personnel, and strove for stability of employment, as impervious as possible to the vagaries of the economy.

Understaffing became a way of life at Dow. Measured in sales per employee, earnings per employee, or similar measures, Dow employees then and later invariably were far ahead of other chemical companies the world around in this respect.

The debacle of 1958, and Dow's sudden about-face in hiring practice that year, did great damage to Dow's reputation on the campuses. It was in many cases years before Dow recruiters could rekindle warmth in their relationships with their campus contacts.

Mark Putnam, who as general manager was director of the 1958 cutback, felt it should be executed within the company without publicity outside its gates. Amazingly, this old-school, no-publicity approach worked fairly well and there was very little publicity about Black Friday outside the company, in spite of the wild rumors that raged in Dow towns from coast to coast. The whole matter was over in a few weeks, and by early fall the economy was improving again.

At the annual Midland Pin Award ceremonies in early May that year, Lee Doan had spoken of the absolute necessity of what the company was doing without referring directly to the 10 percent population cut. How could the company continue spending for expansion at the same time it was firing employees, employees were asking. How did that make sense?

"We are not on some idle and idealistic crusade," he told 413 veteran employees gathered to receive pins for 20 years of service and more. "These things are an absolute necessity because we are today in the most fiercely competitive market we have experienced since the depression of the thirties."

"We could save a lot of money by just sort of stopping everything," he said. "Stopping construction, abandoning programs that are designed to maintain and improve our position in the market and so on. But then when things turned up we would find that we had lost ground and were not in a position to take advantage of our opportunities. If some of our expenditures or investments seem incompatible with economy, consider that they probably are aimed at the long range—not at the short."[41]

By the end of the year the recession was over and Dow was back in its usual mode of vigorous growth. Company sales in the last quarter of the year had recovered to prerecession levels and the last quarter had been "one of the best in history in terms of volume," Doan said in a year-end statement. Dow was introducing two new products at the National Association of Home Builders show in Chicago in January 1959, he noted.[42] The bloodbath of 1958 had been only a detour in the road.

"What a lesson that was, when the bottom fell out of everything and Dow fired 10 percent of everybody across the board," Ted Doan said later. "We had never fired anybody in our lives as a company, and this made all the universities mad at us. It was good in the sense that it gave a lot of people the determination never to let that happen again."

It was a period of change. When Lee Doan became the company's chief executive John Crider, last member of the board of directors commuting from Cleveland to Midland for board meetings, was still serving on the board, as he had since 1908. A board that had begun as an "outside" board, with all of its members except Herbert Dow living in Cleveland and not full-time employees of the company, was now an "inside" board, with all of its members full-time company employees except Crider and Alden Dow, the architect son of Herbert Dow.

Crider retired in November 1950, and was replaced by Ray H. Boundy; when W. R. Veazey, another grizzled veteran, retired in 1953, Boundy became the company's first full-time director of research. In 1952 Carl E. Allen of Muskegon, Michigan, a banker, became the only "outside" director (aside from Alden Dow); he had been associated with the National City Bank of New York and had known some of the Dow directors for many years; Allen left the Dow board in 1957 to become president of the Federal Reserve Bank of Chicago.

A new generation, Herbert Dow's grandsons, took seats on the board of directors—Willard's son Herbert H. Dow II, now staff manager of plastics fabricated products, and Herbert D. (Ted) Doan, Lee Doan's son, manager of the chemicals department. Robert B. Bennett, son of the indestructible Earl Bennett, had become treasurer. Also joining the board were Bill Schuette, the rising star of the Midland Division, and Ben Branch, the young lion who was now president of Dow International. Russ Curtis of the Western Division retired after 37 years and Ed Barstow, with 59 years of service, became honorary board chairman. Dow was becoming young at the top.

As an experiment, Willard Dow had begun to sell Dow stock to the company's employees on a payroll deduction system late in 1948. An employee who owns stock in the company he works for has a deeper interest in its operations and problems, he reasoned, and will have more team spirit. The company became one of the major pioneers in employee stock ownership.

When the first experimental offering of Dow stock was made to employees that year, 19 percent of the employee population subscribed. That seemed an encouraging result, so in early 1950 it was tried again; this time 29 percent subscribed. In 1951 the figure went up to 42 percent. In 1952 45 percent subscribed, and there wasn't enough stock in the 45,000 shares allotted to the program to go around; the issue was oversubscribed.

In the first (1948) plan the stock was offered to employees at a 5 percent discount from the market price (at date of offer); this was boosted to 15 percent in the second plan and 26 percent in the third and fourth. The fourth offering (1952), for example, cost employees $82.50 a share when the market price was $112.125. Over the years the discount has settled down to about 15 percent of the market price and the Dow Employee Stock Purchase Plan (employees are restricted to an amount equivalent to 10 percent of wage or salary, and directors are excluded from participation) has long been one of the most popular fringe benefits of working for the firm, a relatively painless way of acquiring the stock of a blue-chip company, one that has not missed or reduced its dividends since 1911.

The company has over the years devised various other ways of bringing its employees into the stockholder rolls, and virtually every Dow employee is also a Dow stockholder; the exceptions are those who have sold their holdings. Cheering somewhere in the shadows is Herbert Dow, who bought company stock on his own account for his secretary, Flo Thompson, at the dawn of the company.

Carl Gerstacker, who helped establish the employee stock purchase plan in 1948, often said that in his opinion every Dow employee ought to own Dow stock, even young women who didn't expect to work very long, and hourly workers. "They ought to be deep in debt and have their investment only in Dow stock and own no other investment," Gerstacker said. "Then, by golly, they would be like H. H. Dow, who had his whole life involved in this company. If the company did well, the employees would come out rich. If the company did poorly, the employees would be poor and they would deserve to be poor. But I think they would succeed. Nothing works like working for yourself. We are all full of self-interest."[43]

When the first employee stock was offered in 1948, union members asked Local 12075 in Midland if it was all right to buy it. Was it OK with the union? (Union officials have generally been cool to stock purchase by employees on the theory that it tends to make them company supporters, not union supporters). That first year, the question was not answered; but in succeeding years, the union membership were told flat out that the union did not object.

Harold Bowers, president of the local at that time, said he saw no weakening of the union's position as a result of stock ownership. "We have exceptionally good labor relations here," he said. When there was a strike in 1948, he remembered, the first in the company's history, a veteran employee who held $75,000 in Dow stock worked in the union's soup kitchen and exhorted the strikers to "stick it out."

Bowers showed a reporter visiting his union hall the portraits hanging on its walls of John L. Lewis, the union's founder, G. Mennen Williams, a four-term Democratic governor of Michigan, and of Willard Dow, "probably the only company president to be thus honored by a union with which he dealt," the reporter wrote.[44]

Willard Dow had not always been a union favorite. He had come into the headquarters building one morning in 1948 and saw that the lobby had not had its usual overnight cleaning. "What's going on?" he asked Minnie Keil, the receptionist. "Is Charley sick?" The union local had gone out on strike, she told him. "Well, we'll just have to do it ourselves, then," Willard said. He went to the broom closet and took over Charley's job, sweeping out the lobby for the duration of the strike.[45]

When he retired from the company, one of the letters Lee Doan treasured most came from Carl J. Mitchell, president of the Midland local for many years. "You have emphasized the importance of and the preservation of such old-fashioned virtues as friendly, informal cooperation among the employees and a genuine concern for each other's welfare," Mitchell wrote.

> Traditions like these must never vanish from the Company. At least for nearly 30 years that I know of Dow plant life, it was only through the thinking of all the employees that these virtues were present in the company's planning, that created the dedication and the desire of the large majority of employees who want to be the best operator, chemist, craftsman, salesman, technician, janitor, superintendent, etc., that it was possible for him to be, and I am of the opinion that these ingredients must be present and understood if there is a reasonable chance of Dow developing. . . . What have we accomplished, even if we are successful, if we sacrifice the very foundations that hold family, community and country together?[46]

Another milestone in employee relations that occurred in Willard Dow's last year was the founding of the company's Pension and Profit-Sharing Plan, established with a first company contribution of $800,000 in 1948. In August 1949, the contribution was $1,315,665.91.

In the 1950s there also began another revolution at Dow—the gradual change in employee skin color that followed the civil rights activities that stirred the nation in those years and later. When Lee Doan assumed the presidency of the company in 1949, the black population of Midland County, its home base, consisted of one family, a couple who ran a restaurant out in the countryside. Black chemists and chemical engineers were extremely rare, and Dow did not have any.

In the 1950s there began the long, often arduous change that opened the ranks of the company to blacks and other minorities, sometimes over the opposition of the white workforce. Some of the early black employees would get telephone calls in the night proffering threats of various kinds. After a few die-hards had been ferreted out and warned, that kind of activity faded out. The real race for Dow to catch up in minority employment came later, however.

The company's transportation system also began a radical change. Lee Doan became the godfather of the Dow marine fleet, which pioneered the shipment of chemical cargos on the high seas. In 1953 Dow leased a tanker, which was remodeled to carry bulk liquid chemicals and nothing else. Called the *Marine Chemist*, it operated principally out of Freeport, Texas, carrying cargo to Dow terminals on both coasts of the United States. Three years later, encouraged by the experience, Dow commissioned the *Marine Dow-Chem*, the first vessel designed specifically to transport chemicals; it was built at Quincy, Massachusetts, by the shipbuilding division of Bethlehem Steel Corporation and operated for Dow by Marine Transport Lines, Inc. The two vessels carried (and transshipped) Dow cargos to Dow's coastal terminals and divisions and plants in Texas, Louisiana, and California, to Allyn's Point, Connecticut, and up through the St. Lawrence Seaway to Michigan.

This shipping was so successful for Dow that the company commissioned a third ship from the Quincy yards in 1959 that it called the S.S. *Leland I. Doan*, a clone of the *Marine Dow-Chem*. Belle Beutel, Dutch's wife, broke the traditional bottle of champagne on the ships's prow when it was launched on March 31, 1960.[47] In March 1961 the *Leland I. Doan* sailed through the Golden Gate on its maiden voyage with a crew of 39 officers and men, carrying a cargo of Texas division chemicals to Oakland and Pittsburg, California, with a stop at Los Angeles.[48]

An honor of another sort came to Lee Doan in November 1957 when he was cited by *Forbes* magazine as one of America's "fifty foremost" business leaders, based on a poll of its subscribers and business associations. It was a particularly happy occasion for Doan; Willard Dow had received the same award just 10 years before. "A visionary of the expansion of his company," the citation read, "following the hard-driving tradition of its founder while firmly grasping each new opportunity to build his company's business, he has never lost sight of human values or failed to be fully aware of industry's social responsibilities. It can truly be said that through his untiring efforts, progress has become arbitrary at Dow."[49]

The most widely publicized event of Lee Doan's tenure as Dow president was surely the White House ceremonies marking the official opening of the U.S. government's seawater conversion plant, a U.S. Department of Interior demonstration plant at Dow's Plant A in Freeport, Texas, using Dow technology to transform saltwater into fresh.

The day before the event Lee Doan and Dutch Beutel received phone calls from the White House, the gist of which was: "The President of the United States requests your presence in his office tomorrow." Beutel had arranged for the vice president, Lyndon B. Johnson, to preside over the ceremonies at Freeport along with Stewart Udall, secretary of the interior.

Instead, Doan and Beutel scrambled to Washington, where they discovered they were the only invitees for a White House event at which Pres. John F. Kennedy would press a button (made of Dow magnesium) to activate the first seawater conversion plant in Texas. "Beutel and Doan—which one is which?" Kennedy greeted them, and a few minutes later, flanked by the two, made his speech and pressed the button to activate the plant in Texas while photographers recorded the scene for history.

Beutel was warmly impressed by the president.

This guy does everything well. And he does it easily, with no unnecessary pomp or strain. When he pushed the key, ending the ceremonies, there was a lot of confusion as the photographers started to work. Mr. Kennedy posed at least three times at the button for pictures, and then he asked, "You boys want any more?" When they were satisfied, the president shook hands with us, thanked us for coming, and said he appreciated our efforts and our company's part regarding the Freeport water conversion plant. Then Dr. Doan and I were shown out. As we were leaving, I saw one last item that went right along with the president's relaxed and informal manner. It was a little baby carriage parked outside one of the White House rooms.

Meanwhile, in Freeport, Dow Chairman Carl Gerstacker and Division General Manager Earle Barnes hosted the Johnsons and Secretary Udall and applauded as fresh water gushed from a specially designed pipe when the president pressed the button in Washington. Later on, Lady Bird and Lyndon put on an impromptu performance for a fascinated crowd attending a Democratic reception at the Riverside Country Club following the dedication.[50]

In 1959, as Lee Doan's 65th birthday approached, the question of who should succeed him as CEO came to the fore. As he talked to other members of the executive committee about it, they agreed that it was time for "one of the young fellas," as Earl Bennett phrased it, to take over. Their consensus was that it should be Bill Schuette, who had amply proven he could work effectively with men much older than he and breathe new life into an organization, as he had the Midland Division. They began to discuss how to set the stage for this event.

Then on November 8, 1959, the 47-year-old Schuette suffered a massive heart attack, and suddenly was dead. It was the day before Lee Doan's 65th birthday.

"Bill Schuette was the first modern Dow manager," Ted Doan said later, "and I believe Bill Schuette would have run the company, had he lived, because he was a consummate manager; if he hadn't died, I wouldn't have been executive vice president. He would have been. And I would hope he would have been president."[51]

Lee Doan decided to stay on awhile. Almost exactly a year later, on November 6, 1960, Mark Putnam stepped onto the bathroom scale to check his weight one morning and fell dead, also of a heart attack, at age 68. That made the matter suddenly urgent, and it also made it logical to move the heir apparent, whoever he might be, into Putnam's slot as executive vice president.

Within a matter of days the new executive vice president was named. It was not, as many had speculated, the company's brilliant financial vice president, Carl Gerstacker, then 44; it was Herbert Dow (Ted) Doan, Lee Doan's son, then 38. Instead, Gerstacker moved up to board chairman; Earl Bennett, at 80, had decided to retire. Young Doan, as executive vice president, "appears to be in line for the job now held by his father," reported *Fortune* magazine and other publications.[52]

"My father, Lee Doan, set up the organization," Ted Doan said.

I would be proud to set it up the same way; it was a dandy. Gerstacker was chairman and I was president and Branch was executive vice president. He just stuck those guys in there. I wasn't privy to this. I am convinced that he was out selling me. I think he probably had great difficulty doing that. My suspicion is that he had previously indicated to Gerstacker that he would be president of the company. I think my father wondered where the hell I came from, but I think he did that with considerable pride. He loved to see all this going on, but I think he had to make a switch of horses somewhere along there. I think Gerstacker handled that exceedingly well. I don't know how he handled it personally but in terms of the effect on others the way he handled himself was good.[53]

"I probably thought I should have been the chief executive instead of Ted," Gerstacker said many years later,

but I think part way through the experience I began to believe that he was better than I would have been. Today, I think that he was better than I would have been. I would not have been as willing to have a triumvirate or troika, or to listen to other people as much as Ted did. I think he was actually better for the company. His willingness to use Branch and me made it a better system than if I had been the chief executive officer or if Branch had been the chief executive officer. I think it is a great ability that Ted has that was well used. That is an honest, sincere evaluation.

The changing of the guard was formalized at the 65th annual meeting of stockholders, at which Lee Doan made his farewell speech. "Dow stands on the threshold of a new era in its history, with ample reason for enthusiasm for the future," he told the stockholders, who did not yet know it was his retirement speech. Ted Doan was formally elected as the new president and chief executive officer at the customary board huddle after the meeting, just three days past his 40th birthday.

Macauley Whiting, another youngster at 37, became vice president for international operations (Schuette's successor as Midland division manager, Whiting had married Helen Dow, Willard's daughter). Herbert H. Lyon, 43, took over as corporate controller.[54]

A few months before, the top three officers of the company had been aged 68, 80, and 68. Now they were aged 40, 44, and 47, younger by an average of 28 years. The Dow leadership had not been that young since 1897.

Among the letters Lee Doan received was one from S. D. (Steve) Bechtel, chairman and president of the Bechtel Corporation in San Francisco, who was also being succeeded as chief executive by his own son, Steve Bechtel Jr. "Can any two Dads be luckier than Lee Doan and Steve Bechtel?" he asked. "The future is certainly bright."[55]

Lee Doan continued to serve as chairman of the executive committee while the "young fellas" learned the ropes, and continued to receive honors and acclamations; in 1964 he was awarded the Society of Chemical Industry Medal for contributions to chemistry. The company he had taken over in 1949 when it had less than 14,000 employees and $200 million in annual sales now had 31,000 employees and $890 million in sales. The number of shareholders had quintupled in that time, from 19,000 to more than 100,000.

Now it was up to the new guard to show what they could do.

Notes

1. Many marriages were celebrated that spring as the United States entered World War I, including those of Herbert Dow's two eldest daughters. The United States declared war on Germany in April 1917. W. J. Hale and Helen Dow were married on February 7, and L. I. Doan and Ruth Dow on April 7.

2. Gerstacker quoted in "H. D. Doan New Dow President," *Saginaw News*, September 13, 1962.

3. See "Mrs. Leland I. Doan, 1895-1950," *Dow Diamond* 13, no. 1 (February 1950): 2. She was the daughter of Herbert Dow, sister of Willard Dow, wife of Leland I. Doan, and mother of H. D. (Ted) Doan.

4. For complete text, see "Good Will Testimonial Given Dow's President," *Midland Daily News*, April 6, 1950.

5. "For the Voters to Decide—Two Issues," *Detroit Free Press*, March 26, 1951.

6. Summerfield, a Flint (Michigan) Chevrolet dealer, had planned an attempt to launch Saran Wrap on the national market but returned the product to Dow when he joined the Eisenhower team. It was widely believed within Dow that Summerfield and Eisenhower had a gentlemen's agreement in 1952: if Eisenhower had been defeated for the presidency that year, he and Summerfield had agreed, they would fall back on a plan to take over Saran Wrap and promote and sell it nationwide, settling for financial rather than political success.

7. See "Dow Chemical Announces Half Billion Expansion Plan," *Cleveland Plain Dealer*, May 18, 1951. The figures were $84 million in 1947, $49 million in 1948, $43 million in 1949, $29 million in 1950, and $80 million in 1951.

8. See, inter alia, "Dow Chemical Gets Check for $100,425,000 For Debentures Sale," *Wall Street Journal*, July 23, 1952; "Dow Chemical Gets $100,425,000 Check," *New York Times*, July 23, 1952; "Chemicals—The Next 1,000 Years," *Time* magazine, August 4, 1952. Doan noted that 61 years before, Herbert Dow had receive a check for $75 with gratitude, saying, "I think this will last us quite a while," the same sentiment Doan voiced in relation to the $100 million check in 1952. For an overview of Dow's postwar expansion see "The Dow Expansion," *Fortune* magazine, May 1952, 104.

9. Nelson Dow Griswold was the son of Thomas Griswold Jr. and a nephew of Herbert Dow. Beutel was frosty to Griswold when Willard Dow first sent him to Freeport, suspecting he was a "Dow family spy," assigned to report back to Midland on Beutel's activities; but the easy-going, hard-working Griswold soon dispelled these notions and became one of Beutel's most trusted lieutenants. Griswold served on the Dow board of directors for many years. Stein, son of Earl Stein, a veteran Dow production superintendent, had been one of the early transfers from Midland to Freeport.

10. For details see Louisiana Plant Site Study, May 22, 1956.

11. From "Louisiana Division Construction Project," with Appendix, report by J. R. Stein, October 10, 1956.

12. Governor Kennon to L. I. Doan, April 9, 1956.

13. "Louisiana Division Ships First Chemicals," Dow Internal News Service, *Advance Information for Management*, July 30, 1958.

14. For more on development of salaried operations in Louisiana, see Shirley Van Meter, "A Curious Blending of Yesterday and Tomorrow," *Elements* magazine, The Dow Chemical Co., 1, no. 2 (1973): 36-43.

15. "Dow Announces $165 Million Expansion Program," news release, Dow Texas Division, August 28, 1974.

16. Magnesium has always been a boom or bust business, for Dow and other producers, with very few booms. At the end of World War II the industry shut down flat; there was so much war surplus on the market at three cents a pound that it was1947 before most of it was worked off. When production did resume, only Dow returned to ingot production.

17. "Dow Dedicates Madison Magnesium Mill," *Brinewell* 12, no. 17 (June 2, 1954): 1.

18. Richard Elwell, financial editor, *San Francisco Commercial News*, October 30, 1953.

19. "New 'First' for Magnesium Introduced," *Brinewell* 13, no. 19 (January 26, 1955): 3.

20. "What U.S. Business Leaders Think . . ." *Newsweek*, April 13, 1953.

21. L. I. Doan, "Chemistry's Role in Better Living," *Commercial and Financial Chronicle*, June 18, 1953. The prediction seems to have emerged from the Manufacturing Chemists' Association in Washington. See "Doan Cites Chemistry's Big Strides," *New York Herald-Tribune*, May 16, 1953.

22. Oral History, Millard J. Hooker, June 10, 1992.

23. See "Another Forward Step," *Dow Diamond* 17, no.3 (September 1954): 2, and "Medic," pp. 28-29 same issue. For details of Sylvania Awards, see Deems Taylor to L. I. Doan, November 12, 1954. For Saran Wrap history see Max Key and Eugene E. Perrin, "Saga of Saran," unpublished manuscript, 1984-85, Post Street Archives.

24. "Happy Smiles Are the Order of the Day," *Brinewell* 16, no. 21 (July 23, 1958): 1.

25. The lab was first installed in an ancient schoolhouse, the First Ward Elementary School (also called the Dow School), which stood in the middle of what was becoming the Dow research campus; a new nuclear lab was built shortly. Alden W. Hanson succeeded Grebe as lab director in 1954. See "The Idea Man," chap. 5 in this volume.

    The Dow-Detroit Edison project involved a consortium of about 20 companies. It generated from these companies $1 - $2 million annually in development funds, which it used to work toward electricity from nuclear power.

26. *Denver Post*, March 24, 1951. See also Whitehead, *The Dow Story*, 222-24, and "Dow to Operate Atomic Unit for AEC," *Brinewell* 12, no. 9 (March 27, 1951): 1 .

27. Oral History, Leroy Hampton, June 16, 1992.

28. James H. Hanes, general manager, Rocky Flats Division, 1972-75.

29. "Rocky Flats Receives First President's Safety Award," *Dow Corral* (*Round-up of Rocky Flats News*) no. 14 (July 1, 1960).

30. The author was privy to these matters as an early recruit to the Schuette team, and in 1956 became public relations manager of the division and member of its operating board.

31. Oral History, H. D. Doan, July 29 and August 2, 1988, and January 17, 1989.

32. See L. I. Doan, "Basics Producer Increasing Attention to Consumer Sales," *New York Journal of Commerce*, November 24, 1959.

33. For origin of the name "Zefran," see Whitehead, *The Dow Story*, 235–36.

34. "Tempest on the Tittabawassee," *Forbes* magazine, September 15, 1956.

35. "Top Officials of Dow Visit Fiber Plant," *Newport News* (Va.) *Press*, August 19, 1959.

36. The plant at Bennington, Vermont, which produced Christmas and other gift wraps, was sold by Dow a few years later.

37. Oral History, H. D. Doan, July 29 and August 2, 1988, and January 17, 1989.

38. Citations from L. I. Doan, "New Forces Spurring U.S. Expansion Overseas," *Journal of Commerce*, April 6, 1960; and (apparently same text) "Dr. Doan Tells of Foreign Markets," talk by Doan to Midland branch, American Association of University Women, *Midland Daily News*, January 22, 1960.

39. "Banquet Surprise—Dow Founder of Norfolk Descent," *Lynn News & Advertiser*, Norfolk, England, May 16, 1960; "Head of Giant U.S. Firm Visits Their Lynn Site," *Eastern Daily Press*, Norwich, England, May 16, 1960.

40. Papers of L. I. Doan, April 1, 1961. See also "Spain Gives Honor to Doan and Branch," *Bay City* (Michigan) *Times*, May 28, 1961.

41. "Frugality Absolute Necessity, Doan Tells Pin Award Classes," *Brinewell* 16, no. 16 (May 14, 1958): 1. See also "Dow Cutbacks: Not the first time," *Midland Daily News*, March 14, 1993, and Oral History, H. D. Doan, July 29 and August 2, 1988 and January 17, 1989.

42. "Doan Sees Improved Business Climate In Outlook for 1959," *Brinewell* 17, no. 7 (January 7, 1959).

43. Oral History, Carl A. Gerstacker, July 21, 1988.

44. "They All Own a Slice of Dow," *Business Week*, August 23, 1952, p. 76.

45. Willard Dow's more or less instinctive reaction to Dow's first strike set the pattern for Dow management's response to strikes ever since. The 1948 strike concluded with recognition of the United Mine Workers of America as bargaining agent for Dow's hourly paid Midland workforce. Up to that time a "company" union had represented the employees.

46. Carl J. Mitchell, president, Local 12075, District 50, U.M.W.A. to L. I. Doan, October 16, 1962.

47. "New Dow Chemical Tanker Named for Dr. Doan, Company President," New London, Connecticut, *Day*, December 1, 1959; "Name New Dow Tanker S. S. Doan," *Midland Daily News*, November 27, 1959; "New Dow Tanker Is Named for Company's President," *Western Paint Review*, December 1959; and other publications.

48. "Chemical Cargo Carrier Due Here on Maiden Trip," *Oakland Tribune*, March 2, 1961. The cargo included styrene, caustic soda, chlorothene, trichlorethylene, ethylene glycol, diethylene glycol, propylene glycol, and the soil fumigants Telone and Vidden-D. For an account of Dow water-borne shipment and its role in linking chemical products to the eventual consumer, see William B. Seward, *East from Brazosport* (Midland, Mich.: The Dow Chemical Co., 1974).

49. "The Expansionist," *Forbes*, October 1957. See also "Dr. Doan Cited as U.S. Business Leader," *Bay City* (Mich.) *Times*, November 8, 1957; "Dr. Doan Honored as 'Fifty Foremost' Meet," *Dow Texan*, November 13, 1957; and other publications.

50. This June 21, 1961 event was nationally reported. For A. P. Beutel's account of it, see "Beutel Terms Phone Call 'A Shocker,'" *Dow Texan*, July 5, 1961. Reporters speculated at the time that JFK, then on

crutches and travel-restricted, did not wish to be upstaged by LBJ, who was scheduled to give the main speech at the Freeport ceremonies, and set up a competing attraction, a White House press "show," at the last moment.

51. Oral History, H. D. Doan.

52. "Businessmen in the News," *Fortune*, January 1961, p. 52.

53. Oral History, H. D. Doan.

54. "Herbert D. Doan Elected Dow President; Other Top-Level Changes Announced," Dow news release, September 12, 1962.

55. S. D. Bechtel, Bechtel Corp., San Francisco, to L. I. Doan, December 12, 1960.

PART FIVE

DOW GOES
GLOBAL

Dow

1964—Dow sales surpass $1 billion for first time.

1965—Lirugen, Dow's one-shot measles vaccine, is introduced in February, dominates market by year-end. Company launches reorganization as global firm with Dow Chemical Europe, Dow Chemical Latin America, Dow Chemical Pacific, Dow Canada, and Dow Chemical USA as major units.

1966-69—Protests against war in Vietnam focus on Dow's production of napalm, resulting in hundreds of campus demonstrations in United States, related demonstrations worldwide.

1968—*Apollo 8* orbits moon and splashes down in Pacific, heat shield made from Dow epoxy resin.

1969—New Oyster Creek Division near Freeport, Texas, designed to mass-produce chemicals, goes onstream, featuring world's largest phenol plant.

1970—Ted Doan retires as chief executive at age 48, is succeeded by Ben Branch.

1971—Lead-free gasoline gains rapidly in use; sales of ethylene dibromide for antiknock fluids plummet.

Dow sales surpass $2 billion.

1973—Dow is first foreign industrial firm listed on Tokyo Stock Exchange.

Dow sales surpass $3 billion.

1974-77—Dow is world's most profitable chemical company four years running.

1976—Ben Branch becomes board chairman, is succeeded as chief executive by Zoltan Merszei, architect of Dow's European success.

1977—Lorelco, cholesterol-lowering drug, introduced.

1978—Merszei becomes chairman and is succeeded as chief executive by Paul F. Oreffice.

World at large

1963—John F. Kennedy assassinated in Dallas by Lee Harvey Oswald.

1965—United States sends troops to Vietnam.

1967—Soviet and U.S. astronauts walk in space—10 minutes and 21 minutes respectively.

Hanoi bombed by United States.

Dr. Christiaan Barnard performs first human heart transplant.

1968—Martin Luther King Jr. and Robert Kennedy assassinated.

1969—Neil Armstrong becomes first man on moon.

United States begins withdrawal of troops from Vietnam.

1970—Four students shot and killed in war protest at Kent State University.

1971—United States bombs Vietcong supply routes in Cambodia.

Nixon orders 90-day freeze on wages and prices to curb inflation.

1972—Paris peace talks between Vietnam and the United States.

Nixon visits China and USSR.

1973—Break-in at Watergate investigated.

Vice President Spiro Agnew, accused of taking bribes, resigns.

OPEC oil embargo creates worldwide energy crisis.

1974—Watergate scandal results in Nixon's resignation; Gerald Ford becomes president.

1975—Supersonic passenger service begins with Concorde jet flights from London and Paris.

1977—Oil begins flowing through 800-mile Alaska pipeline.

Elvis Presley dies.

1978—"Year of the three popes" as John Paul I dies one month after election and is succeeded by John Paul II.

TWELVE

THE TROIKA

I.

"**D**ow was this little midwestern, isolationist company," Ben Branch said, remembering back to 1959, "most of whose executives took a very dim view of international trade. I don't know how many meetings I sat in where they said, 'We're not going to spend one cent of our hard-earned American money on international business.'"[1]

That was 1959. In the next 20 years Dow was totally transformed, from an obscure firm that made chemicals for other chemical companies into one of the most aggressively international-istic and widely known of U.S. firms and one of the world's half-dozen largest chemical giants.

This feat was accomplished by a three-person executive group called "the troika," the Russian term for a vehicle drawn by three horses abreast. It is quite rare for a business organization to be run by a troika, even rarer for such an arrangement to work well; indeed, it never happens at all without an exceptional team of horses.

This was that kind of team—Ted Doan as president and chief executive, Carl Gerstacker as chairman of the board, and Ben Branch as executive vice president and chief operating officer. Ted Doan proposed straight off that they split up the company among them. "Gerstacker had finance and marketing and Branch had everything else, operations and international. I had more to do with research than either of the other two."[2]

"We spent a fair amount of time together," Ted said. "We tried to meet Monday mornings about two times a month. We would go off once a year to Caneel Bay in the Virgin Islands and the three of us would have a management meeting." The management meeting usually took place on the beach at Caneel Bay, just three men in beachwear and stacks of papers. "People would come along and ask if we were writing a book," Ted remembered.

In these meetings on the fine white sand under the palm trees, "we worked very hard on the people aspects of the company," Ted said. "We really got that organized—we put together all those personnel evaluation systems that are more or less used to this day in Dow." Each year the troika returned from Caneel and laid out the strategy for the company in the year ahead, in addition to having evaluated the performance of each of the company's top 300 managers during the previous year and having decided as a result on key personnel changes and promotions in the top reaches of the firm.

"We had what I thought then, and I think today, was the best management in American business," Ben Branch said.

Ted was the president; he was the one that set the philosophy of the company. Ted Doan invented the matrix system of management, which was awkwardly called "the business concept," for lack of any other name. He implemented this business concept when he became president. Ted also handled the difficult political problems—not political in the sense of politics, but the problems we were exposed to with napalm and that sort of thing.

Carl Gerstacker was Mr. Outside. Carl was an absolute magician with the financial community. I think that Carl could get more mileage out of fewer numbers to prove Dow's greatness than any financial executive I've ever known. He was also directly responsible for the marketing organization and for purchasing.

And I was Mr. Inside. I was the one that was responsible for manufacturing and international and research. It was really a troika, and I think we did a damned good job.

Ted Doan, the leader, was christened Herbert Dow Doan after his grandfather at his birth in 1922 but was always known as Ted. He was the youngest of Lee and Ruth Dow Doan's three children. "I always thought they named me Herbert and immediately thought that was an awful thing to hang on a kid and that they could do something better, so they invented this Ted," he said. "I was Ted since I was a foot long, and nobody would admit they knew why or where it came from."

He was eight when grandfather Dow died. Some time before, having heard that magnesium burns, the boy decided he wanted to see just how it burned, so he got a chunk of magnesium and put it on a lit stove in the kitchen until it caught on fire. "Of course, once it was on fire, nobody could get it out," he remembered. "It damn near burned the whole place down." Like his grandfather, he had strong mechanical interests, and as a youngster tinkered with cars and motors.

When he was old enough his parents packed him off to Cranbrook, a prep school north of Detroit, where he did well both as a student and as a member of the school wrestling team, wrestling in the 105-pound class. He also met his first wife, Donalda (Donnie) Lockwood, who attended Kingswood, the sister school for girls. Then he went on to Cornell, intent on earning a degree in chemical engineering.

When World War II broke out he volunteered for the U.S. Air Force, expecting to become a pilot, but flunked the eye test and wound up spending most of the war in the Pacific as a meteorologist in the Air Force weather service. "I kept moving during the entire war because

I was always installing or repairing weather equipment," he said. "If somebody had trouble or if they had to put in a new installation they would send for me."

On Bougainville he was narrowly missed by a Japanese shell that ripped through the tent in which he was sleeping. "None of that was very frightening," he said. "I don't know why it wasn't frightening. That is probably why people can fight wars, because it isn't as frightening as it sounds like it ought to be."

He did some boxing in the air force and when he returned to Cornell to complete his degree he joined the Cornell boxing team, having now progressed to the 145-pound class. He graduated and came to Dow in February 1949, a few weeks before his uncle Willard, the company president, was killed and his father unexpectedly succeeded to the presidency. He began in the student training program, moving on to technical service and development and then to purchasing. In 1953 he and young Herbert H. Dow II, Willard's son, who had just joined the company, were elected to the board of directors, and Doan joined the staff of Ray Boundy, vice president for R & D.

His first big project had to do with oil shale; Ken Coulter was doing some promising research in the Physics Lab on high-temperature retorting of shale. Ted and Paul Meeske of purchasing negotiated the purchase of 800 acres of prime oil shale land in Colorado from the Columbia Oil Shale and Refining Company, for $2 million. In the end the oil shale research did not pan out, and Dow eventually sold the property for $50 million to Tosco-Sohio. (Tosco-Sohio later sold the same property to Exxon for $500 million.)

"Ray Boundy," Ted said,

was so quiet and retiring that you could hardly tell he was around, and there were a lot of people in the company who couldn't figure out what he was doing, or why he was there. At the same time, guys like Branch and I made a big hero out of him, because we thought he was the best there was. He was the ultimate in participative management; he wouldn't make up his mind until he had talked and talked and worked things over. He would want the minimum to do a job. He was never looking for an empire. Beutel was the empire builder and Boundy was the minimalist. He said, "If I can run the whole thing with one man, I'd rather do it that way than have 100."[3]

One day Dave Pye of Western Division research showed up in Boundy's office with a little jug of polyacrylamide, which he said would do wondrous things. He took a beaker full of muddy water and threw the stuff in it and the water and silt immediately separated, beautifully. "There's got to be a thousand uses for this product," Dave said. Ted Doan said to Boundy, "This is the kind of thing I've been talking to you about. Let me try this as a business."

Polyacrylamide, under the trade name Separan, became a prototype experiment for the organization of business teams, an approach later applied across the company, with basic functions—research, production, sales—working together to develop a product and a market. When there was just a big marketing department and a big research department and a big production plant, Doan theorized, communication in the launch of new products was extremely difficult, up through the organization and back down again and across; the business team cut neatly through all the big-company bureaucracy.

"What I was working on mentally at the time was how to organize this monster, and this was an experiment," Ted said. "We were talking to more than one outside company about how in the hell they did it. The more the company was successful and grew, the less communication there was between these groups."

At this time in Dow, Doan said, Donald K. Ballman, who was head of sales, and Dutch Beutel were almost the entire business team by themselves. "Beutel would call up Ballman and say, 'I'm going to build a glycol plant.' And Ballman would say, 'Hell, I can't get rid of any more glycol.' Beutel would then say, 'Well, you'd better, because I've already got half the plant built.' My fear was that a lot of things were going to drop through the cracks with such a casual arrangement between two big bosses. What's going to happen to diphenyl oxide, for example, when neither of them care anything about it?"

Separan launched Ted Doan's career as corporate organizational guru. In his tenure as chief executive he would steer the company through the only complete stem-to-gudgeon reorganization of its first hundred years—a reorganization of both its geography and its matrix.

Looking at the way Dow was organized in the mid-1950s, he was struck by the fact that the company had a plastics department and an agricultural chemicals department, but no chemical department. Chemicals, the core of the company's business, were considered everyone's concern, but no one's exclusively. He suggested to Boundy, and then to Putnam, that this was a serious sin of omission—there should be a chemical department. Mark Putnam, then the general manager, agreed that a chemical department should be formed, and asked him who ought to head it up. Doan made up a list of a dozen or so candidates, and when he and Putnam had prioritized the list he went to see Bill Dixon, their No. 1 candidate. Dixon turned it down. Jack Chamberlain turned it down. Doan worked on down through his list. No one wanted the job. Putnam finally said, "Well, why don't you try it yourself?"

"I got that job because nobody would take it," Doan said. "They just didn't want it. It was an experiment. So we started this new department in a rather casual way, in an office in the basement of one of the laboratories. I had to do a lot of stumbling around to get started. It was a reasonably miserable start."

The new chemical department, launched in 1956, concentrated on the development of new chemical products because, Ted Doan said, "the rest of the chemical business was working OK." It turned out to be an organization that was badly needed, and quickly became the primary center for encouraging the development and overseeing the launch of new chemical additions to the Dow product list.

When the Finance Committee of the company, still headed by Earl W. Bennett, made studies showing that Dow's optimum growth rate was 7 percent per year, Ted decided to do his own studies with the help of Don Kearney, an analyst in the economic evaluation group. "Let's take the company apart and see what we can do by way of building up a growth company," he told Kearney. When Doan and Kearney were through they came up with a composite growth rate of 12 percent per year and Doan took his case to the board of directors. Working at a blackboard with a piece of chalk, as was the custom at that time, he told the board how the company could grow at 12 percent a year if the company would organize properly to do it, and said the growth rate of 7 percent being tossed around, "should not be treated as though it were the word of God." The board did not adopt his plan, but he had made his point.

Ted Doan's work in the chemical department also led Dow into the pharmaceutical business. He knew Dow sold special chemicals to pharmaceutical firms, but he noticed that Dow did not make a great deal on those sales and he began to look at Dow's relationship to the pharmaceutical houses. "I went over to Kalamazoo [Michigan] and talked to Dick Schreiber, who was director of research of Upjohn," he said. "I said, 'Here is my problem; it's very simple. Dow supplies chemicals to you, and two years later we haven't got any business left that's worth anything, even though we might spend a lot of money getting started on it. How do we make money? How do we arrange things with the pharmaceutical companies so we can make some money?' Dick Schreiber said, 'There is no way you can do it. You are either in the pharmaceutical business or you aren't. If you are going to make money, you aren't going to do it selling to us, you are going to make it by being in it.' I thought that was really good advice. The only way to get the profits from pharmaceuticals is to invent the stuff and sell it."

A half year later he talked to the G. D. Searle Company in Chicago and told Jack Searle, the chief executive, of Dow's interest in the pharmaceutical business and "the fact that we'd probably have to acquire somebody to get in it." Did Searle have any ideas? Searle agreed that Dow ought to acquire a pharmaceutical company and said, "maybe Searle ought to be the one." The problem was that drug stocks were exceptionally high-priced at the time, with Searle having a price/earnings ratio of perhaps 50. "I never even proposed to anybody that we take a serious look at Searle," Ted said. "It was just too big a chunk."

"We wound up buying Pitman-Moore," Ted said.

It was a little company in the animal health and human vaccine business; it still is a name in animal health. That part of the business has passed from hand to hand. They had a product called Lirugen which really wiped out measles. But this company was very small, quite old, and not very up-to-date in research facilities. They had some good people. There was Anton Schwarz, one of the best virologists, probably one of the best in the world in working with vaccines. But there weren't many good people; it wasn't a particularly good acquisition.

It was the start of Dow's pharmaceutical business, however, and Dow was to be a power in that industry until 1995.

By the end of the 1950s, with heart attacks carrying off Bill Schuette and Mark Putnam, Ted Doan was emerging as a legitimate contender to succeed his father as chief executive.

"There was a two-year negotiation that went on," he said. "At some point along the line I declared myself in as a candidate and an active candidate. And the reason was I didn't like any of the alternatives."

The alternatives, he said, were Calvin A. (Tink) Campbell, who thought he should be president, wanted to be, and "did a little politicking" for the job; Dutch Beutel, who undoubtedly thought of himself in that job, but "I don't think anybody else did because of his management style"; and Carl Gerstacker.

"There aren't many people who know this was a disputed election, settled by a vote of the board," he said.

The debate went on for two years, and the issue was never resolved, so they needed to have a vote. I think it was the first time in the history of the company that happened. I think Gerstacker and I handled ourselves reasonably well, in the sense that we debated between the two of us all the way through this thing. We didn't upset the organization, we didn't cause a schism, and the thing came out the way it came out.

My feeling at the time was not so much that I was good and should have the job, but that there wasn't anybody else. There just wasn't anybody else. And the prime candidate was, in my opinion, a steward rather than a builder. So, I did everything I could do ethically. And he as well. There was not one shred of bad business that I'm aware of done in the process of that two years. When that election occurred, and when the dust settled, Ben and Carl and I started working together.

In 1959 Lee Doan had persuaded Ben Branch, then running the plastics department, to take over and run Dow International. "Here was this isolationist saying, 'Now let's go after the international business,'" Ted Doan said,

and that was brilliant. That was a great decision and Branch was the right guy to put in it. And Branch said to him, "I'll do it, but I need to run pricing." Pricing at the time was controlled by Don Ballman, and controlled to a very extreme degree, so that when Ballman said, "I run pricing," he meant "I run pricing, and nobody should fiddle around with that." And he meant he personally was going to approve every price of every product sold by the company. There were no degrees of freedom.

"Lee Doan would pay attention to Ballman on anything," Ted Doan said,

He would do exactly what Ballman wanted to do. Ballman was his protege. And here was Branch saying, "I've got to have pricing." Doan knows his own boy is just going to go right through the roof when he hears that, and Doan said to Branch, "I told you you had the job. You've got it, including pricing. Go ahead." He would never run around and tell Ballman, "I just gave that to Branch." He wouldn't tell Ballman, but he said to Branch, "The first time heads start rolling, come to me and we will settle it." And that's exactly what happened. It was a very unusual transition.

Branch took off, of course, like a skyrocket and did his own thing. Again, nobody told him what to do, and he did a superb job. The best in the chemical industry.

II.

One of Ted Doan's early projects as chief executive was a carefully crafted piece of business philosophy issued under the title "Dow's Objectives" (1965), the first time the company had committed them to writing.[4]

"We had been trying to produce objectives for some time," he said.

I had been encouraged to do it by a lot of people and I wasn't getting very far with it until John Gardner wrote a book called *Renewal*. If you read *Renewal* and the statements of Dow's Objectives you'll find more plagiarism than you can shake a stick at. But Gardner, who is much too liberal for me and ran Common Cause and does a lot of silly things, is a very good thinker and a wonderful person. That book provided the way of going at a statement of objectives as far as I was concerned.

It was a matter of "setting the tone," he said. The objectives were distributed throughout the company and, he said, "I saw it on the wall of every office I went into. You could find it in the janitor's office. You could find it all over the place."

"I think it is important that people know what your philosophical base is," he said. "They will find that out without words, and it is important that what is said at the top matches up with what people see."[5]

To many in the generation of the 1960s profit was an ugly word. In the hundreds of talks Doan gave before Dow employees in the succeeding years, dozens of them based on the statement of objectives, he defended the notion of profits vigorously.

He believed in the theory of management by objectives, he said, and believed each unit of the company should have known objectives. "If you state where you're going, it's easier to get there," he observed. "If you don't know where you're going, as someone has said, any road will do."

"If we want a 'Great Society,' we have to make or create the economic support for our desires, and the 'profit system' happens to be the most effective way of generating that support," he said. "We're in business to make a profit, and it's hard, challenging, satisfying work."

He especially liked the final paragraph of the objectives, probably its most often quoted phrase: "We will strive to make such contributions in products and philosophy that society as a whole benefits because Dow is in business."

"This is the ideal," he said. "It also makes great economic sense. We can measure our success in making a contribution such that society benefits, and that measure is our profits—not the quick buck; I mean the measure of increasing profits over a long period of time which can only be done by making a contribution to society."[6]

As it turned out, 1965 was a prelude to the Vietnam War protests, and in particular the protests against Dow's production of napalm for that war, during which the firm was frequently and violently accused of profiting from the war, and of having no ideals at all.

In the decade that followed, during which Dow (reorganized in 1965-66) became a global firm, it encountered a series of complex questions: What were its objectives in going abroad? Were they simply out to exploit opportunities for profit? How would Dow deal with the governments of host nations? Would it take sides in the elections of those countries? Would it treat the foreign nationals it hired abroad the same as U.S. employees, or if not, what distinctions would it make? How would it deal with a welter of different cultures, customs, and laws, and how would it protect its technology in these countries? Would it adopt different standards for environmental practice and safety and financial practices in different countries?

As these questions came up, the troika tried to deal with them, one at a time. Eventually, by the time Ben Branch was the company's CEO, they decided the company needed to codify its basic "International Business Principles" in writing, or risk drifting into different practices in different countries at different times. Branch asked Herb Lyon, the administrative vice president, to take on this codification with the help of the company's top executives around the globe.

The "International Business Principles" was published in the summer of 1975, translated into various languages, and provided to Dow employees around the world. It was longer than Lyon and others wanted, but it answered many if not most of the questions that were being asked of multinational companies in that period of ferment, and provided some idea of what Dow stood for to government officials and prospective employees in the countries where the company now began to put down roots.

A third major effort to state the company's guiding values was launched in 1985 by Paul Oreffice, then the chief executive, who like Ted Doan and others found the statement of corporate objectives and other documents too long. With David T. Buzzelli and Keith R. McKennon as its principle architects, this resulted in a statement only a dozen lines long called "Dow Core Values" (See appendix C, Key Dow Documents).

Buzzelli and others asked Dow employees around the world what they perceived the company's core values to be, and what they felt its core values should be. "The core values statement is a concise, philosophical tool for guiding the company, while our objectives deal with specific business goals," Buzzelli said. "Objectives can change; the core values are permanent."

"This statement applies to every Dow employee at every Dow location," Oreffice said. "It is not a 'program' or a 'campaign.' Rather, our core values are the written description of the way we at Dow operate. We expect that by clarifying our core values in a clearly stated form and widely publicizing them, they will serve as a continuous reminder of our company's principles, and as an encouragement to each employee to keep these values in mind in every aspect of conducting Dow's business."[7]

In 1994 Frank Popoff and his colleagues remodeled and updated the statement once again, and reissued it under the title "Dow Values."[8] The new statement was printed and once again appeared on the walls of Dow offices everywhere as a guide for conduct.

III.

In 1964 the Dow Board of Directors met in Europe for the first time. "At least half the directors had never been outside of North America before," Macauley Whiting said.

> We organized a full week of events for them in Zurich and Terneuzen and other places. The Europeans, some of whom were suspicious of Dow, were delightfully surprised by this group of directors who came over and who were not dandies or "good old boys," but solid chemists and marketers and real working people; so they were very well received overseas.
>
> At the same time the Dow directors were figuring out, "I kind of like this place. It looks like someplace we could do business." In my mind that was a milestone in changing Dow dramatically from a very insular company. It solved the problem of attitudes at the home office; another part of it was getting acquainted with foreigners and discovering that they were real people, too.[9]

The buildup of the pharmaceutical business continued. It had begun with Pitman-Moore, and now continued with the acquisition of Ledoga, parent firm of the Milan-based international pharmaceutical house Lepetit. Further additions were the Bioscience Laboratories in Los Angeles, and LIFE in Ecuador.

The building of new plants was now taking on very much of an international flavor. The company's first large integrated chemical complex in Europe, located at Terneuzen, the Netherlands, at the mouth of the Scheldt river, was dedicated early in 1965. Dow invaded the homeland of the German chemical giants that year, building a small plant at Greffern on the Rhine. It was also building plants in New Zealand and Argentina. A new plant at Cartagena, Colombia, was scheduled for completion in mid-1965.

Things were speeding up in so many places and on so many fronts that the troika called the first "Dow Management Conference," gathering together about 40 top managers of the company from all over the world for a two- or three-day discussion of strategy and progress. Ostensibly these were planning sessions, but occasionally hard decisions were reached.[10]

The 1965 Dow Management Conference was one of the most productive in the company's history. To get the participants away from interruptions it was held in the Kellogg Center on the campus of Michigan State University about 90 miles south of Midland. It opened with a presentation by Macauley Whiting, who had taken over from Ben Branch as president of Dow International; Whiting proposed nothing less than a new worldwide organization for Dow.

Dow was now a global company, or rapidly becoming one, too big and farflung to be run efficiently out of one Michigan headquarters, Whiting said. It was time to decentralize Dow, and the most logical way to do this was to put a local headquarters on each continent to administer the company's business there. He proposed separate, freestanding managements in Europe, Latin America, and the Pacific, with the sprawling Pacific area embracing all of Asia, Australia and New Zealand, and the Pacific basin. These managements should be independent and self-sufficient for all matters best done locally, he said; research and other things best done at a central location should not be changed.

In the next two days the group in the Kellogg Center completely reshaped the company following the Whiting Plan. They decided that Dow Europe, where a separate organization was already well advanced, would be established as of January 1, 1966, and that Dow Latin America and Dow Pacific would be established as separate entities effective July 1, 1966. These moves opened the way to establishment of a separate Dow USA as well. Dow Canada had been in place for many years. By the time the meeting was over a new Dow had emerged, with corporate headquarters still in Midland, but now coordinating separate geographical headquarters on the various continents and generating and driving an overall plan for developing Dow's business throughout the world.

With the troika's complicity and encouragement, Whiting put specific names in the blanks on his proposed organization chart as general managers of these new area headquarters—Zoltan Merszei (who was already doing it) for Dow Europe; Paul Oreffice, then Dow's country manager in Spain, for Dow Latin America; and Robert W. Lundeen, a relative unknown at the time, for Dow Pacific. Their assignments would be to locate and organize area administrative groups in their assigned portions of the world. With these appointments the new world organization was launched.

Carl Gerstacker told the assembled managers that the troika was genuinely committed to this new organization. "We are going to make a few mistakes as we adjust our system of values and get used to thinking global," he said, "but I can promise you this, and I speak for Ben and Ted as well as myself: we are here to see this new system work and we mean to see that it does work, and we promise you a genuine, concerted effort to make it work."[11]

In the aftermath, as Dow International dissolved and was replaced by these new area headquarters, Whiting found himself without a job. "I could have proposed myself into one of the foreign jobs, but that just didn't seem appropriate," Whiting said. "I acted on blind faith that something good would happen, that there would be a job for me somewhere in the organization. I guess at the time I was harboring a notion that I might become the U.S. area general manager, but that was not to be."

Ted Doan quickly came up with a new job for Whiting. Petroleum resources and energy requirements were becoming a major problem for the company, and he wanted a hydrocarbons and energy department put in place to plan for Dow's needs in basic raw materials and the energy field. He asked Whiting to head it up, and that became his new assignment.

Dow was blessed with a group of bright young marketing stars at the time, such as Oreffice and Charles Doscher, "eager to sell and eager to find customers," Whiting said.

They just swarmed the globe, which was very hungry for chemicals; there was a global short-age of chemicals at that time. This corps of salesmen was hugely effective, backed up by won-derful logistics.

Dow used the telex system much more effectively than other companies, and was able to be much more reliable in deliveries to Frankfurt, for example, than the German chemical compa-nies were, in part because of the telex and in part because of the terminal in Rotterdam that had been developed following the same procedures Beutel had used to serve eastern U.S. markets.

It all "kind of grew out of the business," Whiting said. "Ben Branch had been promoted to executive vice president and was an advocate for international business in the right place at that time." Studies to determine the potential of Dow's international business showed that within 10 years the market could grow from 10 percent of Dow's sales to 50 percent of sales, even while the other 90 percent was still growing. "That prediction was realized," he said. "It seemed that kind of a market could not be served by surplus production; it had to be served by stuff made locally."

These studies came from Robert W. Lundeen, who was in the planning group at the time, Whiting said. "He came up with the business development procedure which was an organized way of making market studies, relating that to manufacturing capabilities, relating that to raw material availability, and in a modeling way putting it all together without ever having designed or built a plant. When the potential was established, we went back and tried to find somebody in manufacturing and engineering who would actually build the plant."

Another product of the 1965 management meeting was the creation of what came to be called technology centers. These grew out of a "buzz group" session in which representatives of U.S. manufacturing asked representatives of Dow International, "How can we help you guys? What aren't we doing for you that we should be doing?" A major complaint of the inter-nationals was that when a plant was built overseas there was no very good way of being cer-tain it incorporated the company's newest and best technology. "And how are we going to be sure we're keeping up with advances in technology once we have built that plant?" they asked.

Max Key, who had just become the company's director of manufacturing, was handed a new task: to devise a series of repositories of know-how for the main products of the com-pany. He set up a network of technology centers, product by product, appointing as managers the people most expert on that product.

"Everybody thought it was impossible to do because the Texans would never agree that Midland should be a technology center (for one of its products) and the Midlanders would never agree that the Texans should be," Whiting said.

But one by one, it was decided where the site of competence was, and that site of main com-petence was then to be responsible for technical supervision of all the existing plants and all the new plants, was to see that new plants were properly staffed to begin with, that there was a manufacturing representative to deal with the engineers, and that the people were properly trained, even though that would be happening in a foreign place under a foreign leadership. They were responsible for the start-up of the plant and delivering capable people there to get the plant started up and running as quickly as possible.

The technology centers, Whiting said, were "one of Dow's really great secrets in expanding over the globe that quickly, providing a direct contact with the center of practice in the United States and every one of the plants overseas." By 1969 technology centers had been established for 33 of Dow's key products under the management of Walter E. Roush and a small staff in Midland.[12]

Beginning in 1986 the technology centers established an annual awards competition to recognize employees or groups of employees "who invent and successfully implement new technology that results in a cost reduction or profit improvement of at least $1 million annually."

The technology centers have been one of the company's most dazzling successes. In 1993 it was reported that in their first eight years Technology Center Awards had been made to 2,674 Dow employees for their achievements in 587 projects that had contributed $1.4 billion in economic value to Dow.[13]

IV.

Two of Dow's financial officers during its first century were legends in their own time. The first was Earl Bennett and the second was Carl Gerstacker, his pupil and successor. First one and then the other, every year or so, would take the train to Wall Street and return with the millions of dollars needed to finance the next stage of mushrooming growth for this little-known chemical firm in central Michigan.

From the time he was five, in 1921, Gerstacker and his sister Elsa began spending the summers with their childless Uncle Jim and Aunt Elsa Pardee "up in Midland." "It was like having a second set of parents," he said. His mother and Mrs. Pardee were identical twins.

When he was a small boy he told Herbert Dow that yes, he could play checkers, and Dow offered to play him one day. "He beat me rather badly, and then he beat me again," Gerstacker said. "I remember thinking I was just a little kid and this grown man would surely throw me a game, somewhere along the way. But he didn't; he just clobbered me, game after game."

From the time he was 17 he worked summers at Dow, beginning as a helper in the Physics Lab. When the company organized a student training course and opened it to employees who scored highest on a special exam, he asked to take the test, open to both high school and college graduates. Young Gerstacker, high school graduate, scored highest of all the people who took the exam.

When he left for college he asked what he should take if he wanted to come back to Dow to work. The Dow people told him, "We hire only scientists and engineers, so even if you're going to be a salesman or an accountant, take science or engineering." Chemical engineering seemed to combine both of these categories, he decided. "I didn't like chemistry and I didn't like engineering, but I took chemical engineering," he said.

His real love was finance, which he learned from his father, an engineer with the Cleveland engineering firm Bartlett & Snow, and from Uncle Jim. "My father was a mechanical engineer, but what he loved was finance and investment," Gerstacker said. "During the 1930s depression, he subscribed to advisory services. We would read the magazines and talk in the evening about what stock would be a good investment. We made every mistake anybody could make, but we did it with very small amounts of money. He taught me more than any college course. He loved finance."[14]

During the depression his father told him Dow stock, having fallen to $75 a share, was a great thing to buy, and the boy took the money he had earned delivering newspapers and sank it all in Dow stock, which promptly fell to $50 per share. "I think that was the greatest experience of all, my father having me gamble all of my assets on one thing," he said. "Very few people go through an experience like that. You can go to school and play with things, but when it's your paper route and you've saved your money and you've given up and sacrificed buying things you wanted, you care and you pay attention."

In 1938, armed with a chemical engineering degree from the University of Michigan, he returned to Dow and completed the student training course. His pay was now $115 per month, a great improvement over the $15 weekly (for a 44-hour week) he had been paid as a student.[15]

He was assigned as an accountant with Dowell, the company's oil well servicing subsidiary, and found himself working alongside a young man with a high school education who turned out more work than he did. "This really bugged me, so I began to cheat by going in at night," he said. "I would work at night so that I could catch up and be better than this competitor." One night he found that the competitor was also working after hours, and they both laughed about it.

He had taken Reserve Officer Training Corps (ROTC) training at Ann Arbor ("because you got paid 20 cents a day and that seemed like a lot of money in those days"), and in December 1940, he was called to active military duty.

The army trained him as an artillery expert and sent him to a bankrupt company that had a contract to make artillery for the British. "I was put in charge of teaching them how to do it and seeing that they did it right," he said. From there he became an expediter and "hatchet man" for the artillery, working with companies that switched over to making artillery and other military gear during the war. "It was a wonderful job because I spent all my time working with the companies and their executives trying to accomplish these things administratively. It was a great education."

He returned to Dow as a 30-year-old major in 1946 and was assigned to the purchasing department, where he again became a troubleshooter. At every chance he worked closely with the financial part of the company, which, as he said, "was really where I wanted to be." In 1948 Willard Dow called him in and told him, "Mr. Bennett (Earl Bennett was then the treasurer of the company) is a wonderful man and very smart, but he leads me around like there is a ring in my nose. He makes me do things I don't want to do. He won't tell me what's happening in the financial part of the company, and I don't think that's right. I'm starting a Finance Committee so other people can find out what's going on with the finances of this company, and I'm putting you on that committee."

Within a few weeks Gerstacker was named assistant treasurer of the company and became Bennett's deputy. He also became a director of the company. He was 32. "I guess I was the most aggressive one on the committee," Gerstacker said. "I pushed harder, so Bennett began to adopt me after a while and accept me. I did argue with him, which he loved."

Bennett was "an amazing financial genius," Gerstacker said. "He liked to start with the answers and work back. He would say, 'Carl, I think we ought to do such-and-such,' and give me some reasons. I used to look at the reasons and see that they didn't make sense; they were absolutely wrong. It finally dawned on me that he had only filled in some things to fit the conclusion he had started with. It didn't matter what the facts were, he knew the right answer. That was the way he did things."

Gerstacker also learned other things from Bennett. "When a security analyst would come in to ask him about the company," he said,

> he would let me sit there and listen so I could learn. The guy would ask a question like, "Epsom salts are doing poorly, aren't they, so is that a bad product?" Bennett would sit there and nod and start to answer the question, but he would never get to the question. Instead he would talk about the latest Dow invention until the outsider's eyes would light up and get really interested in what Bennett was saying. Pretty soon the security analyst had forgotten his question and he would never get back to it. He would be off talking about this other new thing. It was just marvelous. Bennett was something!

Bennett also convinced him that debt was a smart way of life. "My parents thought debt was immoral," Gerstacker said. "My father felt he couldn't walk down the street with his head high until he paid off the mortgage. You didn't owe money, that was terrible! Dow and Bennett believed that the more money you could borrow, the better. They thought you should always be in debt, because then you used other people's capital and you paid them interest, which was tax deductible. Bennett and I used to have lots of arguments over this policy, but he convinced me he was right and that all my past education had been wrong."

So well did he learn this lesson that by 1981, when he retired from the board and from chairmanship of the finance committee, Gerstacker had led Dow to a pinnacle of long-term indebtedness—$4.36 billion in debts, the high for its first century.

When Willard Dow's plane crashed in 1949 and Earl Bennett became chairman of the board, the 32-year-old Gerstacker, who had only been assistant treasurer for a few months, became treasurer of the company.

"They needed a treasurer and I was all they had," he said. "Dow Chemical never believed in going outside the company to hire, luckily for me, or they certainly would have. But nobody worried too much because Bennett was still there and everybody knew he was going to boss the thing anyway." One of Gerstacker's innovations as treasurer was a new method of borrowing, using commercial paper. "Commercial paper is a short-term way of borrowing where you just write an IOU for a million dollars or some sum, and somebody else who has money lends you the money for a short time," he explained.

> Goldman Sachs were the big people in that kind of deal, but up to that time it had only been used by poorly financed textile companies for financing their accounts receivable and inventory. A salesman from Goldman Sachs said to me, "Why shouldn't industrial companies use it?" The interest rate from the banks was 3 percent at the time, and he said he could do commercial paper for 1 $^1/_2$ or 1 $^3/_4$ percent, short-term. It sounded great to me, and I went to Bennett, who said, "The banks will get mad at us and we need the banks; this is cutting into their business and we can't do that."

Gerstacker persisted, and eventually took his proposal to the board of directors with Bennett's support. "We immediately sold about $50 million worth of commercial paper at an interest rate of one and a half and one and five-eighths," Gerstacker said. "We were the first industrial company ever to do that and we pioneered the way for a financing method that today runs into billions of dollars. It was only because Bennett was willing to try something, willing to support somebody. He was fantastic."

The company also adopted a rather unique method of financial reporting devised by Gerstacker and Bennett. The board meetings were held on the second Tuesday of the month, and the financial reports to the directors could never include the preceding month because it was too soon to have the books closed. "We were giving the directors old data all the time; we gave them data not for the previous month, but for the month before that," Gerstacker said.

> We had to find a way to tell the directors what the profits were within a few days after the end of the month. We found ways of estimating inventories and a lot of other things and made a quick estimate that never varied more than about 5 percent from the true profits, which were calculated a month later. For their purposes, being within 5 percent was all they needed to know to make any great decision anyway. When the actual profits came in, it didn't matter much.

"I think that was unique among all the companies that I had known," Gerstacker said. "That system went on for years," until computers arrived and quick closings became possible.

In 1955 he became a vice president of the company, and in 1957 a member of its executive committee. In 1959 he became chairman of the finance committee, a position he was to hold for 22 years. By that time he was a candidate to succeed Leland Doan as chief executive. When Earl Bennett stepped down at age 80 in 1960, Gerstacker became chairman of the board, as his Uncle Jim had been before him. Two years later, the troika was formed and he became one of the threesome that ran the company.

Years later, when he retired as chairman in 1976, Gerstacker paused to look at what had occurred in the company during that turbulent quarter century, 1950–75. Some of the highlights, as he saw them, were that:

- The number of Dow employees grew from 14,000 in 1950 to 53,100 in 1975.
- The cost of wages, salaries, and benefits per employee grew from $4,300 per employee in 1950 to $18,500 per employee in 1975, "probably the highest in the chemical industry worldwide and among the highest for any company of any type, anywhere."
- 44 percent of its employees were Dow shareholders in 1975, including 22 percent of the hourly workforce and 68 percent of the salaried workforce.
- In 1950 Dow had 1,200 employees working in research and development at a cost of $7 million annually. In 1975 the company had 5,200 employees working in R & D at an annual cost of $167 million. By 1975 the R & D group was earning an average of a patent a day in the United States alone.
- In 1950 the company paid $20 million in income tax to governments; in 1975 it paid $475 million in income tax to governments.
- Dow sales grew from $220 million in 1950 to $4.88 billion in 1975. Its purchases amounted to $100 million in 1950 and $3.5 billion in 1975.
- The selling price of Dow products increased an average of only 2.5 percent annually in the 25-year period.
- Dow exports from the United States grew from $18 million in 1950 to $465 million in 1975.[16]

As the company expanded and became a global firm in the 1950s and 1960s its need for financial services expanded exponentially. One of the earliest and most pressing of these needs was the problem of handling dozens of different currencies around the world, especially in Europe. Changing funds from Swedish crowns to Italian lira or Spanish pesetas entailed a substantial commission each time and was costing Dow heavily. "Dow was paying the full retail rate for wholesale volume," as John Van Stirum put it. Van Stirum, a Dutch national with a banking background who had joined the company in Europe, suggested that Dow buy into a European bank specializing in cash management.

Van Stirum specifically nominated the Mendes Gans Bank in Amsterdam, 80 percent owned by the giant Philips organization headquartered in the Netherlands, which had encountered similar problems. Gerstacker and Robert Bennett, Earl's son, who was now the Dow treasurer, became enthusiastic supporters. In 1962 Dow bought 40 percent of Mendes Gans from Philips. The Mendes Gans Bank become the financial turntable for Dow in Europe, saving the company millions. All receipts in European currencies were channeled through its venerable old building in Amsterdam, and it became Dow's financial clearinghouse in Europe. A further advantage was that through its services Dow knew at any time how much of what currency it had available in Europe.[17]

From there it was only one step more for Dow to get into the banking business itself, although Gerstacker issued a disclaimer to the banking community at the outset: "Let me stress that Dow is in the chemical business; we have no desire to compete with bankers."

The notion of a Dow Bank grew out of some early 1960s legislation by the U.S. Congress indicating to Dow observers that an embargo on U.S. investment abroad was around the corner. Alarmed, the troika decided to park some money in Europe so the company would be able to fund the construction projects it had on the books there even if this happened. (As it happened, the ban on investment abroad never occurred.) Bob Bennett and Van Stirum scurried off to Europe to look for a home for $50 million so that the company would not get caught short. Instead, they came back with an idea that blossomed into the Dow Banking Corporation. Gerstacker agreed with their idea, if it could be done without antagonizing the banking community in the United States and abroad, on which Dow depended, and if it could be done profitably.

The Dow Banking Corporation, merchant bankers, opened in Zurich in 1965. It was one of the first of the "Eurobanks." Its emblem was a map of Europe without borders, advertising its status as a bank that crossed national boundaries and did business in many currencies. Van Stirum, now an assistant treasurer of Dow, became the first general manager.

The bank was capitalized at 100 million Swiss francs ($23 million) and was a success from the start, making a profit even in its first year, 1965, though it was open only part of the year. It began by serving Dow's industrial customers and expanded rapidly; it did not accept individual accounts nor accounts from Swiss corporations; its specialty was corporate customers in the United States, Canada, Japan, and Europe, providing them, in the words of Van Stirum, "all of the sophisticated financial services in banking and underwriting required in Europe by the multinational corporations."

This was a period of frantic growth for foreign firms in Europe, and "Eurobanking" prospered mightily. By 1979 the Dow Bank was the largest foreign-controlled Swiss bank, with $729 million in assets (1.68 billion Swiss francs); it was, in fact, the eighth largest bank in all of Switzerland.

Why was the Dow Bank so successful? Van Stirum said it was know-how: "We provide in-depth banking services based upon our know-how and experience acquired over many years with Dow," he said.

> We really understand the overseas financial problems of American corporations. In addition to financial advice, we can also draw on Dow's worldwide technical competence in industry. This combined knowledge is rather unique in a merchant bank and is available to our American customers seeking to expand in Europe. Our smallness helps to further the personal and confidential relationship so important in merchant banking, especially when it comes to such delicate tasks as financial acquisitions and mergers. We strive for competence and excellence. [18]

In 1980 the bank went public, issuing shares equal to about 25 percent of its capital for public subscription in Switzerland. The Fuji Bank of Japan acquired 10 percent of Dow's holdings. Branches were opened in Hong Kong, Buenos Aires, Bogota, London, Singapore, and Miami. The bank entered into a working relationship with Kuhn Loeb Lehman Brothers, the New York investment banking house; Kuhn Loeb had been building expertise in the Japanese financial world since 1907.[19]

Dow's meteoric career in the banking business fizzled out rather abruptly in 1986. As Gerstacker had said 21 years earlier, Dow was in the chemical business, not in the banking business, and Paul Oreffice decided to sell the bank, "as a key element in a program to realign Dow's financial activities and resources in full support of the company's activities" in its basic businesses.[20] In 1969 Gerstacker had asked Oreffice to look into the possibility of a worldwide banking institution, but Oreffice had advised against it. Once again Dow had devised a tool that didn't exist, and then abandoned it when it was no longer needed.

The bank's buyer was the Royal Trust Bank, one of the oldest and largest of the Canadian banks, with 115 offices in Canada and a staff or more than 12,000. As of September 18, 1986, the Dow Bank became the Royal Trust Bank (Switzerland). The Dow board members, including Leslie Merszei, the bank's manager, resigned, and Royal Trust installed a new management team. One of two holdovers on the board was Ed Faessler, a Swiss who had a 35-year banking career with Dow.[21]

It was not all skittles and beer, Faessler said. The bank lost $20 million in a fraud case involving the Equity Funding Company in Los Angeles, and also lost heavily on the Mattel toy company, which almost went bankrupt.

"You had to watch yourself," Bob Bennett said. "A lot of people got into a lot of trouble in foreign banking, because the rules are different. We tend to think that a bank is a bank is a bank, but it's not true. There are all kinds of banks, and the laws involving foreign currencies are a lot different than they are here [in the U.S.].

"It wasn't that bad a nightmare, though."[22]

V.

While he was a student at Western Reserve, Ben Branch was conned into playing Ping-Pong for money one evening with a visitor who carefully concealed how well he could play. Stakes were to be five cents a game, doubling after every game; the player who was behind could quit and pay up, but the player who was ahead could not quit without his opponent's consent. Ben lost every game to this sharper, but refused to give up. Before long he owed the man over $100,000, his brother Harry said. But Ben kept on playing. Midnight came, and 1 A.M., and 2 A.M., and still Ben kept playing, and losing, and the sum he owed was astronomical. Finally, around 3 A.M., totally exhausted and by now barely able to hold up a paddle, the visitor threw in the towel and said, "OK, the bet's off—keep your money." Ben wore his opponent out, the only way he could avert disaster.

THE UNIVERSAL BIOHAZARD SYMBOL

One of Dow's contributions in the 1960s was the universal biohazard symbol, which resembles a ball of serpents' fangs colored fire orange. It has since become a warning sign seen daily in doctors' offices, medical establishments, laboratories, and anywhere else a biological hazard may be present. Beware, it says; this could be injurious to your health.

The symbol was developed by a Dow laboratory in Zionsville, Indiana, in 1966, and adopted worldwide in the decades that followed.

Congress approved a special $10 million appropriation for the National Cancer Institute in 1965, and as one result what was then the Pitman-Moore division of Dow won a $1 million contract to develop controls for biohazards in virus research. The assignment was to design, build, and test the containment facilities that would be needed at the NCI's proposed virus laboratory and animal facility at Bethesda, Maryland—facilities to protect the personnel working in the laboratory from the highly dangerous and infectious materials to be used and prevent cross-contamination in the experiments to be carried on.[1]

The $1 million contract to do this was not a munificent amount even by 1965 standards, but the result was probably one of the biggest bargains in contract research the U.S. government has ever enjoyed; the universal biohazard symbol was a by-product.

The Dow contract was assigned to Dr. Lawrence C. Weaver and his Environmental Bio-Engineering group in the Dow Life Sciences Laboratory at Zionsville, Indiana. Weaver and his team quickly realized that the containment facilities would need to be marked with a symbol indicating where biological hazards were located, and Larry Weaver proposed to Dr. William W. Payne at Bethesda that Dow develop such a symbol as part of the contract. "Good idea," responded Payne, and the Dow team set to work.[2] The familiar radiation hazard symbol had been developed five years earlier, in 1960, by the American Standards Association, helped by at least four federal agencies and numerous professional organizations, and this set the stage for a biohazard symbol as well.

Chuck Baldwin, environmental health engineer on the Dow team, was assigned to develop a symbol, which he proceeded to do after receiving an OK to spend $2,055 on travel and research. Baldwin recruited help in other branches of Dow, and before long several Dow departments were helping him out. D. F. (Del) Macaulay of Dow's Package Engineering & Design group in Midland sketched possible designs, and Bob Williams in the market research group investigated the proposed designs for their memorability and meaningfulness. The Dow patent department checked out the designs for possible infringement of registered copyrights.[3]

Baldwin found a motley collection of symbols being used by individual agencies at that time to signal biohazards. The U.S. Army used an inverted blue triangle bearing the term "BIO" to warn of biological contamination; U.S. Navy laboratories used a rectangular hot pink label with radiating yellow bands to mark areas containing infectious organisms; the National Institutes of Health used a red and black sign to mark restricted areas; the Universal Postal Convention used a white caduceus on a violet field, emblazoned with the French word *dangereux*, to mark infectious materials during transit. None of these was used beyond the sponsoring agency.

Macaulay and other Dow artists created more than 40 designs, most of which were discarded in informal preliminary testing. Six of their designs seemed to stand out, and were selected for intensive testing. Williams and his market research team conducted a nationwide study in 25 cities, with the six candidates mixed in with 18 other commonly used symbols. A week later the people tested were visited and tested again, this time being shown a group of 60 symbols, among which were the 24 they had been shown earlier. The symbol finally adopted clearly emerged as most meaningful and most readily remembered.[4]

The rest, as they say, is history. The new fire-orange symbol was evaluated for six months at NCI and other laboratories engaged in studies of hazardous materials, including the U.S. Army Biological Laboratories and the U.S. Department of Agriculture laboratories. It was accepted everywhere it was used, and the National Institutes of Health recommended its use as a general biological hazard warning.[5]

Along the way, Baldwin worked with the National Safety Council, the American Standards Association, the U.S. Army Biological Laboratories, the NIH Safety Office, Dow's Environmental Health laboratories, the University of Minnesota Division of

Environmental Health and Safety, and a host of individual scientists. In 1967 he and Robert S. Runkle, project manager at Bethesda, presented a paper at the American Association for Contamination Control in Washington describing the evolution of the new symbol. It was already a success.[6]

The Dow team duly completed its $1 million task of designing hazard controls for the Emergency Virus Isolation Facility, or EVIF, as it became known, and the basic work accomplished under the contract was installed and then either forgotten or replaced by newer information and designs over the next 30 years.

The by-product of the work, the universal biohazard symbol, in contrast, is not only going strong, but seems to have a very long life ahead of it.

1. "Dow's Pitman-Moore Gets Contract to Study Cancer," *Oil, Paint & Drug Reporter,* July 26, 1965, p. 42.
2. Dr. Lawrence C. Weaver to William W. Payne, Deputy Associate Director, Field Studies, National Cancer Institute, National Institutes of Health, Bethesda, Maryland, November 16, 1965; W. W. Payne to L. C. Weaver, December 27, 1965.
3. Oral History, Charles L. Baldwin, August 4, 1995.
4. "A Study of the Meaningfulness and Memorability of Various Symbols," Robert J. Williams, Marketing Research Dept., Dow, March 1966. Also, same subject, R. Williams to C. Baldwin, explanation of statistical basis and analyses this study, August 2, 1966, and "Biological Hazards Symbol, Graphic Design Opinion Survey," D. F. Macaulay, Package Engineering and Design, Dow, January 1966.
5. The summary report on the symbol was Study No. 20, Biohazard Warning Symbol, NIH Contract No. PH43-65-1045, to W. W. Payne from Guy C. Mattson, administrative manager, Zionsville Research Center, Pitman-Moore Division of Dow, 1966.
6. Charles L. Baldwin and Robert S. Runkle, "Biohazards Symbol: Development of a Biological Hazards Warning Symbol," *Science* 158 (October 13, 1967). See also "Making It Safe for Research," *Dow Diamond,* no. 4 (1968).

His father worked for the U.S. Department of Agriculture, and the family moved frequently. Ben was born in Omaha and graduated from high school in Cleveland. Inspired by a high school chemistry teacher, he entered Western Reserve University there to study chemistry, won a scholarship, and spent his junior year in Heidelberg studying with Karl Johann Freudenberg, who was, he said, "maybe the greatest organic chemist in the world at that time."

The Nazis were already in power in that year of 1935-36, he said, and "the persecution was already overwhelmingly evident." He heard Hitler speak on three different occasions, and remembered that Hitler's impression on his audience was "visible." "He played them like an organ," Branch said. "It provided incredible evidence of the power of the spoken word to move huge masses of people."

He was the middle of three sons and the only one to finish university. "All of us started, but I was the only one able to finish because money was pretty skimpy." When he graduated in 1937 the nation was entering a recession and he considered post-graduate studies. On the advice of a banker friend, however, he made an unannounced trip to Midland, of which he had no previous knowledge, and asked to see Earl Bennett, the treasurer. Bennett quickly decided he liked this brash young man. "I think I was one of eight people Dow hired that year," Branch said. "I got in [to Midland] in the morning, and went over and saw Mr. Bennett. They hired me that afternoon, and Mr. [James T.] Pardee, one of the directors, was driving to Cleveland that day. So he drove me back, bought me dinner on the way, and delivered me to my fraternity house door. I thought, 'Boy, this is really a terrific outfit.'"

When World War II came on he was sent to Texas to help supervise the construction of styrene plants for the wartime synthetic rubber program. He returned to Midland at the end of the war with a high regard for Texans. "Texans are a breed by themselves," he said. "If you want to be sure a job gets done, hire a Texan. They're really something special."

Don Williams, then director of sales, proposed that he become manager of coatings sales, "a grand-sounding title which turned out to be a one-man department." His assignment was to develop the postwar sales of Dow's coating materials, including the new saran coating resins and vinyl chloride monomer (used in the production of polyvinyl chloride plastics) and what was to become the most important of them, styrene butadiene latex.

He worked with L. L. (Zip) Ryden and Elmer Stilbert in the development of the latex business on a national scale. Ryden, for whom a Dow laboratory was later named, was a principal inventor of latex for paper coatings and latex paints. Latex, which revolutionized the paint industry, grew into one of Dow's greatest worldwide businesses, and young Branch's role in developing the product and the sales network for it marked him as a man with a future in the company.

Branch was also given responsibility for sales of saran, although it was not a coating material, and that brought him into close contact with Charles Strosacker, the "father of saran." Branch liked to tell of arranging for Strosacker, an ardent teetotaler, to throw a cocktail party.

> I went to Stro and said, "Stro, I've got a problem. You know National Plastics is coming." He said, "Yes, wonderful customers." I said, "Well, I've got them taken care of except for Sunday afternoon, and I need your help." And he said, "What do you want me to do?" I said, "I want you to throw a cocktail party." He looked at me as if I'd taken leave of my senses and said, "I wouldn't even know how to do that." I said, "Well, if you'll provide the space and some hors d'oeuvres, I'll take care of everything; let me talk to your maid." So he said, "Okay." Stro provided enough hors d'oeuvres to feed an army, and we had a great time, and I think that was one of the most illustrative stories I know about this fantastic man.

Strosacker and Ephraim Winer, president of National Plastics Products Company, were the two greatest promoters of saran, and Winer was the one who really made saran a commercial success, Branch said. Winer and his family owned National Plastics Products.

In 1952, when Ray Boundy became the company's director of research, Branch was tapped to succeed him as head of the plastics department. "Business is a lot like the roll of the dice," he said. "It always turned out that seven came up when I was asked to be transferred, because it was always to what was a really hot part of the business. And plastics at that time was by far the fastest-growing part of the Dow business and, as a matter of fact, of the whole world of chemistry."

Branch was always candid about the mistakes he had made and the money he had cost the company. "I have never felt uncomfortable with any job I've had, and I think that's the really great thing about The Dow Chemical Company," he said.

I always felt that whatever they asked me to do, that I had the job of doing it. I used to be able to say I'd lost more money for Dow than any employee they'd ever had. I can't say that anymore because the stakes are so much higher. But every time they picked me up and dusted me off and sent me back in.

I think the greatest thing about the Dow I grew up in is that the executives knew that you had to make mistakes in order to have the humility to be acceptable to your peers. You had to have successes to give you the confidence to make decisions. So they encouraged you to take chances without penalty. I tried to characterize my own career in this respect. I've made so many mistakes, and invariably they would assure me (they didn't use these words) that this was a learning process that was necessary in your development. They told me what a great young man I was and sent me back to fight a new battle. There is no way you can get confidence and humility without undergoing these experiences. There is no textbook that will do this.

When Lee Doan asked him to leave the plastics department and become president of Dow International, Branch told him, "Lee, absolutely no one could do anything with this operation if it's going to be run the way it's been run. Please don't ask me to do it unless you're willing to let me really run the thing." Doan said, "Ben, I'd like to have you take this job." He took it with full authority to build Dow's business in a global sense.

In tracing the extraordinary growth of Dow's international business later, Branch saw that as the first reason for his spectacular success as architect of Dow overseas—"we had Lee Doan's backing, and he was like a rock." It was a period when business was poor in the United States—Dow had just emerged a year before from the 1958 shock of a 10 percent cut in personnel—and the company was paring down the payroll rather than increasing it.

"Every year you were supposed to go in and meet with Lee Doan and Carl Gerstacker and explain why you didn't have too many people or why you needed the people you were asking for," Branch remembered. "I went into this first meeting and told them I wanted this many people, and Carl said, 'Well, prove you really need these people,' or something like that. I said,

'Look, all I can tell you is, you give me these people, I'll do more with them than if you give them to somebody else.' Lee Doan said, 'That's good enough for us.'"

A second factor in Dow's international success, Branch felt, was Dow's Texas Division, "which was assuredly the lowest-cost producer of commodity chemicals in the world at that time." Because business was soft in the United States, Dow had a great deal of overcapacity, "so we had the economic muscle to be able to establish a position."

A third factor, in his analysis, was the way Dow organized to do business abroad. The company undertook a study at this time looking closely at the weaknesses of its competitors. "We decided their biggest weakness was that they weren't close enough to their customers," Branch said. "Almost every other (chemical) company in the world, even the Germans, operated out of a central office with traveling representatives reporting back to that office. So we very quickly established a decentralized marketing organization, especially in Europe, but really throughout the world. We moved the sales people out close to the customers."

He spent his first month as the head of Dow International working out a general philosophy, Branch said—in respect to geographic distribution, geographic organization, and marketing decentralization—and decided on a policy of using U.S. sources to build the market. "When our captive market abroad would become big enough, we would first build end-product plants and then gradually move backward (toward raw materials)," he said.

A key manufacturing struggle was that there was room for one big ethylene plant in Europe at that time, and Union Carbide (then the second largest U.S. chemical company after Du Pont) was also attempting to line up enough business to build this plant. "We managed to get the business which with our own needs was sufficient to justify this one plant," Branch said. "We built the plant, and I think if there's any single reason why Carbide's now out of Europe and we're in Europe is that we were able to pick up that key piece of business. That became the real core of our manufacturing operation in Europe."

Another key decision Branch made was not to develop joint ventures in various countries, "which was a thing that many of our competitors did," he said. "If possible we were going to go it alone. We had already inherited some joint ventures, which we gradually got out of." Japan was the only exception to this rule. "I thought then, and still think today, that you cannot be successful without being in a joint venture in Japan," he said. "But in the rest of the world where it's possible to do so, we have gone 100 percent Dow, and I think that was another wise decision."

"We had a zestful, productive bunch of nuts in this Dow International group," he said, "and everybody had a hell of a good time in addition to doing a hell of a lot of business."[23]

Developing sales of a given product in a geographical area and then building a plant to supply those developed sales in that area became the policy and the pattern. "[Dow International] just duplicated that with product after product in a very deliberate and what seemed at the time to be an excruciatingly slow way," Ted Doan said. "In the meantime, other companies were running around making deals and doing big things and buying companies and setting up joint ventures, most of which fell apart over a period of time. And what Ben built was built so solidly that it just kept growing, and when it got a head of steam it just took off. It was a wonderful thing."

Branch's "implementor" of much of this policy was Zoltan Merszei, Doan said. "In fact, I don't know to this day how much of the policy would have come from Zoltan and how much from Branch. But knowing both men, I attribute it to Branch. I think Branch was the strategist of that whole thing and that his execution arm was this very capable guy, Merszei."[24]

When Lee Doan retired in 1962 and Ted Doan became the chief executive, Ben Branch moved up to executive vice president of the company and the troika was in place. Branch continued to be more intimately related to the international business than his two colleagues, and Dow's growth in the world continued apace.

In 1970, at the annual troika meeting on the beach at Caneel Bay, Ted Doan told Carl and Ben that he felt his job had been completed. He was going to resign, he told them, and he wanted Ben to become president. "I suspect he and Carl had talked about it ahead of time," Branch said, "but I don't know. As a matter of fact, I tried to convince him not to do it. I still think we had the best management team in American business, and I really had deep regrets about breaking it up."

Later that year, at the annual meeting of stockholders, Ben Branch became the first chief executive of the company not a member of the Dow family since Albert Convers, and Ted Doan, at the ripe old age of 48, became Dow's senior statesman.

"I've had the unique pleasure of really enjoying every job I've ever had," Branch said, looking back on it.

> And I've also had the unique pleasure of not once in my career being told by anybody what to do or how to do it. I've never attended any of the sessions that are supposed to improve your ability to lead people. And I've never had the feeling that what I was doing wasn't fun. I had no particular exhilaration about becoming president of the company because I was having a ball with what I was doing, and I thought we were an extraordinarily effective group of three people. I had no illusions that I could do it any better than it was being done. As a matter of fact, everything that I thought needed to be done was being done. So it was practically a nonevent. It was obviously a great honor, but not something I had sought, nor was I exhilarated by its occurring.

During Branch's presidency of the company, from 1970 to 1976, the expansion abroad continued at a breakneck pace. In 1964 Dow sales had reached $1 billion for the first time, and sales outside the United States accounted for 23 percent of that billion. In the next dozen years Dow sales quintupled to $5.65 billion and sales outside the United States accounted for 45 percent of that amount.

In 1974 Dow had probably the best year of its first century. It achieved a mark that would have seemed barely conceivable a decade before: it became the world's most profitable chemical company—more profitable than Du Pont, more profitable than the German Big 3 (BASF,

Bayer, and Hoechst), more profitable than Britain's Imperial Chemical Industries, all of which were substantially larger than Dow in total sales. It was to hold that distinction for four years.

Sales in that one year, 1974, increased by an almost unbelievable 61 percent from the year before, from $3.07 billion to $4.94 billion. Net income soared from $275.6 million to $557.4 million. These were the company's biggest one-year jumps in modern times.

Branch and Gerstacker felt like celebrating, and they proposed that the company as a special bonus give a month's pay to every employee in the company except officers and directors. "I walked into the board meeting and said I'd like to give everybody this bonus," Branch recalled. "They said, 'What will it cost?' I said $55 million, and they said, 'Good, let's do it.'" Everyone connected with the company shared in the bounty. Dow's pensioners were each given $2,000 in bonds and $300 in cash. Dividends on Dow stock were increased by 40 percent.

Branch received thousands of letters from the grateful recipients (Dow had 53,300 employees and 94,120 stockholders in 1974), a few of which he published in the company's 1974 annual report. One from Joe L. Tod, Texas Division employee relations, said:

> How can I express to you how much it means to work for a company like Dow? Many years ago, I was individually the beneficiary of Dow's generosity when I was kept on the payroll although hospitalized for a year. [Tod had been a polio victim.] And now, this special award to all employees—this must be the ultimate example of a corporation's expression of its feeling about its employees.... However, I found I was wrong. It was my pleasure and humbling experience to take the special award check to the parents of Mary Cruz. Mary was a young Mexican-American employed in the Texas Division purchasing department until her death in mid-January this year (1974). Believe me, there is no adequate way I could ever describe how her parents feel toward a company that would remember her in this way.[25]

With Ted Doan now taking a backseat (he continued as an active director until reaching age 65 in 1987), Branch and Gerstacker continued as a close-knit team throughout this period. Board chairman Gerstacker served as "Mr. Outside," the company's ambassador-at-large to the outside world, and President Branch as "Mr. Inside," the driving force behind the company's operations and progress. The company had no further executive vice presidents until 1975. Because Gerstacker was so visibly the spokesman for the firm and was always accessible to the press, speaking authoritatively without consulting Branch, outsiders frequently assumed him to be the chief executive, which amused them both.

Branch, who hated and avoided public speaking appearances, liked it that way. It was only toward the end of his career that he began to be recognized by the business world at large as one of America's premier chief executives. In 1975 he received an award from *Dun's Review*, which cited Dow as one of the nation's "Five Best Managed Companies." In 1976 he was named "Chief Executive of the Year" by *Financial World*. "We have the best executives of any company I know," Branch told the magazine, "partly because we try to hire people fresh out of college and teach them our way of doing business. We let them make larger and larger decisions, larger and larger mistakes, and larger and larger successes."[26]

In 1989, many years after he had retired and become honorary chairman of the board of Dow, *Financial World* selected a "CEO of the decade," and it asked 2,500 chief executives and securities analysts for their votes. The winner was Sam Walton, chairman of Wal-Mart Stores; the runners-up were Chrysler Corporation chairman Lee Iacocca and Branch.[27]

The devotion of the troika to the company was passionate and absolute and all-consuming. They were married to Dow. Not surprisingly, all three were divorced during their period at the top of the company. Shirley Branch (she and Ben had married in 1939, and had seven children) was a homebody who shunned the limelight. So did "Donnie" Doan, who pleaded with her husband Ted, in 1953 to refuse appointment to the Dow board of directors because it would, she felt, "change our lives." It did. Twenty years later, discouraged and depressed, she left him. Jayne Gerstacker suffered off and on from mental problems, and although he fought the idea a long time, in the end she and Carl also divorced.

Branch was famous among Dow managers for his love of poker. "We'd have an evening out with a bunch of Dow managers plus some other people and the evening would break up at 10:30," Ted Doan said.

> Branch would say, "Now, fellows, let's go in and play a little poker." By that he meant until four in the morning. I would personally tell him (and I think Gerstacker told him the same thing), "You can't do that. If you are interested in that, fine; go find some of your buddies to do it with, but don't impose that on people who are working for you. That's just unconscionable." He wouldn't buy that. I mean, it was just blinders. He thought that was being friendly with the troops. In fact he was exhausting the troops and he didn't need any sleep at all. If he was up playing poker at four in the morning, he would be at work at eight with a long list of things to do for the day. He had some very irritating faults.

VI.

According to a public opinion survey, Richard M. Nixon was "the most admired man in America" in 1969. Billy Graham, the evangelist, came in second, and Vice President Spiro T. Agnew third.[28] On the social scene, protests against the war in Vietnam, and a women's fashion, the miniskirt, both reached new heights. The year's most historic event occurred on July 20, when *Apollo XI* and a young Ohioan named Neil Armstrong landed on the surface of the moon.

Dow technology played a small role in the moon landing; its epoxy resins were used in the spacecraft's heat shield. The resins were charred during re-entry to the earth's atmosphere but effectively absorbed the 5,000-degree heat and protected the astronauts from harm. Dow's contributions to the lunar flights were accomplished through Catalytic-Dow, a short-lived joint venture (with the Catalytic Construction Company), based at the Kennedy Space Center in Florida.

In March of that year Earl W. Bennett retired at age 89, closing out a career that had spanned almost the entire history of the company to that point. Somewhat later the company dedicated its new Midland headquarters building, which it named the "Earl W. Bennett Building." A dedication plaque noted that Bennett's "financial genius, industry, and sense of humor . . . will remain permanently stamped upon the company's personality."

A 91-year-old Bennett, now blind, attended the ceremonies on the arm of one of his eight children, his son Robert B. Bennett, the company's treasurer. The Pulitzer Prize winning writer Don Whitehead, writing a history of the company in 1968, tried several times to tap Bennett's memories of the early years of the company and came back frustrated. "I just can't get him to talk about the past," Whitehead said. "He only wants to talk about the future."

The Dowell division opened an oilwell servicing base at Prudhoe Bay in 1969, the first facility of its kind on the Alaskan North Slope, and a new crop of Dow pioneers began to wear fur hats.

In the autumn of 1969 the last and biggest chunk of Ted Doan's global reorganization plan snapped into place, with the formation of Dow Chemical U.S.A., and his remapping of the Dow world was complete. Earle B. Barnes, Beutel's successor as leader of the Texas Division, moved to Midland to become first chief of the U.S. area of Dow, and Barnes instituted his own troika, with J. M. (Levi) Leathers as operations chief and G. James Williams as marketing chief for Dow U.S.A.

In the years to follow there were adjustments to Dow's worldwide organization—notably the establishment of Dow Chemical Mideast/Africa as a separate unit in 1977, and the split off of Dow Chemical Brazil from Dow Chemical Latin America in the same year—but the basic organization remained unchanged until 1995.

The troika made its share of mistakes, too. One of their biggest was the purchase of a German textile firm, Phrix-Werke A.G., at Hamburg, Germany, in 1967. The purchase was a joint effort with Dow's German partner in the fibers business, Badische Anilin- und Soda-Fabrik, or BASF; Dow and BASF were joint owners of the Dow Badische Company at Williamsburg, Virginia.

Phrix had the glow of gold when Dow and BASF purchased it, but quickly began to take on the tint of a lemon. It was principally a producer of rayon fiber, and German fiber prices began to plunge almost simultaneously with Dow's investment. The French franc was devalued and the German mark revalued, and a wage increase of more than 20 percent was negotiated for the Phrix workforce in late 1969. All of this had a negative effect on the firm. Nothing went right. Soon Phrix was losing several million dollars per month.

In 1970, having exhausted all other remedies, the Dow board decided to write off its entire investment in Phrix, amounting to $43.3 million. It was the most humiliating case of color blindness the company had ever suffered.

After being singed by the Phrix case the company's enthusiasm for the entire fibers business began to cool. Dow's attitude toward fibers thereafter was much like that of Mark Twain's famous cat, which having once sat down on a hot stove would never sit on a stove again, even when it was reasonably certain the stove was cold. In 1978 Dow sold its half of the Dow Badische company to BASF and closed the books on its fiber business.[29]

The company was also learning a great deal in the consumer trade during this period. A typical example was Liquid TireChain, launched commercially in 1968. It was a wintertime spray for automobile tires developed in the Dow laboratories; you sprayed it on your tires, it immediately hardened, and with the traction it provided you could drive easily through winter's ice and snow. Apparently the general public did not care to squat in a snowbank and spray its auto tires, however. After three years of strenuous effort the product was dropped for lack of sales.

Another product that didn't sell was Dow Domes: giant domes made of plastic foam, quite inexpensive, suitable for water or sewage plants or any kind of building, including residences. A gigantic whirligig machine turned in a gradually narrowing circle and worked Styrofoam plastic foam into a domed shape. A great many Dow Domes were built, but not enough to justify staying in business.

In 1969 the company introduced a series of new consumer products—Aztec sun-care products and Touch of Sweden hand lotion. In both cases Dow was bucking the powerfully entrenched wizards of U.S. consumer marketing. The moment Aztec products were introduced in a given sunny clime, the already established sun-care product marketers immediately would launch concentrated, heavy-expenditure advertising campaigns of their own in the same area. To establish Aztec in a given market thus required an enormous investment in advertising and promotion. After a few years of trying to beat this game, Dow gave up on both Aztec and Touch of Sweden.

Most of the new products that Dow introduced at this period did very well, especially those that involved an entirely new concept rather than an improvement on an existing product. In 1970 Dow launched Ziploc bags, the now-familiar plastic snap-lock closure bags for freezers, leftovers, or any of a dozen other uses. With no competitors, Ziploc did very well. Within 10 years after introduction it held a substantial portion of the household bag market and was attracting its own imitators.[30]

Other new products included Dursban insecticide, an important insecticide useful in forest management, nurseries, greenhouses, home gardens, and other applications, especially effective against mosquito larvae and cockroaches. Zectran insecticide was cleared by the U.S. Environmental Protection Agency in 1971 after seven years of tests by the U.S. Forest Service for use against the spruce budworm, a widespread forest pest. It is also useful against lawn and garden insects. Tordon herbicide was introduced in 1970 with a state registration in Texas; it is used primarily for rangeland brush control, and for the control of brush on utility rights-of-way.

Other new products in the 1970s were caustic soda beads, a new wrinkle on one of the company's oldest products; chlorothene solvent, a safer and better vapor degreasing solvent; N-Serve nitrogen stabilizer, a farm product that prevents nitrogen from washing away with the rain; chlorinated polyethylene (or CPE) pond liners; the IRMA (for Inverted Roof Membrane Assembly) roofing system; Polyethylene D for bananas (a plastic bag incorporating an insecticide to protect the fruit during growth); electro-conductive resins; Voraspring plastic foam for furniture; Saranex two-ply packaging films; urethane foam backing for carpets; and Derakane vinyl-ester resins for corrosion-resistant piping and tanks.[31]

Some of these were at the root of social revolutions of a sort. The banana bags, for example, sold in Central and South America and, draped over the banana stem early in its development, made it possible to deliver immaculately clean and insect-free bananas to supermarkets around the world; the result was substantially increased banana consumption. Dow's work in carpet backing virtually eliminated the felt carpet pads that previous generations had laid under their carpets.

Some of these developments began in unusual ways, as was the case, for example, with Dow's position in urethanes. Jim Leenhouts, of the Technical Service and Development Laboratory, noted in a postwar report that urethanes were "going to be a first-class product," and that Union Carbide was already selling products in that area. Malcolm (Mac) Pruitt, then a researcher in Texas, wrote Leenhouts a letter, saying, "If nobody else from Dow is involved, I'm going to become the urethane man in Dow and I'm going to develop that technology for our company."

He did. That was the beginning of Dow's involvement in urethanes. One of Pruitt's early urethane products was called Nutrifoam. It was a plant growth medium; he and Joe Baggett put nutrients in a foam structure and plants grew in it without touching dirt. Pruitt, who eventually became the company's research vice president, had a Christmas cactus that grew in a urethane foam pot for 14 years, sustained solely by the addition of water. The product was reasonably successful but no money-maker, and Dow finally dropped it.[32]

In a parallel development, many of the older Dow products were being introduced in new areas around the world. By 1979 Styron polystyrene plastic was being produced in 19 plants around the globe; Styrofoam plastic foam was made in 16 factories worldwide.[33]

The emphasis on building a Dow pharmaceutical house continued. In 1967 Dow reorganized its pharmaceutical business as a separate Life Sciences Department, which included Allied Laboratories and its Pitman-Moore subsidiary; Lepetit, S.p.A., Italy's largest pharmaceutical house; Bio-Science Laboratories at Van Nuys, California, a leading specialist in developing and marketing sophisticated laboratory testing methods for medical doctors; LIFE, Ecuador's largest pharmaceutical house; and (in 1969) the Cordis-Dow Corporation, makers and marketers of Dow's small, disposable artificial kidney.

William R. Dixon, the corporate director of marketing, became the first head of Dow's worldwide pharmaceutical business, the only Dow business without geographical boundaries, and took on the task of organizing a coherent pharmaceutical business out of the jumble of companies that had been assembled. Lepetit, for example, had branch offices and small plants scattered about the globe. Uncoordinated research efforts were being conducted in virtually all of these firms. For more than three years, Dixon spent virtually all of his time on the road, traveling about the world trying to organize a pharmaceutical business.

When his health cracked in 1970 and doctors said he had to stop his globe-trotting, Ben Branch switched Dixon to an administrative post in Midland and nominated Julius Johnson, the company's research and development director and a corporate vice president, to be his successor. Under the tutelage of Dixon and Johnson, the company began to pursue a leadership position among the world's pharmaceutical houses and to forge a reputation for innovative new human health products.

Lirugen one-shot measles vaccine, was introduced in 1965 and was instrumental in virtually wiping out measles as a health threat in the United States. By 1969 Lirugen had a 70 percent share of the U.S. market and was licensed for manufacture around the world—in Sweden, Great Britain, Mexico, France, and Japan. Hundreds of millions of the world's children were (and are being) inoculated against measles using this product. It was developed by Anton Schwarz and his colleagues at Pitman-Moore.

Another major discovery was rifamycin, an antibiotic developed by Gruppo Lepetit in Italy and introduced commercially in Europe and Latin America in 1968 and registered in the United States in 1971. Also known as rifampin, rifampicin, and by the Dow trademark Rifadin, rifamycin rapidly became the drug of choice against pulmonary tuberculosis. It is also used against leprosy, viral diseases, leukemia, sarcoma, and trachoma.

Rifamycin was discovered by Dr. Hermes Pagani, a Lepetit research microbiologist, who picked up some soil samples in a pine forest on the French Riviera in the area of St. Raphael while he was on vacation there in 1957. When he returned to Milan, the samples were routinely checked for antibacterial microorganisms in a soil-screening program. The sample from the St. Raphael pine forest yielded the microorganisms from which the new antibiotic rifamycin were derived. Working with Hermes Pagani's soil sample, the Lepetit research laboratories under Dr. Piero Sensi worked for three years to develop an effective antibiotic. They succeeded, and rifamycin quickly became and remained the biggest seller in the Dow pharmaceutical arsenal.

Lorelco cholesterol-reducing drug was introduced nationally in the United States in 1977, and also became a big seller.

An old mural in the Midland County Courthouse, painted by Detroit artist Paul Honoré in 1926, shows Herbert Dow striding the earth, sowing seeds that spring up as new products and new factories to produce chemicals. A half-century after it was painted his descendants and successors were literally doing that.

In the 1970s new plants and chemical complexes were coming onstream continually—the Oyster Creek Division in Texas, in 1971; the world's largest phenol plant, at Freeport, Texas, in 1971; the world's largest chlorine plant, also at Freeport, in 1972; the big new Stade complex near Hamburg, Germany, Dow's second largest in Europe, and the Korea Pacific Chemical Company, at Ulsan and Yeo-su in South Korea, all in 1972; a major chemical complex centered on the island of Krk, in Yugoslavia, begun in 1972 and essentially completed in 1979; a major, world-scale petrochemical complex in Alberta, Canada, begun in 1973; another world-scale complex built at Aratu, Brazil, beginning in 1974; and a large plant near Bangkok, Thailand, in 1977. The company opened its first office in mainland China in 1979.

The road to the future could also be read into two other events of 1971. In February Ted Doan retired and was succeeded by Ben Branch, and Carl Gerstacker pushed for adoption of a new rule by the board of directors and had his way. Henceforth, directors of the company would be required to relinquish line responsibilities at age 60. At 60 they would go into a "deceleration" program, serving as senior statesmen, and reach mandatory retirement at age 65. The aim was to force the advancement of younger persons in the top management ranks and hasten the departure of older executives before they had outlived their usefulness. Executives who had not had five years in their most recent position (Ben Branch being the conspicuous example at the time) were made an exception to the rule.[34]

The other notable change of 1971 was that women became officers of the company for the first time. Lois J. Hoerlein and Gertrude Welker, both veterans of the executive suite, were made assistant secretaries of the company. The first woman member of the board of directors since Grace Dow had served was Barbara Franklin, of the University of Pennsylvania, in 1980; she later left the board to serve as secretary of commerce in the administration of George Bush, returning to the board in 1993 following Bush's defeat by Bill Clinton.

VII.

One day in November 1971, Carl Gerstacker found a note from his secretary, Elsa Carlson: "Mr. Herbert W. Kalmbach, Washington, D.C., is planning to see you tomorrow at 2 P.M. He will be flying into Detroit this evening from California for a breakfast meeting, and will stop here on his way back to Washington."

That was Dow's introduction to the Watergate scandals of the early 1970s, in which the company had happily but a minor role. Kalmbach, President Richard Nixon's chief political fund-raiser, was to become a key figure in the Watergate investigations a year or two later.

Gerstacker and Frank Harlow, then Dow's tax counsel, listened in their best poker-face form as Kalmbach outlined how he was contacting "60 distinguished business leaders"— Gerstacker was on the list—to raise funds for the president's re-election in 1972. They were being asked for $100,000 each; he had visited about half the people on the list, and all but two "had given"—he did not say how much. In 1968 the Nixon forces had spent $34 million in the election, he said; in 1972 it was going to cost a great deal more. (In the end the G.O.P. raised $55 million to re-elect Nixon in 1972, $19 million of it "executive" gifts.)[35]

Eighteen months later Gerstacker told the Watergate investigators (the "Senate Select Committee on Presidential Campaign Activities,") that after Kalmbach's visit he had a follow-up telephone call on the subject from Maurice H. Stans, chairman of the Finance Committee to Re-Elect the President (CREEP), and that he had sent a personal check for $2,000 to the Stans Committee. Stans, who had been Nixon's secretary of commerce, also became a prominent Watergate figure.[36] In July 1973, when many of America's blue-chip corporations were admitting they had made illegal contributions of corporate funds to the Kalmbach-Stans duo, Gerstacker told the press he had felt Kalmbach was asking for funds from him personally, not from the company.[37]

Asked about other Dow executives and their contributions to CREEP, Gerstacker told the investigators Harlow had made up a list of candidates whose 1972 campaigns he felt Dow executives ought to support, and had contacted or written (on his own stationery) a total of 111 of his Dow colleagues. Harlow said 74 of the 111 made political contributions, all by personal check, including 26 checks totaling $11,685 to the Committee for Re-Election of the President.

That was it, except for one minor glitch. During his campaign that year President Nixon made a yo-yo plane stop at the Tri-City Airport serving Midland, briefly addressed an enthusiastic rally gathered on the tarmac there, and flew off again. During the investigations it was discovered that a Dow employee who was a member of the rally committee had borrowed a truck from the Midland plant, and some rope and cable, to deliver empty refuse drums to the airport for the rally. No one had thought to consult anyone in authority at Dow about it, and everything was returned after the rally, but when the incident was uncovered, an intensive company investigation ensued and the incident was duly reported to the Watergate committee as its only finding of improper activity by Dow personnel.

For the business world the Watergate era continued on into the mid-1970s with investigations of corporate activities involving other types of improper payments, and like other large firms Dow was investigated again. Companies such as Dow which had been growing vigorously abroad had all encountered business methods that were by American standards not only unsavory but illegal. Local business practices differ wildly around the globe. Custom, religion, and the degree of corruption or honesty of the current governing group are all factors in the relations between business and government; perfectly ordinary and ethical practice in one country may be a jailable offense in another.

Dow people became quickly and sometimes painfully aware of these problems as they opened up offices and built plants in foreign lands. Should Dow pay a small bribe to the local customs inspector to "facilitate" the entry of a Dow shipment into the country, as was customary in some countries? What about the official who set the tax rate on a Dow plant and let it be known that he expected lavish gifts at the holidays, as he received from other local firms? What was proper conduct for a straitlaced midwestern company like Dow in cases of this type?

One response to these recurring problems was the formulation of Dow's "International Business Guidelines," which were distributed to the overseas personnel of the company to tell them how the company expected them to do business.[38]

The company's adherence to this policy was regularly repeated and reinforced. Zoltan Merszei, for example, "reaffirmed" this policy in a letter to all Dow supervisory employees in August 1977, "in view of the recent emphasis on questionable payments":[39]

"We sell our products on the merits of price, quality and service," Merszei said in this letter. "We do not want business obtained through deviation from this principle.

> There is no need to offer expensive gifts, bribes or any other kind of payment or benefit to representatives of customers, suppliers, competitors, governments or government agencies . . . to obtain business or special treatment of any kind. Any employee should be able to determine what is legitimate business entertainment by noting our standard rules on business entertain-

ment and expense account reporting. . . . In cases where the propriety of the payment is not clear or the alternatives might be harmful to the employee, the matter must be cleared at the highest possible level in the Area management. . . .

Any kind of subterfuge—including the making of payments, allowances or discounts to agents or other third parties for questionable activities of any sort—is strictly forbidden.

Closing one's eyes to any activity which appears to be questionable does not make for a defense. In addition, no payments are to be made to others for any purpose other than that described in the documents supporting the expense. There must be no false entries in any of our records, and no cash or other assets can be maintained for any purpose in any unrecorded or "off the books" fund.

Violators will be subject to discipline up to and including discharge from Dow employment. . . .

Merszei's sweeping policy statement followed what was probably the most intensive internal investigation of wrongdoing in the company's first century. It began in early 1976, at a time when the nation's newspapers and TV screens were full of stories of corporate misdeeds. Ben Branch, alarmed by these reports, appointed a Special Investigating Committee under the chairmanship of Dale A. Bywater, the company's auditor, "to look into the possibility of questionable payments by the company throughout the world." Was there hanky-panky going on despite of the clear rules laid down to Dow employees, he wanted to know? He asked the committee, which also included Robert E. Jones, a senior attorney, and Angelo Coccalatte, controller of Gruppo Lepetit, to find out.[40]

Four months later, having interviewed the 235 Dow people worldwide "most likely to have knowledge of questionable payments if they occurred," the committee presented a full report of its findings covering the period from January 1, 1970, to June 30, 1976. The audience including not only the corporate audit committee (Ted Doan, Herbert H. Dow II, and Carl Gerstacker) but other key management—Branch, Merszei, Lyon, and Groening among them—and Richard E. Goff and Raymond Spindler of the audit firm Haskins & Sells.

Nowhere in the world were any high-level machinations discovered, the committee reported, and in the United States only one improper payment could be found at any level— a $3,400 bill for campaign cards and posters for local candidates paid by the Louisiana Division in 1971. Noting that it had been able to interview all the personnel it targeted, "except certain ex-employees of Gruppo Lepetit," the committee acknowledged that "the already-known problems in Lepetit were confirmed"; indeed, the great bulk of the improper payments uncovered, $2,886,100 of a total of $3,259,300, were turned up in the Lepetit organization. "Dow has been actively trying to work on the Lepetit problem since its acquisition."

In the main, two kinds of questionable payments occurred: (1) bribery to obtain business, and (2) "grease" payments to expedite normal activities, the committee said. Most of the payments to obtain business were to minor officials where sales to their institutions were possible only if payments were made, "which appears to be the accepted practice in these countries. . . . In our opinion these payments are more an extortion for the right to do business than bribery on the part of our subsidiaries." In Iran, the committee said, Dow's pharmaceutical subsidiary reported a drop of 70 percent in its sales when these payments were discontinued.

The single most troublesome matter involved what were usually called "commissions" to government officials—Dow called them extortion—in connection with Dow business. "In several countries [various health officials] receive a majority of their remuneration from these payments and their government pay is adjusted accordingly," the committee observed. "Commissions" of this kind accounted for about two-thirds of the irregularities uncovered by the investigation.

In 1974, for example, Lepetit obtained a large rifampicin order from the Spanish Social Medicine system involving payment of a $139,000 "commission" to the chief of the National Tuberculosis Agency. In Ethiopia, where Lepetit was closing down its subsidiary, a tax official threatened a heavy termination tax bill unless he was paid off. Various amounts were extorted in Egypt, Greece, Morocco, Nigeria, and Zaire.

The most serious problems were in Brazil and Mexico. "Commission" payments to hospital officials, usually those in charge of purchasing, were prevalent in Brazil, and a thorny problem in Brazil was the common use of "despachantes," a species of expediter who helped foreign businessmen get things done, often by the judicious placement of a bribe or two. In Mexico, the investigators observed, "no business is done with government agencies without commission payments to someone in the organization"; from 1970 to 1976 Lepetit Mexico paid $583,000 in such commissions, the "commission" averaging about 10 percent of the transaction. Even the secretary of the Lepetit Mexico labor union was paid a "commission" —about $500 annually—"to help maintain labor peace."

Latin America was by far the most troublesome area for improper payments. Ecuador got a clean bill of health, but commission payment occurred in most of Latin America— Venezuela, Bolivia, Colombia, Costa Rica, and Honduras.

In the Pacific area the problem was relatively small. Hospital "commissions" were used in Malaysia. A "grease" payment ($7,500) was extorted in Indonesia for the installment of a telex machine not available otherwise. Small payments to customs agents were customary in Thailand.

The $2,886,100 in shady payments by Gruppo Lepetit was another matter, and it took years to clean up these practices in the firm. When Dow had begun to invest in the Lepetit pharmaceutical house, based in Milan, Italy, which it eventually acquired, it was a big, reputable pharmaceutical house, the largest in Italy, a going concern, with branches all over the world, and Dow purchased 49 percent of it in 1963 after it had indicated an interest in affiliating with an American company. Afterward Dow executives acknowledged that they had gone into it without knowing very much about the business practices of Lepetit, run by a flamboyant Italian high-roller, the Baron Guido Zerilli. Eventually Zerilli was bought out, Lepetit's business practices were brought up to Dow's high standards, and the Lepetit pharmaceutical empire became a key piece in Dow's pharmaceutical arm, Marion Merrell Dow.

The Bywater Committee's investigation and report became a watershed event in the company's worldwide growth; it established once and for all the ethical basis on which the company was going to do business around the world, and how it was going to deal with "commissions," "grease," and the other forms of polite extortion that prevail in many parts of the world.

In the years that followed the report Dow personnel were required, every year or two, to complete a questionnaire and certify that they had not and were not engaging in such activities. The questionnaires, devised by Donna J. Roberts, who succeeded Herbert Dow II as corporate secretary in 1987, were collected individually from about 10,000 employees—all those in positions where they might be exposed to participation in such practices—and became a prime element in the effort to stay a squeaky clean business firm.

Notes

1. Oral History, C. B. Branch, November 12, 1988.
2. Oral History, H. D. Doan, July 29 and August 2, 1988, and January 17, 1989, is used extensively in this section.
3. Ibid.
4. Objectives, The Dow Chemical Company, March 15, 1965 (See appendix C, Basic Dow Documents).
5. Oral History, H. D. Doan.
6. H. D. Doan, talk, new employee orientation, Midland, February 2, 1967.
7. "Core Values: Basic Principles for All Dow Employees, 'A Written Description of the Way We at Dow Operate,'" *Dow Today*, July 15, 1986. (See appendix C)
8. *Dow Values*, July 20, 1994. (See appendix C)
9. Oral History, Macauley Whiting, August 13, 1990, is used extensively in this section.
10. These meetings were held annually from 1964 to 1967. No official record was kept of the 1964 and 1965 Dow Management Conferences, but the 1966 record ("Dow Management Conference, March 30-April 1, 1966, East Lansing, Michigan") includes a review and summary of the 1965 conference by H. D. Doan. Complete records of the 1966 and 1967 conferences were kept (by Prof. Vernon C. Michelson of Case in 1966 and E. N. Brandt in 1967), both classified "Dow Confidential."
11. Carl A. Gerstacker, "The New Role of Top Management," Dow Management Conference, East Lansing, Michigan, March 16-18, 1965. See also untitled second Gerstacker talk delivered at this meeting.
12. "Directory of Technology Centers," issued by Central Research Index, The Dow Chemical Company, October 15, 1969, marked "Restricted: For use within The Dow Chemical Company."
13. See "Technology Center Awards Nominations Due," in *Dow Today*, internal company news bulletin, no. 116, November 24, 1993.
14. Oral History, Carl A. Gerstacker, July 21, 1988, is used extensively in this section.
15. Even when he was earning $15 per week, Gerstacker was intent upon saving money, and did so by dining in his room each evening on the cheapest meal he could find, two quarts of milk and a candy bar; like Herbert Dow, he kept meticulous records of his expenditures for most of his life.

16. Carl A. Gerstacker, "A Look at the Record, Dow 1950-1975," annual meeting of shareholders, Midland, May 5, 1976.

17. Oral History, Edmund P. Faessler, July 7, 1989. Dow sold the Mendes Gans Bank in 1995.

18. Dow had two assistant treasurers at this period—Roe E. Withrow Jr., in charge of "BMG Operations" (Bank Mendes Gans), and John Van Stirum, in charge of "DBC Operations" (Dow Banking Corporation). See "Why Dow Chemical Got Into the Money Game," Burroughs Clearing House, December 1968.

19. "Dow Banking Corporation," in *Special Edition, Dow Europe Now*, published by Dow Chemical Europe, Horgen, Switzerland, December 1977, provides considerable information concerning the Dow Bank. See also "Dow Banking Corporation Goes Public in Switzerland," *Dow Today*, October 22, 1980.

20. *Dow Annual Report*, 1968, 19.

21. "Circular Letter" issued by Dow Banking Corporation, Zurich, August 1986.

22. Oral History, Robert B. Bennett, August 24, 1990.

23. Oral History, C. B. Branch, November 12, 1988, is used extensively throughout this section.

24. Oral History, H. D. Doan, July 29 and August 2, 1988, and January 17, 1989.

25. *Dow Annual Report*, 1974.

26. "Chief Executive Officer of the Year: C. B. Branch, President, Dow Chemical," *Financial World*, March 15, 1976.

27. "Wal-Mart Founder Cited As CEO of the Decade," *Detroit News*, March 24, 1989.

28. Nixon and Agnew both left Washington in disgrace, of course, some time afterward.

29. See *Dow Annual Reports*, 1970 and 1971.

30. *Dow Annual Report*, 1977.

31. For listings of new products, see *Dow Annual Reports,* 1970, 1975, and 1979.

32. Oral History, Malcolm E. Pruitt, September 9, 1988, and March 15, 1996.

33. *Dow Annual Report*, 1978.

34. *Dow Annual Report*, 1971.

35. From penciled meeting notes, Carl A. Gerstacker, November 30, 1971.

36. Gerstacker to David M. Dorsen, assistant chief counsel, Select Committee on Presidential Campaign Activities, U.S. Senate, "Questionnaire Regarding Political Contributions in 1972 Presidential Campaign," and "Questionnaire for Corporate Officers," August 29, 1973.

37. See inter alia "Inquiries into Nixon's Re-election Funds Turning Up a Pattern of High Pressure," *New York Times*, July 15, 1973, and "They Gave at the Office," *Chemical Week*, August 23, 1973, 19.

38. See appendix C for "International Business Principles," 1976.

39. "Company Policy Against Questionable Payments," Merszei to all Dow supervisory employees, August 19, 1977.

40. See "Investigation of Questionable Payments," in Proxy Statement, The Dow Chemical Company, March 25, 1977; and in Prospectus, Employee Stock Purchase Plan, The Dow Chemical Company, April 22, 1977.

THIRTEEN

THE FLOWER
CHILDREN

I.

In the time of the flower children Dow became a household word. "Dow Shall Not Kill," their picket signs said, or "Napalm, Johnson's Baby Powder," a reference to Pres. Lyndon B. Johnson and "his" war in Vietnam. "Napalm kills," they chanted, "save the babies," throwing the chant back and forth, waving a picture of a crying infant suffering terrible burns.

In 1965, just before the protests began, an Opinion Research Corporation survey showed that only 38 percent of the American public had "heard of" The Dow Chemical Company. Four years later the same survey indicated that 91 percent of the public "knew something about" Dow—about the same level of the populace that could name the sitting U.S. president. What made the company famous was the war protests in which it was involved, which were front-page newspaper and TV news fare throughout that period.

Indeed, a generation of American young people grew up knowing little else of the company except that it made napalm, that awful stuff that was used in that awful war in Vietnam. Because of the deep-seated resentment of Dow those war protests engendered, there is still a stigma of anti-Dow sentiment abroad in the world a generation later.[1]

By the Vietnam War era Dow was making 800 different products, the great majority of them chemicals or plastics sold to other business firms and only two or three of them familiar to most Americans, the best known being Saran Wrap and Handi-Wrap, common kitchen items. In the next few years napalm became the company's best-known product; at the height of the war Dow was the only producer.

Flamethrowers had been used in warfare since the ninth century A.D. Napalm, the modern version, had its origin in World War I flame-throwing devices designed to stop tanks, a new invention introduced in that war. The World War II version, a kind of "jellied gasoline," was used to dislodge the Japanese from their bunkers in the Pacific islands. By the Vietnam War era it had been developed into an awesome firebomb often launched by aircraft and used by American troops against the Viet Cong's hiding places in tunnels and other concealments. The war protesters claimed it was also used indiscriminately against innocent civilians, including women and children; the military authorities denied this.[2]

Its use was immoral and inhumane, protesters argued; making it was a crime against humanity, and Dow should stop making it or be prevented from doing so. During the years 1966 to 1970 the company was involved in at least 221 major anti-Dow demonstrations on American campuses. Off the campuses there were dozens of other incidents, ranging from the bombing of the company's office in Frankfurt, Germany, to the trashing of its office in Washington, D.C. Protesters around the world marched to Dow Chemical installations to voice their anger against the war.

In 1964 the U.S. Air Force had developed a simplified new form of napalm, Napalm "B," at its Eglin, Florida, Air Force Base, and began looking for manufacturers to make it for the war in Vietnam in which the United States was becoming increasingly involved. The formula for Napalm B was simple—about 50 percent polystyrene, 25 percent benzene, and 25 percent gasoline—and making it was just as simple. It was what is called in the chemical trade "bath-tub chemistry"; just mix up the ingredients and you've got it.

All 17 U.S. producers of polystyrene were asked by the Department of Defense to bid on lots of napalm, usually in 25 million pound increments. As the leading manufacturer of polystyrene, Dow routinely turned in a bid (through its newly established government affairs department) and in July 1965 became one of the producers of napalm for the defense establishment.

To fulfill its contract the company set up a small mixing line at its Torrance, California, plant—a tankage system for the three ingredients and for mixing them—and assigned a crew of 10 employees to make napalm. The operation never got much bigger than that, and it was only in operation, sporadically, for about four years. Dow never made more than $5 million worth of napalm in a year, but it became possibly the most widely known operation in the company's history. It was such a small piece of business that when the protests began no member of the troika was even aware that the company was making the material.[3]

Gen. Earle G. Wheeler, chairman of the U.S. Joint Chiefs of Staff, said napalm was used because many of the Viet Cong defensive positions were built with a layer of logs and earth overhead. "To get rid of a Viet Cong or North Vietnamese trooper who's in one of these protected holes you have to have a direct hit practically on top of the thing if you are using high explosives," he explained.

> Napalm, by virtue of its splashing and spreading, can get into such defensive positions. It's also especially effective against antiaircraft positions, because normally the enemy digs a hole—a protected position—and puts his machine down in the hole. . . . Again it takes a direct hit with high explosives in order to destroy it. The napalm splashes in and incapacitates the crew and sometimes destroys the weapon.[4]

In March 1966, the United Technology Center, or UTC, a subsidiary of United Aircraft Corporation and at the time the principal contractor for napalm—it had won the biggest contract and Dow the second largest when the first napalm bids were opened—began to experience protests at the Redwood City, California, plant where it was located; war protesters were lying down on the railroad tracks leading out of the plant to prevent shipments of napalm. In New York, Witco Chemical, another producer, found protest pickets marching at its April annual meeting. The air force quickly clamped a security lid on the napalm program but it was too late; the napalm controversy had already begun.

Presiding over the Dow annual meeting that May, chairman Gerstacker stuck a statement of the Dow position on napalm in his pocket in case pickets showed up, but none did. It proved to be the calm before the storm. The first demonstration against Dow took place in New York City a fortnight later, on May 28. About 75 protesters representing Citizens' Campaign Against Napalm, Women Strike for Peace, and other New York peace groups gathered at the Dow offices in Rockefeller Center and handed out leaflets urging housewives to boycott Saran Wrap. "Napalm burns babies, Dow makes money!" they chanted.

Dean Wakefield, Dow's Eastern public relations manager, handed out copies of the Dow position statement—the same one Gerstacker had been prepared to read—to the press at the scene. The statement, widely used by the company during these years, said:

> The Dow Chemical Company endorses the right of any American to protest legally and peacefully an action with which he does not agree.
>
> Our position on the manufacture of napalm is that we are a supplier of goods to the Defense Department and not a policy maker. We do not and should not try to decide military strategy or policy.
>
> Simple good citizenship requires that we supply our government and our military with those goods which they feel they need whenever we have the technology and capability and have been chosen by the government as a supplier.
>
> We will do our best, as we always have, to try to produce what our Defense Department and our soldiers need in any war situation. Purely aside from our duty to do this, we will feel deeply gratified if what we are able to provide helps to protect our fighting men or to speed the day when fighting will end.

To some this sounded like the "Nuremberg defense," the defense used by German industrialists at the Nuremberg war trials after World War II, who said they "just followed orders."

As Ted Doan, who became the company's principal spokesman on the napalm issue, pointed out, the two situations were not comparable. "We reject the validity of comparing our present form of government with Hitler's Nazi Germany," he said.

> In our mind our government is still representative of and responsive to the will of the people.

Further, we as a company have made a moral judgment on the long-range goals of our government and we support these. We may not agree as individuals with every decision of every military or governmental leader but we regard these leaders as men trying honestly and relentlessly to find the best possible solutions to very, very complex international problems. As long as we so regard them, we would find it impossible not to support them. This is not saying as the critics imply that we will follow blindly and without fail no matter where our government leads. While I think it highly improbable under our form of government, should despotic leaders attempt to lead our nation away from its historic national purposes, we would cease to support the government.

Our critics ask if we are willing to stand judgment for our choice to support our government if history should prove this wrong. Our answer is yes.[5]

The New York demonstration was heavily covered by newspapers and the national TV networks and wire services. On that same day more than 100 pickets representing Students for a Democratic Society (SDS) and the Freedom Now Committee staged a protest march at the Torrance plant. Counterpickets representing the Victory in Vietnam Association also marched at the plant, the first but not the last instance in which pickets favorable to Dow also showed up at the napalm demonstrations.

A few weeks later, in August 1966, the war protest groups organized "August Days of Protest"—"four days of nationwide demonstrations against the war in Vietnam"—and Dow was one of the many targets. Protesters converged on Midland from the University of Michigan, Wayne State University in Detroit, the University of Toledo, and 12 Detroit-area anti-Vietnam War groups, but these strange, unwashed, long-haired visitors were coldly received in Midland and not much happened. The *Detroit Free Press* called their demonstration "a flop."[6] The protest group asked for an appointment with the president of Dow, and one was granted. Another demonstration was held at the Torrance plant the same day.

In New York that day, a mass of pickets tried to reach the Dow offices on the 37th floor of Rockefeller Center. Police were alerted and arrived promptly. In the confused melee that followed, the police arrested 29 pickets and charged them with disorderly conduct. Again the event was widely covered by the TV networks and the press.

On August 22, as a follow-up to the Midland meeting, Ted Doan met with four representatives of the SDS who asked for a full explanation of Dow's policy, and they talked for an hour. Statements made by him at this meeting—twisted and bent out of shape as they were passed along in the protest movement's underground—appeared in protest literature across the country in the next several years.

The first of the campus protests occurred at the beginning of Dow's 1966 campus recruiting season, at Wayne State University in Detroit, where the Wayne Committee to End the War in Vietnam organized an October demonstration against the Dow recruiters. A similar event at Cornell quickly followed. The University of South Florida, UCLA, and Berkeley were not far behind.

Most of the anti-Dow activity in the ensuing years took place on American campuses and was aimed at preventing the Dow recruiters who visited the campus from interviewing prospective employees. The SDS and kindred organizations wanted to localize their antiwar protest, and the Dow recruiter arriving on campus made an ideal target. Recruiters for the military and the CIA also were popular targets but often deflected the protests by moving their recruiting interviews off-campus; Dow insisted on staying on-campus with the other recruiters. "You don't solve a problem by running away from it," Ted Doan said. "We're not going to hide off-campus somewhere."

At Princeton the local SDS chapter demanded that the university ban Dow from recruiting there, and a heated and widely publicized debate ensued. The president of Princeton, Robert F. Goheen, in the end rejected the SDS demands. Pickets showed up when Dow recruiters arrived on the campus, but the Dow recruiters completed their job interviews on schedule anyway. The Dow recruiters always had a full schedule in that time; the publicity given their arrival virtually guaranteed it.

By the fall of 1967 anti-Dow activity on campus was so intense that the company began publishing a newsletter designed to keep key company personnel up-to-date on napalm-related events. (There were 133 separate campus incidents involving Dow recruiters that school year.) Called *Napalm News*, it circulated to about two dozen executives to keep them posted on where Dow was recruiting that day, where trouble was expected and the nature of it, and which Dow representatives were on the scene there, doing what. The first issue appeared on November 8, 1967, the last on March 25, 1969.[7]

In one not untypical incident that year, a recruiter from Dow's Western Division, Hans Beetz, and Dow's West Coast public relations manager, Jack Jones, went to Los Angeles State College, where five students had signed up for Dow job interviews. (A Dow public relations man often accompanied the recruiter to a campus when trouble was expected.) Three IBM recruiters were also interviewing at the college that day. Before the interviews could start, demonstrators poured into the building, threw stink bombs, and generally rendered the building unsafe and unsuitable for recruiting. A college official led Jones and the four recruiters to an adjoining building and asked them to lock themselves in a room there, pointing out a rear window they could use as an emergency exit. The five men barricaded themselves in the room as a student mob pounded on the door. Thirty-five minutes later the door was starting to come off its hinges and a college official appeared at a window in the room and said police wanted them to leave by the rear window. This they did, and promptly found themselves in the midst of the student mob with neither officials nor police anywhere in sight. They made their way through the mob to a car as well as they could and after much pounding, thumping, and rocking of the car, managed to drive away, still with no help in sight. Later Jones discovered that 50 Los Angeles police were prepared to come to the scene if called, but had not been called. To Jones's astonishment the college president told him that in his opinion the situation had "not gotten out of hand."

Reporters were on hand throughout this small riot. On December 15 the Russian Communist Party newspaper *Pravda* described the incident, or one loosely resembling it, in an article entitled "Save Yourself Through the Window, Mr. Jones!" The final paragraph of the *Pravda* article said: "Mister Jones admits that his nerves are beginning to give out. And it is no wonder. This year he has already visited more than 100 colleges. And he has been forced to save himself by flight from 46 of them."[8]

In the 1966-67 school year there were 55 such events involving Dow, almost half of them at West Coast schools. Perhaps the worst of the 1966 incidents occurred at the University of Wisconsin, where a "peace march" was being watched quite benevolently by the local police until a rock came flying out of a crowd of marchers and struck an officer full in the face. In the ensuing ruckus several students and police were injured, none seriously; during that school year the demonstrators and the peace movement at large was generally pacific, and not given to violence.

A year later the demonstrations and the picketers turned violent; peaceful protest, many of them argued, "had not worked." Student violence at Wisconsin, for example, was even more severe in the fall of 1967 than it had been a year before. Protesters took the Dow recruiter, W. L. (Curly) Hendershot, prisoner by preventing him from leaving the room where he was working; 200 or 300 students sat down in the hallway outside the room to prevent him from interviewing any students. After the university administration had appealed to the demonstrators repeatedly to leave quietly, they called on the police to "clear the place out." At sight of the police the students locked arms. The police tried to pull and pry bodies loose, with only moderate success. Then billy clubs appeared. Violence began immediately, and it was considerable. Fourteen policemen and 47 demonstrators were injured, and 71 students arrested.

In 1965, 5 of the 17 U.S. producers of polystyrene invited to bid for napalm contracts had done so. UTC quietly dropped out after completing its first big contract for 100 million pounds. Witco Chemical dropped out too. By 1967 Dow Chemical was the only contractor still willing to make napalm, although not without considerable debate within the company.

The Dow board of directors meeting of March 1967 was one of the most extraordinary in the company's first 100 years. Chairman Gerstacker opened it by raising the napalm question. "I told them we might not be aware of how much controversy there was about the moral and ethical considerations involved and that we should discuss whether we should continue or modify our supply of napalm," Gerstacker said.

The meeting adjourned several times during a two-day session. During the adjournments the directors gathered in small groups, consulted others in the company, or talked to clergy. Gerstacker himself discussed it with his close friend the Rev. T. M. (Ted) Greenhoe of Midland's Memorial Presbyterian Church. Ted Doan said the napalm question "received very open-minded treatment" at this protracted meeting.

> It was a very open debate. There were no set positions. Frequently the board broke into small groups for very intense discussion. Members talked back and forth. At the end of the first day, with nothing firmly decided, but with three or four members looking as if they might take a stand against napalm, everyone went home and must have had a very troubled sleep. The next

morning each of these men individually came to my office and said that after careful and troubled consideration they agreed that the company should continue what it was doing. I am not sure of any exceptions on the board today (1968); maybe one at most.[9]

Once the board of directors had decided that the company would "stand up for what it believed in," the debate within the company was over; Dow would continue to do what it perceived as its duty to its country. "Our sons were serving in that war," Gerstacker said, "and we felt a strong obligation to support them."[10]

In the fall of 1967 the author (then Dow's public relations director) requested an audience at the Pentagon to discuss whether the Defense Department should not, as inventor, buyer, and user of the material, initiate its own vigorous defense of napalm rather than continuing to allow Dow to take the full brunt of the war protest focused on napalm, unaided in any way by the military forces.

Invited to appear at the Pentagon, the writer and David L. Coslett, Dow's press chief, found themselves facing a panel of five full colonels, who grilled them for an hour or two about just what it was they were accusing the armed forces of doing. In the end the panel said it would take the matter under advisement, and they were dismissed.

The trip to the Pentagon was not a complete loss. Shortly afterward Ted Doan received a letter from Secretary of Defense Robert S. McNamara saying that the campus protests were misdirected, that napalm was necessary to the war effort, that it was used with great care, and that Dow was performing a great service for the armed forces. McNamara told Doan the letter could be used in any way Dow wished.[11]

"Along with you," McNamara wrote Doan, "we deplore the isolated instances where demonstrations have gone beyond mere protest to the point of interfering with the rights of students to discuss employment opportunities with any prospective employer."

In that same spring of 1967 it was also becoming clear that the stories of use of napalm against civilians were only a fabrication. "It has been told so often, in so many publications and on so many TV programs, that no one ever thinks to question one of the more shocking horror stories of the Vietnam war: that thousands of Vietnamese children have been savagely burned by U.S. napalm," reported *Time* magazine.

> Only last week a CBS-TV program on the war showed a supposed victim. Dr. Benjamin Spock has not only made the accusation in print; he has also helped to form a "Committee of Responsibility to Save Vietnamese Children." The trouble with the story, says *New York Times* medical columnist Dr. Howard Rusk, is that it is not true. Reporting from Saigon last week after a painstaking investigation, Rusk said he was unable to find a single case of a child who had been burned by napalm, and he heard of only a few.[12]

A physician in Dow's medical department in Midland, Dr. H. Charles Scharnweber, went to Vietnam as part of the Volunteer Physicians for Vietnam (VPV) program of the American

Medical Association and spent two months as a volunteer surgeon at a provincial hospital in Tan An, on the main highway between Saigon and the Mekong Delta. He was one of some 500 physicians to do so. He did not see a single napalm victim during his tour of duty, nor did any of the 10 doctors who were on tour at the time. Dr. Pat Smith, a woman physician who had practiced for 10 years in the central highlands of South Vietnam, told Scharnweber she had never seen a napalm burn victim.

Dr. Charles H. Moseley, project director for VPV, said no more than two percent of all the physicians participating in the program had seen any napalm burns. Other medical groups touring Vietnam hospitals came to the same conclusion. A Medical Appraisal Team headed by Dr. F. J. L. Blasingame of Chicago, a former executive vice president of the AMA, made per-haps the most thorough of the studies, paying especial attention to civilian casualties and burn victims. "The (burn) cases were relatively limited in number in relation to other injuries and illnesses," the Blasingame Committee reported, "and we saw no justification for the undue emphasis which had been placed by the press upon civilian burns caused by napalm." The committee blamed careless use of gasoline for most burns.[13]

The peak of the napalm demonstrations came in the spring of 1968, when college-age youth were on the rampage around the world. The top-grossing film of that year, "The Graduate," had a memorable scene in which Benjamin Braddock (played by Dustin Hoffman) received some career advice: "I just want to say one word to you. Just one word: Plastics." It reminded many of its viewers of Dow, then much in the news.

It was one of the most tumultuous springs in U.S. history. On April 4, Martin Luther King was assassinated in Memphis. On June 5, Sen. Robert F. Kennedy was assassinated in Los Angeles. In between times, Dow held its annual meeting in Midland in the midst of a con-certed effort to persuade the company to stop making napalm. Billed as the "March on Midland," the demonstration was advertised for several months ahead on campuses and among the antiwar organizations.

About 300 students and clergymen (some accounts estimated as many as 500) arrived in Midland by car and bus on May 8 after a rally at the University of Michigan the evening before. Students came from five Midwest states for the event. Dow reminded them of the rule that only shareholders, employees, and newsmen would be permitted to attend the meeting, held in what was then the largest auditorium in town at the Central Intermediate School. About 300 stockholders had attended the 1967 meeting; the 1968 version attracted 1,150.

The protest was loosely coordinated by a New York organization that called itself "Clergy and Laymen Concerned About Vietnam," or CALCAV, headed up by a New York minister, Rev. Richard R. Fernandez. In the morning, Doan and Gerstacker met Fernandez and four of his colleagues in a spirited discussion at the Presbyterian church across the street from the school, open to as many as could cram in. Speaking for the protesters were a group composed of two clergymen, a stockbroker, a housewife, and a nun. Meanwhile, small groups of protest-ers went door-to-door in the neighborhood to canvass local opinion about the war. One group reported going to 14 houses before anyone answered the door. A young housewife cautiously opened her door and saw a young man with shoulder-length red hair, who said: "Madam, we'd like to discuss the Vietnam War and Dow Chemical Company's role in it."

"You don't believe in the war?" the woman said. "I do, so I'm sorry." She slammed the door.

The area in front of the school resembled a carnival as the demonstrators sat on the lawn singing folk songs and debating U.S. foreign policy. A girl sang an antinapalm song to the tune of "Nobody Knows the Trouble I've Seen." A Roman Catholic priest played American folk songs on a Scottish bagpipe. Others played guitars; most wore black armbands (for the Vietnamese babies and women who had died by napalm). As the stockholders filed in to the meeting they waved signs at them reading, "Dow Know-How In Every Drop of Napalm," and, "The War is Wrong and so is Dow."

"You are talking to the wrong people; if you want to stop the war why aren't you talking to legislators?" Gerstacker asked Fernandez. He said the attempts to "embarrass Dow" were simply clouding the real issue—ending the war in Vietnam. "Companies don't start wars, and companies can't end them," he said. "I want the war over, too."

He was critical of CALCAV's tactics. He didn't receive a widely publicized letter from 13 U.S. bishops protesting Dow's manufacture of napalm until three days after he read about it in a newspaper, he said. Fernandez, angry, said, "This isn't a game for us. We are here because we love our country, not because we hate it."

A group of 17 counterpickets representing Central Michigan University and Northwood Institute (now Northwood University) were allowed to march on the opposite side of the street. Their picket signs said, "We Want Peace, Not Appeasement," and, "Send More Napalm to Help Our Men." A young man from Midland who said he had just returned from the Vietnam War carried a sign that said, "I Back Dow, I Like My V.C. Well-Done."

Some 27 of the protesters who were shareholders or armed with proxies carried their fight to the floor of the meeting, and a dozen addressed it. John Ross, an instructor at Massachusetts Institute of Technology, introduced a resolution that would have taken Dow out of the napalm business. Gerstacker said it was legally out of order but asked for a show of hands. It was soundly rejected.

The Rev. James Laird, a Quaker clergyman with the American Friends Service Committee in Philadelphia, asked the Dow officials to "examine their consciences," and said, "we must not surrender to government the right to make moral judgments."

Daniel J. Bernstein, a Scarsdale (New York) stockbroker, said he was advising his clients to sell their Dow stock, "because it will cost Dow hundreds and hundreds of millions of dollars to rebuild its image as a maker of chemicals for progress instead of chemicals of destruction." He nominated Marriner S. Eccles, a former Federal Reserve Board chairman and a militantly antiwar figure, to the Dow board. Eccles received 1,212 votes; the management's nominees received more than 25 million.

To avoid lengthy speeches, Gerstacker instituted what became known to succeeding Dow stockholder meetings as the "Gerstacker rule": "If it takes more than five minutes to ask it, it's not a question but a speech; if it takes more than five minutes to answer it, it's not an answer but a speech; and either one will be gaveled down."

When two young men who said they were from Purdue University attempted to take over the microphone for a rambling diatribe, they were booed by the stockholders, who yelled that they were trying to use the meeting as a "propaganda platform." Several stockholders moved for adjournment, but the motion was lost in a wave of applause, and the young men retreated. "My main problem," Gerstacker observed later, "was to try to restrain the employees and local people who wanted to throw these people out physically."

Gerstacker reserved for himself the last word: "You can harass us. You can hurt us—and we already have been hurt. You can intimidate us. We won't strike back because we respect your right to dissent. But as long as our democratically elected government sends draftees to die in Vietnam, we're going to support those men." The meeting ended in prolonged applause. As the stockholders filed out, the pickets on the lawn serenaded them with a rendition of "We Shall Overcome."[14]

As Richard Nixon moved to end the war and peace talks began in Paris, the demonstrations against Dow began to decline. In the 1968-69 school year there were only 29 of them, and in the 1969-70 school year only 4.

A group calling themselves the "DC-9" broke in and ransacked Dow's Washington offices on March 22, 1969. It was a Saturday, and the guard at the entrance left his post when the emergency boiler alarm rang; it had been activated by a "mysteriously loosened" fuse. While he was investigating, nine persons proceeded to the fourth floor and broke into Dow's offices, accompanied by two photographers—the offices of the *Washington Post* were across the street. They included six Catholic priests, a nun, a former nun married to one of the priests, and a young layman from Detroit.

Armed with jars of bright red blood and heavy metal hammers, the group moved through the dozen inner offices, systematically wrecking them. They splashed blood on the walls, ceilings, and carpet, overturned desks, broke windows, and threw a cascade of company correspondence and literature out onto the street below; paper was four inches deep in some places, the *Baltimore Sun* reported.[15]

Eighteen minutes later police arrived—by this time the protesters had been joined by a dozen newsmen—sorted them out from the newshawks, and led them away in handcuffs as they sang the "Battle Hymn of the Republic," anthem of the peace movement. The group left a lengthy statement explaining their reasoning:

> By this action, we condemn you, Dow Chemical Company, and all similar American corporations. We are outraged by the death-dealing exploitation of people of the third world and of all the poor and powerless who are victimized by your profit-seeking venture. Considering it our responsibility to respond, we deny the right of your faceless and inhuman corporations to exist: You, corporations, who under the cover of stockholders and executive anonymity, exploit, deprive, dehumanize and kill in search of profit. . . .[16]

The next day a group of three dozen pickets marched outside the Dow offices to protest the arrest of the DC-9. They carried signs saying, "Dow, your product is death. Your market is war." Ted Doan responded that the incident had gone far beyond the bounds of reasonable protest. "Any group that feels it has the right to destroy the property of others has quite clearly gone beyond the limit of legitimate dissent," he said.

It was hardly over, however. On November 7, 1969, a group of eight persons calling themselves "Beaver 55" (because, they said, they were "a group of people gnawing away at a wrong") broke into a Midland building that housed Dow computers and computer records, then being kept on magnetic tape, in the middle of the night and announced to the world that they had, "destroyed Dow's napalm data and records." The same group had broken into an Indianapolis Selective Service office a week earlier to destroy draft records.

What the group actually destroyed, it turned out, were principally the records of Midland's blood bank, which were stored on Dow's computers; there were no computer records for napalm in Midland. All eight of the members of Beaver 55 served prison terms for the break-ins.

As the napalm protests wound down, Carl Gerstacker paused to sum up the experience. "During the hundreds of incidents in which we've been involved some strange things have happened to Dow people," he said.

Our recruiters have been locked up in their recruiting rooms many times—the collegiate record for that is still held by Harvard, by the way, at nine hours; our people have been robbed of their papers and briefcases and other belongings; sometimes they've had to leave by the back door, and once or twice they've had to escape by leaping out of a window; we've had a number of bomb threats, and two actual bombings; but during all of this we have never had any Dow employee suffer actual physical harm—at least none worse than being spit upon, although I'm sure that's bad enough.

He said Dow's recruiting efforts, the original target of the protest movement, had not been hurt at all.

Where we have been hurt is that we have in effect been cut off from a segment of society, the size of which is indeterminate, which has blocked us out emotionally because they see us as a symbol of the hated war in Vietnam. So we may have lost some recruits that we really would have wanted, we may have lost some sales that we would otherwise have had, we may have lost some stockholders that would otherwise have purchased and held our stock. The number of Dow shareholders dropped from 95,000 to 90,000 during the napalm demonstrations although only a couple dozen stockholders specifically informed us that they were selling beause of napalm. We suspect a good many of the 5,000 we lost reacted at least in part to the napalm stories, but we have no way of determining just how many.

Gerstacker said the general image of Dow, a matter of great concern to the company, had apparently not declined as much as he had feared. A 1970 study by Opinion Research Corporation showed that in the general population the number of people who viewed Dow either "very favorably" or "mostly favorably" declined from 64 to 60 percent in the five-year period from 1965 to 1970. "During the same five years the percentage of persons who viewed the chemical industry favorably declined from 55 percent to 43, so we were actually bucking a trend," he said. "Additionally, Dow was one of only 2 companies of 58 studied that was significantly better known in 1970 than it was in 1967 (the other was ITT). Surely this familiarity must be connected with the fantastic amount of publicity generated by the napalm demonstrations; there is no other way to account for it."[17]

It became something of a badge of honor during this time for a college student to have been interviewed by a Dow recruiter. Gerstacker liked to tell the story of a Dow recruiter who was interviewing for jobs at a California school and had a line of students waiting for him. In the interview booth next to him was a recruiter from Standard of California who had no interviews at all. The Standard recruiter fiddled with his papers and finally, when he had stood it as long as he could, he went out and addressed the waiting students in the hallway: "Ladies and gentlemen, I think you should know that we supply the gasoline to Dow Chemical that it uses to make napalm," he said. "Now, wouldn't some of you like to interview with me?"[18]

II.

In 1970 much of the world seemed to be unhappy with Dow. The napalm hubbub was winding down on the campuses, but only to a somewhat dampened degree of turmoil. In that year the mercury crisis occurred, and Dow was sued by the state of Ohio and the province of Ontario as well as the commercial fishermen of the Great Lakes. Just beginning was what was to be the longest-running controversy of them all, the "Agent Orange" case and the dioxin crisis linked to it. The notoriety Dow had gained from napalm was making the company a favorite target for pickets of all kinds.

Cesar Chavez, the charismatic leader of the migrant farm workers in California, telephoned Ted Doan, collect, one Sunday night in Midland, and they talked for 45 minutes. "Look, I'm not opposed to Dow," Chavez said. "I think Dow is one of the best companies out there, but they're such an easy target." Doan told him Dow was "not even in it out there in California." Chavez's organization, the United Farm Workers Organizing Committee, was striking one of California's major lettuce producers, Bud Antle, Inc., growers of "Bud" lettuce, and organizing a nationwide boycott of lettuce and grapes. "You are landowners," Chavez said. "I don't care what you are doing, you are just an easy target and I've got to use you."

Soon Dow offices and plants were being bombarded with inaccuracies and half-truths that would indicate, as a Dow communique put it, "a nefarious conspiracy between Bud Antle, Inc., and The Dow Chemical Company to grind the migrant workers deeper into their misery, and to harass and punish Cesar Chavez for defending them."[19]

Dow had been working with the Antle firm to perfect a process for the field-picking of lettuce, using Dow's Trycite polystyrene film. Crews rode and walked across the lettuce fields, picking and wrapping lettuce in plastic wrap, in one sweep readying it for shipment to the supermarkets; it is a practice that has since become standard. In the course of this developmental work Dow had purchased $1 million of the firm's stock—6.6 percent of the total outstanding—and Chester F. Weaver, the Dow auditor, had become a member of the Antle board of directors.

A few weeks later pickets appeared at the Dow headquarters in Midland on one of the coldest days of a cold Michigan winter and took up a frigid vigil on Abbott Road, separated from the Dow headquarters by a quarter mile of lawn; on the other side of Abbott Road was an uninhabited woods reserved for future company expansion. No one had picketed Dow in such isolation before.

Piqued by humanity—the pickets did not appear to be dressed for the rigors of a Michigan winter—and by curiosity—Dow headquarters in Midland seemed quite remote from the lettuce field battles in California—Dow people invited the pickets to come in and get warm. Over coffee, Herbert H. Lyon, chief administrative officer of the company, asked them about their grievances.

The pickets explained in Latin accents that their strike was against the big lettuce growers in California, not against Dow, but they needed all the help they could find to win their fight and they hoped to persuade Dow to use its influence. Lyon asked if they were aware that Dow's total stake in the lettuce business was a $1 million investment in the Antle Company, making it very much a minority voice in Antle and giving it no voice at all with the other lettuce growers. "We are told you control the things," one of the pickets said. "No, we don't tell them what to do; it's their company, not ours," Lyon said. "But you are bigger than they are," another of the pickets said, with a tone of finality.

The UFWOC picketing continued for a few days, and also popped up at Dow locations in California. It stopped when the lettuce strike and the boycott finally concluded.

Agent Orange was a much bigger problem.

In 1962 the U.S. military launched a massive campaign to defoliate the Vietnamese forests in which the Viet Cong were concealed, to deprive them of hiding places and prevent ambushes in which American troops were regularly being slaughtered; from 1962 to 1970, when the program ended, the United States sprayed some 3.5 million acres of Vietnam under this program. The spray it used, most of it shipped in drums painted with an orange band and called Agent Orange, contained as its main ingredients the herbicides 2,4,5-T (2,4,5-trichlorophenoxyacetic acid) and 2,4-D (2,4-dichlorophenoxyacetic acid). It was provided to the armed forces by 11 different U.S. companies. Dow, among the 11, was the largest single supplier, and because of its napalm notoriety the news stories about Agent Orange often identified the makers as "Dow and 10 other companies."

The villain in the Agent Orange case was dioxin, an impurity that occurs in trace quantities in the manufacture of 2,4,5-T. There are 75 dioxins (although only a few have been isolated and studied), but the one causing the trouble was 2,3,7,8-tetradichlorodibenzoparadioxin, usually known as TCDD, or just plain dioxin.[20]

A second defoliant widely used in Vietnam was Agent White (shipped in drums with a white band), whose active ingredients were Tordon, a Dow herbicide designed for tree and brush control, and 2,4-D. Tordon, or picloram (4-amino-3,5,6-trichloropicolinic acid) was introduced by Dow in 1963, and Vietnamese defoliation was its first massive use. Agent White required precision spraying because it would also kill food crops, and it became doubly controversial for this reason; the North Vietnamese and the war protesters claimed it was being used to starve the enemy by killing his rice plants and his vegetable gardens. Agent White never gained the fame of Agent Orange but was just as controversial.[21]

The North Vietnamese complained that the defoliation sprayings caused widespread illness among the people, mostly civilian peasants, exposed to them; and soon they were blaming the American invaders and their spraying for every illness that occurred in their wake. They called the sprayings "war crimes." The scientific and medical minds of the West did not believe the claims of the North Vietnamese, which they dismissed as propaganda, but in the years that followed many of the U.S. veterans of the Vietnam conflict also began to suffer illnesses of mysterious origin, and to blame them on Agent Orange as well.

On October 29, 1969, President Nixon, through the White House science adviser, Dr. Lee A. DuBridge, ordered restrictions on the use of 2,4,5-T domestically, principally restricting its use to areas of low population; a halt to its military use in Vietnam followed shortly. This move was based on tests by the Bionetics Research Laboratories, Inc., at Kansas City, Missouri., for the National Cancer Institute, indicating that 2,4,5-T was a teratogen—it caused birth defects. It later developed that the Bionetics research was seriously flawed—it had used "dirty" 2,4,5-T with abnormally high dioxin levels—but the damage was done.

On December 27 the federal Office of Science and Technology summoned a group of Dow scientists to Washington to tell them all they knew about 2,4,5-T. The Dow group told a panel of distinguished scientists among other things about a new methodology to determine TCDD level recently developed by Rudy Stehl of Dow. The Bionetics sample of 2,4,5-T contained a much higher level of dioxin than normal, they reported (it was later revealed that the Bionetics sample had come from the Diamond Shamrock Corporation). "If Bionetics had selected a Dow material or that of almost any other manufacturer, the teratogenic effect would not have been detected," said Warren B. Crummett, one of the Dow experts.[22]

In the 10 years that followed, Dow stubbornly attempted to defend the product, contending that 30 years of science had shown 2,4,5-T to be a safe and useful product, and that it was the dioxin contaminant that was the mischief maker. Dow had greatly improved its process for making the product after the dioxin problem became apparent in 1964, and the dioxin content of Dow's product was negligible, the company said. It offered to make these process improvements available to other manufacturers.

"If we let them ban a product that has 30 years of studies behind it that says it's safe, what happens to the next product, and the next product, and the next?" asked Oreffice some years later. "How many products would have been banned with no good reason if we hadn't fought for 2,4,5-T? I don't know the answer; nobody knows."

In 1979 the government slapped such severe curbs on the use of 2,4,5-T that Dow stopped making it. Finally, in October 1983, Dow abandoned the battle and junked its 2,4,5-T plant. It had spent about $10 million in the fight to save the product.[23]

In the interim more than 17,000 U.S. Vietnam veterans (plus thousands more in other countries) had filed claims for disability payments related to Agent Orange, and by 1984 some 9,600 of them had been hospitalized and about 1,300 claims had been paid, all for illnesses ascribed to reasons other than Agent Orange.

Additionally some 9,000 of the veterans filed suit against the companies that supplied Agent Orange to the military, seeking a total of about $44 billion. It was the largest product liability case in history to that time, the first of the mass tort class-action cases. The plaintiffs were represented by more than 200 lead attorneys and about 1,000 other attorneys.

Paul Oreffice, then the CEO, called in one of his top lieutenants, Keith R. McKennon, senior vice president and a director of the company, and said, "Keith, put all your other duties on hold and get on this problem. We've got to deal with dioxin and Agent Orange, and I want you to take charge of it. You have experience in that field, and we're in trouble."

In the meantime, the dioxin crisis was developing among the civilian populace of the United States as well. In two highly publicized cases—Love Canal, in the Niagara Falls area, and Times Beach, in northern Missouri—the U.S. government evacuated entire communities and moved out their residents when high levels of dioxin were discovered in the soil.[24]

Oddly enough, the measurements of the infinitesimal quantities of dioxin involved were made possible by instruments and science developed largely at Dow. In the early 1950s chemists were able to measure chemical content accurately only in parts per thousand; they could measure some chemicals to parts per million, but only in an approximate way and only for certain chemicals. Dow was the first to develop an analytical method for dioxin sensitive to parts per million, for example, and that was in 1964.

The advances in this field were largely the work of Warren B. Crummett, a brilliant analytical chemist who headed up this work at Dow. By 1976 Crummett and his colleagues could measure dioxin content to parts per billion, a real scientific breakthrough. By 1980 he could measure one part per trillion and identify which form of dioxin it was. By 1983 the Dow analytical chemists were working in parts per quadrillion. That's parts per 1,000,000,000,000,000. It has been calculated that if you counted the hairs on the head of every person living on earth today, it would come to about one quadrillion.[25]

After Times Beach was evacuated in 1982 the television program *Sixty Minutes* sent a CBS TV crew to Midland to interview the residents about it; Midland was reportedly the next town that would be evacuated because of dioxin contamination. "They (the TV crew) came (to Midland) on the busiest single weekend of the year," Keith McKennon remembered, and they couldn't even get a motel room in Midland. They got rooms in Saginaw and came to Midland to find the few beleaguered, bedraggled folks remaining and ask them if they had any aches and pains and how soon they were leaving town. The traffic in Midland is humongous, and everybody's laughing and having a big time at the art fair, and the antique show you have to see to believe. The tennis tournament is sold out and there are cars all over the place. They're having trouble finding beleaguered folks. To make a long story short, with the exception of a couple of environmentalists from a local organization, they gave up. That story just went away because they could not find any substance for their story line.

The Agent Orange case, moving ponderously, with all the majesty of the law, because of the complexity of dealing with thousands of plaintiffs and multiple defendants all represented by counsel, finally came to trial in 1984 in the Brooklyn courtroom of U.S. District Court Judge Jack Weinstein. "Then the whole thing got resolved in a series of meetings that started at 5:00 on a Friday afternoon and finished in time for a 9:00 Monday morning dismissal of the prospective jurors who were assembled for the purpose of trying the definitive case," McKennon said.

The settlement established a $184 million compensation fund for the veterans, funded by the seven major producers of Agent Orange—Dow, Uniroyal, Monsanto, Hercules, Agricultural Nutrition, Diamond Shamrock, and Thompson Chemical. Judge Weinstein called for that amount to be disbursed to the veterans and their families over the succeeding 10 years. Disabled veterans received from $256 to $12,800, and the families of deceased veterans from $340 to $3,400; eventually about 39,000 veterans received money from the fund, and about 28,000 claims were denied. Veterans were required to show that they had been exposed to Agent Orange during the war. At the end of the 10-year period for filing claims, in January 1995, about $21 million still remained in the fund.

"I'm proud of the way that ended up," McKennon said. "I think it served everyone involved, including the veterans who genuinely believed they'd been harmed. The lawyers didn't take it all, as is so often the case in some of these things. I'm proudest of the Dow team involved. Leonard Rivkin, our outside attorney, from a small law firm in Long Island, essentially dominated all the big law firms and all their pontificators and great lawyers."

McKennon was involved as a senior management person, and most of the other companies did not have such a person. "This represented an important advantage because as we finally got the thing in focus, none of the other defendants wanted to step up to paying their share," McKennon said. "I was able to call Oreffice immediately and get him to call the other defendants' CEO's and say, 'Hey, guys, we've got to get this done. Do us a favor and tell your guys it's okay.' It worked and that thing was resolved in a long weekend. It was quite a remarkable achievement; it resolved the first of the major mass tort national controversy cases."[26]

Judge Weinstein's decision essentially defused the Agent Orange-dioxin crisis, and over the succeeding decade it gradually diminished, but did not die.

During the interminable dioxin controversy, which still drags on today, Dow sustained a number of black eyes, some of them caused by attempting to put its foot in its mouth. In one case nine women living in the rural community of Alsea, Oregon, had suffered miscarriages that they claimed resulted from their area having been sprayed with 2,4,5-T. A scientific study that seemed to confirm their claim proved to have serious scientific flaws. Asked about it by a clergyman, Dow's brand-new chairman of the board at that time, Earle B. Barnes, wrote the gentleman a long letter:

"Serious scientific scrutiny of the data allegedly supporting claims concerning miscarriages in northern California and Oregon, some months after spraying the forests, shows no valid relationship between the spraying and miscarriages," Barnes wrote.

> There is one other piece of information you need to know. There is a flourishing business in northern California and other northwestern states in growing marijuana in open spaces and in forests. Law officials in California have estimated the value of the crop, in three northern California counties alone, at $900 million. Marijuana is very readily destroyed by 2,4,5-T and the U.S. Forest Service has been using it to kill underbrush and the marijuana is also killed. So, Reverend, there is a lot that doesn't always meet the eye in a newspaper article.[27]

It was the first and only time Dow used that argument. Barnes, in his initiation to board chairmanship, said he had thought he was writing a personal letter to a clergyman and hardly expected it would wind up in the newspapers, which it promptly did.

In the summer of 1985 the worldwide environmental organization Greenpeace sailed up the Tittabawassee River in two small boats (the second carrying the press) and stopped opposite the Dow plant in Midland, where it proceeded to plug up the plant's outflow to the river as press cameras recorded the event. Dow had been tipped off that this would happen and all was peaceful. The Greenpeace representatives were then routinely arrested and booked at the Midland County Jail. During their brief stay one of the Greenpeace women tested positive on a venereal disease test at the jail, and although this was confidential information, the word spread fast. A Dow security guard learned it from a crony at the jail and soon the general manager knew it, too.

The general manager, Robert R. Bumb, then made a mistake; he suggested to his public relations manager, Phillip L. Schneider, that he tip off the local Greenpeace contact so that the lady would know she needed treatment. Schneider called Diane Hebert, the leader of Environmental Concerns of Midland (ECOM), and told her. It was one of his last acts as a Dow public relations manager, and one of Bumb's last suggestions as a Dow general manager. An outraged Hebert went to the press with the story, and in the resulting furor Schneider left the company and Bumb, a Ph.D. scientist, quickly changed jobs. Dow published a full-page apology for the incident in the local newspaper.

There were three lessons in this for Dow, the *Wall Street Journal* commented: (1) Don't discuss illegally leaked information with anyone; (2) Get your story straight—in this case, when the test was readministered, the first test proved to be erroneous, and there never was a case of VD; and (3) When you fail to heed lessons (1) and (2), it "can result in government investigations, lots of unwanted newspaper coverage, and a bad image." The *Detroit Free Press* called the Dow action "base orneriness."[28]

Sometimes it seemed as though Dow just could not help getting in trouble. In March 1983 the Environmental Protection Agency in Washington prepared a fairly routine document summarizing the dioxin situation, a resume of information from many sources, none of it especially new or startling. John Hernandez, the deputy EPA administrator, sent it to Dow experts Ronald O. Kagel and Joseph E. LeBeau for scientific review, a standard procedure by which specialists in the technical field involved are asked to comment on a piece of work before it is made public.

The Dow people pointed out some errors in the paper and suggested corrections, hardly startling in view of the fact that Dow had done more research and written more research papers on the subject than anyone else, over a longer period of time. In short order this routine incident exploded onto the front pages of the nation's newspapers. Valdas Adamkus, the EPA's regional director in Chicago, charged that the EPA, through Hernandez, was having its reports and recommendations "edited" by Dow Chemical.

That precipitated a long, ugly fight in the national media and television news shows, with most of the press opposing Dow rather violently; the press knew very little about "peer review," but they were expert on the subject of editing copy, and they were convinced that was what Dow had been doing. On March 17 the *New York Times* published a story saying Dow had refused to provide the EPA with information on what it was putting in the river at Midland. The story was erroneous but it was immediately picked up and used across the nation, and greatly fueled the notion that Dow was an evil and powerful force pulling the strings of government behind the scenes.

The issue became a political one as Congressman James Scheuer charged that Dow had also been given "a private review" of an EPA report on dioxin contamination in the rivers and lakes near Midland. For months the dioxin situation bounced from crisis to crisis, with hearings in Congress, investigations of various sorts, and charges of all kinds by environmental activists, politicians, and the press. The *Detroit Free Press* assigned five reporters to full-time duty looking into dioxin in Michigan.

Explanations from Dow received little or no attention. The press generally was convinced that Dow had been caught red-handed trying to manipulate a governmental agency, the EPA, and all it wanted was material that would confirm this.

At the EPA itself there were wholesale firings and resignations. Almost none of this was related to the publicity accorded Dow's activities, which had also triggered a major crisis within the agency itself. Seventeen top officials of the agency were drummed out of the service during this episode; one, Rita Lavelle, received a prison sentence.

During this period Dow once again revived the practice of a crisis publication. This one, called *Dioxin Dialog*, was telexed to some 200 Dow managers worldwide during the dioxin crisis. The company also published a monthly newsletter called *Scientific Update*, providing information about dioxin, Agent Orange, and their possible health effects, and a regular

Dioxin Media Coverage report, which reviewed what the press was saying. Dow established a dioxin management group and hired extra public relations help.

"The political aspects of the dioxin episode dominated everything else to the almost total exclusion of science," said one Dow observer. "You would not have known, in fact, that this was at base a scientific argument. It was really an argument between Republicans and Democrats disguised as an investigation into the activities of the EPA."[29]

In the long run Dow appeared to be to a large degree vindicated. As had happened in the napalm case, reporters finally began to look seriously at the science of the case. Jon Franklin, a Pulitzer Prize-winning reporter for the *Baltimore Sun* (in 1979 and 1985), was one of them.

Franklin, who as a college student had participated in protests against Dow, was assigned to Agent Orange coverage in 1982 and approached the story with "the righteous fervor that is the armor of the crusading reporter," he said; but when he had finished he concluded there was no medical evidence that dioxin had caused the cancers, birth defects, and other medical calamities that its critics had alleged. The Agent Orange story, he decided, was "a myth" manufactured by antiwar protesters, capitalized on by Vietnam veterans, and widely disseminated by an unquestioning media. He found himself swimming against a powerful current. After some years, Franklin quit the newspaper business and took a job teaching journalism at the University of Oregon.[30]

Still another controversy concerned a product called DBCP. The scriveners of picket signs quickly dubbed it "Dow's Baby Child Preventer." Chemically it was 1,2-dibromo-3-chloropropane, and it was the active ingredient in Dow's Fumazone and other fumigants used against nematodes, microscopic worms that often attack the roots of soybeans, fruits and vegetables, and other crops. There was no alternative method of fighting these pests.

In the spring of 1977 a group of production workers at the Occidental Chemical Company in Lathrop, California, hunched over their lunch boxes one day, wondering how it could be that no one in their department had fathered any children recently, and it occurred to them that it might have something to do with the DBCP they were working with.[31]

They asked for an investigation, which when completed showed that their sperm counts were so low that they were in effect sterile, apparently from working with DBCP. In late July 1977, Occidental passed its preliminary findings on to Dow and Dow began its own investigation.

Dow's sole production plant for DBCP at the time was at Magnolia, Arkansas (although the material had been made at Midland from 1957 through 1975), and Dow quickly tested the sperm count of the employees involved at Magnolia. When several of the first men tested showed low or no sperm counts, Dow on August 11, 1977, suspended production and sale of the product and notified its customers, the government agencies, and the press of this action.

It was a different kind of investigation; persuading macho males to volunteer for sperm tests is a delicate undertaking at best (obtaining a sperm sample for evaluation is a key problem). A related question was, "what is a low sperm count?"; there were no standards for a "normal" sperm count.

Dow presented its findings at a California inquiry into DBCP on October 13, documenting what was already suspected—DBCP could make men sterile. Absorption of the material through the skin appeared to be more significant than inhaling it, two Dow scientists reported. Dr. Perry J. Gehring, director of Dow's Toxicology Research Lab, traced Dow testing on DBCP from 1954, 28 studies in all before the new ones. Dr. Etcyl H. Blair, director of health and environmental research, said Dow had marketed the product only after six years of testing and research. Dow's industrial health standards based on these studies called for a maximum exposure to the material of one part per million, and this was being maintained, they said. Asked whether they knew of any effects on DBCP users in the field, they said Dow knew of none, that farmers and growers use DBCP infrequently, and unlike chemical industry production workers making the product, did not work with it on a daily basis.[32]

In Midland, about 350 employees were identified, with help from the union local, as having worked with DBCP over the years, and 249 of them agreed to participate in a testing program. They were compared to a 77-person control group of employees who had never worked with it. Dr. David B. Johns, Michigan Division medical director, who directed the study, reported that there did not appear to be a problem among the Midland employees. "On the basis of the sperm count results and comparison of the two groups I don't see any group abnormality," he said. "What I do see is a group pattern that to me appears normal."[33]

Publicity concerning DBCP continued for several months, but the picketing against Dow was by this time subsiding, and it gradually faded from the public consciousness. Continuing research showed that the men who had been exposed to the product regained sterility as time went on, and suffered no further ill effects.

Notes

1. See, for instance, the comic strip "Cheeverwood," January 12, 1986, *Houston Post*, in which mother says to son, "Honey, have you decided what you're going to do after graduation?" Son: "I'm going to take that job with Tao Chemical . . . Imagine! I could actually be helping to feed the world, lengthen lives and make the planet a better place for EVERYONE!" Mother: "Wow!" Son (reflects and a look of horror comes to his face): ". . . or I could be making napalm . . ."

2. The word "napalm" was coined from the naphthenic and palmitic acids mixed with gasoline to make the jellied form.

3. During the Vietnam War Dow was never higher than No. 75 on the list of U.S. Defense Department suppliers by dollar volume. At the height of the protests, in 1968, it was No. 98 on this list.

4. General Earle G. Wheeler, chairman, Joint Chiefs of Staff, statement to press on use of napalm in Vietnam, February 27, 1967, Washington, D.C. See also *U.S. News and World Report*, February 27, 1967.

5. H. D. Doan, "Why Does Dow Chemical Make Napalm?," *Wall Street Journal*, December 8, 1967 (reprinted and widely distributed by the company).

6. "Dow Chemical Company," Harvard Business School Case Study 1CH 12G29, BSI 73R (Harvard College, 1968), 10.

7. The 37 issues of *Napalm News* form a diary of Dow's misadventures during this period and are a rich source of information concerning the napalm demonstrations.

8. B. Strelnikov, "Save Yourself Through the Window, Mr. Jones," *Pravda*, December 15, 1967.

9. Oral History, H. D. Doan, July 29 and August 2, 1988, and January 17, 1989.

10. Oral History, Carl A. Gerstacker, July 21, 1988.

11. Undated letter, circa December 1, 1967, Robert S. McNamara to H. D. Doan. The approach to the Pentagon was of course undertaken with the knowledge and approval of the troika; it was typical of Dow to entrust responsibilities of this magnitude to youthful underlings.

12. "The Napalm Story," *Time* magazine, March 24, 1967.

13. "A Doctor Looks at Vietnam," *Dow Diamond* 31, no. 4 (1968). An article in *Ramparts* magazine, December 1966, claimed that one million children had been wounded or burned in Vietnam in the previous five years. The *Ramparts* article was the basis of many of the protests against the manufacture and use of napalm.

14. There were many accounts of this meeting. See, e.g., "Dow Chemical Meeting Backs Production of Napalm; Antiwar Protesters Rubuffed," *Wall Street Journal*, May 9, 1968; "Dow Plays It Cool on Napalm Production Protest," *Toledo Blade*, May 12, 1968; "Dow Refuses to Yield on Napalm Policy," *Tucson* (Az.) *Daily Star*, May 9, 1968; "Dow Protesters Fail," *Minneapolis Star*, May 11, 1968; "Placards and Proxies at Dow Chemical's Meeting," *National Observer*, May 13, 1968.

15. "Antiwar Protesters Wreck Dow Office," *Baltimore Sun*, March 23, 1969.

16. Ibid.

17. Carl A. Gerstacker, "Living With Confrontation," talk to New York Financial Writers, New York, June 3, 1970.

18. The incident was doubly ironic in that Standard of California had been the principal supplier of napalm during World War II through its subsidiary, the Oronite Chemical Company, leading producer of the naphthenic acid used to make it.

19. "Answers to Some Questions Regarding Dow and Bud Antle, Inc.," Dow Internal News Service, December 23, 1970. See also Oral History, H. D. Doan.

20. 2,4,5-T is made by treating 1,2,4,5-tetrachlorobenzene with strong caustic at high temperatures for several hours. Manufacturing processes that do not carefully control temperatures and alkalinity increase the probability of dioxin formation.

21. See Monsanto scientists George R. Harvey and Jay D. Mann, "Picloram in Vietnam," *Scientist and Citizen*, September 1968.

22. Warren B. Crummett, "Dioxin: Molecule or What?" (unpublished ms., 1994). The author is grateful to Dr. Crummett, a retired research fellow of Dow, for permission to read this journal of his long and intimate association with dioxin and the crises attendant to it.

23. See Cindy Crain Newman, "Dow Chemical Withdraws from 2,4,5-T Business in the U.S., a Case Study," Dow internal document, October 14, 1983, Post Street Archives. Oral History, Paul F. Oreffice, August 1, 1988.

24. Oral History, Keith R. McKennon, June 9, 1993. At Times Beach, Missouri, in 1982, the United States moved out all 2,240 residents and then bought out and destroyed the town's buildings, at a cost of $240 million. The official who recommended this action, R. Vernon Houk, director of the Center for

Environmental Health at the Centers for Disease Control, said in 1994 that "it looks as though the evacuation was unnecessary." At Love Canal, where toxic wastes had been buried, dioxin was a major concern, but not the only one. In 1995 the government began moving people back to the Love Canal area.

25. Crummett, "Dioxin: Molecule or What?" The ability to analyze materials in parts per quadrillion, it should be noted, poses a whole new series of problems for mankind; we do not know the "normal" content of the elements or compounds we may find in air or water samples at this level, for we have never been able to measure this precisely. We do know, for example, that it is now virtually impossible technically to comply with the U.S. law (the "Delaney clause" of the Food and Drug Act) requiring a zero content of any cancer-causing material in any foodstuff. As this incredibly fine analytical ability is perfected it will pose new problems of this nature.

26. Oral History, K. R. McKennon.

27. Earle B. Barnes to Rev. Robert E. Roos, chancellor of the Roman Catholic Diocese of Albany, November 1, 1979.

28. Dale D. Buss, "If this Is How They're Beginning Their Campaign, How Will It End?" *Wall Street Journal*, October 4, 1985.

29. E. N. Brandt, "Dow and Dioxin, A Case Study," Public Relations Seminar, Boca Raton, Florida, May 13-16, 1984.

30. David Shaw, "Controversial Stories Go Against the Grain," *Los Angeles Times*, September 11, 1994.

31. DBCP was manufactured by Dow, Occidental Chemical, Shell Chemical, and the Dead Sea Works of Israel.

32. See "Q. and A. on DBCP," Dow news release, August 25, 1977, and "Dow Participates in California Public Inquiry on DBCP," Dow news release, October 13, 1977.

33. "DBCP Update" and "Michigan Division Fertility Study Results," *Brinewell* 36, no. 6 (November/December 1977): 4-6.

FOURTEEN

DOW IN EUROPE

I.

Clayton Shoemaker, in the spring of 1952 the newly minted president of a newly minted organization called Dow International, had his first goal firmly in mind: to establish a Dow bridgehead in Europe. Dow's worldwide sales had reached $200 million three years before, but exports to Europe accounted for only $1.5 million of that sum, and he saw Europe as a glorious opportunity.

Ted Knapp, a member of Dow's three-man export department in Midland, had been visiting Europe two or three times a year since 1949, dealing with the distributors of Dow products there, but with the constantly increasing travel back and forth, consuming up to 11 months per year, he had told Shoemaker, "Traveling all the time is not a civilized way to live. Why don't I just move to Europe?"[1]

Shoemaker readily agreed, and pondered where to establish the first Dow office in Europe. He narrowed the choices to Brussels and Zurich. Both had good airports and good banking, and they were the only two European cities at the time that had telex service, critical to Dow for long-distance order handling.

"I think we probably would have ended up in Brussels except that on his last night in Brussels, when he went there to evaluate it, two things happened to Clayton Shoemaker," Knapp said. "He found bedbugs in his bed, and he lost his briefcase. That's how we ended up in Zurich."

In Zurich Shoemaker talked to John Van Stirum, owner and manager of American Business Counselors, who had an office over a Movenpick restaurant at 21 Dreikonigstrasse downtown. A few months later Van Stirum closed his operation and Dow took over the premises, including Van Stirum's secretary, Erica Widmer, and Dow Chemical Europe was formed there with three employees—Knapp, Widmer, and Bob Kincaid, who had recently joined the export group.

When Dow expanded into Latin America two years later, Kincaid was sent to Montevideo to open the first Dow office in Latin America. Van Stirum, a Dutch citizen, shortly became a Dow employee himself and rose to become assistant treasurer of the parent company and president of the Dow Bank.

The first knotty problem faced by the infant firm on Dreikonigstrasse was obtaining work permits for Switzerland. Even with L. I. Doan and the top management of the company backing the effort, plus the sponsorship of such people as the managing directors of the Ciba Company and the Union Bank of Switzerland, it took nine months to get work permits for Knapp and Kincaid.

Two years later, when Dow asked for a third work permit—for young Zoltan Merszei, who had arrived from Toronto to become the plastics sales manager for Europe—the Swiss objected. "You are asking to increase your workforce by 50 percent," they told Dow. Merszei and his wife, Illy, and their three small children spent the next nine months living at the Hotel Wedebruge in The Hague, during which time an unhappy Merszei lobbied for the removal of Dow European headquarters to that city.

Growth of Dow Chemical Europe was very slow in those early years, and Knapp and his colleagues continued to sell through sales agents or representatives all over Europe, as Herbert Dow had done a half century before. By 1958 the Dow population in Europe was 10, and when headquarters decreed a 10 percent cut in manpower that year, Knapp had to fly to Midland to save cutting the force by one person.

The expanding world market for Dow plastics fueled the early growth. In 1954 Dow built its first polystyrene plastics plant in Europe jointly with The Distillers Company Ltd., and the new firm, called Distrene Ltd., began production at Barry, South Wales, in August 1955. (Dow took over sole ownership of Distrene in 1968.)[2]

In 1955 Dow Europe took another big step forward with establishment of "the Botlek"—in a section of the Rotterdam port called by that name—the rationale being that Dow needed a central warehousing point in Europe for the growing amounts of product it was importing to the continent. Dow's products would flow from the United States, mainly from Texas, to the Botlek, and be shipped from there to customers across the continent.

Formally known as Nederlandsche Dow Maatschappij N.V., or "NDM," with Van Stirum as general manager, it served as Dow's main gateway to Europe for many years, until the company began to build its own major production plants on the continent. The Botlek area was being reclaimed from the sea by the Dutch, as they had been doing for centuries, and the land on which Dow now began building storage tanks and production plants had been under 30 feet of seawater only three years before. The first small production facility, a latex plant, was built there in 1960.

Dow's acquisition of the Dobeckmun packaging firm in 1957 had a marked impact on Dow Europe. Dobeckmun had production and marketing facilities across Europe for the metallic decorative fiber called Lurex, including a plant in Amsterdam (its European headquarters), a showroom in London, and plants at Windsor Forest in England and St. Etienne, France. Some of the early Dow offices in Europe were housed in these facilities.

Growth began in earnest in 1958. Early that year Dow opened its second European sales office at Rotterdam, handy to the Botlek. In March a third office was opened, at Stockholm. That same year the first agricultural chemicals operation was initiated with the formation of Dow Agrochemicals Ltd., which broke ground for a plant at King's Lynn, England. Offices were opened the next year in London, and in Johannesburg, South Africa, the first Dow office in Africa.

The company's first operations in France began in 1959 with the formation of Plastichimie, owned jointly by the Pechiney Company and Dow. It built a polystyrene plant at Ribécourt, France.

There was also a palace revolution in 1959. One fine morning Ted Knapp was Dow's general manager for Europe, with Zoltan Merszei, plastics marketing manager, as one of his lieutenants. By nightfall, Zoltan Merszei was Dow general manager for Europe and Ted Knapp was one of his lieutenants. This coup was engineered by Merszei with the blessing of Ben Branch, president of Dow International, but quickly and quietly accepted by Knapp.

"It's unusual, I think, for someone to have people working for you who then become your bosses," Knapp said later. "Quite often, when that happens, one or the other leaves, usually the person who has been stepped over, but that never bothered me particularly. I wasn't about to spend 20 hours a day competing with those people."

Ted Knapp, the first Dow European, was one of those unusual persons who have often popped up in Dow. His coworkers described him as a loner, "reserved and rather distant," a bibliophile and a gourmet cook, and said that in many ways he became "more European than the Europeans."

"I left the U.S. because I liked the European way of life," he said, "and I liked Switzerland particularly, where there wasn't the materialism that there is in the U.S. Unfortunately, Europe became just as materialistic as the U.S.; everyone wanted a washer and a freezer and a car."

"I like to be alone, and I like nature," he said. "You see more of the country when you walk than if you ride. I'm just a hiker. I've hiked from easternmost Switzerland to westernmost Switzerland, northernmost Switzerland to southernmost Switzerland, half a dozen times, and I've walked all the major rivers, from their source to where they leave Switzerland."

When he retired in 1982 he was asked to name his best experience during his 30 years with Dow Europe. "My best experience," he said, "was any time I flew out of Midland on my way back to Zurich."

Knapp and Kincaid built a core of mainly Swiss employees (the work permit rules strongly encouraged it) who became the old faithfuls of Dow Europe: Henry Schoch, who took charge of Dow's relationships with Swiss governmental units and spent his entire career with Dow; Heidi Baur, who moved over from Credit Suisse and became Dow's first inside saleslady in Europe; Ed Faessler, who became a key executive of the Dow Bank; Peter W. Meier, who became Dow's first manager in Germany, and later in Brazil; Luc Wortmann; and Max Friedli. Most of them were recruited through want ads in the local newspapers; Meier came from a distributor firm.[3]

By 1960 Dowintal, as it was known, had opened offices in Milan, Italy, and Frankfurt, Germany, its sixth and seventh in Europe, and was just getting started.

When Ted Doan and the troika reorganized the company globally in 1965, Dow Chemical Europe was suddenly no longer simply Dow's branch office in Europe but a freestanding headquarters of its own, with its own prerogatives and president. By this time there were growing young Dow organizations in most of the key European nations, and Europeans had been recruited and were assuming key positions as "country managers," heading up the Dow organizations in these countries.

Mac Whiting called a general meeting of Dow International that year to plan the changeover and draw blueprints for the new era. "The Brunnen meeting," as it was called (it was held in Brunnen, Switzerland) marked Dow Europe's coming of age.

A photo of the meeting shows the 45 participants who were to build Dow Europe into a major force on the continent in the next 20 years. They are mostly Americans, but already a third are Europeans, with an admixture of Canadians and other nationalities. There are a few veterans—Bob Helfenstein (Swiss), Manuel Maza (Cuban), Art Young (British-born American)—but they are for the most part youthful-looking and eager. In their midst is their leader, Zoltan Merszei, dapper and confident as always. Eight of the participants sooner or later became members of the parent company board of directors. Many of the others became country managers in Europe or elsewhere, and all enjoyed positions of considerable trust and success in the company.

The only non-Dow participant in the photo is Prof. Vernon Michelson, a scholarly, soft-spoken business professor from Case-Western Reserve University who was an outside consultant to Dow—probably the most influential outside consultant in the company's history. His assignment was to observe the goings-on at Brunnen and make suggestions concerning any oversights or errors he perceived.

It was Vern Michelson who proposed what became known as the "bird-watching" program. The Europeans who were becoming Dow leaders in their countries needed to spend time in the United States, he told Whiting, to get acquainted with the company's culture, its leaders, its methodology; otherwise, he said, a Dow France or a Dow Hellas a few years from then might not resemble Dow U.S.A. or anything Dow at all.

He proposed that these young managers spend at least six or eight months, mainly in Midland, as a learning experience, not doing a specific job but just soaking up know-how, and then return to their native European heath and to their usual jobs. They should spend their time in the United States, he said, "watching closely, and perhaps learning something." "Just like bird-watching," Whiting said.

The first shipment of bird-watchers arrived in Midland in the fall of 1965, half a dozen of them with their families. They were provided houses to live in, usually the homes of Dow managers who were on an overseas assignment somewhere, and assigned a heavy regime of meeting Dow people and learning about various products and operations. In the first group were Duco Akkerman (Dutch), Nils Hernborg (Swedish), Yves Crepet (French), Rene Wildi (Swiss), and Peter Meier (Swiss); others followed at later dates.

The program was full of surprises for the Europeans (and their families, many of whom spoke little or no English), who were put through such programs as sensitivity training and who spent an intensive week or two in this department or that, followed by an intensive week or two in another department, "learning the ropes." Hernborg told Whiting he felt useless not doing an actual job, and a few days later found himself assigned to a sales desk in John Henske's chemicals department, selling chemicals in the United States for the remainder of his sojourn.

Christiane Crepet (Mrs. Yves) asked a newfound Midland friend why Americans did not have decent table salt. "It's so coarse, and you have to pick a lot of impurities out of it before you can use it," she said. It turned out she had bought rock salt, used for melting snow on sidewalks.

For all its simplicity, "bird-watching" worked. The Europeans quickly soaked up "the Dow way" of doing things, and returned home to build Dow Europe.

II.

The first shipload of Dow products from the United States arrived at the Botlek in early February of 1955 aboard the Dow charter vessel *Marine Chemist*. With a product pipeline in place, Dow's presence in Europe began growing with vigor. By 1957 the Botlek was the second largest consumer of steel drums for repackaging in all of the Netherlands.

In 1961 the first Botlek production plant, a latex facility, came onstream. The Rotterdam sales office, opened only three years before, was moved to Brussels and became the West Europe hub of the company, its sales center for Belgium, France, Holland, Spain, Portugal, and North Africa.

Ben Branch, heading up Dow International, had even bigger ambitions. He wanted to build a major chemical complex in Europe. "We designed a plant and called it the Benelux plant [named for Belgium-Netherlands-Luxembourg] because we didn't know in which of these countries it was going to go," recalled Hunter Henry, who became its project manager. "Dow looked at a number of plant sites and eventually selected one in Terneuzen, on an estuary of the Wester Schelde. They put together a project team to build this plant on 86 hectares of polder land, all below sea level."[4]

Terneuzen became Dow's largest chemical complex in Europe. Henry went on from this assignment ultimately to become president of Dow U.S.A. and executive vice president of the parent company.

Before he went to Europe Henry was an unheralded young chemical engineer, assistant superintendent of the ethylene oxide and glycol plant in Dow's Texas Division. When his superintendent turned it down, he was offered an opportunity to go to Terneuzen as project engineer for the ethylene glycol and related plants to be built there, and accepted it. Henry and three other engineers (John Savaso, George McDaniel, and Roy Walker) were to build Terneuzen as assistants to the project manager, Robert H. ("Texas Bob") Smith, who would then become works manager.

On the Monday morning they were to begin working on the project they gathered in Rotterdam, but Texas Bob did not show up. "About four o'clock in the afternoon, Bob came in; he'd been ill over the weekend," Henry remembered.

Tuesday he didn't show up. Then I got a call from Ed Hensley, the chief engineer for Dowintal, who said, "Hunter, you are acting project manager. Bob is ill; we're going to have to take him home." I was scared to death. Here I am, I'm 33 years old, and really, what do I know? I remember I went to open the bids from the contractors to build Terneuzen, and I'd never opened bids before. I asked whether I was supposed to open them here, or am I supposed to open them somewhere else? "You open them here," somebody said. I was pretty green.

Afterward one of the contractors approached him and said he realized Henry didn't understand "how these things work," and that he would like to "fix up my bid to be in better tune with what you want." Henry said he was sorry but the low bid was Fluor-Schyflot, "and that's who I'm going to award the bid to."

He called Hensley to warn him he might get a visit from an unhappy contractor, and told him of their conversation. Hensley said, "You did the right thing. He'll come see me." The contractor flew to Midland and told Hensley that Henry just didn't understand the bid process. Hensley told him, "No, Henry gave you the right answer." He asked Hensley, "Who's your boss?" Ed said, "I can tell you who it is, but he's going to tell you the same thing."

"I had worked in the plants, but you don't learn lessons like that in the plants," Henry said. "That was really my first lesson on what the Dow Chemical Company stands for in terms of doing what's right."

Henry found himself serving not only as project manager for Terneuzen but as its general manager later. From there he went on, at age 36, to be vice president of manufacturing in Zurich.

"First thing you know, Ben Branch and everybody in Dow International thought we were the greatest," he said. "He called us 'those young guys down there in Terneuzen, slopping around in the mud.' Branch was so proud of his young troops, and we couldn't do him any wrong. I kept telling our folks, 'Let's don't start believing all that press, because we aren't that good. They're looking for somebody to solve their problem, and we look like we're solving their problem.'"

The first six production plants started up at Terneuzen late in 1964, and that November the Dow board of directors came to Europe. During the trip, the city of Terneuzen dedicated the road leading to the Dow plant as "Herbert H. Dow-Weg" in the presence of two of Herbert Dow's grandsons, Herbert Dow II and Ted Doan.

Both the Botlek and Terneuzen continued to expand in the following years. Units to produce brake fluids, antifreeze, and saran resins were built at the Botlek. Terneuzen had 14 major production plants and represented an investment of $250 million by 1971 and was still growing. By then Dow was planning on more land for expansion and was projecting the taking from the sea of a new polder to be called Mosselbanken.

On May 24, 1965, the Terneuzen complex was formally dedicated by Prince Bernhard of the Netherlands, who arrived in a helicopter to be greeted by Zoltan Merszei; Colin Robertson, Dow's country manager for the Netherlands; and several hundred other officials.[5]

Ben Branch told the assemblage that Dutch global corporations such as Shell and Unilever had led the way to international success and that "Dow is following the same pattern. In the United States," he said, "Shell is considered as an American, not a Dutch company. This is in my opinion an example worth emulating. We are proceeding in this pattern ourselves."

Prince Bernhard punched out a message to Ted Doan in Midland on the telex machine in the Terneuzen front office with the help of Merszei and Robertson: "I am pleased to advise that the official opening of your new Terneuzen plant took place a few minutes ago. I wish you and your company good luck for the future. Bernhard."[6]

Dow had been recruiting local personnel accustomed to "hard werken," in the Dutch phrase, in the previous months and training them to run a chemical plant, and most of them were delighted with their new way of life. Piet Michielsen, for example, who became a "jack of all trades" in the new plant, had been a greengrocer in the area, selling vegetables to housewives in the time-honored way, door to door with a horse and cart. As a greengrocer he had risen each morning at 4 A.M. and worked until 7 P.M.; now, in his new Dow job, he worked from 7:30 A.M. to 5 P.M. Piet told a local newspaper he "never wanted to leave" his Dow job.[7]

May 24, the local newspaper said, was "een grote dag [a great day] in Terneuzen."

Ed Faessler, a Swiss, was hired and sent to the Netherlands to work with Van Stirum as a "switch expert," a specialty that was needed because after World War II most countries did not have dollars with which to buy U.S. goods, and the United States was the only country producing many of the products the world needed at the time. A host of bilateral trade agreements were substituted, and trade imbalances were rectified through "clearing accounts," which could be bought at a discount by companies such as Dow and sold against dollars to enable the purchase of U.S. goods such as chemicals.[8]

Later on the situation eased—in 1963 Dow bought an interest in the Mendes Gans Bank in Amsterdam, which became its principal clearinghouse for exchanging European currencies—and Faessler moved back to Zurich, where he helped build the Dow Bank.

The centerpieces at Terneuzen were its two giant naphtha crackers, each with a production capacity of 400,000 metric tons annually. The first, built in 1967, was Dow's first big hydrocarbon cracker outside the United States. The second, added in 1975, made Dow a major force in the European chemical world, providing raw materials upstream and permitting expansion of the product line downstream.

In 1973 Dow built its first plant in Belgium, at Tessenderlo, a facility to produce polystyrene and high-density polyethylene plastics.

By the early 1990s Dow's styrene capacity at Terneuzen had stabilized at about one million tons per year, even though Styrene IV (Styrene production unit No. 4) had been damaged by a fire on June 4, 1992—fortunately there were no casualties or environmental damage—and knocked out until late summer 1993.

Terneuzen also became a world factor in the benzene aromatics field with 900,000 tons of annual capacity. It is Dow's only benzene facility in Europe.[9]

Why did Dow grow so rapidly in Europe? Zoltan Merszei once said he had six basic rules for Dow Chemical Europe:

1. Be tops in technology, even in Europe, the cradle of chemistry;
2. Be more efficient than your competitors;
3. Import from the United States only products and know-how that have been successful there;
4. Keep the product line simple by being selective;
5. Create a multimarket organization, working with many languages and legal structures, for this simplified product line; and
6. Avoid business frills by limiting unneeded support functions.[10]

Charley Doscher, who as Dow's marketing chief in Europe for most of this period of growth (1961–80) was in a position to know, said there were three main factors in Dow Europe's success. "The biggest advantage we had in Dow Europe," he said,

was the support of Ben Branch; without that Dow Europe wouldn't be here today. Europe would have been involved with Dow in a much smaller way. The second was that we had Zoltan. And the third was that we took the attitude, perhaps in some respects naively, that the Common Market actually existed. The Europeans didn't take that view; to them the Common Market really didn't exist. They were aware of the Common Market, but not that they would act as though it really existed.[11]

"For instance, when we looked at where we should build the first big petrochemical plant," Doscher said,

we selected Terneuzen. We didn't worry that it was in Holland, a very small market. One could ask, "Why don't you build in the biggest market, in Germany?" What we did is take the whole market and said, "Where is the most advantageous place to locate this plant, because this plant is going to supply the whole Common Market?" A European company wouldn't have done it that way. They would have said, "We're Germans, we'll put this plant someplace in Germany." Or, "We're French, we'll put this plant someplace in France; look at the home market first." But we didn't have a home market. The home market for us had to be all of Europe. I think that was the next biggest reason for success, because then we placed the plants where the logistics were the most favorable, where employment was the most favorable, where quality of labor was the most favorable, where you would have it on the water so you could make shipments by water, where you had good people, and where you were sort of in the middle of the total market. That was a tremendous advantage.

Another key factor was building a market position by importing from the United States before building a European plant to produce it. "We also had the big advantage that some other companies may not have had in that we had the Texas Division," Doscher said. "The Texas Division was the division that was behind the growth of Dow Europe, because of their location and because of the size of their production," he said. "They generally had incremental production capacity vis-à-vis the ship to Europe, so we thought we ought to build a market position first in the downstream products and then back that up later with plants."

"We decided that if we're going to build a polystyrene plant, for example, we'd eventually want to put in an ethylene plant, so we might as well pick a site and build a downstream plant on the site where we could build the upstream plant eventually," he said, "It seemed quite simple to chemical people."

Compared to other companies, Dow was willing to invest in these big commodity plants where others were not, a major difference in Doscher's view. "I remember that we talked with Union Carbide, for instance, for years about selling them ethylene, because they were very reluctant to put up an ethylene plant in Europe. They didn't have the management conviction to do that. That was their major mistake. They didn't do that, and eventually they withdrew from Europe."

Another reason other U.S. companies failed to take advantage of the European opportunities was that they sent people to Europe on short-term assignments. "What we did in Europe was to transfer people who knew the company's business from Midland or some other place in the States and we would leave them in Europe as long as they were doing well," Doscher said.

> Carbide sent people over for two years. We used to watch the turntable. A guy would come, and it would take him a year to understand where Antwerp is and where the markets are. The second year he'd start to produce and before he could produce much they'd transfer him back to the States. The new guy would come and start the thing all over again, whereas Dow people stayed. The tour of duty was open-ended. Our people got to know the territories and the executives in the business. Often a customer would say, "You know, it's amazing how long Dow people stay in Europe."

III.

In his *History of the World, 1914-1991*, the British historian Eric Hobsbawm terms the period from 1950 to 1973 the "Golden Age" of the twentieth century.[12] For Dow Chemical in Europe it was very much a "golden age," and the meteoric growth of Dow Chemical in Spain was the very model of that success. Starting at zero, the company grew to become the largest chemical firm in the country.

The principal architects of Dow's achievement in Spain were Paul Oreffice and Ignacio Artola.

In his travels about Europe in the 1950s, Dr. Wilhelm Hirschkind, special assistant to Dow President Leland I. Doan, had met in Bilbao with friends at the Union Quimica del Norte de Espana—Unquinesa. Hirschkind reported to his Dow colleagues that the Spaniards were interested in renovating an aging business and moving into plastics, and Ben Branch and Zoltan Merszei began to explore those interests.

Early in 1960 Dow purchased a half interest in Unquinesa, changed its name to Dow-Unquinesa, and began to plan its future. Branch proposed to Oreffice, then Dow's manager in Brazil, that he move to Spain and become commercial director of the firm.

"I was not thrilled," Oreffice said, "for two reasons. One was Franco—I was worried about going to a fascist-type dictatorship, and I perceived it as being a very tight dictatorship. I later learned that it really wasn't. And second, I would be going in as commercial director and reporting to a Spaniard running the show and I was worried about what I could do." When he told Branch of these concerns, Branch said the key Spaniards, the two managing directors, were in town and were invited to a cocktail party at Lee Doan's house at five o'clock that day.[13]

"You're invited to the party too," Branch told him, "if you accept the job. If not, you can't come." Oreffice swallowed his concerns and responded that if Ben thought it was the right thing to do, he'd do it, and went to the party to meet his new Spanish bosses.

"I found out that what Ben had told me was absolutely right," Oreffice said. "While Franco had started out as a very tough dictator, he was smart enough in his later years to let loose of the reins. In Spain, you never knew you had a dictatorship; he was the smartest dictator around because dictators become more and more centralized, and he was the opposite." Oreffice arrived in Bilbao after some delay—finding his successor in Brazil took more time than expected—and in the interim he was given a mandate to "clean the place up."

I found a company with about $8 million in sales and 3,100 employees, shot through with corruption," Oreffice said. "All the insurance was in the hands of the brother of one of the managing directors. All the shipping was in the hands of a brother-in-law. The company was overpaying for all of its services. There were 28 Mercedes with 27 chauffeurs at the disposal of management. On one floor the two managing directors had their offices and living rooms where they received people—6,000 or 8,000 square feet for two people. No wonder we were losing money.

Their way of not showing a loss was that they did not depreciate, and they paid essentially no taxes, he discovered. "The first meeting I attended, at which they decided what to do with the profits of the year, went something like this. 'How much do we want to pay in dividends? How much do we distribute to the directors? How much do we give the government in taxes? Ten? No, that's too much. Five? Two, two. Give them two. Is there anything left for depreciation? Yes, maybe there's two left for depreciation.' It was obvious we were decapitalizing the company, because we paid big dividends, off the top."

Oreffice went to the Count of Cadagua, the chairman of the board, "a wonderful gentleman, one of the most marvelous human beings I've ever met." He told him the company was decapitalizing, "so we've got to do some proper accounting, cut the dividend to zero, shut down a bunch of plants that are inefficient, and fire the two managing directors who are the founders of the company, because they set the example for everything else."

After several hours of questioning, the Count said, "Senor Oreffice, I have three roles. I am the board chairman of the company; I am chairman of the Banco de Vizcaya, the largest single shareholder aside from Dow; and I am the largest individual shareholder. As a shareholder I'm ready to back your program 100 percent, but in my other two capacities I need to ask more questions." The two men met the following evening, and the evening after that.

At the end of the third evening the Count said he was ready to back Oreffice and that he personally would take care of disposing of the two managing directors. The two men then set about their program.

One of the difficulties, Oreffice said, was that in Spain (as in other European nations) you cannot dismiss an employee without cause, but from $8 million in sales and 3,100 employees the company moved in Oreffice's three years there to $30 million in sales and 1,600 employees. This trend continued; by the 1990s sales were up to the $400 million level and the employee population was still around 1,600 or 1,700.

Oreffice went to the Minister of Industry, Gregorio Lopes Bravo (later Spain's prime minister), and said, "We have a huge problem. I've got to get rid of a lot of people. Under the law I can't do it. Help me."

Under a program that the two devised, Dow-Unquinesa told people, "Here's five months pay. You're out of a job here, but go to so-and-so; they have a job for you." Lopes Bravo put pressure on industries in the area to take people from Dow-Unquinesa. "We were able to dispose of almost a thousand people that way," Oreffice said. This could be done because at that time, "there were plenty of jobs and no unemployment in Spain," as Artola explained it.

"We shut down all the small, old plants while we built plants for new (to Spain) Dow products like Styron and polyethylene," Oreffice said. "It was a terrible time, a very difficult time. The company we had bought was really a pig in a poke, but it gave us a base. We're the biggest chemical company in Spain now, and we couldn't have done it without that base. But it was a base; we were known; we were not just foreigners walking in."

In 1961 Dow-Unquinesa began construction of a polystyrene plant at Bilbao and it came on stream in October, 1963. In 1964 the firm acquired a plant site at Tarragona, near a new government refinery in the highly industrial northeast of Spain, and began to plan an ethylene unit there. Groundbreaking took place in 1965 and a polyethylene plant came on stream in April, 1966.

A new generation of Dow leadership was forming during these building days in Europe. There Oreffice formed close relationships with Bob Lundeen, a later board chairman, who had become business development manager for Dow International and was a frequent visitor to Spain. Hunter Henry, later president of Dow U.S.A., was project manager for the big plant

Dow was building at Terneuzen in the Netherlands. Zoltan Merszei, future CEO of the company, was in and out of Spain from Zurich.

In August 1965 Oreffice was called to Midland. Macauley Whiting told him Dow was considering a far-reaching global reorganization, and that the plan called for geographical area headquarters to be established in the four corners of the earth; the two relatively undeveloped areas to be organized (or reorganized) were Latin America and the Pacific. "Sometime around the middle of next year," Whiting told him, "we'd like to set up Dow Latin America, with you as general manager, and Dow Pacific, with Bob Lundeen as chief." Armed with this intelligence Oreffice quietly began to organize a staff for the new Dow Latin American headquarters and to prepare to leave Bilbao. Joe Pinotti arrived to succeed him in Spain, as he had once before in Italy, and continued the clean-up Oreffice had begun.

Ignacio Artola, the other main pioneer figure in Dow Espana, had fought in the Spanish Civil War (1936-39) as a 16-year-old volunteer. A Basque, an aristocrat and a monarchist, he had survived two years of combat, "on the side of Francisco Franco against the communists." After the war (he was the 4th of 12 children), he took a law degree and then followed his father into banking, beginning at Banco Bilbao in 1945 and spending three years in London with the bank. In 1955 he founded an import-export business, Compania Atlantica de Transacciones, CAT, with a partner. The partners wrote a list of American companies they obtained from the U.S. embassy, saying they wanted to import fertilizers, and received a response from Dow, saying, "We don't make fertilizers, but here's what we do make," enclosing a catalog of Dow products.[14]

Realizing that Dow did not have a sales representative in Spain, Artola responded by asking to become Dow's agent. A few weeks later Zoltan Merszei arrived in Madrid and engaged CAT as Dow's Spanish sales representative. CAT began selling Dow styrene to the Unquinesa plant at Bilbao, and Artola was subsequently instrumental in the formation of Dow-Unquinesa (of which he became a director), and also in a public tender made later by which Dow became full owner, the first public tender made in Spain.

Tarragona rapidly grew into the hub of Dow production in Spain, outdistancing Bilbao even though plants for some key Dow products—such as latex and Styrofoam—were built near Bilbao. Bilbao was also the only place in Europe where Dow made titanium oxide. Some 60 or 70 percent of the Spanish plastics industry and market is located in Spain's Catalan northeast, however, and that was where the greatest growth occurred. Soon Dow was branching into other products there, such as Coyden, the coccidiostat. In 1980 it bought one of two crackers that Empetrol, the Spanish government refinery, had built in Tarragona; one, it had turned out, was enough for the refinery. In 1967 Franco himself came to Tarragona to dedicate the Dow-Unquinesa polyethylene plant.[15]

In 1966 Artola left CAT in the hands of his partner and moved over to the Dow payroll. Soon he was engaged in selling off some of the surplus pieces of Dow-Unquinesa, such as a plant at Mataporquera, in the mountainous north of Spain, which made calcium carbide (for a nearby Solvay plant) and ferroalloys, with 250 employees. When Solvay switched to a different technology the plant was left with no market for its product, and plans were made to dismiss the 250 employees. Artola was able to find a business group who converted the plant and its furnaces completely to ferroalloys. "We paid them money to take over the plant," Artola said, "but we paid them perhaps half a million dollars and saved $2 million."

"We sold a plant that made phenolic and formaldehyde resins, used for making glues, to Borden Chemicals, and we sold the sulfuric acid plant in Bilbao to a consortium, always with the condition that they took over the people with the plant," he said. "We made a profit on one of the subsidiaries of $22 million," Artola said. "With what we got by selling the subsidiaries, we paid for the expansions."

Dow took an option on a 500 hectare (1,250 acre) site in the southwest of Spain at Huelva, "a beautiful piece of land, with a mile of white sand beach," Artola said, with salt domes beneath it, and began to plan a $1 billion project involving some 30 plants with a cracker, to produce chlorine, chlorinated solvents, and vinyl chloride monomer, the whole based on propane. Dow drilled and confirmed the salt deposits. Branch and Merszei took the Spanish proposal to the Dow board and reported back that they had an "Oklahoma guarantee" (a promise to approve, in Dow vernacular). "The price of the propane was going to be $30 a ton cheaper than in the United States," Artola said.

In Huelva Dow encountered the serious opposition of Explosivos Rio Tinto Company (ERT), one of the largest firms in Spain and the dominant firm in the Andalusian area, where it had mines, a refinery, fertilizer production facilities, and other interests. "ERT traditionally had the field to itself in that area, so they wanted to stop our operation," Artola said. "Do you know what they did? You had to present the details of a project locally, and when we presented the Huelva project they made a copy of it the same day, and the next day hand-delivered (to the government) a project that was a copy of ours. One is an American company and the other is a Spanish company, so the Spanish company would have preference. I tell you, the fights were great; I bled myself there. Finally we won, but we fought like hell."

For a variety of reasons, however, the Huelva project was never built. ERT later went "belly up." "They were so crazy that they went bankrupt," Artola said. "They agreed with their creditors that they would pay their debts at a reduced rate and they committed to sell assets to repay the creditors. They owed Dow some money, but not much. Out of that Dow and Empetrol took over a low-density polyethylene plant in Tarragona, half and half."

Frank Popoff, who had supported purchase of the cracker at Tarragona (which had become very profitable for Dow), also supported purchase of the polyethylene plant. (Popoff, who had become president of Dow Europe in 1981, was a future chief executive of the company.) "One day when we wanted authorization to go ahead with the polyethylene plant I was in Frank's office (in Horgen) and he was talking to Oreffice (in Midland)," Artola remembered. "He passed me the telephone and I said, 'Paul, I commit to pay back this plant in one year.' He said, 'Well, I authorize it, but only on that basis, that you pay it back in one year.' We paid it back in eight months."

When he moved to Dow in 1966 Artola agreed to spend 18-24 months with Dow in the United States to get acquainted with Dow and Dow methods, and he spent that time at the

Dow Latin American headquarters in Coral Gables, Florida, working with Bill Fletcher in business development there and taking Dow orientation courses in Midland. "Sometimes I felt very old because I was 45 at the time, and I was taking those courses with boys," Artola said, "but I was very happy working with those boys."

In 1970 he became Dow's country manager in Spain and remained in that position until his retirement in 1984. Charley Doscher, Dow's chief of marketing in Europe during that time, said Artola was not only the most powerful of Dow's country managers in Europe but the best.[16] There was never any question who was in charge of Dow's business in Spain; it was Artola.

At three-month intervals Artola would meet with the union stewards in Bilbao and Tarragona to detail the quarterly results. "My policy was for the company to be transparent," Artola said. "Spanish companies, if they make money, tend not to tell the union about it. I told them the truth, the same thing you would say to the shareholders, because I believe in being honest, and if they believe you, you can work with them. I personally made the presentation, with slides and all, and answered their questions. Usually I went out to lunch with the union afterward, and after lunch we would often play cards. I had very good connections with them."

In Bilbao, where the employees were predominantly Basques, the retirees from the old Unquinesa firm had ridiculously small pensions, many under $100 a month. In Spain there is a so-called minimum salary, which at the time was roughly $300 per month. Artola got Popoff to authorize him to raise the pensions of all the retired people to the minimum salary. "That was a great achievement," Artola said. The union's reaction was "fantastic."

In 1978, when Dave Schornstein was transferred to Midland and the presidency of Dow Latin America was vacant, Artola became a leading candidate for the post with the active backing of most of the top executives of Dow Europe. Instead, the job went to Enrique Falla, who became Dow's chief financial officer a few years later.

"That was my biggest frustration at Dow," Artola said.

> I went to Dow too late. I think if I had gone to Dow earlier I would have reached a higher position and would have been on the board—not because I am more clever than others, but because of my drive and hard work. I was working in a chemical company and I was concerned that I didn't know anything about chemistry. You realize at the end that if you have common sense you can go anywhere—assuming you are willing to take risks—but there are very few people like that.

When Artola retired the Spanish government awarded him its highest civilian honor, the Great Cross of Civil Merit, for his contributions to the Spanish chemical industry. Among other distinctions it entitles him to be called "Your Excellency." "I'm glad it was a Socialist government who gave it to me, the minister of industry of a Socialist government," he said, "The minister knew perfectly well that I was very much of an anti-Socialist because I never hid it from him."

THE GHOST OF MERRELL DOW

Dow has had its comeuppance many times during its first century, but perhaps nowhere was the experience as much of a slap in the face as it was in Ireland in the late 1980s.

The Killeagh project seemed to have everything in its favor. The Irish government had for years been urging Dow to build a plant in Ireland; an ample supply of qualified personnel was available; there was a new and exciting product to be made; and there were no discernible environmental problems.

Through its Industrial Development Agency, or IDA, the Irish government in the 1980s was wooing new industry to the East Cork region, an area of high unemployment even for Ireland—and Ireland's overall unemployment rate was 17.7 percent in July 1989, the highest in Europe. Merrell Dow, as the company's pharmaceutical arm was then known, was looking for a manufacturing location for its newly developed nonsedating antihistamine, terfenadine, the active ingredient of what is now sold as an antiallergy drug under the trademark Seldane—the first such medication against hay fever and kindred ailments that does not make the patient drowsy.

A Merrell Dow site selection team went to work with the IDA and looked at 25 potential sites, including several in the East Cork area, hub of the Irish pharmaceutical industry; 26 pharmaceutical plants were already located there, representing most of the world's top drugmakers. Dow was leery of East Cork, however, because its harbor had a long-standing pollution problem.

Instead, with its traditional preference for small towns, Dow chose a freestanding site 23 miles from the harbor at the village of Killeagh (pronounced "Killa"), on the main road between Cork and Waterford, and took an option to buy a 90-acre farm just outside the village. On July 15, 1988, Merrell Dow formally asked the Cork County Council for "planning permission" to develop plans for the site, and six weeks later the council approved the request.

Terfenadine made in Killeagh would be shipped to the United States for formulation. The initial investment would amount to 40 million Irish pounds—later upped to 50 million pounds ($80 million)—and provide permanent jobs for 90 people at start-up and 200 within 10 years; there would be 300 construction jobs available during the building phase.

Ireland's Institute for Industrial Research and Standards, better known as Eolas, immediately began work on an environmental impact statement, as the law required.

Killeagh is picture postcard Ireland, fine green farmland that in 1988 nourished some 3,000 cows—there was a butter factory in the neighboring village of Youghal—and 3,000 acres of vegetables, destined mostly for a local Campbell Soup subsidiary, and barley to make the Irish whisky distilled in nearby Midleton.

To the surprise and annoyance of the IDA, opposition to the project began to be heard almost immediately, minor at first and then swelling in volume. Joan Vaughan, a Killeagh mother and housewife, organized the Womanagh Valley Protection Association (the Womanagh River wends its way through the area on its way to the coast). An industrial plant in the middle of our Killeagh? Not on your life, she said. She began recruiting neighbors who agreed with her that such a plant would destroy the character of the area and repel the tourists who constituted one of its main sources of income. Chemical fallout from the plant would taint the milk of their cows and kill their vegetables, she asserted. A second organization, Concerned Citizens of East Cork and West Waterford, later joined the battle, and then a third, Citizens Against Merrell Dow.

Soon there was also founded the Killeagh Pro Industry Group, an organization of people backing Merrell Dow and favoring the building of the plant, who argued that change was inevitable and that the Merrell Dow plant would bring to the area the very jobs that it needed. Citizens were quickly polarized as either pro-jobs or pro-environment; few saw the possibility of reconciling these concerns. Before long it was neighbor against neighbor, brother against brother, father against son.

Arriving in Ireland soon after planning permission was granted, Tom Kennedy, dispatched from the United States as project manager, found himself in the middle of a donnybrook. In August 1988, barely a month after Merrell Dow had decided to go ahead with the project, he was assailed by local farmers in a meeting at the Killeagh community hall. "Ye are not going to pollute us here in Ireland," an old farmer told him. "Ye can take your pollution back to the United States where ye belong."

A group of four farmers backed by the Womanagh Valley Protection Association appealed the decision to grant planning permission to An Bord Pleanala, the Irish planning appeals agency. Letters to the local newspapers said they had raised a fund of 60,000 pounds to hire prestigious legal counsel to fight the case.

A local authority told Kennedy not to worry—the opposition was coming from "at most" 168 persons, highly vocal though they might be.[1] Kennedy nevertheless asked headquarters to send a communications expert in as soon as possible to mount a program to explain the Merrell Dow program to the increasingly fractious populace. Jerry Ring, a veteran PR man, arrived on the run from Midland, and the program he and Kennedy set up was promptly dubbed the "Tom and Jerry Show" by the opposition. It was keyed to "information meetings" at the Killeagh hall, but these were rendered ineffective when objectors packed the meetings and shouted down the speakers. Organized mailings to the neighborhood did not fare much better. It was the first time a foreign company had attempted to take its case to the Irish public.

On February 27, 1989, An Bord Pleanala upheld the Cork County Council's decision to grant Merrell Dow planning permission. The decision was promptly appealed to the High Court of Ireland by the farmer plaintiffs. On April 3, Merrell Dow opened an office in Youghal (pronounced "you'll") and launched a sober, low-key program of response to questions and complaints.

By this time the fight was becoming bitter and determined on both sides. Citizens Against Merrell Dow, the most radical of the opposition groups, proposed to "take the battle to the streets," with public mass meetings and demonstrations. Concerned Citizens of East Cork and West Waterford was raising funds to run a professional media campaign.

Unwittingly, Merrell Dow had become a litmus test for Ireland's future: which did Ireland want more—industry or tourists?[2] Any other choice seemed to the opponents to be excluded, although as the *Irish Times* pointed out, industrial plants had been scattered about the Irish countryside for years, and no one had paid much attention.

Merrell Dow commissioned a "baseline study" of the area, to provide reliable future answers for the question, Is the environment getting better, or worse? Highly competent professionals would study all aspects of the present environment, including the wildlife in the area, the company reported. The project was dropped when the farmers on whose land the study would be made refused their cooperation; in the end, almost none of them cared to defy what was by now the popular opinion against the plant. (Wags in the local pubs asked: "Have ye seen the badger man, Paddy? Has he been around to inspect the badgers on your place? It's part of the baseline study, ye know.")[3]

The death knell of the project was probably sounded on June 3, when Concerned Citizens of East Cork and West Waterford called a press conference in Dublin. Nick Loughnane, a farmer member of the group, said his organization had commissioned an opinion poll of people living within 20 miles of Killeagh, done in early May, and they were now able to announce the results.

Jack Jones, chairman of the country's largest polling agency, Market Research Bureau of Ireland (MRBI), said the poll showed 56 percent of the people in the area against the project, 29 percent in favor, and 15 percent with no opinion. In the farming community, 62 percent opposed it.[4]

Loughnane and his colleagues also presented a petition opposing the plant that had been signed by 10,000 local residents during the preceding month. The petition and a copy of the study were delivered to Charles Haughey, the Irish prime minister, the following day.

Jerry Ring, reached back in Midland by the Irish press, said he was somewhat surprised that public support for the Merrell Dow project wasn't higher, but that this was undoubtedly because the company had not yet started its public information campaign to explain the plant to the public at large. The program—featuring info advertisements in local newspapers—started on schedule a week later.

A few days later Ring told the press that of the 50-million-pound proposed investment in the plant, 15 million or 30 percent of the total would be spent for environmental protection. Padraic White, general manager of IDA, said publicly that Merrell Dow had been "more responsive" to environmental concerns than any firm his agency had ever dealt with. Neither statement seemed to register with the protesters; it was as if they had already voted.

For the next two months the battle for and against Merrell Dow raged on Ireland's front pages and radios, and TV screens. In July Dow appointed John H. Oberlatz, a seasoned manager then running the Dow plant at Allyn's Point, Connecticut, to be its first country manager for Ireland, and Oberlatz, who was scheduled to become general manager of the Killeagh plant, headed for East Cork. On July 22 Kennedy threw a welcoming party for him at the Youghal Golf Club, inviting local officials and businessmen to a lunch and golf match to make his acquaintance.

Oberlatz was also welcomed to Ireland by several dozen protesters from the Concerned Citizens of East Cork/West Waterford, who jeered and hurled verbal abuse at the automobiles arriving at the Youghal Club. "Welcome to East Cork, Ireland's Bhopal," their picket signs said, and "Chemical Plants Kill—Keep East Cork Green." "No Welcome for Merrell Dow in Youghal, Go Back Home," the biggest sign read.

It was a rather peculiar lunch; following their demonstration the protesters moved into the main bar next to the dining room of the modest clubhouse for their own lunch and took down the names of those attending the Merrell Dow event. Tom Kennedy canceled the after-lunch golf match, "to ensure that no one would get hurt." His golf shoes had disappeared in the confusion anyway.[5]

That night there was a nasty fight at 3 A.M. between two Merrell Dow supporters who were cutting down a 20-feet-high sign that said, "East Cork Says No to Merrell Dow," and two opponents who arrived to give them battle. All four suffered cuts and lacerations.[6]

A few days later, on July 27, the Irish High Court in Dublin ruled in favor of Merrell Dow and against the Womanagh Valley Protection Association and the four farmers who had objected to the plant. "Court Gives Green Light to Merrell Dow Plant," said the headline in the *Irish Independent*. Jerry Ring told the press Merrell Dow was anxious to get going and that site work for the plant would begin in September.[7]

Roger Garland, who had been elected Ireland's first parliamentary deputy from the Green Party a few weeks before, on June 15, called the High Court's judgement "an absolute disgrace." The Killeagh fight, he said, was "the biggest environmental issue in

Ireland." He and the opposition groups declared they would "fight Merrell Dow to the last ditch."

Mary Harney, the junior environmental minister for Ireland, announced she would visit East Cork to meet with both sides, but said she herself favored the objectors' side. She visited the site on August 24 and talked with both sides. The minister for industry and commerce, Desmond O'Malley, met with Oberlatz and Kennedy the same day.

Meanwhile, the Merrell Dow board met in Cincinnati on August 29. On July 18 Dow had announced that it was purchasing the pharmaceutical business of Marion Laboratories and combining it with Merrell Dow; the new entity, called Marion Merrell Dow, was to come formally into existence on August 25. One of the board's first decisions on August 29 was that the Killeagh plant was no longer necessary.[8]

H. Fred Plagens, operations vice president of Merrell Dow, flew to Ireland over the Labor Day weekend and on Labor Day he and Jerry Ring convened a press conference in the city of Cork to announce that Dow was scrapping the project.[9]

Merrell Dow's pullout was a bombshell in Ireland, and front-page news across the nation. Prime Minister Haughey called it a "major disappointment."

"We have to give full consideration to the unacceptably high level of unemployment and emigration in this country," the prime minister said. "At the same time we have to protect the health, welfare, and safety of populations in local areas and their environment. It is essential to get the balance right. We have to get the jobs, cut down on unemployment and emigration, and on the other hand protect people from environmental risks and hazards."[10]

Plagens said the environmental ruckus was not a factor in the decision to kill the project. "The environmental controversy had nothing to do with it; we are leaving because the formation of the new (Marion Merrell Dow) group completely changes the economics of the Irish project as a freestanding entity," he said. The company had invested about five million pounds in the project ($8 million) to that point and more than half of that, he estimated, was "money down the drain."

"When Merrell Dow announced its intention to set up in Killeagh it immediately ran into a credibility problem on guarantees about the environment," the *Cork Examiner* commented. "When they announced their intention yesterday to abort it, they found themselves with another credibility problem. Very few people believed the reason proffered for their dramatic change of mind."[11]

The *Examiner* carried a photo of Joan Vaughan labeled: "The Victor." Breda Prendergast, chairperson of the Pro-Industry Group, said angrily that "we abhor the gross hypocrisy of a group who are clearly unaware that a huge unemployment problem exists in this area, but are nonetheless setting themselves up as saviours of our community. They should forget about their triumphalism, and shut up for themselves."[12]

The fallout from the affair continued to plague the East Cork area for years afterward; the wounds were slow to heal. Local politicians felt the area was "paying the price" for the Merrell Dow pullout; after that event it had become difficult for East Cork to attract other new firms that would provide the jobs it needed.[13]

In the aftermath it was generally agreed that the affair clearly demonstrated that Ireland needed an Environmental Protection Agency, the institution of which was "by far the most important new legislation in this area since the Planning Acts were introduced nearly 30 years ago," Mary Harney said. Ireland's new EPA, established in 1990, became in a sense a memorial to Merrell Dow and its Killeagh project.

When unemployment relief was debated in the area, as it continued to be, the ghost of Merrell Dow often haunted the meetings. "The Ghost of Merrell Dow lives on!" the *Cork Examiner* proclaimed in 1990, reporting on a meeting at Youghal described as "an embittered and acrimonious debate throughout which the Merrell Dow saga was the dominant theme." One councillor wondered if they really wanted new industry coming to the town. The Youghal council's chairman, John Brosnan, noted that the IDA "had brought 39 industrialists to Youghal last year but unfortunately nothing has come of that to date."

"There is nothing to be gained in prolonged embittered discussion on Merrell Dow," Brosnan said.[14]

1. "Merrell Dow opposition totally exaggerated," *Echo*, Cork, July 22, 1989. For interviews with objectors, see Robert Allen and Tara Jones, *Guests of the Nation: People of Ireland versus the Multinationals* (London: Earthscan Publications, 1990), 124-59. Values in this section are expressed in Irish pounds, worth $1.60 in 1989.

2. See "Merrell Dow, A Test Case for Chemical Investment," *Business & Finance*, Dublin, December 1, 1988, pp. 10-14.

3. See, inter alia, "Merrell Launch major environmental study," *Cork Examiner*, July 19, 1989; "Merrell Dow orders million pound check of site," *Irish Independent*, July 19, 1989; "Million Pound Merrell Dow Study 'Arrogant,'" *Irish Times*, July 19, 1989; "Merrell Dow Unveils Environmental Study," *Imokilly People*, July 20, 1989.

4. "Poll Shows Majority Is Opposed to Chemical Plant," *Irish Times*, June 5, 1989; "Majority Oppose Merrell Dow Plant," *Cork Examiner*, June 5, 1989. The poll was based on a 500-person sample.

5. "Merrell Dow Chiefs get Stormy Reception," *Cork Examiner*, July 22, 1989. See also Ann Cahill, "Merrell Dow: Right or Wrong?" *Irish Press*, July 27, 1989.

6. "Tension Is High after Scuffles at Merrell Dow," *The Sunday Press*, Dublin, July 23, 1989.

7. *Irish Independent*, July 28, 1989.

8. "Merrell Dow Will Not Proceed With Killeagh Project," news release, Merrell Dow, September 4, 1989; "Background on Merrell Dow Project at Killeagh, Co. Cork," news release, Merrell Dow,

September 4, 1989; and "Merrell Dow and Marion Laboratories to Combine Pharmaceutical Business," news release, Merrell Dow, August 25, 1989.

9. "Merrell Dow May Locate Here Yet," *Cork Examiner*, September 5, 1989; "Time Now for Scars to Heal," *Cork Examiner*, September 5, 1989; "Merrell Dow Project Scrapped," *Echo*, September 5, 1989; "East Cork Taken By Surprise," *Cork Examiner*, September 5, 1989; "A Double Blow By Merrell," *Irish Press*, September 5, 1989; "Merrell Dow . . . Why It Pulled the Plug," *Irish Press*, September 5, 1989. See also editorial, "The Lessons of Merrell Dow," *Irish Times*, September 5, 1989.

10. "Plant Decision 'Disappointing,'" *Cork Examiner*, September 7, 1989.

11. "Credibility Problem for Dow," *Cork Examiner*, September 5, 1989.

12. "Site Opposers 'Hypocrites,'" *Cork Examiner*, September 6, 1989.

13. "Region 'Paying the Price' for Merrell Dow Pull-Out," *Cork Examiner*, April 19, 1990.

14. "Ghost of Merrell Dow Lives On!" *Cork Examiner*, May 15, 1990. See also "Merrell Dow haunts UDC meeting," *Cork Examiner*, January 14, 1992.

IV.

Dow's experience in Greece was heavily influenced by the turbulent postwar history of that country.

Civil war had broken out in Greece in 1946 when Communist guerrillas attempted to take over the country. Warfare continued until October 1949. Following upon World War II, this new war devastated the country and it was several years before Greece began to recover under the durable conservative government of Constantine Karamanlis.

Dimitri Papageorgiou, who became Dow's managing director in Greece, spent 16 years in the Greek Navy during this long period of conflict, reaching the rank of commander and serving with the top Greek naval officers of the war, including Admiral P. Voulgaris, head of the Royal Hellenic Navy (1943-45), and the Greek prime minister for a time in 1946. After the war Papageorgiou became assistant naval attaché in London and took night courses for three years at the London School of Economics; he also held a law degree from the University of Athens. When he left the Greek Navy in 1956 he took a master's degree in business administration at Western Reserve university in Cleveland. With his background in economics, law, and business, Papageorgiou became Dow's top man in Greece almost from the start, and remained so for 21 years.[17]

In July 1960, Dow had acquired a site for a plastics plant at Lavrion, 33 miles from Athens, and incorporated Dow Hellas to run it. When Ted Knapp, who had now become director of personnel for Dow Europe, came to Athens looking for people to run the projected plant, Papageorgiou answered the want ad Knapp ran in the newspapers and was one of four men Knapp hired, the others being chemists and chemical engineers. Papageorgiou was immediately named commercial director of the new enterprise.

The ancient Greeks mined silver and lead in Lavrion. It is a pleasant and historic place, an area rich in archeological treasure, connected with Athens by a little train that runs up to the big city. The town had fallen on hard times, and the Karamanlis government was seeking to locate new industry there to counteract high unemployment. One of its attractions for Dow was its location on deep water, and the company built a terminal there through which to import styrene from the Netherlands.[18]

Ground was broken for the plant on May 14, 1961, with Ben Branch presiding, and the plant began to produce its first Styron in November 1962. Bob Reinker, then Dow's general manager in Greece and Italy, visited regularly while the plant was being built, and the day before it was to be completed he and Zoltan Merszei told Papageorgiou they wanted him to be the plant manager.

"Don't do this," Papageorgiou told them. "Put a production man in to be the production manager. I'm not a technical man." Merszei told him, "Don't worry. We'll make you into one. We'll give you all the support you need." Said Papageorgiou, laughing, later: "And I became one."

The plant came onstream at the end of 1962 and in 1963 a reform coalition under George Papandreou took over the government. A period of confusion ensued in Greece; Papandreou was dismissed by King Constantine in a dispute over who should control the army. Then a group of extremist army officers accused Papandreou's Centre Union Party of plotting to turn the country over to the Communists. Remembered as "the Greek colonels," they organized a coup and took over for a period of dictatorship that was disastrous for Greece, from 1967 to 1974.

It was a period characterized by terrorism, turmoil, and corruption. In 1968 a bomb was planted in the Lavrion plant, placed there, it was determined later, by terrorists resisting the colonels. The next day an army unit came to defuse and remove it, and it exploded, killing an army officer.

During most of these years, Papageorgiou said, the Lavrion plant simply fought for survival. In the early years it had severe technical problems, but learned to manufacture top-grade polystyrene. Customers were never a problem, he said; Dow had the customers before it built the plant, and quickly captured 80 percent of the polystyrene market in Greece. "When you say plastics in Greece, people think of Dow," he said.

During its first five years the plant lost money, and Colin Robertson, the treasurer of Dow Europe, wanted to close it down. "He was not happy because we were spending money without having any profits," Papageorgiou said. Clyde Boyd, the manufacturing manager for Dow Europe, instituted a debottlenecking program that soon turned it into a moneymaker, and Zoltan Merszei never wavered in his support. "The contribution of Merszei and Boyd to the survival of Dow Hellas was critical," Papageorgiou said. "Otherwise I don't know if we would have survived."

When it came time to expand the operation, it was extremely difficult to get the permits to do so from the government; expansion in this historic place was adamantly opposed by the government's archeological department. Merszei came down and presented Dow's case to

Andreas Papandreou (son of George), prime minister of Greece off and on into the 1990s. Papandreou, strongly anti-Common Market and anti-American, refused to budge. Merszei emerged from their private meeting in an unhappy rage.

"We tried to calm him down, because there were other ways we could go at it," Papageorgiou said—avoiding use of land designated by the antiquities experts was a key—and the expansion eventually was effected. Lavrion added polystyrene foam plants for the production of Styrofoam and Pelaspan and a technical service laboratory, and enlarged and modernized its Styron plant. Lavrion, he said with pride, became one of the most profitable operations in Dow Europe.[19]

"The Dow management warned us to be careful and to be ahead of the environmental problems," Papageorgiou said, "and in environment and safety considerations we tried to be 20 years ahead of the rest of Greek industry. That is the reason government and other industries respect Dow as one of the pioneers in this matter, and we're very severe in this."

Although his wife is the daughter of an ex-prime minister and a brother-in-law has been minister of justice and held other cabinet posts, Papageorgiou himself has never run for political office. "Politics is too much for me," he laughed.

He retired from Dow in 1982, and at the request of two banks became president and CEO of the Metall Company, the Common Market's only producer of nickel and a company heavily in debt to the two banks. Four years later he retired to a life of teaching and consulting.

In 1964 Dow opened a sales office in Athens, its ninth in Europe, headed by the aptly named Tom Sparta, an American, as regional sales manager for the Eastern Mediterranean. Athens quickly became the jumping-off point for Dow's sales invasion of the Middle East. Marketers from the Athens office journeyed to Israel, Iran, Iraq, Egypt, Saudi Arabia, and Lebanon.

"You had to have two passports, one for Israel and one for the Arab countries," recalled Roberto Sabbioneda, one of the Middle East trailblazers.

> In Egypt they asked me what was going on in Israel, and vice versa, in a friendly way. I sold jet fuel additive to Aramco [the Arab American Oil Company in Saudi Arabia] at the end of nowhere, in the desert.[20]
>
> We had good customers in Israel for insulating material for refrigerators—and they were producing good refrigerators. We had a good plastics business in Teheran, also with refrigerator companies, and with packaging firms; there was a lot of high-density polyethylene for milk bottles too. In Teheran we even sold the last inventory Dow had of PVC (polyvinyl chloride)— we had a thousand or two thousand tons, and I sold it there. We had a good business in Turkey, also, for plastics and refrigerators and packaging, and polyethylene for film.

When the Voranols (a key component of urethane foams) came in they were highly successful throughout the Mideast, where small factories sprang up to manufacture soft mattresses from the material. Plastic foam plants that made bedding became commonplace during this time in most of the Third World.

In Israel, where Dow had outstanding local representatives in the Jacobson family, sales amounted to more than $1 per capita (sales were $1.8 million there when the population of Israel was less than 1 million), the first place where this occurred in the entire European/Mideast/African area.

This pioneering activity paved the way for the formation of the Mideast/African area administration, a subarea of Dow Europe, in 1977.

V.

Dow's route to success in the United Kingdom was roundabout and unorthodox. The amazing thing about it, coming as it did in a chemical market totally dominated by Imperial Chemical Industries (ICI), one of the world's largest chemical firms, was that it was a success at all.

It began with Robert de Greeff, who became Herbert Dow's agent in London in 1905. Dow relied on him greatly during the bromine wars; it is likely that he helped Dow purchase and repackage bromine and sell it in the German market during those days when Dow was fighting for his corporate life against the Bromkonvention. The two men remained lifelong friends, and R. W. de Greeff & Company remained the company's principal British agent for more than 60 years.[21] The relationship began to change only in the 1950s, when Dow commenced building manufacturing facilities in England, including the Distrene facility at Barry, South Wales, in 1954, and Dow Agrochemicals at King's Lynn, in Norfolk, in 1958.

Dow engaged another London firm, R. H. Cole & Company, as its agent for plastics sales at the end of World War II, and Cole's son Anthony later became Dow's agent in Milan, Italy. Paul Oreffice moved into Tony Cole's offices for a time when he went to Italy to open an office as Dow manager for the Mediterranean in 1955.

The de Greeff and Cole families were only two of the distributor firms who served Dow, faithfully and well, in its early days in Europe. As the Dow firm moved its own sales force into place in the 1960s these firms were pushed aside—gently, for the most part—and Dow direct marketers took over.

When Dow acquired the Dobeckmun firm in 1957 it acquired with it a Lurex operation in Windsor Forest, England, and a sales organization in London under the managership of Robert H. Gregory, whose main concern was marketing Lurex to the fashion trade. Two years later Dow opened a sales office in London and the combined group was renamed Dow Chemical (U.K.) Ltd. Gregory, as managing director, became Dow's top man in England.

Gregory's offices were in a rambling, gracious old house just off Berkeley Square in Mayfair, the fashion district of London, done up in velours and draperies as a fashion backdrop. He presented fashion shows regularly in a large ballroom on the ground floor. The first Dow Chemical offices in England were in the attic, run by John Morris, the chemical sales manager, whom Gregory lured away from Shell Oil. "In Gregory's eyes selling chemicals was a lot less important than the rag trade," explained Stan Buck, one of the early inhabitants of the garret.[22] The salesmen in the attic would sometimes bring their customers to the fashion shows on the ground floor; the chemical crowd found them vastly diverting, Buck said.

Gregory, a self-made millionaire, was well known in London high society and anxious to impress Dow visitors with his knowledge of the British business world. Ben Branch remembered meeting Calouste Gulbenkian, the Armenian oilman who was one of the world's wealthiest men, at one of Gregory's parties. Gregory's agent for Lurex in the Indian subcontinent was Sadruddin Aly Khan, cousin of the Aga Khan; because of the traditional silver and gold wire wedding and ornamental dresses favored in that part of the world, it was a major market for Lurex, and the prince "handled it very well," Buck said.

For a time, Gregory was the only serious rival to Zoltan Merszei as Dow's top manager in Europe, but Gregory died in May 1963, and from then on Merszei was secure in the job.

Because of Great Britain's special relationship with the British Commonwealth nations, Dow U.K. operated independently of Dow Europe in the early years, reporting directly to corporate headquarters in Midland. Dow Europe stopped at the channel. The reason was Great Britain's "imperial preference" rule for the Commonwealth nations, thanks to which Dow U.K. could import product duty-free from Dow Canada; product imported from the United States (or any other non-Commonwealth nation) was subject to a 33-$^1/_3$ percent duty.

The independent status that "imperial preference" conferred on Dow U.K. rankled Merszei deeply (Dow Chemical Europe imported from Dow plants in the United States, mainly Texas) and he mounted a persistent campaign to annex it to Dow Europe. His wedge was pricing. While he knew the British market was different, he told Midland, Dow U.K.'s pricing policy was interfering with his pricing on the continent, and this conflict was reducing Dow's overall returns. After a while he obtained a "coordinating" role for pricing in Europe, including the U.K. "That eventually became full control because price controls the business," Buck said. In 1964 Dow U.K. became a formal subsidiary of Dow Chemical Europe in Zurich, and Dow Agrochemicals was merged into Dow U.K.

When Philip Laird arrived in London in 1963 following Gregory's death, he instituted a housecleaning. Lurex had been folded into the Dow textile operations in 1958, and in 1966 Dow's textile operations were in turn folded into the Dow Badische Corporation, a joint venture with BASF, and Dow itself went out of the textile business. (In 1978 Dow severed its last link to textiles, selling its half of Dow Badische to BASF.)

Laird quickly decided the Mayfair mansion was no place to sell chemicals and plastics. He painted it white, installed bright lights, and tried to make it look like a traditional office, even though the fashion shows continued. When Lurex was melded into Dow Badische, the Windsor Forest operation was closed and moved to King's Lynn, and Windsor Forest was sold. Before long Laird found new and, he felt, more appropriate offices for Dow U.K. on Wigmore Street.[23]

The Distrene operation also had its zany side. It had been built in the middle of a Distillers plant site, and when Distillers soured on the chemical business (as a result of its involvement in the thalidomide scandal), Dow bought out its partner. Distillers sold the rest of the Barry site to British Petroleum (BP), and Dow's Distrene operation became an island in a BP stream, entirely surrounded by BP plants and dependent upon BP for steam, power, services, and practically everything else. It had its own rights of way within the complex, but in spite of BP's being eager to buy it, Dow held on to the little Distrene plant as a stand-alone, one-product site. While small, it has been a highly successful, low-cost unit. Dow established its European polystyrene research and development center there, and Ellis Davies, the center's manager, became Dow Europe's first associate scientist.[24]

The King's Lynn plant, in the middle of England's east coast farm area, started as a producer of Dowpon grass-killer and grew into a medium-sized chemical-producing operation as new units were added—glycols for antifreeze, and latex for paints and carpet backing.

By 1976, Eric Huggins, who succeeded Laird as regional manager, could report that Dow was selling some 250 different products in the U.K., about 75 percent of the volume being brought in from Dow's producing plants on the continent. About 40 percent of production at Barry and King's Lynn was exported.

Huggins called Dow Agrochemicals "one of Dow's silly mistakes," even though it turned into a good plant and Dow U.K. into a good company. Walter Ripper, who had a reputation as one of Britain's outstanding agrochemists, he said, "was persuasive and fast talking, and he came to Midland and talked somebody into letting him build a Dowpon plant. Of course the Dowpon plant really was just an exporter; I don't think we ever sold more than about half a ton a year of Dowpon in the U.K. It was exported to the Middle East and Malay."[25] After Dr. Ripper's death in 1961 the operation expanded into other products.

The major use for King's Lynn Dowpon, Huggins said, was the Malaysian rubber plantations, where a rubber seedling takes seven years to grow to maturity before it can be tapped for rubber. Dowpon kills the tropical grasses that would otherwise choke it out, and allows the rubber seedling to grow.

In 1965 the company opened its second sales office in England, at Wilmslow, a suburb of Manchester in the industrial northland. Other offices opened in Birmingham and Leicester. Corcoran & Company, in Dublin and Belfast, continued to be the company's sales representative in Ireland, as it had been since 1956.

During the oil crisis of the 1970s Dow, as a large petrochemical firm, moved urgently to protect its sources of petroleum feedstocks. It became active in oil exploration in the newly discovered North Sea oilfields off northern England through the Sovereign Oil Company, a small oil company financed by Dome Oil of Canada, with which Clyde Boyd (then president of Dow Europe) had become acquainted during his term as president of Dow Canada. Dow bought some North Sea oil properties, funded oil exploration there by Sovereign, and bought a landing point for the pipelines that it expected to bring oil in from the North Sea.

Through Sovereign Dow also bought an oil rig, the *Sovereign Explorer*, for North Sea exploration. With a price tag of $118 million, it was built at a strike-ridden shipyard in Cheshire and dogged by trouble from the beginning. It was launched late and had to be taken to Sweden for completion. By the time it was ready to operate the bottom had dropped out of the oil market. Dow tried to sell it, but there were no buyers. By the early 1990s it was idling in the Gulf of Mexico, having been operated for a time by Exxon.

"Dow's had this fear and intrigue with protecting feedstock and going back to crude," said Buck, for many years the company's principal hydrocarbons buyer in Europe. "We were a very tiny minnow competing with big sharks."

As a result, Dow's forays into the oil business have invariably been disappointing and costly, he said, and the lessons expensive. The *Sovereign Explorer* was only one example.

VI.

The early managers of Dow Italia were Italian Americans. They were succeeded after a few years by native Italians.

Paul Oreffice, born and raised in Venice, was the first of them all, sent to Milan in 1955 because there was no Swiss work permit for him, to open what was grandiloquently called Dow's Mediterranean area sales office—actually Oreffice's hotel room.[26]

Oreffice was succeeded a year later by Roger Zoccolillo, his close friend from the Edgewood Arsenal in Maryland, where both had served during the Korean War. Zoccolillo spoke Italian Neapolitan style, and the Milanese were astonished to meet an American who spoke Italian with a Naples accent. When Dow acquired the Ledoga-Lepetit firm in Milan in 1964, Zoccolillo moved over to manage the Dow interests in that firm and was succeeded by Joe Pinotti, whose family came from the Genoa area.

The native Italians hired by these Italian American forerunners—Enrico Aliboni and Roberto Sabbioneda led the parade—followed in their footsteps. Dow Chimica Italiana, as it was called at first, became Dow Italia, but it never seemed like an outpost of an American firm.

In 1967 Aliboni and Sabbioneda took Tom Sparta, another Italian American who had succeeded Pinotti, to the airport. "Yankee, go home," they told him. Sparta was the last of the first-generation American expatriates to head Dow Italia.

In January 1960 Sabbioneda had spotted an ad in Milan's *Corriere delle Sera* saying, "Leading American company opening office in Italy and starting a new plant for plastics production." A plastics salesman himself, he proposed to his boss that he answer the ad, "to find out what company was involved," and shortly found himself offered and accepting a job with Dow Chemical.

His job was to sell the polystyrene plastic that would be made at the new Dow plant. Zoccolillo and Merszei, polystyrene sales manager for Europe at the time, picked Livorno (Leghorn) as the site. Southern Italy was full of bribery and corruption, they felt, so they avoided it and instead chose a central Italian site on the water, since styrene would be shipped in as the raw material. The Livorno site was purchased in 1961, ground was broken in 1962, and the plant came onstream in July 1963. Robert E. Reinker, a young plastics engineer, was dispatched from Midland as manager.

Everything went smoothly. Livorno turned out to be the right place for the plant. Sabbioneda and a staff of three sold the entire output.[27]

Acquisition of Gruppo Lepetit S.p.A., Italy's largest pharmaceutical maker, changed Dow's status in Italy dramatically. Lepetit had plants all over Italy and 21 subsidiaries around the world, some of them producing items quite remote from pharmaceuticals. One, for example, was a Lepetit line of cosmetics, "Biobeauty," which Dow later sold. Lepetit marketed its products—$145 million worth in 1970—in more than 100 countries.

Lepetit headquarters was a handsome building in Milan (located on via Lepetit), whose lavishly appointed top floor, irreverently called by underlings "the nightclub," housed the executive suite. The company owned a villa in Rome used solely for visiting customers. The company was run single-handedly by a Sicilian nobleman, Baron Guido Zerilli, who had taken over command at the end of WWII in a vacuum of leadership; Emilio Lepetit, son of the firm's founder, Robert Lepetit, had died in Hitler's Dachau concentration camp in 1945. He left a small son also called Emilio, and this Emilio eventually became the firm's chairman, and occupied that position for many years.

Dow's business in Italy grew rapidly. In 1960, before Livorno and Lepetit, sales were only $1.8 million. By 1964, after Livorno had been inaugurated, the Dow employee population had risen to 130: 100 at the Livorno plant and 30 in Milan. A quarter century later, in 1989, Dow employed 2,500 in Italy and annual sales were $650 million.

In the years before Livorno the Dow Italians tried to ship product in by rail from the Botlek, in Rotterdam, but that was a disaster. "Rail cars would leave Rotterdam and you didn't know where they were," Sabbioneda said. "They could be in Germany, Switzerland, France—you didn't know; and we had customers waiting for products. With 90 percent of the material coming from the United States, the beginning was not easy. We got organized step by step."

A squadron of police came to the Dow Italia office on April 1, 1978, announcing that they had arrest warrants for Tito Montessori, the managing director, and Giuseppe (Pepe) Violini, his alternate. They arrested Montessori in his office and whisked him by train all the way to Brindisi, on the Italian heel, where he was clapped in jail incommunicado. Television cameras and radio crews were waiting for the train in Brindisi and the case immediately became a sensation in the Italian and international press: "Manager of American Chemical Firm Jailed in Brindisi."

The arrest was made by the Guardia di Finanza, the Italian fiscal police, who accused Montessori of violating the Italian law against export of capital; at the time Italians could only take the equivalent of about $1,000 maximum with them when they exited the country. Dow and Montessori were accused of exporting rifampicin from Brindisi at a price higher than that in Italy, so that Dow could then collect funds and keep them outside the country—thereby perpetrating illegal export of capital, the Finanza said.

The Dow managers were astounded. "None of us felt any guilt at all," Sabbioneda said. "We had been following normal commercial practices."

Meanwhile, people at Dow's Milan office were trying frantically to track down Pepe Violini, who had gone up to the Dow Europe offices in Horgen, Switzerland; if he returned to Italy he would be jailed, too. Horgen reported he had left there. "He's on the train to Italy," they said.

Sabbioneda and Maria Pia Travostino, Violini's secretary, sped by auto to Lugano to try to intercept him. Travostino boarded every train arriving from Zurich and searched for him until 2 A.M. Sabbioneda stayed at the frontier, hoping to intercept him before he crossed, if he arrived there. It turned out Horgen had successfully reached Violini at a station closer to Zurich with an urgent message not to go to Italy, and he was safely back in Zurich.

Fearful that they too might be arrested, Emilio Lepetit and Enrico Aliboni, officers of Dow Italia but not named in the arrest warrants, fled to Switzerland by auto the same day, and the three refugees stayed there, waiting for things to cool down.

Montessori languished in jail for a month while Dow attorneys from Italy, Switzerland, and the United States worked to unravel the accusations of the Finanza and get him out on bail. The case dragged on in the Italian courts for years. "The file on the case got so big there were almost 100 kilograms of paper [220 pounds] in it," Sabbioneda said. "They sent the Italian police to the Far East, where they searched for this invoice or that document in Hong Kong, in Tokyo, in Bangkok; after every trip the file got bigger. No judge wanted to be involved in such a complicated case because none of them understood intracompany pricing and that sort of thing. It was a mess."[28]

The case also messed up the lives of both men listed in the arrest warrants. A year after being jailed in Brindisi, Montessori, suffering from prostate cancer, died in Rome a few hours after surgery. Pepe Violini, after a sojourn in Switzerland, went to Midland and spent the next few years as Lepetit's liaison there. When the case finally folded, inconclusively, in 1986, and he was free to return to Italy, he did return, and retired, to Lugano.[29]

Despite streaks of brilliance, such as its discovery of the major antibiotic, rifamycin, Lepetit had a major problem: it was grossly overstaffed. R. William Caldwell, who took over the general managership from Zoccolillo, found employees whose sole duty was to serve coffee. The two main divisions, Gruppo Lepetit and Richter, were quite independent of each other, so that everything was duplicated; there were two administrative centers, two research centers, and the like. There was a large advertising department; the firm had its own print shop for labels and inserts; a movie group making scientific films; and a complete cafeteria service, with its own cooks and servers. There were 115 general services personnel for building mainte-nance—electricians, plumbers and other services—and a staff of five chauffeurs.[30]

Merszei sent down Andrew Butler, an Englishman who later became president of Dow Europe, to help sort this all out and to begin shaping Lepetit into the "lean, mean" Dow image. "By the time the rest of Dow came to grips with Lepetit it had exploded with peo-ple," Butler said. "I think they added a thousand people in the year before Dow Europe got involved. The costs were out of sight, it was losing money, and it was a dreadful mess. We just had to do something to make this stop."[31]

It was typical of Baron Zerilli that when he went down to Morocco to get the government's permission to build a pharmaceutical processing unit there, he took the plans for the plant with him and showed them to the King of Morocco. "The King gave him a white stallion," Butler said. "Baron Zerilli was a great horseman. In return for this Baron Zerilli quadrupled the size of the plant he had committed to build." The plant, built at a rather remote spot on the Moroccan coast called El Jadida, "four times bigger than necessary," Butler said, "was a millstone around our necks ever afterwards."

One of the research centers was closed—of 400 personnel there, only about 150 were actually researchers—and the other was rebuilt and modernized. The staff in the new research center, inaugurated in 1986, included 160 persons, all researchers.

Paring down the 4,100-person payroll of Lepetit became a long-term project. For a time Dow reduced the staff by an average of 70 to 80 people per month. "You cannot fire people in Italy," Sabbioneda explained. "We had to convince them one at a time to leave, to resign, to come in and sign a letter of resignation, so it was not an easy task at all."

"Our job was to stop the hemorrhage, which we did," Butler said, "but we had to get rid of a lot of people there, which was extremely difficult because the government laws were against it."

The Italians, Butler said, "are incredible people; they never lose their capability to smile and enjoy their lives. There were seven porters in the lobby—seven!—and they knew that there was only going to be one when we had finished, because nothing's secret in Italy, but every morning I'd go in and they'd all smile and say, 'Buon giorno! Buon giorno! Come va?,' knowing that six of the seven were doomed."

During this time Butler commuted from Horgen to Milan every week. "Every plan that Horgen hatched was always accepted in Milan with smiles and they'd say, 'What a brilliant idea! My God, how can you guys be so clever?' They'd listen to you all week, then you'd go away, and of course when you left they'd just go on doing exactly what they were doing before. They're marvelous; I loved them, I really loved those guys," he said. "It was a very tough time, but we did what needed to be done."

The Dow people set up a special office with a private telephone and briefed those whose resignation was solicited on where and how to apply for a job, with this office available for their use. "You have to go visit potential employers," Sabbioneda told them. "Take a taxi. We'll reimburse you." The company also provided expert advice on investing the funds they would be receiving in severance pay.

"I had to call people into my office and offer them as much as three years' salary to leave the company," he said. "That was not easy, because some of these people were almost 50 years old and were not able to find another job easily."

Other companies began to come to Dow and ask it to share its expertise on handling such a situation. "We tried to do it in a humane way," Sabbioneda said.

VII.

France being the world's fashion capital, it was appropriate that Dow France should have begun through a product aimed at the fashion market. The product was Lurex, a metallic fiber invented during World War II by the Dobeckmun packaging materials firm in Cleveland.

The prewar world capital for metallic yarn was Lyons, France, and American textile mills imported the French yarns, often made of real gold and silver—which they wove sparingly into special fabrics, a thread here and there, to give them a metallic sheen—until France was cut off from U.S. trade during the war. As a wartime substitute Dobeckmun devised Lurex—laminated aluminum foil between two layers of plastic, fine slit to a very narrow width—and sold it as a novelty replacement for the metallic yarns no longer available. The product became quite sophisticated and developed into the world's best-selling metallic yarn.

Yves Crepet, son of a French silk ribbon manufacturer, traveling in England after the war to try to locate his father's prewar ribbon customers and help revive the war-interrupted family business, was immediately interested when he heard about Lurex. Could he have the agency for Europe, he asked? Dobeckmun hired him as "technical sales advisor for France, Italy, Spain, Portugal, and Benelux," and he set about developing a European market for Lurex. By 1956 the business was big enough that he established a small plant to make Lurex himself at St. Etienne, the ribbon capital of France and his hometown.

Crepet took aim at the fashion business, set up a workroom and some looms, and began creating high-fashion fabrics that incorporated Lurex in them, which he showed the textile manufacturers who dealt with haute couture. The second year he tried it, he hit the jackpot; all the new collections in Paris and Rome featured Lurex. Dobeckmun built a new plant to make the material at Amsterdam.[32]

One day in 1958 Crepet received a telex saying that Dobeckmun had merged with The Dow Chemical Company. A few months later he went to Dobeckmun's European headquarters in London and met Zoltan Merszei and Ted Knapp. "What do you do in France?" they asked. "I run a company you've just acquired." "Oh, we have a company in France?" "Yes, you have."

Merszei asked the name of the company. "Dobeckmun France? If so, first of all, we should call our company Société de Produits Chimiques Dow. Why not?" Crepet said, "Well, it's a Société Anonyme." "What does that mean?" Merszei asked. "It means we need a board of directors. We need a president," Crepet replied. "We need a president?" Merszei asked. "You'll be the president." Crepet thus became president of Société de Produits Chimiques Dow S.A. at age 28.

That same year, 1959, Ben Branch led Dow into a joint venture with the Pechiney Company, forming Plastichimie as a joint enterprise in France and building a facility at Ribécourt. A polystyrene plant went onstream at Ribécourt in 1962 and a saran plant in mid-1963.

In the summer of 1962 Dow decided to open a sales office in Paris, and Crepet closed up the little plant in St. Etienne (Lurex proved to be a feast-or-famine business, depending upon the dictates of fashion; one year you could not make enough of it, the next you couldn't give it away) and moved to Paris, where he became the manager of Dow's eighth sales office in Europe. It now changed its name to "Dow Chemical International (France)"; at the end of 1965 Dow standardized the names of its European subsidiaries and it became "Dow Chemical France"; later on it was simply "Dow France."

The joint-venture plastics plants in Europe turned out to be a mistake. "We had real problems with the joint ventures because the joint ventures could sell wherever they wanted to, and we (Dow) could hardly go into their home territory and compete with them," said Paul Stroebel, Dow's plastics manager in Europe at the time. "We had a Styron plant in England (Distrene) and one in France (Plastichimie)" Stroebel recommended selling out the plant in France to the Pechiney partner, and buying out the partner (Distillers) in England; in 1968 Dow quietly purchased the other half of Distrene, and in 1970 it sold its half of Plastichimie.[33]

Business grew rapidly in France, and beginning with about $5 million in sales in 1963 ($3 million of that being Lurex), it grew in the next 25 years to more than $700 million in sales. A second sales office was opened in 1969, at Lyons, and three more in 1970, at Strasbourg, Bordeaux, and Lille.

In 1959 Stroebel and Elmer K. Stilbert went to Europe to look for a general plant site (the Botlek site at Rotterdam was already becoming crowded), and their top nomination was the area of Strasbourg, France, on the Rhine River. Their recommendation was forgotten for the moment, but in 1968 Dow bought a 375-acre site at Drusenheim, on the river near Strasbourg, and twinned it with another across the river at Greffern (now called Rheinmunster), in Germany.

The Drusenheim-Rheinmunster Dow plant, straddling the Rhine, became a pioneering venture and a portent of the future, with French and German employees swapping back and forth across the river and working in tandem. On the French side it is right on the Maginot Line (of World War II fame), and the plant site includes a bunker of that line, a memento of the last great war between these two traditional enemies, still used today as the plant's sample house.[34]

The municipal authorities in Drusenheim, France, told Crepet they saw no problems in the arrangement so long as Dow never put a German in charge on the French side. "The first thing we did, of course, was to put a German in charge of the plant," Crepet said. "This was Hans Fink, and it went so well; Hans made those people work so hard. Hans Fink became the best friend of the local hotel owner, who had warned me about Germans, and he became the best friend of the mayor, who had told me the same thing."

Drusenheim-Rheinmunster became a unique example of German-French cooperation. Wages are slightly higher on the German side than on the French, and there are other problems, but productivity has been "extraordinary," Crepet said. By the early 1990s the plant manager at Drusenheim was an Italian.

The original reason for building the plant across the Rhine was a patent problem. The first product was Coyden, a coccidiostat, for which the main market was in France, and to protect the patent it had to be manufactured in France as well as in Germany.

Drusenheim today specializes in the manufacture of foams and films for the European market. In 1970 a Styrofoam plant was built, and then an Ethafoam plant, and then plants for Saranex and Trycite films.

Crepet worked hard to get a major Dow chemical complex for France. He told French government officials Dow would need a major source of salt if it were to locate a large unit in France, and in 1974 Jacques Chaban-Delmas, the prime minister, suggested a site at a place called Le Verdon, where the Gironde River empties into the Atlantic north of Bordeaux. Southwest France is not heavily industrialized and there were major salt deposits at Bayonne.

Crepet and his Dow colleagues looked at it carefully but there was one overpowering problem: the salt was at Bayonne, and Dow would have been obliged to build a 100-mile-long brine line from Bayonne to Bordeaux. Soon afterward Dow announced it would build a big chloralkali complex at Stade, near Hamburg, in Germany, and there was only going to be one of those for Dow in Europe; that ended the search for a major chemical site in France.

When Dow acquired Lepetit in 1975, the acquisition had unexpected repercussions on Dow Chemical France. In France Lepetit had a manufacturing plant at Seclin, near Lille, plus a rather lavish headquarters and marketing building in Paris. "Dow suddenly found itself with two headquarters buildings in Paris," Crepet said, "its own, which was rather frugal, and the Lepetit building, which was beautiful."

Also, he said, Lepetit had a lot of people in its Paris offices, "a lot of people we didn't need." Crepet proposed that Dow not use either of the two Paris headquarters but instead seize the opportunity to "get Dow out of Paris," which was a pleasant place indeed, but increasingly high-priced and crowded for a business firm. His first idea was Strasbourg, to be near Drusenheim, but he was also attracted by a new "scientific park" being opened up at Sophia Antipolis, 15 miles from Nice on the French Riviera.

When he recommended to Andrew Butler in Zurich that Dow move its French headquarters to Nice, Butler laughed at first but agreed. "You're even crazier than I thought," he told Crepet. Clyde Boyd, then the president of Dow Europe, said to his surprise, "Go ahead and do it."

Crepet had polled the 120 employees in France, and 48 wanted to go to Sophia Antipolis; "48 was exactly the number we needed to operate," he said. "We moved 48 people from Paris, and to all the others we said good-bye." Dow Chemical France moved into its new headquarters and service center there in 1981, and the dedication was presided over by Michel Rocard, then minister for planning, later the French prime minister.

When he made a trip to the United States a few months later, Rocard visited Midland and had dinner with the Dow board of directors, some of whom were dubious about dining with a Socialist politician. Paul Oreffice delivered the main speech, saying, "Mr. Minister, I thought I was the only maverick economist, but you are also a maverick economist." "Somebody told me he was a Socialist," one of the directors said, referring to Rocard, "but he's a liberal." Rocard told Crepet it was the best evening he had ever spent in the United States.

Sophia Antipolis has become the premier scientific park in Europe, second in the world only to Silicon Valley, in Crepet's view. Dow was one of the first companies to move into the area, and has seen the working population of the complex climb from about 300 to 10,000. It is today the home of DowElanco; with the passage of time, Dow France has moved its offices back to Paris, the capital of all things French.

Crepet had a discerning eye for "picking good people." By the 1990s there were some 45 French managers scattered about the Dow world, virtually all of whom had been hired and had worked for Crepet.

Right from the beginning, we insisted on a university recruiting program, and one of my real objectives has always been to hire only people who can take a top job, never to hire somebody fitted for just one job. We are going to have tremendous growth in Dow Europe and we can afford, I'm sure, to give a job to those top people. The second part of this has been to try to send French people abroad. In order to achieve this I started to diversify my staff and have foreigners working for France. If all my managers were Belgian, Swiss, American, Dutch, Italian, Dow France could export some French. I'm convinced it was good for the image of France to have foreigners working in Dow France.

Not many of the traditional French companies are operating in this way, Crepet said. "The French companies are just starting. It's like the Italian companies—if you're an Italian you can succeed in them, if you are French you cannot. In France it's a little different, but they are changing; France is really changing." A sign of the times: in 1989 the Dow recruiter, visiting the universities of France looking for new Dow employees, was a young German. "That's revolutionary," Crepet said. "Ten years ago we could not have done that."

He was also proud of another aspect of Dow France, and liked to tell French government officials about it. "We are good citizens," he said. "Dow France is small but it is among the 60 biggest taxpayers of France. We are a four billion French franc business, but we give 200 million francs to the government, so we are a real, true French company."

VIII.

In the early days of Dow Europe, unlikely people frequently did unlikely things. Philip Laird, horticulture graduate of Ontario Agricultural College, was an unlikely candidate to pioneer the Scandinavian area for Dow, but in 1954, despite the 27-year-old Canadian farm boy's total ignorance of matters Scandinavian, Clayton Shoemaker sent him to Stockholm to start building Dow's business in northern Europe.

Laird had been recruited out of college to sell agricultural chemicals for Dow Canada, based in Toronto. When Dow International was organized, he was assigned temporarily—"a couple of months," they told him—to close down the Dow Canada export department, whose personnel were moving to the new organization; the department manager, Zoltan

Merszei, was leaving for Europe. When this task was completed Laird packed up the departmental files, put them in a suitcase, and took them over to Zurich. There he was recruited to Dow International, and didn't return to what he had started out to do—sell chemicals for Dow in Canada—for 21 years.

For no particular reason except that someone was needed there, he was assigned to Dow International's "northern Europe area desk" in Midland; at the next desk was Paul Oreffice, whose area was southern Europe. Two years later, in the summer of 1956, when it came time to send someone to Stockholm, Laird was as qualified as anyone.

Phil and Edie Laird had four children under the age of six when they left for Stockholm. "Stockholm was totally underbuilt at that time," Laird said. "To get space, you had to pay what was called 'key money'; you'd pay someone five thousand kroner for the right to rent their place. Dow had only a million and a half dollars' worth of business in Scandinavia, and I was just one person with a girl who was going to work for me. I didn't want to spend a lot of money on office space getting started in Stockholm."[35]

He finally found space in an apartment building where an elderly woman had a large apartment she was willing to share. "She had been able to subdivide it so that one half was hers and one half was for rent; that was all that was available," Laird said. "I put a little sign on the door that said 'P. Laird'; that was our office. Ring once for the very elderly lady, two rings for Laird. That's how we started. We hired another girl and I think we even had three inside salesmen in that little space until we finally moved out of it."

Merszei had awarded the Dow distributorship in Sweden to Thorsten Lilja, a friend and former colleague in the Dow Canada export group who had set up a Stockholm firm called Trebec A.B. Laird began by traveling with the Trebec salesmen, building his own contacts and relationships, and both firms prospered.

For legal reasons it was not until March 1958 that Dow could operate in Sweden under the Dow name. In the interim, everything was done in the name of P. A. Laird. At the changeover Laird went to his furniture supplier and ordered a substantial amount of furniture and equipment for a new office, and asked if they would bill it to Dow Chemical A.B., the name of the now finally official Swedish branch, instead of to P. A. Laird.

The furniture man said, "Sir, we've been dealing with you a couple of years now and we know you, but we don't know this Dow Chemical. If you'll guarantee them, we'll process the order."

"His asking me to guarantee Dow Chemical was the greatest thrill of my life," Laird laughed.

The business was routed through Thorsten Lilja until an incident with Dow's largest phenol customer in Sweden caused the relationship to sour. Lilja pressed Dow for a low price for a large order for this customer, and Dow met the price and shipped the order. Laird then discovered that Lilja had ordered considerably more at the rock-bottom price than the major customer needed, and that he was selling the balance to other customers at the regular price and pocketing the difference.

Laird told Merszei about it and they fired Lilja, although they made him a generous parting arrangement. "Zoltan could not stand that," Laird said.

He thought Thorsten was a close personal friend. If Thorsten could do that to him or to the company, that was it. So we fired him and went out and hired our own sales force as fast as we could. We hired some of Thorsten's own men, because he had built up a sales force to sell Dow products, but as far as Thorsten was concerned, he was out. We went into direct sales in Scandinavia, except for Finland, shortly thereafter.

In Norway Laird hired Per Christiansen, and then Gunnar Ulfsrud, later Dow's top man in Scandinavia. He opened an office in Oslo in October 1964, and in Copenhagen two months later. To run it he hired Bro Jorgensen, a Dane.

On one of Ben Branch's trips to Stockholm he came to family dinner with the Lairds, and Judith, the eldest daughter, was asked to say grace. She said the grace she had heard many times:

> Come Lord Jesus, be our Guest,
> Bless this food, Which Dow hast given us.

Branch exploded in laughter, and the incident became one of his favorite stories.

By 1963, after seven years in Sweden, with their children speaking Swedish and going to Swedish schools, the Lairds decided it was time to move on or become permanently Swedish. He asked for a transfer, and they soon moved to London.

His successor was Nils Hernborg, who became the paterfamilias of Dow Nordic, as the company is known in Scandinavia, for the next generation.[36]

Hernborg, forced to go to work when his father died of a heart attack, had started as a 14-year-old office boy, continuing his education at night school. During World War II he was part of a contingent sent above the Arctic Circle to guard the Swedish border with Finland in weather as cold as -43°, Celsius. He was second-in-command at Andren & Soner, a well-known Stockholm representative firm for chemicals and plastics, when Laird proposed him as his successor.

Hernborg turned the job down at first; he was happy working with his old friend Bo Andren, and he didn't like Thorsten Lilja, whom he knew as "Mr. Dow." When it became apparent that Andren was bringing his oldest son into the firm as heir apparent, however, and when Lilja was fired, Hernborg changed his mind. He went to Zurich to talk to Merszei. How much freedom would he be given if he were to become Dow's chief in Stockholm, he asked?

"If we want to hire you," Merszei said, "it's because we think you're one of the five best guys in this profession in all of Scandinavia. If we hire a guy of that kind, who should be able to give him any directives? You will know everything about your territory better than anyone will know down here in Zurich."

Hernborg's wife, Margit, told him, "If you want to do it, you should do it." Hernborg began with Dow on November 1, 1962, as field salesman for plastics; Merszei promised that within a year or two he would be Dow's sales manager for Sweden.

On the first working day of the new year he went to see Lilja, who was to turn over the Dow customer files that day. As a parting gift for 15 years of service, Branch and Merszei had given Lilja an overlapping commission on everything Dow sold for two years. Lilja refused to give him anything at all.

"It was a bad meeting," Hernborg said. "I finally gave him the option either of turning over the customer files to me, or I would ask Branch and Merszei to cut him off without a dime."

"He finally came to his senses," Hernborg said, "and we took over." In the fall of 1963 the Lairds went to London, and Hernborg became sales manager for Sweden, and eventually regional manager for Dow Nordic.

It was difficult to get the northern nations to work together. "The Danes and Norwegians have a sort of big-brother complex toward the Swedes," Hernborg said. "but we are obliged in many ways to work together. If Gunnar Ulfsrud wanted to build a plant in Norway he was talking about a market of 4.5 million people. Bro Jorgensen in Denmark had even less. I argued that we had to go to Horgen with a market of 25 million people—the combined population in these countries—or they would not listen to us." Over the years this argument prevailed, and in 1970 the Nordic region of Dow Europe was established.

The first Dow manufacturing plant in the area opened in the spring of 1974, a latex plant at Norrkoping, Sweden, primarily producing paper latex for the paper mills in northern Sweden and Finland.

It was tough to get Dow management to agree to plants in the area, Hernborg said. "We were perceived as being more socialistic than we have ever actually been, and our wages were among the highest in the world, sometimes the highest," he said. "Ben Branch was against any plants in Nordic. 'We can never earn a dime from a plant in that country with their high wages,' he said." It did not help that Olof Palme, perceived in the United States as a radical, was prime minister of Sweden at the time.

Hernborg was proud that within two years after it opened the Norrkoping plant was profitable. By the early 1990s it had been the most profitable of Dow's 18 latex plants around the world, for four years in a row.

As soon as the latex plant was open, Dow Nordic began to press for a Styrofoam plant at the same site. Hernborg found a skid plant—a Styrofoam plant on skids—in the Netherlands. It had been used in Holland and in France, and was now lying idle. It was moved to Norrkoping, and began to produce Styrofoam for insulation and roadbeds in the Nordic market.

The Swedish state railway became Norrkoping's biggest customer. It had installed fast trains (over 200 km./hr.) and found that to sustain high speeds properly, a layer of insulation underneath the rails was required.

The Finns, Hernborg said, were "always on their own—that's one of the things I admire them for." "As long as we have a decent living here and can keep the Russian Army away from our border," they told him, "we don't care. You can do what the heck you want in Sweden, Norway, and Denmark."

Since 1952 Dow's agent in Finland had been Algol (named for Albert Goldbeck-Lowe, who founded it in Helsinki in 1894), and if there was an agency relationship anywhere in the world that Dow was happy with, it was with the Algol agency in Finland.[37]

In the Finnish business world, everybody knows everybody, Hernborg said, and Algol had excellent personal connections with all the important Finnish industries. Eric Bargum, its board chairman, "knew everybody and anyone of any importance."

When the latex plant at Norrkoping had been completed, Hernborg said, the logical next step was to build a latex plant in Finland, "before any of the German, French, or Canadian competitors were smart enough to get in and build one"; Finland is an even bigger market than Sweden for paper latex, the biggest single product for Dow Nordic. Hernborg also knew he could not get a plant authorized in any nation where sales were in the hands of an agent, which meant only one thing: canceling the contract with Algol.

When he broached the matter to Bargum, Bargum said, "Well, you're making a fantastic mistake, Nils Hernborg," and told him how much business Dow would lose as a result. "And he was probably right," Hernborg said.

In Zurich he talked to Doscher and Merszei about the problem, and they agreed that there had to be a parting, which should be made as pleasant as possible. They would agree to an overlapping commission, they told him.

Frank Popoff, newly returned to Horgen as executive vice president of Dow Europe, suggested to Hernborg that he go lock himself up somewhere with his best friend in Algol, Bjorn Biese, its chemical sales manager. "You're the only guy who can handle Bjorn when he gets mad," Popoff said.

Hernborg invited Biese for a weekend at his big house out in the Stockholm archipelago—Margit was away—and for two days and two nights they talked only about one thing: the cancellation letter. "He was furious and screaming and carrying on," Hernborg said, as they went for long walks in the islands. Instead of an overlapping commission, leading to a protracted separation, they agreed to calculate a percentage of the sales Algol would make for Dow, as closely as they could estimate, and this sum would be paid by Dow at separation. A few weeks later Popoff and Hernborg handed over the check, and Algol signed the cancellation papers.

The question of building a plant in Finland could now proceed, and eventually, in 1989, Dow opened a latex plant in Finland at a place called Hamina, close to the Finnish border with Russia. The relationship with Algol continues to be friendly, and the two companies continue to work together. Frank Popoff was an honored guest at 1994 ceremonies marking Algol's centennial.

IX.

In the years after the Brunnen meeting, Dow Europe's growth was one of the most dazzling shows ever put on in the chemical industry. Dow's sales in Europe multiplied tenfold, from $150.8 million in 1967 to $1.5 billion in 1976, 85 percent of it produced in plants that were built in Europe. The Dow employee population climbed from 2,000 to 11,600, scattered across 14 European countries, and 99 percent of them were Europeans. Thirty different nationalities were represented on the Dow European payroll.[38]

This was such a spectacular achievement that its architect and leader, Zoltan Merszei, was to leap from there to become chief executive of the entire company in 1976. We will return to that subject shortly.

Let us first look at West Germany, always the largest European market for Dow. In the chemical industry, where other chemical companies are a chemical company's best customers, and with three of the world's largest chemical companies in Germany—Bayer, Hoechst, and BASF—Germany easily outpaced the other nations of Europe in Dow sales. By 1976 Dow sales in West Germany had reached $225 million (compared to $25.7 million in 1966); the next highest country totals in Europe were for Spain and Italy, at about $180 million each.

Dow opened its first German office at Frankfurt in April 1960, and Merszei installed Milan Ondrus, a Czech, as country manager. In 1964, as previously noted, it purchased a production site at Greffern, on the Rhine opposite the Drusenheim site in France, and broke ground for latex and Styrofoam plants there in 1965. (Since the later amalgamation of three small towns including Greffern, it has been called Rheinmunster.) Greffern/Rheinmunster became the incubator for Dow's first generation of German managers—Egon Michel, Wolf Rittershausen, and Bernhard Brummer.

As sales grew, Dow began to plan for a major chloralkali complex in Europe—the Terneuzen site with its big naphtha crackers had no salt deposits—and it looked at sites in England, in northern Germany, in southwest France, and in northern Holland. As usual, it wanted a site near salt domes, close to a large waterway, away from heavy industrial concentrations, and Dow has always favored small towns. After studying the alternatives it chose a site at Stade (pronounced "Stahd´-duh"), on the Elbe River about 25 miles from Hamburg in northern Germany. The site itself, Butzflethersand, had once been an island in the Elbe but the river had shifted over time and it was now part of the mainland, protected by dikes from the annual floods.[39]

Stade, founded in 994 A.D., a jewel of a small medieval town set in walls dating from the Middle Ages, lies in a triangle formed by the North Sea and the Weser and Elbe rivers. In 1648 the region was captured by the Swedes in a religious war, and during their period of control the Swedes made Stade the headquarters for the triangle and established government agencies and courts there. It remained a regional center when the Swedes left, and when Dow arrived it was still an administrative center populated chiefly by government employees. In the 1960s the government of Lower Saxony, at Hanover, decided to use the spacious open land available nearby to attract large industry. The Dow complex was the first to arrive, followed closely by a large aluminum works operated by Vereinigte Aluminium Werke AG and the Reynolds Corporation, and within 10 years more than $1 billion in new industry was built in the area, transforming it entirely. Over the years the Dow investment alone would exceed $1 billion.

The Stade operation was the brainchild of Clyde Boyd, manufacturing director for Dow Europe and later the successor to Merszei as Dow Eurochief. In October 1968 Boyd casually mentioned to T. J. (Ted) Walker, one of his chief lieutenants, "By the way, Ted, you're going to build and manage our new plant at Stade," and Walker became its founder and manager. Ground was broken a year later, on October 22, 1969.

Wolf Rittershausen, then the Styrofoam superintendent at Rheinmunster, and Joachim Schnell, the latex superintendent, were sent off to Texas for training. Egon Michel became the Rheinmunster general manager, succeeding Mike Marshall, and Bernie Brummer stayed on as epoxy resin superintendent.

Stade and Terneuzen soon became the bookends of Dow European manufacturing, and Dow's major production complexes on the continent. Dow and Stade developed a symbiotic relationship, and Dow found itself the leading supporter of a neat, prosperous, medieval city. (In 1989 taxes paid by Dow made up two-thirds of the city's budget.)

"Stade was so poor as an administrative city that it couldn't afford the basics such as a hospital and modern schools, and today Stade is the richest city in Lower Saxony," Brummer, a later general manager at Stade, said.

> It became an advantage for Stade to be poor so long, because after the war it was considered modern to tear down everything that was old and build for a new future. A lot of ancient houses were just torn down as part of the drive to forget the past. Stade never had the funds to participate in this drive so it had to keep its old buildings, and when Stade became rich the philosophy had changed. So Stade preserved a lot. If you walk through the town today you will find a lot of sixteenth-century architecture. The heart of Stade is still in the Middle Ages.[40]

The first plants at Stade came onstream in 1972, just in time for the OPEC energy crisis of 1973. Dow built its own cogeneration facility and started up the site with five gas turbines, becoming an energy island independent of outside power needs. The site developed steadily, with first-phase investment of 400 million DM, and by 1989, two billion DM. Like other Dow sites, it developed an energy conservation program in response to the OPEC crisis. By 1989 it was using 35 percent less energy to produce the same amount of product it had in 1974.

The first major crisis at Stade occurred when the local population, to the surprise and consternation of the project managers, began to protest the building of the plant. The first plants were copies of plants Dow had already built in Texas, Louisiana, and Michigan, with thoroughly proven technology, and the only people on the site were engineers. "They were all very responsible people," Brummer said, "but we had not advanced to the degree that we thought we owed anything to the public except building safe plants. That we were convinced we had done, and that is what we thought the public would expect, but we didn't think we needed to inform our neighbors what we were doing or to explain to them the hazards involved."

All that was changed by the crisis at Stade. It began with start-up of the first chlorine plant and a release of chlorine gas. "We burned a big hole in a chlorine line and released a bunch of chlorine," Brummer said.

> It was blowing toward the Elbe River, which was a good thing. I was in charge at that time. That evening I called one of my colleagues and told him, "Stop the traffic on the Elbe River, because I don't know what may happen." He stopped the boats on the river, and that's when the public became sensitized. From then on we received a lot of public attention. Newspapers and radio stations and all the media began to watch us, and we still didn't really do any public work. We thought if we fixed the pipe, that was the main thing. We didn't respond, and the criticism became pretty severe. There was something negative in the paper very often, until we realized we had to do something; we had to speak out.
>
> We were busy working on the plant, but we were not busy explaining to people what we were doing to get things under control. You would hear interviews with all kinds of people about this except the Dow people. Eventually it became so severe that we started speaking up and explaining things in a full-time way. It was a bitter experience we went through, and we had to struggle for many years for more acceptance by the public. Today I believe we have it. It took us a long time.[41]

When Dow decided to build a second chlorine plant at Stade, a petition opposing it was signed by 2,800 local voters. At this juncture Egon Michel, who had succeeded Ted Walker as plant manager, asked Brummer to step out of his production duties and head up plant services, including response to the protests. Brummer suddenly found himself learning "the hard way" about what he called "the peripheral necessities of the manufacturing job." "I'm sure I could never have done as good a job as a general manager of this site if I had not served in this position for three or four years," he said. (He returned to production in 1976 and became general manager in 1979.)

"We started addressing ourselves to the public, explaining what industry was about," Brummer said.

> I found myself in front of all kinds of groups, explaining what we wanted to do, and I often felt very uncomfortable with these groups. You have to understand that Stade had never had industry before. There was no industry experience. It was only natural that we had to go through this period. It would have been better if we had foreseen this rather than letting it go for years and then picking it up and changing it. Today I think we are accepted here, and people have a lot

better understanding of the chemical industry. We invite our neighbors in and do all those good neighbor things.

Some of it became very personal, he said, with people throwing dead fish on the porch of his house, and acts of that kind. He was concerned about the pressures on his children at school. "The teacher told them we were dropping our effluent into the river in the night, and that my children should ask their father about it and report back the next morning—things like that," he said.

"We worked to improve our environmental performance, reduced emissions and spills, improved our safety record, presented it all in public," Brummer said.

This experience, carried on during the time the "Green" Party was becoming a political force in Germany, led Dow to project Stade as a site without any waste at all, a goal it ultimately achieved in 1990. "We developed and patented technology here at Stade to become a site without waste," Brummer said. "We have published this in Germany and it's talked about. We have earned a lot of respect for this because waste disposal is much more of a problem here in a country only a third the size of Texas but with about four times the population of Texas."

Stade also developed containment technology for highly hazardous materials, and was proud to be the first plant in Dow and in Germany to accomplish this. This grew out of the need to make and consume phosgene in the manufacture of polycarbonate plastic (phosgene was one of the poison gases used in gas warfare in World War I). All the phosgene-containing equipment was put inside a giant containment unit 125 feet high and 75 feet in diameter.

Operating in the shadow of Bayer, Hoechst, and BASF, the Big 3 of world chemical companies, Dow Germany has been under close scrutiny from the bigger, older firms. "They haven't yet accepted Dow as a full member of the club," Brummer said, "but they accept and respect Dow for Dow's performance. They know what we do and how we perform. They have no problems with our way of doing things; they envy us in many, many respects. They are willing to say publicly, 'We want Dow's safety performance,' and things like that. In Germany they would like to keep us small and humble. But we will get there; we will work ourselves up there, and win recognition and acceptance in Germany."

X.

Could a profit-hungry capitalist chemical company from the American Midwest find happiness in the embrace of a rigidly controlled communist economy? That was the question when Dow undertook a major project in tandem with Tito's Yugoslavia in the 1970s, the first and as it turned out only undertaking of its kind.

It was Dow who went courting. By 1972 its sales in Yugoslavia were large enough that the company considered establishing a production facility there; Yugoslavia, it felt, might be a good place to make polystyrene plastic. The Yugoslavs, who since 1948 had been pursuing a course increasingly independent of Stalin and the USSR, had adopted a law some years earlier actually permitting joint ventures, and they greeted the idea with enthusiasm. In short order (for a proposal involving a country behind the Iron Curtain, where such negotiations usually dragged on forever) the two parties agreed to such a joint venture. They announced on September 18, 1973, that they envisioned a $25 million plant at Zagreb, the capital city of Croatia, to produce some 36,500 tons of plastic products annually—including polystyrene and Pelaspan polystyrene foam beads. As the child of Dow and Organsko Kemijska Industrija, it was promptly dubbed the "Doki" project, from the initials of the parents.[42]

A detailed agreement was signed at the end of January 1974 by Zoltan Merszei for Dow and Zdravko Sakac for OKI, and Doki came into being. It was an exception to the rule by which Dow insisted on control of Dow technology; Dow owned 49 percent of the enterprise, the Yugoslavs the rest. Even though it came onstream two years late, in mid-1978, Doki worked well, and everyone was pleased.[43]

Earlier, as Marshal Tito had initiated his effort to court Western industry, Gillette had launched a $10 million joint venture to make razor blades in Yugoslavia, but Doki was the largest investment yet under this program, and its success stimulated the Yugoslavs to try for even bigger fish. Vladimir Lemic, head of Industrija Nafte Zagreb (INA), sounded out Merszei. Would Dow be interested in a share of a really large petrochemical complex?

Merszei knew that INA, Yugoslavia's largest industrial enterprise, ran the nation's biggest refinery operations at the Adriatic port of Rijeka. A pipeline linked Rijeka to Hungary and Czechoslovakia, and there were persistent rumors that it would soon be extended all the way to the Soviet Union. Crude oil arrived there from Libya, Kuwait, and other suppliers.

Did Dow want to take on another big petrochemical complex? Ben Branch, then Dow's CEO, was hardly intimidated. He said he would very much like to find out whether it was possible for a company like Dow to work constructively with the Soviet satellite nations; if Dow could work with a socialist economy such as Yugoslavia, it ought to be able to work anywhere in the Soviet bloc. Go ahead, but don't get Dow too far out on the limb, he advised Merszei, and let's see what happens.

In May 1974, as the OPEC oil crisis was easing, Dow began negotiating with INA and the Yugoslav government for what would turn out to be the largest capitalist-socialist joint venture ever, unmatched in any of the Eastern European countries. As these plans shaped up, Dow would build and operate a major petrochemical complex on the island of Krk (pronounced "kirk"), opposite the Rijeka deepwater port. The negotiations revolved around Velimir Rajkovic, economic minister in the Croat government and president of Petrokem, the association of Croat petroleum and chemical enterprises, and Paul Stroebel, Merszei's business development chief in Horgen. The project was dubbed "Dina," again for the parents' initials, and again the ownership was 49 percent Dow, 51 percent Yugoslav.

"We spent a lot of time negotiating the terms of the contract [with Rajkovic]," Stroebel said.

We knew the risks, working with an entirely different type of economic system. Theoretically you had a worker for your partner. Presumably the workers benefited from the project through jobs, but also through the concept that they were actually co-owners. The government put a tremendous amount of incentives into it. They built a bridge, the longest single-arch bridge in Europe, to link Krk to the mainland; they gave us the land, and all sorts of monetary incentives. They wanted Dow as a partner; they wanted to develop their industry with the best petrochemical technology. If we ever pulled out the worst we could do is get the money back that we put into the project. Along with it we got a very good naphtha contract; they supplied us with naphtha at a preferential price for our Terneuzen crackers.[44]

In addition, Yugoslavia had bilateral trade agreements, especially with East Germany and the USSR, which gave Yugoslav enterprises, including Dina, special access to their markets. "The Yugoslavs needed the hard currency that could come from a venture like this," explained Herb Lyon, then Dow's administrative vice president in Midland. "If material could be produced there and exported to other Eastern European countries, not necessarily socialist countries but countries where they could sell their product and get hard currency, they needed that currency back home badly."[45]

The Yugoslavs had a hard time selling the resultant package to some of their government ministers and their people, Stroebel said. "Rajkovic was very capable and he got things done politically. He was able to convince the ministries to go along with it," he said.

On March 26, 1976, the contract was signed with appropriate fanfare. It called for a $700 million petrochemical complex to be built in three stages over the next half-dozen years. Over the next few years the estimated price tag rose to $950 million, and then to $971 million.

U. S. President Gerald Ford, who had met with Tito the year before to discuss U.S.-Yugoslav trade ties, hailed the Dina accord as "an important step forward in the further development of economic relations between our two countries," and said it would "improve general relations between Yugoslavia and the United States."[46]

Stage one, to begin production at the end of 1979, projected plants to make high-density polyethylene, vinyl chloride monomer, and ethylene dichloride. Two years later, stage two would add low-density polyethylene and styrene plants, and stage three, in 1982, would add a 400,000 metric ton per year ethylene facility and associated hydrocarbons.

The agreement was signed (by Lemic and Merszei) in Zagreb, with board chairman Carl Gerstacker and Dow Europe president Clyde Boyd leading the Dow delegation. Gerstacker told the gathering somewhat prophetically that he was looking forward to returning three years hence to celebrate the opening of a fully operating plant. When that took place, he said, concluding his remarks with a few phrases in the Croat language, he would have proof that "na djelu poznaju junaci"—"by their deeds you know the heroes," a Yugoslav proverb.[47]

The $700 million financing plan included $107.1 million from INA, in land and cash; $102.9 million from Dow, in know-how and cash; $406 million from the Privredna Banka Zagreb, and $84 million in Dina borrowings. Manufacturers Hanover Bank subsequently approved a $300 million loan to Privredna for the project in 1979, the largest loan to a Yugoslav borrower to that time.

Perhaps the most worrisome aspect of the project for the Dow negotiators was what would happen to the project (and to Yugoslavia) if and when Josip Broz Tito were to die, although he appeared in vigorous health in 1976, still going bear hunting and belting down the vodka at age 84. Stroebel went to talk to Sir Peter Carey, permanent secretary in the British government's Department of Industry and a leading expert on Yugoslavia, and Sir Peter was reassuring. "He felt sure that President Tito's death would not cause significant changes in the Yugoslav system, and that the mechanism of electing Tito's successor from the members of the Presidency, composed of the presidents of each republic and the two provinces, was a sound way of achieving a consensus," Stroebel said. Stroebel concluded that Marshal Tito's end would probably not disrupt Yugoslavia's economic and social progress.

For most of a decade after Tito died in 1980 that was the case, but then the country began rapidly to unravel. In 1991, long after Dow had left the scene, what is now called "the former Yugoslavia" fell apart and 4 million former Yugoslavs became displaced persons in a protracted, vicious, confusing war.

After the Dina agreement was signed in 1976 Dow sent project teams to work on the project. A. L. (Bert) Holliday, who had been manager of Dow's Torrance (California) plant, became Dow's Yugoslav country manager. Branimir Strenja, director of INA's Rijeka refinery, became DINA's general director, and Holliday became assistant general director. Strenja was also president of an eight-man "business board" that was to be the key decision-making body; the Dow members were Holliday, Stroebel, Alex Crossan, Dow Europe's eastern regional general manager (and a vice president of Dina); and John Scriven, a Dow attorney who later became the company's general counsel.

"One of the first obstacles we had to overcome internally at Dow was to understand and accept the concept of the legal structure of a joint venture, Yugoslavian style," said Robert E. Monica, a Dow plastics executive.

> In Yugoslavia, the foreign partner invests in the Yugoslav partner, and the resulting joint venture is a BOUW (Basic Organization of United Work), forming a unit within the domestic partner. When we saw the legal structure in the frame of a partnership agreement and realized that the resulting BOUW could be established as a distinct legal entity (albeit contained within our partner's organization) with its own accounting system and its own management, and liability limited to its own assets, we accepted the fact that although different in form, it gave us all the essential conditions we required.[48]

Another matter of concern was the Workers' Council, Monica said, "since they are the supreme authority over the joint venture. However, since the Workers' Council must ratify the joint venture agreement, they permanently delegate to the joint venture management those functions and responsibilities which are agreed upon in the joint venture agreement."

The 157 square miles of the island of Krk began to stir from its historic past; there were bridges and other relics built by the Romans still to be seen there, and it was devoted largely to fishing, figs, grapes, and olives. Merszei, who became quite close to the Yugoslavs during this period, bought a vineyard on the island and became a gentleman vintner.[49]

Actual site work began in early 1978, two years after the signing ceremonies. "It took three years of talks and planning and finally the personal intervention of Marshal Tito to get approval for the Dow Chemical Company's joint venture at Krk," *Business Week* reported, "but work did start this month on the $700 million project."[50]

Delay piled on delay as the project slowly and painfully proceeded. Work on the plant itself could not get under way before the bridge to Krk was completed, and the Dow crews did not willingly suffer these delays. The Dow side had one major setback itself. Bert Holliday was "tremendously capable, not only as far as engineering and accomplishing the physical aspects of the project," Stroebel said, "but he also had a real knack for developing relationships with people. Unfortunately, as the project was coming along, he died of a heart attack. That was a real blow to the ultimate success of the project."

The basic problem, Herb Lyon felt, was that "the Yugoslavs could not be realistic in the way they viewed their own capability to produce and generate cash flow; they couldn't understand the need to be realistic on what was going to happen to their own inflation rate."

Inflation was around 100 percent per year in the country at that time. "Consequently, as the construction of this petrochemical facility began to move, the engineers could look across the fence at a customs impoundment, with materials and equipment ready to come in. But they couldn't release the papers because there was no money available on the part of the Yugoslavs to get the stuff released in volume."

Dow had already exhausted its commitment of funds to the project. "We weren't prone to go at it with more money," Lyon said, "and the project kept moving in a sideways direction for quite a period of time."[51]

It was Frank Popoff, who by then had succeeded to the presidency of Dow Europe, who finally called a halt to the project. "Frank finally got to the point where he was saying, 'We just can't continue this way. It would be a lot better for us if we bail out before this thing gets to the point of going down.' So we bailed out. We brought our people out."

The first part of the Yugoslav experiment, the Doki plastics plant, probably worked, Lyon felt, because the Doki unit, "was so much smaller in total money requirements and space and all the other requirements than the Dina project. They could stomach that with the small Doki project and the thing would not get topsy-turvy because of inflation rates as Dina did."

On November 23, 1982, Dow informed its Yugoslav partners in writing and announced publicly that it was terminating the Yugoslav venture effective January 15, 1983.[52] In the months that followed Dow sold its share of the project to INA and signed a contract with INA to help the Yugoslavs get the project started.

In November 1984, Dow sent specialists from its Oyster Creek, Texas, Louisiana, and Ft. Saskatchewan (Canada) operations to assist in start-up of what was now the INA vinyl chloride monomer plant at Krk, fulfilling that part of the contract. The unit had been scheduled for start-up five years before as a Dina plant.[53]

"It could have been a great project had Yugoslavia been something different than it is today," Popoff said. "It started to come apart because the economy began to suffer problems in the aftermath of Tito's demise and caused a lot of political instability. Still, Yugoslavia hung together. I think they could have made it, although I'll bet that's a minority opinion.[54]

"The demigoguery set in only after the economy failed, and when the economy failed Croat began to believe that Slovene, or Serb, or Bosnian had it better than he did, the Serb believed that the Macedonians and the Croats were getting all the goodies, and the Bosnians knew that everybody else was doing better than they were. Then it was ripe for the demigogues."

Yugoslavia was "a wrenching experience," Popoff said, "because it was potentially a great project. As it turned out, we probably should have pulled out six months earlier."

Notes

1. Citations in this section are from T. E. Knapp, "Interview with Ted Knapp Regarding Dow Europe," 1982.

2. For early dates and developments in Dow Chemical Europe, see Luc Wortmann, *Dow History - European Area*, June 5, 1966. See also extensive memo, Wortmann to T. E. Knapp, "Corporate Structure in Europe—Implementation of 1966 System—Basic Rules & Questions," November 4, 1965.

3. Oral History, Robert F. Kincaid, July 8, 1991; Oral History, Heidi Baur, July 25, 1989; Oral History, Edmund P. Faessler, July 7, 1989; and Oral History, Rosemary Boswell, July 10, 1989.

4. Oral History, Hunter W. Henry Jr., September 11, 1980.

5. See Dow Press Kit, Terneuzen Plant Dedication, May 24, 1965, with copies of speeches delivered and other materials. Also *Dow in the Netherlands*, brochure published on this occasion by Dow Chemical Internationaal N.V., Rotterdam.

6. Prince Bernhard message from *Provinciale Zeeuwse Courant*, Terneuzen, May 25, 1965.

7. *Provinciale Zeeuwse Courant*, Terneuzen, May 21, 1965.

8. Oral History, Edmund P. Faessler, July 7, 1989.

9. See "Terneuzen Aromatics Complex to Be Renovated in 1994," *Dow Today*, March 2, 1993, and "Styrene IV in Terneuzen to Restart Next Summer," *Dow Today*, October 26, 1992.

10. Alex Groner, "Making It with Dow Europe," *Dow Latina*, Dow Latin America, Coral Gables, Florida, August 1974.

11. Oral History, Charles M. Doscher, July 12, 1989.

12. Eric Hobsbawm, *The Age of Extremes: A History of the World, 1914-1991* (New York: Random House, 1994).

13. Oral History, Paul F. Oreffice, August 1, 1988.

14. Citations in this section are from Oral History, Ignacio M. Artola, July 19, 1989. See also *Dow in Spain, 1960-1972*, brochure (Bilbao, Spain: Dow Chemical Europe, 1973).

15. "New Dow Plant in Spain Dedicated by Gen. Franco," *Dow Diamond* 30, no. 2 (1967). See also Alan Allott, "In Spain, it's Dow-Unquinesa," *Dow Diamond* 34, no. 2 (1971).

16. Oral History, Charles M. Doscher, July 12, 1989.

17. Oral History, Dimitri V. Papageorgiou, July 7, 1989.

18. During the Greek classical period Athenian silver coins were called "owls of Lavrion"; they bore the likeness of an owl and were made of silver mined at Lavrion. Lavrion is mentioned by Demosthenes, Aristophanes, Thucydides, Strabo, and other Greek writers. For early Dow history in Greece see Memo, Luc Wortmann to T. E. Knapp, "Corporate Structure in Europe," November 4, 1965, and Wortmann, *Dow History, European Area*, June 5, 1966.

19. See "Lavrion: A Backward Glance," and "Dow in Greece," interview with Papageorgiou by Mark Batterson, *Elements* magazine (English edition) no. 10 (1975).

20. Oral History, Roberto Sabbioneda, July 20, 1989.

21. See H. H. Dow to R. W. Greeff, May 13, 1930, and H. H. Dow to Edward de Greeff, May 23, 1930.
   At a later date Robert Helfenstein, longtime managing director of R. W. de Greeff, retired to his native Switzerland and raised a family there. Dow, looking for people who knew the European chemical industry (and who didn't need Swiss work permits), hired the retired Helfenstein, and later, his son Jack, who became executive vice president of Dow Europe.

22. Oral History, W. Stanley Buck, July 12, 1989.

23. Oral History, Philip A. Laird, August 20, 1990.

24. See "Dow at Barry," *Dow Europe Now, Special Edition*, United Kingdom and Ireland (Horgen, Switzerland: Dow Chemical Europe, August 1976).

25. Oral History, Eric Huggins, September 20, 1994.

26. Oral History, Paul F. Oreffice, August 1, 1988.

27. Citations in this section are from Oral History, Roberto Sabbioneda, July 20, 1989.

28. Ibid.

29. Regarding Montessori, see "The Pioneer," *Dow Diamond* 34, no. 2 (June 1971): 28-31.

30. Regarding Gruppo Lepetit S.p.A., see William Carnahan, "Lepetit—Progress Through Research," *Dow Diamond* 34, no. 2 (June 1971): 36-40.

31. Oral History, Andrew J. Butler, May 5, 1995.

32. Citations in this section are from Oral History, Yves L. P. Crepet, July 5, 1989.

33. Oral History, Paul G. Stroebel, July 2, 1992.

34. See Eugene V. Epstein, "Astraddle the Border: Greffern-Drusenheim," *Elements* magazine (English edition), no. 6 (1972).

35. Section VIII cites extensively from Oral History, Philip A. Laird, August 20, 1990.

36. Section VIII cites extensively from Oral History, Nils Erik Hernborg, July 17, 1989.

37. See Magnus Bargum (chairman, Algol) to Frank P. Popoff, September 13, 1994; "Algol, A Major Industrial Supplier" (English language version), Espoo, Finland, 1994; and Raul Hendriksson, "Algol, Serving Finnish Industry for 100 Years," (English language version), Espoo, Finland, 1994.

38. *Profile of Dow Chemical Europe*, brochure published by Dow Chemical Europe, Horgen, Switzerland, July 1977.

39. See Hans Peter Held, "The Stade Concept," *Elements* (English edition), no. 6 (1972). The issue is devoted almost entirely to Dow's activities in Stade and Germany.

40. Oral History, Bernhard Brummer, July 24, 1989 is quoted extensively in this section.

41. For a detailed account of this episode see Wolff Balthasar, ecologist of Dow's Stade complex, "The Stade Ecology Story," *Elements* (English edition), no. 7 (1973).

42. "Dow Announces Joint Venture in Yugoslavia," *Dow Today*, September 18, 1973. A popular Yugoslav joke of the time had Tito arriving at a fork in the road, the road on the left marked "Socialist Economy" and the one on the right marked "Capitalism." "Which road should I take?" asked his chauffeur. "Signal vigorously that you are turning left," responded Tito, "and turn to the right."

43. "Dow Signs Contract for Yugoslav Venture," *Dow Today*, January 31, 1974. See also Stanley Mason, "Yugoslavia," *Elements* (English edition) 2, no. 1 (1974).

44. Oral History, Paul G. Stroebel, July 2, 1992.

45. Oral History, Herbert H. Lyon, August 7, 1990.

46. "U.S. President Ford Congratulates INA and Dow on Petrochemicals Accord," *Dow Europe Now*, March 31, 1976. See also "Yugoslavia's INA, Dow Agree on Joint Petrochemical Venture," Dow news release, March 26, 1976.

47. Carl A. Gerstacker, address at signing of Dina agreement, Zagreb, March 26, 1976.

48. Robert E. Monica, "Dow Investment in Yugoslavia," World Trade Institute, New York, N.Y., May 5, 1975.

49. "Dow-Yugoslav Joint Venture to Produce Petrochemicals," by Herbert H. Lyon, vice president, and Paul G. Stroebel, director, corporate product dept., slide presentation to U.S.-Yugoslav Economic Council, New York, New York, December 7, 1977.

50. "Yugoslavia: A door slightly ajar for U.S. investment," *Business Week,* February 6, 1978.

51. Oral History, H. H. Lyon.

52. "Dow to Terminate Yugoslav Venture," Dow news release, Texas Division, November 23, 1982.

53. "Dow to Provide Yugoslavian Assistance," *Creek Communications*, Oyster Creek Division, Texas, November 29, 1984.

54. Oral History, Frank P. Popoff, November 16, 1995.

FIFTEEN

DOW AND LATIN AMERICA

I.

Dow's Latin American organization is "the house that Paul built"—Paul Oreffice, a later chief executive of the company, became founding father of the organization when it formally became a division of Dow in 1965—but he was preceded by a small group of trailblazers who first carried the Dow diamond to the South American continent.

In the days following World War II Dow's tiny export department at company headquarters in Michigan consisted of an export sales manager, Howard Ball, and two salesmen, Ted Knapp and Russell Zick. The latter divided the world between them; Knapp took Europe and Africa, and Zick chose Latin America and Asia. They each made an annual trip to these distant places, where Dow products were sold through local distributor firms. Dow's total export business in 1950 was about $10 million, 5 percent of total sales.

Only with the formation of Dow Chemical International and Dow Chemical Inter-American in 1952 did the company begin to emphasize foreign sales. Clayton Shoemaker, who urged creation of these new entities and was named their president, became the spearhead of the new move abroad and immediately decided to open Dow offices overseas, beginning in Europe and Latin America.[1]

That resulted in the opening of offices in Zurich, to which Knapp soon moved (see chap. 14), and in Montevideo, where Zick settled down.

In 1954 Shoemaker decided to open offices in Mexico City and Tokyo. H. L. (Lee) Clack, who had gone to Montevideo with Zick, was sent off to establish a new Dow office in Tokyo, and Zick moved to Mexico City. Bob Kincaid, who had joined the group in 1949, moved from Zurich to the office in Montevideo. These were the first major moves in a game of personnel hopscotch which later became commonplace in Dow International.

Dow's first Latin American office was installed in Montevideo, Kincaid said, because Argentina and Brazil, the dominant South American economies, were controlled by powerful dictators, Juan Peron and Getulio Vargas, at the time. Montevideo, in the small country of Uruguay between these two giants, was "a peaceful, quiet, inexpensive place to live, with fine people," Kincaid said, and he and his wife, Nancy, and their children loved it.[2]

Zick hired two key people for the Montevideo office, Carlos Kolungia, an Argentine and former admiral of the Argentine navy, who had joined Dow on leaving Argentina, and Cedric Hendrickson, who had worked for the Dow distributor in Chile.

One of the oddities of the business was that the revenue from the caustic sales in Argentina and Brazil that formed the bulk of Dow's sales in the continent could not be repatriated to the United States, and Dow was accumulating large sums in "blocked pesos."

"We had a good agent in the Argentine called Williams Quimica that we ended up buying half of with these blocked pesos," Kincaid said.

> We sold a lot of caustic. We also sold things like glycol for dynamite production. We had a great business in Brazil on one-pound cans of methyl bromide, which is a fumigant. Brazil has this great big ant which makes ant hills 18 to 20 feet high called "sauva." The only way you can really kill them is to introduce methyl bromide into the ant nest. We could sell millions of these cans. The agricultural business in general was a good business; sugarcane was a good ag business for us.

Business was so promising that in 1955 Dow decided to station a full-time resident in Brazil, and Kolungia was dispatched to Sao Paulo to open the first Dow office in that country. Then events began to move swiftly.

Juan Peron was toppled from power by a military junta on September 19, 1955, and fled to neighboring Uruguay, an event that dramatically altered Argentine and Latin American history and also had lasting repercussions on The Dow Chemical Company.

Kolungia, the admiral who had also been his nation's minister of the navy three different times, had opened the company's first office in Brazil just a few months before. Kolungia rented a small office on the fifth floor above the First National City Bank of New York in downtown Sao Paulo and hired a secretary, Phyllis Gibson, born in Sao Paulo of American parents, who was to become his right arm and the den mother of Dow in Brazil until her death at the age of 56. She helped the young Brazilians who soon peopled the office with their English, and counseled them on working with the gringos.

In his brief stint as Dow's Brazilian manager, Kolungia concentrated on building the company's sales of caustic soda, for which Sao Paulo was a thriving market, but left the other Dow products undisturbed; they were then being marketed by the Schilling Hillier firm, which represented both Dow and Union Carbide in Brazil.

When Peron fell from power Kolungia was summoned back to Buenos Aires and became Argentina's navy minister once more. His departure prompted the search for a new Brazilian Dow manager that eventually ended when Paul Oreffice took the office. Kincaid had sent Hendrickson to Sao Paulo to replace Kolungia but, he said, "it didn't work out," and he began to look elsewhere. "You could see that Brazil was someday going to really be something."

In 1956 Russell Zick died of a heart attack in the Mexico City office and Kincaid unexpectedly found himself the top Dow official for all of the Americas south of the Rio Grande. Later that year Oreffice arrived in Sao Paulo from Milan, Italy, with his new bride, Franca Ruffini, to become the new Dow manager for Brazil. A new chapter in Dow's Latin American history was about to open.

II.

Clayton Shoemaker knew Dow International would eventually switch to selling through its own sales force, following the model of the Dow organizations in the United States and Canada, rather than relying abroad on local distributor firms such as Schilling Hillier. Why not use Brazil as a testing ground for the change from distributor to direct selling? Oreffice, seeing the opportunity to build an organization from the ground up, welcomed the idea.

When Oreffice arrived in June 1956 an interim sales manager, Richard L. Staples, and an accountant, Francisco Antunes, had been added to the small staff. He inaugurated direct selling almost immediately, running a want ad for a chemical salesman and as a result hiring Salvador Pinto, who became the first Dow field salesman in Brazil and eventually a renowned specialist in selling caustic, Brazil's "Senhor Caustica."[3]

The personnel changed rapidly. Oreffice fired Antunes, whom he found loud and abrasive. Staples came into an inheritance and returned to the United States.

Business grew slowly, however. Sales were difficult because of the necessity of dealing with import licenses and also because of the fabulously high rates of Brazilian inflation, which ran between 25 and 80 percent a year during those years; the currency was regularly devalued by that much.

"It soon became apparent that you couldn't just sell by bringing shipments in from the U.S., and only the largest customers could go through the process of applying for dollars," Oreffice said. "If you were really going to do business, you had to bring products in yourself and sell them there in local currency."

"You needed lots of money, running the risk of devaluation from a currency that was devaluating rapidly," he said.

The only way you could bring products into Brazil was to buy dollars or other foreign currencies at auction, from the stock exchange on Tuesdays; every Tuesday all the stock exchanges in Brazil sold currency instead of stocks. You had to buy the currency; once you had the currency you could apply for an import license; and if they gave you the import license, you could then place the order and bring stuff in. It took six months roughly from the time you put up your money. I kept trying to figure out a way to finance without the risks of devaluation.

Oreffice soon discovered what he was looking for. "What would happen if Dow loaned the Banco do Brasil [the government bank] some dollars in the U.S. and they simultaneously loaned us some cruzeiros in Brazil," he asked a banker friend, "same period of time, no exchange involved, but they would pay us the dollars, we would pay them the cruzeiros?" This became the basis of what were known as "swap loans," and all of Dow's business in Brazil from 1957 to about 1969 was financed through swap loans.

Oreffice had a harder time selling Dow on the swap loan idea than he did the Brazilians. He went before the company's finance committee in Midland to explain "why I thought they should give me half a million dollars so we could make a swap loan." Carl Gerstacker, the chairman, listening to the presentation of this 29-year-old, finally said, "I don't really understand this deal but I think we owe it to Paul to have enough confidence in him to go ahead and do it." The committee approved.

What Oreffice then did was to take the cruzeiros he got through swap loans and go to the stock exchange every Tuesday. "I never missed a Tuesday at the stock exchange to buy dollars," he said. "We'd import goods. We got so good at this and we got so big at it because we could offer product there, where others had to go through the import license procedure, that around 1960 or 1961 we had a ship coming down from Texas and Louisiana every 20 days loaded with Dow products. We would sell them, most of the time, while the ship was still on the water. Just in case, we also had a leased warehouse."

By 1962 Dow had grown from the tiny office on the fifth floor in Sao Paulo to the second largest chemical company in Brazil in sales volume. The total Brazilian import market for caustic soda was 120,000-140,000 tons per year; Dow's sales of caustic climbed from about 1,000 tons per year to more than 70,000 tons per year.

Oreffice became known on the exchange as "O Rey da Soda Caustica," the king of caustic soda. "When I'd walk into the exchange, people would say, 'here comes the king,'" he recalled.

"It was a tremendous learning experience for a young guy, running your own show, independent as can be," Oreffice said. "Ted Doan used to say I had the most independent job in the company. When anyone called [from Midland] I just said, 'What? Can't hear you!' You couldn't get a phone in Brazil. The only way you could get a phone was to try to buy one from someone. When our office was able to buy two lines it was a big achievement."

During his seven years as general manager of Dow Quimica do Brasil its sales climbed from about $1 million per year to around $20 million per year, and it became the largest importer of chemical products to Brazil.[4]

It was such a standout performance, in a country with galloping inflation, that when it came time to establish Dow Latin America as a separate entity a few years later, Oreffice was the obvious choice to be its first president. Some years after that, when Gerstacker was looking for a successor as the company's chief financial officer, he brought Oreffice to Midland and groomed him for the job.

Oreffice's successor as Dow's manager in Brazil was Andre Landau, a Brazilian who had opened and headed the Dow sales office in Rio de Janeiro. He was a micromanager and a proud man; the office boy remembered that where Oreffice had just leaped into the manager's

Ray H. Boundy, Dow's first research vice president.

Ralph M. Wiley, discoverer of the saran plastics.

R. R. (Bobby) Dreisbach, the somewhat eccentric key inventor of polystyrene plastic.

O. Ray McIntire, who discovered Styrofoam while looking for something else.

Dow provided "Dowmetal" gondolas for the early space race between the U.S. and Russia. Here a U.S. Army Air Corps crew inspects a gondola nearing completion at Midland. Left to right: Capt. Albert W. Stevens, Maj. William E. Kepner, Capt. Orvil Anderson. On Nov. 11, 1935, Stevens and Anderson piloted a balloon-borne gondola to a height of 22.066 kilometers (13.71 mi.), the world's altitude record until the Soviet Union launched Sputnik in 1957.

Clayton S. Shoemaker, first president of Dow International.

Mark E. Putnam, general manager of the company, 1949-60.

A. P. (Dutch) Beutel, who established the chemical industry on the Texas Gulf coast.

Wilhelm (Doc) Hirschkind, the "wizard of the West."

William H. Schuette, who was scheduled to become Dow's CEO but died of a heart attack in 1959.

Leroy D. (Roy) Smithers, key figure in the history of Dow Canada.

The "Troika." C. Benson (Ben) Branch, left, was president and CEO of the company, 1970-76; Carl A. Gerstacker, center, was chairman, 1960-76; and H. D. (Ted) Doan, right, was president and CEO, 1962-70. Jointly they presided over the company throughout this period.

The "Brunnen meeting" of 1965 gathered the pioneers of Dow International at Brunnen, Switzerland, and established a basis for "globalizing" the company. Left to right, first row: Duco Akkerman, Marianne Schoen, Bob Helfenstein, Art Griswold, Bill Groening, Ed Hensley, Tom Sparta, Jack Stearns, Colin Goodchild, John Van Horn; second row: Lew Sellers, Manuel Maza, Nils Hernborg, Yves Crepet, Bob Forsythe, Art Young, Elmer Stilbert, Rene Wildi, Zoltan Merszei, Harold Page, Jack Thorsberg, Dick Gettings, Fred Mantel; back row: Joe Pinotti, John Myers, Macauley Whiting, Paul Oreffice, Hunter Henry, Prof. Vern Michelson, Roe Withrow, Milan Ondrus, Eric Huggins, Andre Landau, Bob Bennett, Bob Lundeen, Steve Marshall, Roger Zoccolillo, Bill Dixon, Bruce Rowell, Jim Jones, Colin Robertson, Julius Johnson, Phil Laird, Charlie Doscher, John Van Stirum.

Clyde H. Boyd served as president of Dow Canada and Dow Europe and was among the candidates to become CEO.

Joseph G. Temple Jr. presided over growth of Dow's pharmaceutical branch, Marion Merrell Dow, and its 1995 sale to Hoechst for $5.2 billion.

J. M. (Levi) Leathers, its hydrocarbons guru, was a company hero during the world oil crisis of the early 1970's.

Gen. Golbery do Couto e Silva, the "gray eminence," chairman of Dow Brazil, left the company in 1973 after forming a new Brazilian government.

Robert W. Lundeen, father of Dow's Pacific area operations, later became board chairman.

Earle B. Barnes almost left company in Merszei era, then became chairman and part of the "LOB" (Lundeen-Oreffice-Barnes) top management group.

David L. Rooke, president of Dow U.S.A., was part of a later "LORK" (Lundeen-Oreffice-Rooke-Keil) top management group.

Robert M. Keil continued custom of serving as company's top financial officer without formal financial background.

Zoltan Merszei, president and CEO, 1976-78.

Paul F. Oreffice, president and CEO, 1978-87.

Frank P. Popoff, president and CEO, 1987-95.

William S. Stavropoulos, president and CEO, 1995-

car—it was customary for Brazilian managers to have a car and driver—Landau insisted the driver open the car door for him. "He ruined the chances of a Brazilian heading up Dow operations in the country again for many years to come," one of his Brazilian colleagues said.

When he became the first president of Dow Latin America at the end of 1965, Oreffice faced a new set of problems, beginning with the location and organization of a new area organization. Several places in South America had been suggested as Dow's Latin American headquarters city. Those considered seriously were Lima, Peru; Sao Paulo, Brazil; Mexico City; and San Juan, Puerto Rico. The growing Cuban contingent at Dow, particularly Manuel Maza and Jorge Casteleiro, began to lobby for Miami as an added starter. Macauley Whiting, the president of Dow International, wanted Lima; it was equidistant from most points in Latin America, he said, and he wanted a place where the gringos would be forced to learn Spanish and communicate with the Latinos. This would not, he contended, be the case in Miami.

Oreffice appointed a three-man site selection committee (including Casteleiro) to analyze the advantages and disadvantages of the candidate cities. At the conclusion of its studies the committee recommended the Miami area, based on a variety of findings; it was quicker to fly to most parts of South America from Miami than it was from any city in South America, for example. Also, telephone communications in most parts of South America were at that time rudimentary.

Oreffice and Casteleiro visited the three finalists—Lima, San Juan, and Miami.

In Lima Neville Holmes, a Canadian managing the Dow office there, gave them a tour of this magnificent old city and then took them to his home. Oreffice said he would like to make a quick phone call to Midland. Holmes, flustered, admitted he didn't have a phone. "I've been asking for a telephone for four or five years," he said, "but in the residential areas there have been no new ones." A friend about a mile away had a phone Paul could use, he suggested.

Oreffice and Casteleiro looked at Lima no further, and took the next plane back to Miami. San Juan did not fare much better: it was expensive, and had limited direct flights to South American cities. Many flights from San Juan went through Miami.

In Miami Casteleiro assembled a group of Latin Americans to talk to Oreffice, carefully excluding Cubans, to demonstrate that Miami had representatives from every Latin American country and was not a a Cuban enclave. The Miami business community, with Esso and Gulf Oil leading the charge, told Oreffice of all the advantages they had found in locating there. "Miami," Oreffice in the end told Casteleiro, "is the ideal place for our headquarters."[5]

Oreffice chose offices at 120 Giralda in Coral Gables and the headquarters became operational in September 1966. Four years later, it moved a few blocks to 2801 Ponce de Leon and bigger quarters. For the next 28 years "Coral Gables" was to be synonymous within Dow with "Latin American headquarters."

Most of the communications, travel, and traffic problems within the South American continent improved greatly over time, and the organization itself also matured. The Latin American headquarters of Dow moved to Sao Paulo in 1994.

Dow's business in Brazil flourished so well that by the late 1960s the country was a candidate for a major Dow production facility. In 1969 Dow geologists began looking for a major salt deposit in the country; one would be needed as a raw material source if Dow were to establish a major chloralkali complex in Brazil. After much scouting around, Harold (Foxy) Foxhall, the Texas Division's chief geologist who supervised the search, decided the best prospect was a remote spot on the northwest coast of Brazil, Matarandiba Island. It was a pleasant, primitive little island covered with palm trees and tropical vegetation and no roads, inhabited only by a few fishermen in a small village. Foxhall said there was salt under this island, and challenged Dow to drill a salt well there to prove it.

It was an arduous and expensive undertaking. As Jarbas Carvalho, one of the Dow Brazil pioneers, described it, in those days you took a plane to Salvador, the nearest major city, and then a ferry boat to Itaparica Island; today a bridge has replaced the ferry and it is a well-known resort area. From Itaparica the only way to get to Matarandiba then was to hire a thin black man with one arm who took you across in a canoe. With General Golbery's help (General Golbery became a figure of legend in Dow Brazil, and we will return to his story shortly) Dow obtained permits to drill for salt, and then engaged the only driller in the entire area, a heavy-drinking American vegetating there who had an ancient, rusting oil-drilling rig, and began moving men and machinery out to the isolated island.[6]

Getting bulldozers, heavy equipment, and all the other necessities to the drilling site, and setting up a camp there and a radio station, was a whole saga unto itself. The drilling went well except for two details. One was that the heavy-drinking American seldom showed up for work; his job was eventually taken over by a Dow man, Roy Walker. The other detail was even more serious: it seemed they had drilled a dry hole. The Dow Brazil group was crushed. Hunter Henry, then president of Dow Brazil, was one of the few who wasn't that unhappy, he said later; the Bahia Blanca project in Argentina was making good progress at the time, and Dow did not need two major projects in Latin America. The Matarandiba project seemed to have perished.[7]

Into this scene of gloom and doom rode Walter Hange, a geologist in Foxhall's Texas group, who became the hero of Matarandiba and the man who raised it from the dead. Hange, who had experience drilling for oil in Colombia, came down from Freeport to try to find out what had gone awry, and why Dow had drilled a $150,000 dry hole when geologically there should be salt there.

He studied all of the geological maps he could find, up and down the Brazilian coast—at Petrobas, the Brazilian oil company, at other oil companies, at the Schlumberger and Halliburton oil well servicing company offices, wherever he could find geological maps of the area—and discovered fault lines on the ground not shown on some of the maps. He concluded that Dow had simply suffered the misfortune of drilling into a fault that was not on the map. Dow had to try again, he urged, this time avoiding the fault lines.

Sergio Goloubeff, another Dow Brazil pioneer, remembered a conversation with Hange over a drink. "How can you be so sure about it, Walt?" he asked. "We spent so much money on that first hole. If we miss it this time, we're dead. We're only going to have one more try."

"Look, Sergio," Hange said. "I've done a lot of oil drilling, and you have to be lucky. You have to have guts, and you just have to do it. I'm confident this is the right thing to do."

Hange and Goloubeff enlisted Bob Andrews, the business development manager for Brazil, and the three went to Henry with a proposal for drilling up to three holes at Matarandiba, at a maximum cost of $450,000. Henry was dubious but they finally convinced him; OK, but not a cent over $450,000, he decreed.

Hange told the drilling crew they should hit rock salt about 1,100 meters down. They hit it at 1,058. Goloubeff remembered that he and Andrews found their way to a bar the night they hit the salt, intent on celebrating. At 5 A.M. the next morning they staggered out to the beach to watch the sun rise and sat on some rocks, feeling quite philosophical. "Well, what do we do now?," they asked each other. "We've found the salt."[8]

Once they had the salt the pieces began to fall in place. A plant site was selected on the mainland not far from Matarandiba, at a place called Aratu. Dow began to plan a major complex there, and withdrew from the Bahia Blanca project (to which it would return a quarter century later, at the end of 1995). A long, costly pipeline was laid from the island to carry salt brine to the plant site.

Don Carlo Morales, governor of the federal district of Bahia, signed the papers for Dow's purchase of the Aratu site in a small ceremony with Bobby Caldwell, the Dow Latin America manufacturing chief, in 1973. There were still problems with some squatters on the site who were reluctant to leave, and there were questions as to whether they would have to be expelled from the site by force, but Bobby couldn't wait; he climbed on a bulldozer and drove it onto the newly purchased land himself, pushing some bushes out of the way and breaking ground for the Aratu petrochemical complex, which has become Dow's largest in Latin America.

Dow has expanded in Brazil for some 40 years and Brazil has become the keystone of Dow Latin America, with a staff of about 3,200 in the 1990s and manufacturing plants scattered across the nation—at Guaruja, Aratu, Franco da Rocha, Santo Amaro, and Jundiai. Partly by luck, partly by pluck, Dow has become one of the most successful of the international companies active in Brazil in the last half of the twentieth century, and in many ways, the most successful.

Indeed, by many measures, Dow is today the No. 1 firm in the South American continent in chemicals and plastics. When the Latin American area was established in 1965, Dow's sales there amounted to $45 million; in 1990 they surpassed $1 billion for the first time, and profits (before taxes) amounted to $167 million.

Dow was so successful in Brazil that the rest of the Latin American continent suffered from what they called "Brazilitis." "A lot of managers in Latin America—Enrique Sosa was one, when he was manager of Dow Venezuela—complained about 'Brazilitis,'" said Ernesto Ramon, a later president of Dow Latin America.

Nobody was paying attention to the possibilities of growth and investment in the rest of the Latin countries. If you look at the total capital investment in Latin America at the time, Brazil was 90 percent of it. Where are people going to put the emphasis? On a big thing, at a time when the markets in Brazil were up, up, up. So the emphasis was on Brazil and let's make that big investment grow. Venezuela, Mexico, and Argentina, you'll come later.[9]

Dow managers in the rest of Latin America began to complain that Brazil was getting the lion's share of the development funds and attention. The result of these complaints—the separation of Brazil from the rest of Latin America—"was the right thing to do for awhile because Latin America grew like hell," Ramon said. "People said, 'Our business is Spanish-speaking Latin America. Forget about those guys that speak that funny language (Portuguese, the language in Brazil)—they'll report to Midland.'"

About 10 years later the separation came to an end.

Ernesto Ramon said,

We put a team together to analyze the whole thing, and we said, "This doesn't make any sense anymore. We are not putting $600 million anyplace right now, not in Latin America or in Brazil. We have to manage and avoid duplication, and take advantage of the Brazilian experience and manufacturing base to back up the rest of Latin America and help its growth." So we put it back together, which saved Dow a lot of money and a lot of wasted time.

Casteleiro said the secret of Dow's success in the region was reliance on Latinos to deal with Latino problems. Dow, he said, avoided a mistake made by many U.S. and foreign companies—Japanese, German, British, and French. "They send nationals down there who don't speak the language and never are able to get the customers as Dow can, because Dow now has all Latino managers—not a single American in the top positions in the region."

In Argentina, as this is written, Dow has an Argentine manager; in Chile, a Chileno; in Peru a Peruvian; in Colombia, a Colombian; in Mexico, a Colombian; and in Brazil, a Cuban. "We know people and they trust us," Casteleiro said. "In Latin America, if you are trusted by the customer because you are a national, even if they don't know you personally very well, they will buy from you rather than buy from another company who has a foreigner as head of the marketing department; they prefer to do business with the nationals. That's something that you just can't erase or forget."[10]

III.

In June 1965 a letter from a Chilean government agency landed on Macauley Whiting's desk in Midland, asking if Dow would be interested in a venture in Chile. A study of Chile's petrochemical potential had recommended that plants for low-density polyethylene (LDPE) and polyvinyl chloride (PVC) be built in the country, and Dow and other private firms—18 of them in all, Dow discovered later—were being invited, "to study your possible participation in the companies that would own these plants."

Was Dow interested? No more than a bee would be interested in flowers. Whiting, then president of Dow International; Elmer K. Stilbert, manager of Dowintal's planning group; and Rafael Miquel, manager of planning for Latin America, quickly agreed that Dow was. The company had a new polystyrene plant just going onstream in Colombia that month, and was ready for a new venture. In the case of Chile it was to be one of the more dramatic adventures in company history.[11]

The company at that time mainly sold agricultural and mining chemicals to Chile—xanthates, flocculants, and other chemicals for the country's copper mines—and sales had grown from $320,000 in 1954 to $1,390,000 in 1964 through a local distributor, Duncan Fox, Ltd., an old British firm. The Duncan Fox manager for Dow products, an energetic young Chilean named Jorge Booth, had been in Midland the year before, talking up the great chemical potential of his country. He had also called on his friend Eduardo Simian, then general manager in New York for ENAP (Empresa Nacional del Petroleo, the Chilean government oil firm), but shortly to become minister of mines in the Frei government.

Eduardo Frei, the new president of Chile, a progressive moderate, had been elected in a landslide in 1964 with 56 percent of the vote over his nearest rival, the Socialist Salvador Allende, who received 39 percent. The country had a long record of stability and democracy. Frei, having taken the helm, was pressing to keep his campaign promises to modernize the country and raise its standard of living.

Miquel, one of many Cuban refugees who had signed on with Dow at this period, headed for Chile. Among the officials he talked to was Raul Saez, chief operating officer of CORFO (Corporacion de Fomento de la Produccion—Corporation to Foster Production) and the person who had signed the letter to Dow. Dr. Saez, one of Latin America's most highly regarded economists and a key adviser to President Frei, said CORFO was already narrowing the field to two or three firms with which to pursue the two projects, and that he would like a prompt letter from Dow expressing interest if it was there. Miquel phoned Stilbert and urged that such a letter be dispatched immediately.

Within a few days Miquel had his letter, with attachments. One of them described Dow's extensive background in polyethylene manufacture; another was an analysis of possible financing and ownership of the plant. Dow said it preferred to own 100 percent itself and would always wish to have more than 50 percent of the venture.

By September 1965 the candidates to build the LDPE plant were down to two—Phillips Petroleum and Dow—and only one candidate was left for PVC—Esso. In early December Dow dispatched a team to Santiago to open negotiations. The Dow group was headed by Stilbert, supported by William Fletcher of the Dow planning group, Miquel, and Manuel Maza, another Cuban, Dow's manager for Argentina and Chile. Later the team added Jorge Casteleiro. An agreement was slowly hammered out. In April 1966 the Chileans informed Dow that a new government corporation was being established, Petroquimica Chilena Limitada, or PQC, to coordinate the nation's petrochemical activities. Eduardo Simian was leaving his post as minister of mines to head it up. Negotiations were suspended as the government began a review of its policies. That same spring Dow established a separate Latin American area and Oreffice was appointed its first general manager; Dow used the pause to review its own stance in Chile.

As Fletcher and Oreffice discussed the Chilean situation they began to ask whether Dow should not be interested in the PVC plant as well. Dow decided to prepare a proposal, and quickly put one together. That summer it became apparent that Dow was the only candidate left in the race for the LDPE plant. The negotiations now concerned "New Company," as it was referred to for many months, how it would be owned and managed, how its sales would be organized, its relations with Chilean government agencies and firms, and the like. Eventually it was agreed that Dow would have 70 percent ownership of New Company, with PQC holding 20 percent and ENAP 10 percent.

Oreffice joined in the negotiations from time to time. At one meeting he was asked, "Why should Dow be so much more expensive for its know-how than anyone else?" Oreffice responded, "Because it's the best. You want the best, you pay for it."

Formal signature of the final agreement took place at La Moneda, the presidential palace in Santiago, on November 14, 1967. Chile was represented by President Frei; Eduardo Simian; Fernando Salas, general manager of ENAP and captain of the Chilean negotiators; and several cabinet ministers. Dow was represented by Ted Doan, who signed for Dow; Oreffice; and the members of the Dow negotiating team.

Earlier in the year, at Maza's suggestion, Dow had established a sales subsidiary in Santiago called Dow Quimica Chilena, and had hired Jorge Booth as sales manager. In the interim Ben Branch and Carl Gerstacker had both visited Chile and been impressed by its leadership and potential.

The final agreement called for four plants to be built by Dow near the Chilean government's petroleum refining complex at Concepcion: an HDPE plant and three plants leading to polyvinyl chloride—an ethylene dichloride plant, a vinyl chloride monomer plant, and the polyvinyl chloride plant itself. It was Simian who suggested a name for "New Company"— "Petrodow," formally Petroquimica Dow S.A.—a name that was quickly adopted.

In March 1967 Oreffice sent Herbert E. Engelmeyer, a New Yorker and graduate of the City College of New York, to be Dow's country manager in Chile. Not long after his arrival in Santiago, Engelmeyer found his photo on the front page of the Communist newspaper, El Siglo, describing him as the newly arrived oppressor of the working class. Engelmeyer, whose grandfather had been an organizer for the International Ladies Garment Workers Union in New York, was miffed; he had always considered himself, he said, a "born and raised Eastern liberal Democrat."

It was an anxious time in Chilean politics that summer, with internecine warfare within Frei's Christian Democratic Party and by-election gains by the Socialists, whose chief, Allende, had become president of the Senate. There was dissatisfaction with some of the sweeping reforms Frei was ramrodding through, particularly his expropriations of farm acreage for a land redistribution program. Engelmeyer went to Washington to talk to

Radomiro Tomic, Frei's heir apparent, then the ambassador to Washington. Tomic described his ideas as "communitarian"; he projected a rather broadened Israeli kibbutz system for a future Chile. Engelmeyer thought he detected a strong undercurrent of Marxism in these responses and began to worry that Dow might be committing itself to a major investment in a country moving swiftly leftward. Engelmeyer and Fletcher both began to talk to Chileans about where the country was headed. Simian was unshakably optimistic. Carlos Urenda, senior attorney for Dow's Chilean law firm, said there was nothing to worry about. Dow proceeded nervously with its plans.

A Petrodow board of seven directors was organized with five representatives of Dow and one each from PQC and ENAP. By the terms of the agreement Dow was investing $8 million in cash and was receiving $2 million in stock for its input of know-how; PQC and ENAP were subscribing $4.3 million for their 30 percent holding.

Miquel, who had now moved to Dow's Washington office, found financing for the project at the Export-Import Bank, which approved a $14.2 million loan to Petrodow; another $2 million came from Bank of America. CORFO willingly became the guarantor of both loans. The $31 million Petrodow project was now fully financed until start-up of its operations, scheduled for late 1970.

Both sides were happy with the arrangement, and Dow rapidly developed a close, harmonious relationship with the Chilean government and its agencies. As the four plants were being built the Chilean government asked Dow if it would also consider making mining chemicals in Chile—the xanthates, flocculants, and collectors so vital to its copper industry. Dow agreed to do so, and began planning a plant. As events were to unfold, however, the plant never was built.

Hunter Henry, Dow's manufacturing chief for Latin America, began to put a production team together. Alfonso Suarez, a Colombian who had been highly successful in managing the new Dow polystyrene plant at Cartagena, was tapped to become manager of the Petrodow complex. Earl Smith, a Dow construction expert who had been a professor at the University of Illinois before joining Dow, became project manager. Ground was broken in January 1969. Suarez set to work screening some 500 applicants for engineering jobs with Dow, selecting a first group of 10 who were sent, with their families, to undergo intensive training at Texas and Midland while the plants were being built. Eighteen Chileans were sent to the United States in all; most of them became key supervisors in the Petrodow complex.[12]

On their return to Chile these supervisors had the job of selecting from about 1,000 applicants the first 86 workers at the complex, who in turn began their training to be foremen, key operators, and maintenance personnel. Almost all of them were high school graduates or better. As Suarez observed, "there is a frustrated group of fellows in these countries who have had about two years at the university and then become bank clerks or government workers. They are easily educated and they make good plant operators."[13]

The Dow marketing group also was making progress. The company's sales in Chile were booming—$1.8 million in 1967; $3.6 million in 1968; $4.2 million in 1969. Chilean consumption of LDPE had risen to 7,400 metric tons in 1967, and consumption of PVC to 5,400 tons. This was still far from Petrodow's projected output of 20,000 tons of HDPE and 15,000 of PVC, and Booth and his group were busily developing new uses for these materials in Chile. Prospective buyers were flown to the United States to be initiated into the mysteries of fabricating plastic products, and the potential of exports to other Latin American nations was explored. In April 1969 the first conference of Andean plastics industries was held in Santiago under the auspices of the Chilean Association of Plastics Industries. Petrodow was to be the largest plastic producer in the southern cone of Latin America.

The core group of Chilean supervisors and operators worked long hours as the plants neared completion, totally absorbed in this great new development of which they were a part. Guillermo O'Reilly, manager of Petrodow's technical service and development group, said: "We were like an island; we were isolated from the rest of the world. We always thought that Petrodow was different, that Dow was different, that we had a very, very high technology. We knew what was going on inside Dow, and we lived for that, more than 12 hours a day, even 18, or whatever was necessary. We were so concentrated that what was going on outside in the world didn't have too much of our attention."

What was going on in the Chilean world was increasingly worrisome to the Dow people. There was increasing unrest—strikes, bombings by extremist groups, violence of various kinds—much of it loosely related to the Chilean presidential election scheduled for September 4, 1970. (The Chilean presidential term is six years, and a president cannot succeed himself.)

The 1970 candidates were three: Jorge Alessandri, 73 years old, a stern old patriot and father figure who had once before been president; Tomic, nominee of Frei's Christian Democratic Party; and Allende, who had patched together a group of leftist parties called "Unidad Popular." Allende was running on a 20-point program that included nationalization of copper, nitrates, coal, iron, banking, communications, and transport. As Engelmeyer analyzed it later, a revolution of rising expectations was occurring at this time in Chile, rising out of the Frei reforms:

> When a man is unable to feed his family, he is really not a political factor at all, because his entire being goes toward feeding his family. When you've given him enough to feed his family, however, and a portable radio or a TV set, so that he can see clearly the better life, you awaken in him a realization that for the first time he and people like him represent a political force, and that's where the danger comes. That's when the fellow who can make those wild promises will have a receptive audience.

Election day was bright and sunny, and many Chileans went to the beach rather than to the polls. The world was stunned by the results the next morning: 1,075,616 votes for Allende, or 36.3 percent; 1,036,278 votes for Alessandri, or 34.9 percent; and 824,845 votes for Tomic, or 27.8 percent. The Western Hemisphere had its first elected Marxist president. The Petrodow plants were over 90 percent completed at the time, but not yet in operation. When he heard the news, Dave Schornstein, who had recently succeeded Oreffice as general manager of Dow's Latin American area, went out and bought a copy of the Communist Manifesto.

Technically, with no candidate gaining a majority, the election result was thrown into the Chilean legislature, but shortly after the election Tomic pledged his support to Allende. On October 22, two days before the legislature was to make the vote official, right-wing extremists assassinated General Rene Schneider, commander in chief of the Chilean army. In the wave of unrest that followed, the nation closed ranks behind its new president, Salvador Allende.

The guard was changing at Dow's Chilean headquarters as well. Engelmeyer's assignment had been completed, and he was replaced by Isaac Budd Venable, called Budd, a veteran of Dupont and Dow who had been manufacturing manager of the Rocky Flats (Colorado) plant operated by Dow for the Atomic Energy Commission.

Dave Schornstein called Venable and Booth to Coral Gables to discuss what Dow should do; Dow had never worked with a Marxist government. Should Dow continue pouring dollars into Chile and complete its plants there, or should it cut its losses and pull out immediately? Venable told Schornstein, "Let's not close our eyes to the possibility that the environment is one we can live in, even though that's not probable." The decision was that Dow would indeed try to get along with the new regime. Petrodow's construction continued on schedule.[14]

It was clear that having elected a Marxist president, Chile would never be the same. Simian and Salas both resigned their positions and left Chile. They were replaced on the Petrodow board of directors by Hector Donoso, a Marxist engineer and a friend of Allende's, and Pedro Campbell, a 32-year-old Socialist who had been in East Germany studying economics.

Venable and Alfonso Suarez became convinced it was possible to work with the Chilean Socialists and Communists; after all, they reasoned, they needed Dow's technology as much as the previous government had, and Dow's agreement with the government was fully and clearly spelled out. They began by inviting Donoso and Campbell to a series of meetings to familiarize them with the plants, and tried to work with them smoothly. Both seemed to respond favorably.

With help from Dow technicians the government's ethylene and chlorine plants (raw material suppliers to Petrodow) went onstream, and the Petrodow polyethylene plant also went into production in December, soon followed by the vinyl chloride and PVC plants. It was an exceptionally trouble-free start-up, and the government seemed highly pleased about it. Chile was now a major plastics producer.

At start-up there were about 250 employees at Petrodow, only 11 of whom were not Chileans. As Chileans proved able to run the plants, the number of non-Chileans shrank to three—Venable, an American; Suarez, a Colombian; and Guillermo Carr, an Argentinian, the controller.

THE GRAY EMINENCE

As early as 1961 Paul Oreffice dreamed of a big chemical manufacturing complex in Brazil. The country was consuming large and growing tonnages of caustic soda, all of which had to be imported; manufacturing it within the country would not only make sense but benefit the development of Brazil, he reasoned, and under Dow's tutelage other key chemicals could also be produced in one large facility. His dream had come to naught, blocked at every turn by the government bureaucracies, and he had gone on to other things.

In 1968, now president of Dow Latin America, he tried again. He went to his friend Edmundo Safdie, president of Banco Cidade de Sao Paulo (Sao Paulo City Bank), in which Dow was a minority shareholder. "We want very much to build a plant in Brazil and to be a contributing part of the Brazilian economy," he told him, "but we just can't get through the government red tape involved. What can we do?"

Safdie was a close friend of Roberto Campos, one of the most distinguished Brazilians of his generation, a writer, government official, and one-time ambassador to Washington, and Safdie asked Campos if he would be willing to become the chairman of Dow Brazil and head the effort to get the approvals through the Brazilian bureaucracy. Campos said he did not have the time, but did have someone he would like to suggest.

A few days later, on August 16, 1968, a man named Golbery phoned Dow's Rio de Janeiro office and said he would like to drop by for a chat. He did and talked to Renato Hauptmann, the business development manager. "I knew who this man was and what he had done," Hauptmann said. "I didn't know as much then as I later learned. He asked a bunch of questions and took the projects that we had prepared to submit to the government. When he left I walked with him to the bus stop and he got on a bus, carrying these projects."[1]

This was Dow's introduction to one of the most unassuming and powerful men in Brazil. Herbert Engelmeyer, general manager of Dow Brazil, quickly hired Golbery as consultant for government relations, and in short order he became the chairman of Dow Brazil and its chief strategist for the next half-dozen critical years.

General Golbery do Couto e Silva had headed Brazil's war college and organized the Brazilian army's intelligence unit, the equivalent in Brazil of the CIA, FBI, and military intelligence rolled into one. He had retired in disgust when João Goulart became president of Brazil in 1961 and was one of the three men who had subsequently overthrown the Goulart government. The leader of this group was Castelo Branco, who then became president. When Castelo Branco was killed in a plane crash, Golbery found himself appointed to administer the military retirement fund. Then he was appointed judge in a federal auditing court. This required him to live in Brasilia, however (Brasilia being the brand new capital of Brazil, under construction inland, several hundred miles from the big cities on the coast), and he wanted to move back to Rio; that was his situation when Campos called him about Dow's problems.

Out of the war college that Golbery ran, made up of the top military people in the country, came the plans that were the basis of Brazil's success in the following period. "After the military took over they implemented the plans that were developed at this war college almost completely," said Dave Schornstein, who as president of Dow Latin America worked with the general in those years. "This is what caused the huge success of Brazil beginning in the late 1960s and going through until about 1975. General Golbery was referred to as the Gray Eminence. He had a very good mind, and he literally wrote the modern-day constitution of the Brazilian government. He did not want to be president; he really was more of a gray eminence."[2]

He looked not at all like a general, more like a Casper Milquetoast, in Schornstein's opinion. "He was kind of short, gray-haired, slight," he said. "He spoke in very hesitant English; English was not his strongest language. He read books all the time in six or eight different languages, English being one of them."

He was "a little cautious" about becoming chairman of Dow Brazil, Schornstein said,

because his fundamental interest always was and to his dying day was Brazil. Since he was kind of a modern-day George Washington of Brazil, he didn't want to do anything that would damage his reputation or his ability to be part of the government. Working in a joint venture of a foreign company was not going to endear him to certain segments of Brazil. But he kind of liked Dow because of our open style and involvement of people. If it had been a different company I'm not sure he would have accepted that.

The nice thing about the General, he said, was that

he knew the government so well backwards and forwards that you'd sit down and explain what the problem was, and he could tell you exactly how to go about it to get it approved, and in the right sequence. After that, we were getting those plants approved. He may have used some of his personal influence, but basically it was because we were using the knowledge that he was giving us about how to go about getting it approved, and who to watch out for here, and how to change your pitch over there, and all that type of thing.

One of the first things the general pointed out to his new Dow colleagues was a loophole in Brazilian law that opened a six-month window in 1969 during which a foreign company was allowed to buy land on a harbor. "The general found out that we could do it," Schornstein said. "Nobody else did it. He found out that there was this gap, and we got permission to buy this land (the Guaruja plant site and the Sao Mateo terminal site across the bay from it) during this six-month period. Of course, once you had it, you were always grandfathered. So that's where we put those plants."[3]

"This man was incredible," said Hauptmann, who worked with him closely for five years. "This man had read anything and everything that you could think of and many things that you couldn't think of. He understood philosophy, history, art, music, politics. He knew very little about business, but it didn't take him too long to understand what the game was about."

"Like most military people," Hauptmann said, "he was a man of very limited means. All the money he had, he spent on books. When he died, he left a library of over 30,000 volumes and he'd read them all. It's not just that he had them, but he had read them, some of them two or three times."

Engelmeyer and Golbery became Dow's team in Brazil. "Herb understood the general and the general understood Herb in terms of what each could do for each other and for the company," Hauptmann said. "As a result of that, it was a unique combination."[4]

Doors that had been locked and barred began to open for Dow in Brazil. Marine terminals were an example. Brazil had what Jorge Casteleiro called a "port monopoly." "They had given the marine terminals of all Brazil to a group of politicians and you had to do business with them to pass through any port with your merchandise. Dow, of course, wouldn't stand for that, so he [Gen. Golbery] was able to get us for the first time ever our own marine terminal in Guaruja. Dow now has four or five marine terminals because Brazil is enormous; it's bigger than the United States in territory."[5]

"We got our first projects approved and they were really substantial," said Hauptmann. "We started to become a real company and not a flimsy import and reselling company. We started to gain substance. We started to grow, really grow. As early as then, [the general] tried to convince Dow to go to joint ventures. He understood as early as 1970–71 that that was the way to go. He knew that long-term growth could only be achieved 'in the system.'"

The General would come to his Dow office in Rio by 9 A.M. and would never leave before 7 or 7:30, sometimes much later. "He'd make the calls with us and he saw the people," Hauptmann said. "He was ostracized in terms of power, but he had all the right connections and he knew how to get to the right people. He knew everybody. He had the access, the credibility, and the mind to understand what Dow wanted and to make it palatable to the environment."

When the terminal at Guaruja was inaugurated, on May 27, 1971, Dow invited 400 customers, government officials, and other notables to a sit-down barbecue. General Golbery and the minister of transport made the main speeches. It was the first bulk terminal ever built in the port area of Santos, on the coast east of Sao Paulo City.

"It took a lot of work and ability, mainly by Jarbas Carvalho, the man who spear-headed it," Hauptmann said. "This terminal became a very important part of the Dow strategy." Carvalho, who worked with Golbery in obtaining the authorizations needed for the terminal, said the general would send him to see a lower-down official who was to actually issue a permit after talking to "the big shots of the government." "He used to tell me, 'I talked to this guy, now you go talk to this other fellow. But you know beforehand that I've talked to his boss,'" Carvalho said.[6]

In the fall of 1973 General Ernesto Geisel became the new president of Brazil and immediately invited General Golbery to return to government. Golbery became head of the civil cabinet in the Geisel administration, the civil cabinet including everything in the government that was not military (that was the military cabinet), and thus arguably the second most powerful person in the nation.

For several weeks the employees in Dow's Rio office looked on in amazement as the highest and mightiest personages of Brazil came by to visit their colleague the general, who used his modest Dow office as his base while he shaped the new Brazilian government. He worked half-time for Dow and half-time for the government for awhile, and then at the end of calendar 1973 closed his relationship with the company.

In February 1974 Dow gave a dinner party to say good-bye to him. Ben Branch, the company's chief executive, came down from Midland and gave the main talk. Branch said he was honored to have had the chance to know and work with the general and that he was envious of Brazil having someone like the general in a key position. He wished there were people in the United States with the same stature and understanding of the world and of human beings as the general who could be attracted to positions in the government of the United States, he said.

In that same February 1974 came word that the Brazilian government had approved Dow's giant chlorine-caustic project in the far northeast of the country, near Matarandiba Island. It would be a 100 percent Dow-owned facility, something unheard of in modern-day Brazil.

The Aratu plant, Dow's largest manufacturing facility in Latin America, became General Golbery's legacy to Dow. "He was convinced that Brazil needed to be opened up, that Brazil needed competition," said Ernesto Ramon, who arrived in Brazil as Golbery was leaving.

People tried for years to connect him with corruption and wrongdoing, but they couldn't. We at Dow suffered substantially in the late 1970s and early 1980s. The press, who wanted to hurt him and Geisel, couldn't get anything against him; they all said he was the great power behind the whole Geisel movement, so they tried Dow. Every time they ran a Golbery picture they used a picture of the Guaruja opening when he had a Dow hat on with the Dow diamond, depicting him as a Brazilian politician trying to help a multinational company, because they couldn't get anything else against him.[7]

"The last permit he got was for a 2,4-D plant," Ramon said. "He handed me that permit when I got the job in Brazil in 1974, and then we never got a single permit from 1974 until the mid-1980s."

While Dow suffered because of its relationship with Gen. Golbery, Ramon said, "on balance it was tremendous. There's no question: the guy put us on the map."

1. Oral History, Renato Hauptmann, March 13, 1991; Oral History, Paul F. Oreffice, August 1, 1988.
2. Details of General Golbery's background and career mainly from Oral History, R. Hauptmann; Oral History, Dave W. Schornstein, March 15, 1991; Oral History, Jorge Casteleiro, March 13, 1991; Oral History, Sergio Goloubeff, March 27, 1991; and Oral History, Jarbas Carvalho, March 25, 1991.
3. Oral History, D. W. Schornstein.
4. Oral History, R. Hauptmann. Unfortunately it must be noted here that Engelmeyer, a lover of fast cars, was later killed, along with his wife, Irma, in a tragic automobile accident.
5. Oral History, J. Casteleiro.
6. Oral History, J. Carvalho. For general history of Dow Chemical Latin America see *Dow Latina, Veinteavo Aniversario* (Dow Latin America, twentieth anniversary), booklet, Dow Chemical Latin America, Coral Gables, Florida, 1986.
7. Oral History, Ernesto Ramon, August 21, 1995.

Within a few weeks after start-up the plants were supplying the Chilean market with high-quality products; a year or so later the polyethylene plant was operating beyond its design capacity (20,000 metric tons per year) and the PVC plant was running at 80 percent of capacity (15,000 metric tons per year), remarkable for new plants. Small amounts were already being exported to other Latin American countries.

Relationships with ENAP were harmonious but soon began to sour with PQC, a new organization that became the scene of political infighting. Some of the executives installed there by the new regime quickly acquired a reputation for being more interested in political than in technical matters.

What was more troubling was that the new regime began to ignore the terms of the agreement with Dow. The government failed to pay the last installment on its 30 percent share of Petrodow. Allende issued a decree that foreign companies such as Petrodow could not borrow money from Chilean banks for working capital, and Petrodow suddenly had to scramble for cash. Fortunately Dow Quimica Chilena was selling all the polystyrene it could make at the time, and it lent cash to Petrodow. Surprisingly, Donoso permitted ENAP to sell ethylene to Petrodow on credit for months on end, and Petrodow was also able to stall its payments for chlorine to PQC.

Officially the government contended that its differences with Dow were simply "varying interpretations of the master agreements," not breaches of contract. Campbell and Donoso argued that some of the arrangements in the master agreement had favored Dow too much and Chile too little. Oreffice said, "it was obvious from the beginning (of the Allende administration) that we were going divergent ways. It was like living under a mountain and on top of the mountain was a huge rock that was sort of loose. And one of these days it might fall on our heads."

Allende's ministers found ancient laws still on the books authorizing "the intervention of the central power" in industries failing to meet "norms" imposed by the government, and these were used as pretext for the expropriation ("interventions," they were called) of both Chilean and foreign business firms as Allende launched his nationalization campaign. The Ford Motor Company and others left Chile before this activity began. Dupont, General Motors, and others sold out or were taken over. Before 1971 was out, 37 firms had been expropriated and 116 others were scheduled for similar treatment.

Allende froze prices, handed out wage increases of up to 60 percent, ran the government mint overtime (more than doubling the amount of money in circulation in his first year), and provided make-work jobs for large numbers of the unemployed in the government or the expropriated industries. He raised military pay substantially, blunting for the moment the possibility of armed force hostility.

All of Chile went on a brief spending spree with the new income, but there was still mounting unrest, particularly in the countryside, where for his land redistribution program Allende expropriated more farms in seven months than Frei had taken over in his six-year term. Bands of armed peasants, led by extremists of the MIR (Movimiento de la Izquierda Revolucionaria—Movement of the Revolutionary Left), known as the "MIRistas," helped the land distribution scheme along in their own fashion; these outlaw groups seized farms and turned them over to their own members. The government turned a blind eye to these practices, the MIRistas being among its supporters. Squatters took over some 5,000 apartments, ignoring the government's own housing program. Anarchy was on the march.

By late 1971 Petrodow and its 250 employees were the only privately operated industrial concern in the entire Concepcion–Talcahuano region. Then, in December, the government asked Dow to open formal discussions with the objective of increasing the government's share in the enterprise from 30 to 51 percent. The rock on top of the mountain was wobbling.

After considerable debate, Venable and Dow decided to dicker with the government. It had been four years since the formal agreement had been signed with the Chilean government and more than a year since the plants had gone into production. Dow's immediate response was that the government should begin complying fully with that agreement, as Dow had, before talking about changing it. So it asked first for a demonstration of good faith in living up to the old agreement. In respect to 51 percent ownership, the company was adamant about retaining management control of the complex.

"You can't run a successful high-technology plant without having management control," Schornstein said.

> We have to have control of the manufacturing facilities and the financing; we've got to be able to choose the people; we've got to meet our safety standards and our environmental standards; we have to bring in the technology; and we need to manage marketing. Your creative ideas come out of both your environment and the needs of your customers. You can run a plant for a period of time without being in contact with your market, but in three or four years your market will change so much you'll be out of date.

The first of several formal meetings with the Chilean government on revising the agreement was held in February 1972, with Venable and Alberto Orrego, an attorney, representing Dow. Dario Pavez, the new general manager of CORFO, became the chief negotiator for the government. Schornstein and Hunter Henry came down from Coral Gables and discussed the situation with Pedro Campbell, who was a CORFO representative at the meetings. Ben Branch, now Dow president, also came down and joined the meetings. To a suggestion that Dow's ownership be reduced to 49 percent, Branch replied, "You want 51 percent? Take 100 percent." Pavez quickly reassured Branch that the Chilean government and Dow had the same interests, that Chile really wanted the number of Dow plants and products increased, and that Chile recognized that Dow worked for a profit.

Venable told Pavez that Chile had saved $4 million of its shrinking foreign exchange by not having to import 12,000 metric tons of polyethylene and 4,200 tons of PVC. The growing exports of the plant would bring in $3.5 million to Chile in 1972 for 9,000 tons of polyethylene and 5,000 tons of PVC. Petrodow was selling surprisingly high amounts of product to Argentina, Uruguay, Peru, Bolivia, Colombia, and Ecuador. It had become a shining economic success in a Chilean economy whose entire horizon was filling with failures. Unfortunately it was not the right time for a private firm controlled by a large U.S. parent to become a shining success.

Among other problems, the maintenance crew had balked at going on a four-shift schedule to make maintenance personnel available around the clock, and this became a touchy issue. Government representatives met with the union personnel. The maintenance group raised its demands higher. On September 25 the plant was halted by a wildcat strike, illegal by Chilean law. Rene Garcia, the industrial relations manager, Alfonso Landeros, the polyethylene plant manager, and Jorge Zapata, the maintenance superintendent, met with union representatives. Suarez talked to the government partners, and they too wanted a settlement of the dispute. On September 29 the Concepcion newspaper reported ominously that the Petrodow workers had voted for government intervention, "to bring order to the administration of Petrodow."

The plant supervisory group responded to this action in a joint letter signed by 42 of the 43 engineers and supervisors in the plant. Addressed to Pavez, the letter explained the necessity of putting the maintenance department on four shifts and stated their own "firm conviction" that the "highest interest of the country" was being served by the present company administration. The lone unsigning holdout was Sergio Hidalgo, an engineer in the polyethylene plant. Negotiations continued, both on this front and between Suarez and the government partners concerning the latter's desire to own 51 percent of Petrodow.

Suarez wrote a letter to all employees stating management's position. The union leadership, he felt, was communicating fully to the rank and file neither the demands being made by the union nor management's position and offers. In response to the growing union demands for worker "participation" in the management of the firm he told them: "Let's differentiate between the concepts of co-management and participation. . . . There is no doubt that there is an ample field for participation, e.g., in the fields of well-being, recreation, safety, and discipline. However, we are not in favor of allowing access to the procedure of selection, hiring, or promotion of personnel."

It became evident that neither the union leadership nor the government officials involved were much interested in a settlement. The government mediator twice invited both sides to meet with him and then failed to show up.

These events were suddenly overshadowed by a key event in the history of the Allende regime, the "paro nacional." It began on October 10 as a trucking strike. Allende was proposing to nationalize the trucking industry through formation of a state trucking company. Most of Chile's truckers, the vast majority of whom owned just one or two vehicles, violently opposed a state trucking monopoly, and called a strike. The government immediately arrested the top officers of the Confederation of Truck Owners. The public reaction was swift and widespread. The strike quickly spread from truckers to construction workers, shopkeepers, physicians, lawyers, and other representatives of the middle class who did not want to be "nationalized." Violence broke out across the land, but especially in Santiago and Concepcion. The government declared a state of emergency, seized the nation's radio stations, requisitioned the strikers' trucks, and put most of the country under military control. The country's economy slowed to a crawl, virtually paralyzed. The strike lasted several weeks.

During this time there were no trucks available to deliver Petrodow's products. Dow's offices in downtown Santiago looked out on the site of daily battles fought with water jets, rocks, and tear gas between government troops and strike supporters. Early in the strike

Venable decided for safety's sake to send home the Dow office workers, keeping only a skeleton crew. They asked customers to come to the Petrodow warehouse in Santiago in their own vehicles, if possible, to pick up orders of plastic materials. The polystyrene plant was still running all out, and the warehouse was full. Customers began to arrive at the warehouse in their own cars and trucks; a few even came in taxis.

On October 16 Venable heard rumors that a government requisition of the Petrodow plant was imminent, although negotiations were still under way. On Wednesday evening, October 18, as a meeting of the Dow staff in Santiago was breaking up in Venable's apartment, they heard over the radio that the government had requisitioned both Petrodow and Dow Quimica Chilena—the latter a complete surprise to both Venable and Jorge Booth.

The group at Venable's decided they had no choice but to go to the office early the next morning to prepare for the takeover, and at about 10:30 A.M. the receptionist announced, "Mr. Venable, there is a very strange-looking group of people here, and they want to talk to you." "Send them in," Venable said.

The "strange-looking group" included the two persons who had been named "intervenors" by the government, two other government officials, and two carabineros. Venable asked Orrego, the attorney, to receive the group with him, and accepted the papers they offered—orders whereby the government requisitioned the plants, offices, equipment, inventories, supplies, and bank accounts of Petrodow and the offices of Dow Quimica Chilena, and appointed intervenors to take charge of and operate the two companies.

Appointed general intervenor for the Petrodow operation was a stranger named Dario Figueroa, and another stranger, Jaime Dassori, was named intervenor for DQC. The intervenor of the Petrodow plant was Saul Casanueva, one of the government negotiators with whom Dow had been dealing, who had addressed the Petrodow union members at one point about the benefits of working in "the social sector"—that is, as an employee of a requisitioned firm.

A notary was called in to make an official record of the proceedings. Venable protested that the reason given for the requisition—that Petrodow was paralyzed by a strike and in consequence materials vital to the nation were not being delivered—was wrong. The fact of the matter was that Petrodow's products were being delivered and were available for delivery, he asserted.

When the formalities were complete, Venable took the intervenor to another room and introduced him to his assembled staff as their new boss. Afterward, he phoned Schornstein in Coral Gables. "Well, it just happened," he announced.

The intervenor asked Venable to stay on for a few days to facilitate the transition, and Schornstein agreed this was the civil thing to do. The DQC files had already been removed, and he planned to make his own apartment into Dow's Chile offices as a focal point for communications, Venable said. Yes, he would get in touch with the U.S. ambassador. Venable and Booth went off to a sorrowful lunch, and then to Orrego's office, where they tried to make sense of the situation. They surmised that the takeover was temporary; Petrodow had simply been caught up in the sweeping actions the government was taking in reaction to the paro nacional. It would all be over in a week or two. They could hope that, anyway, they agreed.

They went back to the offices and Venable called the staff together one last time. He thanked them all for their services and told them how sorry he was that their relationship was ending so badly and so abruptly. Then, under the pressures that had been building up for weeks, he broke down and sobbed.

Down in Concepcion, 350 miles away, Suarez was also waiting that day for the intervenor to arrive. Early in the afternoon he called a meeting of all Petrodow employees, the striking union members as well as the supervisors. He told them what he knew, and that the intervenor would be arriving later in the day. What is Dow going to do, they wanted to know? Suarez responded: "As soon as I have surrendered the plant to the custody of the intervenor, I will walk out and Dow will leave with me. Dow will never accept an arrangement of this kind, especially if it is shoved down their throats." Most of the union members refused to believe this statement, having been assured by Casanueva that Dow was interested only in the profits the plants could earn and that they would shortly negotiate a settlement under which their profits would continue.

Suarez urged the employees to cooperate with the new management and to keep the plants running. "Political systems come and go," he said. "The only real thing you have is the plant, and it is up to you to look after it and produce for the good of your country." He thanked them all for their help since the opening of the plants.

The secretaries, one by one, came to Suarez and took somber and tearful farewells. "All of a sudden," Suarez said, "from a very happy community, a very efficient operation, it had been converted into nothing. They saw the specter of insecurity, and they were angry at the stupidity of the government people."

Toward 6 P.M. Juan Antonio Garrido, the regional manager of CORFO, telephoned to say that the intervenor would arrive around 8. Suarez said it had been a long, hard day, and why didn't they wait until the morning to change the command? Garrido said no, the government wanted to start getting the plants back into operation that very night.

The intervenor and his assistants did arrive around 8, with no police escort. The workers, one of whom was Casanueva's brother, ran the flag up the flagpole and saluted him with cheers, laughter, and hugs. The engineers and supervisors were not as happy; many of them had known their new boss as a mediocre chemical engineering student at the University of Concepcion, and later as a fanatical Socialist.

The papers were being read to Suarez and he was signing them when a group of supervisors came in, shouting that their cars were being searched, inside and out, at the plant gate. Casanueva simply nodded, but Rudolfo Mulach, a production engineer in the PVC plant, grabbed him and continued to protest. He had been a classmate of Casanueva's at the university. "The workers are searching our cars and our personal belongings," he told him. "What does this mean? We were promised our rights would be respected." His grip tightened and moved to Casanueva's throat. Frightened, Casanueva said he would straighten it all out. He called the guard at the gate and said, "This is Saul Casanueva speaking. This is an order. Leave the engineers alone. Let them leave without any problem." By 10 P.M. the formalities were over, and everyone went home.

The superintendents met that night at Rene Garcia's house to discuss these events. "I'd like your opinions," Garcia said, "on how long Petrodow will function without Dow." Zapata, the maintenance chief, responded, "I give it six months. Then it will shut down for lack of spare parts." After a long discussion along this line, Garcia proposed they get together with the new bosses on the morrow, "and tell them the things we have discussed tonight."

Casanueva laughed at these predictions of doom. Dow would soon be back, he said, or they'd change the technology of the plant. The Rumanians would come in and change things and make an entirely different kind of polyethylene and PVC. Or parts could be fabricated in Chile; this was just one more challenge facing the Chilean people in freeing themselves from the imperialist yoke of the United States, he said. Later, when a new labor contract was presented to him by the union, he simply agreed to it. It called for a substantial wage increase, a fund of three million escudos for a housing project, and the right of the union to market and keep the proceeds of all the off-grade polyethylene produced in the plant.

This last provision caused consternation among the engineers when they learned about it. Since the workers could specify which material was off-grade, it was a virtual license to steal and a death blow to the incentives for producing a quality product, they pointed out. Casanueva assured them that the workers now had major responsibilities and would be loyal to the broader cause of the welfare of the Chilean people.

The Suarez family packed their belongings for the return to their native Colombia. "I worked on the Petrodow project for five years," Suarez said, "and they were five of the most productive years of my life. What hurt me most was to see the anguish of all these people, the employees and their wives. We had great dreams for Chile, and everything was coming along well. It was hard to say goodbye."

After publication of the requisitions in the official journal, Dow filed an appeal to the Special Tribunal and to the Controller General, an autonomous government agency set up to rule on the legality of acts of the administrative branch of the government. Dow and its attorneys felt they were on firm legal ground on a number of counts. If the Controller General ruled against the Allende government, howerver—as it did two months later—the matter would then be thrown into the Chilean courts and drag on for years. In the event, the government simply ignored the Controller General's ruling.

The Santiago employees of Dow and Petrodow decided on a "brazos caidos" (arms folded) policy—report to the office but not work. A day or two later Jose Pablo Dulanto, the chief accountant, phoned Venable and said he'd been chosen by a meeting of the supervisory employees to ask what Dow was going to do. "We're going to oppose the requisition in every way we can," Venable told him. "We're going to fight them."

In Santiago the telex machine chugged out a message from Schornstein in Coral Gables. "I want to personally thank each and every one of you for your unwavering support in what has been a deeply troubled period for our enterprise in Chile," it said. "We intend with all legal means available to oppose the intervention which we consider to be an unjustified action. The current crisis facing all of us is certainly the most difficult we have had to face together since the start of our endeavor. However, we have faced difficult problems before and together we have resolved them. Hopefully the same ingenuity, creativity, and hard work can get us through this difficult crisis. . . . We will continue to be with you as long as it is in our power to do so."

The telex operator in Coral Gables then queried, "How received, Santiago?" The response from Santiago read: "Received perfectly. Thanks very much, Dave, on behalf of all members of Dow Quimica Chilena and Petrodow. It's fantastic, and this impacts us emotionally to know that we have a real boss and gentleman in charge. This gives us new strength and courage to continue with our act. . . ." The telex was cut off at that point, deliberately.

In a later meeting the more than 50 Santiago employees decided they needed to coordinate their plans with their colleagues in Concepcion, and elected a committee of five to go to Concepcion. Enrique Larroucau, Sergio Robledo, Andres Concha, Jaime Nieto, and Gonzalo Petchen took a plane down and were met by Alfonso Landeros. In the evening he took them to a meeting of the Petrodow employees at a farmhouse belonging to Fernando Diaz, superintendent of the PVC plant. Of the 58 nonunion employees of Petrodow, 54 attended.

The Santiago delegation said they were ready to go on strike against the government indefinitely rather than accept the interventions. What was the feeling of their colleagues in Concepcion? After long and lively debate 49 of those attending voted to stay away from their jobs until the intervention was ended. The dissenters were quickly won over. By the time the delegation returned to Santiago, the vote to strike against the government was supported by all 58 of Dow's nonunion employees in Santiago and 73 of 76 in Concepcion.

This astonishing development—a group of supervisors striking against a Marxist government—caught just about everyone by surprise except the concerned group of supervisors. Probably the most astonished of all was the Allende government itself. In no other enterprise the government had expropriated had the supervisory employees taken such a step.

The striking employees proceeded to form an employees' association, appoint committees and spokespersons, and seek meetings with the appropriate authorities. One of their first acts was to place advertisements in the form of an open letter to the minister of the economy in two of the Santiago newspapers. The ads, which were tantamount to a declaration of principles, voiced their concern for their jobs, their industry, and their country. They supported Dow's position in the intervention and said Dow's help was vital if the plants were to continue to be successful.

The government responded swiftly. It canceled the labor contracts of four members of Venable's staff, including Concha and Larroucau, and threatened the same treatment to the remainder. A day or two later, in the night, the intervenor had all the locks changed, locking the employees out of their offices. Although they were frustrated, the strikers made certain that the press was invited to witness employees pounding futilely on the doors, and the public saw this on television. A neighbor firm promptly offered the use of office space and equipment, though it could only accommodate 20 people, and this was accepted.

Venable asked Jorge Casteleiro, chief legal counsel of Dow Latin America, to come down and observe what was going on, and Casteleiro quickly became the liaison between the striking employees and Dow. He carried a pledge from Schornstein that they would all be reinstated if the government returned the plants.

In afteryears the employees involved liked to tell about an elderly cleaning woman in the Santiago office who had been working for Dow for three years. The intervenor proposed that since Dow was gone she go to work for him, doing the same thing she always had. She refused, saying, "I will never get used to working with other people in the places of people like Dow." He offered to double her salary but she rejected it, telling him, "There is no money that can make me change my mind." She walked out and went to the offices the Dow people were using temporarily, offering to clean them free of charge.

The strike against the government was much discussed and admired around the Dow Company. "It was a wonderful, courageous, and inspiring act," commented Carl Gerstacker, the board chairman. "They have chosen to put their own lives and well-being at risk for what they believe, and it's this type of action that gives me great confidence in the future of the Chilean people." It also introduced an entirely new factor into the Chilean situation for Dow management. Schornstein and Hunter Henry went to Chile to get first-hand information about the situation, and decided the only ethical position Dow could take, in view of the sacrifices the striking employees were making and the very real jeopardy they were in, was to try to get the plants back and then work out an accommodation with the government. "In making a business decision, the most difficult type is that in which you're weighing intangible moral values against calculable, known economic values," Schornstein said.

Schornstein went to Midland to brief Ben Branch on the situation, describing the courage of the striking employees and the position Dow was taking. He added that this also meant an added exposure to risk of several million dollars for the company. "There are things more important than money," Branch said.

The government intervenors attempted to restart the plants. Sergio Hidalgo, the only Dow engineer who had refused to sign the letter to Pavez, assured Casanueva that he could accomplish this himself, with help from the union operators. The result was a thunderous explosion that woke up much of the Concepcion area; it was a "decomp," an occasional problem with polyethylene plants. Petrodow had had four of them in the early days of start-up, but none as violent as this one. Police and navy personnel rushed to the plant to find the personnel shaken, but unhurt. Hidalgo replaced the burned-out motor with another. Improperly assembled, it burned out too.

Hidalgo and Casanueva put ads in the papers the next day, signed by most of the union personnel, saying everything was normal at the plants. "Last year Petrodow exploded four times," the ad said, "and no one said anything because it was something normal and expected.

But now that Petrodow is under the workers' control, the explosion in the polyethylene plant has tended to produce a public alarm."

Petrodow, in the words of one employee, began to resemble a jail. No employee meetings were permitted. Dulanto, the accountant, was shocked to hear about the "new accounting system" being used at Petrodow. "All they do is issue checks—they don't even classify the type of expense," he said. He heard of shipments made without invoices or records of withdrawal, of millions of escudos in cash lying around the office, with no daily or monthly balance being kept.

The striking employees, through their employees' association, formed teams that competed with each other to raise money. Some bought fish at the seaside and farm products from the countryside and marketed them in the city at a profit. Others taught English or math, or repaired cars or TV sets. A group of secretaries in Santiago made and sold sandwiches. Others became dealers in eggs, fruit, or chickens. One team made and sold zuecos, a type of wooden shoe popular in Chile. Guillermo Carr, controller of the Dow companies, one of the first fired by the government, became the group's treasurer; the escudos were turned in to him and then distributed to the employees as a percentage of salary, with those who had been lower paid receiving a higher percentage of their former salaries. It was share and share alike; the foes of socialism had become more socialistic than their enemies.

Alicia Crichton, an order coordinator in the Santiago office, said, "Many other groups had gone on strike to protest government policies. A lot of them lacked organization. But we just worked very hard, and we knew we must get used to last year's dress."

In a meeting the employees' association finally obtained with Fernando Flores, one of Allende's many ministers of economy, they presented their conditions for going back to work. Flores promised the government would try to settle the problems and lift the requisitions. His promises boosted the strikers' morale, but nothing further happened except that from time to time the government would fire a few more of the Dow employees. There were a total of 50 firings in the first 50 days of the strike, and then, mysteriously, they stopped.

The government also used various tactics of deception. Officials would whisper that Budd Venable was negotiating with the government for Dow's return, and that Dow was accepting a 49 percent share. Once a government official told Dulanto that Venable was at that very moment negotiating with them in Santiago. Venable was able to prove that he had spent the entire week in Buenos Aires.

Employees and their wives were subjected to threatening phone calls in the middle of the night. After one of these a shaken Mary Venable, Budd's wife, talked to the American ambassador, and the Venables moved in with an embassy family for the duration.

The employees' wives also formed a group and taught each other what they knew; there were classes in budgeting, clothing repair, and the like.

One question posed when the intervention occurred was whether the company should continue to sell its other products to Chile, most conspicuously the badly needed mining chemicals for the copper industry. Hunter Henry and others decided the answer was yes;

refusing to sell these products to Chile would have political overtones, and the company had always tried to stay clear of politics. "Vindictiveness doesn't get you anyplace," said Henry. "It gets you ulcers. We are very unhappy about what happened, but we don't want to punish the Chilean people because of what the Chilean government did." The striking supervisors heard continuing reports of the deterioration of the plants. Replacement parts were in desperate supply. Parts were being cannibalized from one part of the complex to another, and some plants were shut down a good deal of the time. Overall, they estimated that the plants were running at 35 to 40 percent of capacity. Their customers were on quota and often received only parts of their orders. Exports were out of the question.

Worker participation was in full bloom at Petrodow, and the operators were free to do as they pleased. Supervision could not be sure whether an order would be followed or not. The union did not seem to be getting much benefit from the rule giving it all the off-grade material produced; product not up to grade was labeled "prime" for domestic consumption.

The workers did get their housing project, with 50 houses begun in the first year, but there was growing dissatisfaction with promotions based on politics and with a spy system practiced both on the job and off. Some of the older employees formed an opposition union called the FUT (Frente Unido de Trabajadores—United Workers Front), and some of the younger workers began to join it as well.

In January the strike committee met with a new minister of economy, Orlando Millas, a Communist. He was quite friendly, but again nothing happened. As the strike dragged on the question of members of the strike group leaving Chile came up with increasing frequency. Rene Garcia, the industrial relations chief, and Emilio Assef, administrative services manager, were the first to go, moving to key positions with Dow in Brazil. The strike group, worried that over time this policy might decimate their ranks and kill their effort to get the plants back, asked Schornstein about this. Schornstein and Henry explained that they had not tried to increase the flow of people out of Chile, but at the same time they did not want to deprive these people of "the opportunities for promotion that would have come along whether there had been a requisition or not."

When the Allende forces made slight gains in the 1973 elections to the legislature (evidence of extensive election fraud was uncovered later), the strike committee was forced to face the fact that there was no sign change was going to take place in Chile. Following an unsuccessful effort to arrange a meeting with the minister of labor, they gloomily voted to disband their strike, which had gone on for five months.

Over this period their ranks had remained intact. Three people in Santiago and two in Concepcion had gone back to work for the government-run operations, but the other 130 had held out to the end.

The strikers moved quickly to a new chapter in their lives. About half left Chile in the following weeks, and of this half about half went to work for Dow in other countries. A committee of the employees' association helped others find jobs in Chile, and most of them did. A few, scraping by on whatever jobs they could pick up, had to survive as best they could.

By now Chile was by all ordinary measures a bankrupt nation. It could not pay its foreign debts; its inflation rate was the highest in the world; profiteering and black markets were widespread; and industrial production moved lower and lower. Allende's critics were crying that he was trying to kill democracy by stifling the economy; some were jailed for voicing such comments. His government had taken over more than 400 firms. Only half of the 120 companies owned by U.S. interests were expropriated, but that half accounted for about 90 percent of total U.S. assets in Chile, or some $900 million, according to a study by the U.S. Embassy.

Soon the government had to order food rationing, but even this program was politically motivated. Run by neighborhood "Councils of Prices and Supplies," controlled by the party faithful, the program would, for example, bring in a shipment of food to a local supermarket in the night. In the morning, however, the residents would find that truckloads of strangers had been brought in from other neighborhoods and were lined up and ready to buy the entire shipment.

Violence began to sweep across the nation. When Allende went on the air to appeal for calm, terrorists contrived to knock out the power in most of the country, leaving him with virtually no audience.

The crisis came to a boil nine days after this aborted broadcast, when the Chilean Congress passed a resolution declaring that Allende was acting outside the Chilean Constitution. The Allende government, this resolution said, "habitually violates the guarantees which the Constitution grants to all inhabitants of the republic, and allows and abets the creation of illegitimate parallel powers. . . . The government is not merely responsible for isolated violations of the law and the Constitution; it has made them into a permanent system of conduct."

There was talk of civil war. The Chilean military, by long tradition apolitical, was still reluctant to move, but it changed its mind when it became clear that in the midst of this chaos the cadre for a revolutionary army was being trained and equipped. Chile was becoming a laboratory for revolution.

The crisis came to its climax on September 11 when military forces surrounded and attacked La Moneda. Within a few hours the battle was over and Allende lay dead in the shell of a bombed-out presidential palace. In the evening the country was introduced on television to its new leaders, the chief of whom was the Chilean army commander, Gen. Augusto Pinochet. Pinochet was to be Chile's dictator for many years to come.

The military, which had planned well, quickly brought the nation under control. In Concepcion not a shot was fired. At the Petrodow plant a brief fight broke out between the new union, the FUT, and those still loyal to the Allende regime. Like all the other fights, this one was won by the antigovernment forces, and the FUT in jubilation raised the Chilean flag to the top of the pole in front of the plant.

A few days later the new ruling junta replaced the intervenors with "delegados"—temporary administrators selected for their background and experience in the plants they were to run, and for their opposition to the Allende administration. José Dulanto, the former chief accountant, was appointed temporary administrator of Petrodow, and Andres Concha, one of the key figures in the strike committee, of Dow Quimica Chilena in Santiago.

Dulanto, who had been working at Channel 13 TV in Santiago, headed for Concepcion. Escorted by navy vehicles, he drove to the plant. The naval commander called out all the workers, presented Dulanto, told them all politicking was over, and warned against sabotage. He took about 20 of the workers aside and promised that every fifth one of them would be shot if there was deliberate destruction or theft of equipment. He gestured to two grenades in his belt and added, "If there's any discussion, these are my arguments." There was no discussion.

Dulanto called a meeting in the cafeteria the next day, distributed the bonus traditionally given on the anniversary of Chilean independence, and told the workers to go on vacation until they were called. He began checking the books and files and found them in woeful condition, with many records missing. When they heard Dulanto had been appointed administrator, Franco Brzovic and Oscar Brain and others of the supervisors left other jobs to come back to Petrodow. The workers were also called back, with few exceptions. Some left the company of their own volition, and a few were arrested. Saul Casanueva, who had disappeared shortly after the coup d'état, was found some days later and confined on nearby Quiriquina Island along with the eight or nine plant workers who had been arrested.

Dulanto began the delicate, painstaking work of getting the plants restarted. The polyethylene plant was soon running at 65 percent of capacity. The PVC plant, in worse shape, got up to 45 percent and then had to cut back to 10 percent because of severe corrosion of its equipment. Dow did what it could to restore the plants to operation, issuing orders in its own name for the fabrication of replacement parts, although there had not yet been any suggestion or invitation to the company that it return. It scoured its own plants for parts as well.

At the polystyrene plant, Concha, joined by a handful of returning technicians, was soon able to get the plant running at about 80 percent but was unable to sustain this rate because of a shortage of styrene, the basic raw material. He found no spare parts, no financial records, no sales program, and no plan for raw material resupply. Total personnel had increased from 45 to 85, much of this accomplished by splitting jobs in two, allowing one man to work and another the freedom to attend political meetings and rallies. Styrene had been imported without paying customs duties. Loans had been made to employees without keeping records. Tools, typewriters, adding machines, safety goggles, and hard hats had disappeared. Oscar Infante, the former general manager, estimated the cost to resume production at from $300,000 to $500,000.

Many workers, particularly those unqualified for their jobs, left when Concha took over. He asked Dow for replacement parts and for styrene, which was in worldwide shortage. Dow sent two men from Argentina and two from Coral Gables to help him restore the financial records.

The junta quickly brought Eduardo Simian back from exile and asked him to oversee the resumption of normal activities in Chile's oil and petrochemical industries. As a former board chairman of Petrodow, Simian was keenly aware of the need to get Dow technology back, and he triggered an invitation to Dow to send a team of experts to Petrodow to assess the condition of the plants.

"I got a call from the second naval attache at the Chilean embassy in Washington," Schornstein said. "I guess he was one of the guys who was loyal to the military and not to Allende. In his broken English he explained who he was. His next words were, 'We want you back,' meaning Dow. As far as I know, we were the first company they contacted to come back."

Dow readily accepted the invitation, and before the end of September had dispatched the first technical team to arrive in Chile since the change of governments barely two weeks before. The team was headed by Bobby G. Caldwell, Dow's director of manufacturing for Latin America. The technical report it issued was a litany of missing, damaged, or broken parts and equipment, unsafe conditions, and slovenly housekeeping and maintenance.

Caldwell walked around the plants with one of the top operators and asked him, "Why did you let things get into such a mess, Ricardo? Didn't you guys have any pride? Didn't you realize that if things kept going the way they were, pretty soon you wouldn't even have a plant?" The operator responded: "Well, after a while you get tired of beating your head against a wall. Everybody was jockeying for position or attending political meetings. Nobody worked too hard. So finally you just decided to do what they did."

Schornstein went to Chile in October for a look at the plants and a visit with Simian. Simian asked: "What are your conditions for coming back?" It was barely six weeks since the junta had taken over.

Schornstein was prepared with an answer. Dow had three conditions for returning, he said: (1) maintenance of the original 1967 agreement with the Frei regime; (2) abrogation of the labor contract giving the union the right to sell all off-grade product; and (3) government recognition that Dow had invested large sums in Petrodow over a period of several years and had got very little in return. This recognition, he explained, might be reflected in favorable government action at the appropriate time in respect to export incentives; tax exemptions; entry permits for spare parts, replacement equipment, and raw material imports; and foreign currency availability for payments.

The government asked Dow to have its attorneys draw up a declaration of intent to take the plants back, detailing these terms and conditions.

Within another fortnight an agreement was reached for the return of both Petrodow and Dow Quimica Chilena to the original owners, and Dow named a new man to take charge of its operations in Chile—Harry Mohlmann, a 40-year-old who had six years of experience with Dow's Latin American operations in Brazil and Colombia. Mohlmann set about his first task, the hammering out of a detailed understanding with the Chilean government, and a new agreement was signed early in 1974, by which time the work of rebuilding and restoring Dow's Chilean companies was proceeding in earnest.

"Chile recovered very nicely," Schornstein said, many years later, "but there was a definite split (among the personnel) after we got the organization back and running; there were those who had been there during the intervention, and those that weren't."

Mohlmann soon rebuilt the staff, hiring 60 new employees, promoting 53, and transferring many to new jobs. In the 10 months after Dow returned, the Chileans surpassed the previous one-year sales record. "The Chileans have again shown their extraordinary professional talents and dedication," Mohlmann said.[15]

In the years that followed, Dow increasingly came under fire in the United States for working with and thereby implicitly supporting a harsh dictator, General Pinochet, who became increasingly autocratic with his years in power. "We were invited down to Chile by the Frei government, kicked out by Allende, and then found ourselves in bed with a military junta that became a dictatorship," Gerstacker commented.

"All of us," Branch said, "feel an intense pride in our Chilean employees' integrity and courage as human beings. They have set a remarkable and touching example for Dow employees everywhere."[16]

"You have to give Pinochet some credit," Schornstein said. "I think he set up a pretty good economic system; they took some pretty hard steps. While he was taking those steps he was a dirty dog, but now that it's working, it was a miracle. People really forget how bad things were down there."

IV.

In 1959 Kincaid sent Thomas G. Johnson to Bogota to explore Dow's affairs in Colombia. Dow was doing a brisk business in agricultural products in that area through Caja Agraria, a Bogota distributor that imported Dow's 2,4-D herbicides and other materials and marketed them to local farmers. Was it perhaps time for Dow to build a herbicides plant in the region?

Johnson recommended building one and in 1960 opened an office in Bogota, where he established Dow Quimica de Colombia. It was quickly successful and within a year or two the staff had grown to a dozen people and was selling Dow's products in all the Bolivarian nations—Venezuela, Ecuador, Peru, Bolivia, and Colombia. Johnson hired a young Colombian chemical engineer, Rafael Pavia, who had been working for Ecopetrol, the Colombian national oil company—Pavia was unhappy in the jungle of Ecopetrol's bureaucratic politics—and assigned him to build a small herbicides formulation plant at Bogota.

Pavia remembered traveling to Midland from Bogota and trying to find the office of Max Key, the Dow manufacturing chief. "Can you imagine a guy from Colombia going to Midland and getting on a bus and seeing a plant as large as a city?" he asked.[17] He returned to Colombia and built the first herbicides plant in the country. Harry DeLong, a 2,4-D expert, came down to help.

The plant did so well that within the first year after it was in operation Shell and Schering and two local Colombian companies all contracted for Dow to produce herbicides for them as well; the plant produced under their labels in addition to Dow's. Dow in effect had 100 percent of the market, and once the plant was in production the Colombian government increased duties on the products it produced and in practice no one else could import them.

"It was a very small investment and the one that gave life to Dow Colombia because it was making money like crazy," Pavia said. Two years later Dow decided to add an esterification plant. Schering and Shell built their own formulation plants but Dow was the only one with a manufacturing facility. In the late 1960s Dow built a duplicate of this plant in Venezuela.

While this was going on Tom Johnson went back to Midland (he left Dow to join Monsanto some years later) and Fernando Gil-Zorrilla, a Uruguayan, became manager of Dow Colombia. When Gil-Zorrilla left in 1964, Manuel Maza, a Cuban, came to Bogota as country manager for Colombia.

Maza became Pavia's hero: "my professor, my inspiration, my discipline," he said. "I remember when he came to Colombia for the very first time, he asked all of the engineers and all of the employees to have the Dow name on the door of their cars. It said 'Dow,' to tell the people while we're driving in the city that we are Dow. He really loved Dow," Pavia said.

Maza noted that Dow was importing large amounts of polystyrene plastic to Colombia and asked Pavia to make a rough market study of polystyrene consumption in Colombia. "Rafael, is there enough market to support a plant?" he asked. When Jack Stearns, executive vice president of Dow International, visited Bogota, Maza put the question of a plastics plant in Colombia on the agenda.

Pavia remembered the Saturday meeting with Stearns at which Maza presented his project. "But Colombia's very risky," Stearns objected. "There's drugs and violence and all that."

Maza banged his fist on the table. "Risky, you say? Risky is Europe. Have you ever seen a world war in Colombia? In Latin America, a world war? Never! Colombia being destroyed like Germany? Colombia being destroyed like France? Do you think there's risk in Colombia compared to that?"

Stearns said, "You're right. It is more risky in Europe than in Latin America."

"I was almost crying, hearing this argument," Pavia said. "This Manuel Maza was a real fighter."

The plant was built at Cartagena, the historic old port in the north of the country, once colonial Spain's principal bastion in the new world and site of the largest slave market in the Caribbean, from whence galleons laden with gold and emeralds had sailed for Spain. Dow became the vanguard of a crew of pioneers who now made the area of Mamonal, south of the city, the nucleus of a new world chemical community.[18]

The plan was to import styrene monomer from the United States as raw material for polystyrene. "Colombia wanted to promote the industrialization of places outside Bogota because almost everything was locating in Bogota, and issued a ten-year tax exemption for industry locating in Cartagena," Pavia said, "and the tax incentives plus Cartagena being a very good port was why the decision was made. We looked at Barranquilla, a river port in the coastal area, but Cartagena had the tax incentives."

A new company, Dow Colombiana S.A., was formed for the polystyrene business, and the plant was dedicated on July 9, 1965, with Dr. Raimundo Emiliani, the Colombian minister of justice, and Dr. Carl Gerstacker, Dow's board chairman, officiating.

As with the herbicides plant, imports to Colombia were permitted before the plant was built, but once it was producing, imports were no longer permitted and duties were raised. Knowing this, Dow's competitors imported at least a year and a half's worth of consumption before the plant started up. By the time of the start-up the country was glutted with polystyrene.

Six months later, Maza and Pavia were summoned to Midland and told they had to moth-ball the plant. There were no sales from it, no income from it, only expenses. The Latin Americans explained what had happened—competitors flooding the market before the start-up—and asked for six months' grace. "It's not good business for Dow," they were told, "close it down." Finally it was agreed to keep the plant open a few months longer. An export shipment of 1,000 tons to Hong Kong at this critical juncture helped. Finally, as the excess stock in the country was worked off, sales began to pick up, and then the plant took off like a rocket.

"Dow told us, 'you have to create a market,' and sent us a guy named Joseph J. Rabideau, who knew all about polystyrene uses," Pavia said.

> He showed them how to produce new things, and he still is a man they remember in Colombia because the plastic industry in Colombia was being born in those days. It was kind of a garage industry, the plastics converters. He came from the outside and taught them how to use poly-styrene—not theory, but how to do things. Those were very nice days because you could see how new applications improved sales, and the market was growing and growing and growing. The participation of a fellow like Joe Rabideau was vital to the market in Colombia.

The Cartagena facility started as a small plant—3,500 metric tons per year—and that was doubled, and then doubled again. By 1985 the plant had gone through its fourth expansion, and its capacity had grown to 45,000 metric tons. It became one of Dow's top polystyrene plants in Latin America. About half the annual capacity is exported, mainly to other countries in South America; the Colombian market absorbs only 20,000-25,000 tons yearly.

In 1966 Pavia was sent to the United States for a training assignment, principally to acquire know-how in polystyrene, and on his return to Colombia was offered a position in sales. He found himself traveling the Bolivarian region, selling plastics.

At first he found this galling. "When you went to a customer and you had to wait a half-hour or an hour, I got mad," he said. "Why, after studying chemical engineering, master's degree and all that, do I have to wait half an hour for this son-of-a-gun who doesn't want to receive me because he's busy?" But after his first sales he became enthusiastic about his new career.

"For me, it's like a fight with gladiators," he said. "You and I are the two fighters. He fought his position and I fought mine. There is nothing like selling. I say to young people, 'When you sell something, you have to feel like an orgasm.' You have to really get into it. What counts is your ability to negotiate and to get the order. I said, 'This is what I want to do in life.'"

The other countries in the region began to develop their own independent status. Oscar Novo, a Cuban, went to Venezuela as general sales manager. In Quito, Ecuador, a German Dow employee, Helmut Bloch, took over. Pavia became general sales manager in Colombia, succeeding John W. Mowitt, one of the rare Americans in South America. Ron Bollen, a Canadian, became the country manager.

In 1966 Dow became a 50-50 partner with Ecopetrol in building Colombia's first poly-ethylene plant. The project became known as "Policolsa" (short for Poliolefinas Colombianas S.A.). Ecopetrol wanted to manufacture ethylene and produce low-density polyethylene plas-tic from it for the South American market. Dow was the winner out of about 10 companies who bid on the project; Pavia's experience at Ecopetrol before joining Dow was useful.[19]

Bob Lundeen headed the Dow team that negotiated the contract with Ecopetrol for the joint company. "The negotiations lasted a long, long time, because we negotiated every single paragraph of the contract," Pavia said. "Bob Lundeen had a lot of patience to negotiate that but finally we signed the contract."

Policolsa was to take ethylene from Ecopetrol's plant and make it into polyethylene. Unfortunately, once it was built the ethylene facility did not produce up to its expected capac-ity and the plant looked to be a disaster in the making. Dow had designed a plant to make 40,000 metric tons of polyethylene, but when it was completed the ethylene plant made avail-able only enough raw material for 15,000 to 18,000 tons. It appeared that the only answer was to sink more capital into the ethylene plant to increase its capacity, but Dow declined, saying, "No, we don't want to put in more capital; it's your problem, not ours."

In the end Dow decided to sell its share of the project to Ecopetrol. Eventually the prob-lems were worked out, and by the 1990s Policolsa was considering how to expand its capacity.

In June 1972 Ron Bollen took Pavia and their wives to dinner, ordered wine, and lifted his glass in a toast to Pavia. "Here's to Dow's next head man in Colombia," he said. "I had thought of such a promotion, but I'm not sure I was expecting it," Pavia said. "I almost broke into tears."

Except for a three-year hitch as general manager of Dow Quimica Argentina, he was to remain Dow's "head man in Colombia" until his retirement in 1993.

When Branch made a swing around Latin America in 1973, he and Dave Schornstein stopped in Colombia to call on the nation's president, Misael Pastrana, along with Pavia. They were planning further expansion in Cartagena, they told the Colombians.

By this time Dow had become the top petrochemical company in the country. "You go to Colombia and you say, 'I work for Dow,' they open all the doors," Pavia said. "It's a very well known company; it is a very good name."

In 1975 Schornstein sent the 42-year-old Pavia back to school, to Harvard University's Advanced Management Course, a three-month on-campus cram course for senior managers to which Dow occasionally has sent representatives. Pavia found it a "shocking" experience— "you realize you don't know anything and that you have to learn a lot more"—but said "it really has helped me a lot in my career."

When he returned to Colombia he began laying out long-term strategies, 5 to 10 years ahead. In the early 1980s he fashioned a "Quantum Leap" strategy for Colombia designed to hold and build on Dow's position as the nation's petrochemical leader.

He made a presentation to Bill Stavropoulos and his staff in 1984 (when Stavropoulos was president of Dow Latin America) on "how Dow Colombia is going to look in 1990." Stavropoulos "thought it was kind of a mania," Pavia said, "but finally agreed to listen." After that Pavia presented a yearly report comparing actual accomplishment to this plan. Dow continued to invest in the country, notably for a new polyols plant that started up in 1990, and for expansion at Cartagena.

Dow's sales and profits in Latin America are highest in Brazil, but Colombia is second in both categories, Pavia was proud to point out, "even higher than Argentina and Mexico."

"Now the other countries are really waking up," he said in 1991. "Venezuela and Mexico are on our heels now, so it's going to be difficult to maintain the position."

V.

Mexico was always a special case for Dow. In the 1940s and 1950s, when the company began to expand outside the United States, it had been one of the most promising markets for Dow products anywhere, possibly the best in Latin America, but over the years the Dow presence in the country grew only fitfully and stubbornly, in the face of great obstacles.

"We never could get anything cracking in Mexico," Bob Kincaid said, "and I think that was for lots of reasons. The Mexican government controlled and isolated for itself basically all the petrochemicals business," a practice that continued into the 1990s. "It's a hell of a market, but to build and get into that market with the regulations I knew about was very difficult."[20]

To the company headquarters in Michigan, Mexico seemed a far-off, foreign country, but to Dutch Beutel in Texas it seemed an inviting, next-door neighbor, and much of the early history of the company in Mexico reflected this dichotomy, which gradually became a serious problem.

Beutel, who had started his career as a mining engineer, liked to visit Mexico and look at mines and mining properties, and because of its proximity began to consider it a kind of extension of his Texas territory. By the late 1950s Dow's manufacturing manager in Mexico—supervising several small production plants—was reporting to Beutel in Texas while the Mexico City sales manager reported to Midland, though they were housed in the same offices.

"The only problem was that Dutch wanted us to sell the chemicals that they made (in Texas) and he wasn't gonna pay us any commission," said Jack Thorsberg, Dow's Mexican manager at the time, "so this got to be a hot argument. It ended up in a meeting between Branch and Beutel," and was straightened out, he said, but Beutel never lost interest in Mexico.[21]

When a Latin American headquarters was established in 1965, Mexico City was one of the candidates to become Dow's Latin American headquarters, an idea promoted by Rodolfo Santamaria, a Mexican who had been manager of Dow's Mexican office and then moved to Midland to work with Elmer K. Stilbert's Latin American development group. Largely because of its shortcomings in travel and communication facilities, however, Mexico City was only an also-ran in the contest.[22]

Dow "got into Mexico [in a manufacturing sense]," Thorsberg said,

> because a man promised us that if we could get a big shipment of caustic soda he could get the license to get it to Mexico City. So we shipped it to Tampico. He never did get the license, and it ended up being washed into the Gulf of Mexico in a storm. But he did end up a partner of ours in a joint caustic-chlorine venture; we bought probably the oldest caustic chlorine plant in the hemisphere. We picked our partner through a marketing contract, not through a manufacturing contract. In those days, Dow International would ask the manufacturing people to send someone down there to help them technically. We got involved in an aspirin plant at Tlalnapantla in much the same way, and Bill Williams used to go down there maybe three times a year; Ralph Hunter went down for the caustic chlorine plant.

Thorsberg, Dow's Mexican manager following the death of Russell Zick in 1956, remembered that Howard Ball, Dow's long-time export manager, made his first (and only) trip out of the United States on a trip to Mexico City soon after he took over. "He was the best, or could have been, the best goodwill man for Dow in the whole wide world," Thorsberg said. "People in Mexico still remembered Howard Ball 8 or 10 years later. He did little things. For example, one morning he walked into the office in Mexico City, and the sun was shining, and he looked around the office and said, 'There should be a vase of flowers on every secretary's desk in this office. Why don't we brighten this place up?' So we got them (they sell flowers down there very cheaply), and after that, every Monday morning every secretary's desk got a fresh bouquet of flowers."

Ball, he said, "had a horrible time making a decision; you had to make a decision for Howard, and he wanted everything to be fair and honest and aboveboard. He had a hard time understanding competition and price cutting and those things. He never believed that Monsanto would openly cut a price on Dow to get an order. He had a hard time with the difference between the real world and where he was brought up."

In 1958 Thorsberg got married, and his parents held a reception in Midland to introduce his new wife. Ball telephoned the day of the party to say he would not be coming; he had been fired by Dow that day, he said, and he was "afraid that if he came he'd embarrass the people who were there, so would you please excuse me?"

"I went to see him the next day and he was just as kind as he could be and six months later he was dead," Thorsberg said. "The Episcopal minister in the funeral service said 'from a broken heart,' and I'm a little inclined to agree. Because the Dow Chemical Company was Howard's whole life existence."[23]

Dow research was exploring fluorine chemistry during this period of the middle 1950s, and Beutel's geologists discovered a Mexican fluorspar deposit, south of Texas's Big Bend Park, as a source of fluorine. Beutel formed a company, La Domincia S.A. de C.V., to mine the fluorspar, which at first was trucked over to Dow's Texas Division during the dry season, when the trucks could drive across the parched Rio Grande River without difficulty.[24]

As this business grew, Beutel decided a bridge across the Rio Grande was necessary to make deliveries possible year-round, and proposed that the Dow board authorize the cost of building one. Carl Gerstacker opposed the bridge strongly, saying a little basic planning would make it unnecessary. The board authorized the expenditure anyway, with Gerstacker dissenting, and when the bridge had been completed some time later, Beutel invited Gerstacker to the opening ceremonies. With a big grin Beutel watched as a bronze plaque was unveiled at one end of the bridge. He had arranged for it to be called the "Carl A. Gerstacker International Bridge."

In the end Dow did not need the fluorspar and sold La Domincia to Dupont, the largest user of the material.

At the end of 1992 Dow announced that it was combining Mexico with its other North American properties to form Dow North America. The formation of the North American Free Trade Area (NAFTA), which followed about two years later, provided a formal political matrix for the alignment the company had already adopted.[25]

Dow had been one of the companies urging adoption of the NAFTA legislation, well before it was passed by the U.S. Congress and adopted by the three North American nations. Not surprisingly, the company's sales in Mexico improved markedly once NAFTA came into being.

VI.

Dow's early love affair with Argentina, where it first projected a major Latin American chemical complex, quickly turned rather sour. It was a frustrating story of political jockeying by Argentine officialdom and interminable waits for permits to build plants, but was spiced by one of the more unlikely events in Dow's history, a challenge to a duel with pistols between two board members of its Argentinian affiliate.

In the days following World War II Dow engaged a young American in Buenos Aires, Thomas J. Williams, to market its products in that country. Williams "knew everyone" in Argentina, and did very well at this, and he and Dow prospered. Williams was especially well known among the military crowd, and he wined and dined many high-ranking officers; among them was Col. Juan Peron, who a few years later became the country's president and dictator.

Peron, among other presidential acts, impounded the Argentine peso, and Dow was soon piling up pesos which could not be spent anywhere except in Argentina. Williams suggested a solution; why didn't Dow use those blocked pesos to purchase a half-interest in Williams Quimica y Tecnica, his firm? Dow accepted and sent its own man to Buenos Aires to work with Williams. He was Theodore F. (Ted) Thorsberg, a Midlander who had once taught school in Puerto Rico and had married there. The firm became known informally as "Dow-Williams," although it was never incorporated as such.

Williams and Thorsberg made increasingly ambitious proposals to the Argentine government in respect to its imports of chemicals, and in October 1953 Williams went to Peron with Dow-Williams Program No. 3, which among other items called for imports of 100,000 tons of caustic, 10 million pounds of phenol, large quantities of weed killers, and five million pounds of Dow polystyrene—$14.6 million worth of Dow products in all. When Peron approved it, Williams asked about getting it past the Central Bank, which took a very long time to review and authorize such programs.[26]

Peron—his popular wife, Evita, had died the year before, but he was still at the peak of his power—showing what a dictator can do for an old friend, called a special meeting of the cabinet to consider this matter. Williams laid his program before them, and won their approval.

At this meeting the minister of defense suggested that Williams ought to be appointed one of the directors of Atanor, the largest Argentine chemical company and a key supplier to the military, Atanor being a "mixed" company owned partly (44 percent) by the government and partly private industry. This was speedily accomplished, and Williams also became a major stockholder of Atanor. Dow wound up owning 22.5 percent of Atanor's stock.[27]

This was the background against which two members of the Atanor board of directors traveled to Midland in January 1954, to propose a major expansion of their firm with Dow's help. They were the Italian-born Dr. Ladislao Reti, who had founded Atanor 10 years before, its chemical brains and managing director, and Eduardo Francheri Lopez, a Spanish aristocrat who was the firm's syndic, representing the Argentine government's interests on its board.

Reti and Lopez made a tour of Dow's U.S. installations, stopping for three days of talks in Midland, visiting Dutch Beutel in Texas, and going on to Dow Western to visit Dr. Hirschkind, who knew Reti and the Atanor plants in Argentina well and whose friendship with Reti provided strong support for the Dow-Atanor relationship.[28]

Atanor wanted to expand by manufacturing the weed killers 2,4-D and 2,4,5-T, pentachlorophenol wood preservative, carboxymethyl cellulose, and vinyl and polyvinyl chloride, and the two companies arrived at an agreement whereby Dow would provide engineering and operating data for plants of this nature and the two companies would jointly explore their construction.[29]

Reti and Lopez were not particularly good friends to start with, and this extended trip together, lasting several months, rapidly became intolerable for them both. By the time they returned to Buenos Aires they had become mortal enemies, speaking to each other only to deliver insults. Once they were back in Argentina the Atanor board meetings became the theater of their feud, and nothing constructive could any longer be agreed upon by the Atanor board.[30]

In July, Lopez, one of the best pistol shots in Argentina—he wore a medal proclaiming his prowess—challenged Reti to a duel. His honor, he said, had been offended by Reti's remarks at a board meeting, and this was the only way it could be restored.

A duel in Argentina is a serious affair. The chances of Dr. Reti, one of his nation's best chemists, against Francheri Lopez, one of his nation's best pistol shots, would not have been good. Although dueling was illegal, there was a "finca" (or plantation) near Buenos Aires, "where arguments could be settled in this manner without interference," Ted Thorsberg noted.

Thorsberg said the affair was triggered by an event that occurred while the duo was in New York. Lopez met "a representative of the Pan American Union," who wanted to confer medals on them both. When he told Reti about this, Reti said the Pan American Union did not confer medals so there must be some mistake. An investigation revealed that the "representative" was actually Alberto Vidaurre, a Peruvian, and that his organization, "the Inter-American Union for Freedom and Democracy," of which he was the sole member, did not even have an office. Reti recommended they forget the incident and the medal, but Lopez became angry and claimed his information was a lie—it was just that Reti didn't want him to receive a medal.[31]

Reti wrote Hirschkind that at subsequent Atanor board meetings, "I had to listen to the vulgar insults and explosions of hate" of Lopez, who some months later, "provoked me to a duel."

"He sent me his seconds and I had to nominate mine in this stupid and disgusting parody of an affair of honor," Reti said. "They settled matters without bloodshed, reinstating both adversaries in the honorable condition." This was accomplished by printing a Public Notice in the Buenos Aires newspapers, which said (in part):

> In Buenos Aires, on the 23rd day of July 1954, Mssrs. Colonel Pascual Semberoiz and Dr. Luis Veneroni, on behalf of Mr. Eduardo Francheri Lopez, and Mssrs. Brigadier General Alfredo Intzaugurat and Dr. Dario Sarachaga, on behalf of Dr. Ladislao Reti, having exchanged their respective powers, Mssrs. Colonel Semberoiz and Dr. Luis Veneroni stated that they were charged by their principal to request from Dr. Reti a recantation of the expressions attributed to him regarding the mission carried out by Mr. Eduardo Francheri Lopez in the USA in his capacity as Director of Sociedad Mixta Atanor, or, failing this, a reparation by armed duel. The gentlemen representing Dr. Reti stated that, considering the circumstances under which the events took place, during the course of administrative functions, the appreciation of which, by Dr. Reti, was not made with the intention of offending or defaming in any way the honour and dignity of Mr. Lopez, the correctness of whose conduct, both private and political, he is pleased to acknowledge, they have in consequence no objection to declaring that Dr. Reti had no intention of being disrespectful to Mr. Lopez, whom he recognizes as an honourable official and gentleman. . . .[32]

Unfortunately for Dr. Reti, his 10-year contract as managing director of Atanor was coming up for renewal at the following board meeting, on August 16. Reti had been pushing unsuccessfully for board approval of the Dow agreement since his return to Buenos Aires in March. At the August meeting the Dow matter was postponed once again, this time for six months, in effect killing it, and the board then proceeded to fire their company's founder.

"The representatives of the government declared that, in consideration of my undisciplined behavior and my opposition to the authority they represented, under no condition should my contract be renewed," Reti told Hirschkind.

Reti's departure also, in the end, spelled Dow's departure from Atanor. Some months later Reti became chairman of the chemical industry division of the United Nations Economic Council for Latin America. Williams, who had prudently stayed out of the line of fire, continued to market Dow's products in Argentina.

It was almost 10 years later, when the Latin American area was launched, that Dow started over again in Argentina, taking the funds that had been invested in Williams Quimica and Atanor and establishing Dow Quimica Argentina, which had no relationship to its predecessors. John Van Horn, a peppery product developer, was sent down from Midland to be its first president.

Up to 1971 and the discovery of salt on Matandariba Island, it was Dow's intention to build a major chemical complex in Argentina as the keystone for its Latin American operations. The company purchased a small plant at Aldo Bonzi in 1959. By 1968 Van Horn had progressed far enough with the project that a Dow terminal at La Plata went into operation, and in 1970 the first Dow-built plant in Argentina was inaugurated at San Lorenzo.

The San Lorenzo plant made two products—Zoalene, a coccidiostat (to prevent coccidiosis in poultry), and latex. "That was a good little plant," said Schornstein. "That was Bobby Caldwell's baby; it was all his show."

Caldwell, who later became manufacturing manager for Dow Latin America, was gung ho to build a big plant in Argentina and was looking at Bahia Blanca, 400 miles down the coast from Buenos Aires, as the best available site. In April 1968 the company announced that Caldwell had been named project manager for Dow's Argentine petrochemical complex and would have complete responsibility for designing, building, and running the plant.[33]

The project never got far off the drawing board, although the strong-minded Caldwell threatened several times to move into the plant site with bulldozers and get construction started while he waited for the Argentine government to provide the permits. The projected complex was called PNP—Petroquimica Nord-Patagonica SAIC y F. In August 1970 Caldwell brashly announced the lineup that would build the plant, a dozen seasoned Dow managers being brought in from Dow installations in Florida, Texas, California, the Netherlands, Louisiana, Midland, Colombia, and Chile. He said some 20 Argentine engineers and chemists would be trained at Dow operations elsewhere in the world for periods of from one to two years in preparation for taking on key posts at Bahia Blanca, and that two Argentine chemical engineers were already in training at Dow's Louisiana Division.

"It was a good petrochemical site," Schornstein said. " Basically we were looking at what we would ultimately build in Brazil."

"Things started going from good to bad and from bad to worse in Argentina," he said.

When it started to get bad, Bob was worried about it; I was worried about it. When we finally sat down and talked about it, we decided the only thing to do was to kill the project. This was after we had about three years of work into it. Then I had to go up (to Midland) and tell Branch that we were doing it, and he was happy. He was happy that we arrived at the decision ourselves. It was a tough project but we finally had to pull the stopper on it.[34]

Jorge Casteleiro said Argentina was difficult because of the bureaucracy.

The Bahia Blanca project was going to be a super-duper thing—$500 million. Dow committed the error of appointing Bobby Caldwell as project manager before we had obtained approvals for the project. Bobby was a doer—the guy you'd have to get in to build the complex of plants once you had everything ready; then he would build the plant in so many months and he'd kill anybody if it weren't done. But he wasn't the guy to go to Argentina and be nice to the government people to try to get them to authorize the project because he was very impatient. He went ahead and bought land and facilities and spent a lot of money; he moved many Dow persons down there. He moved over 20 Dow engineers from the States and got houses for them and their families. He bought the land for the whole complex, built the piers because it's a deepwater port—that's why Dow picked it.

But the whole problem was the government agencies. They kept fighting with each other. Each government entity supposedly had their own experts, their own economic wizards.

The incredible thing about the Argentines is that these presidents can't get their own cabinet to work as a team with them. Impossible! I used to go down there every month and stay there a week or two negotiating with this minister and the other. The moment they saw that we were approved by the minister of whatever, the other guys would reject it. Finally, Dow pulled out and moved to Brazil.[35]

"The Argentine has been an enigma to me forever," Bob Kincaid said. "Kolungia said that the problem with the Argentine is that there are no true Argentine patriots, and until they solve that problem they will never get anyplace. It's a rich country; the people are well educated, but they don't go anyplace; they will not make these personal sacrifices."[36]

The great potential of Argentina remained very much alive, however, and a quarter of a century later, under the more stable regime of President Carlos Menem, a modern-day Peronist, Dow went back to Argentina and recaptured the Bahia Blanca project it had envisioned in the impatient, gung ho days of Van Horn and Caldwell. By then the Peronists had become Argentina's most powerful party and Bahia Blanca had become the country's main petrochemical complex, its largest producer of ethylene and a major producer of caustic, chlorine, and polyvinyl chloride.

When in 1995 the Argentine government decided to privatize Petroquimica Bahia Blanca (or PBB), as it was then known, Dow organized a consortium of firms (also including the Argentina energy giant YPF and Itochu, Japan's largest trading company) and submitted a bid for the complex. Its bid of $357.5 million won the pot, and the consortium acquired PBB, giving Dow "a strong polyolefins position in the important four-nation Mercosur trading bloc of Argentina, Brazil, Paraguay, and Uruguay."[37]

Dow also acquired full ownership of Polisur S.A., a producer of low density polyethylene and linear low-density polyethylene.

The wheel of history had come around full turn, and another chapter was beginning for Dow in Argentina.

Notes

1. In late 1951 the U.S. Congress altered the tax laws by adopting the so-called Kennedy provision, which allowed U.S. firms to accumulate earnings abroad tax-free until they were repatriated. The Western Hemisphere was treated separately under this provision, and for this reason Dow, in taking advantage of it, established Dow Chemical International and Dow Chemical Inter-American as separate firms.

   Shoemaker appears originally to have projected Dow offices for these firms in Brussels, Montevideo, and Hong Kong. See "Dow Goes Abroad," outlining this structure, in *Dow Diamond* 15, no, 2 (April 1952): 6.

2. Oral History, Robert F. Kincaid, July 8, 1991.

3. Early history of Dow in Brazil from Oral History, Salvador Pinto, March 20, 1991; Oral History, Francisco Barraconi, March 20, 1991; Oral History, Jose Franco de Moraes, March 19, 1991; Oral History, Dave W. Schornstein, March 15, 1991; Oral History, Anibal Galhardi, March 21, 1991; Oral History, Jorge S. Casteleiro, March 13, 1991; Oral History, Luis Valeriano Moro, March 25, 1991; Oral History, Paul F. Oreffice, August 1, 1988; Oral History, R. F. Kincaid; Oral History, Jarbas Carvalho, March 25, 1991; Oral History, Hunter W. Henry Jr., September 11, 1990; Oral History, Ernesto Ramon, August 21, 1995.

4. Oral History, P. F. Oreffice.

5. For a fuller account of the site selection, see Jorge S. Casteleiro, "A Gables Beginning" ("El Comienzo"), in *Dow Latina*, Veinteavo Aniversario, published by Dow Chemical Latin America, Coral Gables, 1985.

6. Oral History, J. Carvalho; Oral History, Sergio Goloubeff, March 27, 1991.

7. Oral History, Hunter W. Henry Jr., September 11, 1990.

8. Oral History, S. Goloubeff.

9. Oral History, E. Ramon.

10. Oral History, J. S. Casteleiro.

11. See "The Nation-State and the Multinational Corporation in Lesser-Developed Countries: Dow's Experience in Chile," talk by Carl A. Gerstacker at a seminar on the nation-state and the multinational corporation in lesser-developed countries, Aspen, Colorado, September 15, 1973. (Text had been distributed to attendees prior to the military coup d'état in Chile of September 11, 1973).

12. Oral History, H. W. Henry Jr.

13. Alex Groner, "Petrodow, The Story of an Industry Caught Up in the Turmoil of Political Upheaval," 1974, a book-length account of Dow's experience in Chile during the Allende regime, was commis-

sioned by Dow Latin America in 1973 but for various reasons, primarily political, never published. Mr. Groner, now retired, kindly made the manuscript available to the author, who gratefully acknowledges this assistance. "Petrodow" is quoted extensively in this section.

14. Oral History, D. W. Schornstein, is quoted extensively in this section.

15. "Report 74," published by Dow Latin America, Coral Gables, Florida, May 1975. For other Branch comments see President's Letter, *Dow Annual Report to Stockholders, 1973, 1974*, and *1975*.

16. See Herbert E. Meyer, "Dow Picks Up the Pieces in Chile," *Fortune*, April 1974.

17. This section relies heavily on Oral History, Rafael Alberto Pavia, March 11, 1991.

18. See "Cartagena: After Many Centuries, a Friendly Kind of Invasion," *Dow Diamond* 33 (June 1970): 22-25.

19. Discussions of Ecopetrol project in *Dow Annual Reports* to stockholders, 1966 and 1967.

20. Oral History, R. F. Kincaid.

21. This section relies heavily on Oral History, John W. Thorsberg, September 7, 1994.

22. Oral History, J. S. Casteleiro.

23. Ball was one of the victims of Dow's 1958 "Black Friday" episode, when the company reduced personnel by 10 percent across the board. He was a nephew of Grace A. (Ball) Dow.

24. See "Economic Study of Mining and Milling Domincia's Fluorspar Reserves," W. H. Blaney to H. G. Roebke and C. M. Shigley, Dow, Texas Division, September 3, 1956, and related studies.

25. The bridge, originally designated the "Heath Crossing Bridge," is located near Marathon in Brewster County, Texas.

   For Dow's position regarding NAFTA, see, e.g., "A Call to Action: NAFTA Countdown," *Dow Center Line,* No. 42, October 27, 1993.

26. T. F. Thorsberg to Carl A. Gerstacker, "Dow-Williams Program No. 3," report dated October 28, 1953.

27. For history and activities of Atanor, see Dun & Bradstreet Co. (Argentina) report, July 22, 1952.

28. Most of the records of the Dow-Atanor relationship are found in the papers of Wilhelm Hirschkind; Hirschkind and Reti were regular correspondents during these years. For details of the tentative Dow-Atanor agreement (never approved by the Atanor board of directors), see L. I. Doan to L. Reti, Summary of Agreement, March 25, 1954.

29. See "Visit to Midland of Dr. Ladislao Reti, managing director, and Senor Eduardo Lopez, director of Atanor, compania para la industria quimica S.A. Mixta, Jan. 6-9, 1954," Hirschkind papers.

30. L. Reti to W. Hirschkind, September 5, 1954.

31. T. F. Thorsberg to C. A. Gerstacker, August 30, 1954.

32. Public Notice in *La Nacion*, Buenos Aires, July 26, 1954 (translation by Thorsberg). Col. Semberoiz, Lopez's second, was also a director of Atanor.

33. "B. G. Caldwell Named Project Manager for Dow's Argentine Petrochemical Complex," Dow news release, April 16, 1968.

34. Oral History, D. W. Schornstein.

35. Oral History, J. S. Casteleiro.

36. Oral History, R. F. Kincaid.

37. *Around Dow* 2, no. 2 (March/April 1996); *Dow 1995 Report to stockholders.*

SIXTEEN
DOW IN ASIA

I.

In 1943 a young second lieutenant, Robert W. Lundeen, was dropped into remote southeast China, at a place called Suichuan, as a weather forecaster for the U.S. Air Force. It was his introduction both to life in China and to life as a manager. Some months later the Japanese ran all the Americans out of southeast China; the defeated Americans regrouped back in Kunming (the capital of Yunnan Province in south China) and started over again to build U.S. air bases in China. Lundeen and two other officers were handed the task of rebuilding the weather service.

"We had to organize and staff and provide the apparatus and the people to rebuild the whole air force weather service in China," Lundeen said. "We had a lot of problems, but it was one of those rare managerial experiences for a young man that is extremely hard to get in industry. It proved a great asset when I came to work at Dow."[1]

When the war was over Major Lundeen turned down a promising military career and joined Dow Chemical. Twenty years later he was asked to organize and staff Dow's organization in the Far East, of which he became the founding father.

In his early career Lundeen was planning director for Dow's Western Division and often helped present California projects to the Dow Board of Directors in Midland. In 1961 Ben Branch asked him to come to Midland and join the team that would put Dow International on the map. He became an assistant to Elmer Stilbert, the Dowintal vice president for business development and new projects.[2]

Four years later, when Branch and the other members of the troika decided to divide the world up into geographic regions, Lundeen had become the business development director of Dowintal and was well acquainted with the Dow board; as he had in his California days, he now brought Dowintal projects to them for authorization. He was also the only major Dow manager with experience in the Orient. Branch and Mac Whiting, who succeeded him as president of Dowintal, chose Lundeen to become the first general manager of Dow's Far Eastern Area Administration, effective January 1, 1966.

Lundeen took charge of an area that encompassed almost half the earth—all of Asia, west to India and Pakistan, south to Australia and New Zealand, east to Japan and the Philippines—and more than half the world's population, including the world's most populous nations, China and India.

Dow had been doing business in Asia for many years. Its first shipment of bromides to Japan had left Midland in 1908, and from 1916 on it had become a major factor in the indigo market in China, the world's largest market for what was and still is the standard clothing-material dye in China. The Dow "chop," a flying tiger bearing a Dow diamond in its front paws, had been carried all over Asia on indigo pails.[3]

In 1966, however, Dow's sales volume in the Asian area was only $30 million, about 2 percent of total Dow sales. The company had sales offices in Tokyo, Hong Kong, Osaka, and Sydney. Its only manufacturing plants were operated in Japan by the Asahi-Dow management. There was another small operation in Australia. All in all, Dow was a negligible factor in the Asian marketplace and Asia was a negligible factor in Dow's overall business. Lundeen's challenge, and opportunity, was to change all this.

In a period of six months, at the end of 1965 and the beginning of 1966, Dow International disappeared and the new world organization came into being. Lundeen chose Hong Kong as headquarters for the Far Eastern Area Administration and established temporary offices in Hong Kong's Hilton Hotel, where key aides began to assemble. The 13 rooms used as offices were soon crowded with 16 expatriates and 12 local staff. "The file boxes had to be stacked on top of the bathtubs," recalled Dave Kwok, the first manager of economic evaluation and pricing.

"Hong Kong didn't seem a strange place to me. It was just a more economically advanced version of the life in China I had experienced 20 years previously," Lundeen said. "The people were as cheerful, hard-working, and responsible as the Chinese people I had come to know and admire as a young officer in the U.S. Army."

"We knew so little about Asia; I guess some of us thought Hong Kong was a part of Japan," said Arnold L. (Bud) Johnson, first controller and treasurer. Husbands and wives were given an orientation course before leaving the U.S., and some language training. "Imagine about 30 adults sitting around the table trying to learn how to count to 10 in Chinese," Johnson said.[4]

The British schools were greatly overcrowded when they arrived, so the expatriates established their own. It opened in September 1966, with 38 students (including children from other American companies in Hong Kong) and six teachers. Dick Gettings, the first industrial relations manager, served as headmaster for the first year in addition to his Dow duties. The school opened as the Hong Kong Extension of Midland High School and as other expatriates arrived grew up to become Hong Kong International School, the city's leading school for the children of expatriate Americans.[5]

Some of the new arrivals were not sure what they were supposed to do in the vast virgin territory to which they were assigned. Johnson and Vince Buckley, the first area legal counsel, shared an office, and one day Clyde Bryant arrived from Texas as the newest staff addition. Bryant came in and said, "What are you guys doing, and what do you think I'm supposed to do?" They spent the next few hours discussing it.

Jim Harris, a pioneering marketer, said most of the early business was polystyrene or polyethylene plastics, used in Hong Kong mainly for making a new product, artificial flowers, then often called "Hong Kong flowers." Caustic sales in drums were a big item. The agricultural chemicals business was growing, and mining chemicals were booming.[6]

"I got some great people to come work with me," Lundeen said.

I also wound up, not surprisingly, with a few turkeys who'd been palmed off on me; it took me a few months to find out who they were. Oh, calling them turkeys is overstating it; they just weren't up to the demands of doing what we needed to do in Hong Kong. They were fine as district sales managers in Boston or someplace like that where they had a lot of supporters and a lot of resources around. But in Hong Kong they were the resource and the doer all in one, and it was a lot different business. That combination hurt them; there aren't a lot of people who handle that combination readily.

After a few years of "teething troubles," as he called them, the organization took on a momentum of its own, Lundeen said. "The territory was very spread out. We had to have a Dow manager, a person who knew his stuff, where the action was. I had to have complete confidence in the local manager so he and I could level with each other, because I depended on him almost entirely to ease the local situation," he said.

The first key to success in the Pacific was "some very good people in the right places," Lundeen said,

stalwarts like Eric Huggins in Japan, a Canadian who was one of our pioneers in Asia; Colin Goodchild, an Australian, who retired after being president of Dow Pacific; Lee Dupuy, who put Dow's business in Korea together and did an absolutely spectacular job of that; some other fine managers like Bernie Butcher, who came from Dow Europe as director of marketing; Bud Johnson and Bill Schmidt on the accounting and finance side; Ted Menerey, employee relations manager; and Louis Shelton, from Texas, director of manufacturing.

Early on I got the key geographic and functional managers together at frequent intervals and we came up with a list of things we needed to do. We decided there were some territories that were relatively unexplored and that we had better put a Dow presence there. That was one of our best strategic moves. We felt, "We're never going to know whether there's any business in these places unless we get a Dow person there and find out." We could fiddle around with traders and agents from now until hell freezes over, but they've got a lot of other things on their plate. Until we get a top-flight Dow person in the territory to try to move Dow products and thus give us ultimately a base to build a factory and have a really big presence, we're never going to be a success. So we'll make the investment in people.

Lundeen called Jim Harris, then the chemical sales manager, to his office in Hong Kong one day. "Jim," Lundeen said, "we've got to find out whether there's any business worthwhile for Dow in Thailand. We're fooling around with ag products and chemicals down there but nobody knows much about the place. We'd like you to go and see if this is a place where Dow could do business. Would you like to go to Bangkok and do that?" Harris, a young bachelor, said "Great!" Lundeen said, "Okay, get yourself a Thai resident visa and airplane tickets and go, and then let us know what you need."

Lundeen rapidly spread a network of Dow people and offices across Asia. Growth was slow at first, and the area did not reach the $100 million mark in annual sales until 1972. But by 1974 it had reached $200 million, and by 1978 the $400 million level. By the early 1990s sales had surpassed the $1.5 billion mark.

For a dozen years Lundeen himself was almost constantly on the go. "Each month I literally spent a week in Hong Kong, a week in the United States, a week in Hong Kong, and a week somewhere else in Asia," he said.

But it was a good way to run the business in those days. As we started to get some presence in these countries, we got some good local people because they want to come to work for you once it looks like you're going to stay. That's how we really got the business going, by investing in human resources where our judgment told us we ought to, nurturing those things that looked good, having a competent central staff that could provide resources, making sure the business was controlled, and then having a chief executive who had time to do what he needed to do.

Having an excellent group of senior managers in Hong Kong, he said, "freed me up to personally spend a hell of a lot of time in the field. I went out and sniffed the air, met the people, and talked to the governments. I would immerse myself, talk to government officials, meet our customers, and spend time with our salesmen in the territory. I didn't have to be in Hong Kong to run things, because I had fine managers who could do that."

The staff stayed in the Hilton for most of a year and then moved to the new, 14-story New Henry House office building on Icehouse Street in central Hong Kong, where the Dow people rubbed shoulders with the Asian emissaries of IBM, Swissair, and Rank Xerox.

Life in Hong Kong was seldom dull, and was enlivened by riots and bombings in 1967. For a time there was a severe water shortage and water was supplied for four hours every fourth day. Harris remembered having dinner at a Wanchai restaurant while police experts defused a bomb planted nearby. "The restaurant owner told us to enjoy our food, and he would let us know when it was safe to leave," Harris said.

Hong Kong became more than Dow's Eastern headquarters in 1973, when Dow built a world-scale polystyrene plant on Tsing Yi, an undeveloped island in the Hong Kong harbor. Dave DaSilva, the first Hong Kong regional sales manager for Dow, was a key player in this move. "We had nurtured the idea of building a polystyrene plant in Hong Kong for some time," DaSilva said, "so as soon as the Hong Kong government decided to offer land for industrial development in the early 1970s, we moved quickly to secure land for our plant. It is a well thought out investment and I am proud that it has proven to be very successful for Dow." DaSilva later became president of Dow Chemical China Ltd.

The Tsing Yi Plant was Hong Kong's first major chemical plant. In spite of being more than a little risky—Hong Kong is a free port, with no tariff protection for its manufacturers—it has proven to be a good bet.

II.

Eric Huggins, son of a London bobby, had joined Dow Canada to sell plastics out of Toronto after an apprenticeship with R. H. Cole, Dow's agent for plastics in England. In 1953 Clayton Shoemaker of Dow International and Russ Crawford, general manager of Dow Canada, asked him to go to Tokyo to establish Dow's first office in Asia, and he became a roving salesman covering most of the continent.

The military occupation of Japan had ended. MacArthur had been sacked by Truman and gone into retirement, and the government handed back to the Japanese. "There weren't many foreigners there," Huggins said. "It was a bit of a ghetto in that respect. It was extremely difficult to find acceptable housing for us, but then it was difficult for the Japanese to find housing, too. If the job hadn't been so interesting I think I would have quit, because it wasn't easy living, not at all." He and his wife went to YMCA evening classes to learn Japanese, which turned out not to be as difficult as they had thought.[7]

From Japan he covered the territory all the way to Afghanistan. "I used to go to Australia and New Zealand either via Taipei or Manila, so it meant that on that trip I was away about eight weeks," he said. "Those were the days when flying was really flying, and it took about 16 hours to get down to Sydney. From Vancouver or San Francisco it took 22 hours to get to Tokyo. It was an eight or nine weeks' trip to get into Calcutta, New Delhi, Karachi, Bombay, and down to Madras and Bangalore. Then I used to do what I called the short trip, and that was Malaysia, Indonesia, Singapore, and maybe up into Burma."

Even obtaining food was difficult for those accustomed to a Western diet. "Any weekend I was home I would spend driving a car 30 or 40 miles around Tokyo just to get groceries," he said. "The only baker was the German bakery in the center of Tokyo, and if you wanted bread, that's where you went. If you wanted bacon, it meant driving 25 miles to get a pound of bacon."

In October 1956 Huggins was sent to open a new office in Hong Kong, which 10 years later became the area headquarters. "I opened all the early offices in the Far East," Huggins said, "Tokyo, Hong Kong, Sydney."

Once Japan had become one of Dow's biggest customers, a status it reached by the mid-1980s, there was lingering debate over who had been responsible for establishing the Asahi-Dow Chemical Company, the foundation for Dow's business in that country. Zoltan Merszei was given credit for it, and so were Max Key and Jack Chamberlain. All of them contributed to this development but the basic truth lay elsewhere, Huggins said: Asahi-Dow was invented by the Japanese.

The idea came out of MITI (the all-powerful Japanese Ministry of International Trade and Industry), said Huggins. "Japan was heavy in natural fibers and textiles—silk, cotton, jute, hemp—but in the postwar era had no synthetics," he said. "MITI decided that Japan must have synthetics and they designated companies to go out and get them. They designated somebody to go out and get nylon, somebody else to get polyethylene, somebody to get polypropylene, and they fingered Asahi-Kasei to get saran."

Several Japanese companies had expressed an interest in saran, so Lee Doan and Ray Boundy sent Jack Chamberlain, Dow's plastics research manager, on a fact-finding mission to Japan in the fall of 1951. Chamberlain had come back recommending Asahi Chemical Industry Company as the best partner for Dow.

Asahi Chemical was the biggest chlorine manufacturer in Japan, and saran was high in chlorine content, so MITI told them, "Go and get saran," Huggins said. Thus both partners had chosen each other before the courtship began, making for a brief courtship. A three-man Asahi delegation headed for Midland late in 1951 but arrived instead at the Dow Canada offices in Toronto, unable to get into the United States.

"They couldn't get visas because of Manabu Enseki," Huggins said. "Enseki had been the first minister in Washington at the time of Pearl Harbor and he was not acceptable to the United States."

"They sat in Toronto for six weeks and bugged me constantly," Huggins said. "I phoned Midland every other day asking, 'Please, what's happening?' I diverted them in various ways, and got to know them reasonably well. Eventually Enseki got a visa and I drove them to Midland."

Max Key, then production manager for saran, was involved in the negotiations and became a long-term board member of the new firm, as did Huggins. Yoshio Tsunoda of the Japanese trio became its president, and later chairman. The hero of the negotiations, Huggins said, was the third member of the Dow negotiating team, Bill Groening, then assistant general counsel of the company.[8]

"Groening did an absolutely masterful job of putting the agreement together," Huggins said.

The agreement specified that all the profits would be paid equally to the two shareholders annually. As a consequence there has never been an argument about money with Asahi, or with Asahi-Dow; and as you know, in business that's where most arguments start. Once a year they declared a dividend, paid Asahi, and paid Dow. It meant that the company never had any cash, which was a very good thing, because any time it needed any capital it had to come to both parents and ask for money. It wasn't until later years that we allowed the company to borrow money. It worked extremely well. I was at every board meeting and never once did I hear an argument about money.

Dow was also very fortunate at the start in enlisting Nichi-Men (literally "Japan Cotton") as its agent in the country. It was Zoltan Merszei who had found and signed up Nichi-Men during a trip he made to Japan in 1949 at Lee Doan's behest. "They were totally reliable," Huggins said. "What I liked about them was that they said that they could do something and they did it, or they said, 'No, that's not for us. We can't do it.'"

Asahi-Dow Ltd. was inaugurated in 1952 with initial capital of $1.1 million. In its first year sales were less than $1 million—the market for saran filament for fishing nets, its first product, was not great—but it grew rapidly, eventually producing the entire range of saran products, including Saran Wrap, and then branching into Styron and the styrene-related products, latex, and Styrofoam, and then into the polyethylene-related products such as Ethafoam, and Clorothene (1,1,1-trichloroethane). From modest beginnings it became a truly outstanding example of successful business cooperation between Japan and the United States.

By 1979 Asahi-Dow was the largest polystyrene producer and the most profitable petrochemical company in Japan. It had nine plants scattered across the Japanese islands from Sapporo in the northeast to Fukuoka in the southwest, and offices in Nagoya, Osaka, Sapporo, and Fukuoka, as well as in Tokyo. It had a 70 percent share of the Japanese Styrofoam market, 70 percent of the household film market, and a third of the polystyrene market. From total investments of about $8 million Dow had already received some $27 million in Asahi-Dow annual dividends and it owned a $94 million share in the firm's equity. Asahi-Dow's sales amounted to $600 million.[9]

Asahi-Dow had also built up a research and development operation, established originally to modify Dow technologies and products for the Japanese market, and then moving into the creation of new products and technologies. Two of the developments of which it was most proud were Xyron, an engineering plastic used in the automotive and appliance industries, and Copolene, an ethylenic resin with uses in packaging, business forms, golf balls, auto bumper-guards, and footwear.

In December 1971 Bob Baker, plastics marketing manager for Latin America, was entertaining some Japanese guests at his house in Coral Gables (trying to sell them vinyl chloride monomer for a plant the Japanese were building in Nicaragua), when a telephone call came through from Bob Lundeen in Hong Kong. Frank MacRae, the general manager of Dow Chemical in Japan, had had a heart attack and he needed someone there quickly, Lundeen said. Would Baker like to be Dow's head man in Japan? "Think about it and talk to Dottie and call me back," Lundeen said. "Hold on a minute, Bob," Baker said. He extracted Dottie from the party and said they were being given the opportunity to go to Japan; would she like to go to Japan? "Do YOU want to go to Japan?" she asked. "If all the people are like Kanagawa and Watanabe and Kosaka," he said, naming the principal guests at their party, "let's go." She said, "Okay." Baker went back to the phone in the bedroom and told Lundeen, "Okay, we accept." "Wait a minute," Lundeen said, "don't you want to think about it?" "No," Baker said, "we've already thought about it." Fifteen days later he was in Japan, leaving Dottie behind to sell the house, the car, and their other belongings.[10]

They shipped a trunk to Japan containing their clothes, two bowling balls, and two bicycles. "The bowling balls were mistakes," Baker said, "but the rest was all right. We didn't even move into a hotel. We moved into Frank MacRae's old house. In the interim Frank had had another heart attack and they had put him on a plane and got him to a hospital in Honolulu."

His first three years in Japan "were blurs," Baker said. He was working six days a week, 10 hours a day. The key Japanese employees (90 percent of the staff were Japanese) told him they felt Dow would never succeed in Japan, "as long as we were the branch of a foreign company; there were no roots, and they couldn't feel comfortable that their jobs would continue."

As a result Baker proposed the formation of Dow Chemical Japan, Ltd., and it was incorporated in August 1974, the first 100 percent foreign-owned company authorized by the Japanese government to manufacture and sell chemicals and plastics in Japan. DCJL and Asahi-Dow then began a period of parallel growth. "Up to then all our business in Japan had been done by trading companies and distributors," Baker explained. "We sold nothing direct. But we couldn't just stop using them, so we started a program with some of the distributors where we could sell direct but would still commission them. Within a period of six years or so, 63 percent of our business was direct and the rest through distributors."

To provide additional Japanese "roots," Dow bought some land and built a laboratory at Gotemba, in the foothills of Mt. Fuji, to house its technical service group, the beginnings of the "Dow Japan Lab." It also began to develop small, high-technology plants, the first of which was a polyol plant at Kinu Ura, in the Handa area. Land is extremely expensive in Japan, often costing as much as the plant on the land. The Kinu Ura site cost $70 million, but as the first Dow-owned and -operated site it was a milestone in Dow's history in Japan.

"Once we had our own plant in Japan we could begin to recruit at the universities in Japan and interview the kids who could speak English and offer job opportunities directly to college graduates instead of getting them through a newspaper ad or as a second job," Baker said. "We were able to get some very outstanding people and get them into the Dow system."

By the early 1980s sales from Dow technologies in Japan were approaching $1.2 billion, the bulk of it at Asahi-Dow, whose sales amounted to $880 million in 1981.

During the severe worldwide recession of 1982 (during which, it will be recalled, Dow withdrew from major projects in Yugoslavia and Saudi Arabia), Asahi-Dow suddenly came apart, to the astonishment of most observers of Japan business; Dow sold its share of Asahi-Dow to its Asahi partner for $231 million. The agreement also gave Dow 100 percent control of three Styrofoam plants, "because that product is a critical part of our specialty business in Japan," as Paul Oreffice, then the CEO, put it.[11]

What happened? As Lundeen saw it, the break had actually begun two years before, during some discussions between Baker, Andrew Butler, then president of Dow Chemical Pacific, Lundeen and Kagayaki Miyazaki, one of the three Japanese who had originally come to Midland to negotiate the birth of Asahi-Dow (who had now advanced to president of Asahi Chemical) and some of the senior members of his staff.[12]

"It became evident during the course of this meeting that Miyazaki's lieutenants, who had been rather recently promoted to their positions and knew little about the almost 30-year history of the Dow and Asahi Chemical relationship, were intent on Asahi Chemical's having a much larger role in the management of Asahi-Dow than its Japanese parent had previously taken," Lundeen said.

The nub of the issue was that Asahi Chemical had decided to compete with Asahi-Dow in a field of technology which Dow had proposed to develop in Japan with Asahi-Dow, and they were opposed to Asahi-Dow's concluding the deal with Dow. Asahi-Dow's and Dow's interests in the joint company were to be subordinated to Asahi Chemical's, and Asahi-Dow was to be treated more like an Asahi Chemical subsidiary than a fifty-fifty enterprise. This was an unprecedented policy clash.

There ensued a series of discussions that lasted more than a year. "Many of them were continuations of the one-on-one meetings which Miyazaki and I had been having several times a year for over a decade," Lundeen said. "Despite the cordial and productive personal relationships which we had and the high regard in which we held each other, and despite the personal intervention of Paul Oreffice, it was not possible to break the logjam."

Just at this time Dow had to review its global investment posture, and it was concluded that the company's interest in Asahi-Dow, except for the Styrofoam business, "should be included as a candidate for asset disposal," he said.

In February 1982 a team of Asahi Chemical executives led by Miyazaki and a team of Dow executives led by Lundeen gathered at the Stanford Court Hotel in San Francisco and spent five days hammering out the terms of sale. "It had been extraordinarily difficult to get Asahi Chemical to even discuss the possibility of the breakup of Asahi-Dow," Lundeen said. "Since Miyazaki had been involved in the negotiations that put it together 30 years before, a great deal of face was involved. Besides, such arrangements were very unusual in Japan—almost like a divorce, or breaking up the family."

The final agreement was a good one for Dow, and good for Asahi Chemical, Lundeen said, "but it was tough on the loyal Asahi-Dow employees who had built their careers in the company and now had an uncertain future as Asahi Chemical employees. One of the most difficult tasks I ever faced as a manager was to fly to Tokyo and personally explain to Fukashi Hori, the chairman of Asahi-Dow, and Yoshio Tsunoda, its president for many years, both long-time personal friends, why Dow had to make the difficult decision to disengage after 30 years of a fruitful and happy business relationship which had so many warm and meaningful personal friendships as part of it."

"However, those are the responsibilities that go with the territory," he said.

Dow's relationship with Japan has sometimes been rocky but always special. It traced back to 1914, when Sanko & Company became Dow's sales agent in Japan through Herbert Dow's acquaintance with Dr. Joichiro Takamine, a wealthy Japanese businessman and chemist who was the firm's main shareholder. Dow visited Japan twice himself and in 1922, fascinated by Japanese gardens, brought a well-known Japanese gardener, Paul Tonow, to Midland, where he made his services available to Midlanders interested in this avocation.[13]

In later years Carl Gerstacker became a well-known and highly regarded figure in Japan (perhaps better known in Japan than in the United States) as chairman of the U.S.-Japan Business Council. The council was the arena for much of the criticism of Japan for exporting aggressively but being loath to permit Americans to sell their products in Japan. During one hot and heavy debate on this matter Gerstacker called a halt to matters and said to the Japanese: "Gentlemen, I believe what my American colleagues are saying to you is that you have been playing with a handicap of about 15 or 16, and you really should be using a handicap of about 8."

The room went silent, for the Japanese are passionate fans of golf, and the analogy was perfect and timely. "It stopped everything," Baker said. "Carl Gerstacker became famous in Japan for it. The Japanese loved him, as they should have; he was a good, very open supporter of theirs."

A dozen years later Dow and Asahi Chemical buried the hurts of the 1982 divorce, resumed a constructive dialogue, and in October 1994 formed a new joint venture that went into operation at the beginning of 1995. Called Styron Asia Ltd. (or SAL), it spent its first year marketing polystyrene in Asian countries outside of Japan. It was SAL's plan that the two partners would then build a polystyrene plant together. The long-lasting Dow and Asahi partnership had revived, and was again alive and well.

III.

The exuberant growth of the company in the late 1960s, once its worldwide reorganization was complete, depended on mutually reinforcing factors—able administrators, astute financiers, resourceful manufacturing engineers, imaginative researchers, hard-driving marketers, and a web of service organizations supporting these basic functions. Receptive governments, satisfied customers, and a climate of public acceptance were vital.

It also required a dirty-fingernails type of person, the mucker and digger willing to travel strange territories for extended periods of time in search of unknown and unsuspected markets, almost literally beating the bushes for sales. Successful early employees of Dow in Asia spoke of "the thrill of going where no Dow person had ever gone before," as they explored the chemical and plastics markets of Afghanistan, Burma, and Sumatra.

One of these was Gustav A. De Groot, a Dutchman who positively relished the challenge of going into new territory and who did so all over the world during a 30-year career in which he toiled for Dow in North and South America, Asia, Africa, and Europe. Gus, it was said, would disappear into some exotic part of the world and reappear in a few weeks with a fistful of orders for Dow goods and a recommendation that Dow open an office there.

He was born in Schiedam, near Rotterdam, and as a youth decided he wanted to see the world, all of it, especially the United States, the land of opportunity. He became fluent in English, Spanish, French, and German as well as his native Dutch, and when he was 30, married and a father, made his way to the United States, where he got a job at Colonial Williamsburg, Virginia. There he wore a three-cornered hat and buckle shoes and fired off muskets and cannon for the amusement of the tourists.[14]

One day he visited the nearby James River Division of Dow and asked about a job. To his amazement the employment manager, George Maharens, provided him an airline ticket and invited him to fly up to Midland for interviews with Dow International. A week later he was hired as a product flow coordinator, moved his family to Midland, and began to learn the worldwide Dow product flow system.

"It was such a gung-ho operation, and there was so much enthusiasm," De Groot said,

you could hardly avoid being excited as well. The sky was the limit in those days. There were all kinds of interesting people in Dow International; there were Japanese; there were Dutch; there were Germans; there were Hindus. The customer could be in Buenos Aires, Mexico, Japan—anywhere. Everybody had to work hard and you could not afford to make too many mistakes—they counted the mistakes. They had a weekly meeting and told you, "Here's where you went wrong again," but the ambiance was always positive. You did not get much guidance or training, there was no time for it; you had to ask your colleagues and you had to sort of swim and survive. I knew some who fell off the sled. They just couldn't make it.

There were some language problems, too. De Groot remembered in his first week calling the propylene glycol plant and asking, "Can I have 20 drums of propylene glycol for next week for Mexico?" "The guy said, 'You bet!' I didn't know what that meant, and I didn't know whether I had it or not, so I asked the guy next to me, 'I asked him for 20 drums and the guy said, 'You bet!' What does that mean?" He said, "You've got it."

De Groot was startled at the amount of responsibility thrust upon him and the decisions he was called upon to make. One day Jack Stearns, a Dowintal vice president, called him and said, "Gus, I have some questions about caustic soda in Brazil. Should we leave the price the same? Should we raise it? Or should we lower it, and if so by how much?"

De Groot looked over his papers and went to Stearns's office, where there was a person he had never met. "Gus," Stearns said, "this is Paul Oreffice from Brazil. Tell us your answers to the questions I gave you." De Groot said, "No increase. No decrease. The price should stay the same." Jack said, "Paul, there's your answer. Thanks, Gus, you can go now."

"I compared this way of doing business with the way I was used to in Europe, where I could never really make any decision," De Groot said.

In a big European company they told you what to do. Right or wrong, that was the way it was. For me this was so much easier and more motivating. The first time I wrote a letter I went to my supervisor, Keith Ward, and said, "I wrote this letter to a customer. Can you sign it, or approve it?" Ward said, "No, I'm not reading it, and I'm not signing it. It's your business. If we get any complaints I'll come to you, yes, but you write the letter, you sign it."

After a couple of years he was promoted out of what was called "the fruit cellar"—the production coordination group was in the basement and was named for its file cases, which sported bright colors corresponding to various geographic areas of the world—and became a staff assistant working for Glenn Prielipp, later the marketing chief in Hong Kong.

It was Prielipp who invited him to join the staff at the Hilton Hotel in Hong Kong as a marketing manager. Discussing with his tiny staff how they should tackle the problem of "blank" territories—countries where Dow had no sales offices, which at the time was almost all of Asia except Japan and Australia—Prielipp suggested that each marketer, in addition to other duties, choose some more or less "blank" area, concentrate on it, and report back to him what Dow should do there. De Groot chose Indonesia, Malaysia, and Singapore; another man chose Pakistan and India.

It turned out that De Groot, with his language skills, wanderlust, and five years of experience in Dow products, was a natural for this activity.

"The first thing I always did in the hotel upon arrival (in a new place) was to take the Yellow Pages, if any, and look for chemical companies or plastic producers. Then I just took a taxi and went to see them," De Groot said. "My experience was that once you had visited one who was a reasonable contact, he would lead you to others. It was actually easy."

He went to Singapore and Malaysia on his first trip, and reported there was easily the potential there for $10 million in Dow business. "That sounds reasonable," Prielipp said. "What do you suggest?" "I think Dow should open an office in Singapore, centrally located for southern Asia, and go from there," De Groot said. "We think that's a good idea. Who do you think should do that?" "I think I should," De Groot said. Prielipp and Lundeen agreed. "Go do it," said Lundeen.

Armed with a check for $50,000, De Groot in 1970 moved his family to Singapore, opened an account with the Chase Manhattan Bank there, and set up for business. While Nell De Groot enrolled the children in school and looked for office space Gus ran an office from a Volkswagen automobile, and they sent telexes from the post office.

They put an ad in the newspapers for a secretary and interviewed candidates in their room at the Ladyhill Hotel, hiring Jeanne Ow, who "did everything," De Groot said. Installed in an office on Stamford Road, De Groot canceled the agreement with Dow's local agent and hired Anthony Tan, who had been handling Dow's business in Malaysia. From then on Tan concentrated on Malaysia and De Groot on Indonesia.

In that first year Dow sales in the area were $350,000; only three years later they were $17 million.

Dow already had roots in the Malaysian capital of Kuala Lumpur, where Huggins and F. M. (Milt) Hunt had established an office three years before. "Malaysia had two very stable industries," Huggins said, "rubber and tin. These were good solid industries. Dow had a very handsome market in Malaysia for Dowpon, the grass killer, because it was the one selective grass killer that handled a grass they have, *dospalum conjugatum*, which has a swordlike leaf. It grows rapidly and is very difficult to cut down because of its swordlike capabilities; it cuts through your skin if you rub against it."[15]

Huggins was soon selling 3,000 tons of Dowpon per year to the Malaysian rubber growers, "and there weren't 3,000 tons of Dowpon sold anywhere else." One of the earliest manufacturing projects of the new headquarters in Hong Kong when it was founded was a Dowpon plant in Malaysia, which it built at Shah Alam, near Kuala Lumpur, and incorporated as Pacific Chemical Berhad, Dow's Malaysian company. It went onstream in 1970.

Arriving in Jakarta, De Groot rented a taxi for the day and as he was traveling about to his list from the Yellow Pages he saw a mule cart in the traffic bearing a sign that said, "Asahi-Dow Polystyrene." Looking again, he told the taxi driver, "Follow that mule cart, because he's going somewhere I have to be."

"This happened by luck, plain luck," De Groot said.

We arrived at a Chinese company called Pioneer Plastics, the number one plastic converter in Indonesia, thousands of tons a year. I went in and the guy said, "Explain to me. We already buy Dow products; we get them from Asahi-Dow in Japan. Are you competing with your own product?" I said, "In a way. It's the same product, but we don't make it in Japan, we make it in the U.S. and we make it in Europe." The guy said, "Well, this fits very well because the country is running out of foreign currency. We can no longer import from Japan but we do have U.S. aid dollars." He had something like $1 million in U.S. aid. "I'll buy 500 or 1,000 tons of this product," he said. That's how we started the Indonesian business."

De Groot quickly discovered he wasn't supposed to compete with Asahi-Dow, but "because of the U.S. aid which Asahi-Dow could not comply with, it was not a problem in the end," he said.

He went to Indonesian paper mills and sold Separan. He went to paper mills and sold Tydex 12 flocculant. "They were not used to seeing a supplier from the U.S. or Europe come knock on their doors right in their own backyard," De Groot said. "They really appreciated it; they would do anything to give you an order. American companies were practically unknown at that time. The Europeans by tradition were there, but we easily competed with them because they were not very active then."

In Surabaya, East Java, where Dow later opened an office, he sold propylene glycol humectant to a "kretek" factory, where 200 women made cigarettes by hand on small machines. Sweet-smelling clove "kretek" cigarettes are highly popular in Indonesia but almost nowhere else.

One of the biggest markets, as in Malaysia, was the Sumatran rubber and palm oil plantations, where Dowpon again was an immediate success, this time in the control of alang alang weed. In 1974 Dow built a plant near Medan, in northern Sumatra, where 45 Indonesians were by 1975 employed in making Dowpon and Dalapon grass killer chemicals.

Two years later Dow brought a plant to produce Dursban insecticide onstream at the same site. "We had a big Dursban insecticide business in Indonesia," Colin Goodchild said. "Indonesia is a huge rice grower. We were supplying about $10 million of Dursban to the rice industry in Indonesia."[16]

It was not all cocoa and cookies, however. "The influence of the central Indonesian government is strong in Jakarta," De Groot explained,

> but in Sumatra, where the Medan plant is, its influence is quite limited. You have to deal with the provincial government. When they were constructing the Medan plant an officer of the Indonesian Army with about 200 or 300 men came to the plant and said, "Your plant may be in danger, and we are here to protect this investment by the United States and your company. You are, of course, grateful to us." We said, "Yes, we are very grateful for this, but what is the price?" I think the guy asked for 5 percent of the shares and a supply of rice for his people and several hundred bicycles. I don't think the project manager, James Hubbard, gave them the shares but probably gave them money or rice or bicycles, because they could easily cause problems. The central government does not have that much power in the outlying regions.

Lundeen recalled making a trip to Banda Aceh, the capital of Aceh Province in northern Sumatra, and stopping to call on the provincial governor at Lhokseumawe. There he, Goodchild, and Peter Walker were blockaded by a group of angry villagers upset with the governor. "Those were the things that added spice to life," Lundeen said. "Aceh is 100 percent Islamic," De Groot explained, and has long been an area of considerable unrest down to the present day.

Until the end of WW II Indonesia had been the Dutch East Indies, and many of its leaders were Dutch educated, so it was relatively easy for the Dutchman De Groot to adjust to the Indonesian way of doing business. "When projects go through government offices they move very slowly," De Groot said. "You go there once a week and you say, 'Mr. Chung, how is it going?' Mr. Chung says, 'Well, let me see. Yes, I think next week.' So you say, 'Yes? Okay, let's go for lunch and talk about things.' You hope that next week it will move forward a little."

It was not that easy for the hard-charging American businessmen Dow sent to Hong Kong. Thomas J. Scott, manager for agricultural chemicals, came to Jakarta to try to speed up the Medan project and De Groot went with him to the ministry of agriculture.

"I know Indonesia needs this investment urgently and we are willing to do it quickly," Scott told the department undersecretary, "but you have to cooperate. I would like to see the minister of agriculture tomorrow morning and get this all arranged. I'm leaving for business in Thailand and other places."

"This doesn't work," De Groot said. "The guy will not even talk to his minister, but he will never say no. He will say, 'Yes, I understand. We will see, but I feel that the minister is probably very busy tomorrow.' You already know this means 'no.'"

Scott made another "especially serious" mistake, De Groot said. "He put his feet on the table, and this they don't like at all." De Groot closed the conversation as gracefully as possible and went back after a few days to try to repair the damage.

He told the official, "I know exactly how you feel, but I want to explain that this man comes from a completely different culture and this is the way business is done there. We were not trying to make you angry. We really are friendly people. We want this investment and you want it, so let's forget this difference in culture and just continue between you and me." He said "Okay." A month later the project was approved and signed.

Sometime later the undersecretary told him,

Gus, this country has survived 5,000 years without a Dow agricultural products plant and we could probably survive another 5,000 years without one. You should tell your American friend that Indonesians like to be in harmony with nature and with people. We do not like conflict, and definitely not confrontation. If you ask an impossible question where you know that the answer will probably be no, we don't ask such a question. Some of you Westerners think we are liars because we don't say yes and we don't say no, but if you try to understand, you listen, and then you know whether it's yes or no.

The government printing office in Jakarta used cleaning solvents to clean its printing machinery, and was using trichlorethylene purchased from a German firm; it was cheaper than Chlorothene, Dow's brand of inhibited 1,1,1-trichloroethane, the competing product, although Chlorothene was considerably safer to use. De Groot learned that government regulations provided that workers using trichlorethylene were to be given extra food, and the office could not work more than two shifts of eight hours because of safety regulations. "But with Chlorothene you wouldn't need the extra food and you could work three shifts," De Groot told the manager.

Even though the Dow product was more expensive, it was more economical and safer. "On that basis we sold Chlorothene to the GPO, and this was at that time, a big order for me," De Groot said, "200 tons of Chlorothene a year."

There were also the "tricks" of the trade. At first Dow could not sell glycerine in Indonesia, for instance; Japanese-produced glycerine appeared to be cheaper. Indonesian buyers traditionally purchased glycerine by the drum and paid no attention to kilos or liters. De Groot discovered that the Japanese, knowing this, sold glycerine by the drum but filled the drum only perhaps 80 percent full; Dow drums were full.

"So I would explain to them that our price per kilo or liter was actually lower than the Japanese," De Groot said. "Once you explained this to these people, they started thinking and realized they were being taken."

The South Asian marketplace at that time was a contest between the Europeans, the Japanese, and the Americans, De Groot said. "The local people were trying to achieve a balance and things were out of balance; the Americans were weak in this area. So there was a tendency to welcome more American involvement. They didn't want too much of the Europeans because of the colonial past. They had a dislike of the Japanese due to their World War II experience. So the timing was right for the American companies."

Another trailblazer in South Asia was James W. (Jim) Harris, whom Lundeen had dispatched to Bangkok to establish a Dow sales office. Harris arrived in Bangkok in late 1967 and hired a local woman, Vachi Charoensook, as administrative secretary and interpreter. He too discovered that going out into the boondocks was the only way to build the markets, and he too found the experience rewarding. He recalled visits to remote sugar mills to sell Separan flocculants, selling plastic resins on sales calls made by boat, and traveling to Phuket to sell Dowpon grass killer there before it became a Thai tourist paradise with big modern hotels.[17]

His territory also included Myanmar, then called Burma, and, "many times I was the only hotel guest at Rangoon's famous Strand Hotel," Harris said. "For many years with one or two guests it remained almost fully staffed. Even though I was the only guest I was still requested to wear coat and tie after 5 P.M. in the lounge and dining room."

Lepetit, which Dow acquired in 1963, had a pharmaceutical plant at Bangkok and was a major force in the pharmaceutical business in that country. In 1975 Dow built a polystyrene plastic plant at Phrapradaeng, near Bangkok, and it went onstream in 1978. It was named Pacific Plastics Thailand, and became a great success. In the late 1980s Dow began making further major investments in Thailand, including a styrene monomer facility and a polyols plant. They were run by new Dow entities in Thailand—Siam Styrene Monomer Company, Siam Synthetic Latex Company, SD Group Service Company.

By 1991 Michael D. Parker, an Englishman who had become president of Dow's Pacific area, was forming new joint ventures in South Asia. "Perhaps the most significant development of all (in South Asia)," he said, "has been the diversification of large, financially strong Asian companies into chemicals and plastics. These new entrants from Korea and Taiwan, and now from Thailand, Malaysia, and Indonesia, are the new competitors, and some are also our partners in the joint ventures we are forming to build new plants in Korea, Thailand, and Indonesia."[18]

India was the first Asian country Dow went into west of Japan; Dow established its first venture there in 1952 just after it formed Asahi-Dow, its first joint venture abroad. Unfortunately India was to become a resounding business disappointment.

In that first venture, Polychem Ltd., which built a small styrene and polystyrene plant in Bombay, Dow owned a quarter of the shares, the enterprising Hindu Kilachand family another quarter, and the Indian public the other half.

"Frankly, our partners weren't much," Lundeen said.

In my view they were a very unsatisfactory group of people. One of my initial ideas (in 1966) was to see if we could use Polychem as a base to expand our business in India. It seemed logical. But our partners the Kilachands wouldn't allow Dow to do any of the management and insisted that it was their company to run. I was not willing to put any good Dow stuff into that company if the Kilachands were going to run it because I didn't trust them. We had many fierce and sometimes very unpleasant discussions about that, and we never put anything more into Polychem and eventually sold our whole interest in the company.[19]

Dow tried a number of other ventures in India, including Indian Detonators Ltd. (IDL) in Hyderabad, whose foreign share it purchased from ICI; it eventually sold IDL as well. At the time it fit in with an explosives business Dow was attempting to develop in Minnesota.

"We also tried an agricultural pesticide plant in India and I don't know how many other things," Lundeen said. "After about 10 years of investing a lot of manpower I issued one of the few edicts, maybe the only edict, I ever issued in my career at Dow. I said, 'We're not going to screw around with anything more in India. Don't bother me with Indian projects. We have spent 10 years now and have invested some of our best people, and we've produced nothing. We're not going to waste any more time. So don't bother me.'"

IV.

Until 1959 Australia was the great outback for Dow, completely unexplored territory. Up to then it had hardly seemed worth exploring, really; total Dow sales in Australia and New Zealand amounted to only $850,000 that year. Furthermore, the Australian chemical industry, though little developed, was totally dominated by ICI (Imperial Chemical Industries), the British behemoth, which would not easily give up its stranglehold on an attractive market.

Eric Huggins, Dow's advance man in Asia, still in 1959 the lone resident representative of the company in this whole vast area, with the title of "manager of the Far East office, Hong Kong," began serious exploration of Australia's potential and decided, with Clayton Shoemaker's support, to establish an office in Sydney.[20]

Huggins put a want ad in the local newspapers and hired Colin Goodchild, a fellow Briton, as Dow's first employee in the Australian commonwealth. Goodchild, a native of Surrey, had studied chemistry at London University and served with the King's African Rifles in Uganda for three years. Armed with this background he had then signed on to sell plastics for Monsanto back in London and had promptly been shipped out to Australia, where Monsanto built a polystyrene plant that came onstream in 1955.

Goodchild, selling Lustrex, the Monsanto equivalent of Dow's Styron, had met Huggins, and the two became friendly competitors. When Goodchild answered his advertisement Huggins hired him and Goodchild opened an office in Sydney consisting of himself and a secretary, Beverly Ralph Campbell; both were to spend their careers with Dow.

Goodchild plunged directly into discussions that had been going on between Huggins, Shoemaker, and CSR Chemicals, a small joint venture at Rhodes in Sydney owned by The Distillers Co. Ltd. of England and the Colonial Sugar Refining Company of Australia. CSRC wanted a license to manufacture Dow polystyrene. (It may be remembered that Dow and Distillers had been partners in the Distrene joint venture at Barry, Wales since 1954.)[21]

In April 1959 the two firms agreed to form CSRC-Dow Pty. Ltd. for the production of styrene. Its plant would form part of the new Altona petrochemical complex, the first petrochemical venture in Australia. The complex was based on an oil refinery in Melbourne jointly owned by Mobil and Esso. It included a naphtha cracker and facilities for production of ethylene, and a number of companies were formed to process the downstream products, CSRC-Dow among them. A few months later it added ethylene dichloride, which was sold to B.F. Goodrich to make PVC. Union Carbide bought ethylene from the cracker to make polyethylene. The CSRC-Dow styrene was sold to a synthetic rubber company, which bought butadiene from the cracker and made styrene-butadiene rubber. [22] The complex negotiations for all this (and more) went on for almost two years. The CSRC-Dow enterprise added a small chlorine-caustic plant along the way.

Altona thrived, and within a few years Dow was eager for growth. The Dow managers saw opportunities for latex and epoxy resins and agricultural chemicals, but hesitated to put plants for these products into the CSRC-Dow partnership. The partnership was working well, but the partner was a sugar refiner and had no technology or markets in the chemical field. "The contribution from our partner was zero," Goodchild said.

By 1968 Goodchild and Lundeen decided they had to make a move. They told Colonial Sugar Refining they would like to buy out CSR Chemicals and convert Altona into a fully owned Dow company that Dow would then use as its Australian manufacturing base. After some dickering CSR accepted. Altona continued to prosper and in the 1990s was Dow's largest manufacturing site in the Pacific basin.

CSRC-Dow was merged into Dow Chemical Australia, and this gave Dow strong manufacturing sites in New South Wales and Victoria. Altona (Victoria) rapidly added plants for latex, epoxies, and polyols, and expanded its polystyrene capacity. Later an agricultural chemicals plant was added at Smithfield (New South Wales), near Sydney.

A large proportion of the Dow manufacturing managers in the Pacific area got their start at the Altona complex, and in later years Australian-bred plant managers were popping up at Dow locations around the world. "The Australian mafia," Lundeen called them.[23]

"So we were becoming a force in the chemical industry in Australia," Goodchild said. "The industry was still dominated by ICI, but companies like Union Carbide, Monsanto, and Dow were now getting very strong."

Dow had products that fit well with the Australian economy. It was strong in the animal health business in these years, and with the help of some research expertise was soon marketing large quantities of these products to sheep and cattle ranchers in Australia and New Zealand. Dow had a new sheep dip, the first of the anthelmintics, and when Goodchild told Midland how much of it he'd need in Australia the ag chemical people there found it hard to believe. Unfortunately for Dow, within a year some researchers at Merck, Sharp & Dohme discovered a product that was even better and after that Dow was only an also-ran in that use.

Another big product was Tordon, the Dow brush killer, which was used to kill the eucalyptus trees that cover much of the country. "In the big cattle territories, in the northern territory in Queensland in particular, you could develop more pastures if you could just kill the trees," Goodchild said. "You didn't necessarily have to fell them, but you could increase the pasturage by killing the tree. We found that small amounts of Tordon introduced into ax cuts would kill the tree. The growth of the leaves would stop, you'd let in more light, the pastures would grow, and you could carry more cattle."

"Millions of trees were treated," he said. "You wouldn't notice it if you drove through or flew over Queensland, there's so much land and so many trees, but it did open up a lot of the country."

As was frequently the case in other parts of the world, though, Dow's most successful product in Australia was caustic soda. Australia is blessed with large deposits of easily mined bauxite; in some places it can just be scooped up with bulldozers. When you treat bauxite with caustic soda you produce alumina, the raw material that can then be smelted to aluminum. Some of the world's largest alumina refineries have been developed in Australia, and they consume vast quantities of caustic soda.

Goodchild's first target for caustic sales was Queensland Alumina Ltd. (QAL), at Gladstone, and he scored a bullseye. On November 18, 1966, the largest vessel ever to enter the Freeport, Texas, harbor, the 34,000-ton *Naess Crusader*, loaded on 31,500 long tons of 50 percent caustic soda and sailed for Australia via the Panama Canal, a 33-day voyage of 9,234 miles. It was the largest single shipment of caustic ever made to that time.[24]

A second big shipment to QAL sailed in January 1967, and a third about the size of the record shipment in May. Dow's contract with QAL has gone through many phases in the past 30 years, but is still in operation.

This success generated a further idea: why not build a Dow chlorine/caustic facility at Gladstone and avoid the huge cost of shipping caustic halfway around the world? The liquid chlorine produced could be shipped northward to Japan, which was chlorine short.

"In theory it all looked very good, and we spent a fair bit of money developing this project," Goodchild said, "but the environmental difficulties of moving large volumes of chlorine into Tokyo Bay were insurmountable."

Looking at other possible uses for the chlorine, Goodchild turned his attention to a place called Redcliffs, in south Australia, which had a large natural gas system coming onstream. "If we could extract the ethane and crack that, we'd have a cheap form of ethylene; we had hard salt fields nearby in the form of salt lakes; we had the caustic market in Australia; and we had an ethylene dichloride market of huge volumes in Japan. So we worked on that project in the early 1970s," he said.

Redcliffs bloomed into a project for a huge Dow petrochemical complex, but was finally done in by politics, competitors, and a decline in the market for hydrocarbon products. "We came to a critical point and backed away," Lundeen said. The end came when the Gough Whitlam government came to power in Australia, the first Labor government in many years.

"At the Ministry of Mines and Industry Whitlam had an ex-union leader by the name of R. F. X. O'Connor, known to his intimates as 'Strangler' O'Connor," Lundeen said. "The

Redcliffs negotiations had been going on for seven or eight years when we got to this critical point, and it looked like the Labor government was going to stomp on us." He asked for
an urgent meeting with O'Connor.

Lundeen flew straight through from Midland to Melbourne. When he arrived there was a
strike—"there are always strikes in Australia," Lundeen said—and a Dow salesman drove him
the remaining 300 miles to the capital at Canberra. He had been on the road for 36 hours.

"We arrived at Parliament House on schedule," Lundeen said.

> I'd had a night's sleep which got me back from being a zombie. Goodchild and Geoff Norris
> (a key manager in Australia and later Dow's country manager there) and I went in to see
> O'Connor. O'Connor was a big, craggy man who stood about six feet four. He met us by him-
> self in his office, wearing a baggy old gray sweater and red galluses. He had a very rumpled
> appearance and a big shock of white hair. "What the hell do you guys want?" was the gist of
> his opening remark.

O'Connor then proceeded to "lambaste us up one side and down the other," Lundeen said.
"Why did we foreign companies expect any concessions from the Australian government? Just
what did we think the Australians owed us? Plenty of good Australian companies could do
this project, and so on, and so on. Finally he took a deep breath and allowed us to say something, but it was already apparent that ICI was going to get the nod, and they did. But ICI
never did anything with the project; the project has never been done."

It was probably good "that we didn't spend more time on it," Lundeen said in retrospect
some years later—he felt there was a strong possibility Dow could have moved forward with
Redcliffs when the Conservative Malcolm Fraser government came to power—"because it
was one of those things whose time had really passed by the time we were ready to do something with it, if you look at the long flow of events. We had to get O'Connor's blessing
because as minister of mines he controlled exploitation of both the natural gas and salt we
needed; but he wasn't going to have anything to do with us, and that was the end of
Redcliffs." It was one of only two cases in his experience, Lundeen said—Korea was the
other—where a major Dow project was killed for nationalistic reasons.

Then there was the Great Queensland Fertilizer Caper. It began in the early 1960s when
Don Ballman, senior vice president for marketing, established "VIFCO" (Ventures Investment
Finance Company) under Robert Prince, an entrepreneur/promoter whose assignment was
to ferret out unusual investment opportunities for Dow.

On a trans-Pacific flight Prince sat next to an executive of Chicago's meatpacking Swift
and Company, then a major factor in the fertilizer field. By the time they had flown from
Sydney to Chicago the two had hatched a plan for a joint Swift and Dow fertilizer enterprise
in Australia. Swift had a new concept for selling fertilizer in Australia that would floor the ICI
people, who had been selling fertilizer in Australia for a century. (Someone should have seen
a blinking caution light right there, Lundeen said, but no one did.).

Out of this beginning came Austral Pacific Fertilizers Ltd., a Dow-Swift venture that built a plant on Gibson Island near Brisbane, a $70 million investment. It produced 650 tons/day of ammonia, 700 tons/day of urea, and marketed a full line of fertilizers, all based on natural gas as feedstock. Brazenly, the plant was just across the Brisbane River from an ICI fertilizer plant.

"As you can imagine, this development didn't sit well with ICI," Lundeen said. "They had a monopoly on fertilizer in Australia, and they didn't think this was a very good idea at all. Not only did we build this magnificent new facility with a fantastic headquarters office in Brisbane, but we had these terrific distribution centers spread all over Queensland with modern, painted trucks."

Austral Pacific Fertilizers rapidly turned into a financial disaster and to the dismay of Bob Vandegrift, transferred from Midland to run the company, was soon about to go bankrupt. When a desperate Vandegrift had to borrow money from Dow to meet his payroll, Lundeen flew to Australia and he and Goodchild went up to Brisbane to look at the situation.

They decided their only reasonable option was to make peace with ICI. "We were killing their business and they weren't going to let us come back to life," Lundeen said. "They were going to make sure we were stillborn, but in the process we were going to ruin their business. We knew ICI was feeling a lot of pain because we had screwed up their market to a fare-thee-well."

Lundeen and Goodchild went to call on Tom Swanson, the managing director of ICI. "We put our cards on the table and said, 'Tom, we have a big mess on our hands. We'd like to sort it out. How can we rationalize our efforts?'" Lundeen said.

Swanson, an astute businessman and in Lundeen's eyes a first-class gentleman, said, "Well, about the only way we can do that is to combine the companies. You guys have already spent all the money." They sat in Swanson's office and roughed out a plan for shrinking Australia's fertilizer production capacity and the number of personnel employed in it.

"We didn't think we'd get into any antitrust troubles, either," Lundeen said. "Of course, doing something like that, joining forces with a competitor, is something you never do in the United States."

The rough plan developed in Swanson's office at this meeting was then refined and eventually approved by Dow, Swift, and ICI. It called for the consolidation of four Australian fertilizer firms, from which would result Consolidated Fertilizers Ltd., CFL. At ICI's request Goodchild took a year's absence from his Dow job and became the first managing director of CFL, and "by golly, in a year's time he straightened it all out," Lundeen said. "He rationalized the business." At the end of the year he returned to his position as managing director of Dow Chemical Australia.

Many years later, Lundeen was pleased to observe that CFL "is doing just fine." Dow still owned 20 percent of the firm. "That was the Great Queensland Fertilizer Caper. I'll never forget it," he said.[25]

During the anti-Vietnam War protests of the late 1960s Australian crowds marched on the Dow offices in Melbourne and Sydney from time to time. In Melbourne Goodchild was burned in effigy by one crowd. "It was a strange feeling to watch yourself being set on fire because you were the reason why Dow was burning babies, or so it was said, in Vietnam," Goodchild said.

Another time he was sitting in the ICI Building, talking to Tom Swanson in the top floor boardroom, where they looked down on a crowd marching up the street toward the ICI head-quarters. ICI, as a weapons manufacturer, was not popular with the protesters either. As they watched the antiwar crowd marching toward them Swanson turned to Goodchild and said, "Are they coming for you, or for me?"

They both shuddered at the time, Goodchild said, "but now you recall those incidents and smile."

V.

A great many Americans alive at the time remember even today what they were doing the day of John F. Kennedy's assassination on Friday, November 22, 1963. For a handful of Dow people negotiating in Midland that day—Chet Otis, Lew Sellers, Bob Lundeen—it was also the day Dow acquired half of an agricultural chemical firm in New Plymouth, New Zealand. The new firm born that day is called Ivon Watkins-Dow and while small by world standards is the biggest agricultural chemicals firm in New Zealand.

The firm started as Ivon Watkins Ltd. in 1944, and was operated by Dan Watkins, the entre-preneurial half of two Watkins brothers. Dan's ambitions and his ideas, it was often said, "were too big for his geography." In November 1963 the brothers doubled the capital of their com-pany and Dow bought all the new shares. Colin Goodchild brought Dan Watkins to Midland, and there the deal was consummated and the firm became a joint venture with Dow, with Watkins as managing director.

"Dan Watkins was a fine man, and Ivon Watkins-Dow went along in a pretty nice way for a few years," Lundeen said.

> Then, in about 1967, Dan decided that we ought to expand the scope of Ivon Watkins to petrochemicals. He wanted to do big things; Dow didn't want to do big things until we'd done a few small things successfully. We had a lot of fun with what we jokingly called "Freeport on the Tasman," because off-shore at New Plymouth where the main factory of Ivon Watkins-Dow is located is the Maui Gas Field; this was going to be the basis for all these petrochemi-cal raw materials.[26]
>
> We did a lot of work trying to develop a petrochemical scheme using cheap Maui hydro-carbons as a source for plastic petrochemical production. To make a long story short, it never really made much sense. The costs of getting the gas to shore were high; it didn't have enough ethane and propane in it; we couldn't negotiate a proper deal with the people who owned the gas; and there were a lot of other reasons. Dow decided it had better places, like Alberta, Canada, and other locations, to buy natural gas.

Dan got pretty frustrated over time. He made a number of unrelated acquisitions at Ivon Watkins-Dow—a timber firm, a film and packaging outfit—little companies that didn't make any sense, stuck around for a while, and kind of frittered away. Finally, we had to take the management over.

"That was one of the more difficult personal negotiations I ever had," Lundeen said.

Dan had started this company, and he was such an enthusiastic and decent person. The company was on fairly hard times when Dow had finally to make the decision to take it over; otherwise, it wasn't going to be good for Dow, nor for the New Zealand shareholders. This was no longer a company that Dan Watkins owned; it was a listed company on the New Zealand Stock Exchange.

The nice thing about it was that the New Zealand public directors were astute businessmen and real gentlemen. They agreed with Dow that we should take the management over. They were extremely helpful in getting Dan disengaged. He became chairman of the company, Dow put in its own manager, and it worked out all right.

At that point Dow became owner of 51 percent, and in 1988 purchased the remainder of the company, one of Goodchild's last acts before retiring.

Goodchild had hired Jack Fisher to open Dow's first office in New Zealand, at Auckland, soon after the Hong Kong office was established, and Jack started to develop the Dow business there. By 1981 the firm had offices and distribution centers at Hamilton, Palmerston North, Wellington, Christchurch, and Dunedin.[27]

"It was a very happy and close relationship that we had in New Zealand," Goodchild said. "Although the market was relatively small, the penetration Dow had in New Zealand was one of the highest of any country in the world."[28]

"New Zealand has been difficult," according to Bernie Butcher, a later marketing director for Dow in the Pacific and board member of Ivon Watkins-Dow. "Big agricultural opportunities, that's what Ivon Watkins-Dow really has. We've made a lot of money there, but it's always been difficult because it is a small market, and it is still all agricultural."[29]

VI.

In 1966 what were to become the "four tigers" of Asia—four of the world's fastest-developing economies in the late twentieth century—were still slumbering industrially, content to be classified as underdeveloped nations. Their awakening coincided to an amazing degree with Dow's arrival in the area. In 1966 Singapore withdrew from Malaysia and began a period of rapid growth; much of the phenomenal development of Taiwan, Hong Kong, and Korea began at this same period.

"Yes, we arrived at the right time," Lundeen said.

When Lundeen moved to Hong Kong in the summer of 1966 a prescient Huggins told him, "Bob, we've got to do something in Korea. That place is going to be like Japan." Lundeen agreed, and they made a date to go to Korea in November.[30]

"Korea was a crummy place in 1966," Lundeen said. "Nobody in his right mind went to Korea." Dow's longtime agent in Seoul, S. N. Kim, met them at the plane. There was talk of the government putting together a petrochemical complex, and they were immediately interested. They hired Tom Sheehan, a friend of Jim Harris who was working at a trading company in Seoul, and Sheehan opened Dow's first office in Korea.

Development of the projected complex moved slowly, but by 1969 was taking shape, and Dow began to look for a seasoned manager to take over and develop an enterprise in Korea. Dutch Beutel flew to Titusville, Florida, where Dow's contract with NASA was winding down, and talked to Lee Dupuy, Dow's manager there, about the job.

"I always kept a room for him at one of the motels in Titusville," Dupuy said. "He drank Wild Turkey and I always had a bottle. He'd come down in a Lear jet by himself and I'd meet him at the airport. We'd go over to the room and open the bottle of Wild Turkey, drink a lot, have some supper, and usually the next day he was out of there. It was great! I remember going home around one o'clock about two-thirds lit and waking my wife and saying, 'Guess what? I've got a new job in Korea.'"[31]

Beutel arranged for Dupuy to see Lundeen, whom he had never met, and the Dupuys and their four children moved to Korea in 1970.

He moved in with Sheehan's small sales force in Seoul and set about forming a company, the Korea Pacific Chemical Company, a joint venture owned half by Dow and half by Chungju Fertilizer Company, which was 100 percent owned by the Korean government. KPCC was to make and sell low-density polyethylene and vinyl chloride monomer, building these two plants at the government-planned complex near Ulsan, on the southeastern coast just north of Pusan.

Living in Korea posed problems for many foreigners, said Dupuy. "You had to be willing to live in a very rough society," he said. "It was dirty and ugly, and there were no good places to shop. My wife used to devote two full days a week to shopping for food, and you'd have to go place to place to place. Seoul was a madhouse. Parking was just wall-to-wall people. It was difficult, but if you're young enough and you're interested in strange things, you can do it with enthusiasm."

They took a four-week total immersion course in Korean in Miami before leaving, "one of the most difficult things I've ever done in my life," Dupuy said. "I never got to be really fluent in Korean, but I could speak and understand enough to keep them honest when they were speaking Korean in the meetings."

As the Korean economy began to pick up, KPCC flourished with it, and when the government began planning a second, larger petrochemical complex at Yeosu in south central Korea, Dow was the first foreign company to express interest; Dow proposed to build a chloralkali plant to provide chlorine for the complex.

"We were doing so well with the two plants we had that we wanted to build additional factories," Dupuy said.

> The problem was that Dow was unwilling to license its chlorine technology to a joint venture, and wouldn't license it to KPCC. So the only way we could get a chlorine plant was to go 100 percent Dow. This was contrary to Korean government regulations, which insisted there be Korean participation. However, because they wanted the technology so badly, they stretched the point and we got permission to form a 100 percent company, Dow Chemical Korea, Ltd., and built the chlorine plant. In addition we built another very large vinyl plant at Yeosu.

Dow had been eager to build a chloralkali complex in Japan, but insistence on its being a 100 percent Dow-owned operation made the Japanese "come apart at the seams," as Bernie Butcher, then the marketing chief in Hong Kong, put it. "The Koreans," Butcher said, "called us and said, 'If they won't let you build it in Japan, why don't you build it over here?' That's how we ended up in Korea with the chloralkali operation."[32]

Dow was becoming a major player in the Korean economy. Within a few years it was the largest foreign investor in the country.

As these new plants were being built, Dupuy moved to Hong Kong to become a vice president of Dow's Pacific area but continued to have responsibility for Korea until he left Asia in 1980. He was replaced on the scene first by Gerry McCoy, who had been the business development manager in Hong Kong, and later by Ed Craigsman and L. F. (Lee) Wretlind.

The world economy pitched into a pronounced downturn at this point, sparked off by the 1973 oil crisis, and since Korea had no oil sources of its own, this crisis was devastating for the Korean petrochemical ventures. Demand for the products of the petrochemical complex plummeted just as new capacity was about to come onstream. What had started out as "a very happy early experience," as one Dow manager called it, suddenly became a nightmare, a matter of riding out the storm.

In addition, the Korean government changed, and with it its attitude toward foreign investors. After a period of turmoil the ultranationalists took over. "We had an outstanding business going there," Lundeen said. "Perhaps the single thing that I personally negotiated of which I was most proud was helping Korea put together a viable petrochemical business. Dow was the major foreign player. Lee Dupuy really did all the work after the initial agreement negotiations, and managed it for us. Things went along fine, and then Park Chung Hee was assassinated. Chun Doo Hwan came in."

> When Park Chung Hee was president the management of the country's economy was very tightly controlled by the Blue House staff. That was like the White House staff [in the U.S.]. Very powerful senior secretaries on the president's staff were the czars of industries in Korea. To make something happen you had to negotiate a deal with the people in the Blue House,

who by and large were extremely able individuals. So we had negotiated in the Blue House and with the Korean entity they designated.

This fellow Chun Doo Hwan had a very different idea about how Korea ought to be managed. Let the cabinet do things, he said. As best I could tell, in the old days the policy was decided in the Blue House and the cabinet then implemented it, but the cabinet ministers didn't have a lot to do with negotiations. Chun Doo Hwan said, "Okay, now you cabinet ministers will do things, and furthermore we're going to have a lot less state intervention. Let the private sector do private-sector things." Chun Doo Hwan's supporters were the new people that came into the Blue House, and they were very nationalistic, younger army officers.

At the same time business in Korea got into a lot of trouble economically. The world market prices for petrochemicals dropped off. It was not unique to Korea, but Korea was particularly hard hit because of the very high price of energy in Korea. We used a lot of chlorine in our products and we had this new chlorine plant at Yeosu. It was clear to us that the only way we could straighten out the mess was to consolidate our two companies in Korea, one of which was a 100 percent-owned company (the chlorine-caustic company) and the other fifty-fifty owned with what was de jure a Korean public company but de facto a government-controlled company.

By this time Lundeen was back in Midland as executive vice president of the company, and then in 1982 as chairman, but his portfolio of management responsibilities still included Dow Pacific, of which Andrew Butler was now president. John L. Hagaman took over as Dow's top man in Korea.

"Korea Pacific was a joint venture but was really controlled by the Korean government," Hagaman said.

Ostensibly the officers seconded to Korea Pacific from the Korean side came from the Korean partner, but really they came from the Korean government. Early in the life of Korea Pacific the government had seconded business-oriented people from the ministry of chemical industries, or business or business-oriented people. Before I went up there the government changed and started seconding retired military officers. Military officers have a different mind-set than business people, and that was an overall factor.

The second factor was that when the second generation of plants came onstream in Yeosu, we went from a situation of fairly significant undersupply, an inability to supply the market, to a position of oversupply, to not being able to run your plants at capacity. The third element of stress was the fact that we had Dow Korea as a 100 percent [Dow]-owned company and Korea Pacific as a 50-50 owned company, yet they were totally intertwined in raw materials; the chlorine came to the joint venture from the wholly owned company. All those things started exerting stress, and the relationships began to sour over time.[33]

The Korean operations began to lose money, and the losses began to climb. In 1980 and 1981, Dow Korea lost a total of $42 million and KPCC lost $18 million.

"Andrew Butler and I were confronted with the problem," Lundeen said.

What the hell do we do? Finally, with the help of a lot of very able people in Midland and Hong Kong and Seoul, we came up with a bailout scheme that would treat the minority share-holders fairly; half of this company was owned by the public. If we brought it all together, we had to make sure these public shareholders weren't disadvantaged. Dow really would own about 75 percent of this thing once it was rationalized.

We had a scheme we thought was very fair, but there was a Korean general running this so-called public company, put there by the Ministry of Commerce and Industry, and he decided he didn't like this scheme. He was a friend of Chun Doo Hwan, he was very nation-alistic, and he didn't know anything about business. So we thought we'd have to appeal to the Ministry to straighten out this difficult general.

Lundeen vividly remembered calling on Kim Dong Whie, South Korea's minister of com-merce and industry, to explain Dow's problem. "We wanted to rationalize the company, we wanted to make it successful, and to do so we had to implement our scheme. This general was standing in the way. He just wouldn't come to the party. 'So why don't you do something about it, Mr. Minister?'"

"The minister said, 'Mr. Lundeen, I hope you understand that His Excellency the President's new program involves noninterference in the private sector. As far as I can see this is clearly a private-sector dispute. Korea Pacific Chemical Company is a private company and the Dow Chemical Company is a private company; the government has nothing to do with it. I hear what you're saying. It sounds very reasonable, but I'm afraid I can't do anything for you.'"

Lundeen said, "Mr. Minister, you know and I know that all of the [Korean] directors of Korea Pacific Chemical Company were put there by the government; every single one of them is a government appointee. We didn't have anything to do with it, nor did the share-holders have anything to do with it. You know that and I know that. If you put them in, you can take them out. And until you do we're going to have an impasse."

Minister Kim repeated his remarks on private sector affairs and added, "We can't interfere. I'll do my best but I can't hold out any hope."

"They never did anything, so we got out," Lundeen said. "We sold our interests."

Before that happened Andrew Butler applied some pressure in an interview with the *Asian Wall Street Journal*, Hong Kong-based sister publication of the New York original. Butler told a reporter that Dow's partner in Korea had turned life into an "aching" process of continual arguments. "It's like being partners with cotton wool," Butler said; the Korean partner brought nothing to the venture, having no experience, clout, technology, or money. The partner's top executives included retired Korean army generals who "haven't even run a garage." During a visit to the joint venture, Butler said, "all my antennae said, 'This is a government office.' Everyone was sitting around reading newspapers. This was what this two-star general called a marketing organization."[34]

Once they had decided to get out, Butler and Lundeen let nothing stand in the way. When the Koreans opposed the sale of Dow's interest, Dow took the government of Korea into court for breach of contract. "We took them into court in Pusan, the court of first jurisdiction," Lundeen said.

> The judge wouldn't hear the case. That was no surprise, but we had an arbitration clause in the contract that said if we couldn't resolve disputes we would take it to international arbitration in Geneva. So we said, "Okay, sports fans, hang on, here we go." Very nicely we let it be known that we were quite prepared to haul the government of the Republic of Korea into arbitration in Geneva with a serious complaint by their then biggest private foreign investor. With that, Chun Doo Hwan decided the problem somehow could be solved.

Dow sold its interests for $60 million (its investment was estimated at $145 million) to Korean Explosives Group, a private company. "They took and used our reorganization formula exactly," Lundeen said. "Consolidated, the two companies ran like gangbusters, making all kinds of money. That was nationalism. That's the only really tough nationalism problem we ever ran into in Asia, aside from the Redcliffs project in Australia."

The Korean blowup left both the Dow people and their Korean partners with conflicting emotions. Hagaman, whose tenure there ranged from the peak of Dow investment to the departure, was quite disappointed. His whole family loved Korea. "A lot of people thought Korea was a hard place to live at that time, but we liked it immensely from the time that we got there," he said. "If you went to my wife today and asked, 'Of all the places that you lived in Asia, which did you enjoy the most?' she'd say, 'Korea, clearly, hands down.'"

"You can really get to know people," Hagaman said of the Koreans. "They're very individualistic, emotional but warm, very personable, very interactable, very approachable, really fine people."

Hagaman, who was president of the American Chamber of Commerce in Korea during his time there, said different kinds of investments were viewed quite differently.

> If you're a Motorola and you come in and utilize Korean labor to make semiconductors and send those semiconductors back to the United States, you're going to be very well treated in Korea; they like that. If you're Nike shoes and you come in and make a zillion pairs of tennis shoes and send them back to the United States and employ a lot of people, you're going to be very well treated and very well thought of. But if your objective is to come in and participate in the Korean economy and make money by participating in the Korean economy and ship dollars back to a New York bank, that is seen as raping and pillaging the country; they don't like that at all. There are two totally different mind-sets.

Dow was in this second category, Hagaman said. "We were there to bring technology in and be a good citizen, but we were there to make products to sell in the Korean market and make money which we would send back to the U.S. You're not nearly as welcome when you're in that mind-set as when you're in the mind-set of making something to export to make money for Korea."

Neither side was pleased with what had happened. "Breakup of Dow Chemical's Joint Venture With Koreans Leaves Both Sides Unhappy," said a headline in the *Wall Street Journal*. Korea, seeking to overcome a reputation as a difficult place for foreign investors, was left with a conspicuous international black eye. Dow was also criticized severely, in Korea and elsewhere.[35]

Lee Tae-Sup, chairman of the commerce committee of Korea's National Assembly, told the *Journal* that Dow employees, "acted like they thought they were doing business in California," ignoring local custom by going public with their complaints before touching all the right bases privately. (Dow responded that at that point, "we had nothing left to lose," by going public). "We're going to have to do a lot better job of showing we're open to foreign investment," Lee Tae-Sup said.

In the aftermath, foreign investment in Korea dropped off markedly; foreign investors complained more, and invested less.

Ten years later, however, Dow was moving back into Korea rather strongly. "I think it was unfortunate that we left Korea," said Colin Goodchild, who became president of Dow Pacific a year after the departure.

> I can well understand the reason for doing so; the company was suffering and Dow was losing money, and we had troubles with our partners. In retrospect we would have been better off to have stayed, but I say that with the benefit of hindsight. We did go back in again. We formed a joint venture to make latex, and that plant is now [1993] onstream. We maintained our sales, and we have expanded even further. So we're going back into Korea and we should be in Korea. It's a very important market.[36]

Korea, said Goodchild, is an important place to be for anyone in the chemical business, for "what is happening in Korea, Japan, and China these days is a major part of what's now happening to the chemical industry in the world."

VII.

He was disappointed in just two countries in Asia, Lundeen said. India was one and the Philippines was the other. "It was just too corrupt," he said of the Philippines. Dow established an office in Manila in 1964, even before it had an Asian headquarters, and began to explore possibilities for the company there.

"Of course, if you were going to do something serious in the Philippines one of Ferdinand Marcos's friends was involved," Lundeen said, "because they had their hands in everything big."[37]

"We really didn't do any business in the Philippines," Goodchild said. "We had a sales office there and a pharmaceutical operation, but the Philippines was a difficult place. It was very mercurial and it was also corrupt, particularly in the early days; later it became politically unstable."[38]

"We tried there," said Lee Dupuy, "but the Philippines was the most corrupt society that I ever ran into anywhere in the world. And they were blatantly corrupt."[39]

Dupuy remembered going both with Lundeen and alone to discuss manufacturing projects with Filipino officials. "This was during the Marcos regime," he said.

> They were promoting a petrochemical complex near one of their refineries, and they were essentially offering the factories out on a competitive basis, so I went over to explore that. The government people I talked to said, "It will cost you so much money up front if you want to do it." "Who does the money go to?" "It goes to Mrs. [Imelda] Marcos." A lot of the other Asian societies were corrupt, but in a subtle way; maybe I'm naive, but most of the time in other countries I didn't even know it. But in the Philippines, man, it was out on the table. "It will cost you so many millions of dollars. If you want this project we'll give it to you, but this is the up-front money if you want it." There was no doubt it was going into the Marcos's pocket or one of their relatives.

On one visit Dupuy and Lundeen went to see the head of the Philippines national oil company, the country's petroleum czar, Geronimo Valasco. "When he got through telling us all the things we were going to have to do and all the people we were going to have to pay off in order to do business in the Philippines," Dupuy said, "Bob and I walked out of his office, looked at each other, and said, 'Outta here!' It was terrible."

After that incident Lundeen handed down the second edict of his career. "We are not going to invest any money in the Philippines," he decreed. "This is a place we're going to have nothing to do with."

It was really too bad, Lundeen said, "because the Philippines were a country with a lot of fine people and good resources, even though they were just horribly managed. But we aren't a social reform organization," he added. "We are a business organization."

VIII.

Sitting in the shabby splendor of the Cho-sun Hotel in downtown Seoul one evening in February 1972, Bob Lundeen and Lee Dupuy watched a television broadcast of Richard Nixon's history-making visit to China. As they witnessed the amazing sight of Nixon and Mao Zhedong toasting each other, ending the hostility between the two countries that had existed since 1949, they excitedly realized that great change was in the air and that a new door was opening. "We sat looking at the TV and talking about the opportunities that might now present themselves in China," Dupuy said.

Up to that time "I couldn't see it for sour apples," Dupuy said, "and no one in Hong Kong was promoting it within the Dow system; we didn't have any China projects we were interested in."[40]

In his early days in the Pacific it had been almost impossible for an American company to get an invitation to the Canton Trade Fair, Lundeen remembered. "Since in those days that was where most Chinese business was conducted, it was essential to get an invitation," he said. Lundeen wangled one through Ricardo Moratti, Southeast Asia manager for Dow's Italian subsidiary, and went as a business consultant to the Italian firm, Gruppo Lepetit. "In later years, after we had established the vital personal relationships with Chinese purchasing people, doing business there became less of an adventure," he said. Sales to China out of Hong Kong began in 1970.[41]

China officially adopted an Open Door Policy in 1979, and that year Dow opened its first Chinese office in Guangzhou. Dave Schornstein, who succeeded Lundeen as president of Dow Pacific in 1978, witnessed this major change. "There was a world of difference between the attitudes in China when I first arrived and when I left in 1980," Schornstein said. "By that time there was a growing openness in dealing with China and things looked good for our marketing potential."[42]

During the 1980s Dow opened four more sales offices and signed a pair of technology licensing agreements with China. "We decided to open sales offices and sort out later whether we had opened them in the right place," Goodchild said. "The important thing was to get in."[43]

As the opening of China continued, Paul Oreffice visited China with Goodchild in 1987 to see for himself. "That was a gamble at the time," Goodchild said, "because China was developing pretty fast then and Dow was interested in getting more involvement. Oreffice came away an enthusiastic supporter of our aims in China."

These aims included formation of a joint venture with the Chinese, and in April 1989 that came to fruition when Mike Parker signed documents forming the Zhejiang Pacific Chemical Corporation, owned half by Dow and half by Zhejiang Chemical Factory. Zhejiang Pacific was to build plants to make propylene oxide, propylene glycol, and polyols at Ningbo in Zhejiang Province.[44]

It looked as though all this might come to naught, however, when quite unexpectedly, two months later, on June 3, 1989, occurred the event that has become known as "Tiananmen Square"; Chinese troops fired on and killed hundreds of students demonstrating in favor of democracy on Tiananmen Square. They had erected a home-made replica of the Statue of Liberty. The government's brutal crackdown shocked a watching world and set off a period of great turmoil in China.

Dow's office in Beijing, like the rest of the city, was closed for several days after the event. Dow put the $50 million Ningbo project on hold, "to study the situation," knowing that general violence might break out across China, but a few months later, after things quieted down, cautiously proceeded.[45]

By the time of Tiananmen Square, Dow's sales in the People's Republic of China had reached the $120 million per year level and Dow had 30 employees resident in China and another 50 working on Chinese business in Hong Kong. Installed as country manager in 1988 was China-born and U.S.-educated Michael Lung.

In addition, China had growing economic problems. An "official" inflation rate of 18.5 percent was estimated by Lung to be "more like 20 to 30 percent," and with inflation came corruption. "Because of the fast growth of the economy, corruption set in," Lung said. "Inflation now becomes not just an economic problem but a political one. In order to control corruption they have to control inflation."

Five years later, as the Chinese economy continued to lurch forward, the company decided it was time to express its confidence in China's future, and in a rather bold move it consolidated its operations in the People's Republic of China, Hong Kong, and Taiwan into a single Greater China operation. Lung became general manager for Greater China, and Loh Shai-Choon, who had been country manager for Taiwan, became general sales manager for Greater China.[46]

It was a natural move because of the increasing interaction between the PRC, Hong Kong, and Taiwan. Denis Wilcock, who had succeeded Mike Parker as president of Dow Pacific, saw it as practical and positive. "It will optimize Dow's presence in Greater China, which represents a significant growth opportunity," he said, "and make better use of Dow resources."

In December 1991 the Asian headquarters of Dow paused to celebrate its 25th birthday with a party at the Hong Kong Hilton, where the first offices had been located. Lundeen came from his retirement home in Washington state to give the keynote talk. "Being president of Dow Pacific was the greatest job I had in Dow," he said. "It was more fun, it was more challenging, and it was filled with more exciting people than any other position I had before or since."[47]

Frank Popoff, the company's CEO, told the celebrants that the Pacific area, "is and will continue to be Dow's principal opportunity for rapid growth. The work ethic, innovation, creativity and flexibility that characterize Hong Kong and its people are a model for the whole of the Dow world."

At the same time the Pacific headquarters celebrated a move to new offices, located in the top five smoke-free floors, 47 through 51, of the Sun Hung Kai Centre, in the Wanchai area of Hong Kong. From there, Dow could see far into Asia.

Notes

1. Oral History, Robert W. Lundeen, October 14, 1988, is quoted extensively in this section.

2. Dow International had four vice presidents at the time: John C. H. Stearns, V.P. marketing; Max Key, V. P. manufacturing; Elmer K. Stilbert, V.P. business development; and Arthur M. Griswold, V. P. special assignments.

3. Herbert Dow considered building an indigo plant in China in 1919, but the project fell through. Dow's principal agent in China was the Wah Chang Trading Corp., Shanghai.

4. Oral History, Arnold L. Johnson, August 26, 1993.

5. See "Dow Sets Up High School in Hong Kong," *Chemical & Engineering News*, April. 3, 1967.

6. *25th Anniversary, Dow Pacific*, brochure published by Dow Chemical Pacific Ltd., Hong Kong, 1991.

7. This section quotes extensively from Oral History, Eric Huggins, September 24, 1994.

8. "Establishing the Asahi-Dow Operation in Japan," talk by Max Key, Commercial Chemical Development Association, Bedford Springs, Pennsylvania., October 7, 1954. Also Oral History, William A. Groening Jr., July 22, 1988.

9. See Yoshio Tsunoda, president, "Partnership at Dow: Status and Outlook at Three Joint Ventures," Part 3, Asahi-Dow Ltd., November 1979.

10. Oral History, G. Robert Baker, March 13, 1991, is quoted extensively in this section.

11. See President's Letter, *Dow Annual Report to Stockholders*, 1982.

12. Oral History, R. W. Lundeen.

13. H. H. Dow to Prof. U. P. Hedrick, Geneva, New York, February 3, 1914. Dow told Hedrick that Takamine had introduced him to Japanese food: "The Japanese dinner was the most beautiful to look at of any meal I have had the pleasure of witnessing," he wrote. "We started off with raw fish, eaten with chopsticks. The fish itself was absolutely fresh and when dipped in a sauce was no more objectionable than raw oysters. I got so I could handle a slippery mushroom with the chopsticks without dropping it, and mushrooms seemed to be an important part of a number of dishes. The most pleasing thing was their beauty. . . ."

14. This section quotes extensively from Oral History, Gustav A. De Groot, June 1, 1992.

15. Oral History, Eric Huggins, September 22, 1994. See also "Dow in Southeast Asia," *Dow Diamond* 33 (June 1970): 2-5, and "Assignment: Overseas," an account of a Dow family transferred to Kuala Lumpur, *Dow Diamond* 32 (June 1969): 16-20.

16. Oral History, Colin Goodchild, May 1993. See also "New Presence in Indonesia," *Pacific Friends*, employee publication of Dow Chemical Pacific, Ltd., Hong Kong, no. 6, December 1973.

17. *25th Anniversary, Dow Pacific*.

18. Ibid.

19. This section quotes extensively from Oral History, R. W. Lundeen.

20. Oral History, E. Huggins.

21. Oral History, C. Goodchild, is quoted extensively in this section.

22. See "Associated Company Formed," *Dow Diamond* 22, 1 (April 1959): 32.

23. Oral History, R. W. Lundeen.

24. "Caustic Soda Goes Down Under," *Dow Diamond*, no. 2 (1967). See also "Australia Views Its Challenges," *Dow Diamond*, no. 4 (1967).

25. One of the negotiators in Brisbane was Donald Kelly, then treasurer of Swift, who later became a world-scale leveraged buyout artist and amassed an enormous personal fortune. "He had a great sense of humor, but was absolutely hard as nails," Lundeen said.

26. Oral History, R. W. Lundeen.

27. *Welcome to Ivon Watkins-Dow Limited*, brochure published by Ivan Watkins-Dow, New Plymouth, New Zealand, 1981.

28. Oral History, C. Goodchild.

29. Oral History, Bernard B. Butcher, June 11, 1992.

30. Oral History, R. W. Lundeen.

31. Oral History, Leonce F. (Lee) Dupuy, September 1, 1993.

32. Oral History, B. B. Butcher.

33. Oral History, John L. Hagaman, May 18, 1992.

34. Oral History, Andrew Butler, May 5, 1995.

35. "Pitfalls of Partnership: Breakup of Dow Chemical's Joint Venture with Koreans Leaves Both Sides Unhappy," *Wall Street Journal*, January 5, 1983; "Korea Tries to Limit Effects of Pullout by Dow Chemical, but Cynicism Persists," *Wall Street Journal*, October 28, 1982.

36. Oral History, C. Goodchild.

37. Oral History, R. W. Lundeen.

38. Oral History, C. Goodchild.

39. Oral History, L. F. (Lee) Dupuy.

40. Ibid.

41. Oral History, R. W. Lundeen.

42. Oral History, Dave W. Schornstein, March 15, 1991.

43. Oral History, C. Goodchild.

44. *25th Anniversary, Dow Pacific.*

45. See "Dow's Business in China Goes On," *Midland Daily News*, September 17, 1989.

46. "PRC, Hong Kong, Taiwan Become Greater China Unit," *Dow Today*, February 3, 1994.

47. "Dow Celebrates 25 Years in the Pacific," *Dow Today*, January 17, 1992.

SEVENTEEN
ZOLTAN

I.

In early 1975, Ben Branch, looking ahead to his 60th birthday and what Dow calls "deceleration," took an informal poll of his board of directors, asking, "Who should succeed me, when I go, as CEO?" It was no contest; a clear majority favored the succession of Earle Barnes, a well-liked 35-year veteran of the company, then 58 and president of Dow Chemical U.S.A., the company's largest operating unit. Three others received votes—Paul Oreffice, Zoltan Merszei, and Clyde Boyd.[1]

The Dow pattern was that Branch would become board chairman during his "deceleration" period, beginning at age 60, serving in that capacity until retirement at age 65. His successor would be recommended to the board at the proper time by Branch, Gerstacker, and Doan, who for a dozen years and more had jointly guided all major decisions in the firm.

The differences between the candidates were quickly apparent as the three men mulled them over. Barnes had spent his entire career in the research and manufacturing sectors of Dow, in the United States; he had no background in marketing, finance, or the foreign field. Merszei, in stark contrast, had no experience in the United States, none in manufacturing, and none in research. Only Boyd, president of Dow Chemical Canada, had both foreign and U.S. experience and a rounded background in the company. Oreffice, although perceived as a future CEO, was only 47.

As they discussed the matter, Doan, Branch, and Gerstacker came to the conclusion that Barnes and Merszei were considerably ahead of Boyd in leadership qualities and that Oreffice needed more seasoning, so it became for them a two-horse race between the popular American veteran without foreign experience and the brilliant young European without U.S. experience, at a time when the company's business was quite evenly split between U.S. and foreign sales and likely to remain so. Was it possible in some way to put this dazzling duo together at the head of the company, to take full advantage of both their talents, and if so, how?

All three were aware that Merszei had been openly broadcasting his ambition to hold "the top job in Dow" for almost 25 years now and that he wanted this job, as he said privately, "violently";[2] Barnes was more quietly and controllably ambitious for the post. They were also aware that if Barnes became president and served to age 65, Merszei would then be but a few months shy of his 60th birthday and too old, by the Dow rules, to be the CEO; choosing Barnes would thus in all likelihood preclude Merszei from the presidency of Dow forever.

Barnes as CEO, Merszei as executive vice president? Merszei as CEO, Barnes as executive vice president? The options were carefully considered.

As their conversations heated up, other considerations were trotted out: Barnes, with his long U.S. experience, would probably be more "dependable" as CEO; there would be little risk of his making major mistakes. On the other hand, why replace Branch with a man only a year or so younger? Then again, selecting Merszei, foreign-born and with experience solely on the foreign side of the firm, would provide a major lift to the ambitions and acceptance of the rapidly growing force of foreign nationals within the company, around the world, and tapping a younger man—Merszei was 53—would be vastly encouraging to the "young tigers" around the firm.

The matter of risks was a major concern. Merszei could be a spectacular risk, one argued; "he might lead the company into a new period of great progress and innovation, and then again he might blow it entirely." But the time to take such risks, another said, is precisely when the company has so many strong, solid people around, and "we have so many good sound people today that they could fix the mistakes." Then, too, there was a risk of splitting the board of directors by nominating Merszei, since a majority of the board had informally expressed their preference for Barnes, and Merszei had trailed in third place in that poll.[3]

They decided Doan would talk to Barnes about the situation, and Branch would talk to Merszei, before they tried to arrive at a decision.

In April Ted Doan called Barnes in for a chat that lasted three hours, asking Barnes who should be the next president of Dow. Barnes said the company should move control to a younger team in the near future, and said he saw Paul Oreffice as presidential material, and also Zoltan Merszei, and Dave Schornstein and David Rooke as well, but it would be better for any one of them to take over while Ben, Ted, and Carl "were still around." His first choice, he said, was Oreffice.

Doan asked about Clyde Boyd. "Too old," Barnes said. He asked about Merszei. Barnes said Merszei got good results but that opinion of Merszei in the company was "bad." He is like Dutch Beutel in some ways, Barnes observed, a "driver"; people work for him even if they don't like him as their leader. Like Beutel, Merszei doesn't handle people well, he said, "but he gets things done."

Could Earle work for Zoltan, Ted asked? Barnes said no, he couldn't ever work for Zoltan, and for that matter he was finding it difficult to work with him. Would Earle quit if Zoltan became CEO? "At my age," Barnes said, "probably not."

"Now tell me about Barnes as president," Ted suggested. "I'm too old," Earle said. "For another thing I'd worry day and night whether I'm capable of doing the whole job. I can understand marketing and financial concerns, but I couldn't run those functions myself; I don't know enough about them. I can run research and manufacturing and business in the U.S.A., but everything else I'd be worried about.

"But, even understanding these concerns of mine, please don't count me out," Barnes added. "I would just love to have that job, and I'd give it everything I've got."

Suppose we were to set up an arrangement with Barnes as president and Merszei as executive vice president, Doan asked. Barnes said he couldn't by any stretch of the imagination be comfortable with an arrangement of that kind. "I'd want to pick my own team and structure it to get the job done."

In the meantime Branch was in Europe to talk to Merszei. He started by telling him he'd come in third in his poll on the succession to the Dow presidency. Why should that be, Branch asked; why did Zoltan think his fellow directors would rank him only third among the prospects?

Merszei said there were of course reasons he might not be considered the best candidate. He was not a chemist or a chemical engineer, and leadership by a chemical man was traditional in Dow, he knew. He was not a production man, either, and that was probably against him. He was perhaps too international in his outlook to suit a lot of people, and for some he was perhaps too autocratic, which was the European style. "When I give orders I expect them to be followed," he said. "I admit that." He realized Dow was an American company, and he wasn't an American. He knew that some people criticized him because he was goal-oriented, relentlessly goal-oriented, and he knew he had been criticized for running a lean organization, too lean, some felt.

Then he went on to detail for Branch what he felt he could bring to the Dow presidency. "Investors like me," he said. "So do stockholders. I'm an innovative, courageous businessman. I'm a good leader. I pick good people. I can handle the problems of working with Socialist governments and governments of all kinds, which is of great importance to Dow in today's world. And I'm 53-$1/2$ years old—young enough, but old enough."

He repeated to Ben how "violently" he wanted the job, more than he had ever wanted anything in his life, he said, and he had been working for it ever since he had come to the company, 26 years before. "I can be a good leader for Dow—better than good. I've proved that in Europe, and I'll prove it in the rest of the world as well. I can provide continuity to the company by making it a truly international company, which is what it is trying to be and is destined to be."

When Branch returned to Midland the talks among the three men continued, with Barnes still the consensus choice. In July Doan reported to Branch and Gerstacker on further talks with Levi Leathers, Clyde Boyd, and others, including Barnes and Merszei. He had told Leathers, the company's Texas-born manufacturing vice president, that Barnes and Merszei were being considered as the next CEO; what did he think? Leathers said it would take him and the rest of Dow "about five years to get over the shock," if Merszei got the nod. There is great communication in Dow now, he said, and "what I hear" is that Dow people in the

United States "worry" about Merszei—"they're not sure they trust him." After thinking about it at more length, though, Leathers said he thought either Barnes or Merszei would be OK. He personally preferred Barnes, but was not really opposed to Merszei.

Clyde Boyd also said he preferred Barnes but was not anti-Merszei. He said he didn't in the least envision Zoltan as courting disaster for the company if he became its CEO. Zoltan may be "afraid to chew out production people," he observed, "but he's a good manager."

Doan said that among the people he had talked to, Merszei was generally perceived as the best manager, but unfortunately that experience was restricted to Europe. Merszei was also conceded to be a "tough manager on costs," always a prime Dow virtue. The basic question, he thought, was whether Merszei had an understanding of all types of people—not just Europeans—and how to motivate them, and the same could be asked of Barnes and his understanding of non-Americans.

Merszei was seen as flexible, but not a risk taker; Barnes was seen as weak in planning: "he solves problems on the fly," one said. The psychology of Merszei becoming chief executive would be bad, said Gerstacker; Merszei was perceived as Branch's boy, almost his son. "You'd have the same kind of nepotism problem you had with Ted Doan succeeding his father as Dow CEO. A lot of Dow people will see Ben and Zoltan as one entity."

But Gerstacker, in spite of this, was now leaning strongly toward Merszei, arguing that Earle Barnes, if he were CEO, "wouldn't use Branch," who would be relegated to a minor role in the company; this would not happen with Merszei, and Branch should understand this and try to cope with it. Branch would be a lot more comfortable with Merszei, he said. Doan, laughing, accused Gerstacker of loving the "ham" and the salesman in Merszei, and the "exotic, foreign flavor" he represented.

Branch said he was also now less inclined to support Barnes than he had been before, that he couldn't see that Barnes's people skills were very good, and that he was familiar with at least three cases of top executive moves that had been, in his view, mishandled by Barnes. Barnes seemed to be able to develop only technical people, Branch said, "and he really has no comprehension at all of the foreign field." There were cases, in fact, where he was convinced Barnes had been "devious." For these reasons, Branch said, he was switching his support to Merszei.

Within a few more minutes, there was unanimity in the troika; they would nominate Zoltan Merszei as the next president and CEO of The Dow Chemical Company.

At the next meeting of the board, on August 7, one of the most thoroughgoing shake-ups of the top Dow command in its history—the "summer of '75 shake-up"—took place on the recommendation of Branch, Doan, and Gerstacker.

Two new executive vice presidents of the company were elected at that meeting—Earle Barnes and Zoltan Merszei. Merszei was to make immediate arrangements to move to Midland; Boyd was appointed his successor as president of Dow Chemical Europe. Oreffice, who had been the chief financial officer, became Barnes's successor as president of Dow U.S.A.

On that same day, in another startling move, G. James Williams, attorney, marketing director, and general manager of the plastics department, but without previous financial experience, was appointed the new chief financial officer of Dow, succeeding Oreffice. The troika had elected the high-risk option in this case as well.

This big summer shake-up also set the stage, and put all the players in place, for the second act of the changeover drama, which took place at the annual shareholders meeting of May 5, 1976, in the big new Midland Center for the Arts. At that meeting, the first in Midland in three years, before a packed house in the 1,500-seat auditorium, Gerstacker announced his retirement as chairman (his 60th birthday occurred on August 6, 1976), Ben Branch was elevated to the chairmanship, and Zoltan Merszei was elected the new chief executive officer.

"I have been planning for many years to retire at age 60," Gerstacker told the stockholders at the conclusion of the meeting. "I will be 60 years old this year, and it is time to turn things over to others." He noted that he would remain a director of the company and chairman of its finance committee. "After almost 40 years it is easy to leave active work with a company when you have complete confidence, as I do, in the men who will be doing the work you have been doing," he told a press conference later.[4]

In the organizational meeting of the board, which traditionally takes place at Dow immediately following the annual meeting at which board members are formally elected, the election of new officers was accomplished within a few minutes and the new president emerged to face his first press conference, accompanied by Gerstacker and Branch.

"Don't expect any major policy changes," Merszei said, pointing to Dow's spectacular performances in the previous two years. "It will take some doing to improve on that record. If we just follow on the path of our predecessors we'll be doing all right."

He told *Fortune* magazine a few days later that Dow would continue to operate with a troika type of leadership, with himself, Branch, and Barnes as the threesome. Barnes would "hold down the fort" at Midland while Merszei and Branch spent most of their time on the road. "I have never believed in the kind of supervision that requires your presence all the time," he said. "If you have confidence in the people who work for you, if you don't look over their shoulders, it's amazing how much more comfortably they can do their jobs."[5] He expected to spend perhaps 70 percent of his time on the road, as he had in Europe, he told another reporter.

As a counterpoint to the dawn of a new era in its history the company's shareholders also overwhelmingly approved a two-for-one stock split on that May 5.[6] The company's ability to accomplish the split and its accompanying dividend increase (from 20 to 25 cents quarterly), Gerstacker told the press, had been brought about by Ben Branch's exemplary leadership over the past half-dozen years, and thus the "Branch split" was in a very real sense a salute to one of the nation's great chief executive officers.

Yet most of these signs of continuing progress and prosperity in the company were quite lost in the hubbub that attended the surprise election of Zoltan Merszei, non-American, non-chemist, unknown to a great majority of Dow's U.S. employees and friends, to the presidency of the company. Until six years before, the Dow family had always supplied the chief executive; Ted Doan's mother had been Herbert Dow's daughter Ruth. Ben Branch had been the first CEO from outside the family. Now suddenly the chief executive of this midwestern American chemical company was a handsome young Hungarian who was a citizen of Canada, related to no one, and who, most alarming of all, had no credentials in chemistry.

II.

There were two Zoltan Merszeis, perhaps even more. One was a handsome, charismatic business leader who single-handedly led Dow to success in Europe, accomplishing positively brilliant feats unparalleled in the business world. Another was a philandering, ill-educated egomaniac, blithely threatening to lead his company to destruction.

"He is not Attila the Hun, nor is he the Second Coming of Christ," Frank Popoff said.

> If you listen to Zoltan, from his breast evolved the company, or certainly [the components of it in] Japan, Canada, and Europe, and—if they'd only listened to him—the United States. If you listen to other people he was potentially the ruination of the company. Neither of those is true. He was a colorful guy and a good leader, but he was bending the company in a direction that probably threatened research and the historic Dow Chemical Company. Some of that was maybe a good idea, but in excess it would have been a horrible situation.

Merszei's ego, said Ted Doan, "was, and is to this day, completely out of hand. Everybody has an ego; it's the problem of how you handle the ego that counts, and Zoltan never was able to handle his ego. . . . Ben Branch spent a considerable amount of time trying to counsel Zoltan in getting his ego under control."

Merszei was born in Budapest, Hungary, in September 1922, and although his family was Calvinist attended the Jaszo Premontrei Gymnasium just outside Budapest, run by the Roman Catholic Premonstratensian Brothers. He speaks with particular fondness of his maternal grandfather, a country doctor at Debrecen, with whom he spent summers and holidays. In 1939, as World War II was breaking out, his mother sent him to Switzerland to continue his schooling and in 1941 Hungary, joining with Nazi Germany, declared war on the Soviet Union.[7]

One of about 60 Hungarian schoolboys in Switzerland during the war, he says he met Allan W. Dulles, later chief of the CIA but then U.S. consul general in Zurich, and was recruited for the Office of Strategic Services, forerunner of the CIA. Another acquaintance of this period was Richard Helms, also a later chief of the CIA. "This is a chapter of my history that for various reasons I can't talk about even today," Merszei says.

This period of his life has always remained murky. He lists a bachelor of architecture degree from the Federal Polytechnic Institute in Zurich (1944) in his curriculum vitae, and a bachelor certificate in civil engineering from the same school (1945), but the school has no record of his attending classes there. ("There was a fire and my records were destroyed," Merszei says). His early colleagues at Dow believed he never had any education beyond the high school level. His first wife, Illy, told friends she met him for the first time when he came to her father's house to plant trees and bushes for a landscape architect her father engaged. She even claimed, in a public dispute with him, that he had never been in Switzerland at all until he was sent there by Dow in the early 1950s. (They divorced after he left Dow in 1979, and he remarried.) If he had no college training at all, as seems likely, it did not hold him back; Merszei eventually acquired honorary doctorates in law, in science, and in chemical engineering.

"People used to tell disparaging stories about Zoltan," Frank Popoff said, "but people saw him as their guy, a fighter for Dow Europe, very human, with all the failings that humans have, but a fearless, tireless campaigner for the best interests of Dow Europe."[8]

His womanizing was legendary. Ted Doan remembered.

> That may be too strong a term, but not much too strong. I know Zoltan well enough to know that that [particular] gal was probably seduced right then. She didn't mind it, but that didn't go with everybody else. I have watched him get airline tickets out of a person in Heathrow Airport where he seduced the girl with his eyes and his talk into doing things that she knew were against the rules and she wouldn't do for anybody else. It was part of his technique. If he had a woman, he could take her to the cleaners if she had the slightest inclination. However, that didn't impress the women around here [in Midland]. Most of them didn't like it at all. The men liked it even less. And in the [American] South you don't do that kind of thing.[9]

Tom Sparta, one of his longtime colleagues in Europe, remembered going to lunch with Merszei to meet an American correspondent newly arrived in Zurich to report on American business activities on the continent. Their waitress was a blushing, fresh-faced teenager. It seemed to be her first day on the job, and Merszei struck up a ferocious flirtation. He spent much of the luncheon describing for the American correspondent the joys of introducing nubile young ladies to sex. "Once you have trained them a little bit they are really very, very good," he said.

After the correspondent had gone his way Sparta said, "Zoltan, don't you think it was a bit much, going on that way?" "Maybe," said Merszei, "but I'll tell you one thing, that correspondent will not soon forget who is Zoltan Merszei."[10]

"He was an amazing fellow," said Frank Popoff. "His strength was, he could read Ben [Branch] and anticipate him, and Branch spent a lot of time [in Europe]. He saw Dow Europe at its best. We were always on parade when Ben was anywhere in the vicinity. Ben respected Zoltan as an implementer. Zoltan wasn't bashful, either, about what he did or what he asked other people to do, and that's what was needed at the time. He had no delusions that he was charting a course for [Dow] Europe; that was being done, and it was principally Ben's vision. Zoltan was very effective in getting the resources and implementing the plans. He was a very important guy to Dow's development."

Merszei operated Dow Europe primarily through three lieutenants, Popoff said; Dick Bechtold, the business chief; Charles Doscher, marketing and sales; and Clyde Boyd, manufacturing. Merszei "would drop those guys in the bear pit and they would flail around, slash, cut, argue, and fight, and from that would come a consensus which Zoltan would harvest and say, 'This is what I have decided we will do.' It was a classic management technique, I guess."

"The bottom line," Popoff said, "is that for all his foibles Zoltan Merszei was instrumental in building up Dow Europe."[11] "He was just a genius thrown into the wrong slot," Ted Doan said.

III.

When Zoltan Merszei took over the helm of the Dow company in 1976 it was sitting pretty, the world's most profitable chemical company for the third year running.

Even Dow insiders had a hard time believing the company's sensational success of 1974. Earnings after taxes more than doubled from the year before—from $271 million to $563 million—and 1973 had been a banner year. For the first time Dow surpassed Du Pont, the biggest company in its business, in profits, and Du Pont was twice as big as Dow in sales.[12] It was an accomplishment no one at Dow would have deemed possible 10 or 15 years before, when Dow was the fourth largest U.S. chemical company, struggling to reach the billion-dollar-a-year plateau in sales.

To prove its 1974 triumph was no fluke, Dow did even better in 1975. Its earnings came in at $632 million, again leading the world's chemical industry. In 1976, Merszei's first year as top man, earnings flattened out at $612 million, and in 1977 tumbled back to $555 million, but in both years the company was still the world's most profitable chemical firm, and in the eyes of many expert observers, the best.

Then before the annual meeting of his top management at Ocean Reef, Florida, in January 1978, Merszei proposed an audacious goal—Dow must double its earnings in the next five years, he said.

On January 20, 1978, he wrote his top lieutenants (the names of Barnes, executive vice president, and Leathers, manufacturing vice president, did not appear on his list, however) a follow-up letter to this meeting, calling attention to a summary of "improvements we need to make if we are to improve our performance. . . . I want to be sure you understand that [these] are more than just recommendations," he wrote. "They represent decisions, and I urge you to proceed with their implementation immediately. . . . As soon as possible I want to receive follow-up reports from you on what you are doing to improve your particular situation."[13]

On the surface, Dow was running in top gear, continuing to outperform the rest of its industry. Merszei's captaincy was beset with behind-the-scenes problems almost from the outset, however, and the situation rapidly grew worse.

The first rumblings against the "one-man rule" Merszei was perceived as imposing were already being heard. Barnes told Doan he was being "left out of everything," and that he was contemplating early retirement. He said he wasn't alone in this feeling, and he thought the troika should know that the company was going to lose some of its best managers if something weren't done. Oreffice was among those telling friends he was ready to quit.

The company was rapidly splitting into two camps—Merszei loyalists, and those who felt he was destroying the "real Dow" of independent thinkers and doers, judged on their achievements and not on their loyalty to a central authority. "People are tearing each other down," rather than working together, Ted Doan soon decided, after talking to trusted friends.

Zoltan had brought some of his closest European associates with him to Midland. One was Alfred (Freddy) Hunziker, his chauffeur and general "gopher," who picked up Merszei's laundry, carried his luggage, and performed similar duties. In Europe, such a personage at the side of the chief executive was commonplace and accepted; in Midland it was an aberration. A person playing that role had never been seen in the town.

Another was W. Mark Batterson, Zoltan's talented public relations director, who helped him with speeches, letters, meetings with the press, and other chores, including planning for social events. Top managers discovered they could not always determine when a request ostensibly carried to them by Batterson on behalf of Merszei actually originated with Merszei, or when it was Batterson's own idea. If they questioned it, as some did, Batterson could reach Merszei, and get his approval on the matter and his assurance that the request truly came from him, before the questioner could; on the rare occasions when Batterson did not get there first, Merszei would call, chuckling, saying he had "forgotten" he had asked Batterson to do it. As time went on Batterson's abuses of power became more frequent and flagrant.

(On February 8, 1979, the day Merszei resigned as board chairman and left the company, Batterson was called in by Herb Lyon and fired. "There was no question it had to be done," Oreffice said later. "There was just the question of who would have the privilege." Batterson was listed on the books as having taken early retirement.)[14]

H. C. (Curt) Stephens, another Merszei aide, performed miscellaneous chores, especially as manager of a facility at the Midland Country Club, the "Dow Club," where top-level visitors were entertained by Dow executives. Merszei liked to introduce Stephens as "my pimp," which never failed to shock sedate, conservative Midlanders.

One of the directors drew up a balance sheet for Merszei at this time on a scrap of paper that he kept. On the plus side he noted: "Loves Dow, wants Dow to be No. 1, wants to be No. 1 at Dow; will do anything to succeed; works harder than anyone; great self-confidence; great intuition." On the minus side he wrote: "Impossible ego; Batterson; acts like a dictator; won't listen [underlined twice]; people lack confidence in him; "wild" image; doesn't understand Dow R & D, manufacturing, or finance; doesn't understand USA."[15]

By March 1978 there was growing revolt and a consensus among the directors, as they talked about it behind closed doors, that "we made a mistake" in electing Merszei. Some of them, and others in the company, began to urge upon Doan, Gerstacker, and Branch that they were "the only ones who could do anything about it"; they had "put Zoltan in," they could also "take him out."

The veteran threesome met and quickly decided action was in order. But what action? They agreed Merszei was not doing a good job, and they even more painfully agreed there was no possibility that anything Merszei could do to change would cure the problem. Therefore, they agreed, Zoltan should no longer be the chief executive and should be relieved of that position in the near future—in the next few months. The annual meeting of stockholders was only a few weeks away; it would be preferable to take action before then.

This turn of events put Ben Branch, especially, in a distressing position. In 1976, after becoming board chairman, he had moved his main residence to Switzerland, where he was chairman of the Dow Bank and director of several European subsidiaries, and informally he had become an advisor to the president of Dow Europe, with an office at Dow's European headquarters. Once a month he flew back to Midland, where he kept a small apartment, to preside over the board meetings. He had also purchased a residence at Marbella, in the south of Spain, where Merszei had a place. He spent much of his time traveling to Dow installations all over the world, an activity he hugely enjoyed and at which he excelled. With Branch in Europe and Doan and Gerstacker coming in only for the monthly directors' meetings, Merszei had literally been running the company single-handedly.

Now Branch felt as though he were being fired himself, he told Doan and Gerstacker, and he didn't like it. Should he have spent more time in Midland, "helping Zoltan"? Probably, but it was too late to worry about it now. He suggested an arrangement in which there would be no CEO; Branch would remain as chairman, Merszei as president would become chief planning officer, and Oreffice would be executive vice president and chief operating officer. Neither Gerstacker nor Doan liked the idea.

Gerstacker suggested an arrangement with Branch as chairman, Merszei as vice chairman, and Oreffice as president. Doan and Branch did not like the idea. Their first duty, they concluded, was to talk to Zoltan and let him react and make suggestions. "He deserves this," they agreed.

The next day Gerstacker met with Zoltan to tell him of the situation. "There is near open revolt in the company," he told him bluntly. Zoltan's leadership, he regretted to tell him, "wasn't working"; he and Ben and Ted had agreed that the situation wasn't reparable, and in consequence they had painfully reached the conclusion that Dow had to have a new CEO within a matter of months.

Merszei's reaction was amazement, shock, and disbelief. "I can't believe you and the others could feel this way," he exploded. "How can you suddenly decide such a major thing? Why haven't you told me before if you felt I was doing some things wrong? Not one of you has. If you felt I didn't have Dow people with me as their leader, why didn't you say so before, and help me?"

Dow was his "whole life," he said, and he had always done well at Dow; how could this change so suddenly? He did not believe it could; there must be some rumors flying around or some intrigue going on, and they had been taken in by it. He had had nothing but compliments on his performance and he just couldn't believe key Dow people would want to see a change in CEO—nor should Gerstacker, Doan, and Branch.

He said he had made some difficult decisions, capital questions and manpower questions, but the CEO must make difficult decisions sometimes, which hurt some of his people, and he had not been afraid to make such decisions, although he knew full well there were Dow people who opposed some of these decisions. People like Carl and Ben and Ted should support him in difficult times as well as good and not just decide he should be replaced if they thought something had gone wrong somewhere. "After all," he said, "Dow is still the world's best, most profitable chemical company, and that to me means it has been the best-managed chemical company in the past two years. How can you talk to me this way?"

At a meeting the same evening, Branch said he realized a CEO should not have to be trained on the job, but there was no gainsaying the fact that Merszei had "lost his people." He said he truly wished there was a way he and the others could be proved wrong on this; could Zoltan think of one?

Merszei said that as it happened a worldwide personnel survey was being undertaken, with all 53,000 Dow employees being asked all sorts of questions in respect to problems and morale. You three are all wrong, he said, but surely if the kind of problem you tell me about really exists it will show up in this survey. The results, he said, were due by September, five months away. It was to be a thoroughgoing job, he said. Branch said things could not possibly wait that long. Could we do a survey of perhaps the top 500 people in the company, he asked, and do it pronto?

Merszei suggested the questionnaires be mailed back to him personally, "in every language," to speed it up. In the end the idea of a survey was abandoned, only to be revived in much simplified form—a survey of board members only—at the monthly board meeting a few days later.

Those present at this four-person evening meeting would remember a wrenching, emotional outburst by Zoltan, "something like the cry of a wounded stag," that capped this pivotal discussion with the troika. Merszei launched into a wide-ranging harangue that went back to Herbert H. Dow and his problems as CEO and the backing he had received in tough times. "Up until now," he said, "this has been a Dow tradition. What we are talking about never happened before in Dow."

"If you three are against me," he cried, "who is with me? How can you be so sure you are right?"

Then he became calmer. He said he "of course" wanted what was best for the company. "I have a conscience too, you know. I am in your hands."

Events then moved with gathering speed. The survey idea proposed by Merszei some days before was revamped, stripped bare, and placed before the board of directors for their approval a few days later; in final form it would include only the 18 members of the board of directors. Doan, Branch, Gerstacker, and Merszei would not be interviewed. The interviewers would be

Herb Lyon and Julius Johnson, both scheduled to go on the deceleration program and perceived as scrupulously honest and impartial. Each would interview a group of seven of the directors (six plus himself) on whether Zoltan should remain as CEO; if there should be a new CEO, who; if there should be a new chairman, who; and any other top management changes they wished to propose. This was to be done by the end of April, when the board was scheduled to meet in preparation for the 1978 annual meeting of stockholders on May 3.

This approach, the board felt, should "clear the air" concerning the future of the company and its current management. The directors agreed to be in Midland, "for full discussions, should they be needed," the weekend of April 28-30, leading up to a full meeting on Monday, May 1.

Merszei emerged from the meeting where this plan was approved smiling and looking his usual buoyant self. "This is going to result in a vote of confidence for me from the full board of directors and get this whole sorry thing out of the way," he told one or two confidants on the board. He left almost immediately for a scheduled tour of Dow installations in the Pacific.

Two years before, Paul Oreffice had been an also-ran in the competition to become CEO of Dow. In 1978 he became the front-runner as soon as Zoltan Merszei's downfall became certain. The only other serious candidate was again Clyde Boyd, but Earle Barnes had said Boyd was "too old" two years before; now Boyd was 60 and only four-and-a-half years from retirement.

The notion of Ben Branch taking retirement and being succeeded by Merszei as board chairman quickly gained support. Branch not only had "picked the wrong guy," but, "didn't fix it when it went wrong." Merszei's move to chairman would provide a graceful exit for him, and his unmatched international expertise could continue to help the company in the foreign field. Most saw this as a temporary expedient, though, and favored Merszei moving to the chairmanship "for maybe six months." The names of Earle Barnes, Herb Lyon, Ted Doan, and Bob Lundeen floated to the surface as candidates for a longer-term chairmanship.

Now that he had more "seasoning," Paul Oreffice was the odds-on choice for the presidency. In a popularity vote among Dow employees Oreffice would win in a landslide, it was said, and it was probably true; but in the board of directors he was now favored by a rather narrow margin. Clyde Boyd was again a strong candidate.[16]

When he returned from the Pacific, Merszei resumed what became almost nonstop sessions with Gerstacker, Doan, and Branch. The results coming in from their inquiries, he was told, were a devastating commentary on Merszei's stewardship of high office in the company; on a scale of 0 to 10 he was being given a rating of 5 or less. There was a fairly even split on whether his shortcomings were reparable. He had high marks in Europe but was flunking miserably in the United States. In Latin America, the Pacific basin, and Canada his ratings were mixed. "He has not been accepted in the United States and Dow people in the United States cannot learn to operate under the Merszei style," it was reported. "And he isn't learning because he won't listen."

Zoltan's style of confrontation ("he confronts everyone," it was said), in which he often ridiculed employees before others, promoted distrust, and did not work in the United States.

His ego was unbelievable, so huge that some employees found it laughable. Some said he was not truthful, that his words were not matched by his actions, and that he used others' ideas but never gave them credit.

On the plus side he was seen as superb in dealing with government agencies and with other corporations ("but he may spend too much time in these activities"), as having a high degree of courage ("the man has guts," many employees said), and highly skillful in using the ideas of others, though not an original thinker himself.

In response, Zoltan said he felt the fall in Dow earnings and resultant steep tumble in the price of Dow stock had blinded Dow's "three wise men," as he called them occasionally, to all else. The difficulties, he said, arose from his trying to represent Dow to the outside world and run it on the inside at the same time. Things had worked very well when Ben Branch was "Mr. Inside" and Carl Gerstacker was "Mr. Outside," but he, Zoltan, had been trying to do both jobs at once, without much help from them. The fundamental things that led them to select him in late 1975 had not changed, he said; he still had the same strengths that he had then. This quick judgment of him was unfair; the company would have done even worse without him running it, he said. If there were problems of style, style is always different, and he could change his, he added.

At the board meeting of April 28, inaugurating preparations for the May 3 stockholders meeting, Merszei presented his case at some length. He had tried to do his very best, but it was becoming obvious that he had made some mistakes, and these seemed to loom larger for them than they did for him, he told the board. He spoke of the tough economy in which the company was operating, and the "big transition" for him from European to U.S. culture.

But now, I'm hearing about a lot of uneasiness, that "the troops are in revolt." I was shell-shocked when I heard this, he said; I must have been blind or deaf. I suggested a company-wide survey to get at the bottom of this. And I asked for a job performance review. Herb and Julius have done a great job on this, he said, "my first JPR in 30 years." I have heard a lot of feedback, and you heard about it. There is no rebellion in the troops, but I have learned a lot about my shortcomings and it has been a shattering experience. Maybe I needed that. My style is not understood, or did not fit, and has upset a lot of people, including some of you. I was in a hurry, and I pushed too hard, he said.

The board of directors should protect its leadership from its mistakes, even with a club, if necessary, he said. I expected this kind of help and support from you, but I didn't get it, he said, and I hope you won't mind my telling you this bluntly and reproaching you for it. I will continue to try to do my very best. I can do everything you expected when you chose me to be your leader. Every Dow employee, after receiving a job performance review, is given the chance to improve, he concluded. I need your help and support to do that.

When he had finished the room was silent and he looked from face to face with a little smile. With that the board adjourned for the weekend.

The board meeting of Monday morning, May 1, the "Mayday meeting," was quite brief.[17] A poll of the directors, Herb Lyon reported, conducted by himself and Julius Johnson upon their instructions, showed that a majority of the directors favored acceptance of the retirement of Ben Branch, which had been tendered, and the elevation of Zoltan Merszei to board chairman, succeeding Ben. As president and chief executive officer a majority of the directors had expressed their support for Paul F. Oreffice. Merszei, rising, said, "I don't suppose I should stay for the vote," and left the room.

Later that morning a terse news announcement was issued, announcing Branch's "decision not to seek reelection as chairman." Merszei was replacing him, and Oreffice would become president and CEO, the announcement added. Final action on this realignment would be taken at the organization meeting of the company directors following the annual meeting of shareholders on May 3. "A younger management can more easily cope with these challenging times, so I recommended that these changes be made," Branch said in the announcement.[18]

IV.

The 1978 Dow stockholders' meeting, the last presided over by Ben Branch, played to a full house at the Midland Center for the Arts. It had been a tough year. Jim Williams, chief financial officer, told the assemblage that the effects of OPEC oil price increases, the recession of 1975, and overcapacity in the chemical industry were still being felt around the world and that Dow was "disappointed but not discouraged" by the dip in its 1977 earnings.

Nonetheless the company had spent more than a billion dollars on its massive global building program in 1977, he reported, and more than two-thirds of Dow's gross plant was presently less than five years old. In the world's chemical industry, Dow was still the leader in profits, and it was primed to defend that title.[19]

Merszei presented the "President's Energy Award," instituted in response to the oil crisis, to employees of the Texas Division's Magnesium A Plant, who had reduced their energy consumption by 11 percent in 1977. Oreffice, still president of Dow Chemical U.S.A., accepted on behalf of the Magnesium A employees. The brief ceremony was rich in symbolism, for within an hour Merszei was also to pass on to him the baton of Dow leadership.[20]

In his final "President's Report," Merszei noted that "as soon as your board takes formal action immediately after this meeting, you will have a new president, Paul Oreffice. I will be chairman of the board. It has been my privilege to work closely with Paul from the very early days of his and my career. I know that he doesn't fear the future, as I don't. He is well prepared to cope with change and identify opportunity when others see only adversity."[21]

Of Ben Branch, he said that he "has been a fine mentor, supervisor, and above all, a good friend. We should all remember that it was under Ben Branch's leadership that we became the most profitable chemical company in the world."

In his prepared text he described what he felt were Dow's major strengths, which would serve as a foundation for continued global growth of the company. There were in his view six:

(1) Dow's advantageous positions in energy procurement, reserves, and conservation: Dow has "so many positive alternatives for energy that we are ready to go in any direction required"; (2) "The best people in the business. They produce more sales dollars per person than the employees of any other major chemical company in the world"; (3) Dow's advantageous position in living with an increasingly regulated industry: "We are in a strong position either to find substitutes for products which invite regulation or to make existing products acceptable. We realize that the best way to reduce the size of regulatory agencies is to be responsible"; (4) The company's continuing commitment to expanding research and development, "especially efforts which have taken Dow into markets which demand energy-saving products"; (5) Dow's determination to "stick to the profitable, and what we do best" while maintaining a global manufacturing and marketing mix with well established roots; and (6) Flexibility: "There are some who fear loss of markets as nations face shifting political sands; we have become adept at working with others and understanding their politics and customs."

"Our goal," he said, "is to help build a new technological wealth that will help diminish hunger, disease, and poverty in all its forms."[22]

When he had finished Ben Branch took the microphone for the valedictory remarks of a 41-year Dow career. Draping his lanky six-foot six-inch frame and long arms over the podium as if embracing it, he commented that although he was bowing out as chairman, he expected to remain a director and a full-time active employee until his 65th birthday. "I still have a little more time to help write the history of this company," he said.

Speaking without notes and becoming steadily more emotional as he went on, he delivered a long, rambling review of his Dow career, which had begun in 1937 when Dow was a small, $25 million-a-year firm. He recalled one by one the people he had worked for—Robert Heitz, Art Young, Bill Collings, Clayton Shoemaker, Ken Bowen, Ray Boundy, Donald L. Gibb, William R. Dixon, Leland I. Doan—he had learned from all of them, he said. He paid tribute to those he had worked with closely, "to whom I owe so much"—Gertrude Welker, his long-time secretary, Elmer K. Stilbert, Ray Boyer, Bill Goggin, Buzz Nelson. He praised his colleagues on the Dow Board of Directors. "The work they do is a great bargain for the owners of the company," he remarked.

At the organization meeting afterward Branch was named honorary chairman and, as decided two days before, Merszei became the new chairman and Paul Oreffice the new president and chief executive.[23] This action completed, Branch told the board that Zoltan Merszei would be a fine chairman of the board; he had done "a fantastic job" in Europe, had been the CEO of Dow at a most difficult time, and had grown in the job. He was sure, he said, that Zoltan still had a great future ahead of him.

Oreffice, in a brief acceptance speech, referred to the "American dream" he had brought with him from his native Italy as a boy; it was now coming true for him, he said. He looked forward to working with them all to help the company "keep on expanding," he said.

Two other appointments were made. Lundeen, who a few months before had been named president of Dow Latin America and had moved halfway around the world, from Hong Kong to Coral Gables, Florida, was appointed executive vice president, and would now move to Midland. David L. Rooke, operations vice president, was promoted to president of Dow Chemical U.S.A., replacing Oreffice.

V.

After all the formalities of his fall from grace were over, it proved well-nigh impossible to convince Merszei he had been demoted and that the post of chairman had been offered simply as a means of graceful exit from Dow, an honorable diving board from which he was expected to launch out into another world as soon as he could. He had seen the Ben Branch model of chairmanship, a not unpleasant life, and quickly began to emulate it.

Three days after the stockholder meeting, Gerstacker told him his salary was being trimmed. His 1977 pay from Dow had amounted to almost $500,000; as of June 1 the rate would fall to $300,000, and in six months it would drop again to $250,000, Gerstacker told him. Merszei was dismayed. He said he expected maybe no raises for a while, but certainly not a big cut. He pleaded with Gerstacker not to "disgrace" him, not to "hurt me when I'm down." Gerstacker said no, that was it, but agreed to talk to Oreffice.[24]

A fortnight later Gerstacker tried again, explaining that his new pay rate was based on his job description as board chairman. "If you don't wholeheartedly accept your job description and try to make it work, maybe $250,000 is too much," he said. "Maybe you should leave Dow."

There was more. By July 1 he was to give up his office and apartment in Zurich, and he was to stop using Freddy Hunziker. No personal services would be performed for him by any Dow employee unless specifically approved; no expenses for travel, lodging, meals, or anything else would be paid for him by Dow or any affiliate; and all of his expenses were to appear on an expense report, which would be submitted to Gerstacker as chairman of the compensation committee.

Zoltan, grumbling, accepted. By early fall he seemed to have forgotten his troubles and was complaining he did not have enough to do. He proposed he be named chairman of the nominating committee; that he rejoin the executive committee; that he be appointed to the Asahi-Dow board in Japan. He wanted to be involved much more than he was in the company, he said, and to earn more than $250,000 in annual pay.

Gerstacker told him a better idea was for Zoltan to take early retirement or quietly seek a top job at another company through some "headhunting" firm. Merszei became agitated, said he had spent his whole life with Dow, 30 years of it, and did not want to leave; he had done a great job for Dow, and should be used. It could all be worked out if Gerstacker "forced it" to work, he said.

Gerstacker replied that he couldn't "make it work," and that the kind of thing that was happening to Zoltan had happened many times to others—he mentioned Lee Iacocca, fired at Ford and a hero at Chrysler—and it did not mean Zoltan had failed. He said perhaps Zoltan should respect Carl's judgment and "allow that it may be right."

Typical of Merszei's schedule as board chairman was the fortnight following the October 5 Dow board of directors meeting, over which he presided. He left after that meeting for meetings in Frankfurt, Germany, with Prof. Dr. Matthias Seefelder, board chairman of BASF, and his colleagues. Then he flew to Madrid for a private meeting with the secretary-general of the Spanish Socialist Party, and continued on to his residence in Marbella, which he was selling. At the weekend he flew from Malaga to Pittsburgh for a dinner hosted by the Federation of German Industries. Monday he had meetings at Mobay Chemical Corporation in Pittsburgh, and then flew to Washington, D.C. for a dinner where the speaker was Ambassador Robert S. Strauss, chief U.S. foreign trade negotiator. The next morning he had breakfast with a small group including G. William Miller, Barry Goldwater's running mate for vice president. He had lunch with the ambassador of Yugoslavia at his residence. After lunch the Dow plane picked him up in Washington to bring him back to Midland.[25]

When he got back, he asked Gerstacker what new positions he had been named to in the interim. Gerstacker said he and Oreffice would like to talk to him about that, together. They told him he could not have as important a Dow position as he wanted, and if he could not accept that, he should retire or quit. Zoltan said their judgment of him was wrong, that Dow needed him, and that he was not going to leave. Oreffice should "order people to use him or sell people" on using him, Merszei said. Oreffice said, "That won't work." Merszei said, "Like I told you before, I reject your judgment."

By New Year of 1979, those most intimately involved—Oreffice, Gerstacker, and Doan—were convinced Merszei had no intention of leaving unless he was forced to, and that they had no choice but to force the issue.

Oreffice prepared a letter to Merszei offering him the options of resigning, retiring, or being fired, and giving him until the February 8 meeting of the board of directors to decide which of these options he preferred. On January 9 all three met with Zoltan, and Oreffice handed him the letter. Merszei read it quickly, and said he wanted "time to think about it." No, they said, we've been telling you this for months; we mean "immediately." Merszei said he had to get outside counsel. Gerstacker said Merszei had not accepted the situation very gracefully in April 1978, and that if he did not retire or quit now he would be fired, and being fired was the worst possible outcome for Zoltan.

Merszei again asked for time. I can't be fired "without cause," and he could not see any cause, he said. Oreffice said the February board meeting was the deadline, because that was when the proxy statement for the annual meeting of stockholders had to be finalized.[26] Merszei said he would try to meet that deadline. Oreffice said "trying isn't good enough; that is the deadline." They would be nominating a new chairman at the February board meeting, and would not be nominating him for reelection to the board. Oreffice advised Merszei to begin talking with Herb Lyon about a financial "separation package."

That was January 7. Five days later Merszei met with Lyon, administrative vice president, for a first discussion of separation details. On February 8, the deadline imposed by Oreffice, Merszei handed in his resignation. He had been Dow's chairman for nine months.

The next day a headline in the *Wall Street Journal* said "Chairman Resigns at Dow Chemical, Cites No Challenge." Merszei told the reporter he had decided to resign after he realized that only Dow's president and chief executive officer can chart the company's direction and shape its business. The chairman's job at Dow, he said, is more of a "statesmanlike post of making speeches and shaking hands. That's all right for some people," but, "I'm an operations man and a doer, and the chairmanship just wasn't enough of the kind of work that gives you the possibility to create things. I decided I'd better get out to see if I can duplicate my performance somewhere else," he said. "I haven't really given any thought," to what he might do, he said, though, "I'm very fond of Dow, and wouldn't do anything that might compete with its business."[27]

There was more news out of Dow that day. Earle B. Barnes, who had been sparring with Merszei since 1975, and not very successfully, was nominated to be his successor as board chairman. Nominated to replace Merszei as a director of the company was Paul W. McCracken of the University of Michigan, one of the top economists of his generation, a member of the Council of Economic Advisers (CEA) under President Eisenhower, from 1956 to 1959, and chairman of the CEA under President Nixon, from 1969 to 1972.

Two months later, on April 17, 80-year-old Armand Hammer, the autocratic chairman of Occidental Petroleum Company, announced the appointment of Zoltan Merszei as vice chairman of the company, a newly created position, telling the press that, "when I look at him, I see a lot of myself in my younger days." Three months later, in July, Hammer promoted Merszei to president and chief operating officer, and by October *Business Week* magazine and other publications were reporting that "if Zoltan is patient, he may someday be the CEO of Occidental."[28]

As things turned out, Merszei became just one more in a long string of Hammer heirs, the fourth president and seventh heir apparent at Occidental in a dozen years.

In a farewell interview with the *Midland Daily News*, Merszei told reporter Starr Eby that his leaving Dow "was partly my own fault, because I had a great deal to do with the shaping of the CEO as the central position in the company. I was hoping to make out of my chairmanship something like Carl Gerstacker had, but his position was partly because of his history with Dow."

He said he had no regrets, "about what I've done at Dow. I'd do it again gladly. Where would Dow be today without the contributions I gave it?"[29]

Notes

1. Dates and other information from Carl Gerstacker's personal notes and records, which he made available to the author. Oral History, Herbert D. Doan, July 29 and August 2, 1988, and January 17, 1989.
2. See, for example, Oral History, Eric Huggins, September 22, 1994, and Oral History, Zoltan Merszei, December 21, 1988, April 3, 1989, and June 3, 1994.
3. Carl Gerstacker papers. Gerstacker kept detailed, dated records during this period, most made in pencil during the meetings discussed.

4. Extensive press coverage of these events reproduced in *Dow Press Analysis*, no. 72, compiled by Dow Public Relations Dept., June 14, 1976. See also "Gerstacker Retires as Dow's Chairman," *Midland Daily News*, May 6, 1976.

5. "A Multilingual Chief for a Multinational Corporation," *Fortune*, June 1976, 27. Also Jeanette M. Reddish, "People of the Financial World: Zolton Merszei, Dow Chemical Co." *Financial World*, July 1, 1976, 22.

6. Of 150,556,880 shares voting, only 159,364 opposed the split, almost 1,000 to one.

7. Oral History, Z. Merszei.

8. Oral History, Frank P. Popoff, November 16, 1995.

9. Oral History, H. D. Doan.

10. Oral History, Thomas A. Sparta, September 26, 1996.

11. Oral History, F. P. Popoff.

12. In 1973 Du Pont sales were $6.04 billion, and net income $585.6 million; Dow sales were $3.07 billion and net income $271 million. In 1974 Du Pont sales were $6.98 billion, and net income $403.5 million; Dow sales were $4.94 billion and net income $563 million.

13. Merszei to selected Dow executives, January 20, 1978.

14. Oral History, Paul F. Oreffice, August 1, 1988.

15. Carl Gerstacker Papers.

16. According to Merszei's notes, the eventual vote was Oreffice 9, Boyd 7.

17. The events culminating in Merszei's ouster are referred to in Dow backstairs lore as "the seven days in May"; the actual dates were April 27–May 3.

18. "Branch to Retire as Dow Chairman," *Dow Today*, no. 33, May 1, 1978.

19. Minutes, Annual Meeting of Stockholders, The Dow Chemical Company, May 3, 1978; "Dow Not Pessimistic About Future," *Dow Today*, May 3, 1978.

20. "Texas Division Wins President's Energy Award," *Dow Today*, no. 34, May 3, 1978.

21. Minutes, Annual Meeting of Stockholders, The Dow Chemical Company, May 3, 1978;

22. "Merszei Cites Strengths for Dow's Growth," *Dow Today*, no. 34, May 3, 1978.

23. Minutes, Directors' Meeting, The Dow Chemical Company, no, 34, May 3, 1978.

24. Merszei had received a substantial raise effective April 1, only a month before, approved by the compensation committee the previous January. It brought his base salary to $455,000 per annum.

    Additionally, Dow executives in 1978 were earning bonuses under an incentive plan, the "Executive Award Plan," pegging bonuses to Dow earnings. The awards began when earnings reached $3.12 per share, at which level Merszei would have received a $135,000 bonus; actual 1978 earnings were $3.16. Thus his total 1978 earnings, with bonus, would have been about $580,000, if he had remained CEO.

25. Zoltan Merszei, itinerary, October 5-17, 1978.

26. A corporation's proxy statement, among other legal functions, proposes nominees for the board of directors for the succeeding year and must be filed with the U.S. Securities and Exchange Commission at least three months before the annual meeting of stockholders.

27. "Chairman Resigns at Dow Chemical, Cites No Challenge," *Wall Street Journal*, February 9, 1979.

28. "A Swashbuckler Tries His Talents at Oxy," *Business Week*, October 22, 1979, 176.

29. "Merszei Takes Occidental Job," *Midland Daily News*, April 17, 1979.

PART SIX

THE MODERN
ERA BEGINS

Dow

1979—Dow overseas sales are more than 50 percent of total for first time.

1980—Dow sales surpass $10 billion.

1982—Deepening recession, worst since 1930s, causes another 30 percent drop in Dow income. Dow sells Bio-Science Clinical Laboratories, oil and gas properties, Dow share of Asahi-Dow, reducing payroll by 7,200.

1985—Dow introduces Seldane (terfenadine), nonsedating antihistamine, in U.S.

1987—Oreffice becomes chairman, is succeeded as CEO by Frank P. Popoff.

1989—Dow net profit is $2.5 billion, company's best record in its first century.

Dow and Eli Lilly and Company pool their agricultural chemical businesses to form DowElanco, one of world's largest agricultural chemical firms.

Dow acquires Marion Laboratories, Inc., and forms Marion Merrell Dow Inc., based in Kansas City, Missouri.

1990—U.S. Patent Office study shows Dow has highest number of female patentees of any corporation receiving U.S. patents—354 between 1977 and 1988.

1992—One-time charge of $994 million to adopt new accounting standard results in net loss of $496 million, only loss in century.

1993—Dow reduces workforce by 5,900.

1994—Dow sales surpass $20 billion.

Zhejiang Pacific Chemical Company, joint venture at Ningbo, People's Republic of China, starts up propylene oxide plant, first Dow production in China.

1995—Dow sells its 71 percent stake in Marion Merrell Dow to Hoechst A.G. for $5.1 billion.

Dow takes over three former East German companies southwest of Berlin, plans to revitalize East German chemical production.

William S. Stavropoulos succeeds Popoff as chief executive.

World at large

1979—Shah of Iran is overthrown, Ayatollah Khomeini takes over government.

1981—Iran releases 52 American hostages after 444 days of captivity.

1982—British forces retake Falkland Islands after Argentinian invasion.

1985—Mikhail Gorbachev becomes general secretary of Soviet Communist Party, calls for sweeping economic changes.

1986—Space shuttle *Challenger* explodes moments after liftoff, killing seven astronauts, including teacher Christa McAuliffe.

Chernobyl nuclear power plant explosion sends radioactive fallout across Europe.

1989—East Germans allow citizens to exit country without visas; on November 9, Berlin wall begins to fall.

Chinese students on Beijing's Tiananmen Square demand greater democracy; on June 6, Deng Xiaoping sends troops who fire into the crowd.

1990—Soviet Communist Party endorses Gorbachev proposal ending 72-year hold on power in USSR, signaling end of communism and of cold war.

1991—Operation Desert Storm liberates Kuwait in 100-hour blitz following Saddam Hussein invasion.

1995—Republican conservatives roll back liberal programs during 100-day "contract with America."

O. J. Simpson declared "not guilty" after yearlong trial in century's most publicized murder case.

1996—Clinton elected to second term over Republican Sen. Robert J. Dole.

EIGHTEEN

Don't Tread on Me

I.

Does a company take on the personality of its chief executive? This seems sometimes to be the case, but when Paul F. Oreffice was Dow's chief executive from 1978 to 1987 it was such a close fit that it was difficult to say whether the company had taken on his personality, or he had taken on the company's.

He was brash and feisty and a bit arrogant, proud and patriotic and a whiz at mathematics, and he was determined never to let anyone, no matter how powerful, walk over either him individually or the company he represented. He spoke half a dozen languages fluently, loved athletic contests of all kinds, and refused to be a loser.

Oreffice was born in Venice, in Benito Mussolini's Italy, in 1927. When he was in the fifth grade, Mussolini and Hitler came to Venice, and he and his schoolmates were turned out to cheer them as they passed. They stood in the rain for two hours and then in the hot sun for four or five more, waiting. Oreffice came down with bronchitis and was ill for several months. When he was 12 his father disappeared; eight days later the family learned he had been thrown in jail by the Fascists. Twenty-five charges were filed against him, one of which was that he had said one of his horses was more intelligent than Mussolini. He was released but remained under what amounted to house arrest.[1]

Eventually the family was allowed to leave Italy with only the suitcases they could carry and $500 in money each. They sailed for New York on the U.S.S. *Manhattan* on June 1, 1940; it was the last passenger ship to leave before war closed the ports. "We had just caught our first sight of the Statue of Liberty when the news came over the radio that Italy had entered the war," Oreffice said.

With only temporary visas for the United States, the Oreffice family had to move on. Two months later they sailed again, this time to Quito, Ecuador, where the young Oreffice continued his education, this time in Spanish. Only at the end of the war did the family finally get visas for the United States. An attaché at the U.S. Embassy in Quito had told Oreffice that if he was interested in chemical engineering, Purdue was the best school for it, and he enrolled there without ever having seen it. "I haven't changed my mind about it in all these years," Oreffice said.[2]

"The first few months at Purdue were the toughest challenge of my life," Oreffice said. He was fluent in Italian, German, French, and Spanish, but had almost no knowledge of English. "I'd stay up till two, three, four in the morning with a dictionary on one side and my textbook on the other, trying to catch up with what I hadn't understood during the day," he said. By the time he graduated in February 1949 he was completely fluent in English.

He had only one job offer when he graduated, from Seagram Distillers, and he became a supervisor in a Seagram bottling plant at Lawrenceburg, Indiana. He stayed there until he was drafted into the army in January 1951, and he spent most of his military career in the Chemical Corps at Edgewood Arsenal, Maryland.

At Lawrenceburg he was still, in his words, "painfully shy," and he joined the Toastmasters Club there. "The Toastmasters Club, with its setup where you make short speeches and somebody criticizes them, probably did more to pull me out than any single thing I've ever done," he said. (When he arrived in Midland he promptly founded a Toastmasters Club there.)

In the Chemical Corps he was assigned to a group testing the chemical materials made there, "a considerable amount of wasted time," he said, "but another growing up experience."

In the army he started writing lyrics and music for popular-type songs, and began to consider music as a career. When it came time to leave the army he went to New York and spent six weeks working with an arranger and getting some of his songs recorded. He met Mitch Miller, Percy Faith, and other big names in the music world. "I came to the conclusion that it was such a racket that it wasn't for me," he said, "but I gave myself a chance to do it. Incidentally, I allowed an iron curtain to descend on that phase of my life the day I came to Midland. I never wrote another song."

He had six job offers when he left Edgewood, including offers from Du Pont and Monsanto. Pepsi-Cola, he said, offered the most money, but Du Pont had made a very good offer and was the leading candidate when he went for his last interview, which was at Dow. "As I went through the interviews [at Dow]," he said, "I got a feeling that here was a company that obviously wanted to get in the international business but didn't know a thing about it, and I had something special to offer. It was clear, all through my interviews, that international would be the thing."

Steve Starks, the Dow recruiting chief, sent him a job offer (at a pay rate that was fifth among the six he received) mentioning nothing international, so Oreffice wrote him a letter saying that if there was no clear understanding that his talents would lead him into the international business at Dow he did not wish to join the company, and would accept the Du Pont offer. He received back "the most amazing two-page letter from Bill Dixon, the assistant general sales manager, a masterpiece justifying why the offer had been made in the way it had, and finishing with, 'we want you.' So I accepted the job at Dow."

After a few weeks in the sales training program he was assigned to Dow International, which had been formed only the year before and now had offices in Zurich and Montevideo. He started as assistant on the Latin American desk, working for D. B. McCaskey. A few weeks later he was almost fired when Russ Zick in the Montevideo office asked for authorization to meet a competitive price on polystyrene and no one who could authorize it was in town. In desperation Oreffice finally decided it was better to take the business and wired Zick the go-ahead. The next day, when he told Howard Ball, the international sales manager, what he had done, Ball indignantly told him he ought to be fired and took him into the office of Clayton Shoemaker, saying Oreffice was usurping authority and doing things he was not authorized to do.

Shoemaker stopped him and said, "Let me understand this. If Paul had done nothing the business was lost, right?" "Right." "And Paul, you tried to find so and so and such and such and couldn't?" "Right." "I want you to know, Paul, that without analyzing the actual business decision," Shoemaker said, "you did the right thing."

"What a relief for a guy who thought he was being fired to have the big boss stand squarely behind you," Oreffice said. "It's immaterial that he also agreed with the decision itself. The fact that he was willing to stand by me was an unbelievable thing for me, something that taught me very much how to handle people for the future."

After a year on the Latin American desk he was put in charge of the European desk, and a year after that he was sent to Zurich, bringing Dow's European workforce to four—Ted Knapp, the first Dow European; Ted DeVries, who left the company a few years later; Zoltan Merszei, who wound up living in Holland because he had no work permit in Switzerland; and Oreffice. Dow had only two work permits in Switzerland, and after attempts to get one for Oreffice failed he went to Milan and established a Dow office there.

"I had the wonderful title of Mediterranean Sales Manager," Oreffice said, "which means I was the only Dow person covering France and Italy and Greece and the Middle East. Essentially I lived out of a suitcase. The Dow office was my suite at the Hotel Duomo in Milano."

At that time Dow did not do its own selling abroad. Its own sales force operated only in the United States and Canada, so most of Oreffice's effort to expand Dow's business in the Mediterranean area was done through distributors.

In Milan he met the lady of his dreams and became engaged to marry her. As they were making wedding plans and fixing up an apartment to move into, Jack Stearns, the executive vice president of Dow International, arrived in Milan and asked Paul, "How would you like to go to Brazil?" Dow International had decided that Brazil would be the place for Dow to begin doing its own selling for the first time outside the United States and Canada, and wanted Oreffice to go to Brazil to do this.

Oreffice went to his fiancée, Franca Ruffini, to talk to her about it. "Here I had this lady that I was engaged to, and I had to tell her, 'Stop all the arrangements, fixing up the apartment and so forth, we're going to Brazil.' And I, with great trepidation, talked to her. She said the dream of her life had always been to go to Argentina or Brazil. She said, 'When are we going?' So it was a weight off my shoulders." In June 1956, they were on their way to Brazil. Oreffice was 28.

By the time he was 50 he had fully earned his reputation for feistiness, and was the chief executive of a company that shared this trait, which was epitomized in the case of the well-publicized "spy flights" made by the Environmental Protection Agency over the Dow plant at Midland.[3]

The EPA hired an aerial survey service to make low-level reconnaissance flights over the Dow plant on February 7, 1978, to determine whether Dow was complying with the Clean Air Act, and to double-check the reports the firm was making to the EPA concerning its compliance.

Dow immediately sued the EPA, claiming the overflights amounted to illegal search and seizure, and to taking property without due process. The company's trade secrets could be determined from the photographs, and under the Freedom of Information Act such photographs might be turned over to whoever asked for them, the suit said. High-resolution photography, enlarged to mural-size proportions, reproduces intricate details, and any skilled chemical engineer with the basic knowledge of a certain process could detect Dow's manner of doing business from these photographs, the company alleged.

The flights violated Dow's Fourth Amendment (prohibiting unreasonable searches and seizures) and Fifth Amendment (forbidding the taking of property without due process of law) rights, Dow said.[4] By the time the case came to trial in early 1982 it was a widely celebrated incident, a test case cited as typical of the aggressive personalities both of the company and its CEO.

In the first instance the court held that the EPA had indeed violated Dow's Fourth Amendment rights and had exceeded its statutory authority as a government agency. U.S. District Judge James Harvey prohibited the EPA from future aerial surveillance flights over the Midland plant but also established new legal precedents: "In this age of ever-advancing and potentially unlimited technology, the government should be made aware that it does not possess 'carte blanche' authority to utilize sophisticated surveillance methods to keep watch over citizens or businesses not suspected of any criminal activity," Judge Harvey said. "As the government's arsenal of technologically advanced surveillance equipment expands, so too, the protections of the Fourth Amendment should broaden in response."[5]

The EPA appealed the case, however, and it was later reversed by the Sixth Circuit Court of Appeals in Cincinnati by a 2-1 vote. Dow then carried it to the Supreme Court, where the Cincinnati decision was ultimately upheld by a 5-4 vote in 1986. Jane M. Gootee, the Dow attorney who handled the case, felt the company would have won at the Supreme Court except that its case was joined with a flyover case involving marijuana growing. "If it had been the Dow case alone I felt we would have won," she said.

A few months earlier Oreffice had gotten into another nationally renowned rhubarb, this one with Jane Fonda, and it was perhaps the most celebrated of his jousts. In October 1977

Fonda, the award-winning actress who had sympathized with the North during the Vietnam War, made a swing around the United States raising funds for an organization called "Campaign for Economic Democracy," brainchild of her activist politician husband at the time, Tom Hayden. In a stop at Mt. Pleasant, Michigan, home of Central Michigan University and only 30 miles from Midland, she launched into a rambling attack on corporate power for which she was paid $3,500.

"We have a new body of rulers whose names you don't know and whose faces you don't recognize, but who control your life," she said. "These firms have learned to manipulate the tax laws, to get away from paying their fair share, and the middle class must pay the burden." One of these "economic giants" monopolizing the American economy and making free enterprise "virtually obsolete," she said, was Dow Chemical.[6]

Reading about it in the newspapers the next day, an incensed Oreffice, then president of Dow Chemical U.S.A., immediately wrote to Dr. Harold Abel, president of CMU. "Of course it is your prerogative to have an avowed communist sympathizer like Jane Fonda or anyone else speak at your university, and you can pay them whatever you please. I have absolutely no argument with that," Oreffice wrote.

> While inviting Ms. Fonda to your campus is your prerogative, I consider it our prerogative and obligation to make certain our funds are never again used to support people intent upon destruction of freedom. Therefore, effective immediately, support of any kind from the Dow Chemical Company to Central Michigan University has been stopped, and will not be resumed until we are convinced our dollars are not expended in supporting those who would destroy us.[7]

The Oreffice-Fonda tiff was front-page news across the nation for the next few months. Dow was acting "like a spoiled child who did not get his way," the CMU student newspaper said. Fonda said Dow was practicing "corporate blackmail." Other opinions ran the gamut from warm applause to violent opposition. Oreffice stuck by his guns, contending that business had not only the right but the duty to specify what its money would be used for. That in the end became a basis for agreement—Dow funds given the university would be used only for purposes specified by the donor.

The case was discussed in dozens of newspaper editorials. George F. Will, a widely published columnist, said that

> although Fonda fancies herself bold beyond belief, in this instance, as in most, her behavior was conventional. (One radical free-spirit nonconformist is pretty much like another.) But Dow's behavior was unconventional. It is, alas, unusual for the business community to balk at subsidizing those who detest it. . . . Capitalism inevitably nourishes a hostile class, but there is an optional dimension of this process: American business has been generous with gifts to universities—not too generous, but too indiscriminate. Dow has given the business community a timely sample of appropriate discrimination.[8]

Oreffice kept careful track of the voluminous mail he received on the case. Of the first 500 letters he received he counted 480 praising his action and only 20 opposing it. That was perhaps unrepresentative of public opinion at large, although that still, and surprisingly to many, favored Oreffice. A straw vote in the *Saginaw News* favored the Dow decision by 67 percent (419 votes) to 31 percent (207).[9]

Oreffice walked into the board of directors meeting one day to find a little flag at each director's place. It was an early version of the American flag, born when the nation was still a British colony, displaying a coiled serpent and emblazoned with the phrase, "Don't Tread on Me." Keith McKennon, in jest, was proposing that it be adopted as the official Dow company flag. Oreffice smiled, but the point had been made. A few months later he himself sponsored a task force to study how to make Dow a kinder, gentler company.[10]

II.

Fidel Castro took power in Havana in January 1959 and set about establishing the first Marxist regime in the Western Hemisphere, introducing himself to the world as a "humanist." It was only three years later, on December 2, 1961, that he revealed himself as a Marxist-Leninist and unveiled his plans to bring communism to Cuba. In the meantime the exodus of Cuban professionals to the United States had begun, a trickle at first, then growing to a steady, urgent stream.

"It was obvious that the best of Cuban society had left for the U.S.," Paul Oreffice said. "I'd like to say I knew they were going to be that good, but I didn't."

For Dow the timing was superb. It was just at this period that the company was building up Dow International and Dow Inter-American and preparing to expand into Latin America. The first wave of Cuban refugees began to arrive in Midland to take positions in these organizations in 1960. A few years later Oreffice would recruit the second wave when he organized the headquarters of Dow Latin America at Coral Gables in the Miami area, which by then was becoming "Little Havana."

Manuel Maza was in the vanguard. When Castro came to power he was the marketing manager of Dow's distributor in Cuba, and was importing tank-car lots of Dow products into the country. Maza phoned his friend Bruce Rowell at Dow International and told him, "Look, I don't want you to give me three to six months to pay anymore; from now on you must ask me for an irrevocable letter of credit first. Don't ship me anything unless you receive full payment first." He said he would explain more fully the next time Rowell came to Cuba.

Rowell flew down to Havana and Maza told him, "Look, this is a communist takeover and I don't want to have a bunch of Dow railroad tank cars sitting in my plant waiting to be confiscated when it happens." When U.S.–Cuban relations broke down beyond repair in 1960, Dow lost only one carload of goods.

Maza left Cuba when that happened, 46 years old, with a wife and seven children and no money outside Cuba. He called Rowell from Miami and Rowell told him Dow did not have a job for him at the moment but could get him a job as vice president of Ochoa Fertilizers, its distributor in San Juan, Puerto Rico, if he wanted it. Maza grabbed it, and spent the next 18 months selling Dow products there. San Juan became a way stop for Cubans leaving the country.[11]

Then Rowell called Maza and told him Dow had a job for him, and asked him to come to Midland for training. A few weeks later Maza was installed as general manager of the Dow office in Bogota, Colombia, arriving just in time for child number eight to be born there. Maza got acquainted with Ben Branch and Carl Gerstacker during his time in Midland and began to lobby for Dow to undertake a major expansion in Latin America. In 1963 he wrote a long letter to Macauley Whiting, president of Dow International, outlining the glittering opportunities for Dow in South America. Widely circulated, it was instrumental in moving this project forward.[12]

In South America Maza became a Dow recruiter, recruiting Latinos who would later occupy key positions for Dow in Latin America. Rafael Pavia, a Colombian, then a young engineer with Dow at Bogota, saw him as something of a hero. "He was responsible for the first Dow investment in Colombia," Pavia said. "Then he went to Venezuela, and then he went to Chile, and then he went to Argentina. Every place he went, Dow was emerging from the ground. He was the creator of Dow Latin America. Eighty percent of the initial investment of Dow in Latin America was Manuel Maza's idea. It was his fight. He had a lot of perseverance."[13]

Maza died quite young. Jorge Casteleiro, a lifelong friend who was recruited to Dow by him and became Dow's general counsel for Latin America, said it was diabetes. "He had diabetes as a boy, and it gets worse and worse as the years go by. He was taken to Houston. Dow sent him there. They put in plastic veins and arteries to try to save him, but eventually he died."[14]

Casteleiro was hired when Robert Prince, in charge of acquisitions and mergers for Dow, went down to Quito, Ecuador, with Dow attorney Richard Darger to discuss the acquisition of LIFE (Laboratorios Industriales Farmaceuticos Ecuatorianos), a move initiated by Maza, expecting the negotiations to be conducted in English. Dr. Alberto Di Capua, the principal owner of LIFE, told them his Ecuadoran managers and directors spoke no English and could not read English-language legal documents. "Go on back to Midland and forget about LIFE," Di Capua told them. "I'm not going to negotiate with you people in English."

Prince and Darger went to Bogota to talk to Maza, who told them, "The man you need is Casteleiro, who has law degrees from both the University of Havana and Harvard. He's in Miami. Do you want to interview him?" Casteleiro was hurriedly hired, and successfully concluded the negotiations with LIFE.

Casteleiro, Oreffice said, was "the best businessman/lawyer I've ever worked with. With all due respect to all the lawyers I've ever known, if you had a tough problem to negotiate, Jorge was the man to go to, just a fabulous, fabulous gentleman."

Another of the first wave was German Alvarez-Fuentes, whose father had owned one of the largest Cuban drug companies. He became assistant to William R. Dixon, then in the process of developing a world-class Dow pharmaceutical organization, and was closely involved in Dow's acquisition of LIFE and Lepetit, which had extensive properties in Latin America.[15]

Oreffice remembered that Alvarez-Fuentes, "a marvelous guy who died," was a former Cuban high-jump champion and member of its national basketball team. "When he was in his fifties he was the best athlete we had in Coral Gables," he said. "We had a decathlon with 16 people in it, a great thing to unify a little organization like that. Young Enrique Sosa was also outstanding," Oreffice said. "When you look at the company and you look at the people who worked down there, you find a lot of them are in very big jobs today; we really had a top-notch group." Sosa became president of Dow North America and, like Enrique Falla, a director of the company.

On April 17, 1961, when some 1,500 Cuban exiles trained by the CIA landed at Bahia de Cochinos, the Bay of Pigs, expecting to "liberate" Cuba (a fiasco in which for lack of support the invaders were quickly either killed or taken prisoner), there were three future Dow employees among them—Luis Castellanos, "Chino" Arguelles, and Enrique Falla. They were held prisoner until December 1962. (Dow, already sympathetic with the plight of Cuban refugees through the employees it had recently hired, sent a large shipment of medical supplies as part of the payment Castro demanded for their release.) Castellanos marketed Dow agricultural chemicals in the northern half of South America for most of a long career. Arguelles changed jobs several times and left Dow after a dozen years. Enrique Falla had a brilliant career with the company, becoming an executive vice president and until 1996 chief financial officer.[16] The Cubans who joined Dow were chemists and accountants, attorneys and engineers, salesmen and secretaries and most of them had highly successful careers.

Some of the Cubans, such as Eugenio Farinas, studied at Florida Atlantic University when they reached Miami, and then joined Dow. Cristobal Martinez, member of a prominent Havana newspaper family, worked in a Dow saran plant. Pedro Cejas, a chemical engineer, worked in the economic evaluation department of Dow's Western Division and then worked his way back to DowElanco in Florida. Alberto Adan, one of three brothers with doctoral degrees—his was in pharmacy—became advertising and public relations manager for Pitman Moore; when Dow sold it he became manager of translations. Pablo Valdez-Pages became Dow's general manager in Argentina, and then president of Dow Brazil.

Pedro Martinez-Fonts was Dow's general manager in Costa Rica and Mexico, and then went on to become North American commercial director for epoxy products. Rafael Miquel became Dow International's representative in Washington, D.C.; Hugo Andricain became a major manager in Dow's Louisiana Division; Adolfo Morales became a physicist in Louisiana; and Isidro Quiroga served as a business manager in specialty olefins. Some died young— Danilo Gomez, Oliver Aguero, Jose Jimenez—but the list of Cuban employees was a very long and very honorable one.

What made the Cuban transplants to Dow so successful? Oreffice said that "they're smart, hard working, but very different individuals. There's really no uniformity between them in their style; they've just proven to be terrific people." Bob Kincaid, Dow's first manager in South America, said, "the Cuban is different from the rest of the Latin Americans; they're much more like North Americans are in their mental processes."[17]

Falla said the Cubans had multiple advantages. They were well educated, many being educated in the United States; they knew the environment, the U.S. way of doing business; they were "cheap"—they would work for less than Americans; they were "hungry"—they would go anywhere and do anything; and they were loyal and honest. Cubans, Falla said, are aggressive and business oriented, so much so that they're known as the "Jews of the Caribbean"; "we are proud to be called that and it is really quite an apt description of the Cuban business mentality," he said.

Dow was not the only U.S. company to take advantage of the outflow of talent from Cuba. Coca-Cola was another outstanding example: Roberto Goizueta, a Cuban, became its chief executive officer. Rohm & Haas, in the chemical industry, also did well in this respect.

Ben Branch said the contribution of the Cuban refugees to the Dow Company was enormous. "Dow really ought to erect a statue of Fidel Castro in the center of Midland," Branch suggested, "just to recognize his help to the company."[18]

III.

In September 1978 Oreffice gathered 30 top Dow managers at Shanty Creek in northern Michigan. "Let's talk about the year 2000," he proposed. "What does Dow have to do to be a great company in the year 2000? And what do we have to do in the interim to get there?" Later he would call it "one of the most significant meetings I ever held"; it established the pattern of Dow development for a decade or more.

Diversification became the company's number one target. "Diversification came out as the absolute essential," Oreffice said, although this also implied "putting more resources into some of the businesses we were already in." The leading candidates for this treatment were pharmaceuticals, consumer products, and agricultural chemicals. As it turned out, the competitive barriers were to rise continually over the next 15 years in these fields, but there was no way of predicting that in 1978.

One of his first acts as Dow president had been to call in Sam Berkman, the founder and president of Bioscience Laboratories, a Van Nuys, California, testing laboratory later sold by Dow. "Sam," he said,

> I'd like you to be in charge of a team. Five years from today Dow is either going to be on its way to becoming a major pharmaceutical company or we get out of the business. I'd like you to form a team and start scouting for an acquisition opportunity in the pharmaceutical area.
>
> I felt it was absolutely important for Dow to get away from being strictly a basic chemical and plastic company, that we needed to go downstream. Where was the big action, the big opportunity? We had a base for pharmaceuticals—it was too small, too miserly—but that was

the place we ought to go. So I thought we ought to expand downstream in pharmaceuticals, number one; that was my first priority. And let's put more resources into consumer products and ag chemicals, and into specialty chemicals.

That began "a push to diversify but stay strong in the basic chemicals and plastics," as Oreffice put it. The Berkman team, acting on a tip from an investment banker, turned up the possibility that the Richardson-Merrell Company, manufacturers of Vicks Vapo-Rub and other products, might be willing to shed the ethical pharmaceutical side of its business, the Merrell Company. Eventually, in November 1980, this resulted in Dow's acquisition of the venerable old William S. Merrell & Company, founded in Cincinnati in 1829.

Joe Temple, then the president of Dow Latin America, was Oreffice's choice to take over what was then known as the Dow Global Human Health Group and to form a new Merrell-Dow Pharmaceuticals, Inc., of which he would be president and chief executive. Temple, he specified, would have "51 percent of the votes" in any matter concerning the development of the new firm.

"I knew I'd be in deep trouble if I ever had to use that club," Temple said, "but I was glad he said it."[19]

Temple promptly moved the headquarters of the new firm to Cincinnati, where Merrell still had its major operations, and set about building a major pharmaceutical firm.

At the same time this acquisition was taking place, Dow's consumer products line had continued to grow, reaching the $1 billion annual sales level in 1979, divided among pharmaceuticals, agricultural chemicals, and household products (they were then a single accounting category). The main household products were Saran Wrap and Handi-Wrap, Dow Bathroom Cleaner ("with Scrubbing Bubbles"), and Ziploc bags. In 1985 the household products line doubled its size (from $321 million to $593 million in annual sales) when it added the Texize line of products, acquired from Morton Thiokol, and in 1987 Dow Consumer Products Inc. changed its name to DowBrands. Joseph L. Downey, DowBrands' veteran leader and chairman, became a member of the Dow Board of Directors in 1989, giving it more clout and status than it had ever had before.

Dow's agricultural chemicals business, the other segment of its consumer specialties trade, is one of Dow's oldest and most successful businesses, dating back to 1907, when Herbert Dow began marketing lime sulfur (calcium sulfide) for use as a fruit tree fungicide—the first commercial result of his backyard experiments in applying various chemicals to the apple and other fruit trees he grew there. When he added lead arsenate spray to his product line in 1910, farm chemicals began to be seen as a distinct line of products and the agricultural chemicals department gradually took shape.

The company established its first agricultural field experiment station at South Haven, Michigan, in 1936. By the early 1980s its agricultural chemicals were a $500 million-a-year business, selling, among other products, the best line of weed and brush control chemicals on the market (2,4-D and the other phenoxy herbicides and Tordon); Dursban, the world's best-selling broad-range insecticide; and Plictran, for control of plant-feeding mites.[20]

In 1982 Oreffice called in Keith McKennon, his corporate public affairs director, and gave him a new assignment."We've got an ag business that's having some trouble," he said,"and we need to redefine it in a global context. Why don't you try creating a global ag chemical business? We'll take it out of the mainstream structure to give you a freer hand."[21]

"At the risk of sounding prideful," McKennon said,

that changed the character of Dow's ag business and I am very proud of the way the men and women of the ag business made that work. We went from a bunch of people in different regions of the world thinking first about their region to a bunch of people around the world thinking first about Dow's global ag business. If they had to develop a compound that was second best for them because it was first best everywhere else and we could only develop one because we couldn't afford the cost of developing two, they'd get onboard and we'd do it.

In addition to putting the ag business on a global footing he initiated discussions with Elanco Products Company, Eli Lilly & Company's plant sciences business, about a possible merger. These discussions "did not bear fruit because we couldn't agree on the basis for putting the two companies together," McKennon said, "but we conducted those discussions in such a professional way and with good enough feeling, even though they failed, that Eli Lilly subsequently was willing to reopen the discussion."

By that time McKennon had moved on to become president of Dow U.S.A., and John L. Hagaman had become president of Dow's global ag chemicals business. Consolidation had been taking place in the agricultural chemical industry for a number of years, Hagaman said."Du Pont bought Shell's U.S. ag business. Rhone-Poulenc bought Union Carbide's ag business. Chevron formed a joint venture with Sumitomo and then sold their part of the joint venture to Sumitomo, which in that way took over Chevron's ag business. It went on and on," he said.[22]

In February 1989 Hagaman contacted Edward R. Roberts, his counterpart at Eli Lilly, and said, "You know, the industry hasn't changed. The need for consolidation is still with us. Is there a basis for us to talk again?" That initiated talks. "We had the first talks in late February and signed a preliminary agreement in April. We signed a definitive agreement in August and closed the transaction at the end of October. It went very rapidly," Hagaman said.

The two companies agreed that they would "value" the businesses, "and then set the percentages each owned on the basis of the value of the two businesses," Hagaman said. "It was known at that time that that would result in Dow having a majority share."

The new company, called Dow Elanco (in 1990 it became DowElanco), combined the ag chemical businesses of the two firms. It was launched on April 18, 1989, with Dow holding 60 percent of the shares and Eli Lilly the other 40, which it may sell to Dow if it wishes. One of the largest of the research-based agricultural chemical companies, it had sales of $1.5 billion in its first year, ranking it sixth in the world. In the next few years the reorganization and remelding of the two organizations were completed and it was a comfortably growing corporation. By 1995 sales were $2 billion.[23]

DowElanco began building a new corporate headquarters and research center in Indianapolis in 1989 and completed it in 1994, the largest agricultural and specialty research operation under one roof in the world. It features computer-operated greenhouses that can simulate worldwide growing conditions, ranging from a 40-degree day for winter wheat in South Dakota to a 90-degree day with high humidity for rice growing in the Pacific.[24]

In the spring of 1994 it launched its first major new product, Broadstrike, a multicrop, broad-spectrum, broadleaf herbicide based on the flumetsulam molecule in the family of compounds called sulfonamides. "Broadstrike herbicide is a low-volume/high-value product, part of the new approach to using agricultural chemicals on a grams-per-acre basis," the company said. "Farmers use less of the product to achieve more crop protection."[25]

The product received EPA registration for use in corn and soybeans in October 1993, after only 24 months of data review, a DowElanco record. On the average this process requires five to seven years.

Expansion of the firm overseas had already begun with a 1991 announcement that a world-scale production plant would be built at Drusenheim, France, to manufacture active ingredients for crop protection products. In March 1995 Dow formed a joint venture to build a plant at Lote, south of Bombay, India, to make these same products, beginning with chlorpyrifos, the active ingredient in Dursban insecticide. Their partner, one of India's largest chemical firms, is National Organic Chemicals Industries Ltd., of Bombay, and the venture is called DE-NOCIL.[26]

"It's odd," reflected Frank Popoff in relation to this project, "but we are finding opportunities today in countries and markets where once we said staunchly that we would not and should not be involved." (Bob Lundeen, 20 years before, had declared India was one place Dow should not go.)[27]

The future of DowElanco was looking bright. "I think we can be one of the leading agricultural chemical companies for as long in the future as you want to look," said Hagaman. Dow was forecasting that DowElanco's sales could reach $4 billion by the year 2000.[28]

IV.

As one of the world's premier petrochemical companies, using great quantities of crude oil as a raw material to make chemicals, it was inevitable that Dow would become involved in the planet's premier oil source, the Middle East. The company's ventures into the Arab world were a roller-coaster ride that seemed never to stop.

During the oil crises of the early 1970s Dow was buying its petroleum feedstocks from the Russians, the Algerians, the Iranians, the Kuwaitis, and the French. The big European chemical companies generally had alliances with major oil companies for their oil supply—ICI with Phillips, BASF with Shell, Hoechst with Caltex—but Dow remained independent and played the field.

The Soviet Union became Dow's principal source of naphtha, with Dow buying 1.2 million tons of Russian naphtha annually under a 10-year contract negotiated by Steve Marshall, the Dow purchasing chief in Europe, to feed the big cracker at Terneuzen in the Netherlands. When the price of crude oil began to climb, the Russians frostily informed Dow that they were either going to increase the price or stop shipping—which option did Dow prefer? Dow responded that if the price were raised it would expect a quid pro quo—a longer contract or larger volume, for example.

While this discussion was going on, the Dow purchasing staff scurried about the world buying naphtha wherever it could find it. Dow became the first firm to move naphtha from Iran in bulk; it signed contracts with Kuwait and Algeria as well.

When the Soviet Union carried out its threat to stop shipping, Dow, to the astonishment of the Russians, stopped a payment of $62 million. The Russians could not believe a firm with Dow's reputation would renege on payment. Dow explained that withholding the payment represented an offset against potential loss and that the contract was very clear: "If you pump we pay, and if you don't, we don't."

Popoff led a Dow delegation to Moscow to talk to the Soviets. "I got to go to Moscow on a regular basis until we sorted that out," Popoff said.

> In the process we knew our [Moscow] office was bugged, and yet we weren't always sure. On one occasion we had a very stiff meeting the first afternoon we got together with the Russians, didn't have dinner together, went our separate ways. We Dow people agreed that when we went back to the office we would talk some more and say, "We can't possibly make any concessions. We're not authorized to make any concessions. This is a terrible thing. We have to go back and talk to them but the impasse will go on. We have no flexibility," etc., and we agreed that during this conversation we would refer to Stan Buck as "William," his name being William Stanley Buck but always known as "Stan" (Buck was the longtime chief hydrocarbons trader for Dow in Europe).
>
> The next morning we went in, and the Russians obviously had heard what we said at the office and knew we had no flexibility. They basically needed to get their $62 million back, so suddenly they were not the stiff, formal Russians of the evening before. They were now very cordial, to the point of saying, "And William, how are you!" Keeping a straight face was the hardest thing we had to do.[29]

"Dow came out of it with a compromise that gave us a permanent discount of 2.5 percent," said Buck. "The price of oil then collapsed, and they lost $42 million because of the change they introduced. This rankled for many years and the Russians stopped supplying us."[30]

Ben Branch, then the CEO, was convinced very early that Dow had to expand its petroleum sourcing to those parts of the world where feedstocks were plentiful and inexpensive. That meant the Middle East, where the bulk of the world's oil and gas reserves were located. At the beginning of 1973 he and Merszei had long discussions with their colleagues on the subject. The Mideast countries were inviting chemical companies to come and help them make petrochemicals out of their oil; it seemed clear that Dow should accept the invitation, but should it accept that of Iran, or that of Saudi Arabia?

Merszei and Branch both felt Iran was a more favorable environment for a Dow project because of its westernized Shah, but they decided to pursue both possibilities and later on perhaps choose the one that offered the best chances.

In May 1973 a Dow delegation flew to Saudi Arabia to open negotiations with Abdulhady Taher, governor of Petromin, the Saudi oil giant, who was responsible for such projects. Led by Zoltan Merszei, the Dow task force included J. M. (Levi) Leathers, the company's hydro-carbons guru; Steve Marshall; and two attorneys, Robert E. Jones and Alfred S. (Al) Farha, who spoke Arabic. Their goal was an arrangement under which Dow and the Saudis would build a major chemical complex in Saudi Arabia; this would open the door, they hoped, to a Saudi "oil entitlement" to Dow of 250,000 barrels a day, which the Dow management badly wanted as feedstock for the proposed Crude Oil Processing Plant (COPP) in Texas.

Farha became Dow's key negotiator, and a year later he and Taher signed a Letter of Understanding; this became the basis for a feasibility study then to be made, looking toward a final agreement and the project itself. The process proved to be long and labyrinthine. Farha spent much time in Saudi Arabia and began to get acquainted with the Saudi royal family and government officials, including Prince Saud al-Feisal, later the Saudi foreign minister, and Sheikh Ahmed Zaki Yamani, the kingdom's petroleum minister and a leading figure in OPEC.

In 1975 King Feisal was assassinated by his own nephew and the crown passed to his half-brother, King Khalid. With the new king came a new set of faces, and the Dow negotiations were passed to a new minister, Ghazi Al-Gosaibi. A year later Al-Gosaibi formed Saudi Basic Industries Corporation (Sabic), and it assumed responsibility for all the petrochemical ventures on the Saudi docket.

Also in the chase for Saudi oil and petrochemicals facilities were Exxon, Mobil, Shell, Celanese, and Mitsubishi.

The Dow team continued working on the feasibility study, and on February 15, 1977, reached an interim agreement, the "Sabic-Dow Jubail Petrochemical Complex Interim Agreement," signed with suitable pomp in Riyadh by Al-Gosaibi and Farha. Andrew Butler, now the president of Dow Mideast/Africa, flew in from Geneva for the signing, which went well except that Butler narrowly avoided being jailed.

Accompanied by other Dow people, Butler was snapping pictures of veiled Bedouin women in the Riyadh marketplace when he was pulled aside and arrested by the Saudi police for this forbidden activity. He was escorted to the courthouse steps in the center of the city, where an open-air trial took place with a white-bearded imam as judge. Farha announced, in Arabic, that he would serve as Butler's attorney. The trial was serious, for foreigners were frequently imprisoned for lesser offenses than this in conservative Saudi Arabia, the heart of Islam.

A crowd gathered at the courthouse steps as the trial commenced, and a gaggle of fun-loving children began to call for Butler's execution—for him to be beheaded with a sword. Farha told the judge Butler was "but a humble plastics salesman," and that he was trying to take pictures not of the Bedouin ladies but of some plastic containers on sale in the marketplace. He took the film out of Butler's camera and threw it to the ground, saying that the camera didn't work, anyway. "We were not under oath, you see," Farha said, "so I could exaggerate a bit." As the religious leader pondered his decision, Farha slowly backed away with Butler, saying to the imam in Arabic, "May Allah find favor with you and your descendants for your mercy." They got into a nearby taxi as the crowd jeered, and drove safely away.[31]

The work on the feasibility study dragged on for another two years. It was only in 1981 that a joint venture with Saudi Arabia finally was concluded and on May 20 it was unveiled; it had taken eight years to reach this point.

The complex would be called "Petrokemya," the Sabic-Dow joint company that ran it would be called the Arabian Petro-Chemical Company, and Sabic-Dow would invest $1.5 billion to build petrochemical plants in the Jubail industrial complex of eastern Saudi Arabia. The $1.5 billion price tag made it the biggest project Dow had undertaken to that point.

At the heart of Petrokemya would be an ethane cracker producing 500,000 metric tons of ethylene per annum. The complex would produce 180,000 MTPA of polyethylene. Construction was to start early in 1982, and the facilities would come onstream in mid-1985, as would a 300,000 MTPA ethylene glycol plant.[32]

Jubilant that the years of negotiations had finally borne fruit, the Dow organization sprang into action. The Texas Division of Dow prepared to train technicians and engineers for Petrokemya, the bulk of them Saudis who would first spend 6 to 12 months in language training and "orientation to American life" in Albuquerque, New Mexico. Joe A. Ward, superintendent of Polyethylene 1, was appointed manager of Petrokemya training.

H. H. McClure, general manager of the Texas Division, saying the project was "very important to the future of Dow and the Texas Division," asked Dow employees to "do all we can to make them welcome with true Texas hospitality. These folks will be a very long way from home, in a strange land, and working hard. We can all help to make their time here pleasant and productive."[33]

All of these dreams and plans came crashing to earth in the summer of 1982, when Oreffice told his colleagues that he was sorry but the project had to be killed, and the sooner the better.

That set the stage for the final act. David Rooke, president of Dow U.S.A., flew to Zurich to talk with Colin Goodchild and Dick Bechtold, who had taken over the Saudi negotiations earlier. "We of course concluded that the best position for Dow would be to withdraw from the project," Goodchild said. "This would not be easy: we had made a lot of commitments; we had spent money, of course; the engineering had started; people had been recruited and were getting ready to get into position; we had an office in Saudi Arabia run by a guy named Charlie Jacobs who was representing us on the spot on a daily basis; and of course we had to be careful of our reputation."

Frank Popoff joined Goodchild and Bechtold and they flew down to Riyadh to tell the Saudis. "Frank had to bear the brunt of the major conversation with Al-Gosaibi," Goodchild said, and Goodchild was assigned to "clean up the final details, and that turned out to be not a very easy task." Goodchild and R. William Barker of Dow's legal department, the Dow attorney responsible, closed out that chapter of Dow's involvement in Saudi Arabia.[34]

"I can well remember being called by Frank Popoff on a Saturday afternoon in August 1982, to come to his house and read a letter from Paul Oreffice," Farha said. "The letter was clear and said we should do everything we could to get out of the Saudi project now. Frank did not like that decision, and neither did I, and although a strong effort was made to change Paul's mind, in the end we were left with little choice but to exit the venture in the most acceptable manner."

On December 1 Dow announced that it was withdrawing from the agreement to establish Petrokemya. "During the course of the extensive Dow-SABIC negotiations, the global petrochemical industry has experienced slower growth in demand which has reduced the need for additional capacity," a Dow news release said.[35]

Oreffice was trimming Dow's sails furiously in 1982, one of the worst profit years for Dow on record. In the spring the company sold its interest in Asahi-Dow, its oldest foreign joint venture; it was purchased for $231 million by the Japanese partner, Asahi Chemical. In August Dow sold Sam Berkman's Bio-Science Enterprises, at Van Nuys, California, which was in the business of developing and marketing clinical tests to the health industry; American Hospital Supply Corporation acquired it for $120 million. In October Dow sold its holdings in Dow Chemical Korea and Korea Pacific Chemical Company to the Korea Explosives Group for $60 million. In November it terminated its joint petrochemical venture in Yugoslavia, on the island of Krk (effective January 15, 1983), by giving notice to the Yugoslav partner, Industrija Nafte (INA). In December it dissolved still another partnership, the D-H Titanium Company, a joint venture with Howmet Turbine Components Corporation.[36]

The big shock was the Saudi venture, however, burst like a bubble at the end of nine years. Petrokemya became a wholly owned Saudi project, and eventually a successful one.

"There was a faction, a strong faction on the board and in the company, that felt that that's where Dow's future was," Oreffice said. "They felt that Du Pont had done the right thing by buying Conoco, and that we were going wrong by going downstream—we should be backward-integrating. I wanted to avoid that route."

Dow's relationship with Iran dated from the early 1960s, when W. W. (Bill) Allen, manager of the agricultural chemicals department, persuaded the company to invest $2 million in an Iranian company that was to build a model agricultural development in the Khuzistan region of Iran, using Dow's farm chemicals. John Deere, the farm implement manufacturer, Citibank of New York, and other firms both Iranian and non-Iranian were investors.

When it became clear that the Iranians expected Dow to provide chemicals free of charge, John Deere to provide farm equipment free, and Citibank to lend money interest-free, Bill Allen looked for a way out. There didn't seem to be one, and he finally dispatched Farha to

Teheran with instructions to get Dow out of the company even if he had to lose the $2 million investment.

While Farha was negotiating he met another visitor to Teheran, Hisham Naraghi, a customer for Dow products he knew, who had extensive pistachio and almond plantations near Modesto, California. Naraghi was having even more problems with the Iranians than Farha was, but said perhaps he could help.

The next day Farha was called out of his meeting and offered $2 million for Dow's shares in the company by Naraghi. In consternation the Iranians promptly agreed to buy Dow's shares, to prevent their falling into the hands of Naraghi. Farha returned to Midland with a cashier's check for $2 million. "The enemy of my enemy is my friend," Farha said, an old Arab proverb. It was a lucky event for Dow; a year later the venture went broke.

Dow's exploration of the possibility of a petrochemical complex in Iran did not take as long as it did in Saudi Arabia. Paul Stroebel, Merszei's business development director, already had contacts in the Shah's government, and most of the Dow Iran team members were the same ones pursuing the Saudi project. The Iranian proposal called for a chemical complex at a place called Bandar Shahpur (now called Bandar Khomeini), on the Persian Gulf near the Abadan refinery of the National Petrochemical Company of Iran (NPC).

In June 1974 the managing director of NPC, Baghir Mostophi, came to Horgen to sign a Letter of Intent with Merszei. Dow was to own half of a world-scale ethylene cracker and derivative plants at Bandar Shahpur amounting to a $500 million investment. Dow would put up $50 million, and the rest of the capital would be generated by interest-free Iranian government loans.

The Shah of Iran was in Zurich that day, and Mostophi and Farha visited him at the Dolder Grand Hotel, where the Shah gave his approval to the Letter of Intent with Dow. Merszei and Mostophi then signed the formal agreement and Dow proceeded with the feasibility study.

In June 1975 the Shah abruptly changed his mind and announced that all Iranian projects involving foreign investors would be 75 percent owned by Iran. He thereby contravened the agreements that had been reached with these investors, including Dow. Dow told NPC that in view of the Shah's pronouncement there was no longer a deal. NPC asked Dow to reconsider, and Dow said it would reconsider if Iran kept its word. After a year of discussions Dow pulled out of the Bandar Shahpur project completely in the summer of 1976, and as events transpired it was one of the company's luckier decisions.

Mitsui Chemical Industries of Japan replaced Dow in the project, expanded on it, and eventually invested more than $1 billion in it. When the Shah was ousted in 1979 and the Ayatollah Khomeini came to power, all foreign properties were nationalized. The Bandar Shahpur complex itself was completely destroyed in the war between Iran and Iraq in the 1980s, and Mitsui took a heavy loss that would otherwise have been Dow's.

Another piece of luck involved an old pharmaceutical plant in Teheran built by the Lepetit firm, which was among those nationalized by the Ayatollah. Dow contested the takeover and in the end, under the auspices of the World Court in The Hague, received a $3 million payment from the Iranian government, together with an order for $8 million worth of pharmaceutical intermediates.

One interesting incident that occurred as the Ayatollah came to power in Iran involved a wandering Dow Styrofoam plant. Andrew Butler and Dow Mideast/Africa had decided to put a Styrofoam plant in Iran to serve the needs of the entire Gulf area. (Styrofoam is used extensively in the Middle East to insulate against heat.) The plant had been operating in Canada and was movable on skids; in due course it was loaded onto a ship headed for Iran and arrived there just as the Iranian Revolution was breaking out. In the nick of time Dow called on its newly appointed Styrofoam distributor in Kuwait, Mohammed Said Al-Naqeeb, to get the plant out of danger, and Al-Naqeeb was able to divert the ship and get it and the plant into Kuwait. Eventually the plant was sent to Sharjah, in the United Arab Emirates, where it was set up and went into operation in 1980.

Al-Naqeeb became a key person in Dow's history in the Middle East. Of Iraqi origin, he had both Iraqi and Kuwaiti citizenship; his uncle had been destined to be the king of Iraq, but the British chose the Hashemite King Feisal and the uncle was exiled to Egypt. The family had extensive properties and date plantations in the Basra area; Al-Naqeeb's wife was related to the ruling Sabah family of Kuwait.

Also among the most important of Dow's contacts in the region was Sheikh Ahmed Juffali, often listed among the world's billionaires by *Fortune* and *Forbes* magazines. The Dow people first met him in 1973 in connection with the Saudi project; E. A. Juffali Brothers was the most prominent business family in the Saudi Arabian kingdom. The Juffali family at that time was building up a collection of joint companies with German and American companies, and Zafer Husseini, the Juffali manager in eastern Saudi Arabia where the Jubail project was scheduled to be built, entertained many of the Dow visitors to the area and took a personal interest in the Dow project.

The Juffali firm became Dow's distributors in Saudi Arabia through formation of a joint-venture company. In 1977 Dow and Juffali established joint offices in Jeddah and Riyadh; Dow sales grew from $2 million to $40 million under the direction of a young Palestinian, Souhail Farouki, a Ph.D. chemist from the University of Nebraska. Dow and Juffali built a Styrofoam plant called Arabian Chemicals Company in Jeddah, and a carpet latex plant in Jubail.

Dow's history in the Middle East has suffered more than its share of disappointments, but at the end of its first century the company was still hoping to develop a project similar to the big dream at Jubail that went awry. This one would be in Qatar, on the Arabian Gulf.

V.

Paul Oreffice was not one of those people you could feel neutral about. He had both admirers and detractors, probably more of the former than the latter, although some of the detractors were venomous enough to offset a great deal of admiration.

A nonsmoker, he made the Dow headquarters in Midland a smoke-free area; at first certain areas were set apart for smokers, but soon these too were eliminated, and in 1986 areas outside the buildings were established as the sole smoking areas. The example of headquarters quickly set the pattern for Dow worldwide, and the company became one of the pioneers in providing a smoke-free environment. Oreffice would hardly have won a popularity contest among the company's smokers.

An abstemious drinker, he banned alcohol on the company's executive aircraft, but after considering that people who were not Dow employees were sometimes passengers, he relented and permitted beer and wine.

A straight arrow, he would not abide any degree of dishonesty. "You can't be a little dishonest," he said. "It's like getting half pregnant; there's no such thing. You can't be half honest."

He recalled an instance in his early days as Dow manager in Brazil:

The guy with the sales tax came in and said, "I'm going to shut you down for a couple of weeks if you don't pay me off." I said, "Shut us down." Well, when he didn't get anything two days later, he left. I know of another American company that paid once, and then the next tax guy, and the next guy, and the next guy, was there. It compounds very strongly. They knew Dow wouldn't pay, so they stopped bothering us.

Oreffice "is one of the most dynamic, charismatic and effective people I've ever met," said Keith McKennon, who worked with him as closely as anyone, "but in fairness I'd also have to say that he is a very strong-willed man. He doesn't suffer fools gladly. He's a very proud man who has a lot of conviction in his beliefs and a man who one crosses at one's peril, and particularly in any visible, public way."[37]

Oreffice and McKennon developed "a knack for communication," McKennon said.

He came to respect my judgment, which I was quite free and candid with, but almost always in private. I was one of those people, and there were only two or three, who were quite comfortable with saying, in private, "Boss, I think you got this one wrong. I wouldn't do that. Wouldn't this be better? I see a lot of downsides here." We were somehow able to develop a thing where I was comfortable being a little bitty banana opposite the bunch; but the bunch was very comfortable hearing pretty directly from the little banana and respected what he heard.

The low point in Oreffice's career occurred in the early 1980s when a behind-the-scenes palace revolution threatened, an event in some respects similar to the one that had ousted Merszei a few years earlier. Concerned with his aggressive public stance and other matters, the company's directors began asking each other privately, "Where is Paul taking us? Should he continue on as our CEO?" This crisis was caused partly by the company's miserable financial performance in those years, partly by Oreffice's prickly behavior, and partly by a variety of other reasons.

After a good deal of closed-door debate, the board of directors dropped the matter. "We were just coming out of a recession," Frank Popoff (then president of Dow Europe and Oreffice's eventual successor) said of the incident later, "and my comment was a simple one: The worst thing we can possibly do now is to get involved in some sort of a succession issue in terms of who might best replace Paul, or should anyone replace Paul. A number of us took that attitude and said, 'This is no time for this kind of a deal.' We got past that in pretty good shape."[38]

A chastened Oreffice, to the surprise of many, proceeded to reorient the company to a kinder, gentler path. "That was us," McKennon said, "We were the 'Don't tread on me' company. How far that has changed! The seeds and the elements for that change were planted in that time frame [1983-84]. During that period Dow transmogrified from the company that sets up antiaircraft guns to shoot down EPA flyover planes to the company that exists today."

The changes were proposed by an Oreffice-sponsored task force called "the Futures Group," led by Richard K. Long, later the corporate communications director. The group produced 13 detailed projects, ranging from the "Dow lets you do great things" television commercials (perhaps Dow's most successful television presentations of the twentieth century; they came to a close in 1996) to a heightened program ("Visible Scientists") designed to give Dow scientists an opportunity to present the scientific viewpoint on various issues of the day on which they were expert.[39] Over the succeeding years the "Futures" program made Dow a less combative and more cooperative, conciliatory organization.

"Convincing Paul about that was not the world's easiest assignment," McKennon said,

> because it's quite a different tack than "Don't tread on me." To his everlasting credit, while I wouldn't say that he chose to get up and lead the band, in his own quiet way he said to me, "I'll quiet my rhetoric on the other side of this. You guys go work on the band. Let's go do that." So he was supportive of that and it was a challenge for him to come to that change. And if I am proudest of one contribution, having been there at a moment when we could create, if you will, and make viable, the "Futures" thing, and then let it occur—I really think that changed the character of the company. I think that was one of those changes that are fundamental in terms, and that last—a watershed event.
>
> And where in the 1980s did that occur? It occurred on Paul's shift, with his advice, consent, and tacit support. It made The Dow Chemical Company a different company, and I think, had we not done it, we'd have regretted it as long as there was a Dow. So I felt good about that.

Looking back over his career, Oreffice said that

> what I think has been incredible is the people we have in this company and the vision they've had. When I came to work here [in 1953] everybody in management was a conservative mid-

westerner. How these guys had the vision to understand that the rest of the world out there was something they ought to be doing is incredible. They felt uncomfortable with foreigners; I was "different" when I came here. I spoke with an accent. I combed my hair straight back. (I once was told, by the guy who ran sales, that I'd never make it in sales if I didn't part my hair.) And the change they've been able to bring! How these people were able to broaden is just incredible. When I first went to Brazil I was told by a member of the top management, "Just do whatever business you can, but remember Dow isn't going to put any of its hard-earned dollars overseas." And we went from that attitude to the kind of company we are today. It's really a remarkable achievement.

Top management people "like Gerstacker and Doan," he said, "deserve a huge amount of credit in that they had the guts to take an immigrant like me and do what they did with me."

It's not that I became the head guy; I was on the board of this company when I was 43 years old. That's an unusual age, and I hadn't worked here in Midland except the first two years. I give these people a tremendous amount of credit for doing things like that. Now it's easy; now we're doing it all the time. We're a big international company. We do have people from all over the world. But it wasn't that way 30 or 35 years ago, when they took a 28-year-old guy and slammed him down in Brazil to create a company. I constantly tell our managers today, "I hope you have the guts to do things like that, because it's too easy to get comfortable as you grow and just put people you're comfortable with in different jobs."

It couldn't have happened in any other country, Oreffice said. "No question about that—an immigrant like me could not have become the head guy of a large company in Germany or in Japan or in Brazil or wherever. This could only happen in this country. I've had a ball and intend to continue to have a ball," he said.

Notes

1. The Oreffice family's difficulties under the Fascists in Italy are described in some detail in Ralph Nader and William Taylor, *The Big Boys* (New York: Pantheon Books, 1986), 143-95.
2. Oral History, Paul F. Oreffice, August 1, 1988 is quoted extensively in this chapter.
3. "EPA Flyover Threatens Dow's Trade Secrets," *Brinewell* 37, no. 3 (May-June 1978): 18-20.
4. For further detail concerning the legal issues involved, see "One Picture Is Worth a Thousand Words," interview with Jane F. Gootee, attorney, *Brinewell* 40, no. 6 (Nov.-Dec. 1981): 16-20.
5. "Court Rules EPA Flyover Was Illegal," *Brinewell* 41, no. 2 (summer 1982): 3.
6. Sharon A. Johnson, "'Economic Giant' Dow Attacked by Jane Fonda," *Midland Daily News*, October 11, 1977.
7. P. F. Oreffice to Harold Abel, president, Central Michigan University, Mt. Pleasant, Michigan, October 12, 1977.

8. George F. Will, "The Incandescent Fonda," *Washington Post* and other newspapers, November 3, 1977.

9. "Today's Ballot Box Question," *Saginaw News*, November 2, 1977.

10. Some of the headquarters humor was more pointed. When Oreffice ordered construction of underground parking at the Dow executive wing it was immediately dubbed the PUKE (Parking Underground for Key Employees) project, a name that stuck. Levi Leathers who refused to park there was presented with a garage opener, complete with a plate labeled PUKE, at his retirement.

11. Oral History, Jorge S. Casteleiro, March 13, 1991.

12. "Do we believe in Latin America?" Letter, M. Maza to M. Whiting, September 4, 1963, circulated by Clayton L. Dickey, Advertising/Public Relations, Dow International.

13. Oral History, Rafael A. Pavia, March 11, 1991.

14. Oral History, J. S. Casteleiro.

15. Author interview, Alberto Adan, October 4, 1994.

16. Author interview, Enrique C. Falla, September 28, 1994.

17. Oral History, Robert F. Kincaid, July 8, 1991.

18. Oral History, J. S. Casteleiro.

19. Oral History, Joseph G. Temple Jr., October 28, 1988. For early Merrell history see Henry S. Enck III, "William Stanley Merrell, Cincinnati Industrialist" (M.A. thesis, University of Cincinnati, 1965).

20. See *Global Agriculture Is Our Business*, brochure published by Global Agricultural Products Department, The Dow Chemical Company, 1986.

21. Oral History, Keith R. McKennon, June 9, 1993.

22. Oral History, John L. Hagaman, May 18, 1992.

23. See "Dow, Eli Lilly to Form Global Agricultural Products Company," "Open Letter to the Citizens of Midland," signed by Joe Temple, Executive Vice President, The Dow Chemical Company, April 18, 1989; and subsequent news announcements (*Dow Today*) of April 18, 1989; May 11, 1989; June 28, 1989; August 15, 1989; August 22, 1989; September 15, 1989; and January 17, 1990.

24. "DowElanco: Improving the Quality of Life Around the World," *Dowfriends*, spring 1995, 5.

25. "Launching the Flagship of DowElanco's New Fleet—Broadstrike Weed Control System," *Brinewell* 53, no. 1 (spring 1994): 19.

26. "DowElanco Europe to Build Worldscale Plant in France," *Dow Today*, no. 69, June 12, 1991; "DowElanco Plans New Product Plant in India," *Midland Daily News*, March 6, 1995.

27. Oral History, Frank P. Popoff, November 16, 1995.

28. See "Dow, Eli Lilly to Form Global Agricultural Products Company," *The Dow Quarterly Report* (stockholder quarterly), First Quarter 1989.

29. Oral History, F. P. Popoff.

30. Oral History, W. Stanley Buck, July 12, 1989.

31. Alfred S. Farha, "Dow in the Middle East," personal communication to the author, December 10, 1994. Many details in this account of Dow's history in the Middle East are derived from this document, for which the author is most grateful.

32. "Sabic-Dow Joint Venture to Go Ahead," Dow News Release, Texas Division, May 20, 1981.

33. "Saudis to Train at Dow Texas Division," Dow News Release, Texas Division, July 13, 1982, and "Ward Named Manager of Petrokemya Training at Dow," Dow News Release, Texas Division, July 13, 1982.

34. Oral History, Colin D. Goodchild, May 1993.

35. "Dow Chemical Withdraws from Saudi Arabia Petrochemical Joint Venture," Dow News Release, Texas Division, December 1, 1982.

36. See Dow news releases: "American Hospital Supply to Acquire Bio-Science Enterprises," August 8, 1982; "Dow Agrees to Sell Its Korean Operations," October 11, 1982; "Dow to Terminate Yugoslav Venture," November 23, 1982; and "Dow and Howmet Agree to Dissolve Joint Venture," December 28, 1982.

37. Oral History, K. R. McKennon.

38. Oral History, F. P. Popoff.

39. See "Futures Program, Phase II Report and Action Plans," Richard K. Long to M. C. Carpenter and B. M. Klumpp, December 7, 1983.

NINETEEN

DOWNSIZING

I.

When Paul Oreffice reached mandatory retirement age in 1987, the transition to Frank Popoff at the top of the company was one of the smoothest and least controversial in the company's history, in part because it was prepared well in advance. Joe Temple might have been a candidate to succeed Oreffice, but he was only a couple of years from deceleration, and he was riding the company's most ferocious tiger, the Merrell-Dow pharmaceutical firm, from which no one, including Temple himself, wished to see him dismount. Another likely candidate was Keith McKennon, also an executive vice president of the company, but McKennon refused to be a candidate.

"A couple or three directors asked me what level of interest I would have in being considered for Dow Chemical's chief executive officer," McKennon said. "My position on that was 'Frank [Popoff] is better qualified and better skilled for that job than I am, and I will support him and would not accept a draft. First, I think more people would vote for him, and second, I think they should.'"[1]

As early as 1984, in a conversation at the Inn-on-the-Park in London, Oreffice had talked to Popoff, then president of Dow Europe, about the succession. "If events go as ordained," Oreffice told Popoff on that occasion, "I may be asking you to come back [to Midland] next year. If I do, it's not for your smiling face; it may be as my replacement as CEO." In 1985 Oreffice did ask Popoff to return to Midland, and he spent the next two years as heir apparent.

Popoff was the son of a Bulgarian army officer, a veteran of the Balkan wars of the early twentieth century decorated for valor by Bulgaria's king, Ferdinand I. In the political chaos that followed these wars his father emigrated to the United States and joined the American Expeditionary Forces under General John J. Pershing, serving with the AEF in Europe during World War I and earning American citizenship in the bargain.[2]

547

On a trip back to Bulgaria the seasoned soldier married a student at the University of Sofia, and Frank, their youngest child, was born in Sofia in 1935. When World War II broke out the family set out for the United States. Popoff remembered going through Ellis Island as a small boy and being deloused there by a man who yelled at him in English he couldn't understand.

The family went to Terre Haute, Indiana, where there were other Bulgarians, and opened up a dry cleaning shop, which did quite well. At Wiley High School he played football and basketball. "I could run very fast," Popoff said, "which probably preserved my life on numerous occasions." The chemistry teacher there, "Buck" Weaver, sparked an interest in chemistry.

He followed an older sister and enrolled at Indiana University, where at the end of his third year he was accepted into dental school. "I did very well," Popoff said. "I was third in my class of about 120 students," but in his second year of dental school he went to the dean and told him he thought he'd made a career mistake and wanted out. "I don't think I'm going to make Indiana a very good dentist," he told him. He switched to a new MBA (Master's in Business Administration) program and to chemistry, receiving both an undergraduate degree in chemistry and a graduate degree in business in 1959.

During his last year, having married Jean, a fellow student, the summer before, he worked in the college placement office. He had problems filling the interview schedule for Dow Chemical (in 1958 Dow had abruptly canceled its campus recruiting at the time of the Black Friday incident, and it was in bad odor on many campuses in the spring of 1959), so he signed up for the last slot on the Dow schedule himself. He had already decided to go to work for Reilly Tar and Chemical in Indianapolis, where, he said, "the management seemed rather senior and I thought, 'What a great opportunity for a young man.'"

In the middle of his interview with Fred Peacock, the Dow recruiter, Peacock got a phone call that his wife was presenting him with a child. "Frank," Peacock said, "I can't conclude the interview, but would you come to Midland?" Popoff, feeling trapped, said he would, and wound up entering Dow's sales training program. "I basically came to work for Dow," Popoff said, "by virtue of trying to make sure that this good company wouldn't say, a year or two later, 'Those guys from Indiana didn't fill our interview schedule; let's wash our hands of Indiana.'"

He served an apprenticeship in technical service and development and in the Cleveland sales office, and then became an assistant product sales manager in Midland, responsible for a grab bag of brominated compounds that were by-products of Dow's huge ethylene dibromide business. By his 30th birthday he was the marketing manager for transportation chemicals, mainly antifreeze and brake fluid.

He remembered that

we won the Ford brake fluid business when Mr. Lee Iacocca took a new Lincoln out of the Wixom (Michigan) assembly plant one day equipped with disc brakes, brand new at the time. Apparently Iacocca was riding his brake pedal and overheated his brake fluid and had poor braking performance. The next morning he said, "I want a 450-degree boiling point brake fluid, and I want it now." We said, "Well, we'd have to get SAE [Society of Automotive Engineers, which establishes various standards for the industry] approval for that." He said, "I want the product now. Whoever can do it gets all of our business."

Dow had a fellow named Joe Schrems, blind he was, who came up with a formulation that filled the bill and we got the Ford business," Popoff said. "We've had Ford's business ever since, and it's been a terrific relationship. Thank you, Mr. Iacocca. Maybe more importantly, thank you, Joe, this wonderful man who was absolutely blind but was a genius at formulating brake fluids."

His success in marketing antifreeze in the United States through the major oil companies (Dow-packaged antifreeze was sold at corner gas stations under the gasoline marketer's label) led to an assignment in Europe to introduce the same concept there, and he soon knew the words for antifreeze in German, French, Swedish, and Italian. The experiment was so successful that Dow Europe asked for his services full-time. The Popoffs (he was 32) packed up their three children, ages two, three, and five, took a Berlitz course, and headed for Europe. He and Jim Norbury became the chemicals marketing team in the embryonic Dow Europe organization.

"These were the wild and woolly pioneering days when much of your job was dedicated to making sure you had the product as well as making sure the customer agreed to buy it," Popoff said. "Some of our selling was more internal than external in those days."

Dow in those early days in Europe was seen as "cowboys selling excess capacity," Popoff said. A favorite story that circulated in European chemical circles concerned the Saudi prince who had three sons, he remembered. On his birthday, the oldest son asked for a car, and the prince bought him a new sports Mercedes. The second son asked for a boat on his birthday, and the prince bought him an elegant Italian racing boat. The youngest son asked for a cowboy outfit on his birthday, and the prince bought him Dow Chemical.

"That story was told over and over and over again," Popoff said. "We were called 'the cowboy outfit' by the press and media. If I'm proud of one thing in the 10 years I spent there it was that we went from 'cowboy outfit' to being really prime movers in the industry."

After only 30 months in Europe Popoff, to his astonishment, found himself back in Midland as manager of agricultural chemicals marketing. "I thought I had done something terribly wrong, frankly," he said. "I knew nothing about agricultural chemicals." Within a short time he was working on Dursban insecticide (and Reldan, its methyl analogue) and developing applications for it on Egyptian cotton and paddy rice in Asia.

A year later Earle Barnes decided to merge the agricultural chemicals department and the organic chemicals department, and moved the organics chemicals department into the ag chemicals building. "The original shotgun marriage," Popoff said. "He was very unhappy with the organic chemicals department for reasons that are his own."[3] Bob Naegele and Frank Popoff had the task of reorganizing the department.

It was his first experience with downsizing. "It's never difficult to downsize if you're willing to promote your best people," he said. "We promoted the best people, and found that the next level of people were just as good as the people they were waiting to replace."

"We consolidated a lot of jobs," Naegele said. "We made some of them a lot bigger than they were before, and usually those left over went somewhere else. We had to let some go because we couldn't find a home for them. Most of them were not incompetent; they were just underjobbed."[4]

"The oil shock came along and saved our bacon, frankly," Popoff said. He remembered, for example, Schenectady Chemical, "a great customer for Dow phenol—they were big in phenolic resins for wire coatings and laminates. We took their price from 9 cents to 34 cents a pound in one fell swoop because they recognized we could not supply them at the previous price. Oil was not $2.50 a barrel any more; it was $12.50 or $13 a barrel after the oil shock, so huge increases were needed on all these things."

Popoff went to Clint Braidwood, the president of Schenectady Chemical, and said,

"How would you like to be given a nice piece of ground in Freeport, Texas, free of charge, to build a new plant on, for tearing up the old contract and writing a very competitive, sensible new one?" Braidwood said he'd like to see the property and take pictures of it, after which Schenectady would make a decision. Eventually the deal worked out, and Schenectady Chemical built a satellite plant at Dow's Texas operations. "They have a lovely plant in Texas, and it's going strong," Popoff said. "They've expanded and expanded. It's one of our better satellite facilities there."

When Naegele moved on to become president of Dow Chemical Canada in 1975, Popoff succeeded him as general manager of Ag-Organics; but now his mandate from Oreffice (who had succeeded Barnes as president of Dow U.S.A.) was to preside over the divorce of the two departments. "Hunter Henry picked up organics and John Donalds picked up ag, and I went to Europe in less than a year's time," Popoff said. "It was a better ag department and a better organics department by virtue of the split up."

He spent the next nine years of his career in Europe, rising from marketing manager in 1976 to president in 1981, and joining the Dow Board of Directors in 1982.

Along the way he was picking up a reputation for making tough decisions when they had to be made. In 1979, when hydrocarbon raw materials costs were spiraling out of sight, he went to Clyde Boyd, the president of Dow Europe, and proposed that Dow unilaterally shut down production and stop selling in Europe. Dow did.

"In 1979, naphtha prices had gone off the map," he explained.[5]

The Shah of Iran had fallen, crude oil was costing up to $50 a barrel and naphtha up to $500 a ton. Yet we were locked in on product prices, although our raw materials costs had gone up on a skyrocketing basis to these $500 levels. I knew the Russians (from whom Dow was buying naphtha) and the oil companies wouldn't relent. But we also had done our homework and knew that there was not an excess of chemical capacity in Europe, so we took a gamble, because we knew we could not afford to sell at those prices.

I said to Clyde, "It's your area, but as far as I'm concerned I'd like to give our guys a furlough from selling and send them in to talk to their customers and say, 'Look, we're not here to renege on anything, but you know that we can't sell at these prices considering our raw materials circumstances. We'll relieve you of any contract obligations, but go get the product elsewhere, because this is not a business we can do.'"

Our competitors loved it. People laughed at us and said, "You're cutting your own throats." BASF laughed and made public statements saying, "The cowboys are on their way home." Within two days they realized they didn't have enough product to meet demand. It had been a very hard winter, ethylene supply was diminished. Prices soon went back to an appropriate level. This cascaded from Europe to the U.S. to the other areas, and we [Dow] got a major shot in the arm, a big spike in earnings at that time.

The incident also earned Dow some grudging recognition from the European chemical industry. When a recession hit in 1982 Popoff got a phone call from an executive at a large German firm, asking, "What are you going to do now?" "What are you talking about?" Popoff asked. "You stopped sales and got prices back up in 1979," the German said. "Now we're back in the pits again." Popoff said, "Yes, but this is a different ball game; there's plenty of supply out there." "Well, you have to do something," the German said.

What Popoff did on that occasion was to convene a symposium (at the Dolder Grand Hotel in Zurich) of the entire European chemical industry. The idea was to "see if we can harmonize the premises under which we're managing the European chemical industry." "In a very legal way, a series of studies came out of that meeting," and "by the time 1983 was over, many of the marginal plants in Europe had been shut down." Japan piggybacked on that and "they shut down 30 percent of their ethylene production at the same time," he said.

"I couldn't have called that meeting if we had not made a transition from being cowboys, if you will, to being members of the fraternity, and now we certainly are."

II.

Sea changes in both the political world and the business world began to occur, rather unexpectedly, around 1985. The "global village" became a reality. The end of the cold war in 1989 crystallized and hastened these changes, and the impact upon a worldwide firm such as Dow was intense and immense.

"While we at Dow talked 'global,' and probably meant international in the 1960s and 1970s, globalization became a reality only in the middle 1980s," Popoff said.

Finance and financial products became global only then. It's only in the decade beginning then that you could borrow yen or float financial issues in Japan, or that you could repatriate lira, or that you were welcomed in financial markets in a variety of places which formerly had been denied you, due to currency and investment restrictions. That broke the logjam. In the middle 1980s the financial products became universal and we began to understand that both the movement of money and the velocity of that movement were unprecedented. That, to my mind, preceded the diminution of trade and tariff barriers, which are really rather recent vintage phenomena. GATT and NAFTA are important passages in a process; this world was protectionist until not all that long ago.

The end of the cold war shifted the mindset dramatically, he said.

Raw material and energy prices began to harmonize and logistics made products vulnerable to arbitrage, so that, for example, polyethylene prices in the U.S., Europe, and the Pacific Rim all came together. Intellectual property and know-how and the willingness to transfer technology became a reality because people felt better about being able to protect it. And finally, work and workers began to be more mobile than ever before, and technology facilitated that.

Dow found itself in a suddenly global world, "and now we do need a global strategy," he said, "which is not to say you can have global implementation; you can centralize strategy and strategic planning, as you must, but boy, you better make sure the implementation is done as close to the customer on as local a basis as you know how."

Global competition brought with it pressures to cut costs more severe than even such super-cost-conscious firms as Dow had ever experienced before. Before long those pressures began to translate into what among other euphemisms were called "Rifs" (Reductions In Force), "downsizing" (the most popular term), "rightsizing" (popular with business executives), or "reengineering the corporation" (a favorite of academic writers). Whatever the label, it meant slashing the corporation's working population, often by draconian means. Globalization brought about this same phenomenon in virtually every large company, worldwide, and many not that large, and since the middle eighties downsizing has become a beat that still goes on as a new century approaches.

Following the 1958 debacle, when Dow had fired 10 percent of its workforce in the spring and summer and then began hiring again in the fall, the company's top officers had sworn they would do everything they could to avoid a repeat of that unsavory episode. Twenty growth years later this resolve had faded, and by 1981 the company reached the peak employment of its first 100 years—64,000 employees.

In the dismal economic year of 1982 many large companies laid off thousands of employees. The Dow population dropped by 7,200 that year (a record for the company to that time), but most of the reduction occurred because of divestitures and attrition. The company did offer an incentive program for early retirement, and 2,000 employees chose that option.

"The sweeping layoffs which characterized much of industry in 1982 were avoided by Dow, and we continue to consider that the most unacceptable form of personnel reduction," Paul Oreffice reassured the company's shareholders and employees at that time.[6]

The problems of overstaffing continued to plague the company throughout the 1980s and into the 1990s. At the end of 1985 Dow offered another retirement incentive program, and again about 2,000 employees took advantage of it. "It was a very humane program, but it wasn't effective for our shareholders and didn't achieve what we wanted," Popoff said.

"Then what happened? Business got terrific and I could not prevent the hiring that transpired," he said.

> It wasn't an orgy of hiring, but people saw our business really strong and said, "How can we possibly harvest this business, on this curve that we're extrapolating into the next century, unless we have more people on board?" We hired folks. One year we hired over a thousand more than we should have in the U.S. area. We realized that some of the things we needed to do in terms of internal supply were better done outside the company—outsourcing—that some things shouldn't be done at all, and that competitiveness was now redefined by a new global economy where your competition was not other fat U.S. companies but people that no one had ever heard of, in Taiwan or Thailand or somewhere else not previously renowned for making chemicals or plastics.

So Dow entered this era of global changes "a little overstaffed," Popoff said, wondering whether it could "grow its way out of this." After a lot of agonizing, "we said, 'Let's see what we can do with a combination of less hiring, redeploying people, and addressing performance.' I don't care who you are, at any point in time you have some people who aren't carrying their weight. We did fine on the redeployment, we did fine on the hiring, but our people just had an awful time with the performance."

> People aren't willing to say to you, "Frank, I've been telling you, the last couple of times we've gotten together to evaluate your performance, that your daily work hasn't been as good as it should be. You've made some improvement (or you haven't improved, as the case may be), but I see a leaner Dow on the horizon. I think if the wolf comes close to the door, as he very well may, you ought to be looking elsewhere" [for employment]. That's not a hard thing for me to say, but it must be immensely hard for other people. What they wanted was a program where they could say to somebody, "Gee, Frank, you're a wonderful fellow, so when I see you at the supermarket or the ball game don't be angry with me. There's nothing personal in this, but you gotta go—and the devil made me do it."
>
> We didn't stress performance. Being fired should be a very individual thing; it should not be a collective exercise. The 5 or 10 percent of your people that you lose, that's a real hardship for them and for you, but think about the other 90 percent. Instead of appearing to preserve the viability of the organization and their work, what you're doing is making 90 percent of your organization say, "There but by the grace of God go I. If they are counting off in fives and shooting every fifth person, I may be the next number five."

The Dow Company "has never been altruistic," he said,

we have fired people for as long as I can remember. We've probably fired fewer people summarily today than we ever have before. Today losing somebody is a ritual under the aegis of employment practices and policies. Dutch Beutel never worried about it; he just fired you. "You're outta here. Goodbye." Maybe it's our culture, but I don't object much to what we did—we had to do what we did. We had to ramp up the hiring a little bit on the premise that business was going to continue to be terrific forever. That not being the case, and redeployment and growth not being enough, we had to let people go, but I was not terribly happy with how we did it.

Everybody says to me, "Gee, Frank, you're a good guy; we know it wasn't you." BS; it was as much me as anybody else. I don't want to come out of this as the good guy. My hand was in this as much as anybody else's; but what people recognize is my criticism of how we did it. We didn't do it very well. Some of the best terminations don't look like terminations at all.

Popoff let it be known that any employee who was let go and wanted to talk to him about it was welcome to do so. "I've talked to over 400 people in my office who have been let go," he said.

The problem is a simple one—people aren't ever going to retire anymore; they're going to wait to get laid off. I've talked to tons of people, very good friends and some people I'd never seen before. A supervisor has to be held accountable for not just going through the ritual but for doing it in a way that preserves the dignity and goodwill of the individual, because we're letting some good people go; they're just not the best. We're not firing incompetent people. You know, we're not really firing that many people, but let's call it firing because if I try to call it anything else people are going to say, "You're hiding." We're letting people go who are individually fine, totally adequate, but not the best of the best. If we were losing the best of the best, we ought to shoot the management.

I really hated it. What we have in the training and development of these people is priceless, and not just because they're friends but because they're tremendous assets and investments. I'm sorry we're losing any of them. That notwithstanding, I think we've done a relatively good job compared to other companies, but you can starve to death on comparisons.

The heaviest downsizing at Dow occurred in 1993, when about 6,000 employees were let go. Another 2,000 were shown the door in 1994. In 1995 the global payroll declined by 14,200, but most of that reduction represented the sale of Marion Merrell Dow and the Latin American pharmaceutical business, which employed 11,100, a subject to which we will return shortly.[7]

In both 1995 and 1996 the company hired about 400 new employees, but by the end of 1995 its rolls had shrunk to 39,500 employees worldwide compared to 63,800, the highwater mark at the end of 1981—a decline of 38 percent.

In contrast, over that same span the company almost doubled its sales, from $11.9 billion in 1981 to $20.2 billion in 1995.

The Dow Company culture did not change at all during this time, in Popoff's view.

The Dow folks are special; they really take care of each other. The culture is strong and I hope we never lose it—honestly, it's what sustains us. I don't know how to quantify it and I guess nobody does, but it's as important to our succeeding in China as our technology, our capital, our political connections, or anything else. Dow people will tough it out and get it done. You hate to disappoint them and you don't know how to measure the damage that's done by letting people go.

The only thing I worry about, or ever have from the first day worried about is losing the goodwill of Dow's people. We ain't the classiest folks in the world, with the best pedigree. We don't always have the best technology. We certainly aren't the best capitalized. I don't know what the hell we are. Except we're successful. And I think I understand that. I have asked incredibly difficult things of Dow people. They've delivered. I've never been disappointed by Dow people, and I know I've disappointed them.

He remembered something said, he thought, by Herb Lyon or Max Key: "I don't know if I've ever motivated anybody, but I sure as hell know when I've demotivated people." "That's very, very difficult," he said. "We are a very human company. I hope we never change. That's our culture."

III.

In 1989, that watershed year when the Berlin Wall toppled, the Soviet Union fell apart, and the Iron Curtain crumbled, Frank Popoff and the Dow Company were intent, even as the world changed around them, upon a strategy designed to rebuild the firm into a series of "basic businesses." These would be freestanding, self-governing organizations making and marketing related groups of products. The company's line of consumer products (now called DowBrands), was one of these basic businesses; agricultural chemicals, pharmaceuticals, chemicals and related products, plastics, and hydrocarbons were the others.

Six years later, at the end of 1995, the basic businesses were reorganized into 15 distinct business groups, and these business groups became the global driving forces in a company reacting to a changing world and renewing itself to face a second century.

Two of these "basic businesses" came into being in 1989—DowElanco, the agricultural chemical business (see chap. 18), and Marion Merrell Dow, the pharmaceutical house.

Joe Temple, at the helm of Dow's pharmaceutical operations, was building a world-class ethical drug house in 1989, and he had two acquisition targets—Rorer Pharmaceuticals, with its strong line of over-the-counter pharmaceuticals, and Marion Laboratories, which had a strong in-licensing program and was a marketing powerhouse. "At that time, we said to ourselves that the ideal combination would be we acquire Rorer, we acquire Marion Laboratories, we blend it with what we have, and that would be perfect," Temple said.[8] In the years 1985 to 1989 Merrell Dow was a roaring success; its annual sales climbed from $500 million to $1.3 billion.

Early in 1989 there were rumors that Marion was a takeover candidate, and Temple's colleague Dave Sharrock phoned a friend at Marion, Fred W. Lyons, Jr., its president and CEO. "In the event Marion Laboratories decides to make itself available (for acquisition)," Sharrock told Lyons, "call us. Put us on the list."

Not too long after that, Marion did call, and negotiations quickly got under way. Dow's acquisition of Marion was announced on July 17, 1989, after what Temple called "a horrendous night before," when he and Bob McFedries, the Dow negotiating team, spent all night in the office accompanied by Enrique Falla, Dow's chief financial officer. The Marion Laboratories board was also in an extended meeting, and communications flew back and forth between the two groups all night.

"The Marion people gave us a long lecture about the role of the board of the new organization, and what the composition of that board should be," Temple said, "and we had discussed all that." They wanted to be sure they were run as a pharmaceutical firm, not as a chemical company.

"Look," Temple told them, "we're tired of hearing about the responsibilities of the board of directors. Let's cut it off and either make a deal or not." That was "rather rude," he said, but, "the next morning they ended up making a deal on the terms we had agreed to, and which the Dow board had already approved."

As a first step, Dow acquired 39 percent of the outstanding stock of Marion at $38 per share, for a total of $2.223 billion. Added to other sales and its own holdings, Dow soon had 51 percent of the firm.

A key point in the negotiations was that Temple, then close to his 60th birthday and scheduled to go into the Dow deceleration process, agreed to reverse field and not go into deceleration—the only case where this occurred in Dow's first century.[9]

Instead, Temple agreed to go to Kansas City, Missouri, where Marion was located, as its chief executive, and stay on while Merrell-Dow and Marion merged into a new Marion Merrell Dow. This required his prior retirement from Dow; and to take on these new responsibilities Dow offered him a cash payment in lieu of his retirement pension and other forms of pay, the total amounting to a tidy $5 million.

"I said 'Thank you very much,' and went down to Kansas City," Temple smiled. "I'm not sure it wasn't worth more than $5 million because I've always said that 'Mergers are a bitch.'"

He had not yet met Ewing Marion Kauffman, "Mr. K," founder and grand old man of Marion Laboratories (the firm name came from his middle name), owner of the Kansas City Royals baseball team, who had at first opposed the deal, but the two hit it off extraordinarily well. Kauffman soon became supportive and helpful.

"Marion Laboratories probably had the premier sales organization in pharmaceuticals in the United States," Temple said, "and I think Marion Merrell Dow also had that." It had no research worth the name, however, and fairly mediocre manufacturing facilities. "Manufacturing is just not important to traditional pharmaceutical companies," Temple said.

The early days of Merrell-Dow, born in 1981, had been difficult. The firm made no profits at all from 1981 through 1984 as Dow Pharmaceuticals and Merrell were merged; reductions in personnel, the closing up of old plants, and the selling off of unrelated businesses were the order of the day. Beginning in 1985, however, Merrell-Dow prospered, reaching a sales level of $1.3 billion in 1989. Combined with Marion the sales volume leaped to $2.3 billion in 1990 and then in the following three years climbed rapidly to $3.3 billion. Earnings increased roughly 20 percent per year in 1990, 1991, and 1992.

Marion Merrell Dow was looking like what Dow had always wanted—a big winner in the pharmaceutical field. "It contributed $2.5 billion in earnings to Dow during a lean period in business," Popoff observed. Then the bottom fell out.

What happened, Temple said, was a "revolution" in the pharmaceutical world, set off when Glaxo Group Ltd. of Great Britain acquired the Wellcome corporation in the United States for $15 billion and became the world's largest pharmaceutical house. The pharmaceutical world was turned upside down. "These mega-mergers characterized the change that took place," Temple said, accompanied by a "tremendously focused and increased emphasis on reduction in health care costs, which included pharmaceuticals." Bill Clinton had come to the U.S. presidency in 1992, and health care reform was high on his list of priorities. In the end his reform measures failed to pass Congress, but the national debate on the subject did focus attention on reducing health care costs.

"The belief (in pharmaceuticals) was that you had to be big, rationalize, and spread your research costs across a whole lot more sales, or you were going to be eaten alive by these companies that were going through the mega-mergers," Temple said. Almost overnight the perception was that "if you weren't big, you couldn't succeed." That perception was right, Temple said, "with the caveat that if your research and development is productive and produces at a reasonable rate products which are new and really meet unmet needs, you could be very successful at Marion Merrell Dow's size."

"Our sales got up to $3.3 billion, and that's a good-sized company," Temple said. "We were about the size of Upjohn—their sales are in the same range—but under the new rules, that ain't big enough."[10]

"The definition of 'big' changed," according to Popoff. "The definition of big was a $5 billion company not so long ago. The definition of big now is $10 or $12 billion."

In February 1993, "it became very clear to us that we were not going to make our earnings per share plan for 1993, and we acted right away," Temple said. "We had what we call Rif I [Reduction In Force]—at that time we just called it Rif—and we ended up reducing the population of Marion Merrell Dow by probably 700 people. Our sales and earnings dropped that year and at the beginning of 1994 we decided we hadn't done enough. So we had Rif II and reduced another 700 or more associates and made some other economies." (MMD's workforce at the beginning of these moves was about 9,000.)

THE WIZARDS

A s Dow headed into its second century its reputation for putting up with "odd ducks" remained intact.

Among those upholding this reputation were a dazzling duo known as "the Wizards," probably the world's most outstanding analytical scientists in the field of the dioxins—and the only part of this statement they would disagree with is the "probably." Formally they are Dr. Lester L. Lamparski and Dr. Terry J. Nestrick of Dow's Analytical Laboratories in Midland, but they are almost never formal and wear T-shirts and blue jeans to any event, no matter how dignified. They were once asked to leave a posh Canadian restaurant, upset at this violation of its dress code, when they arrived to dine at the invitation of the Canadian government. The T-shirts they wear often bear a message they consider appropriate to the occasion. Frequently the message, and their language, much of it profane, is critical of their employer, The Dow Chemical Company.

Lamparski resembles a long-haired, red-bearded Viking. Nestrick affects an Apache hair style complete with headband and black mustache. Neither corresponds to the common stereotype of the neatly groomed, white-coated laboratory chemist.

Their arrogance is close to legendary; like Muhammad Ali, the boxing champion, they freely proclaim that they are the greatest. "There's only one person who can do it better than us and He doesn't live on earth," Nestrick told a newspaper reporter.[1]

Nestrick and Lamparski burst onto the scientific scene in the late 1970s—they were about 30 then—when they published some highly original work on the "trace chemistries of fire." They supplied the data necessary for this hypothesis and for developing mechanisms that explain how it is reasonable. This work indicated that the dioxins are ubiquitous—they occur naturally as a function of the burning of many substances—are not new, and are not exclusively a product of chemical manufacturing.

The "trace chemistries of fire" theory was widely questioned by the scientific community at the time, but that did not bother the Wizards. In the intervening years it has slowly won grudging acceptance, and the Wizards have won a widening reputation for sticking by their scientific findings. "We knew we were right," Nestrick said. They went on from there to become the preeminent technicians of dioxin analysis and world-class analytical scientists.

Warren B. Crummett, the Dow research fellow who led the way in trace analysis, turned these analytical "whiz kids" loose on dioxin in 1976 when it was coming to the fore as a national and global issue. In the years since that time dioxin has continued to draw headlines, and the Wizards continue to add to their laurels.

Crummett listed some of their "firsts":

- First to find chlorinated dioxins in the standard urban dust sample (as defined by the National Bureau of Standards);
- First to find chlorinated dioxins in soil and dust from cities other than Midland;
- First to find chlorinated dioxins in automobile mufflers, cigarette smoke, and wood soot;
- First to find chlorinated dioxins in a sealed sample of municipal sewage sludge (which had been exhibited at the 1933 Chicago World's Fair);
- First to discover the presence of 2,3,7,8-TCDD (commonly called dioxin) at the part per trillion level (in fish from Midland's Tittabawassee River);
- First to separate all 22 isomers of tetrachloro-dibenzo-p-dioxins and all 10 isomers of hexachloro-dibenzo-p-dioxins;
- First to determine the 2,3,7,8-TCDD isomer specifically;
- First to analyze water for dioxin at a part-per-quadrillion level, "with repetitive reliability sufficient for the regulation of effluent from an industrial site";
- Among the first to prove de novo synthesis of the chlorinated dioxins in a fire.[2]

Officials of the federal Environmental Protection Agency have called their work with dioxin analysis "unequaled." They sometimes receive mail addressed simply to "The Wizards, Dow Chemical, Analytical Labs, Midland, MI 48640"—from the National Bureau of Standards, from university professors, and from prestigious research institutions.

One of their managers, Lemayne B. (Wes) Westover, officially banned the "Wizards" name, but the mail kept coming and he finally stopped telling them they couldn't use the term. "We've had teams other than the Wizards work on these things, but not with the kind of results that the Wizards get," Crummett said.[3]

The reviewer of a manuscript to be published by the World Health Organization commented that

> The work of Lamparski et al. is first rate. The Dow scientists pioneered much of the analytical work relating to determination of chlorinated dibenzo-p-dioxins (CDDs) and dibenzofurans (CDFs) in the environment and they are still leaders in this area. Their methods have been adapted or modified by many other laboratories and in several round-robin investigations the Dow methods have proven to be among the most effective.[4]

Nestrick and Lamparski criticize Dow management for its "inability to relay their dioxin work to society," which they say contributes to public confusion about dioxin. "We already have world-class science and capabilities," Nestrick said. "Now Dow has to establish it has world-class management."

Nestrick says, "as far as I'm concerned, it doesn't matter if I take something apart and look for dioxin or some other wonderful compound we're interested in. Separation is just something I enjoy."

In their more than 20 years working together the two have learned to trust each other's work even though they frequently have professional disagreements and argue with each other "about two or three times an hour."

They do agree that they are the best research team in the nation. "Everybody's got to be the best at something," Lamparski said. "Right now we don't have any competition," Nestrick said.

1. Julie Morrison, "Wizards at Work—Dow Scientists Lead Nation in Trace Dioxin Hunt," *Midland Daily News*, March 12, 1984.
2. From Warren B. Crummett, "Dioxin: Molecule or What?" an account of the Dow analytical work on the dioxin molecule, unpublished manuscript which the author was privileged to read on loan from its author (1994), 362.
3. Oral History, Warren B. Crummett, April 15, 1993.
4. The paper was "Compound-specific HRGC-LRMS determination of Halogenated Dibenzo-p-dioxins and Dibenzofurans in Environmental and Biological Matrices."

These moves were successful, and excluding any of the impact of the Hoechst acquisition (which took place in the spring of 1995) Marion Merrell Dow's 1995 earnings were "significantly above 1994 and way above plan," Temple said. At the Hoechst takeover the company was "in pretty good shape on a short-term basis, and with research coming around, in my view, and that's very hard to predict, I think the prospects are pretty good," he said.

An added 1994 pressure on Marion Merrell Dow was that it was facing loss of exclusivity on its two big sellers—Cardizem, a medication for high blood pressure and angina, and Seldane, a nonsedating allergy pill. Cardizem (the generic name is diltiazem) was a billion-dollar product, and Seldane (generic name terfenadine) was approaching it.

"The perception was that we had a pipeline that was not going to be productive in the near term and that we were going to lose exclusivity on our two big products," Temple said. "We did not lose exclusivity on either one of these products because we did things that involved a whole myriad of rather complicated steps to extend that exclusivity."

If you create a line extension and do the clinical tests required by the Food & Drug Administration to get it approved, he explained, then you get three years of exclusivity.

We had three-times-a-day Cardizem, two-times-a-day Cardizem, and now the new product was a once-a-day Cardizem, Cardizem CD. A once-a-day drug is much more likely to get compliance from patients than other dosage forms, so we were able, through educating physicians and other techniques of telling our story, to get people switched from the regular Cardizem (called Cardizem SR) to Cardizem CD, and Cardizem today is still a billion-dollar product between the United States and Canada. The patent has expired on Cardizem, but our exclusivity continues.

"Pharmaceutical companies have cycles based on the exclusivity of their products expiring," he explained, and there was much talk of MMD's potential loss with the patents expiring on Cardizem and Seldane.

"What really hurt Seldane," he said,

was that in mid-1992 we had a labeling change which resulted in what they call a "black box"—a box of black type on the label—specifying that Seldane was contraindicated in concomitant use with erythromycin and a product called ketoconazole. Ketoconazole is a very rarely used drug, and that had always been on our label. Our scientific and medical data say it's not a problem with erythromycin but the FDA insisted it was and we agreed to the labeling change. One of the other major products that competes with Seldane has the same problem, but Claritin, our main competitor, didn't apparently have that problem, so their message to doctors is, "Why take a chance?"

No product has ever been approved for over-the-counter (OTC) use with a "black box" on it, and Marion Merrell Dow's strategy had been to take Seldane from a prescription product to over-the-counter, Temple said. "Pre-black box we would have had the largest ever anywhere in the world switch of a prescription product to an OTC product if we took Seldane over-the-counter," he said. "That really hurt. Who knows what causes stock prices to rise or fall, but coincidental to the announcement that we were going to have a 'black box' on Seldane, our stock went down six points."

"We were never able to convince the security analysts or the press or whoever that we had a powerful pipeline which was going to result in big new products in the period 1992 through 1996," Temple said. "That's the period everybody worried about, and we called it 'The Valley.' Our strategy was to fill The Valley. You can only cut costs and reduce people so much, and then you had to go out and get new compounds."

We in-licensed a cholesterol-lowering drug called Lescol from Rhone-Poulenc, and it competes with Mevachor, which is Merck's big drug; Rhone-Poulenc decided to bring Lescol out at half the price of Mevachor, and what they wanted was somebody who had really good marketing capabilities in the United States, particularly in the cardiovascular area. We got another product called Losec from Astra-Merck and we're copromoting Losec with Astra-Merck and its product in the anti-ulcer area that Carafate is in, Carafate [an antiulcer drug] being one of Marion's big products; we have a good franchise in the antiulcer area.

In 1993 Marion Merrell Dow acquired the Rugby-Darby Group, largest distributor of generic products in the United States, with annual sales of $300 million. That gave MMD marketers the capability of packaging together the MMD prescription products and the Rugby generic products, or "bundling," especially to the growing number of health maintenance organization (HMO) customers. "For two or three years now, based on surveys with HMO organizations themselves, Marion Merrell Dow has had either the number one or number two position in regard to their value as a supplier to HMOs," Temple said in late 1995.

In the press, Marion Merrell Dow began to be spoken of as an acquisition candidate. "There were three or four pharmaceutical companies in the United States that for some years people concluded were potential acquisition candidates, mainly because of their size," Temple said. "Upjohn was one of them; they're gone (acquired by Pharmacia, a Swedish pharmaceutical house). G. D. Searle was; now owned by Monsanto. Syntex was another; Roche bought Syntex. Marion Merrell Dow was another. So it was not a big surprise that the street (i.e., Wall Street) would project that Marion Merrell Dow would be sold."

It was Dan Dorfman, Wall Street columnist and TV pundit, who pulled the trigger. Dorfman called Doug Draper of Dow press relations in the spring of 1994 to ask whether Dow was planning to sell its shares in Marion Merrell Dow. Draper phoned him back and said, "Mr. Popoff says Dow's action will be dictated by the best interests of Dow's shareholders." "Does that mean you'll sell Marion Merrell Dow?" "No," said Draper, "it means Dow's action will be dictated by the best interests of Dow's shareholders."

Dorfman concluded that Marion Merrell Dow was available at the right price, and wrote an article saying so.[11] "That sent our stock up, and it ended up with Dow and Marion Merrell Dow issuing a statement in August 1994 saying that both companies had hired investment lawyers to assist in determining what strategic moves Marion Merrell Dow ought to anticipate," Temple said.

In the interim Temple and his colleagues were still studying how Marion Merrell Dow could get "a lot bigger." "You get a lot bigger by acquiring somebody, by a joint venture, or by what executives like to call 'strategic alliances' when they don't want to tell you anything, but that can take any form," Temple said.

Temple assigned a veteran Dow executive, Malcolm Barbour, to "look at all of the non-U.S. companies to find out what company we would like to be associated with, in some way that would make the best fit from a product viewpoint or from a geographic viewpoint or from any other viewpoint." Barbour reported back that Hoechst A.G., the big German chemical company, came out at the top of such a list.

"We found out later that simultaneously Hoechst had done the same thing in-house, and Marion Merrell Dow had come out at the top of their list," Temple said. "Hoechst's number one priority was to take their horrendous position in pharmaceuticals in the United States and fix it, and the way they were going to do that was an acquisition. The main thing Hoechst wanted from Marion Merrell Dow was its presence in the United States, its extremely highly regarded sales force, and its number one position based on surveys with HMOs.

In April 1994 a quartet of Marion Merrell Dow's top executives—Temple, Lyons, Richard Markham (recruited from Merck to succeed Lyons as president of MMD), and Pierre (Pete) Ladell, who ran the firm's U.S. business—journeyed to Midland for a meeting with Popoff and the Dow Operating Committee.

"We had two things we wanted to expose to Dow," Temple said. "One was that we really thought we were going to have to get significantly bigger to be a real player in pharmaceuticals. The other was our assessment of Hoechst as a possible strategic alliance candidate, including, perhaps, acquisition of the Hoechst pharmaceutical business."

The Operating Committee asked them to find out whether Hoechst had any interest, Temple said.

Dick Markham and Fred Lyons sat down and talked with Hoechst, and that's when we found out we were at the top of their list. Then we did the usual thing: they formed a team, we formed a team, and we exchanged information on products, forecasts, etc. That was taking place in July-August-September of 1994, and it progressed to the point where what Hoechst really wanted to do was to buy Marion Merrell Dow. Dow was looking at an $11 to $14 billion acquisition to buy Hoechst's pharmaceutical operations, and in no way was Hoechst going to sell them anyway, but that's the kind of money Dow was looking at.

"That kind of acquisition would have turned Dow toward pharmaceuticals to such a degree that it would have overshadowed everything else in the company," Popoff said.

Starting out with the intention of buying, Dow now found itself in the role of selling. In October Popoff met with Juergen Dormann, chairman and CEO of Hoechst AG, in Switzerland and the two talked about closing a deal.

"Where is our future in Hoechst?" Dormann asked rhetorically. "In pharmaceuticals, pharmaceuticals, pharmaceuticals." "When he said that," Popoff recalled, "I said to myself, 'Oh boy, oh boy, oh boy.'

"I was trying to get a couple more dollars," Popoff said, "but the Germans are tough bargainers, and the negotiations broke off. That kind of spoiled my Christmas. Finally, in February, they called me again. They came partway. They didn't come all the way, but we got our price."

"I'm delighted we sold it, but I'm ambivalent about Dow getting out of the pharmaceutical business after we put so much talent and time into building it up. As we went along in that business every hurdle we came to was higher," he said.

Of the German Big Three chemical companies, Popoff said, both Hoechst and Bayer have long histories in pharmaceuticals. Hoechst has moved most aggressively in the direction of pharmaceuticals, but had major problems breaking into the U.S. market. According to industry observers, before the Marion Merrell Dow acquisition it had only 1 percent of U.S. drug sales.

The sale was made public in March 1995, with Hoechst agreeing to buy all the outstanding shares of Marion Merrell Dow at $25.75 each; for the 197 million shares owned by Dow (71 percent of those outstanding), that translated into $5.2 billion. The new firm, Hoechst Marion Roussel, began to take shape immediately.

In a separate transaction, Hoechst's operating arm, the former French firm Roussel, acquired Latin American Pharmaceuticals, Inc. (LAPI) from Dow for $200 million. LAPI, the former Lepetit businesses in Latin America, had not been merged into Marion Merrell Dow.

Dow was now out of the pharmaceutical business worldwide.

In its second century Dow will continue to play a strong role as supplier to the pharmaceutical industry, Popoff said. The Michigan Division, the big Midland manufacturing plant that was once the entire Dow Company, is strongly oriented to production of pharmaceutical and agricultural specialties. "That is what the Michigan Division will be all about," he said.

"Dow can always be a supplier to pharmaceutical companies," Temple said. "Dow is going to continue to make active ingredients for Hoechst Marion Roussel for awhile; I think they are obligated to do that for five years."

"I think the boat has left the dock though," he said,

as far as Dow ever being in the pharmaceutical business again. If you let many years go by and you think about how big Merck, Hoechst Marion Roussel, Smith Kline Beecham, and Glaxo Wellcome are going to be then, there's no point. And you can't get in that business by inventing a product and starting with one product; you are going to have to acquire something. If you can't come up with $10 or $12 billion now, you probably aren't going to come up with $20 or $40 billion five or ten years from now.

Looking back on it, Temple felt that Dow "did better than any other chemical company that went into the pharmaceutical business. We were held up as the example of how a chemical company should do it. But now we're out of it [we meaning Dow], and I think out of it forever. You should never say forever, but I have to say it in this case."

"It's not a happy conclusion on my part," Popoff said.

Some people are dancing in the aisles and are glad we're rid of it, very honestly, because they never saw us as a big player. Security analysts love us for getting out of it. Some employees who say, "We'll never be what we need to be in polymers, chemicals or ag if we inordinately spend assets to build ourselves up to the right level to be a real player in the pharmaceutical business," are happy. I'm sad because I'm greedy and I had hoped that we could do both.

IV.

The sorry plight of East German industry came to light only when the two Germanies were once more joined together as a nation in October 1990 following the collapse of communism. The chemical industry was a prime example—a dismaying spectacle of aging, largely outmoded, ill-maintained plants, burdened with swollen payrolls, make-work jobs, and the stigma of an environmentally irresponsible attitude and behavior that had contributed no little to the ecological disasters visited on Eastern Europe under communist rule.

The chemical industry in that part of Europe had once been among the world leaders in the field, the pride of its citizenry, one of the foundation stones of their economy and prosperity. The great Buna chemical complex at Schkopau (for which Buna rubber is named) had been a key piece of the I. G. Farben empire and one of the industrial pillars of Hitler's Third Reich. Now, with the cold war finally ended, the question was whether this time-honored industry had decayed beyond redemption. Could it still be rebuilt and restored to the place in the market it had once enjoyed? To do so would require enormous technological skills, supported by massive amounts of money and endless patience.

When German Chancellor Helmut Kohl looked for help to the German Big Three chemical companies—Hoechst, Bayer, BASF—the world's largest in their field, the Big Three had already "picked the plums" in East Germany, as one observer put it: acquired the more desirable chemical properties. "The East German chemical industry is so far gone that it is better that it die," they advised the chancellor.

"The Big Three German companies weren't interested," Popoff said. "Let's be totally candid. I'm sure they were offered this (opportunity) and they said, 'We really don't need that; it's a mess,' compared to Ludwigshafen, Leverkusen, Frankfurt. A lady whom we had known forever, Minister Birgit Breuel, the minister of economy in Niedersaxony, said to Kohl, 'If our German companies won't do it, I know an outfit that will.'" She told him about Dow Chemical, who operated a big plant at Stade, near Hamburg.

"Kohl, who's from Ludwigshafen, where BASF headquarters is located, said, 'How are they compared to BASF?' She said, 'Just as good, and for this I think a little better.' He said, 'Go to work.' So she did, and that's how they came to us."

Elmar Deutsch, Dow's general manager for Germany, came to Midland to report on developments. "Would I be wasting my time if I showed slides of the East German plants and made a presentation to the management board?" he asked Popoff. "Get your butt in there and show them the slides," Popoff told him. The presentation sparked immediate interest. "Everybody at Dow got onboard," Popoff said.

Popoff himself, during his years in Switzerland, had sometimes argued the merits of "greenfield" sites compared to retrofitting old facilities with his friend Armand Hammer, chairman of Occidental Petroleum Company (and its chemical subsidiary, Oxychem), who had done business with the Russians since the time of Lenin and was still the USSR's favorite U.S. capitalist. "Armand Hammer loved to go to a new part of the world, and he always argued that the ideal situation was to have a showcase site on green fields unencumbered by anything else, and to be there by fiat of the number one man in the government," Popoff said. "That's a highly idealized scenario, and it sounds good but it doesn't work. We in contrast had always advocated retrofitting sites and bringing them up to international standards, and since we had been advocates of that (to Armand Hammer as well as others) it helped Minister Breuel convince the Germans that if no German company were available, Dow would be the most logical outfit to invite to the party."

The green field versus retrofit debates took place in the 1970s and 1980s, but Dow had made clear that in its view the answer in Eastern Europe was retrofitting existing facilities, making them economically and environmentally viable. "Please," Popoff said, "let's not walk away from what's on the ground and the workforce that serves it, and get enamored with a greenfield site somewhere else."

Several other parties were interested in the East German plants as well, but Dow was "given the nod," Popoff said, and "we hammered out the deal. The Treuhandanstalt (the agency in charge of selling former East German properties) ceased to exist on December 31, 1994, so we had to renegotiate the whole thing with the German Ministry of Finance in the early part of 1995."[12]

On April 6, 1995, Dow signed an agreement to privatize the three state-owned East German chemical companies, now merged under the name "BSL" (Buna Sow Leuna Olefinverbund GmbH). The agreement was with the successor agency to the Treuhandanstalt, the BvS (Bundesanstalt für vereinigungsbedingte Sonderaufgaben—Federal Institute for Unification-Caused Special Tasks). Dow's "transition team" arrived on the scene on June 1 and began the takeover process that would ultimately result in Dow holding an 80 percent stake in BSL with BvS holding the remainder. Dow has the option of buying the remainder from BvS by the year 2000.[13] Dow and the German government agreed to pour a total of $7.8 billion into the rejuvenation effort, subject to approval by the European Commission at Brussels, set up among other purposes to study state aid projects to see that they are compatible with European Union rules.

Included in the takeover were a steam cracker at Saechsische Olefinwerke GmbH in Boehlen (30 miles south of Schkopau), electrochemical units and derivative operations at Buna GmbH in Schkopau, and polyolefin operations at Leuna-Polyolefine GmbH in Merseburg (20 miles west of Schkopau). Simultaneously Dow announced that it would build a 200,000 ton per year polypropylene plant at Schkopau to come onstream during the second quarter of 1998. It would also build a pipeline from Boehlen to Rostock, on the Baltic coast, designed so raw materials could be pumped to the plants from the coast.

"Typically for Dow," Popoff said, "we said, 'Hm, this isn't on deep water; we don't like things that aren't on deep water.' The Germans said, 'Yes, but this has been here since before the turn of the century.' We said, 'Well the nearest thing to deep water is a bunch of pipelines,' so we decided on a pipeline to the North Sea. That will guarantee us our feedstock situation."

The "restructuring" of the three companies is to be completed by the year 2000. Dow itself will invest close to a billion German marks ($700 million) in plant expansions during the restructuring period, and an additional 1.25 billion marks ($880 million) after the year 2000; Dow's total investment will be about $2.83 billion.

Deutsch told the press Dow planned to build several other new facilities at the three sites, including a Dowlex linear low-density polyethylene plant, an aniline production facility, and an acrylic acid plant, as well as polymer compounding and recycling facilities. The chlorine plant at Buna and the steam cracker at Boehlen would be upgraded, he said.

"This is a tough job," Popoff said, "but it fits our chemistry to a T. It's chloralkali chemistry, it's a cracker, it's olefins, it's aromatics—it's what we do, plus a couple of things that we haven't done before that we're very excited about, such as acrylic acid."

In July a sizable delegation of Germans visiting the United States traveled to Midland to discuss the whole project with Popoff and Bill Stavropoulos, then the company's chief operating officer but scheduled to succeed Popoff as chief executive later in the year. Led by Reinhard Hoeppner, prime minister of Saxony-Anhalt, and Klaus Schucht, minister of economy and technology, the delegation was accompanied by seven German journalists representing the German national print and broadcast media.[14]

Then Dow turned its attention to the final major hurdle, and submitted its revised plan for approval by the European Commission. That came through, after some delay, on November 8, 1995, when the commission approved the proposal and allowed the German government to provide Dow a $6.77 billion subsidy to undertake the modernization of the BSL complex.

"The Commission concludes that the modified proposed plan by Dow Chemical will be viable," the commission said officially. More than half the aid package would be spent even if privatization were not to go ahead and the firms were closed down immediately, the commission pointed out. "Indeed, in such a case, aid schemes would have been applied to cleaning up the heavily polluted sites of all three companies, to demolishing abandoned plants as well as to financing a social plan," it said.[15]

When completed it was the biggest sale of state-owned assets in East Germany since German reunification in 1990.

"It took forever to get it through the European Union," Popoff said,

but we did. They chiseled and chipped away at our program, saying the subsidies were too rich. We knew we would be punished in the media for being subsidized to take this "jewel" off the East Germans' hands. We'll clean up the site, modernize it, and build some plants. By the year 2000 we'll have had those subsidies ($6.77 billion), we will hopefully have modernized the facility, and then we will live with the consequences because profit and loss at that time will accrue to Dow, thank you very much.

The environmental aspects of the BSL project are especially troublesome, Popoff said, a truly major challenge for Dow's newly established environmental business, Radian International LLC. "It makes a good way to get our new environmental business established in Europe, working for ourselves," he said.

By early 1996 the downsizing of the three-company BSL complex was proceeding briskly. The three companies had employed as many as 30,000 during the communist period; their payroll was 26,000 at the time of the merger of the two Germanies, and shrank rapidly to under the 6,000 mark—a reduction of 20,000—by the time of the Dow takeover. BSL sales in 1995 amounted to $970 million.

Dow expected the workforce would settle at about 2,300. By the terms of its agreement with the German government it had agreed to maintain at least 2,200 jobs at the three sites, and would pay heavy penalties if employment fell below 1,800.

From Dow's viewpoint, the arrangement gave the company a major presence close to the East European and Russian markets, expected to be big growth markets in the twenty-first century. Additionally, it gave Dow a new set of employees familiar with key business leaders in that region, versed in their languages and familiar with their ways of doing business.

So here was Dow, at the end of its first century, charging into territory that a century before had housed some of the unquestioned masters of the chemical world and taking on the task of restoring the chemical industry there to its former brilliance.

One hundred years before, the Deutsche Bromkonvention had attempted to snuff out this upstart company from the American Middle West. The little midwestern company had fought the German cartel for five long years, refusing to die, and the Bromkonvention had finally stopped trying. History, as it sometimes does, had now come around full circle. The American upstart had become a major force in the Bromkonvention's homeland and was charged with reviving a moribund chemical industry there that in its turn was refusing to die. Herbert Dow would have been amused, and pleased.

V.

As CEO, Frank Popoff emphasized six issues more than any others, and returned to them time and again in his talks to employees and other audiences around the world. They were issues he saw as critical to the future of the company: competitiveness, trade, environment, education, technology, and corporate credibility. Most of his public utterances reflected these basic, interrelated concerns.

For a company in the late twentieth century, being competitive in the world marketplace was vital to its very survival, he said, and a company that was not competitive, "should just lower its voice and step aside"; but if a company were competitive it should practice that competitiveness "on as broad a horizon as you can; trade globally, export, work for open and free markets."

He agreed with the view of industry that said, "we don't care how competitive you are or how universally you are trading, but if you're doing so in a fashion that is seen as suspect from an environmental perspective, we'll close your plant down. We'll padlock the rascal."

If these concerns were met, then, "the ultimate solution to all of our problems is education, because education should not be seen as competing for the best and brightest or even subsidizing good teachers and teaching. The ultimate challenge for education is delivering an enlightened society, and if you have that, then all the other issues are eminently solvable."

Technology was related, "because education is the process that liberates discovery and technology, and technology and people are what will make us what we desire to be—great, if we are capable of greatness."

The last issue, corporate credibility, meant to him that "everything you do had better be totally aboveboard, because if you're not credible with the public, then your ability to influence issues number one through five is lost because you haven't handled issue number six, corporate credibility.

"While all the other issues are important to the chemical industry, the chemical industry is front and center on environmental matters. We said, 'We can be a voice for education and for technology, and active in trade and competitiveness issues, and hopefully add to the issue of corporate credibility, but it's on the environment that we must be the lead industry.'"

Popoff took the initiative himself in this regard by sponsoring the "Responsible Care" program, a concept that originated in Canada with Jean Belanger, who headed the Canadian Chemical Producers Association (CCPA), supported by David T. Buzzelli, president of Dow Canada at the time.

"It's maybe the most powerful thing that this industry has done for as far back as I can remember," Popoff said. Belanger and Buzzelli contended that "we chemical producers have to show continuous improvement in our emissions to land, air, and water," and they said, "Let's put some teeth in it; let's make it a condition of membership in CCPA that every company has to show a reduction in pollution every year. If you can't do that, you're out of the organization."

Popoff, then chairman of the Chemical Manufacturers Association (CMA) in the United States, carried the program to CMA, and with the support of Robert Roland, CMA president, and after "about a one-year debate," it was adopted by CMA. "We got all 188 members of CMA to sign on, and now Responsible Care is alive and well in over 30 countries," Popoff said, "not necessarily with the same teeth in all the countries, but environmental leadership has become a major concern" for the industry.

"I didn't volunteer but I wound up being sort of the standard-bearer for environmental reform for the industry," he said. When President-Elect Bill Clinton convened a meeting of business and government leaders in Little Rock, Arkansas, to discuss the agenda for his presidency, late in 1992, Popoff attended as a representative of the chemical industry.

As Popoff moved towards his 60th birthday and deceleration, which would occur in 1995, attention began to turn toward the succession, which was a two-horse race. The contenders, both elected to the Dow Board of Directors in 1990, were Enrique J. Sosa, one of the bright, ambitious Cuban refugees who had joined the company in the early 1960s, and William S. Stavropoulos, son of a Greek immigrant who had grown up living above his father's restaurant in the little town of Bridgehampton, on Long Island, New York.

The two were on parallel promotion tracks, and at one point in the late 1970s were jointly commercial directors for Dow U.S.A., with Stavropoulos responsible for plastics and Sosa for chemicals and performance products. By 1984 Sosa was president of Dow Brazil and Stavropoulos was president of Dow Latin America, which embraced the rest of Latin America. Stavropoulos became president of Dow U.S.A. in 1990. When Oreffice retired at the end of 1992 Popoff became both chairman and president and the race entered the home stretch.

In April 1993 Stavropoulos moved out front, becoming president and chief operating officer, the first time that designation had been used in the company; Popoff remained as chairman and CEO. At the same time, the company formed Dow North America, combining Canada, Mexico, and the United States, and Sosa became the first president of this new entity, the largest geographic unit in the company.

The company's move toward a combined North American operation, announced in December 1992, anticipated the NAFTA (North American Free Trade Agreement) legislation by about two full years.

"We had been strong proponents of NAFTA and we thought NAFTA was an inevitability, despite all the political hubris that swirled around," Popoff said.

I was invited to attend the signing of the NAFTA documents. I'll tell you, to see Clinton, Reagan, Bush, Ford, and Carter all standing up and saying, "This is in the best interests of America," was kind of special. Much earlier we had said, "There's a lot of synergy to be achieved by taking a North American perspective." Duplicating in Mexico and Sarnia from a headquarters standpoint what we do in the United States is just part of the equation. We needed to recognize also that the same customers were on both sides of the border, just as we were.

Popoff appointed a task force from the three nations to study the situation, with Denis Wilcock, a British citizen, then the president of Dow Canada, as chairman. "Dow Mexico was totally onboard and wanted to be appended to the United States rather than to the rest of South America," he said. "In the best Dow tradition the task force said, 'It's a good idea, and if it's a good idea a year from now it's probably a good idea to do it now and not wait for a year from now.' So we jumped the gun."

The establishment of Dow North America was a body blow to the Dow Canada headquarters at Sarnia. "Sarnia was fine in an environment where the border between Canada and the U.S. was far more protective," Popoff said, "but it just wasn't economic in a North American sense of the word." While Canada was a big winner on balance, "because of the tremendous resources we've put into Alberta," Popoff said, "if you're working in Sarnia that doesn't do much for you."

The race between Sosa and Stavropoulos formally ended at the annual stockholders meeting in May 1995, when Popoff announced that Stavropoulos would succeed him as CEO on November 1. Three months later Sosa ended his 31-year career at the company. The Amoco Corporation, in Chicago, had approached him a few weeks before and asked if he'd be interested in running its $5 billion chemical business. It was a tough decision, he said, but he'd decided he needed a change.[16]

Sosa had become familiar to Dow North American employees in the previous few years as the Dow executive who traveled from site to site explaining the company's reasons for downsizing. "I felt very fortunate to have eased the pain of the past few years," he said. "I felt that I was helpful in making the need for change better understood."

Michael D. Parker, a Briton from Liverpool and a 27-year employee, succeeded Sosa as president of Dow North America. Parker also headed up 3 of the 15 business groups: chemicals and metals, specialty chemicals, and emulsion polymers.

Popoff liked to joke that the last three chief executives of Dow (Merszei, Oreffice, and himself) had all been foreign-born, so to succeed him the board had compromised by choosing "a Greek kid from Long Island."

Stavropoulos, the "Greek kid from Long Island," had once been a talented semi-pro baseball player on the same team with Baseball Hall-of-famer Carl Yastrzemski and Yastrzemski's father. Carl played shortstop and his father played second base, with Stavropoulos at first. The double-play combination of Yastrzemski to Yastrzemski to Stavropoulos must have been the longest in history, he joked.[17]

Yastrzemski went on to baseball stardom with the Boston Red Sox, and Stavropoulos went on to study pharmacy at Fordham University in New York City, followed by a doctorate in medicinal chemistry at the University of Washington. He started with Dow in 1967 as a research chemist in pharmaceutical research at Indianapolis. After 10 years in pharmaceuticals he moved to Midland to learn the plastics business, and began a rapid climb to the top.

During his two years as chief operating officer Stavropoulos and some of his colleagues set out to analyze the Dow organization, and by the fall of 1995 he was convinced the company needed a thorough reorganization to meet the changing demands of worldwide competition. He was soon busily putting the new organization in place.[18]

Stavropoulos's reengineering of the company—the first worldwide reorganization since the troika had set up the global Dow organization in 1966—took power from the geographic headquarters and put it in the hands of 15 business organizations. "Clearly the businesses have more sway today than they did in times past," Popoff said, "but everybody says appropriately so because it's only recently that the economy has become truly global."

If you ask a Dow person what they are, Popoff explained, they give you an answer that has three dimensions: "I am a plastics salesman in Spain"—Spain the geography, plastics the business, salesman the function. Or, "I'm a production superintendent for chemicals in Stade"—Germany the geography, chemicals the business, production the discipline. "I think people wanted to have the multiple dimensions of their jobs not only better defined, but better brought together so there wasn't an eternal tug on 'Gee, this is good for my business, but is it good for my function? Is it good for my area? Is it good for the company?'"

"What we've been able to implement in terms of changing the matrix organization—not throwing it out, but rebalancing business, geography, and function—has been done with more goodwill and more cooperation than I could have imagined," Popoff said. "Can you imagine what the area presidents [the presidents of Dow Europe, Dow Latin America, Dow Pacific, and Dow Canada] would have done if we had tried this 10 years ago?"

By early 1996 the new organization was in place. Stavropoulos introduced a remodeled, 13-member Management Board (not to be confused with the board of directors), now revamped into a cabinet representing the businesses and geographical areas and functions of the company. Six of the members, including Stavropoulos, its chairman, were also members of the board of directors.

New faces were popping up all over. Tony Carbone, now a group vice president with the eight plastics-related businesses, as well as Dow Pacific, reporting to him, became a member of the board of directors, as did Mike Parker. J. Pedro Reinhard, a Brazilian who became chief financial officer in the fall of 1995 when Enrique Falla embarked on the deceleration path, also became a board member. Geoff E. Merszei, son of Zoltan, was elected company treasurer, an event that would not have occurred in very many companies.[19] Fernando Ruiz, an Ecuadoran, became assistant treasurer.

The powerful long-term trend toward diversity of race, nationality, and gender in the management, begun 40 or more years before, continued unabated as an underlying theme of the company. Dow had become a global melting pot, and it was increasingly normal and unremarkable for a woman or a black to reach the top rungs of management. Kathleen Bader, for example, was the head of Dow's polystyrene business with $1.3 billion in annual sales; Bob Wood, an African American, was the head of Dow's engineering plastics business, with $1 billion in annual sales.

In many ways, these steady and inalterable currents foreshadowed the business realities of the twenty-first century and the shape and working climate of the industrial future for a multinational company.

The company's more than 2,000 products were now organized into 15 specific businesses, most operating quite independently of each other and headed up by an individual responsible for that business worldwide. The annual sales of these businesses ranged from $400 million annually (New Businesses, under Fernand Kaufmann) to $3.1 billion (Polyethylene, under Romeo Kreinberg).

"Our mission," Stavropoulos said, "is to be the most productive, best value growth chemical company in the world. The Dow Chemical Company of today is different than it was just three years ago. And it will continue to change as we pursue our mission. Reactions to these changes in the company range from a longing for the past to uncertainty to excitement about the future."

As the company headed into its second century it had lost none of its verve, excitement and optimism. It was, Stavropoulos told employees, "an exciting, challenging, rewarding place to work."[20]

Notes

1. Oral History, Keith R. McKennon, June 9, 1993.

2. Oral History, Frank P. Popoff, November 16, 1995, is quoted extensively throughout this chapter.

3. It is probably pertinent, however, that prior to the merger the organic chemicals department had sold out its production of several key organic chemicals at bargain basement prices on long-term contracts. When the oil crisis of 1973-74 struck and the cost to Dow of petroleum raw materials for these products skyrocketed, its organic chemicals department found itself in deep trouble, saddled with long-term contracts at prices that did not reflect the costs of producing them.

4. Oral History, Robert E. Naegele, August 6, 1990.

5. As a rule of thumb naphtha sells at 10 times the cost of a barrel of crude oil; $13 a barrel crude, for example, means $130 a ton naphtha. Dow's European operations at this time were heavily dependent on naphtha from the Soviet Union that was processed to make chemicals in the Dow complex at Terneuzen, the Netherlands.

6. *Dow Annual Report to Stockholders*, 1982.

7. See Cheryl Wade, "Dow Cutbacks: Not the First Time," *Midland Daily News*, March 14, 1993. The number of Dow employees at year-end, 1980-95, according to the company's annual reports to stockholders, was:

1980	56,800	1988	55,500
1981	63,800	1989	62,100
1982	56,600	1990	62,100
1983	54,500	1991	62,200
1984	49,800	1992	61,400
1985	53,200	1993	55,400
1986	51,300	1994	53,700
1987	53,100	1995	39,500

8. Oral History, Joseph G. Temple Jr. (II), October 9, 1995, is quoted extensively in this section.
   Around 1984 Dow purchased an equity position in four pharmaceutical firms: Marion Laboratories, Millipore, Rorer, and Morton Thiokol. In the interim before the Marion acquisition it sold its holding in the first three and acquired the Texize Division of Morton Thiokol.

9. See "Dow Announces Tender Offer for Marion Laboratories," *Dow Today*, no. 92, July 24, 1989. As mentioned elsewhere, company rules require Dow directors to relinquish line management positions at age 60 and enter a "deceleration" period; usually they continue as members of the Dow Board of Directors until reaching age 65 and retirement.

10. Upjohn, headquartered in Kalamazoo, Michigan, was a candidate for Dow acquisition in 1983-84 but Dow refused to contemplate a hostile takeover, according to Temple. In 1995 it was acquired by Pharmacia AB, a Swedish firm, and became part of Pharmacia & Upjohn, Inc.

11. Dan Dorfman, "'For Sale' Sign for Marion Merrell Dow?," *USA Today*, June 21, 1994.

12. Birgit Breuel had become president of the Treuhandanstalt.

13. "Dow Signs Agreement with BvS to Privatize Three Chemical Production Sites in Germany," Dow news release, April 6, 1995.

14. "Government Delegation from the Former East Germany to Visit Dow Chemical," Dow news release, July 7, 1995.

15. See "Dow Chemical Gets Funds to Buy Former E. German Group," *Detroit Free Press*, November 9, 1995 (Reuters); and Nathaniel C. Nash, "EC Gives Green Light to Dow–German Government Chemical Deal," *New York Times* News Service, in *Midland Daily News*, November 10, 1995.

16. See Enrique J. Sosa, Letters to Dow Employees, August 28 and 29, 1995; and "Sosa Leaves Dow for Amoco Post," *Midland Daily News*, August 29, 1995.

17. See "Oreffice Announces Impending Retirement; Popoff Elected Chairman; Stavropoulos to Become President and Chief Operating Officer," Dow news release, September 10, 1992; Stavropoulos biography, July 1993; "Small-Town, Big-Time Success," *Midland Daily News*, July 6, 1995.

18. For details concerning the "new" Dow, see W. S. Stravropoulos, "Building for the Next Century," Special 12-page insert in *Around Dow* 2, no. 1 (Jan./Feb. 1996).

19. Merszei had brought both his sons, Leslie G. and Geoffrey E., into the Dow organization during his term as president, giving rise to accusations of nepotism.

20. Stravropoulos, "Building for the Next Century."

EPILOGUE
GROWTH AND RENEWAL

I.

If there was a single defining incident in the early history of The Dow Chemical Company it was the occasion in 1913 when Herbert Dow shocked his colleagues by telling them it was time to get out of the bleach business. The company had been founded to make bleach only 16 years earlier, and that was for a time its only product, but bleach no longer had a future, and when he explained his reasoning they agreed and the company began to phase out of the product. It has vigorously culled out failing products ever since.

To many the loss of its principal product must have seemed a major setback for the little firm in Michigan. In 1912 sales had been just $809,000, and to drop its main product at this point must have seemed to many suicidal.[1] What actually occurred, of course, is that the company began an intense search for other ways to use the chlorine freed up by going out of bleach manufacture, found ways to use this chlorine in a host of new products, as we have seen, and in the succeeding years grew mightily; instead of a setback, the decline of the bleach market became a powerful engine for growth.

Growth and renewal has always been the gospel of the company, and remains so today. Knowing when to stop making bleach is part of that wisdom.

After a journey through 100 years of history we arrive at the truth Herbert Dow knew from the beginning: that healthy growth depends on regularly pruning the tree (not only in a product sense but in a people sense and a venture sense as well), removing the growth that burdens further growth. Renewal springs from new growth and nurturing the central life-giving trunk. The agonizing downsizing of the 1990s, painful as it was, is the curtain-raiser on a new era of growth. A pruned Dow today will be a growing Dow tomorrow.

"The universal truth about Dow is growth," Popoff said. "That's the opiate we're all hooked on and I hope we always are. We've taken huge risks to keep that [fire for growth] kindled. Growth is what every Dow employee is promised, either by direct statement or by implication when they are hired. When you were hired, somebody said, 'Popoff, this is a growth company.' They said it to me and they said it to everybody else, and by God, it had better always be a growth company."[2]

When a security analyst asked him if Dow was still a growth company now that it had reached $20 billion in sales, Popoff said, "We ought to be a $30 billion company." "Why?" asked the analyst. "Because if you get that top line right," Popoff said, "that means you've got the projects and the programs to get you from here to there. We have the people who will implement them, if we have the will to define those opportunities and then go after them."

There is no place in the Dow lexicon for any other option than continued growth, and the only question is how to achieve that growth.

The leaders of the company, from Herbert Dow onward, have universally acclaimed Dow as a growth company, but other characteristics of the company have also been important to them.

Over the years there have been many debates, inside and outside the company, about just what constitutes the "Dow style," the "Dow approach," the "Dow way," and it remains an elusive concept, although there is agreement that growth is a basic element.

Ted Doan said he thought of the "Dow style" as being "opportunistic and quick-witted, and on top of the world at any moment in time and taking advantage of it, whether it is financial or product or what-have-you." At the same time, he said, Dow "has this apparent faith in technology and research and the willingness to spend enormous amounts of money."[3]

There are two countervailing themes in Dow, he said, one being long-range planning and the other an adeptness at "scrambling." "That is a wonderful combination," he said, "because the scrambler will overcome and do better than the long-range planner every time, but the scrambler will run out of things to scramble on if he hasn't got this underpinning being built and generated all the time as well."

Hunter Henry found the ethical and moral values of the company to be critical. "The people who work in this company believe in the inherent honesty and ethical behavior of the company," he said. "It really is a caring company, although I can tell you a lot of people don't feel that way. Fundamentally, the company holds moral values, the moral values that this country holds dear. This sounds like I'm ringing the patriotism bell, and I am to a certain extent."

"I just hope we can carry that on," he said, "and I hope that however I've been seen to do things would encompass some of that. That sounds a little like flag waving and motherhood, and perhaps it is, but that's the way I feel."[4]

Shutting down a bleach plant was not enough, Ted Doan said. The company also became very good at shutting down other plants that need to be shut down.

We had mercury in the St. Clair River and Sarnia [headquarters plant of Dow Canada] was accused of putting it there. We dug into the facts, and sure enough, there's mercury all over the place, and a big source of it is going to turn out to be Sarnia. So we wrote the Sarnia [caustic] plant off. It cost $40 million, and it was Branch who said, "Look, if we're going to do things right, we're going to do them right. Let's write the thing off and get out of it." So we got out of the business; we wrote off $40 million.

"Branch was good at this," Doan said. "We were all good at this."

Another facet of the Dow culture is a scarcity of written rules and instructions. "Dow has a wonderful habit of not writing anything down, including organization charts," Doan said. "There has never been a policy manual in the company; there is no thought of putting one together. Dow has skipped all that kind of thing, much to its benefit."

The reason for "not writing it down," he said, "is fairly well thought out. That simply says you can't forecast what the conditions are going to be and you are better off trusting the people at that time than you are trying to say, 'Here is the way you must act under certain circumstances.' So I don't think [behavior] is institutionalized. I think parts of it will remain in the institutional memory and be applied as time goes on."

The fact of growing up as and remaining staunchly a small-town company is another facet of the Dow character. "The little town has the advantage of allowing one to do one's own thinking," Ted Doan said, "and I suppose develop more loyalty and maybe more honesty in the approach to whatever you're doing and whatever your style is. I think it's hard to stay honest in New York. It's not hard to stay honest in Midland, if only because your neighbor is looking at you. . . . Dow has been very insular for exactly the right reasons."

Bob Keil felt the same way.

If somebody said to me, "You people in Dow are different. I don't know if you're any better or any worse, but I sense that you have your own particular culture," and asked, "In a word, how do you account for that?," I would answer, "Geography." Because we all live in this small town, we see each other all the time. I have often gone to my office five times on the same weekend day; it's like walking next door or down the street. In New York City, it would be the end of the world.[5]

Jim Williams felt it was critical to the company's success (as did many other Dow managers) that it let young employees make important decisions. "We've got ads running today that say, 'Dow lets you do great things,'" he said.

That's been one of the distinguishing characteristics of Dow; they do give their people freedom, they do let them do things. As a young lawyer I was given the responsibility for making some very important decisions. We were striving to make Styrofoam nonflammable, or

at least self-extinguishing. The guys would work their fannies off and come up with something and I had the job of saying, "Okay, this is sufficiently self-extinguishing; now you can
call it self-extinguishing." That's a pretty damn important product and pretty heady kind of
thing.[6]

Another characteristic of the Dow character was what Ted Doan called "taking care of
odd ducks." Since the days of Bobby Dreisbach ("really a nutty guy, but one of the key figures in polystyrene"), he said, "everybody has thought Dow was good at taking care of odd
ducks; that is, taking care of them by letting them live their lives and letting them be comfortable in Dow, and making a hell of a contribution."

J. M. (Levi) Leathers, who rose to be Dow's manufacturing vice president and a board
member, "probably couldn't have been a member of the board of directors of any other
company of comparable size in this country because he was odd in a lot of ways; he had
his own language but was quite a brilliant fellow and made quite enormous contributions
to Dow," said Doan.

Keil said M. H. P. (Pat) Morand was another major Dow executive who would not have
become a major executive in most companies. "He was an enormous guy, weighing probably 350 pounds. You just can't make a body like that look good, and Pat enjoyed the things
that contributed to his overweight condition." Keil saw himself as another example. "Do
you see me functioning in Wilmington?" he asked.

I don't mean to knock Du Pont; they are wonderful people, but there aren't many companies where you could be, say, seriously blind. I was on the board of the company. I would
look across the table and not see the features of the directors on the other side. We all got
so that none of us paid any attention to it; we didn't care; it didn't make any difference. I'm
sure it has happened elsewhere, but it happens here (at Dow) so often—it's easier to do
here, for some reason.

As a director and employee, Keil said he saw his constituencies as, "first, the enterprise,
then the employees, followed by the communities we live in, because they supported us
when we needed them—we should never forget that. Next comes the public, then the
shareholders who originally funded this company, and their heirs, and finally, the transient
shareholders. I realize that if I were in court I would probably be told, 'That's not your
responsibility as a director.' But I care about the enterprise."

II.

"The history of the United States," Woodrow Wilson said, "has been one continuous
story of rapid, stupendous growth, and all its great questions have been questions of
growth."[7] The history of Dow Chemical has been the mirror image of that observation.

Why did Dow grow so big, so fast? We have visited some of the wellsprings of this growth during our survey of a century at Dow, but it may be useful to take a parting look at the research laboratories and related technology-generating apparatus that fueled it.

"Dow is a technology company," said Ed Rainwater, a former general manager of Dow's Texas Operations, repeating a universal sentiment in the company. "Its existence depends upon its ability to compete and its successes in technology spell the real difference between Dow and other companies in being able to provide a strong, healthy company for years to come."[8]

Among the major concepts that have made Dow successful are its technology centers, created by Max Key beginning in 1965, and its business management teams, inaugurated by Ted Doan at that same period; this is the view of Larry Wright and Bob Gallant, both of them key figures in the company's manufacturing arm in recent years. "The creation of technology centers and the business team concept enabled Dow to become a very strong global player in the chemical industry because we had the ability now to transfer technology anywhere in the world and make it work," Gallant said. "The business teams, by bringing together manufacturing, research, marketing, and distribution, enabled us to coordinate these and to do it very effectively. Dow's focus on good technology and applying good technology and emphasizing manufacturing excellence was extremely important and valuable to Dow."[9]

"What made Dow a great company from the beginning was its culture of striving for innovation and improvement in both products and processes," said Wright. "That was the heritage that the founder of this company gave us and it must not be lost."[10]

"Dow Chemical has been dominated primarily by research and production; they held the power in the company" for many years, said Mac Pruitt, the research and development vice president for whom the company's central research complex in Midland is named. "That means we have had strong manufacturing and strong research and strong development of new products. When you swing around the other way," you're in deep trouble. "I hope Dow doesn't go that way, and I've been assured . . . that they're not going to let that happen."[11]

Dow's technology, Ben Branch said, is the base for all of Dow's performance. "Dow hasn't 'invented' many basically new products," he said, "but it is unequivocally better than anyone else in the world at taking the products and developing processes that are better than the competition, and then further improving the processes even more on the next generation of plants."[12]

One of Dow's real strengths, said Rainwater, has been taking technology and making it significantly better. "It didn't seem to me that Dow was particularly strong in the development of new molecules, but I was certainly struck with the ability of Dow to take existing processes and dramatically improve the technology to provide a significant competitive advantage," he said.

The cornerstone of Dow's integrated operations was its hydrocarbons and chloralkali technology, Rainwater felt. "Most of our significant products are downstream derivatives of these two fundamental technologies," he said. "Absolutely paramount," said Wright.

Dow's chlorine cell technology, upon which Herbert Dow founded the company, has continued to improve for 100 years, Rainwater said. "It's just amazing to go back and look at the improvements in the life of the cells and the improvement in their efficiency, which has led to a reduced cost of chlorine, thus providing a competitive advantage to the downstream products that are produced."

"In the chloralkali area," Wright said, "cells and diaphragms are lasting 5 to 10 times as long today as they were several years ago, and that's come from technology and innovation."

As another modern-day example, Gallant cited development of the metallocene catalyst, a Dow research development of the 1990s that he called "a tremendous breakthrough, every bit as significant as the development of the Ziegler catalyst when it came along." "I think that's going to be the most significant single product in Dow's line over the next 10 to 15 years," he said in 1996. "What's amazing is that from the time the metallocene catalyst was first successfully developed and demonstrated in the lab until we were turning out commercial products in the marketplace was only two years—and that's phenomenal."

"We used to think back in the 1960s in terms of catalyst efficiencies of 600 to 800 pounds of polyethylene per pound of titanium tetrachloride catalyst," he said, "and today we think in terms of yields up around 500,000 to a million pounds. Also, this work led to the Dowlex process, and gave Dow what was a preeminent position in terms of product quality, with our Dowlex process and our Dowlex products."[13]

The new metallocene chemistry, called "Insite," was also a vital cog in development of DuPont Dow Elastomers L.L.C., a new joint venture between Dow and DuPont formally launched in April 1996 after a year or two of gestation. The new firm combines DuPont's leadership in the synthetic rubber market with Dow's new metallocene technology. Its first product will be Nordel rubber, or EPDM (ethylene propylene diene monomer), and it expects to make a full spectrum of other rubbers (elastomers, chemically), including Tyrin (chlorinated polyethylene).

DuPont Dow projects $1 billion in annual sales from its elastomer products—$2 billion within five years—and 2,500 employees, with production beginning in the first quarter of 1997. The new venture will also have production facilities at Dow sites in Freeport, Texas, and Stade, Germany.[14]

The "Insite" technology beautifully typified recognition of a research need and successful response to it. Bill Knight, Bill Howell, Ashby Rice, and others in polyolefins research in Dow's Texas complex urged the necessity of a major catalyst research program if Dow were to continue to be a leader in polyolefin products in the future. Fred Corson and Bob Nowak in Midland agreed with them, and asked Jim Stevens in central research to organize a technical team to tackle the project. From the beginning the team included representatives of manufacturing and marketing as well as research. The star research contributors were David Devore, Francis Timmers, David Wilson, and Robert Rosen. This team turned up several catalysts they discovered to have very high productivities in terms of pounds of catalyst per pound of product. The new discoveries translated into action with exceptional speed because existing production units could easily be adapted to the new catalysts.

The "Insite" experience has already become a case study at Dow for bringing different functions together on a project from the outset to produce speedy results and move from idea to commercial sales in a much shorter time.

Dow's growth in technology was paralleled by giant strides in manufacturing capability. In the late 1970s Dow built its first naphtha-based ethylene cracker on the Gulf Coast (it had two of them at Terneuzen, the Netherlands, dating from the late 1950s, but this was its first cracker in North America). "That became a very important plant and we made significant improvements on it," Gallant said.

> In late 1994 and early 1995 we started up on the Gulf Coast a huge new naphtha cracker that cost $700 million and brought it to capacity in one month's time. In Ft. Saskatchewan [Canada] we started up a huge ethane cracker that cost $550 million and brought it up to capacity in two weeks' time. We started up a large vinyl plant in Texas and brought it up to capacity in about three weeks' time. Most people in the industry were taking three to six months to bring these big plants on-line. I think this is a demonstration of how excellent our manufacturing has become.

As Dow in 1996 shifted to a focus on 15 worldwide businesses, Gallant said the movie *Jurassic Park* reminded him of Dow's new business approach.

> There were two really dangerous things in *Jurassic Park*, tyrannosaurus rex obviously, but also the raptors, the small, very efficient, fast predator dinosaurs who always showed up where you didn't want them to show up. In Dow we have now created the business raptors who go out and serve each customer individually in a particular business and can be wherever they are needed; but we also have our tyrannosaurus rex, which is the huge capability for manufacturing, so that between tyrannosaurus and raptor we have the ideal combination to go out and be dominating in the marketplace. I think this is an advantage no other company has been able to put together.

The role of Dow's Technology Centers "will continue to shift as Dow's needs and priorities change," said Don A. Rikard, a former corporate director of manufacturing, "but there will always be a strong need for Technology Centers because we simply can't spend the time and effort repeating developmental work in individual locations."[15]

"Dow's goals today and what they're trying to do is correct," Pruitt said, referring to "the feeling of the present management that the business people should run the company," but, "all I say is if they do, do not let the research and the manufacturing technology get too dominated by the business people. If you do, you'll lose your shirt. Do not lose your technology. It has to have a strong voice, and research and production have had a strong voice at Dow. If we maintain a very strong R&D function in the company, where they can have their say-so and they get their input, then I think we're okay."[16]

III.

It is not possible in a book of this kind to give credit to more than a fraction of the people who built The Dow Chemical Company in its first century. Many of the true heroes and heroines of the company are or were known to only a few.

Some of those who made significant contributions are mentioned only sparingly here—the Julius Burows and Harvey Hackenbergs, the Gene Kenagas and Ray Rigterinks, the Carl Mitchells and Brick Dressels, the Jarbas Carvalhos and Luther Evans. A case in point was the company's number one product in its first century in both sales volume and earnings—Styron, the omnipresent polystyrene plastic that emerged from Dow's Physical Research Laboratory in the mid-1930s to became the first of the modern-day plastics. In the research laboratory it was, as are most modern inventions, the result of a team effort. The creativeness and sweat of Bobby Dreisbach, Larry Amos, John Grebe, Ray Boundy, Ray Boyer, Sylvia Stoesser, Walter Roush, and many others was poured into the invention of Styron and together they opened the door to the age of plastics.

Many at Dow had little faith in Styron in its early days, as has been mentioned. The turning point came in the days just after World War II, when two youthful assistant managers seized an opportunity to put a major push behind the product. The two were Bill Dixon, assistant plastics sales manager, who had been labeled "most likely to succeed" of the University of Michigan class of 1935, and Ernie Mitchell, assistant manager of the plastics department, who had spent World War II helping run the styrene program for synthetic rubber.

In the days after the war's end Ray Boundy, chief of Dow's plastics department, was chosen to go to Germany to inspect the I.G. Farbenindustrie and bring back German know-how for use by the United States, and Don Gibb, plastics sales manager, went on a tour of Dow's sales offices. Dixon and Mitchell, left in charge, promptly asked for an audience with the Dow Board of Directors to discuss the Styron program and its future.

The time was ripe for Dow to leap out ahead of Monsanto and Union Carbide in the plastics field, they told the board; plastics, in the postwar era, were about to experience explosive growth. They recommended a crash program to improve the Styron manufacturing process; purchase of the big wartime government-built styrene plant at Velasco,

Texas; and an aggressive marketing program to establish brand recognition for Dow's Styron.[17]

Charles Strosacker was ecstatic at what he heard, but most of the other board members were at best skeptical. E. O. Barstow asked Dixon (his son-in-law) if he really meant to infer that Styron might possibly one day reach the sales volume of Epsom salts, one of Dow's longtime sales leaders. (Epsom salts at the time was the Dow board's idea of an outstanding product.) "Yes, Dr. Barstow," Dixon said, "that's exactly what I mean." Earl Bennett, the board chairman, who had been leading the grilling of the two young managers, finally excused them, and they left feeling thoroughly beaten. Five minutes later Bennett emerged from the board meeting and found them at the drinking fountain. "Boys," he said, "we've decided to accept your full recommendations."

"That was a shock to us," Mitchell said, "but not as big a shock as Boundy and Gibb had when they got back to town." The two young entrepreneurs had not let their traveling bosses know what they were up to. History, of course, proved them right; later there were periods of Dow history when Styron produced as much as half the company's earnings.

Both Ben Branch and Ted Doan listed Dixon among their nominations for Dow's unsung heroes; Mitchell was listed by others. Dixon, Branch said, "introduced modern marketing methods to Dow."[18] Doan called him "a marketing genius, perhaps the first inventor of advertising to create demand back through the chain of supply."

Bobby Dreisbach, who with Larry Amos and Sylvia Stoesser is generally credited as the principal inventor of Styron, was another nominee as unsung hero by at least two former CEOs. It was Dreisbach's invention of the use of sulfur to inhibit the polymerization of styrene, Branch said, that "led Dow to leadership in the production of styrene monomer, and that affected Dow's entire future, especially in styrene monomer but also, in my opinion, in the polymer industry generally."

Ray Boundy, Ted Doan said, was Dow's first real director of research, was important in the development of plastics, and was "leader of one half the good young men in the company in the 1950s."[19]

Levi Leathers, Doan said, was "the world's greatest chemical engineer, whose hand is all over Dow, including energy saving." Leathers, Paul Oreffice said, was "the best process man in the history of the chemical industry and so recognized inside and outside Dow." Oreffice noted that Leathers spent many of his vacations at a Dow plant somewhere, doing what he enjoyed most—working at improving the process it used. "Many manufacturing breakthroughs came from his fertile mind," he said.[20]

All of them mentioned the uncanny abilities of those who could somehow spot talented young men and women and recruit them for Dow Chemical. Steve Starks led the list; he almost single-handedly recruited top talent for Dow in the 1930s and on into the 1940s. Oreffice said Gordon Clack, who became Starks's assistant at the end of World War II, had the same ability, "a personnel man who had a tremendous 'feel' for what would make a future leader," he said. "When he thought that a young candidate was good, he made sure we hired him almost regardless of what others thought."

In the 1960s, Ben Branch became president of Dow International and brought Bob Baker along to help staff it, a difficult task because the U.S. organization was often unwilling to let its best people go, and frequently offered second-stringers to Dowintal. "Baker had such a deep knowledge of the company's human resources that he was able to pinpoint the future leaders that Dowintal should go after with amazing accuracy," Branch said.

Oreffice remembered asking Baker's advice on people when he was asked to set up Dow's Latin American Area in 1965. "His handwritten suggestions still stand as the most remarkable people document I have ever seen," Oreffice said. "His list of youngsters with potential—Joe Temple, Hunter Henry, Bob Keil, etc.—was a veritable Who's Who of future Dow stars."

Ben Branch also pointed to a number of other innovators: W. L. (Buzz) Nelson, "who found, obtained a license, and put Dow in the Ziploc bag business"; L. L. (Zip) Ryden and Elmer K. Stilbert, who developed the processes and patented the principle uses for styrene-butadiene latexes; and Alden W. (Aldy) Hanson, "whose recirculating tube process for acrylonitrile-containing polymers has been the basis of our Tyril and ABS processes."

Ted Doan singled out Max Key, "a real production professional and the inventor of technology centers"; Glen O'Neal, longtime manager of Dow's St. Louis sales office, "the original non-Midland sales guru, who trained a large group of exceptional people"; W. R. (Bill) Collings, "a true entrepreneur," who became the first president of Dow Corning; John Van Horn and R. A. (Al) Lindsay, who originated "the idea of end-use products, the idea being to balance the chemical commodities with increasing sales of specialty chemicals"; Bob Heitz, "maybe the best laboratory director Dow ever had." "Not only is this not recognized," Doan said, "but most people would disagree with it. His laboratory invented polypropylene, hollow fibers, and water-soluble polymers."

Doan also added a list of people "with large jobs and big names but who are generally unsung." Among them: Tom Griswold Jr., "who made the first attempt at engineering as opposed to puttering"; Bill Schuette, "a world-class inventor of management methods and a bridge to bring Dow into modern times"; Zoltan Merszei, "along with Ben Branch, the builder of Dow Europe—a unique personality"; W. C. (Bill) Goggin, "a strong man in plastics and an innovator organizationally with target teams"; Earle Barnes, "a technical wizard and a manipulator of men, mostly for the good; creator of Texas research"; and Clyde H. Boyd, "a born leader and builder, who rebuilt the magnesium process and built such things as oil and gas in Canada and production in Europe."

Oreffice nominated a similar list of candidates, including Joe Temple, who "fit the pieces together and put Marion Merrell Dow on the way to becoming one of the world's most successful pharmaceutical companies"; Keith McKennon, "a remarkable human being with unusual common sense and a great feel for people, without question a major stabilizing influence in two Dow administrations"; and Robert M. (Bob) Keil, "a man of brilliant intellect who at one point in his career was out of a job because he was too smart for his bosses; a tremendous thinker who helped set the course for The Dow Chemical Company for the next 20 years of this century and into the next one; an excellent negotiator who made hundreds of millions of dollars for the company by adroitly leading the divestiture of some properties and the acquisition of others."

Oreffice also pointed out for special credit the pioneers in Dowintal, led by Clayton Shoemaker, its founder and first president. Shoemaker, Oreffice said, "had the vision to see that the only way to become an international business was to 'be there.' While other companies ran their business out of headquarters in the United States, Shoemaker pushed responsibility to the field and quickly established the precursors to the Dow areas." In Oreffice's opinion, "Clayton Shoemaker never gets enough credit for taking very limited resources and making the non-U.S. business an important part of Dow."

Bob Kincaid, the first sales manager for Dow Europe and the first sales manager for all of Latin America, "set the tone for future generations by pioneering international selling for the company," Oreffice said. "It's easy to get business when you are established, but it's very difficult to do what Bob did, put a medium-size midwestern chemical company on the map in country after country."

Tom Sparta "single-handedly put Dow in the polyurethane business in Europe at a time when there were real questions as to Dow's ability to break into the business," he said. "Against all odds, Tom did everything, including the hands-on job of going to customer plants and showing them how Dow products worked in their machines. Today polyurethanes and their components are one of Dow's largest businesses and consistently one of the most profitable."

Branch said the wives and families of those employees Dow sent abroad deserve "more appreciation than we can ever give them"—the young American families "who left the convenience and security of the U.S. to go to some far-off god-forsaken post like Moscow or Lagos to find out from scratch how to order a typewriter, shop for groceries, educate the kids and build a business for Dow."

"I have wished," Branch said, "that every Dow office around the world could have a plaque stating that so-and-so was the person who started that business and that every subsequent employee was in his or her debt."

Those who played strong behind-the-scenes supporting roles, such as Clara Turner, aide to Herbert Dow; Elsa Carlson, aide to Earl Bennett; Margaret (Peg) Lynch, aide to L. I. Doan; Dorothy M. Bollenbaugh, aide to Ted Doan; and Lucille Dougherty, aide to Carl Gerstacker—certainly deserve more credit than they will ever get as well.

Then there were those tragic cases who died early, before they came to full flower—M. H. P. (Pat) Morand, for one, Bill Schuette for another, Manuel Maza for a third. There were those who for one reason or another left Dow—E. O. Cross, for example, an early employee of the company, whom Herbert Dow wanted to nominate for his board of directors; instead Cross left for the gold rush in the Klondike, and when he came back became a vice president of General Electric instead. Another was John M. Henske, who left Dow and became president of Olin Chemical Company. Then there are more obscure ones, like Jaap Viersen, a Dutchman who suggested Dow take a lease on some land off the Scheldt River that was at the time under water; Dow did, and it now forms part of the Terneuzen plant, which could not have expanded without it.

There are even those who deserve recognition who never worked for Dow at all. One example is Hedde Rijpstra, burgomaster of Terneuzen, who worked tirelessly and effectively to bring Dow to his town. Another is Dave Garroway, the TV personality who helped put Saran Wrap in American kitchens in the 1950s, thus inaugurating Dow's effective use of the most powerful communications device of the late twentieth century. Another was W. A. P. (Wop) John, a school friend of Willard Dow's and one of the founders of McManus, John & Adams, which served as the company's principal advertising agency beginning in 1935; successor firms were continuing the relationship more than 60 years later.

All of these, and so many others, were strands in the fabric that forms the Dow of today.

Notes

1. 1913 was the first year Dow sales exceeded $1 million, and then just barely; net sales were $1,032,000. The devastating Midland flood of 1912—with that of 1986 the city's worst of the century—also was a setback.
2. Oral History, Frank P. Popoff, November 16, 1995.
3. Oral History, H. D. Doan, July 29 and August 2, 1988, and January 17, 1989.
4. Oral History, Hunter W. Henry Jr., September 11, 1990.
5. Oral History, Robert M. Keil, August 8, 1990.
6. Oral History, G. James Williams, August 16, 1990.
7. In "The Making of the Nation," c. April 15, 1897, The Papers of Woodrow Wilson, Princeton, N. J., 1966.
8. Oral History, Edwin L. Rainwater, February and December 9, 1996.
9. Oral History, Robert W. Gallant, February 1996.
10. Oral History, Larry F. Wright, February and December 10, 1996.
11. Oral History, Malcolm E. (Mac) Pruitt, January 15, 1986 and March 15, 1996.
12. Oral History, C. Benson Branch, November 12, 1988 and March 8-9, 1996.
13. Dowlex is Dow's brand of linear low-density polyethylene. Dow (and other producers) had used the Ziegler catalyst in its manufacture since 1954, when Dow was first licensed to make this plastic (see "Wizard of the West," chap. 7).
14. *Dow Annual Report, 1995*; "Breaking Ground for EPDM Plant," *Around Dow* 12, no. 3 (May-June 1996): 32.

15. "Dow Technology Centers: Continuing a 25-year Tradition of Excellence," *Dow Today*, no. 103, September 18, 1990; Oral History, Donald A. Rikard, September 1994.

16. Oral History, M. E. Pruitt.

17. J. Ernest Mitchell, "The Big Push on Styrene & Styron," communication to author, August 1, 1995.

18. C. B. Branch, communication to author, November 13, 1988, is used extensively in this section..

19. H. D. Doan, communication to author, May 5, 1992, is used extensively in this section.

20. P. F. Oreffice, communication to author, July 20, 1992, is used extensively in this section.

ORAL HISTORY
INTERVIEWS

(Interviewee, date, location, interviewer[s])

Akkerman, Duco N., July 8, 1989, Horgen, Switzerland (James J. Bohning and E. N. (Ned) Brandt).

Arbury, Dorothy Dow, January 18, 1989, Midland, Mich. (Brandt).

Artola, Ignacio M., July 19, 1989, Madrid, Spain (Bohning and Brandt).

Baker, G. Robert, March 13, 1991, Coral Gables, Fla. (Bohning and Brandt).

Baldwin, Charles L., August 4, 1995, Midland, Mich. (Brandt).

Ballman, Donald K., September 23, 1988, La Jolla, Calif. (Bohning).

Barnard, Robert D. (Barney), February 21, 1989, Walnut Creek, Calif. (James C. Mackey).

Barnes, Earle B., October 22, 1988, Freeport, Tx. and November 11, 1988, Grand Rapids, Mich. (Bohning).

Barraconi, Francisco, March 20, 1991, Sao Paulo, Brazil (Bohning and Brandt).

Barstow, Ormond E., July 28, 1988, Midland, Mich. (Terry S. Reynolds).

Baur, Heidi, July 25, 1989, Horgen, Switzerland (Bohning and Brandt).

Bennett, Earl W., 1962, Midland, Mich. (Clarence E. [Dusty] Rhodes).

Bennett, Robert B., August 24, 1990, Midland, Mich. (Bohning and Brandt).

Beutel, Albert P. (Dutch), 1967, Freeport, Tx. (Don Whitehead).

Blair, Etcyl H., May 24, 1994, Midland, Mich. (Bohning and Brandt).

Bonter, Theodore, 1993, Mackinaw City, Mich. (Anita Fisk and Jan Jones).

Bosscher, Harold, August 10, 1990, Midland, Mich. (Bohning and Brandt).

Boswell, Rosemary, July 10, 1989, Horgen, Switzerland (Bohning and Brandt).

Boundy, Ray H., September 9, 1988, Midland, Mich. (Bohning).

Boyer, Raymond F., January 14, 1986 and August 19, 1986, Midland, Mich. (Bohning).

Branch, C. Benson (Ben), November 12, 1988, Houston, Tx. (Bohning), and March 8-9, 1996, Houston, Tx. (Holmes H. McClure)

Brandt, E. N., June 17, 1992, Midland, Mich. (Bohning).

Brid, Panama, March 13, 1991, Coral Gables, Fla. (Bohning and Brandt).

Brummer, Bernhard, July 24, 1989, Stade, Germany (Bohning and Brandt).

Buchanan, Ruth Hale, June 13, 1991, Washington, D.C. (Bohning and Brandt).

Buck, W. Stanley, July 12, 1989, London, England (Bohning).

Butcher, Bernard B., June 11, 1992, Midland, Mich. (Bohning and Brandt).

Butler, Andrew J., May 5, 1995, Midland, Mich. (Bohning and Brandt).

Carvalho, Jarbas A. de, March 25, 1991, Sao Paulo, Brazil (Bohning and Brandt).

Casteleiro, Jorge S., March 13, 1991, Coral Gables, Fla. (Bohning and Brandt).

Crepet, Yves L. P., July 5, 1989, Horgen, Switzerland (Bohning and Brandt).

Crummett, Warren B., April 15, 1993, Midland, Mich. (Bohning and Brandt).

Cuervo, Jose R., March 11, 1991, Coral Gables, Fla. (Bohning and Brandt).

DeGroot, Gustav A., June 1, 1992, Richmond, Va. (Bohning and Brandt).

Doan, Herbert D., July 29, 1988, August 2, 1988, and January 17, 1989, Midland, Mich. (Bohning and Arnold Thackray), and November 3, 1989, Midland, Mich. (Judith O'Dell).

Doscher, Charles M., July 12, 1989, London, England (Brandt).

Dupuy, Lee F., September 1, 1993, Tampa, Fla. (Bohning and Brandt).

Faessler, Edmund P., July 7, 1989, Zurich, Switzerland (Bohning and Brandt).

Galhardi, Anibal, March 21, 1991, Sao Paulo, Brazil (Bohning and Brandt).

Gallant, Robert W., February 1996, Midland, Mich. (McClure).

Garrett, Angela Elias Post, August 30, 1985, Saginaw, Mich. (Brandt).

Gerstacker, Carl A., July 21, 1988, Midland, Mich. (Bohning).

Gerstacker, Esther Schuette, April 29, 1991, Midland, Mich. (Brandt).

Goggin, William C., August 20, 1986, Midland, Mich. (Bohning).

Goloubeff, Sergio, March 27, 1991, Rio de Janeiro, Brazil (Bohning and Brandt).

Goodchild, Colin D., May 1993, Wahroonga, NSW, Australia (Brandt).

Groening, William A., July 22, 1988, Midland, Mich. (Bohning).

Hacking, John M., August 22, 1990, Sarnia, Ont., Canada (Bohning and Brandt).

Hagaman, John L., May 18, 1992, Midland, Mich. (Brandt).

Hall, Donald D., August 31, 1973, Midland, Mich. (transcribed oral memoirs).

Hampton, Leroy, June 16, 1992, Midland, Mich. (Bohning and Brandt).

Harlow, I. Frank, September 30, 1988, Midland, Mich. (Reynolds).

Harlow, Ivan, March 12, 1984, Midland, Mich. (Carl A. Gerstacker and Brandt).

Hauptmann, Renato, March 21, 1991, Sao Paulo, Brazil (Bohning and Brandt).

Hay, James M., May 27, 1994, Midland, Mich. (Bohning and Brandt).

Heitz, Robert G., September 26, 1988, Walnut Creek, Calif. (Mackey).

Henry, Hunter W. Jr., September 11, 1990, Midland, Mich. (Bohning and Brandt).

Henske, John M., May 2, 1989, Greenwich, Conn. (Macauley Whiting).

Hernborg, Nils, July 17, 1989, Stockholm, Sweden (Bohning and Brandt).

Hillary, Bertrand B. (Bert), August 21, 1990, Sarnia, Ont., Canada (Bohning and Brandt).

Hooker, Millard J., June 10, 1992, Midland, Mich. (Brandt).

Huggins, Eric, September 22, 1994, Midland, Mich. (Bohning and Brandt).

James, William R. C. (Will), March 15, 1991, Coral Gables, Fla. (Bohning and Brandt).

Johnson, Arnold L. (Bud), August 26, 1993, Midland, Mich. (Bohning and Brandt).

Johnson, Julius E., September 9, 1988, Midland, Mich. (Reynolds).

Keil, Robert M., August 8, 1990, Midland, Mich. (Bohning and Brandt).

Kenaga, Eugene E., May 26, 1994, Midland, Mich. (Bohning and Brandt).

Kincaid, Robert F., July 8, 1991, Williamsburg, Mich. (Bohning and Brandt).

Knapp, Theodore E. (Ted), September 1982, Zurich, Switzerland (Frank P. Hammond).

Kriner, Barney, September 19, 1988, Walnut Creek, Calif. (Mackey).

Laird, Philip A., August 20, 1990, Midland, Mich. (Bohning and Brandt).

Lehman, Freeman R. (Pete), June 12, 1992, Midland, Mich. (Bohning and Brandt).

Look, Alfred T. (Al), October 2, 1990, Canyon Lake, Tx. (Bohning and Brandt).

Lundeen, Robert W., October 14, 1988, Midland, Mich. (Reynolds).

Lyon, Herbert H., August 7, 1990, Midland, Mich. (Bohning and Brandt).

McClure, Holmes H. (Mac), October 1, 1990, Lake Jackson, Tx. (Bohning and Brandt).

McIntire, O. Raymond (Ray), June 7, 1993, Midland, Mich. (Brandt).

McKennon, Keith R., June 9, 1993, Midland, Mich. (Brandt).

Merszei, Zoltan, December 21, 1988 and April 3, 1989, Greenwich, Conn., and June 3, 1994, New York City (Bohning).

Mitchell, J. Ernest, May 4, 1995, Charlotte, Mich. (Bohning and Brandt).

Monica, Dorothy Garrett, July 9, 1991, Midland, Mich. (Bohning and Brandt).

Moraes, Jose Franco de, March 19, 1991, Sao Paulo, Brazil (Bohning and Brandt).

Moro, Luis Valeriano, March 25, 1991, Sao Paulo, Brazil (Bohning and Brandt).

Naegele, Robert E., August 6, 1990, Midland, Mich. (Bohning and Brandt).

Neely, William J., October 10, 1995, Midland, Mich. (Bohning and Brandt).

Oreffice, Paul F., August 1, 1988, Midland, Mich. (Bohning).

Pankratz, Paul M., May 26, 1994, Midland, Mich. (Bohning and Brandt).

Papageorgiou, Dimitri V., July 7, 1989, Horgen, Switzerland (Bohning and Brandt).

Pavia, Rafael A., March 11, 1991, Coral Gables, Fla. (Bohning and Brandt).

Peterson, Norman R., June 10, 1993, Midland, Mich. (Brandt).

Pinto, Salvador, March 20, 1991, Sao Paulo, Brazil (Bohning and Brandt).

Popoff, Frank P., November 16, 1995, Midland, Mich. (Brandt and Thackray).

Pruitt, Malcolm E., September 9, 1988, Midland, Mich. (Bohning), and March 15, 1996, Lake Jackson, Tx.(McClure).

Rainwater, Edwin L., February, 1996, Rockport, Tx. (McClure), and December 9, 1996, Rockport, Tx. (Bohning and Brandt).

Ramon, Ernesto, August 21, 1995, Coral Gables, Fla. (Brandt).

Rikard, Donald A., 1994, Lakeway, Tx. (McClure).

Ritzer, Joseph E., April 19, 1991, Midland, Mich. (Brandt).

Rooke, David Lee, October 3, 1990, Kerrville, Tx. (Bohning and Brandt).

Roush, Walter E., May 15, 1989, Lake Jackson, Tx. (McClure).

Rubens, Louis C. (Bud), August 19, 1986, Midland, Mich. (Bohning).

Ruules, Roelof, July 14, 1989, Terneuzen, the Netherlands (Bohning and Brandt).

Sabbioneda, Roberto, July 20, 1989, Milan, Italy (Bohning and Brandt).

Sanford, Donald, October 13, 1984, Brighton, Colo. (Brandt).

Schornstein, Dave W., March 15, 1991, Coral Gables, Fla. (Bohning and Brandt).

Scott, Paul D., August 20, 1990, Sarnia, Ont., Canada (Bohning and Brandt).

Sheetz, David P., August 9, 1990, Midland, Mich. (Bohning and Brandt).

Shelton, Louis G., August 5, 1992, Midland, Mich. (Brandt).

Shigley, Claire M., June 15, 1989, Yakima, Wash. (McClure).

Smart, John L., August 22, 1990, Sarnia, Ont., Canada (Bohning and Brandt).

Smithers, Leroy D. (Roy), January 26, 1991, Boca Raton, Fla. (Bohning and Brandt).

Stenger, Vernon A., April 13, 1993, Midland, Mich. (Bohning and Brandt).

Stoesser, Sylvia Goergen, August 17, 1990, Midland, Mich. (Bohning and Brandt).

Straub, Francis W. (Bud), January 31, 1989, Pittsburg, Calif. (Mackey).

Stroebel, Paul G., July 2, 1992, Berwyn, Pa. (Bohning).

Temple, Joseph G. Jr., October 28, 1988, Midland, Mich. (Bohning), and October 9, 1995, Midland, Mich. (Bohning and Brandt).

Thorsberg, John W. (Jack), September 7, 1994, Midland, Mich. (Brandt).

Towsley, Margaret Dow & Dr. Harry A., December 6, 1989, Ann Arbor, Mich. (Brandt).

Van Horn, John C., September 13, 1993, Columbia, Md. (Bohning and Brandt).

Weldon, E. Leonard (Len), August 21, 1990, Sarnia, Ont., Canada (Bohning and Brandt).

Whiting, Macauley, August 13, 1990, Midland, Mich. (Bohning and Brandt).

Wildi, Rene, July 25, 1989, Buelach, Switzerland (Bohning and Brandt).

Wiley, Ralph M., April 14, 1993, Midland, Mich. (Bohning and Brandt).

Williams, G. James, August 16, 1990, Midland, Mich. (Bohning and Brandt).

Winfield, Gertrude, May 25, 1994, Midland, Mich. (Bohning and Brandt).

Wright, Larry F., February 1996, Kerrville, Tx. (McClure), and December 10, 1996, Kerrville, Tx. (Bohning and Brandt).

Yates, William M., June 7, 1993, Midland, Mich. (Brandt).

Ziegler, Earl E., January 12 and March 4, 1996, Midland, Mich. (Brandt).

SOME IMPORTANT DOW CHEMICAL U.S. PATENTS

(List compiled by William M. Yates, chief patent counsel, 1977.)

1. Herbert H. Dow, "blowing-out" process for making bromine, 1891 (U.S. 460,370).

2. Thomas Griswold Jr., bipolar electrode cell for making chlorine and caustic soda, 1911; Louis E. Ward, 1921; Ralph M. Hunter, Lawrence B. Otis, and Robert D. Blue, 1942 (U.S. 987,717; U.S. 1,365,875; U.S. 2,282,058).

3. William J. Hale and Edgar C. Britton, manufacture of phenol, 1926 (U.S. 1,607,618).

4. John J. Grebe and Ross T. Sanford, acidizing of oil wells (basis of Dowell activities), 1932 (U.S. 1,877,504).

5. Robert R. Dreisbach, making styrene from ethylbenzene using superheated steam, 1938; Robert R. Dreisbach and James E. Pierce, distilling styrene without polymerizing, 1941 (basis of Styron plastic) (U.S. 2,110,829; U.S. 2,240,764).

6. John H. Reilly and Ralph M. Wiley, polymeric vinylidene chloride (Saran), 1939 (U.S. 2,160,903).

7. Robert G. Heitz and William E. Brown, manufacture of perchloroethylene, 1948; Glenn W. Warren, 1951 (U.S. 2,442,324; U.S. 2,577,388).

8. Laurence L. Ryden, water-based paint from synthetic rubber latex, 1950 (U.S. 2,498,712).

9. John A. Easley and Harry E. Swayze, Dowetch photoengraving rapid etch process, 1953 (U.S. 2,640,763 to 2,640,767).

10. J. Lawrence Amos, J. L. McCurdy, and O. Ray McIntire, process of making high-impact polystyrene, 1954 (U.S. 2,694,692).

(Additional list compiled by Richard G. Waterman, chief patent counsel, 1985.)

11. Sheldon B. Heath and Forest R. Minger, extracting magnesium from seawater, 1944 (U.S. 2,342,666).

12. Piero Sensi and Pinhas Margalith, rifamycin and rifampicin, 1958 (U.S. 3,743,635, 1973, U.S. 3,979,376, 1976).

13. Henry I. Mahon, artificial kidney, reverse osmosis, 1966 (U.S. 3,228,876).

14. Anton J. F. Schwarz, measles vaccine, 1964 (U.S. 3,133,861).

15. Donald R. Wright, spiral generation of plastic domes, 1965 (U.S. 3,206,899).

16. Ray H. Rigterink, clorpyrifos insecticide (Dursban), 1966 (U.S. 3,244,586).

17. John D. Stewart and Milton E. Heslep, filling subterranean voids, 1974 (U.S. 3,817,039 and U.S. 3,852,967).

18. Clarence E. Habermann and Ben A. Tefertiller, acrylamide catalysts, 1971 and 1973 (U.S. 3,631,104 and U.S. 3,767,706).

19. John C. Moore, gel permeation chromatography, 1972 (U.S. 3,649,200).

(Additional list compiled by Michael S. Feider, patent department, 1996.)

20. Lawrence Sawyer and George Knight, linear low-density polyethylene fibers, 1989 (U.S. 4,830,907).

21. Jonathan Siddall and Thomas Johnson, preparation of superabsorbent polymers, e.g., for use in disposable diapers, 1989 (U.S. 4,833,222).

22. Louis Meyer, James Vanderhider, and Robert Carswell, internal mold release agents, 1989 (U.S. 4,876,019).

23. Jaime Simon, David Wilson, Wynn Volkert, David Troutner, and William Goeckler, bone cancer treatment, 1990 (U.S. 4,898,724).

24. William Kleschik, Robert Ehr, Mark Costates, Ben Gerwick, Richard Meikle, William Monte, and Norman Pearson, active compounds used in Broadstrike and Pronto herbicides, 1990 (U.S. 4,954,163).

25. Osborne McKinney, David Eversdyk, and Michael Rowland, production of ethylene-acrylic acid copolymers, 1991 (U.S. 4,988,781).

26. Duane Treybig, Wendy Harris, and Christopher Thomas, injection molding of linear low-density polyethylene, 1991 (U.S. 5,015,511).

27. Richard Skochdopole, filled blends of polycarbonate resin and rubber-modified styrenic polymers, 1992 (U.S. 5,091,461).

28. Shih-Yaw Lai, John Wilson, George Knight, James Stevens, and Pak-Wing Chum, new elastic substantially linear olefin polymers, 1993; and Lai, Wilson, Knight, and Stevens, 1994 (U.S. 5,278,272).

29. Donald Tomalia, Donald Kaplan, William Kruper, Roberta Cheng, Ian Tomlinson, Michael Fazio, David Hedstrand, Larry Wilson, Chu Jung, and David Edwards, Starburst polymer conjugates, 1994 (U.S. 5,338,532).

30. David Devore, Francis Timmers, David Wilson, and Robert Rosen, Titanium (II) or zirconium (II) complexes and addition polymerization catalysts therefrom, 1995 (U.S. 5,470,993).

KEY DOW DOCUMENTS

1. Objectives, The Dow Chemical Company (H. D. Doan, March 1965)

I. Primary Objective

It is the primary objective of The Dow Chemical Company to produce maximum long-term profit growth.

The achievement of this objective brings with it several essential results:

— Profit growth will benefit the company's stockholders;

— Profit growth will benefit the company's employees by enabling us to offer them greater opportunities for self-advancement, and improved job security;

— Profit growth will benefit the general public and the economy at large by enabling us to contribute more broadly and continuously to the improvement of living standards throughout the world.

II. Corollary Objectives

We will work toward several corollary objectives necessary to the achievement of our primary objective:

We will find, attract, and hire the most imaginative and competent people available, and we will treat them well in every respect, specifically including compensation commensurate with their contributions.

We will provide the equipment and training necessary to achieve maximum productivity with maximum safety.

We will market our products and services based on the optimum in price, quality, service, and delivery; and we will be honest in our claims and advertising.

We reaffirm that continuous innovation is the primary basis of our profit growth, whether it be accomplished through process improvement, through new products, or new uses for existing products, through new ways of marketing products, or through basic research.

III. Supporting Philosophical Considerations

Maximum long-term profit growth can only be obtained by the right kind of people, placed in the right environment, organized in the most effective fashion, approaching the task with the optimum attitude, and generating for themselves and the company continuous self-renewal. Our philosophy in these matters may be summarized in three categories:

A. Attitude

We will encourage the development of skills, attitudes, habits of mind, and the kinds of knowledge and understanding that will be the instruments of continuous change and growth on the part of our people.

We will avoid settled ways of doing things, we will avoid loss of flexibility, loss of innovation; we will avoid too many written rules and precedents. We must recognize that unwanted, unwritten rules are the hardest to identify and avoid.

We will encourage our people to develop self-discipline and enthusiasm for hard work.

We will let ethical ends triumph over means, and prefer substance over form; we will seek the goals we set rather than being preoccupied with the methods or techniques or procedures for reaching them.

We will tolerate some inconsistencies, some profusion of purposes and strategies, some conflict, some differing traditions, some diversity of intellectual positions.

We will tolerate revolutionaries who pursue their objectives with singleness of purpose, encourage a "loyal opposition," and listen carefully to critics who call attention to an area which requires renewal.

We will recognize that there is a balance to be sought between conserving and developing our existing assets, and using them to create new assets; and we will lean, in this balance, toward committing our resources to the goal of continuous self-renewal.

B. Organizational Philosophy

Our purpose in organization will be to give capable, responsible individuals maximum freedom within the context of accomplishing large and complex goals.

We will give our people participation in the management of the business to the highest degree possible.

We will have power widely dispersed rather than tightly held; we will have many decision-making points rather than one; we will have many points of initiation for new ideas.

We will shift personnel to broaden perspectives; and we will redefine jobs to break them out of rigid categories.

We will reorganize when necessary to break down calcified organizational lines.

We will choose flexibility over massive strength.

C. Personnel Philosophy

We will make the development of the individual one of the aims of the organization.

We will organize to give attention to human needs; we will design systems that contribute to the growth and fulfillment of their participants.

We will emphasize the individual and see that the organization places minimum restraints on him.

We expect the individual to earn freedom with the development of self-discipline.

We will make organizations for men, not men for organizations.

IV. General Philosophy

We will orient to the future.

We will accept the notion that the future brings change, and we will believe in our ability to influence the shape of the future.

We will strive to understand and be good citizens of the different societies in which we operate.

We will strive to make such contributions in products and philosophy that society as a whole benefits because Dow is in business.

2. International Business Principles, The Dow Chemical Company (Herbert H. Lyon, et al., August 1975)

I. General Objective

The Dow Chemical Company operates in pursuit of maximum long-term growth in profits through superior performance. The company enters commercial activities in any nation fully aware of its social responsibilities to that nation.

We provide a wide range of products and services through the technology we have developed over many years and we are therefore in position to contribute to improvement of the living standards of many nations in the world.

As a commercial venture, the company seeks within the restrictions of the need for long-term profit growth to employ its resources in countries where its products and services will contribute significantly to those countries' growth and development.

We believe our commercial objectives are complementary to the economic and social growth of our host nations.

II. Relationship with Host Governments

We endeavor to invest for the long-term in those countries where we are wanted, and where use of our scientific and technological base will contribute both to the economy of the host country and to our long-term profit growth.

We comply with the laws and regulations of those countries in which we operate, and we seek to conform to the policies and objectives of host nations. We prefer to do business directly, rather than through intermediary parties, with individual host governments.

We willingly pay our fair share of taxes to all governments. We pursue a policy of open communication on this and other matters with host governments. We resist discriminatory or punitive taxation or regulations on the part of any government.

We abstain from partisan political activity. We do not believe in and will resist becoming an instrument of the foreign policy of any government.

In cooperation with host government authorities, we seek the resolution of any problems that may arise.

III. Responsibilities to Employees

The high technological nature of our processes and product lines necessitates highly talented and skilled people. We seek to attract and hire the most competent and best qualified individuals regardless of nationality, color, sex, or creed, and we compensate them well for their contributions within the framework of host country compensation practices.

We encourage our employees to develop their individual skills, talents, knowledge, and understanding, and we aid them in this endeavor.

We believe that well-motivated employees are most productive and, consequently, contribute most progressively to the efforts of the company. We try, therefore, to grant maximum possible freedom to employees to demonstrate their desire and capability for increasing levels of responsibility. We encourage employees at all levels to become decision-makers in how to best advance the job to be done, recognizing that decisions determining the nature of the job to be done must be taken by management.

We provide recognition and opportunities for growth into positions of increased responsibility for our employees as their competence increases, and we promote the best qualified individual regardless of nationality, color, sex, or creed, consistent with the objectives of our host nations.

We believe the safety of our employees to be of primary importance, and promote a strong safety atmosphere and attitude in our operations in all countries through training, equipment, and the continuing involvement of employees at all levels in the development of safe attitudes and practices.

While we prefer to deal directly with our employees in solving problem situations, rather than through intermediary parties, we strongly believe that each employee should have the right to determine for him/herself whether he/she wishes third party representation.

We believe in providing reasonable autonomy for local managers who know their own country's needs and markets best. We encourage these managers to develop qualified local employees so that they may assume increasingly greater responsibilities in the management of the business.

IV. Some Key Considerations

A. Organization

In organizing the units of the company we favor the existence of many decision-making points, of many points at which ideas may be initiated, and a high degree of decentralized authority; and we will provide to capable, responsible people the maximum possible degree of freedom to achieve desired goals. We do not, however, take maximum freedom to mean unlimited freedom; and consequently we provide appropriate controls to insure the pursuit of our commercial objectives.

B. Investment and Finance

We generate much of the funds necessary for expansion and growth through the accumulation of retained earnings in the countries where we operate.

We believe in the free flow of funds across borders and oceans, but we recognize the right of governments to restrict or stimulate this flow to protect their own economic health.

We seek to preserve our assets, through currency conversion when necessary, but we will not seek through financial transactions to impair the stability of any currency.

We will willingly provide information to host governments on financial matters, as may appropriately be required. We expect that such information will be accorded the confidential handling normally due privileged information, as agreed upon with the host government.

C. Transfer of Technology

We possess superior technology and plan its use carefully. We believe in the flow of technology across borders and oceans, but recognize the right of governments to restrict or encourage this flow under certain circumstances.

When our technology meets the needs and markets of a host nation and it serves our basic objectives, we will actively pursue the opportunity to serve the appropriate markets and to contribute to an economy through the upgrading of its resources.

In introducing our technology to a host nation, we will adapt that technology to the particular or special needs of that nation, consistent with economies of size.

Because of its value to our future we expect to receive adequate compensation for and continued protection of the confidentiality of our proprietary technology, whether patented or not, as a consideration in any investment program.

D. Ownership of the Company

We encourage broad international ownership of the stock of The Dow Chemical Company, and we particularly encourage our employees to become investing shareholders. While we prefer to own 100% of our business ventures, we recognize the desire of host countries for local participation in the ownership, and where conflict between local and foreign ownership may exist, we will always seek constructive solutions with our host nations.

V. General Responsibilities

We respect the social and cultural mores and heritage of the countries where we operate, and intend to be good citizens of all the countries in which we are active.

We are committed to excellence and leadership in the field of environmental protection and safety. We will follow high standards of performance in this regard in every country where we operate.

We recognize and respect the desire of host nations to conserve and upgrade scarce natural resources, and will provide know-how and leadership in this field as may be feasible and appropriate.

We are committed to the concept of product stewardship— that is, to our basic responsibility, to the maximum practical extent, for proper use of our products by our customers, so as to avoid undue exposure, injury, or harm in their processing, transport, or use. We are committed to the training and education of purchasers and users of our products regarding the potential dangers of misuse.

In summary, we strive to achieve the full benefits of the free flow of people, capital and technology about the world, and we try to conduct ourselves in such a way that international understanding is enhanced, and the living standard of the citizens of host nations is raised.

3. Dow Core Values (P. F. Oreffice, D. T. Buzzelli, et al., July 1986)

Long-term profit growth is essential to ensure the prosperity and well-being of Dow employees, stockholders, and customers. How we achieve this objective is as important as the objective itself. Fundamental to our success are the core values we believe in and practice.

Employees are the source of Dow's success. We treat them with respect, promote teamwork, and encourage personal freedom and growth. Excellence in performance is sought and rewarded.

Customers receive our strongest possible commitment to meet their needs with high-quality products and superior services.

Our products are based on continuing excellence and innovation in chemistry-related sciences and technology.

Our conduct demonstrates a deep concern for ethics, citizenship, safety, health, and the environment.

4. Dow Values (F. P. Popoff, et al., July 1994)

Fundamental to our success are the Values we believe in and practice.

PEOPLE are the source of our success. We treat one another with respect, promote teamwork and encourage personal freedom and growth. Leadership and excellence in performance are sought and rewarded.

CUSTOMERS are the reason we exist. They receive our strongest commitment to meet their needs.

Our PRODUCTs and SERVICES reflect dedication to quality, innovation, and value.

Our CONDUCT demonstrates integrity and commitment to ethics, safety, health and the environment.

We live our values by:

- Discovering science and developing technology for products and processes that anticipate market needs and create value.
- Creating an environment that fosters confidence, excitement, accountability and diversity.
- Pursuing quality performance.
- Communicating openly and frequently.
- Measuring performance according to its contribution to business success.
- Protecting people and the environment as part of everything we do and every decision we make.

Selected Bibliography

Aftalion, Fred. 1991. *A History of the International Chemical Industry*. Philadelphia: University of Pennsylvania Press.

Barrons, Keith C. 1975. *The Food in Your Future: Steps to Abundance*. New York: Van Nostrand Reinhold.

_____. 1981. *Are Pesticides Really Necessary?* Chicago: Regnery Gateway.

Blair, Etcyl H. 1973. *Chlorodioxins— Origin and Fate*. Washington, D.C.: American Chemical Society.

Borth, Christy. 1939. *Pioneers of Plenty, the Story of Chemurgy*. New York: Bobbs-Merrill.

Boundy, Ray H., and J. Lawrence Amos, Eds. 1990. *A History of the Dow Chemical Physics Lab*. New York: Marcel Dekker.

Boundy, Ray H., and Raymond F. Boyer, Eds. 1952. *Styrene: Its Polymers, Copolymers and Derivatives*. American Chemical Society, New York: Reinhold.

Boyer, Raymond F., and Herman F. Mark, Eds. 1986. *Selected Papers of Turner Alfrey*. New York: Marcel Dekker.

Brandt, E. N., and Barbara S. Brennan. 1990. *The Papers of Herbert H. Dow*. Midland, Mich.: Northwood University Press.

Campbell, Murray, and Harrison Hatton. 1951. *Herbert H. Dow: Pioneer in Creative Chemistry*. New York: Appleton-Century-Crofts.

Colegrove, William. 1983. *Episodes: Texas Dow 1940-1976*. Houston: Larksdale.

County of Midland, Michigan. 1897. *Official Register, History, Art Folio and Directory*. Saginaw, Mich.: Imperial Publishing Co.

Dalton, Richard F. 1995. *Life and Legacy of Charles J. Strosacker*. Midland, Mich.: Northwood University Press.

DeVorkin, David H. 1989. *Race to the Stratosphere, Manned Scientific Ballooning in America*. New York: Springer-Verlag.

Dow, Joseph. 1893. *History of the Town of Hampton, New Hampshire, from its settlement in 1638 to the autumn of 1892,* 2 vols. Salem, Mass: Salem Press.

Dow, R. Piercy. 1929. *The Book of Dow, Genealogical Memoirs.* Rutland, Vt.: Tuttle.

Dudek, Vic. 1992. *The First 50 Years: Dow Canada 1942-1992, A History of Dow Canada.* Sarnia, Ont.: Dow Canada.

Duerksen, Christopher J. 1982. *Dow vs. California: A Turning Point in the Envirobusiness Struggle.* Washington, D.C.: The Conservation Foundation

Gray, Gib, Ed. 1976. *Dow in the West, 1916-1976.* Dow Chemical, Pittsburg, California.

Griswold, Thomas Jr. 1973. *The Time of My Life.* Midland, Mich.: Northwood Institute.

Groening, William A. 1981. *The Modern Corporate Manager.* New York: McGraw-Hill.

Gross, William H. 1949. *The Story of Magnesium.* Cleveland: American Society for Metals.

Hale, William J. 1932. *Chemistry Triumphant.* Baltimore: Williams & Wilkins.

_____. 1934. *The Farm Chemurgic.* Boston: Stratford.

_____. 1936. *Prosperity Beckons.* Boston: Stratford.

_____. 1939. *Farmward March.* New York: Coward-McCann.

_____. 1952. *Chemivision.* Haverhill, Mass.: Destiny Publishers.

Haynes, Williams. 1954. *American Chemical Industry: A History.* 6 Vols. New York: Reinhold.

Karpiuk, Robert S. 1981. *Dow Research Pioneers, 1888-1949.* Midland, Mich: Pendell Publishing.

Levenstein, Margaret C. 1991. "Information Systems and Internal Organization: A Study of The Dow Chemical Company 1890-1914." Ph.D. diss., Yale University.

Lloyd, Lewis E. 1955. *Tariffs: The Case for Protection.* New York: Devin-Adair.

Morris, Peter J. T. 1989. *The American Synthetic Rubber Research Program.* Philadelphia: University of Pennsylvania Press.

Norris, Peter. 1994. *Arthur Henry Knighton-Hammond.* Cambridge: Lutterworth Press.

Robinson, Sidney K. 1983. *The Architecture of Alden B. Dow.* Detroit: Wayne State University Press.

Seward, William B. 1974. *East from Brazosport.* Midland, Mich.: Dow Chemical Co.

Thompson, Stanley J. 1980. *The S/B Latex Story.* Midland, Mich.: Pendell Publishing.

Warrick, Earl L. 1990. *Forty Years of Firsts: Recollections of a Dow Corning Pioneer.* New York: McGraw-Hill.

Whitehead, Don. 1968. *The Dow Story.* New York: McGraw-Hill.

Yates, Dorothy L. 1985. *William R. Collings, Dow Corning's Pioneer Leader.* Midland, Mich.: Dow Corning Corp.

_____. 1987. *Salt of the Earth, A History of Midland County, Michigan.* Midland, Mich.: Midland County Historical Society.

INDEX

A